ST GREGORY OF NAZIANZUS

ST GREGORY
of
NAZIANZUS

An Intellectual Biography

John A. McGuckin

ST VLADIMIR'S SEMINARY PRESS
CRESTWOOD, NEW YORK
2001

Library of Congress Cataloging-in-Publication Data
McGuckin, John Anthony.
  St. Gregory of Nazianzus: an intellectual biography / J.A. McGuckin.
    p. cm.
  Includes bibliographical references and index.
  ISBN 0-88141-229-5 (alk. paper) — ISBN 0-88141-222-8 (pbk. : alk. paper)
    1. Gregory, of Nazianzus, Saint. 2. Christian saints—Turkey—Biogra-
phy. 3. Authors, Greek—Turkey—Biography. 4. Philosophers—Turkey—
Biography. I. Title.
BR1720.G7 M34 2001
270.2'092—dc21
[B]

2001019144

Copyright © 2001
ST VLADIMIR'S SEMINARY PRESS
575 Scarsdale Rd., Crestwood, NY 10707
1-800-204-2665

ISBN 0-88141-222-8 (paperback)

ISBN 0-88141-229-5 (hardcover)

All Rights Reserved

PRINTED IN THE UNITED STATES OF AMERICA

CONTENTS

CHRONOLOGICAL SYNOPSIS OF THE VITA[1] GREGORII

Date	Events in Gregory's Life	—in the Empire	—in the Church
325	Nonna's conversion of her husband Gregory the Elder from the sect of Hypsistarians.	Constantine Emperor.	Council of Nicaea Anti-Arian Homoousian creed.
326	Birth of Gorgonia, elder sister of Gregory Nazianzen.		
328/29	Gregory the Elder's consecration as Bishop of Nazianzus.		Consecration of Athanasios of Alexandria.
329/30	Birth of Gregory at Karbala, family estates at Arianzum near Nazianzus (DioCaesarea) in SW Cappadocia.	Constantine's Jubilee. Dedication of Constantinople.	Recall of Arius from exile. Birth of Basil (330).
331/32	Birth of his brother Caesarios.		
336			Death of Arius.
337		Death of Constantine. Accession of Constantius II in E.	
342-44	Early studies under Carterios his tutor and Amphilokios the Elder.		Council of Sardica.
345-46	Rhetorical studies in Cappadocian Caesarea.		
347-48	Study tours of Palestinian Caesarea and Alexandria with Caesarios and Carterios. Brief residence in Alexandria.		
348	Departs from Egypt with Carterios for Athens. Storm at sea (November).		

1 This Gregorian synopsis departs at a few chronological points from that established by the pioneering scholars: Sinko, Gallay, and Bernardi. The dating of the Letters and Orations follows their schemata, in the main. The Letters are often more difficult to place precisely than the Orations, as Gallay notes in his recent critical edition. The historical notes to the Orations in the Migne edition are hopelessly outdated. *Letters* 226-238 are the main numbers in the Gregorian corpus whose precise dates cannot be fixed with confidence. They do not feature in the present synopsis, nor do they affect any matter of historical substance.

348-58	Scholarship in Athens (in part with Basil).	355 Elevation of Julian as Caesar.	355 Basil abandons Gregory in Athens. 356 Basil's tour of monasteries.
358-59	Gregory returns to Cappadocia. Oratorical display at Nazianzus (Ep. 3); retreat to semi-seclusion on family estates. Sporadic visits to Basil in Pontus (Epp. 1-2, 4-6).		Synod of Ancyra affirms Homoiousian doctrine under Basil of Ancyra & Eustathios of Sebaste.
360		Julian proclaimed rival Augustus.	Homoian Synod of Constantinople. Eunomios the Neo-Arian consecrated bishop.
361	Gregory forcibly ordained priest by his father.	Death of Constantius (Nov. 3). Julian enters his capital (Dec. 11).	Eunomios publishes his Apologia.
362	His winter flight to Pontus (Epiphany); Possible preparation of original Philocalia with Basil (assigned by some to 358-9); Gregory the Elder signs heterodox confession in his son's absence; local monks withdraw from his communion; Gregory's return at Easter; Apologia to local church (Orats. 1-3); Caesarios' withdrawal from Julian's court (Ep. 7). Orat. 15. & begins Invectives.		Return of Athanasios from third exile. Synod of Alexandria. Consecration of Aetios the Neo-Arian as bishop. Euesebios of Caesarea consecrated. Basil returns to Caesarea.
363	Finishes Invectives: Contra Julianum (Orats. 4-5); Epp. 8-12.	Julian's death in the Persian Campaign.	Basil composes: Adversus Eunomium. His ordination 363.
364	Visit to Basil to advise him on his future in light of alienation from Bishop Eusebios; return to Nazianzus to effect reconciliation with local monks (Orat. 6); writes Epp. 12-15?	Death of Jovian. Elevation of Valentinian & Valens.	
365	Intercedes for Basil with Bishop Eusebios of Caesarea (Epp. 16-19); Epp. 21-24?	Revolt of Procopios. Valens at Caesarea.	Athanasios' fifth exile. Reinstated 366. Damasus Pope in Rome.

368	Death of his brother Caesarios (Orat. 7; Orat. 14); Epp. 20, & 30-36?		367–Death of Aetios at Byzantium. Basil building Hospices.
369/370	Death of his sister Gorgonia (Orat. 8); Epp. 29 & 37-39.		Basil's visit to Samosata.
370	Basil's deception over Caesarean episcopal election (Epp. 40-46).		Basil elected Bishop.
372	Basil appoints Gregory as Bishop of Sasima. Episcopal ordination (Orats. 9, 10, & 11); major conflicts with Anthimos of Tyana; Relations with Basil strained (Epp. 48-50). Retreats to seclusion. Epp. 25-28.	Valens' division of Cappadocia's boundaries (371/372) (Ep. 47). Demosthenes and Modestus at Caesarea. Valens at Caesarea.	Gregory of Nyssa consecrated bishop. Meeting of Valens & Basil.
late 372	Gregory settles in Nazianzus to assist his father as auxiliary bishop (Orat. 12).		
373	Episcopal Preaching. (Orats. 13, 16-17); Epp. 56-60. Epp. 61-62, 245-248. Poem: Lamentation on My Soul.		Amphilokios of Ikonium consecrated; Death of Athanasios. Jerome studying with Apollinaris at Antioch. Alienation of Eustathios and Basil. Eusebios of Samosata exiled (374-378).
374	Death of his father (Orat. 18); Basil in attendance at funeral. Death of his mother a few months later. Epp. 63-71, 79 (Orat. 19).	375: Death of Valentinian I. Accession of Gratian.	
375-378	Gregory's retirement to Seleukia; Monastic life and study in St Thekla's convent. Epp. 72-79. Gregory invited to support Nicene community at Byzantium. Epp. 241, 244?	377: Gothic invasion and depredations of Thrace. 378: Death of Valens and annihilation of Roman armies by Goths at Adrianople.	Basil composes treatise, On the Holy Spirit. Gregory Nyssa exiled 376 (returns 378) Eunomios publishes 2nd Apologia. Diodore consecrated at Tarsus.
379	Gregory travels to be missionary bishop in Constantinople. Orats. 20, 22, Orat. 24 (Oct. 2),[2] 32.	Theodosius raised to the purple by Gratian. Ceases toleration of "heretics." Aug. 3.	Death of Basil (Jan.).[3] Death of Macrina the Younger. Synod of Antioch.

2 Gallay (1943, 132-211) sets the Orations delivered between 379-381 in this order: 22, 32, 25, 41, 24, 38-40, 26, 34, 23, 20, 27-31, 37 & 42.
3 Some set this earlier to 377 or 378.

380

Gregory involved in controversies with Neo-Arians and hostile crowds at Constantinople (Epp. 80-86, 98); After Easter: Orats. 23, 33. Ep.77. Orats. 21 (May 2), 34, 41 (Pentecost), summer–autumn Gregory delivers Theological Orations at the house- church Anastasia (Orats. 27-31).

Strife with Maximus the Cynic (Orats. 25 & 26); November 27: installation of Gregory in Basilica of the Apostles as recognized bishop of Constantinople: Orats. 36, 38, 37.

Theodosius publishes *Cunctos Populos* in February, from Thessaloniki, adopting catholic Christianity as the "Religio Romanorum."

November 24: Theodosius enters his capital Jerome travels to Constantinople to hear Gregory teach.

November 26: exile of the Arian bishop of Constantinople—Demophilos.

381

Orats. 39 & 40. May: opening of Council of Constantinople. June/July president of council after death of Meletios. Pressured resignation: Orat 42. Retirement to Arianzum. Epp. 88-90, 95-97, 99-100, 128-129, 153, 157. & Many Poems.

January: reception of Gothic chieftain Athanarich into Constantinople. Athanarich's death and state funeral.

John Chrysostom ordained deacon by Meletios at Antioch. Gregory Nyssa writing the: "Adv. Eunomium." Jan. 10: Arians ejected from city churches. May: Council of Constantinople opens in Church of St Eirene.

382

Administration of his father's church at Nazianzum; Begins *De Vita Sua* his autobiographical Poem. January memorial Oration for Basil (Orat. 43). Epp. 91-94, 130, 167, 171-172, 224.

Visigothic settlement in Empire. Synod of Rome. [Possible further session of Council of Constantinople.] Attempts by Theodosius to attain a political settlement of the Church's doctrinal conflicts.

382-3

Resumption of duties at Nazianzus (Orats. 44 & 45). Increasing efforts to relinquish the church and find a new Bishop. Epp. 87, 103-124, 126-127, 131-152, 154-156, 158-166, 168-170, 173-181, 183-192, 249.

Eunomios the Neo-Arian exiled by Theodosius, in his final moves against Arianism. Theodore Mopsuestia ordained priest at Antioch.

383	Retirement for treatment at the Spa at Xanxaris; local Apollinarist disputes at Nazianzus, Epp. 101; 125.	
384	Consecration of his relative Eulalios as his successor at Nazianzus (Epp. 157, 182). Ep. 102. 202 Final retirement to his estates at Arianzum. Extensive poems. Increasing ill-health. (Epp. 51-55, 193-196, 224-225).	386: death of Cyril of Jerusalem.
387	Property disputes at Nazianzus (Ep. 203). Final Poems and Letters. Prepares edition of Collected Letters and edits Selected Orations. Epp. 197-201, 204- 223, 235, 239, 240.	Augustine's baptism by Ambrose at Milan. 389: Baptism of Paulinus of Nola.
390/391	Death at Arianzum. Familial bequests: property distributed to church; liberation of family slaves. Gregory's great-nephew Nicobulos acts as his literary executor and editor. Bishop Eulalios, his cousin and successor at Nazianzus, edits and publishes some of Gregory's Orations.	Death of Diodore of Tarsus. Death of Apollinaris.
391	February: Theodosius issues edict prohibiting all forms of pagan worship.	
398		John Chrysostom consecrated bishop of Constantinople.
400		Rufinus translates 9 Orations of Gregory into Latin. He is cited as the arbiter of catholic faith.
431		Gregory is cited as a major theological authority at the Council of Ephesus.
451		Designated "Gregory the Theologian" at the Council of Chalcedon. Becomes, thereafter, the most frequently published writer in Byzantine manuscript tradition.

BIBLIOGRAPHIC ABBREVIATIONS

AAT	*Atti della Academia delle Scienze di Torino*
AATC	*Atti e Memorie delll' Accademia Toscana la Colombaria*
AB	*Analecta Bollandiana*
AC	*L'Antiquité Classique*
ACIBC	*Atti del Congresso internazionale su Basilio de Cesarea* [Univ. di Messina, 1979]. Messina, 1983.
ACO	*Acta Conciliorum Oecumenicorum,* E. Schwartz, ed. (Berlin, 1924-1940; new edn. J. Staub, 1971)
ACW	*Ancient Christian Writers.* New York. 1946-
ANF	*Ante Nicene Fathers.* Ed. A. Roberts & J. Donaldson. [1885-1896; reprinted by: Eerdmans, Grand Rapids, 1951 1956]
ANRW	*Aufstieg und Niedergang der Romischen Welt. Geschichte und Kultur.* Berlin. De Gruyter
A&R	*Atene e Roma.* [Bolletino della Societa italiana per la diffusione degli studi classici]
ASNP	*Annali della Scuola Normale Superiore di Pisa*
BCO	*Bibliotheca Classica Orientalis*
BFC	*Bolletino di Filologia Classica*
BHS	*Berliner Historische Studien*
ByJ	*Byzantinische-Neugriechische Jahrbücher*
ByZ	*Byzantinische Zeitschrift*
Carm.	*Carmen / Carmina.* The Poems of St Gregory Nazianzen. PG. 37
CH	*Church History*
CJ	*The Classical Journal* (Colorado)
CPG	*Clavis Patrum Graecorum.* Ed. M. Geerard. 5 vols, Turnhout. 1974-1987
C&M	*Classica et Medaevalia.* Revue Danoise d'Histoire et de Philologie.
Courtonne	Yves Courtonne (ed. & tr.) *Saint Basile : Lettres.* 3 vols. Paris. 1957, 1961, & 1966
CQ	*Classical Quarterly*
CR	*The Classical Review*
CSCO	*Corpus Scriptorum Christianorum Orientalium.* Louvain
CWS	*The Classics of Western Spirituality.* New York. Paulist Press. 1978-
CTP	*Collana di Testi Patristici,* Rome
DA	*Dissertation Abstracts.* International Abstracts of Dissertations and Monographs. Ann Arbor, MI
DACL	*Dictionnaire d'Archéologie Chrétienne et de Liturgie.* Ed. F. Cabrol. 15 vols. Paris. 1907-1953
DCB	*Dictionary of Christian Biography.* Ed. W. Smith & H. Wace. 4 vols. London. 1877-1887
Diss	*Dissertation* (Unpublished Academic Thesis)
DOP	*Dumbarton Oaks Papers*

DS   *Dictionnaire de Spiritualité*. Paris
DTC   *Dictionnaire de Théologie Catholique*. Ed. A. Vacant, E. Mangenot, E. Amann, et al.
            15 vols. Paris. 1903-1950
EO   *Echos de L'Orient*
Ep.   *Epistle / Letter*
Eph Lit   *Ephemerides Liturgiae*
ET   *English Translation*
EThL   *Ephemerides Theologicae Lovanienses*
FOTC   *Fathers of the Church*. Catholic Univ. of America Press
GOTR   *Greek Orthodox Theological Review*
GRBS   *Greek, Roman and Byzantine Studies*. Duke University, (N. Carolina)
H   *Hermes. Zeitschrift für klassische Philologie*
HThR   *Harvard Theological Review*
ICS   *Illinois Classical Studies*
IRB   *Institutul Roman de Bizantinologie*. Bucharest
ITQ   *Irish Theological Quarterly*
JAC   *Jahrbuch für Antike und Christentum*
JECS   *Journal of Early Christian Studies*
JEH   *Journal of Ecclesiastical History*
JOEByz   *Jahrbuch der Österreichischen Byzantinistik*
JTS   *Journal of Theological Studies*
KK   *Kirche und Kanzel*
KQS   *Kirchengeschichtlichen Quellen und Studien*
LCC   *Library of Christian Classics*. Philadelphia / Westminster
LCL   *Loeb Classical Library*. London, & Cambridge. MA
MCr   *Museum Criticum*
MH   *Museum Helveticum*
MSAF   *Memoires de la Societé Nationale des Antiquaires de France*
MSLC   *Miscellanea di Studi di Letteratura cristiana antica*
MSR   *Mélanges de Science Religieuse*
MTZ   *Münchener Theologische Zeitschrift*
NPNF   *Nicene and Post-Nicene Fathers*. Ed. P. Schaff. et al. [1887 1894; reprinted by:
            Eerdmans, Grand Rapids. 1952-1956.
            2 Series (Nicene & Post-Nicene) 14 volumes each series.
NTT   *Nederland*. Theol. Tijdschrift. Wageningen
OCA   *Orientalia Christiana Analecta*. (Pontif. Inst. of Oriental Studies) Rome
OCP   *Orientalia Christiana Periodica*
OS   *Ostkirchliche Studien*
PBR   *Patristic and Byzantine Review*. New York
PE   *Pro Ecclesia*. Minnesota/New York

PFLS   *Publications de la Faculté des Lettres et Sciences humaines de l'Université de Montpellier*
PG   *Cursus Completus Patrologiae Graecae.* Ed. J.P. Migne. 167 vols. Paris. 1857-1866
PGS   *Program des kl. hum. Gymnasiums Straubing*
PhW   *Philologische Wochenschrift*
PIOL   *Publications de l'Institut Orientaliste de Louvain*
PL   *Cursus Completus Patrologiae Latinae.* Ed. J.P. Migne. 221 vols. Paris. 1844-1855
PMS   *Patristic Monograph Series.* Philadelphia Patristic Foundation.
PO   *Patrologia Orientalis.* Ed. R. Graffin & F. Nau, Paris. 1907-1922
QILCL   *Quaterni del'Inst. di Lingue e Letterature classiche*
QLP   *Les Questions Liturgiques et Paroissiales*
QU   *Quaderni dell'Umanesimo*
RB   *Revue Bénédictine*
RCC   *Revue des Cours et Conferences*
RE   *Realencyklopädie der classischen Altertumswissenschaft.* (Ed. Wissowa-Kroll-Mittelhaus). Stüttgart, 1894ff
REByz   *Revue des Études Byzantines*
RecPhL *Recherches de Philologie et de Linguistique*
RecSR   *Recherches de Science Religieuse*
RHE   *Revue d'Histoire Ecclésiastique*
RHPhR   *Revue d'Histoire et de Philosophie Religieuses*
RITh   *Revue Internationale de Théologie*
RM   *Rheinisches Museum*
RMAL   *Revue du Moyen Age Latin*
ROC   *Revue de L'Orient Chrétien*
RPh   *Revue de philologie, d'histoire, et de littérature*
RPL   *Res Publica Litterarum.* Studies in the Classical (University of Kansas)
RPLHA   *Revue de Philologie de Littérature et d'Histoire Anciennes*
RQ   *The Renaissance Quarterly.* (Renaissance Society of America) New York
RSC   *Rivista di Studi Classici*
RSCI   *Rivista di Storia della chiesa in Italia*
RSLR   *Rivista di Storia e Letteratura Religiosa*
RSR   *Revue des Sciences Religieuses*
RTHP   *Recherches de Travaux d'Histoire et de Philologie.* Bibliothèque de l'Université, Louvain
SBN   *Studi bizantini e neoellenistici.* Associazione Nazionale per gli Studi bizantini. Rome
SC   *Sources Chrétiennes.* Paris
SGKA   *Studien zur Geschichte und Kultur des Altertums*
Sic Gymn *Siculorum Gymnasium.* (Catania)
SIFC   *Studi italiani di Filologia classica*
Stud Clas. *Studii Clasice* (Bucharest)
SP   *Studia Patristica*

Sym. Naz. *Symposium Nazianzenum.* Ed. J. Mossay. (Actes du Colloque Internat. Louvain-La-Neuve. 1981)

SGKA. [*Gregor von Nazianz II.*] Paderborn. 1983.

SVTQ *St Vladimir's Theological Quarterly.* Crestwood, New York

TSK *Theologische Studien und Kritiken.* Gotha.

Tillemont *Mémoires pour servir à l'histoire ecclésiastique des six premiers siècles.* (Mémoires) 16 vols. Paris. 1693-1712.

TU *Texte und Untersuchungen zur Geschichte der altchristliche Litteratur.* Leipzig-Berlin

VChr *Vigiliae Christianae*

WS *Wiener Studien*

ZAC *Zeitschrift Für Antikes Christentum.* (De Gruyter), Berlin & New York

ZK *Zeitschrift für Kirchengeschichte*

ZNTW *Zeitschrift für die Neutestamentliche Wissenschaft und die Kunde der alteren Kirche*

ZPT *Zeitschrift für Patristische Theologie*

St Gregory Nazianzen

Of all the ancients,
You I think I could live with,
(some of the time)
comfortable in you
like an old coat
sagged and fraying at the back,
(its pockets drooping with important nothings
like string, and manuscripts of poems)
perfect for watching you off your guard,
rambling round your country garden,
planting roses, not turnips,
contrary to the manual
for a sensible monk;
master of the maybe;
anxious they might take you up all wrong;
shaking your fist at an Emperor,
(once he had turned the corner
out of sight);
every foray into speech
a costed regret.

Your heart was like a spider's silk
swinging wildly at the slightest breeze,
too tender for this tumbling world
of mountebanks, and quacks and gobs,
but tuned to hear the distant voices
of the singing stars
and marvel at the mercy of it all.

John McGuckin
1996

For Anna

Preludium

St Gregory Nazianzen has not been well-served by English theological scholarship. This is especially surprising given the fact that a long prior tradition of British patristic study has been closely associated with avenues of research and intellectual presuppositions that owed much to a background in Classics. Gregory was, without question, the greatest stylist of the patristic age. He dominated Byzantium and its schools for centuries as the model of Christian rhetoric and philosophy. Perhaps that was his problem. English scholars who looked at patristics from the vantage point of a formal education in Classics preferred their Greek rhetoric from earlier ages. A long-standing prejudice against the Latin writers of the so-called "silver" and "tin" ages had long exiled the reading of patristic texts from the curriculum of schools of Classics, and so it was with the Greeks of the era of Gregory. The age of late Second Sophistic was viewed with some distaste.

Today, such views are rightly outmoded. Nonetheless, the English school of patristics passed over Gregory. Even on the few occasions he was treated with some degree of seriousness as a theologian he was inevitably "lumped in" together with Basil and Gregory Nyssa as one of the Cappadocian Fathers. He tended to be read literalistically, taken for the face value of his words—a fatal way of underestimating the subtlety of an ancient rhetor, who freighted every phrase with a precisely loaded nuance suitable for the occasion. Often little care was taken to penetrate deeper than the surface meaning of his text, and little consideration was afforded to the strongly dialectical nature of his context of argument.[1] There is hardly a study of Gregory's theological relationship with Basil, for example, that does not begin by citing Gregory's *Letter* 58 which addresses Basil with the following words: "I have always taken you as the guide of my life, and my teacher in the sacred doctrines."

But few have gone on to point out how the text is meant, not so much as a testimony that Basil served as his only source of theological ideas, rather as a subtle deconstruction of Basil's pneumatology, seen to be such by its recipient, and an attack on his position which drew forth a furious rejoinder[2] which Gregory then "innocently" protests was an overreaction. As with so much of Gregory's writings one has to listen carefully to the subtext before leaping to conclusions. In regard to Basil, some of his most laudatory acclamations of his friend as theologian are reserved for times when he is setting out to criticize him for his attitude or behavior.[3]

1 Cf. Tsames (1969).
2 Basil, *Letter* 71, Courtonne 1, p. 167.
3 Cf. *Letter* 46, PG 37.96; Gallay (1964) p. 59—where he attacks Basil's arrogance while simultaneously

Although it is undeniable that there existed among these intellectual friends of Cappadocia a shared vision of culture and religion that must not be underestimated, a level of familial interrelations that served as a network to advance and support one another's Christian careers, and a level of mutual inspiration that led all three to develop some of their finest work, nevertheless the extent of "sameness" should not be overestimated. The usual story of enforced harmonisation of three distinctly interesting minds (more if one does not forget Amphilokios of Ikonium and the remarkable women of the families) has led to the neglect of the subtle message of Gregory Nazianzen in favor of his more directly appealing contemporaries.[4]

It was an approach that was to have a long history, and often still determines the treatment of some textbooks, despite its decidedly odd premiss of the three teaching the same theology. In Gregory's case the oddity might become apparent if we remember that he walked out of the Council of Constantinople in 381, partly because it had adopted the Trinitarian theology of Basil as lobbied for by Gregory Nyssa against his advice. He himself was severely disappointed that such a poor result, what he regarded as nothing less than a failed opportunity, should have emerged from the synod. It might have been no small consolation to him to have known that despite the letter of the Creed, it was his own theological construct of the Homoousion of the Spirit that was to win the day, becoming the official interpretation of that creed for later generations, and his own construct that was even to be read backwards into the intention and mindset of Basil himself: a rhetorical device he himself had invented (and published—as soon as Basil had died).

Even when attention was turned towards the Cappadocians as a school, Gregory did not seem to be very successful in commanding the attention of scholars. Gregory of Nyssa was pursued with relish for his apophatic mysticism, regarded as a true oriental exoticism; Basil was felt to be a man of action the West could look up to—a monk reminiscent of the organized Benedict who always remained the favored occidental paradigm. Gregory Nazianzen, on the other hand, almost seemed to be something of a disappointment. Perhaps there was just too much to be read. And his Greek was, after all, rather demanding, especially in the poetry with its Homeric resonances, and very discursive, needing patient editorial skills.

But as to why the Orthodox East had enthusiastically acclaimed him as "The Theologian" par excellence, there seemed to be no small degree of puzzlement. Gregory was thus despatched with a token edition of select translations (none of the poetry was felt to be in order) in the NPNF series, a few mentions in histories of dogma as a

---

pouring rhetorical oil upon the waters, designating him (at the same time in seriousness and raillery) as: "divine and sacred head," "eye and voice of the universe," "palace of eloquence."

4   The recent and highly learned study by Pelikan (1993) similarly shows such imbalance in its treatment. On almost every critical issue discussed, theological statements are given to Basil and Gregory Nyssa, while Gregory Nazianzen is allowed merely to provide local color. He emerges from a very large consideration of the theme as a most shadowy character.

minor member of "the Cappadocian school" fell to his lot, and he was occasionally regarded in the context of Apollinarism and the Christological controversy, though even here his contribution was frequently dismissed as a mere passing place on the way to the clarity of Chalcedon. Even today literary studies, relating to Gregory's poetry, his rhetorical style, or the Greek manuscript tradition of his works, far outweigh the body of work dedicated to his theology proper.[5]

The British scholar G.L. Prestige summed up this whole climate of neglect with the rather patronizing dismissal of him as nothing more than an "inspired popularizer" who preached a theological system allegedly worked out by Basil.[6] A closer study of Prestige's treatment of Gregory[7] reveals the usual story of minimal contact with the actual texts. The work published by Plagnieux several years after Prestige's own popularizing overview had appeared signaled the beginning of the end[8] of this long European misreading of one of the truly great Christian minds of the early centuries. From the middle of this century academic research has begun to make headway into the complexities and subtleties of his thought. Dedicated work by European and American scholars over the last fifty years[9] has subsequently produced a revival of some fine contemporary studies of Gregory's style and theology in the English language.[10] New translations have also begun to be produced,[11] and this has led to a growing interest in Gregory's life and work.

There have, however, been problems that continued to dog the great man, and result in the extraordinary situation that no full-length critical introductory study of his life and thought could be found in English. To begin with his personality was too fussy to command the interest of those who liked their patristic history with some dash. The manuscript tradition of his works was so extensive, and those works copied and cited so often in Byzantium[12] that the text tradition was in a sorry state demanding careful and

---

5 See for example Thematic Guide to the Bibliography, p. 426.

6 Prestige, 1952, p. 234.

7 In an extensive treatment of the major patristic writers in an earlier study (Prestige, 1940) the neglect of Gregory is even more apparent.

8 There were earlier exceptions such as the fine works of Hergenroether (1850), Draeseke (1892, 1906), and Pinault (1925).

9 Especially Althaus, Bernardi, Gallay, Mossay, Moreschini, Sinko, and Szymusiak.

10 Mainly works from American scholars such as Winslow, and Norris, Ruether, and Gregg; and the British scholars Donald Sykes and Neil McLynn. The work of the Scandinavian, Ellverson, has also advanced the field. A new work is also in progress from the scholar Susan Elm.

11 See the listing of the modern translations in Bibliography A given in this study. In citing passages from Gregory I am indebted to the translations of Dennis Meehan (1987) for the autobiographical poems *De Rebus Suis*, and *De Vita Sua* (FOTC 75) and to L.P. McCauley (1953 and 1968) for *Orations* 7, 8, 18 and 43 (FOTC 22). Peter Gilbert has produced some versions of interesting poems in his 1994 CUA Dissertation. I have also learned much from the excellent translation work of Carolinne White (1996) and Donald Sykes (1996). I hope they will all forgive me for having more often than not made my own emendations even when I based myself on them. At many other instances I have made my own version of the texts directly.

12 Cf. Noret (1983).

exact scholarship to resolve the many problems of corrupt passages, spurious attributions, and chronological sequencing.[13] The beginning of that work was disrupted by the Second World War, and with the scattering of the Polish scholars of the Cracow Academy, and the eventual execution of one of the leading lights of Gregorian research,[14] a monumental work was stalled, and took several more decades to resume its momentum.

Perhaps the greatest problem dogging Gregory's heels was the prevalence among European scholars of a scholastic mode of thought in theology. Theologians who approached Gregory in this fashion fundamentally misread his whole systematic intent, and in consequence distorted the theological edifice he was intent on building up. As Wordsworth had said:

> No officious slave
> Art Thou of that false secondary power
> By which we multiply distinctions, then
> Deem that our puny boundaries are things
> That we perceive, and not that we have made.
> To Thee, unblinded by these formal arts,
> The unity of all hath been revealed.[15]

And of no one was this more true than of Gregory. His ability to use Aristotelian distinctions and categories misled many. It was to take a generation after Bertrand, Daniélou, and Crouzel,[16] those who had first begun to realise the extent of the mystical substrate of the great Origen, to begin to appreciate, in a similar way, the importance of Gregory's symbolic imagination, and the subtlety of his rhetorical subtext. By scholasticisation, a great Christian conception of theological culture, that was at once social, ecclesial, and mystical, was often ruined with insensitive and inappropriate categorisations on the part of the commentators.

In the Orthodox world Gregory had always been regarded first and foremost as a theologian. That was usually understood to refer to his work on the foundations of classical Trinitarian orthodoxy.[17] In fact his influence was probably more pervasively felt in the paradigm of Christian Hellenism he bequeathed to nascent Byzantium. Byzantine Christianity, in a real sense, was Gregory's mind-child and masterpiece, partly by design, and partly by his transmission to later Byzantium as the last of the ancients and the first of their "moderns." He was the archetypal patron of the new Christian Byzantine culture that set out to clip the roses of Hellenism of their thorns,[18] and gather them in to

---

13 Werhahn's scholarship has been outstanding in this regard, so too that of Gallay, Bernardi, and Mossay, among others.
14 The story of Leo Sternbach's racial murder by the Nazis is told by Mossay (1970:2).
15 *The Prelude*, II.
16 J. Daniélou, *Origène,* (Paris, 1948); F. Bertrand, *Mystère de Jesus Chez Origène* (Paris, 1951); H. Crouzel, *Origène et la connaissance mystique* (Bruges/Paris, 1961).
17 His *Five Theological Orations* (Orats. 27-31) remain a central part of the basic theological curriculum in Eastern Orthodox schools of theology.
18 See Norris (1984); Beck (1977); Camelot (1966); Coman (1976); Fleury (1930); Guignet (1911);

decorate and color the form of a new world order. As the study of Byzantine theology itself begins, rightly, to take a place in the light, and demand a hearing on its own terms,[19] so too the time is right for a reassessment of this last of the Antique and the first of the Byzantine Christian theologians; and surely one of the finest.

After several excellent modern studies of Gregory's theology, style, and historical context,[20] this book has a lot to live up to. But its justification might be given in the fact that it is now more than fifty years since Gallay's standard critical *Vita* was first written,[21] and even though a new review of the Life has appeared recently in French, from Bernardi's hand,[22] there is still a pressing need for a critical introduction to the life and thought of Gregory in the English language. The desire to introduce Gregory to an audience larger than that comprised by devoted theological specialists alone, is a factor that has dictated the shape of the work and influenced the choice of form in terms of intellectual biography. It has also been of particular interest to use some literary deconstruction in the course of the present work. Twentieth century literary theory, aware of the complexities of text and subtext and their correlation with ranges of meaning, leaves the modern reader in a peculiarly "open" state to the letter, and this might help towards a contemporary reassessment of what this most subtle of ancient rhetoricians wanted to say through the craft of words.

Faithful to the tradition of Gregory, I have tried to present the text as discourse rather than doctrinal treatise. This is not to suggest it is not concerned with doctrinal and metaphysical matters, perhaps too concerned with these things for the tastes of many—yet these were the central passions of Gregory's life, and it is crucial to understand the theology if we are to hope for any insight into the theologian. And *vice versa*. Nonetheless, there are several excellent studies of the doctrinal controversies of the period already in existence, and several works that focus on precise aspects of the theological construct of our author.[23] The present work aims to offer a general view of the theology within the flow of the life. I have been very conscious of the complexity and refinement of the intellectual controversies prevalent during the late Arian period, but this work will attempt to deal with the theological arguments in such a way that the doctrine does not so much war against the history, rather that the biography becomes an approachable and living medium of intellectual analysis and speculation. Those who expect a theological analysis, will, I hope, find enough to satisfy them especially in the analysis of the Orations delivered in Constantinople between 379 and 381. This is dense and compact, and mirrors the manner in which Gregory engaged in syllogistic

---

Kennedy (1983); Kertsch (1978); and Trisoglio (1986).
19 See Ostrogorsky (1989), pp. 1-21.
20 Particularly Althaus (1972); Bernardi (1968); Gregg (1975); Ruether (1969); and Winslow (1979).
21 Gallay (1943).
22 Bernardi (1995). An interesting account but one that does not surpass Gallay.
23 For a general perspective, cf. Hanson (1988); and the bibliography to the present study should provide more than enough reading for anyone who wishes to advance into more detailed areas of Gregorian research.

battle with the Neo-Arians of his generation. It is as clear as I have been able to make it. Since he was first and foremost a theologian of the inner life of the Trinity, that does not mean clarity will always be hand in hand with comprehensibility. If others judge that in this work I have failed to present a sufficiently comprehensive account of the wider political and ecclesiastical condition of Gregory's world, it is perhaps partly because I have approached that world consistently through the lens of his own perception of it, as given in his own literary constructs. The focus here has been first and foremost on Gregory. There are innumerable other, good, surveys of the world of Late Antiquity, but precious little in respect to dedicated biography of Gregory Nazianzen; on his own terms, in his own right.

As was the case with Gregory, it falls to the craft of the writer to present the glimpsed theological vision through the alluring veil of persuasive words—the duty and art of the Rhetor-Philosopher. The choice of Intellectual Biography suggested itself as the best medium for a portrait of a theologian who regarded the inner land-scape of the self as the path to transcendent insight and earthly serenity. It might have been preferable to describe it as psychological biography, but the ancient term Psyche no longer bears the same fullness of range as once when it connoted the religious men-tality and intellectual form of a subject, and such a title might have raised expectations this book can only hope to fulfil in very small part. The intention of this introductory Biography was always that its own text should be self-explanatory, even if the reader will have to go elsewhere, on many occasions, for a more serious pursuit of many of the terms, issues, and controversies turned over in the course of our narrative. The complexities behind many of the arguments will be signalled, when necessary, in the footnotes, which should thus provide (in harmony with the extensive study bibliogra-phy which has been collated for this purpose) a fuller guide to all who wish to delve more deeply into matters that excite their interest. For the innumerable references to Gregory's text which are found in the footnotes, I have consistently used the Migne reference. This is by no means the best edition. There are now various critical editions of parts of the poetry, and most of the Orations can be found in good editions in vari-ous volumes of the SC series. They are, however, very scattered, and all the new critical editions have the common virtue of clearly correlating where in their text the corre-sponding Migne reference is. In short, from a PG reference anyone can locate quickly, and without difficulty, the relevant critical text from a number of better versions, although not every library will hold the complete editions that represent modern criti-cal versions of the Gregorian corpus, nor have all the Gregorian texts used in this work a critical edition other than Migne to which one can appeal. I have also been aware that this present study on Gregory may come to be of some interest and of some use in Eastern European faculties of theology and Orthodox seminaries, where the Migne system is perhaps the only available patristic source for primary materials. Simply to save duplication I have restricted myself, then, to the PG reference which is still the only total or comprehensive system of reference possible.

Biography was a choice of medium that Gregory himself would have approved, did approve, since he couched so much of his work in the genres of autobiography, historical panegyric, and poetry, not least that finely constructed argument that comprises his last and greatest work of theological autobiography, the poem *De Vita Sua*. This review and rehearsal of his whole life, from the perspective of the old man, was a text charged with apologetic intent, designed to present his defense in the aftermath of a humiliating political retirement that was forced upon him in Constantinople in 381. Along with several other autobiographical poems he composed, among which this is the most notable, it is the first ever exemplar of Christian autobiography[24] and one that, like Augustine's *Confessions*, has a doctrinal motive that is never far from the surface.

Along with his numerous Letters and Orations and other personal poetry, the *De Vita Sua* is a splendid resource for reconstituting Gregory's history, and one that gives some dimension and modelling to our modern picture of this fourth century aristocrat. Gregory is unlike any other early Christian father. His inner psychological life is intimately related to the intellectual journeys on which he embarked. Those journeys themselves are fascinating enough. He redesigned the face of Christian theology in his lifetime, and like many another master architect, deserves to be listened to again after innumerable years in which others have added to, ostensibly trying to "improve," his building.

The style with which those journeys are narrated is one of consummate rhetorical mastery. Gregory is an anxious, worried, personality making his way through a rough knockabout world. Much of the character of life in his day emerges time after time in the details of his writings: as for example the way he commended his mother to the admiration (and emulation) of his church congregation when he reminded them, with obvious awe and admiration, how she would never dream of spitting on the church floor during the liturgy. He was a too-sensitive soul, made and ruined at the same time by a privileged aristocratic upbringing. He is highly conscious of his own dignity and allied himself to the Christian cause at a time when most of the other bishops around him were far from models of serene spirituality. His ecclesiastical career took him to the heights and the depths of Christian life in Late Antiquity, and at the end of his life he retreated to a long retirement during which he collated and edited his papers, reviewed his achievements, and took some well-deserved consolation in the beauty of Greek letters; a beauty he had never renounced, unlike the unbalanced Jerome, for all his personal asceticism, but had pressed into new allegiance as servant of the Gospel message.

Trying to argue, throughout his life, that Christianity had a pressing obligation to address and refine its cultural impact, a duty to form and beautify the aesthetic character of the human race as much as the moral, Gregory sometimes felt like a voice in the wilderness; lost between those Christians who regarded culture as a bogeyword, whose faith was propped up by narrowness and bigotry, and those for whom Christianity was all too rapidly being transformed into a merely parallel

24 Cf. Courcelle (1957).

culture as bishops clamoured for more revenues for their sees, and power and venality seemed to win the day. His voice, however, was not really lost on the winds. After Rufinus' translation of the *Theological Orations*, Gregory was ever after regarded as a pillar of orthodox Trinitarian and Christological doctrine.

The Byzantine scholars, who ever loved Greek culture and strove to marry the best of Christian and Hellenic values, heard more of the tone-range of all that he had been trying to say, in their long reading of him through the Greek Middle Ages. In the factional fighting among students and devotees over the burning issue whether Gregory or Basil, or John Chrysostom deserved to be regarded as the finest of all Greek theologians, a compromise was finally imposed, by tired ecclesiastical authorities, that ordered all three to be celebrated and iconically depicted together, as the "Three Hierarchs."

The feast day is still observed in the East,[25] and Gregory thus remains a very popular and well-known saint of Orthodoxy. Of these three leading patristic saint-bishops the Byzantine tradition clearly regarded Gregory as the chief theological intellect of the entourage. The Byzantine liturgical texts for his own, separate, ecclesiastical feast,[26] hailed him as "the most exalted mind of theology" and the troparion, or liturgical poem, of his feast day still invokes him in these graceful terms:

> The shepherd's flute of your theology[27]
> drowned out the trumpets of the rhetoricians,
> For the gift of eloquence was graced to you,
> for searching out the deep things of the Spirit.
> Intercede for us, O Father Gregory,
> with Christ Our God,
> that He might save our souls.

The Byzantines, who could read him easily, and did so extensively, thus cherished his memory and gave him his rightful role as father of the Byzantine Christian oecumene, and a special title which is justly his, and by which he is most commonly known in the Orthodox world: St Gregory the Theologian.[28]

---

25 January 30.
26 January 25. (The Latin church celebrates him on May 9.)
27 Based on Gregory's own description of how he "brought a shepherd's pipe" to the defense of the orthodox at Constantinople; Carm. 2.1.19, v. 65, *Lament on his Calamities*, PG 37.1276.
28 P. Chrestou has advanced a thesis that it is a western bias to continue to call him Gregory Nazianzen, arguing that Gregory himself says that he never accepted the bishopric of the see of Nazianzus, his father's see, and that to ascribe him this episcopal title, rather than that of Constantinople, to which he was elected in 381, reproduces the bias of the Roman-led western Church, which in the fourth century contested his right to the throne of Constantinople. (Cf. Chrestou [1982], p. 366, reproduced by Papademetriou in GOTR 39, 1-2 [1994], pp. 5-6.) There is little in this conspiracy theory of any merit. Despite Gregory's claims late in life that he never was the bishop of Nazianzus (made because he wished to retire and the canons did not recognize the concept), the local hierarchs of Cappadocia clearly recognized that he held title to the church, not least as the resident episcopal occupant, the founder's heir, and main local landowner, and thus waited for him to nominate a successor from his own family: which he eventually did, thus acknowledging his title in passing it over.

I

IN SEARCH OF A SELF

Thence did I drink the visionary power
And deem not profitless those fleeting moods
Of shadowy exultation: not for this,
That they are kindred to our purer mind
And intellectual life, but that the soul
Remembering how she felt, but what she felt
Remembering not, retains an obscure sense
Of possible sublimity, whereto
With growing faculties she doth aspire.

Wordsworth

"My father was noble and honorable man, an old man...truly a second patriarch Abraham."[1]

When Gregory wrote those words he was himself an old man, in ill health, and recovering from a political debacle which had ruined him in the most humiliating fashion. In the great capital of Byzantium, within the space of a single year, he had been hailed by an influential part of the aristocracy as the hero and restorer of Christianity, and then at the very height of his honor, denounced and ridiculed as the silly old bumpkin whose incompetence had demonstrated his unfitness for office. He had even been ridiculed by mummers on the stage at Constantinople in a farce that had brought the house down with laughter.[2] Penning these opening lines to his autobiographical poem in retirement on his estates in Cappadocia was an exercise that soothed his spirit. He had returned home, to Karbala, his private estate. It was a place, and a condition of country squire, against which he had spent much time protesting, arguing over and again his need to flee familial ties and responsibilities in order to fulfil his life's higher calling, and yet it was both geographically and spiritually a domain of security from which he could never quite manage to stand free, and

---

1. *De Vita Sua*, 51, PG 37.1033. "Noble and honorable," translates *Kalokagathon*.
2. Orat. 2, *Apol. De Fuga*. 84, PG 35.489; cf. also Carmen *De Vita Sua*, 865, PG 37.1089; and Orat. 22.8, PG 35.1140. *Oration* 2 generally belongs to 362 but this section, which is full of strong words about bishops' machinations, the election of inexperienced persons, and a very fresh sense of personal injury, clearly relates to his time in Constantinople during 381. If, as seems to be the case, Gregory re-edited and collated his orations and letters in his time of retirement at Arianzum, after 381, then it is natural that he should have reworked his first "Oration after Flight" in the light of some of his experiences after this most recent "flight" from the capital. (Cf. J. McGuckin, "Autobiography as Apologia in St Gregory Nazianzen" in *Studia Patristica* [Acts of the 13th International Oxford Patristics Conference] M. Edwards [ed.] [Peeters: Leuven, 2001].)

I

perhaps never really wanted to. In the grief of his troubles in 382 it must have seemed to him that he had returned to his starting place, his own secure domains from which he could look out over his life, make sense of it, make out of it even a redoubtable statement of apologia to his enemies.

How significant it is that he starts with his father, and how revealing that even when he is an old man himself, his father stands before him archetypally as an older man still. Gregory the Elder never once appears as anything but an old man as far as his son is concerned. The relationship between the two is complex and interesting. Into the strange balance of affection, clan ties, and financial power, that constituted the father-son relationship in Roman Late Antiquity we must also add some peculiarly personal elements coloring Gregory Nazianzen's personality profoundly, and making of him a highly introspective, insecure, and sensitive child. When he came into the full brilliance of his intellectual powers, and was endowed with much of the stubbornness of intent that must have so characterized his father and the stern matriarch who was his mother, Nonna, then the potent mix of Gregory's greatness and fallibility was already formed. The early years on the Cappadocian estate near Arianzum,[3] probably a very extensive *Latifundium* (a hillside station, probably vineyards), explain much about the whole outcome of Gregory's later career. Two related factors are predominant, both of them succinctly stated in the opening sentence quoted at the head of the chapter: social class and family expectations.[4]

Behind his ostensibly dutiful filial statements about his father, and the undoubted admiration in which he held him,[5] the roar of some troubled waters can be heard. Although his writings at times surprise the modern reader by the honesty and freshness of the emotional passion they readily admit, on these matters of his relation to his father Gregory is like a seashell. Its secrets have to be prised from it after the deep swell of rhetoric has subsided.

3. The hillside estate near the village of Arianzum, 14 km S.W. of the town of Nazianzus was called Karbala (Ramsay in 1880 described it as a two-hour horse journey between Nazianzus and Karbala). For its location, cf. Ramsay (1890), p. 285; Gallay (1943), p. 16f and esp. Syzmusiak,(1972), pp. 545-548. Karbala is probably the contemporary village of Guzelyurt in Turkey, (pre-1922 Greek name: Gelvere), on the road between Urgup and Aksaray. It is a specially beautiful place overlooking the snow-clad twin peaks of the mountain Hasan Dagh. Nazianzus was Nenizi, now the village of Bekarlar, to the southwest of modern Aksaray, 100 km S.W. of Caesarea (itself now Kayseri). The site of ancient Nazianzus is today an agricultural plain marked by a tumulus and a Seljuk tomb (octagonal in shape just as the original church there once was) about 1.5 km east of Bekarlar itself. Seven km south and higher up the hillside from Guzelyurt, over a dividing ridge, is the ancient settlement of Arianzum (Sivrihisar).

4. See Kopecek (1973), (1974).

5. Gregory had a deep affection for the old man, and regarded him, genuinely, as "a great man"; this much shines through the moving funeral oration he composed on his account in 374: Orat. 18, PG 35.985f. His most revealing remark, however, is to pinpoint as the most characteristic element of him "his simplicity, and freedom from guile and resentment" (Orat. 18.24, PG 35.1013).

Gregory was one of three children from his parents' marriage. He was born as the second child, but firstborn son, when his parents were in their late middle age, and this would have been in 329 or 330, at the beginning of his father's episcopal career. He remarks on the lateness of his birth, reproducing what was possibly his mother's self-description as a "Sarah" producing progeny beyond expectation. He had an elder sister, Gorgonia, whom he admired, and a slightly younger brother, Caesarios, to whom he was devoted. Both his parents represented the curial class in the Roman province of Cappadocia Secunda. Both clans were comfortably rich.

The marriage caused an immediate clash of interest, for relatives on Gregory's maternal side were longstanding Christians, but his father was an adherent of an obscure sect called the Hypsistarians,[6] not Christian but observing a monist theology of the One supreme God, and following certain Jewish practices in worship and observance. The use of lights and the centrality of fire in their liturgy suggests Persian influence. The ethic of the sect was probably based on the Jewish scriptures, which they accepted. Gregory's mother's family had little objection to her marriage into this circle, but it was not an attitude which was shared on the other side. Marriage into a Christian alliance caused a great rift here, and initially Gregory the Elder was disowned.[7] That he nonetheless pressed ahead with his plans to marry his Christian wife, despite the prospect of being rendered penniless, suggests that while the Christian clan might have been regarded as nouveaux arrivés, they nonetheless possessed sufficient wealth of their own so as not to care. What both clans shared in common, however, was a desire to see the next generation rise from the provincial base to secure high positions in the social hierarchy.

In this case the parental aspirations were successful—all three children of Gregory and Nonna achieved social eminence along different tracks. Gregory, the eldest son, was to make his mark as a man of letters, and achieve international fame in the church as a theologian hierarch. He would never, himself, have cared to define his significance simply in terms of his office as a bishop, for his ecclesiastical career had been too patchy for that, and in any case he clearly regarded the class of episcopate with some scorn. He was an aristocrat to his fingertips and there were simply too many illiterates and dubious characters entering the ranks of the troubled Christian hierarchy in the late fourth century to make the office, as yet, an undisputed mark of

---

6. A mixture of pagan mythology and Jewish observances. Cf. Orat. 18.5, PG 35.989-992. Gregory of Nyssa also speaks of the sect. Cf. G. Bareille. "Hypsistariens," DTC 7.1. 572. Their origin is probably from the *Sebomenoi:* the righteous worshippers—i.e., some kind of Jewish proselyte groups, who continued independently of formal Christian control to merge biblical monotheism with "gentile" worship practices.

7. Gregory the Elder subsequently inherited all his family's wealth, and was obviously forgiven, but there are signs that the rift between the womenfolk of the two clans was not healed, as the younger Gregory states (with some admiration) that his mother refused, all her life, to eat with pagans or have them in her home.

social eminence. A generation after him this might have been the case, but Gregory feels that he bestows honor on the office rather than vice versa.

For him, his eminence is to be expressed by refusing involvement in public service, partly as a result of his ascetical philosophy, something akin to the nascent monastic movement of his time, and partly as a result of a longstanding aristocratic tradition of self-distancing from the *hoi polloi*. Often he has a barely concealed disdain for Christian hierarchs whom he generally regards as his social inferiors.[8] He is at his ease most in communicating with the chief provincial magistrates, and Urban Prefects in Byzantium, acting as *Patronus* and intercessor, in the traditional manner of the Roman gentleman.[9]

As for his younger brother Caesarios, he became an eminent physician at Constantinople, and entered into the ranks of the Emperor's confidants before Julian's anti-Christian policy made it wise for him to withdraw. After Julian's death he remade a brilliant political career and was Imperial Treasurer of Bithynia when he was brought to an untimely death.[10] His residual estate was so considerable that it was an object of rapid pillage by his creditors and domestics, but Gregory secured enough of it to make generous settlements on his surviving relatives when eventually making his own bequests.[11]

His elder sister Gorgonia made a powerful marriage into a high-ranking Christian military family. Like her mother, converting the elder Gregory to Christianity, she herself brought over her husband Alypios,[12] a senior officer and curial official, to her way of Christian asceticism.[13] Their villa at Ikonium, near her aunt's estate there

---

8.   Cf. Orat. 2.8; *Carmen de seipso et episcopis* 2.1.12, vv. 154-192, PG 37.1166-1227.
9.   E.g., Epp. 10, 29, 37, among others.
10. Orat. 7.6-10, 15, PG 35.761-768, 773.
11. Cf. Ep. 29. *To the Prefect of Constantinople*, PG 37.64-65; Gallay (1964), p. 35.
12. Alypios as Gorgonia's husband: cf. *Epitaph* 24, PG 38.22. There are several Alypii mentioned in Gregory's correspondence, and there has been some degree of confusion over the identities of them all. This argument presupposes that Gorgonia and her husband Alypios were the recipients of Ep. 86 of Gregory, PG 37.157-160. Hauser-Meury (1960) is perhaps too cautious in dividing the Alypii into five distinct personages, as only three distinctions are needed: (a) a former Prefect of Constantinople, husband of one Simpliciana (Epp. 207-208). He is (obviously) dead at the time Gregory writes to his widow; (b) an Alypios who has a brother Aerios, to whom Gregory writes in connection with a legacy he expects (Ep. 61); and (c) Alypios who is the recipient of Epp. 82-86. This is a member of the curial class with whom Gregory has a close relationship, and from whom he feels he can expect services. References in Ep. 86 to "the sister" have often been taken to refer to some unknown sister of Alypios, and thus commentators have not thought to identify him as Gregory's brother-in-law. Information given to us from Gregory's funeral oration over Gorgonia can explain the designation, however, and suggests that it was Gorgonia herself to whom Gregory was referring.
13. Orat. 8.8; 8.20-21, PG 35.797. In the Oration the husband is given an identity only in relation to Gorgonia as a Christian ascetic. Gregory is suggesting that in converting him to asceticism, she made him a person. This parallels much of what he says in terms of his own father's relationship with his mother: "If you wish me to describe him briefly, let me say that he was her husband, for I know not what further need be added" (Orat. 8.20, PG 35.813).

(the city which was eventually the important see of their cousin Amphilokios), was an opulent one from which she was able to act as a liberal patron.[14]

The women of the Christian clans of Cappadocia seemed almost like a new breed—powerful as matriarchs, yet adding a decidedly new twist to that power base, for in their radical espousing of the principle that "there is no longer male nor female in Christ,"[15] they passed over psychological and social barriers that still contained their pagan sisters within the social mores of an immensely strong patriarchy. This was not merely the patriarchal *tendenz* of the Late Roman Empire (for it had already demonstrated how powerful the matriarch could be in her own right) but that familial system as lived out in the more orientalized provincialism of Cappadocia.

In this context it is the generation of Gregory's grandmother,[16] mother and sister, as well as Basil's extraordinary female relatives,[17] which gives us an extraordinary picture of a strong sense of feminine identity rooted both in the power base of marriage and that of dedicated virginity. Of his mother's unremitting influence over his father, to bring him eventually into a profession of Christianity which his own family opposed so violently, Gregory says:

> She prostrated herself night and day before God, and begged him with much fasting and weeping, that he would save her "head." She zealously devoted herself to her husband and strove to win him over by a variety of methods; by reproaches, admonitions, blandishments, estrangements, and most of all by her own character and the example of her fervent piety, for this is the supreme way in which another soul can be swayed and softened, and willingly constrained to virtue. It was inevitable that the drop of water inexorably striking the rock, should hollow out the stone.[18]

His sister Gorgonia had evidently learned from a capable mistress, and within a short time had similarly redressed the unequal scales of gender expectation in her marriage to the soldier Alypios:

> Although she was linked in carnal union, she was not thereby separated from the spirit. She did not ignore her first Head simply because she had a husband as head. For when she had served the world and nature for a little, to the extent that the law of the flesh willed it (or rather as He who imposed the law on the flesh willed it), she consecrated herself wholly to God. And what is more excellent and honorable, she also won over her husband and gained, instead of an unreasonable master, a good fellow servant.[19]

14. Orat. 8.12 ("an incredible generosity of attitude," Orat. 8.13), PG 35.801-804.
15. Gal 3:28.
16. Gorgonia the Elder, mother of his uncle Amphilokios and his own mother Nonna, was eventually the mother-in-law of one bishop, and the grandmother of two others.
17. Not least Macrina who brought up and taught (*Adelphe kai didaskalos*) her three brothers, Basil, Gregory of Nyssa, and Peter of Sebaste, and initiated them into the monastic lifestyle. Gregory Nyssa's *Life of Macrina* gives some information about her. As for Basil, nowhere in his voluminous writings does he give the slightest indication of, or acknowledgement to, her influence. Cf. S. Elm, *Virgins of God* (1994).
18. Orat. 18.11, PG 37.997.
19. Orat. 8.8, PG 35.797

In turn, her own daughter, Alypiana, was an eloquent testimony to the influence of her mistress and mother and in trumpeting it abroad and championing the notion of female spiritual and mental equality, Gregory was intending to let it stand as an instruction to future generations of Christian women, who might thereby populate the land with a new kind of progeny of their own education. Alypiana was a favorite niece of Gregory's, and later her son Nicobulos was to be his pupil, his heir and the final editor of his literary opus. Shortly after her marriage her husband Nicobulos the elder wrote, with some humor, to complain how his "little wife" was not strong enough to enjoy his vigorous country pursuits. Gregory replies, in turn, that though she is no match for him in physical stature there is something Nicobulos has left out of the picture:

> But why don't you mention how she is almost planted in the earth because of the force of her prayers, or how she stands always with God in the great flights of her mind. And then where does your greater physical height come into it? Take note when she knows to be silent, but when she speaks always listen to her. Observe her scorn for feminine adornments, and what virile force[20] this woman has. See how she loves her husband and manages the household, then surely you will be forced to admit the point of the Laconian saying: In truth the soul cannot be measured, for the exterior person ought to be judged from what is within.[21]

The impact of these women ought not to be underestimated either on the male children they formed and brought up, or on the husbands they guided, sometimes pushed, into the adoption of Christianity.[22] The significance of the Anima in Gregory Nazianzen's character is marked and, for better and worse, determined the subsequent course of his life.[23] He was always happier away from disputes, seeking gentle companions who affirmed and looked after him and, in a sense, figures who made his decisions for him. A noted aspect of this prioritization of the Anima was not least his lifelong dedication to virginity. Gregory loved to identify himself with his mother, over and against his father, as one of those who were born to Christianity as

---

20. *Andrikon.* see G. Cloke, *This Female Man of God* (London, 1995).
21. Ep. 12.5-6, PG 37.44-45; Gallay (1964), p. 19.
22. Marriage and sexual politics can be a powerful implement of control. Gregory the Elder's ability to produce children materializes only after his agreement to convert to Christianity. The dream which forms the ostensible "opening" to his readiness to change his ancestral patrimony in favor of that of his wife is one in which he hears the psalms being sung (a feature of the worship of his own sect) but which is "properly interpreted" for him by his Christian wife.
23. He more than once describes himself in feminine terms, as when he sends on his nephews to the Rhetor Libanios (Ep. 236, PG 35.380) characterizing himself as "mother" to the latter as "father": "I, their mother, send these children to you their father. I am a mother in terms of nature, while you are a father in terms of eloquence. Look after them as I have looked after them." When he reminds Philagrios of how close they were as students together he learnedly says how they "shared a loving discourse, as Homer puts it." By such a reference to the *Iliad* he characterizes himself in the *persona* of Helen. (*Iliad* 3.175; Greg. Ep. 30, PG 35.65-68; Gallay (1964), pp. 37-38.)

distinct from those who were converted to it. Among these strong women Gregory was brought up to value an aristocracy of the spirit that flowed in the female line and owed no symbolic spiritual allegiance, or subservience, to the male seed.

It was class rank, based on the wealth of the estates in Cappadocia run by slaves and familial serfs, that was the platform for such clan success. The family does not seem to have had a long and ancient lineage, and Gregory seems almost to delight in making this known at his father's funeral, for it underlines his general theme that his father's real nobility derived from his wife. But this also suggests a clue to their financial success in so far as they obviously did not have to manage old estates through the bad times of the economic collapse of the previous century. In the lifetime of Gregory the military situation on the Danube border was signaling clearer and clearer troubles to come for the Imperial government. It was a fraught climate that boded well for Cappadocia as one of the more secure satellite zones of Byzantium. Providing (as it did) high-quality horses for the imperial cavalry was a good trade to make in such insecure times.[24] But if wealth was the necessary platform for eminence, it was education, and in particular rhetorical flair, that was the real key to advancement, and indispensable for anyone who wished to rise out of the ring of provincial magistracies and local responsibilities that were expected of the curial class, to follow a career at the center, in the great cities and especially around the imperial court. Throughout their mature lives both of Gregory and Nonna's male children had their eyes set on the glittering lights of the capital city, Caesarios more overtly, but Gregory also, and it was their successes in the capital that were used, despite Gregory's deprecating protestations, as the touchstone of their careers in the funeral encomia and autobiographical poems that Gregory composed in his later years.

The parents of children from such a class were ready to invest substantially in their offspring's education. As it turned out in the case of the rising Christian clans of Cappadocia, at Nazianzus and Ikonium and Caesarea, their aspirations were remarkably successful. In one generation they produced a school of Cappadocian ascetics and thinkers (rooted in families and allied by clan): Gregory Nazianzen, Basil of Caesarea, Gregory Nyssa, Peter of Sebaste, Amphilokios of Ikonium, Macrina, Theosevia, Gorgonia, Alypiana, Nicobulos, Eulalios; the like of which had not been seen for a hundred years in that province,[25] and would not be seen again. Here was a case where the second generation felt itself ready to move beyond the first, and even though this was seen as a familial success, it was also the cause of no little friction. Both Amphilokios the Elder and Gregory's father resisted their sons' attempts to make an independent life. Basil was spared the problem, and thereby given a much freer hand, by the early death of his father, and the ability to employ

24. Orat. 43, PG 36.497.
25. The memory of Gregory Thaumaturgos, the great disciple of Origen, was vivid in the area. Through Macrina the Elder (Basil's grandmother), who was his disciple, there was a direct familial connection by personal memory.

the finances fluidly. Gregory, for example, held his uncle Amphilokios in high esteem. Certainly he regarded him as considerably more intelligent than his own father and was ever grateful to him for having given him his first instruction in literature,[26] but he has no qualms in wanting it to be graven on his uncle's tombstone that: "he left behind sons who were more eminent than their parents."[27] He had roused the old man's fury by encouraging the younger Amphilokios to make the break from public life and adopt celibacy and a life of ecclesiastical service in the episcopate.[28] It was a public breach with parental expectation he could never quite manage to make for himself, for his advice to his cousin comes in the aftermath of his own father's death, and his ability finally to control the estate.

Gregory clearly loved his father dearly. The very moving tributes which he offers at his father's funeral[29] are not merely conventional. He depended on his father more than he would have cared to admit, and wanted his father's strong and commanding personality to remove all the obstacles from his own life's path, yet he fretted constantly at the imposition of that authority. He wanted to live in a safe dependence, but not in the shadow, and was thus like the eternal dependent; but he could not understand why that relationship exasperated his father so much and at times made the latter determined to interfere in his son's life to the extent of providing him with gainful employment. Equally, perhaps, Gregory's need for his father emanated from a relationship in which he had been much ordered about and much directed, for such is the kind of upbringing that causes great dependency of character, and in Gregory's case that amounted to an almost pathological anxiety and submissiveness. He often speaks of the kindness of his father, but there are other times when he talks of how his notable characteristic was the way in which his temper would blow over in a minute and all his towering rage would be forgotten almost as soon as it had appeared.[30] On another occasion, he exemplified his father's mildness by reminding the townspeople how, unlike other local magistrates, he did not so much use the rack and lash as threaten it to produce a change of behavior, and settled instead for a simple "boxing of the ears" of offenders.[31] In terms of the normal standards of the Late Empire, this was indeed an extraordinary affability, but there is sufficient evidence to suggest that psychologically his father's personality worried and dominated that of his nervous son.

For all his filial affection, and for all his fear of his father's authority, it is also abundantly clear, even though he couches it in words of some sophistication, that he

26. *Epitaph* 104.10-11, PG 38.65.
27. *Epitaph* 103.5-6, PG 38. 64.
28. Ep. 63. PG 37.124-125; Gallay (1964), pp. 81-83.
29. Orat. 18.21, 25, and 26, PG 35.1008-1017.
30. Orat. 18.21; 18.25-26; the local population were in fear of his priestly "imprecations" and Gregory attributes to them recalcitrant villagers' troubles with fevers, violent animals, and dark oppressive dreams. Orat. 18.26, PG 35.1017.
31. Orat. 18.25, PG 35.1016.

knew himself to be superior and resented that parental influence considerably. Behind and beneath his reverence and affection there are some darker currents running. The paternal influence over Gregory was so formative that perhaps even his most personal decisions to depart from the parental plan partly testify to his continuing thrall—not least his decision to adopt the celibate life of the philosopher, a blatant rejection of bloodline ties and a permanent rebuff to his father's aspirations for a lineage that would continue the familial power base.

Gregory's descriptions of his father survive in several funeral panegyrics for various members of his family and in the long autobiographical poem he composed at the end of his career in Constantinople. Often the remarks have been taken at face value—the dutiful son lamenting his father. There is undoubtedly that element present, but it should not blind us to another motif that is carefully crafted into the rhetoric, a current of antagonism and resentment never far absent. But why does this matter? Or is it merely a commonplace of human relations between sons and fathers that devotion and competition so disport themselves? The significance might become more apparent later, but it is worthy of note at the outset that Gregory made it his theological life's work to stand against the theological monism which had been his father's ancestral tradition. He defends his mother's Christological tradition. Moreover, in his opposition to Arianism (that major theological conflict which forms the context of his whole life's work) he argues passionately that the Son's relation to the Father is not one of power over inferiority, but ought to be conceived as a freedom based on mutual love. He describes the Son of God as the one who proclaims and interprets the Father's silence. He was more than aware that, on several occasions, not least the famous *Oration* 16,[32] he had to speak up in the face of his own father's theological "economy" of words. His Trinitarian doctrine insists that the Son is not inferior to the Father solely because he is caused by the Father and that the "coming after" the Father cannot be taken as an excuse for the former's superiority of status. His is a doctrine that teaches the full co-equal glory of the Son, in the face of hierarchical conceptions of paternal dignity and power. These were radical notions running counter to received opinion of the day, and what many felt to be the obvious "inner meaning" of the very terms of the Christian vocabulary. That this series of bold and fundamental conceptions at the heart of Gregory's theology, conceptions that made of his Christological and Trinitarian system the standard orthodoxy of subsequent Christianity, are so intimately related to his notion of a father's relation to his son, is of no small significance. The fact that, in the late Platonic manner, Gregory also regarded psychological introspection as a primary theological

---

32. Orat. 16, *On His Father's Silence*, PG 35.933f. The father's bungling of his relationship with the local monks, a dispute centered on his inadvertent support of the Arian cause (at least insofar as this was interpreted by the fiercely Nicene monks of the locality), was another occasion Gregory liked to cite as evidence of how his father was dependent on him (Orat. 6, *De Pace*, PG 35.721f. See also Orat. 18.35, PG 35.1032).

method (the soul as the mirror of the deity, and its scrutiny as a sure way to discern the still visible imprints of the Creator's touch), also makes his own experiences highly pertinent to his theological construct.

A further point, worthy of note in this regard, which shall be elaborated subsequently, is that Gregory's theological method was particularly characterized by a form of intellectual ambivalence: the holding of apparent opposites in creative tension.[33] This aspect of antithetical method was a recognized form of Hellenistic rhetorical philosophy,[34] and one which Gregory had learned to good effect in his time in Athens, but not since the time of Origen had any Christian intellectual so successfully combined philosophical method with theological speculation, thus rehabilitating his Alexandrian hero's vision of Christianity, and providing a paradigm for the whole future development of the Byzantine church.

In Gregory's hands, antithetical method became a distinctive and original theological style, one in which he worked out large vistas of his doctrine of God, and Christ, and which he used to heal the fractured state of the tradition of Christian theology as it reached him in the twilight of the long Arian conflict. In this method Gregory was not forced to choose an "either-or," he could adopt the "both-and" with sufficient qualifications.

This "creative ambivalence" of his methodology, which was so much a part of his theological genius, provided that essential bond which made it intellectually possible to align the Semitic imagery of the Scriptures with Hellenistic logical process and to forge a genuine Christian Hellenism that could now bring systematic order to a fecund but sprawling biblical theology, yet also avoid the suppression of symbol and mystical insight under the tyranny of logical deduction (a sad outcome that all too often results when theology is monopolized by systematics). In this role as a great bridge-builder between the Semitic and Hellenistic worlds of discourse, Gregory Nazianzen revealed himself as the true heir and successor of Origen of Alexandria. The ambivalence and tentative nature of his personal character: decisive insight and passionate, urgent responses, yet along with this, tortured vacillations and the fine making of distinctions, all prepared and exactly fitted him for his role as intellectual midwife.

This personal ambivalence, it could be argued, is largely the result of his relationship with his father. If we consider those texts where that relationship is in question we can see something of that psychological ambivalence on display. The orations are exquisitely crafted pieces of literature and here, perhaps, it is his subtleties that speak as loud as his overt statements. When his words move the listener by a direct appeal to the emotions it is not a raw sensibility that the orator wishes to touch, it is rather an emotional solidarity in sympathy with the speaker, as evoked by the highest level

33. For a study of this method, cf. Norris (1991); Focken (1912); Tsames (1969).
34. Cf. Lloyd (1966), pp. 15-171; Kennedy (1963), pp. 33-34, 64-66; Norden (1898), pp. 16-23.

of literary art. It is the abstraction and artistic metamorphosis of sorrow into poetry—a life lived as an art, which was Gregory's instinctive aesthetization of all his experiences. This surely means that while the emotional feelings are nonetheless genuine, the implicit critique that lies never far behind his words is all the more consciously deliberated.

To begin at the end, we can see some of these motives at work in the great funeral panegyric he delivered at his father's obsequies in 374. One of the ways of scrutinizing Gregory's coded way of describing his relation to his father is to isolate the biblical references he uses. Instead of having to deduce psychological results from general attitudes, we can instead penetrate more directly to the heart of his compositional style, his rhetorical methodology, where learned allusions form the subtext of the message he wishes his hearers to recognize—to the degree to which their own intellectual finesse allows them to recognize the allegorical truth clothed in the material form of the outward letters. Looking at these texts we should follow the invitation which Gregory is delivering to us, to penetrate beneath the surface level of words, the material form, and discover the "spiritual meaning" where the orator's mind, his deeper self, lies partly revealed before us.

All the biblical references to his father are fashioned on this level of double signification. Some are obvious, as for example the categorization of the Elder Gregory as: "the man who discovered a valiant woman."[35] The wise man of the Old Testament proverb is an ostensible praise of his father which serves, in fact, to subordinate the paternal position to that of the maternal, to define his father's worth in the fact that he was directed by his wife's superior stature.[36] This is a regular refrain of Gregory's. In this oration he dwells on how Nonna was the administrator of the estate in terms of Christian largesse. This should not be taken to suggest that she had control of the legal and fiscal aspects of the estate, which surely must have remained in the Elder Gregory's competent hands,[37] rather that she administered those aspects which the younger Gregory regarded as having abiding significance—the employment of the family's social power and wealth for the purposes of advancing the influence of the Church:

> Although their wealth and readiness to bestow it were shared equally by himself and his spouse, for they rivaled each other in striving after excellence, still for the most part he left the function of dispensing it in her hands, for he believed her to be the best and most faithful steward of such matters.[38]

35. Prov 31:10.
36. Cf. Orat. 18.8, PG 35.993.
37. From what Gregory tells us his father rose to high civic rank, and was local magistrate. Gregory gives enough indications that his father was more than competent in civil and financial affairs, to make any suggestion that he relied on his wife's business sense an unnecessary premiss. Cf. Orat. 18.6, and 18.25, PG 35.992, 1013-1016.
38. Orat. 18.21, PG 35.1009.

In the story of the advancing Christianisation of the empire in the fourth century, this has a greater significance than merely the distribution of charitable largesse by a rich household, for it was by controlling legacies and re-employing landed wealth in active areas of social involvement that the young Christian movement was to consolidate its power base. That movement was already underway before the persecutions of the Diocletianic era, which were, perhaps, more interested in confiscating and neutralizing organized Christian ownership of property than in any making of ideological martyrs.

In the Constantinian settlement the permission given to the Church to inherit estates, to enjoy significant tax exemptions, and to hold and dispense property as a corporate body, were chief factors in allowing the Christians a burgeoning of influence throughout the fourth century. In his own lifetime, by the means of dedicated celibacy, the younger Gregory was able to direct the cash flow away from the self-perpetuating circuit of the estate, away even from family responsibilities, to the Church's use. While he was alive he was able to enjoy and control the distribution of that wealth, in a very welcome condition of tax exemption, as a cleric.[39] Upon this fact his social and ecclesiastical career was founded.

There was no doubt about it; he was a very wealthy and influential man. After his death the estate was passed to the Church's corporate use, after a few familial bequests had been distributed. The financial terms of this Constantinian settlement encouraged celibate commitment among the rich curial classes of the provinces, for the political and personal freedoms it offered. Just as Augustus found he had to penalise the rich Roman aristocracy who refused to marry, so even Christian emperors later had cause to regret the generosity of the primitive settlement and to seek to curtail the right of clerics to avoid curial duties and tax impositions.[40]

At the time of Gregory the possibilities of that freedom were being first explored, and Christian women, particularly of the higher rank, were not slow to seize on the opportunities that widowhood and dedicated virginity could now offer. Within a Christian context, it was now possible to secure personal freedoms hitherto undreamt of. Melania's religious foundation in Jerusalem, and that of Jerome at Bethlehem (built as it was on the wealth of the Roman ladies Paula and Eustochium) are examples of how a redirection of personal wealth, formerly tied in to familial estates, could create a very public and exciting establishment of a Christian presence.[41]

This meant that for Gregory almsgiving was far more than the effete notion of occasional donations to the needy which the word suggests today. One needs to remember how remarkable were the inequities of wealth distribution in the ancient world, and thus to what extent the poor relied on the vastly wealthy landowners who

39. Constantius exempted clergy from all supplementary taxes and levies in 346.
40. See Jones (1986), pp. 96, 894-904 and passim; also Kopecek (1973) and ibid. (1974).
41. For a wider context see: G. Cloke, *This Female Man of God* (London, 1995).

controlled production. For a new religion, such as Christianity, to emphasise the interdependence of the rich and the poor, and to insist (contrary to common religious presuppositions of the time) that the poor were an object of keen interest to the Deity, ensured its political ascendancy. In Gregory's thought the care of the poor is a privilege laid upon Christians which serves to conform them to the Deity[42] a major element in his favorite conception of the Christ-life which he designated as Theosis—the transfiguration into the divine life, of which celibacy, the personal asceticism of a simplified lifestyle, and above all scholarly seclusion (the formation of the human *Nous*), both formed essential parts.

So, when Gregory describes his mother as taking over this element of the estate's finances, it carries a significance beyond the conventional notion of the rich wife dispensing occasional benefactions. Nonetheless, on the smaller and more personal scale, the motif of his frequent subjugation of his father to his mother is clearly present here. If this reference to his father as the wise man who chose the valiant woman is a fairly obvious example of such sub-textuality, there are many other instances where his subtlety is more impressive. At a key moment in his father's funeral oration, for example, Gregory describes how the bishop had first been baptized, and seemed to shine with a wonderful radiance:

> As he came forth from the waters a light shone round him and a glory worthy of the disposition with which he had approached the grace of faith.[43]

This deliberately evokes the simile of his father as a "new Moses," coming from his encounter with God with a face radiant in illumined glory. But for all its ostensible praise, in comparing him to a great patriarch, the subtext of the simile has dark shadows. The attentive reader is aware, for example, that Paul had undermined the image profoundly in 2 Cor 3. There the Apostle tells his readers that the letter kills while the spirit gives life, a text that was fundamental to the whole of Gregory's method of biblical exegesis in the Origenian manner. It is also argued there that the glory of Moses is as nothing before the glory and freedom given to those who have the spirit of the Lord. When Gregory depicts his father as Moses, he is subconsciously portraying himself as a new apostle. Similarly, for Moses is a term which he likes to attribute to his father, he and the reader that knows the text are well aware that Moses was halting in speech and needed to rely on Aaron, the High Priest, to speak for him. The Moses simile, then, carries with it an allusion to Gregory's rhetorical power, the priest who could speak and fashion discourses beyond the range of the stern patriarch.

In 373, on the occasion when the long-awaited harvest at Nazianzus had been destroyed by hail, the elder Gregory was faced with distraught and angry villagers who wanted to know why God had allowed such a disaster to visit them. On that

---

42. See Queré-Jaulmes (1966).
43. Orat. 18.13, PG 35.1001.

occasion the old man was reduced to a depressed silence and Gregory had to rescue the situation both by preaching an oration in the church to explain the disaster theologically for them, and by interceding for his region with the imperial authorities to defer tax imposts. Old Moses had faltered and the silver-tongued Aaron carried the day triumphantly.[44]

Gregory particularly liked to describe himself, often explicitly, as a new Aaron or Samuel. In the autobiographical poem he even puts it into his father's mouth to designate him as such in an imaginary dialogue where he has his father begging his son to return to help him in his church duties. All this is done in a way that leaves us in no doubt as to the superiority of the son over the old man. The whole narrative, of course, represents Gregory's perception of events in a highly stylized way. On other occasions when he is being less craft-conscious Gregory describes the same event in very different terms—as an irresistibly forceful demand from his father, which he resented but was unable to refuse. In this instance, the mental delight the son takes in being "needed" by the old man is all the more remarkable when one considers it is a literary product of Gregory's own advanced age, written more than eight years after his father's death. The prevalent idea of the son as being subject to the father under law is gainsaid here by the context Gregory creates for his imagined dialogue—the figure of the desperate suppliant who in this instance almost (and Gregory introduces that idea by a clever use of a negative suggestion) seems to stand in fiscal need before his heir. In addition the images of Samuel and Aaron, applied to himself, are used as powerful subversive symbols, for both became independently powerful of their patrons (the patriarch Moses, and the old High Priest Eli) along the paths of priesthood and prophecy:

> He entreated me with outstretched hands[45] and touched my beard, with words to this effect: Dearest of sons, your father implores you. The aged father turns to the young man, the master to the servant, servant by nature, and by double law.[46] My child I am not asking you for gold or silver, or precious stones, or estates, or any material goods. I am asking you to set yourself beside Aaron and Samuel.[47]

44. Orat. 16, PG 35.933f.
45. In the *De Vita Sua*, Gregory sets this speech in the context of his refusal to take up episcopal duties at Sasima (PG 37.1055, vv. 371-372). There it stands as a welcome excuse for him to flee trouble and return as assistant bishop to Nazianzus. Historically I think it is a reminiscence of his father's insistence that he be ordained priest as his assistant in 361 (and eventual successor), which Gregory relocates in his customary manner of refuting or appealing to the paternal request as it suited his needs at times of various crisis. It is this demand of his father's which he cites to Basil as the reason (in 359) why he cannot come and live with him in the monastery at Annesoi (cf. Ep. 8.2, PG 37.36; Gallay [1964], p. 11), though he professes he wants to be in Basil's company more than anything else.
46. The "natural law" which made a son "subject to" a father; and the law of inheritance which made the son similarly subject. Gregory is implicitly opposing a concept of "spiritual law" (his right to follow a God-given calling) to the material conception of authority his father is applying.
47. I.e., take over priestly duties alongside him in the church at Nazianzus. *De Vita Sua*, vv. 500-509, PG 37.1063-1064.

"Samuel," however, was above all else, a self-designation that Gregory learned to apply from his mother, who must have told him often about her dream before he was born, when it appeared to her that she was a new Hannah and her unborn child was destined to be a second Samuel. This was a dream that took on the role of a foundational element of Gregory's self-perception, and to which he returns frequently.[48] The subtext of that dream, especially for Gregory, is equally indicative. For the third notable character in the Hannah story, when the mother wishes to dedicate her child to the Lord, is the rather dim and aged priest Eli.[49] When the young Samuel grows up in the service of Eli, in God's house, the contrast between the young prophet who can hear and recognize the voice of God, and the jaded hierarch who represents a past that needs to be superseded, is a marked aspect of the biblical narrative.[50] The relevance to Gregory's domestic situation is obvious.

For all Gregory's rendering of the story to suggest that his father's request was that of a poor old man whom no one with any pity could refuse, the sterner reality peeps through, not least later in this same text when Gregory tells the reader how his father warned him that if he did not obey the summons he would be disowned on the deathbed:

Let me have this favor, or let some other hand lay me in the grave. That is the punishment I determine if you disobey.[51]

And he concludes:

And so, parental fear won the day, and brought me back.

Elsewhere he admits that he feared his father's curse if he did not obey,[52] but the financial implication of a refusal would have been ruination, and Gregory's desire to pursue the monastic life certainly did not involve any option for penury. His decision to take up ecclesiastical duties as coadjutor to his father was more a result of compulsion than he could bring himself to admit, even years later. For his father it was a perceived triumph. If his son had set his face against the continuation of the dynasty by and through the administration of the *Latifundium*, and was using the Church as his excuse for such an aversion of dynastic expectations, then the old man would use the very avenue of church duties to ensure Gregory's submission: forcing him to administer the church at Nazianzus which he himself had built, and which he regarded as an extension of the family *Latifundium*.

Gregory says, in retrospect, that he only agreed to help out his father because the estate had to be administered, both his parents were in extreme old age, and he was

48. *De Vita Sua*, vv. 69-81, PG 37.1034-1035; *De Vita Sua*, vv. 90-94, PG 37.1036; *De Rebus Suis*, vv. 424-466, PG 37.1001-1005.
49. 1 Sam 1:9-16.
50. 1 Sam 3.
51. *De Vita Sua*, v. 515, PG 37.1065.
52. *De Vita Sua*, v. 364, PG 37.1054. He tells in the *Funeral Panegyric* how his father's priestly curses were feared in the whole Nazianzus region (Orat. 18.26, PG 35.1016-1017).

the only surviving child of the family.[53] Put this way he explains why it is that he spent almost all his mature career at home, while ever protesting this was not his intention. The truth is, however, that he is here describing the situation only as it applied from 370-374. He is thereby disingenuously glossing over the point that he was under his father's thumb, despite all his protests, for the whole of the time his father was alive,[54] and not just from 370 onwards.

The manipulative power that the father exercised over Gregory was rooted in the Roman notion of the *patria-potestas*. The father-son relationship was fundamentally one of power and service, and the benefits of inheritance were offered as incentives to those who served well and conformed. As Gregory put onto the lips of his father earlier in his speech, such a notion was rooted in the concept of "law" based on familial relationship, and throughout his life Gregory distrusted it, and tended to regard it as a mode of thought and behavior antagonistic to the spiritual freedom to which he aspired.

In his ascetical program he wished to subject the law of the flesh to ensure the freedom of the spirit. He wished to follow a path of solitude, away from the pressing demands of his father which he found cowed his sensitive soul. In the face of the Roman philosophy of the *patria potestas*, rooted in the notions of law, subjection, and inferiority, the concept of familial love or parental dotage was something very secondary. Such relations pertained primarily to the age of infancy, and were largely the domain of the household's women. At an educable age the Roman child of good family would be taken away from the influence of women, and committed to the care of male tutors. From that time on his education, along with everything else in his training, was designed to prepare him for his role as the eventual successor to his father.

The Comic Poets' stock character of the doting old father who is ridiculously generous to his heir (an image Jesus applied in his parable of the Prodigal Son)[55] was a hilarious stage joke precisely because in real life this was not how things were, despite the fantasies of the younger generation. The idea of sonship based upon law and servitude, was something that Gregory found intimately and distressingly distasteful. In the Gospel, and in the Pauline doctrine of the superiority of the spirit that gives life over the letter that kills, he recognized a new Christian principle that would justify his throwing over of the traces (as far as he ever dared to do so in reality). It was a religious sentiment that grew from the deep soil of his psyche, and in his case it was to prove one of those great ideas that strikes root in the depths of the soul and determines the entire character of a life's work and thought.

If we return to the *Funeral Oration* we see how Gregory applies other "patriarchal" titles to define his father. Again, in ostensible praise he calls Gregory the Elder

53. *De Vita Sua*, vv. 310-320, PG 37.1051.
54. With the exception of a protracted stay in Athens (348-358) which he ever regarded as his golden age, and which he tried to extend as much as he could until his father forced him to return home by cutting off the finances.
55. Lk 15:11-32

a "Second Noah." The fact that the old man had built the church on his own land, and entirely from his own resources,[56] made the very concept of Gregory's flight from family responsibility through the avenue of the Church now an impossibly complicated one. As a bishop, as well as a father, the Elder Gregory could make demands on his Christian son that seemed irresistible. In this image of Noah, the son turns them in his mind and symbolically defuses them.

Gregory applies the Noah title with specific reference to his father's program of church building. He describes his achievement in founding a magnificent Christian building (the power base on which his episcopacy was founded) in parallel terms to Noah building an ark that saved the animals and the human race from the Deluge. The church too rose up like an ark, destined to save sinners from perdition:

> Like the great Noah, the father of this second world of ours, he it was who caused this church to be called a second Jerusalem, a second ark rising above the waters of deluge.[57]

But immediately comes the subtext that radically qualifies and disarms the image, and neutralises any theological power claim that might have been made on the basis of it. The negative qualification of this image is very dramatic. Even those who understood only a little of biblical history would be able to associate Noah with two things, at least. The first was his rescue of creation in his ark. The second was the less creditable story of how he became drunk and through this lapse (a patristic symbol of ignorance and fallibility rather than sexual immorality) was responsible for the disgraceful incest by which his daughters conceived children by him to repopulate the world. Having characterised his father as "great Noah," the following paragraph of his oration immediately turns to talk about one of the great scandals his father had caused in the local church—his unwitting lapse from orthodoxy when he signed a creed that was not recognized by the local Nicene monks and was thought to have sided with the Arians. If he was Noah the ark builder, on this occasion he had grounded the ship. In patristic symbolism the lapse into heresy is often characterised as "fornication" and Gregory explains it away as a result of his father's gullibility (just as Noah's lapse to incest came from the mental oblivion of drunkenness):

> He had been carried away by his simplicity, and in his guilelessness he had not been on his guard against guile.[58]

Nevertheless, the Christian tradition of the fourth century did not regard the adoption of a heretical creed as a matter of a "small lapse," and the monks at Nazianzus immediately denounced their bishop as a heretic and separated from his communion. It was common knowledge that it was the younger Gregory, the great defender of the Nicene cause, who was solely instrumental in effecting the reconciliation by inducing his father to make a retraction. In case his audience at the funeral

56. Orat. 18.39, PG 35.1037.
57. Orat. 18.17, PG 35.1005.
58. Orat. 18.18, PG 35.1005.

had forgotten the incident, Gregory makes sure they now remember, by excusing his father posthumously for it. And just in case they had forgotten his role in the affair, he reminds them explicitly, though with suitably becoming diffidence:

> At the time, if I may speak with the presumptuousness of youth, I was his partner in piety and action. Cooperating with him in every good work, and running alongside him, as it were, I was deemed worthy to contribute a very large share of the labor.[59]

What he means by the last reference is that to the extent his father is regarded as the material founder of the church in Nazianzus, the younger Gregory demands the right to be regarded as its spiritual founder after the ship had come to grief under his parent's piloting, sprawled on the rocks of heresy. The undercurrent themes that undermine a figure who in life was too large for comfort, overshadowing and repressing him, spring up unfailingly in Gregory's literary treatment of his father.

A particularly favored image Gregory has to depict his father is the title of the "new Abraham." In many respects the gray-haired and venerable old man seemed well depicted by the figure of this patriarch. Again, ostensibly it starts out as seeming to be high praise indeed, for Abraham was "the father of the faith" and the progenitor of a new race of the elect. But it is a title which he uses, once more, to introduce several critical undercurrents, not least to shift the focus onto Sarah, Abraham's wife, she who carried in her womb the new hope of Isaac; an obvious symbol of Nonna and Gregory himself. At the end of the *Funeral Oration* he makes such a pairing explicit:

> Let us join our spiritual reflections on these last rites with our spiritual Sarah, the lifelong partner of our father Abraham.[60]

In the *Funeral Oration* for his sister Gorgonia, delivered five years earlier in his father's presence, the same pairing is made:

> Who is there who does not know our new Abraham, and the Sarah of our day? I mean Gregory and his wife Nonna.[61]

In what is an extraordinarily crafted weaving of biblical themes, it is clear that the main subtext of the designation Abraham is one that allows Gregory to speak of his father as an "alien outsider" who is led by the woman of faith. He is the symbol of bondage, she the symbol of promise and freedom, and the fruit of the promise is Gregory himself as the new Isaac.

Once again it seems that for Gregory it is the physical and spiritual tie to the mother that really matters, and it is through her that he implicitly makes his claim to be released from his father's ambit of influence by adopting the life of a Christian ascetic and recluse. She is his justification for breaking free from his father's dominance, just as his father himself broke free from familial allegiance and dynastic

---

59. Orat. 18.18, PG 35.1008.
60. Orat. 18.41, PG 35.1040.
61. Orat. 8.4, PG 35.

expectations when he followed Nonna's direction and renounced his ancestral religion in favor of Christianity. For Gregory this is fundamentally what is conveyed by the Abraham title:

> He was justified by faith[62] and she has dwelt together with the man of faith. He, beyond hope, has been the father of many nations, and she has brought them forth spiritually. He fled from the bondage of his father's gods, and she is the daughter and mother of the free. He went forth from his kindred and his father's house for the sake of the land of promise, and she was the occasion of his departure... Theirs was the promise, theirs a son Isaac, as far as in them lay, and theirs the gift.[63]

The great patriarch Abraham, in Gregory's eyes, is, in his finest aspects, the product of a woman's direction and influence. It is the spiritual, feminine, power which he elevates over the repressive and material dominance of his father:

> This good shepherd was the product of his wife's prayers and guidance, and it was she who taught him the ideal of a good shepherd's conduct. He nobly fled from his idols, and later even put demons to flight,[64] but she would never share salt[65] with the worshippers of idols.[66]

By the use of such subtle symbols Gregory signals, not least to his father who was present on the occasion of the former oration, that in his estimate Christianity has undermined the Roman concept of *patria-potestas* fundamentally. And not only in theory is this so, for in practice the feminine aspects of influence and control have been responsible not only for his own bid to leave aside family duties and seek the quiet of seclusion, but also for his father's own renunciation of his family, a principle to which he now seeks to sacrifice his son. Although he was in awe of his father and struggled against that influence, it was his mother who was the most significant power base he recognized. His admiration and desire to base his ancestry on her needs no disguising. If she, in her own turn as parent, had shackled him, it was with fetters of precious metal:

> My mother had inherited from her ancestors the faith that is pleasing to God. This golden chain she cast around her children, displaying in female form the spirit of a man.[67]

In the son's adoring eyes it was Nonna that was the Sun of the family, setting in the shade the frightening figure of the bluff squire, his father:

62. Rom 4:2, 5f.
63. Orat. 8.4, PG 35.793.
64. Not an attribution to his father of charismatic ability as a thaumaturge or exorcist, rather a conventional reference to his presidency over the church as bishop in charge of the baptismal rites which began with liturgical exorcism.
65. Pointedly, because when Gregory the Elder's mother disowned him because he took up Christianity, Nonna in her turn seems to have disowned his side of the family. By this subversive behavior, justified on the basis of religious principle, she thus became a role model for all of the younger Gregory's struggles to break free of his father's "familial" demands.
66. Orat. 8.5, PG 35.793.
67. *De Rebus Suis*, vv. 118-120, PG 37.979.

My mother was a fit mate for such a man... a woman in body, yes, but in character she eclipsed any man.[68]

In hinting at his father's lack of spiritual sensitivity, in contrast to his mother who dreams and hears voices, and himself who has the power to interpret mysteries, Gregory is depicting himself as the real soul mate for such a mother. It is the sensitive child's perennial trouble. Even in his late maturity he feels compelled to tell his readers that he was the chosen darling of her dreams:

In her sickness she thought she saw me, her darling—for not even in her dreams did she prefer anyone else in the family.[69]

The fact that he speaks like this over his father's sarcophagus, underlines the impact even further. At the end of that panegyric his offer of consolation to his bereaved mother approaches an almost Oedipal level of sentiment in his offering of himself as a substitute, but he is careful, nonetheless, to make it clear that his freedom is now assured by his father's death, not deferred by it:

Do you want someone to care for you? Then where is your Isaac, whom he left behind for you, to take his place in all respects? Ask small things of him, the support of his hand, his assistance, and give him greater things in reward, a mother's blessing and prayers, and the freedom that follows thereafter.[70]

The old *Tyrannos* is dead, the son and heir is king. It had been Gregory's peculiar difficulty, as heir, not that the beloved but overweening figure of his father had to be felled by death before he felt free of the shadow, rather that death had been unable to topple the great oak until it was almost 100 years of age. When he found his freedom Gregory was almost an old man himself, and found it was more a loneliness than a liberation that he experienced. When his mother died shortly afterwards, he took to his bed, ill and depressed, convinced that his own end had also come.[71]

So far, his Abraham and Sarah titles have demonstrated how he has used his narrative to subordinate his father's role to that of his mother. His self-definition as Isaac, however, reminds us that there is an even more powerful undercurrent to this part of his biblical typology.

No one in his audience, educated or not, could have failed to be aware of the most famous stories associated with Abraham. As was the case with Noah, two tales stood out in the common imagination. Thus far Gregory has only treated one of them, Abraham's leaving of his ancestral home. There is, however, another: the awesome story of how the ageing patriarch set his face on the sacrifice of his son. If the Elder Gregory is Abraham, the younger sees himself as the sacrificial victim, led on by an implacable father, and rescued from his clutches only by God on the very

68. *De Vita Sua*, v. 61, PG 37.1034.
69. Orat. 18.30, PG 35.1024.
70. Orat. 18.43, PG 35.1041. The words immediately following, if not wholly for rhetorical effect, might suggest his mother bridled at the remarks: "Are you vexed at being instructed?"
71. Cf. Ep. 64, PG 3.125f; Gallay (1964), pp. 83-84. written in 374 AD.

mountain of sacrifice: "In this case the priest is Abraham," he says, "and the victim an illustrious Isaac."[72]

When he came back, rather shamefacedly, to Nazianzus after his panicked flight from the town, to take up the priestly duties which his father had forced upon him, he tells the congregation that they have witnessed his "immolation":

> These are the gifts given to you by this august Abraham... who today is bringing to the Lord his willing sacrifice, his only son, him of the promise.[73]

That ponderous influence that his father exercised over his son's psychology caused an immense fund of suppressed resentment. It spills out at times in a bitterness that even seems to surprise Gregory for the power of feeling it still evokes in his advancing years. In the *Funeral Oration,* addressing a prayer to his departed father, he moderates his accusation of tyranny against him:

> Guide safe from danger the whole flock, and all the bishops whose father you were called, and guide me who once was overpowered by you and coerced in fatherly and spiritual guise, so that I may not entirely blame you for that tyranny.[74]

On other occasions the softening qualifications are less to the fore. As late as 383 he looks back to the "tyranny" of his ordination with an emotion that is still extraordinarily raw:

> While in this frame of mind (preparing to embrace a life of seclusion) I became involved in a serious crisis. My father was well aware of my thinking, nevertheless he exerted pressure to raise me to an auxiliary throne, so that he might constrain me by the bonds of the spirit, and pay me the highest honor in his power. Why he did so, I cannot say. Perhaps he was moved by fatherly affection, which when combined with power is a force to be reckoned with. Tyranny of this kind (I can find no other word for it, and may the Holy Spirit forgive me for feeling this way) so distressed me that I suddenly shook myself free of everyone—friends, parents, fatherland, and kin.[75]

The moment of breaking point, a rebellion from which he climbed down in due course, and returned to the village church, had come when his father attempted to invade the arena of Gregory's spiritual life, and exert pressure on him as a Christian hierarch as well as a father. It was an invasion of this last "secret place" which Gregory could not tolerate, the domain he had psychologically assigned to his mother's guardianship, and later, as we shall see to the tutelary "female spirits" who appeared to him in his dream at Athens. It was not a domain where the gruff and commonsensical paterfamilias had any role to play.

In a more hidden biblical typology Gregory also depicts his father as an Old Testament King in part of the *Funeral Oration.*[76] He tells the story of how on one

---

72. *De Rebus Suis,* v. 444, PG 37.1003.
73. Orat. 1.7, PG 35.400.
74. Orat. 18.40, PG 35.1040.
75. *De Vita Sua,* vv. 337-349, PG 37.1052-1053.
76. Orat. 18.29, PG 35.1021-1022.

occasion his father was seriously ill, but merited, on account of his upright way of life, a special act of healing from God. Once again this is ostensible praise. The old man's probity is affirmed, as so often throughout Gregory's reminiscences, but there is a subtle subtext: for if the old man is a Hezekiah, then it is clear that Gregory sees himself as the court prophet Isaiah. In his interpretation of the healing it is Gregory, like Isaiah, who hears the Word of God,[77] who stands as the great prophet capable of the divine vision and able to hear the Seraphim crying out,[78] and who is thus able to intercede with God on behalf of his father. His narrative leaves the reader in no doubt that it was the liturgy which Gregory himself was celebrating that was the cause of the old man's cure, and at its end the father is able to stagger to his feet from the bed in his chamber and weakly join in prayer with his son—like Hezekiah who rises from his sick bed to sing a canticle to the Lord,[79] while at that moment his son (like Jesus healing the official's son at a distance),[80] intercedes at the temple altar.

The dynamic of the text again clearly subordinates the figure of the father to that of the son. One wonders if the symbolism could be pressed further? Hezekiah lived all his life in faithfulness to God and devout probity, aspects of religious devotion which Gregory unhesitatingly attributes to his father too. But at the end of the narrative of his cure the Old Testament text sums up his final years, as an old man, as a time when he lapses from his readiness to advance the Kingdom of God because he is only concerned with ensuring the comfort of his own old age.[81] As a rebuke to his limited and self-obsessed dynastic ambitions Isaiah announces to the old man that his sons will be eunuchs in a Babylonian exile. As far as Gregory was concerned, his father's obsessive desires to ensure his son's presence and obedience were not motivated by any sensitivity to the divine word he had received, confirming his prophetic vocation, rather by a need to arrange the security of his old age. Isaiah's rebuke to the old and fearful king is, in substance, remarkably like the decision of the younger Gregory who had dashed his father's dynastic and material hopes by renouncing marriage and by dedicating his fortune to the prophetic service of God.

Even so, the account of how his father had "merited" such a remarkable healing from God serves to enhance his father's status. To offset this, in the flow of his rhetoric, Gregory once more qualifies its significance by immediately recounting a parallel healing which took place for his mother, when she was beset with a fever.[82] The vitality and vividness of this narrative overshadows, deliberately so, that which he had earlier dedicated to his father. Once again Gregory is the central character of the story. The detail of his mother's fever reminds the reader of the story of Jesus' cure of

77. Is 38:4
78. Is 6:1f
79. Is 38:9-20
80. Jn 4:46-54.
81. Is 39:5-8
82. Orat. 18.30, PG 35.1024.

Peter's mother-in-law from a fever, at the village of Capernaum.[83] In the Gospel narrative these cure-miracles signal the start of Jesus' public ministry. After them he orders his disciples to begin their travels for the sake of the Kingdom of God.[84] Hardly had they begun to travel than we find the mother of Jesus, with other members of the family, pursuing him and attempting to make him return to his family and home.[85] In a signal rebuke to his mother and family Jesus made it clear, on the basis of the miracles, and on the proof they gave of his right to proclaim the Kingdom of God in freedom, that familial ties could no longer restrict his vocation.[86] Similar motives are at work in Gregory's text. In his account of his mother's cure he stresses her spiritual sensitivity, a theme which is not attributed to his father. She, like Mary the mother of Jesus, is attuned to her son's spiritual destiny, but still capable of allowing maternal sentiment to make her feel justified in attempting to control it.

Dream narratives have a special significance for Gregory, as windows of spiritual perception and moments of particular revelation. When he depicts his mother dreaming of him he is making some interesting theological as well as psychological statements. Lying feverishly sick Nonna dreamt one night that Gregory came to her bringing prosfora, loaves of white bread from the church, over which he had made the sign of the cross. He feeds her and her strength returns. She takes this for a real event. On the following morning when he comes to her bedside to enquire how she spent the night she is surprised that he does not seem to know, and tells him that he is responsible for her recovery because it was he himself who brought her the strengthening loaves. He marvels at the story but does not reveal to her its mysterious significance at that time.

In the Markan story depicting the arrival of the mother of Jesus, the occasion when she tried to take him back home by force,[87] Jesus gave a teaching that the true disciple is one who hears the word of God and prefers it to familial ties. This narrative of the dream-bread is one of the ways Gregory psychologically realised that aspect of his calling. Feeding his mother white bread signals Gregory's transition from the role of the child fed milk by its mother. Now he has reversed the role, and for milk he returns the finest of bread. It is a biblical code to remind the reader of the Pauline axiom that the true disciple must pass from the stage of suckling milk, which means to live on the basis of natural impulses, to that of solid bread, which means to be able to perceive spiritual values with wisdom and authority.[88] As Nonna receives bread she is summoned to respond to Gregory her son, as Mary was summoned to respond to Jesus, no longer on the old basis of maternal affection, but now

83. Mk 1:29f.
84. Mk 1:37.
85. Mk 3.20-21.
86. Mk 3:31-35.
87. Mk 3:21, 31-35.
88. 1 Cor 3:1-3

on the basis of a true disciple who is able to recognize spiritual truths with a mature spiritual wisdom of her own.

By juxtaposing both healing narratives so closely Gregory has demonstrated his capacity, once he has embraced his vocation as prophetic emissary of God, to return life to those who once gave life to him. On the basis of that parental relationship they made claims over his career. Now, in a time of his life which marks a critical departure from those parental claims (his father's sarcophagus lies at his feet as he speaks), he is signalling his own readiness to take over the role of parental authority: he announces how he raised up a weak and impotent old man, and how he fed his mother, not with milk, but with the finest of wheat, like a healing angel come by night. Gregory's symbolic rhetoric unfastened the straps with which his parents had bound him, straps which in real life he was, perhaps, never so successful in releasing so decisively, and which because of the phenomenal length of his father's life, controlled him until he was well advanced in years.[89]

The formative stress that Nonna imposed on his young psychology is of major and indisputable proportions. It can be synopsised in one overarching and frequently repeated image that Gregory uses, a self-defining image in his rhetorical account of his early self. This is his mother's great dream when she was pregnant with the infant Gregory.[90] It is obviously Nonna who has impressed this narrative on to her son, and with his marked sensitivity for dreams and omens, the impression was a profound one. In her pregnancy Nonna dreamt that she saw the face of her unborn son:

> She was anxious to see a male child in her house, a desire common indeed to many women. But she turned to God and prayed for the fulfilment of her desire. When her mind was set on something she was not easily restrained. God granted this grace, and being thus favored in her prayer she actually anticipated it because of her great longing. A gracious foretaste was given to her, a vision that contained the shadow of her request. My likeness and my name appeared clearly to her, the work of a dream by night.[91]

So, like the aged Sarah expecting promised Isaac, or bold Hannah praying for Samuel, Gregory's mother also receives an indication that her child had a high destiny. If she related the substance of the dream to her young son, he has shaped it rhetorically as an older man, and it is a mark of the impact it had on him in his early days how well he crafts it, and how often refers to it, even in his advanced age. It is a cardinal point in the search for a self-definition. As she has dreamt of her unborn son, on waking she realises that she should name him "Gregorios"—the child of waking visions, the watcher.

89. In Orat. 18.38 Gregory remarks that 45 was the average expectation of life in his time. He himself was 45 when he spoke. His father left him, in other words, when he too was an old man.
90. Cf. *De Vita Sua*, vv. 68-78, PG 37.1034-1035; *De Rebus Suis*, vv. 429f, PG 37.1002; Orat. 18, PG 35.1021-1024.
91. *De Vita Sua*, vv. 68-78, PG 37.1034-1035.

This pre-birth sign relates him, in self-perceived role and status, not only to the biblical figures we have witnessed already (Isaac, Aaron, or Samuel) but even to the prophet Jeremiah or John the Forerunner who were marked for God's service in the wombs of their mothers.[92] As Origen had already speculated, these great prophets were chosen souls, spirits of a refined order beyond the normal range who came to earth possessed still of the pre-existent glory they had with the Logos himself, for the service and salvation of many.[93] If Gregory is influenced by this aspect of Origen's exegesis,[94] the sense of destiny inculcated into him by his mother was indeed profound.

More obviously significant to him was the way in which this presentiment led his mother to "dedicate" him to God's service from his youth. Here she stands like Hannah, Elizabeth, and Mary herself:

When I was delivered from my mother's womb, she offered me to you.[95]

In Nonna's case the formal dedication probably coincided with the rites of initiation of the baby into the catechumenate, but for Gregory they assume a far greater significance:

She dedicated me as a new Samuel in the Temple.[96]

In a speech which he puts onto his mother's lips Gregory describes his chosen vocation as a fulfilment of a vowed duty, a natural result of a pre-birth consecration, and (revealingly) the acting out of his mother's aspirations as well as his own:

Such was my mother's wish and even while I was a child I yielded to her desires. My tender soul began to be shaped in a new mould of holiness, but the seal awaited the will of Christ who so manifestly conversed with his servant. He bound me with holy chastity, and put a rein upon my flesh.[97]

Here, the "seal" with which Christ consummates and perfects the mother's first vision, seems not entirely to be the baptismal consecration to which Gregory of course alludes, and which was to happen later in Athens, but more precisely to another dream which, like a baptism, "sealed" the first, this time his own dream; a supremely formative psychological and spiritual experience in which he felt he had been dedicated to chastity and a life of scholarly pursuits. Its implications will be considered later, for now it is enough to note how its impact as a determining vision, shaping and defining his mature years, is conditioned to the extent that this dream of Gregory is understood as a confirmation and completion of his mother's dream. It is significant how he manages to fix the course of major events in his self-identity

92. Jer 1:4-5; Lk 1:14-15, 40-41.
93. Cf. Origen's *Commentary on John 2:29-31*, SC vol. 120, p. 326f.
94. He makes no specific allusion to it, and generally attempts to reduce the mystically speculative elements of Origen's theology to make them more palatable in the fourth-century Church, though he undoubtedly knows the tradition intimately.
95. *De Rebus Suis*, v. 424, PG 37.1001.
96. *De Rebus Suis*, vv. 431, PG 37.1002.
97. *De Rebus Suis*, vv. 450-455, PG 37.1003.

and life's course by a parallel intuitive method to that of Nonna. She was taciturn, tended not to encourage achievements in herself or her children and controlled the family to some degree by means of the introverted anxiety that motivated her: "Fear was her guide. It is a powerful teacher."[98] She was scrupulous in repressing her emotions in public:

> How extraordinarily admirable is the fact that she restrained external manifestations of grief to such a degree.[99]

In an age when men and women lamented and rejoiced openly and spontaneously as the norm (despite the intelligentsia's flirtations with Stoic ideals) she was indeed extraordinary. All in all, it must have amounted to a very serious childhood in those years when he lived in the women's quarters of the villa, a tendency to which his parents' advanced years when he was born, must have contributed. He says as much himself:

> Already I was taking on some of the dignity of old age, and little by little, like a cloud from out of a cloud, the desire for better things led me on. As my mind developed I made progress, and only enjoyed those books which were concerned with God. [100]

The influence of his parents marked him deeply, then, from his earliest childhood to the declining years of his life. In his own retirement he found himself suffering more and more from moods of depressed distraction. One of his occupations then was to write almost innumerable epitaphs for lost friends and family. The parental formation and expectation seemed to set the pattern of all the family's relationships, even those between the children themselves.

Gorgonia, for instance, seems to have been as forthright and determined as her mother, with a capacity to instill awe and admiration into Gregory, like his father, but perhaps with little warmth or confidence being in evidence. Although she was only a few years older than Gregory it is very much as the "elder sister" that she comes across to us in his writings. Once again we glean most of our information about her from the funeral oration Gregory preached for her after her death in 369. Even allowing for the stock phrases of panegyric, and the common literary custom of praising virtuous women for their sobriety, there is something that is chillingly severe in his remark about her: "Who so derided laughter that the very hint of a smile seemed almost too much for her?"[101]

And this observation from her brother seems all the more notable when one considers his own lifelong delight in good-natured jokes, conversations, and witticisms. On one occasion when Gregory invited his brother-in-law Alypios to spend some time with him he is very circumspect about including her in the invitation. The letter was written at a time when Gregory is worried about the depredations being made on his family's estates. This might be evidence to locate it after the death of

---

98. *De Vita Sua*, v. 67, PG 37.1034.
99. Orat. 18.10, PG 35.997.
100. *De Vita Sua*, vv. 95-100, PG 37.1036.
101. Orat. 8.9, PG 35.800.

Caesarios in 368, and thus one year before Gorgonia's own death. Alypios has written to Gregory wanting to join him for a forthcoming festival, and he replies in a very genial letter promising he would waive any objections purists might have to a soldier in uniform being present at the litanies, and inviting Alypios to come and stay with him for a while. He is very diffident about inviting "the sister." The neutral designation has often been taken to refer to Alypios's own sister, and thus used as evidence for thinking Ep. 86. was addressed to another couple altogether. It is however, explained by other information which Gregory gives us in the *Funeral Oration for Gorgonia*. If, as Gregory knows, Alypios and Gorgonia are by now living together as celibates, then the designation "sister" is doubly apposite as a designation of both his and Alypios's relation to her. In Christian usage of the fourth century "sister" often refers to a spouse.[102]

His eagerness to have Alypios stay with him contrasts with his diffidence in having her join them. In part this may be explained by the ill health which was affecting her in what was, after all, the last year of her life; but even so his words leave the invitation open in a way that suggests no small degree of tact was necessary in dealings with her. He does not want the responsibility of inviting her. Equally he does not want to run the risk of not inviting her:

> So much, then, has my rhetorical skill been put to the service of persuading you to come. As for the sister—I will not suffer any recriminations[103] if she is coming. In fact, if she does not come, both she and I will probably get the blame. Let her come, if she will, without an invitation. It is you whom I am encouraging to come.[104]

There is definitely a sense, although he does not express it in so many words, that the pleasantries of the visit between one Roman gentleman and another, would be much more fun without her. In her funeral oration she appears as too large a figure to permit the usual encomium of a woman who excelled in the feminine arts. To describe her in terms of her role as wife and mother, Gregory says, would be: "to praise the statue for the shadow it casts."[105]

In this oration he makes public the knowledge he had of how she had persuaded her husband to follow a celibate lifestyle with her in the latter part of their marriage. In adopting this ascetical life after producing several children, she was perhaps returning to an early aspiration she shared with Gregory from childhood, to adopt the monastic lifestyle. If so her aspirations had been successfully repressed by her father, and her uncle Amphilokios who must have helped to arrange the marriage to

---

102. Cf. Gregory's Ep. 197, PG 37.321; Gallay (1967), p. 88; referring to Theosevia the recently deceased wife of Gregory Nyssa; cf. Devos (1983). In his *Epitaph for Theosevia* and in *Letter* 197 Gregory uses *Syzygos* and *Adelphe* interchangeably.
103. From those (probably the local monks) who might have objected to a military uniform in church, but would be glad to see Gorgonia present, a known patroness of ascetics.
104. Ep. 86, PG 37.157-160; Gallay (1964), p. 107.
105. Orat. 8.9, PG 35.800.

a family in the latter's own town of Ikonium. In a much later Epitaphion verse Gregory gives a hint of this, something he could not have whispered in the course of her funeral oration with the families all around him. Here he describes her as "Jephthah's daughter,"[106] that is, a cruel and unthinking human sacrifice caused by the implacable obstinacy of her father's vow. It is a very caustic reminiscence.

In the overriding of Gorgonia's desires for the freedom of a celibate Christian life-style, in the manner of Macrina and her sisters at the convent of nearby Annesoi, Gregory must have been overawed by the extent of his father's power over the destinies of his children, but perhaps also forewarned about it. The same would not happen to him, though he was conscious that his own determination to elect celibacy had nevertheless been compromised seriously in the extent of the freedom his father would allow:

> Abraham received a son from God.
> Noble Jephthah received a daughter.
> How greatly both were sacrificed.[107]

In the time of her late married life Gorgonia was adept in the ascetical practices of prostrations, fasting, night vigils, sleeping on the ground, withdrawing from social conversation, almsgiving, and lack of personal adornment.[108] In fact her asceticism has some of the hallmarks of the Egyptian tradition which Gregory deprecatingly mentions in reference to Basil's establishment at Annesoi.[109] His own preferred style of monasticism was significantly different in tone, and spirit. Perhaps he was overawed and even a little upstaged by Gorgonia's severity in that vocation he had elected for himself, and carefully mapped out as a suitable lifestyle for a gentleman, quite different from the wild monks that roamed the streets of such places as the capital, whom he regarded as little better than riffraff. In some parts of the ascetical movement dirt was a sign of dedication.[110] As Jerome once explained to his dubious Western readers, Eastern nuns shaved their heads because they never washed, and this shaving very sensibly inhibited the spread of lice. We must suppose that the "odor of sanctity" in several cases might have passed unnoticed in the welter of other odors. Gregory hints at this in a typically delicate manner when he reminds the congregation of her physical appearance:

106. Judg 11:12-40
107. *Epitaph* 94, PG 38.58.
108. Orat. 8.10-14, PG 35.800f. In 365 Gregory wrote to Nicobulos who had married his niece Alypiana, Gorgonia's daughter. In an exchange of pleasantries where Nicobulos had commented on how small his new wife was, and how their interests differed so much, Gregory replied by reminding Nicobulos that, petite though she was, her life of prayer had made her "almost grafted into the ground," and in her spiritual stature she was more than a match for his manliness. Cf Ep. 12; Gallay (1964), pp. 19-20.
109. It is a playful allusion to the rigours of his stay there, but beneath it all there is a serious intent. For Gregory, monastic praxis did not need to follow all the *mores* of the Egyptian ascetics, several of which he regarded as uncouth.
110. When he sets out to praise his local monks (Orat. 6.2, PG 35.721-724) he mentions their characteristic appearance: "squalid and unkempt hair, bare feet, ugly clothes."

How squalid her body;
Her garments carrying only the odor of virtue.[111]

This was a redoubtable character who must even have given God a rough time; leaving him little room to refuse when she had set her mind on something. To overcome a "strange" illness she took herself to the church of Bishop Faustinos at Ikonium, in the middle of the night and, as Gregory tells us:

> committed an act of pious and noble impudence... placing her head on the altar and pouring out abundant tears... she vowed that she would not leave go of it until she obtained her recovery. Then she anointed her whole body with the medicine she had emitted,[112] even a portion of the antitypes of the Precious Body and Blood which she treasured in her hand[113] and mingled with her tears.[114]

Even though Gregory is impressed by the cure that follows instantaneously after she wipes her body with this mixture of tears and eucharistic elements, he is a little taken aback by her boldness. At one stroke she has invaded the holy of holies of the church where the non-ordained were not supposed to tread, and dispensed with the clergy by ministering illegitimately to herself (perhaps while still a catechumen). What a rich benefactor of the Church could get away with was evidently different to the behavior demanded of lesser Christians.

Gregory also seems puzzled by the nature of an illness that could come and go so suddenly and with such bizarre results:

> She was sick in body and grievously afflicted with a malady of a strange and unusual character. Her body would suddenly become fevered, her temperature rising, and her blood racing, followed by a sluggishness that induced a comatose state, an incredible pallor, and paralysis of the mind and limbs. This used to happen quite frequently at times. The terrible disease did not seem human.[115]

Gregory meant, of course, to imply a demonically caused illness that was miraculously exorcised by the quality of her faith. But even so it was a dubious compliment. Despite his use of the narratives as an ascetic's encomium, there is still in Gregory's attitude a certain hesitancy observable as to the way his sister might be regarded as having been "excessive." From our perspective today it is all too easy to invoke hysterical neurosis to explain her behavior, but the religious psychology of the ancients is far from being an open book. Gorgonia's attitude at the altar, this

---

111. Orat. 8.14, PG 35.805. So I would render the subtle undercurrent of the Greek: *arete monon anthountos.*
112. I.e. her own tears
113. The eucharistic elements were kept in the sanctuary of the church for the (baptized) sick. Gorgonia has committed something of a scandal (a) by appropriating the mysteries perhaps still as a non-baptized, (b) by administering them to herself and, (c) by anointing her body with them as a prophylactic rather than consuming them in the public eucharistic liturgy. Gregory glosses over all of this and focuses only on the "pious motive."
114. Orat. 8.18, PG 35.809-812.
115. Orat. 8.17, PG 35.809.

desperate bargaining for divine favor, and quest for bodily purification in illness, was something that her contemporaries, pagan or Christian, would have found natural. The incised testaments on the walls of ancient Asklepia, the temples of the healing god, provide a vivid parallel. Gorgonia's attitude marks a chapter in the way in which the early Church was already beginning to make inroads into the old religions, ousting several key functions of their shrines and displacing the role of the cults in the popular imagination. Despite this, in Gregory's text a question seems to remain, delicately coloring the narrative. Like Gregory himself, in later life, Gorgonia seemed to have been extraordinarily prone to illness. In his case it amounted to physical sores allied with mental depression; in her case catatonic withdrawal from reality.

For Gregory illness often came at moments when decisiveness was demanded of him. When he felt out of his depth in the politicking at Byzantium, for example, he says:

Fortunately, illness came to my rescue, for it kept me for the most part at home.[116]

But unlike Gregory, even in her sickness Gorgonia comes across as a dominant figure. Her early death occurred on precisely the day which she had previously announced to her family, having learned it, so she told them, in a mysterious dream.[117] She herself, in accordance with common custom at that period, had deferred her baptism until the time of crisis announced by the onset of her illnesses. Even though she had been living as an ascetic she had, for many years, been in the status of a catechumen. Gregory suggests that in her case the baptismal sacrament was more of a "seal" than an initiation, but also gives us the information that she determined that her husband and children should not follow her example. On her deathbed she arranged their baptisms—a very profound intrusion into their subsequent life-patterns, and in the case of Alypios, her husband, a more or less certain prohibition to any subsequent marriage approved of by the Church in that era.

Although Gregory's oration seeks to give his sister high praise as a Christian ascetic, there is very little in his narrative that suggests any personal touch of warmth, and certainly no shared memory of childhood days—things which illuminate his much more affectionate references to his mother and his brother Caesarios. Gorgonia was a figure that the young Gregory could perhaps revere, but not bond with closely.

How different things are with his younger brother Caesarios. Gregory delighted in his company, and their closeness in age meant that they could share the closest of ties for a long period, studying together at home, at the local school in Nazianzus, and then at their uncle's house in Ikonium, before setting off on mutual student travels to Palestinian Caesarea and Alexandria. It was only in Alexandria that

---

116. *De Vita Sua*, v. 1745, PG 37.1151.
117. Orat. 8.19, PG 35.812.

Gregory left his brother who then began his medical studies, while he himself took ship for Athens.

When he delivers the oration for the premature death of his brother, he cannot recall the times he shared with him without weeping.[118] This oration is filled with a warmth and sentiment that is missing from his descriptions of his father and sister. At one instance Gregory recalls: "something quite remarkable that occurred, which gives me the greatest of pleasure to bring to mind."[119]

His story concerned how they had both met up again, as a great surprise, in the streets of Byzantium, when after completing their studies in Alexandria and Athens respectively, they had simultaneously decided to visit the capital *en route* back to Cappadocia. Gregory attributes this meeting to the prayers of their mother, but he also shapes the story implicitly to lead the reader to recognize in the event mysterious evidence for a certain synonymity of spirit which he must have felt with his brother.

However close, the two were very different characters indeed. Gregory leaned upon Caesarios, relied on him to sort out all manner of difficulties, and then likes to give wise advice as though to a son. In short Gregory reproduced his father's attitude to him as a paradigm for relationship. On Caesarios' part there was a deep affection for his brother. He encouraged Gregory's literary skills, and loved to hear him perform. There ran through him a strong desire to protect the elder brother. Caesarios' vivacity and outgoing nature proved a valuable foil to Gregory's own insecurity. His natural abilities took him to high public office,[120] and even in the competitive world of Byzantine politics his liveliness of character made him a general favorite at the court.[121] Even Julian the Emperor admitted defeat in trying to persuade Caesarios to renounce his allegiance to the Christian cause. With a wit that was at once charmingly deprecating, and menacing in its implications for the future, Julian replied to Caesarios' obstinacy with the words: "How fortunate the father. How unfortunate the sons."[122]

Even though Gregory shows some anxiety about whether his brother would be able to retain his Christian integrity in Julian's court,[123] Caesarios had a courage that would not draw back from defying his imperial lord and master when he was serving in his administration, and standing even in his presence.

---

118. Orat. 7.6, PG 35.761.
119. Orat. 7.8, PG 35.764.
120. He is not the Caesarios who appears in Ep. 23 as the City Prefect of Constantinople, but Gregory's Ep. 7 shows that he had risen from the rank of successful court physician to Julian, to become part of the imperial administration under Valens.
121. Orat. 7.10-11. Gregory describes him as "the people's idol" (*De Rebus Suis,* v. 229, PG 37.987); and says: "Poor Caesarios, there was a time when you shone like a morning star in the imperial palace." (*De Rebus Suis,* v. 177, PG 37.983).
122. Orat. 7.13, PG 35.772.
123. Ep. 7, PG 37.32-33; Gallay (1964), pp. 8-10.

Gregory also wrote *Invectives Against Julian*, to stand against his policy and theology, but published them when his protagonist was dead. Such was the difference in bravado between the two. When Caesarios died prematurely, after surviving an earthquake in Bithynia,[124] but then succumbing to the plague that swept the region in the aftermath, Gregory was devastated. Caesarios had died in office as Imperial Treasurer of the Province of Bithynia,[125] leaving a considerable estate. Gregory was overwhelmed by the strategies needed for sequestering and administering it, and much was plundered by those he describes as freebooters of the great man's camp.

Despite Gregory's protestations that everyone who made rapacious claims on the estate was an evil plunderer, there are grounds to think that Caesarios did leave behind him many genuine and angry creditors.[126] The announcement Gregory made that his brother had willed his estate "to the poor" might not only be read as a virtuous act of restitution, a deathbed philanthropy, as Gregory characterises it, but also, perhaps, as an attempt by Caesarios to forestall his creditors by bequeathing his capital assets to the Church—a comparatively safe tax haven (conveniently represented by his father and brother in the present instance), and thus "to the poor" in the sense that the Church would administer any fiscal credit on their behalf. If, in practice we read "Gregory" for "the Church" we can understand why the device might have failed to impress generally.

Certainly, Gregory oscillates between public protests that the money seized from Caesarios' estate had been stolen from "the poor," and more private letters where he presupposes that Caesarios' assets simply revert to the family. At the end of the day perhaps Gregory simply synthesized both notions: applying what remained of the money for his familial church's use while alive, and intending to pass it on for philanthropic purposes once the direct family line had terminated with him. This is exactly what he did do, in drawing up his own will in 381, a testamentary document that has survived. Gregory's complete inability to understand or control the complicated affairs in Byzantium, and the financial mess into which he soon realized he had fallen, compounded his grief on the loss of a fellow-soul.[127] In his eyes it was Caesarios' death which opened the floodgates for all the disasters that soon were to fall upon him:

> While he lived I enjoyed a reputation second to none, wealth or power of any kind being foreign to all my aspirations. But when he died my only legacy was trouble and woe.[128]

From that time the elements of self-doubt and depression, so markedly a feature of Gregory's later years, are never far away from his more private correspondence. He

---

124. Ep. 20, PG 37.53-56; Gallay (1964), pp. 28-29.
125. Orat. 7.15, PG 35.773.
126. Cf. Bernardi (1968), p. 111.
127. *De Rebus Suis*, vv. 165-229, PG 37.982-987; *De Vita Sua*, vv. 370f, PG 37.1055.
128. *De Rebus Suis*, vv. 187-190, PG 37.984; *De Vita Sua*, v. 374, PG 37.1055.

describes Caesarios as "an oak," and "a fence."[129] He was nothing less than: "Greg-ory's right hand."[130]

And his loss was irreplaceable: "Who can ever be like him again? No one, ever, not on this earth."[131]

Even though the general theme of the *Funeral Oration* is to present Caesarios as a model Christian, it is clear that Gregory has some real difficulty in fitting the buoy-ant figure of his brother into the mold of the humble ascetic. Nevertheless, he tries: "He showed to God in the hidden man, greater piety than appeared in public."[132]

If the imperial police were investigating the claims of the creditors as well as Greg-ory's counterclaims, and it was a case that was to drag on for years, it would certainly do no harm to have a text at hand that could be called on to attest for his late brother's saintly character. This is perhaps one part of the motivation for his funeral oration.

Gregory's sense of loss after Caesarios' comforting protection was removed is pathetically revealed in this retrospective he composed in his old age:

Alas, alas, sad dust of Caesarios. He was always ready to ward off the mob from me. He made it possible for me to evade all distress. Never did anyone revere a brother as he did me, giving me respect as if I was a beloved father.[133]

The necessity of being in the thick of personal engagements, and the need of a commanding and decisive personal presence in this financial crisis, left Gregory bruised and battered. He started out administering the affair himself, but had soon been joined by his more practical father, for all his grey hairs. Gregory looked back on the time years later, and sardonically quoted Theognis to sum up his jaundiced view of Byzantine society:

> If we share a bowl of wine
> friends thick around shall press.
> If we try to share distress,
> their numbers fast decline.[134]

The long extent of that dependence Gregory had on Caesarios made its sudden loss, when once it came, all the harder to endure. The sum total of these familial influences, in Gregory's case, made for a character that needed to flourish in the ambit of someone else who could present a more vivid or more determined aspect to the harsh world of everyday reality. Whether that figure was his father, his mother, the sister whom he felt might even have outdone him in the ascetical life, the brother whom he loved to be with, or whether it was to be, as later in life, the father surro-gate of Basil the Great, the need of Gregory for such shelter left him peculiarly

---

129. *De Rebus Suis,* vv. 187-190, PG 37.984 ; *De Vita Sua,* v. 374, PG 37.1055.
130. *Epitaph* 19, PG 38.20.
131. *Epitaph* 19, PG 38.20.
132. Orat. 7.11, PG 35.768.
133. *De Rebus Suis,* vv. 218-222, PG 37.986.
134. Theognis. 5.643-644; Greg. Ep. 13, PG 37.45.

vulnerable throughout his life to the demands or expectations of others. His power of introspection and innate sensitivity came at the price of a plasticity of character, insecure anxiety and vacillation, and also an explosive stubbornness that blew over quickly but often left him with troubles in a long following wake. All these things were to mark his mind and his Church career decisively.

When the time came for him and Caesarios to leave the women's quarters and advance on the next stage of life charted out for him, beginning their preliminary education with Carterios the pedagogue, and Amphilokios his uncle at Ikonium, the young Gregory had little sense of what the outside world held for him. The first encounter, when it came, was a passionate delight in discovering the new vistas. He at last found an arena in which he excelled more brilliantly than in any Palaestra or Gymnasium, more bravely than on any military parade ground. He found a domain where he was superior by far to his bold father, and even his confident brother. He was about to discover that the world of imagination into which he had retreated in the villa, could, paradoxically, help him to master a universe of which he otherwise felt afraid. The young aristocrat, his mother's little Samuel, was soon to be given a new set of horizons, entranced by the power and persuasiveness of words, and wondering at the force with which the seduction inflamed him. He wittily describes it with the fondness of an old man recalling his youth:

> When the first downy beard grew upon my cheeks,
> I was stirred by my first hot passion—for literature.[135]

---

135. *Ton logon d'eros thermos. De Vita Sua*, vv. 112-113, PG 37.1037.

2

"THEN CAME ATHENS AND LETTERS"

What thou lovest well remains,
the rest is dross
What thou lov'st well shall not be reft from thee
What thou lov'st well is thy true heritage...
What thou lov'st well shall not be reft from thee.

Ezra Pound

If, as Gregory tells us, his mother was adamant in refusing to hear even the mention of a Hellenistic myth or pagan practice in her house,[1] then we might deduce that her feelings on Gregory and Caesarios embarking on the next stage of their formation were highly ambivalent. She had little voice in the matter. In common estimate, and certainly in the fixed opinion of her husband Gregory and her brother Amphilokios, the proprieties for the upbringing of Roman gentlemen had to be observed, Christian or no.

After the formative years with the women in the villa, during which time Gregory had clearly absorbed his mother's deep-rooted and visionary form of Christianity, it was time for the children of the Roman upper classes to depart for a patriarchally dominated and male-oriented society, where the skills that would be necessary for their future careers would be absorbed. Such was the theory. In fact that meant that the affluent classes of Late Antique society would follow in the footsteps of their predecessors of centuries before them, and pursue a pattern of education that had little changed in its fundamentals. Literature would be enough to form the basis of a total education, and rhetoric, the highest level of educational attainment, would not only allow a person to practice law and civic administration (perceived as the only fit occupations for a gentleman outside the supervision of his own estates) but would even equip him to embark on philosophical enquiries, of which a little, in moderate measure, was always seen to be an ideal accompaniment to literary accomplishment in the archetypal figure of the Roman intellectual from the Augustan Age onwards.

Gregory and Caesarios would have been sent on their long educational tour regardless of their aptitude or personal feelings, nevertheless they both seemed to have welcomed the change, eager to expand their horizons. Both of them extended their travels to the very limit of the time that was regarded as suitable, and at the end of that period of studies both had determined to make a life for themselves on the basis of their respective professions: for Gregory the life and calling of the philosopher, something that for him was to be a harmonization of the highest attainments of the classical world yet in

1.   Orat. 18.10, PG 35.996.

35

Christian form, "our philosophy"[2] as he calls it; and for Caesarios the practice of medicine, from which basis he moved to a successful political career in Constantinople.

If Nonna was unable to prevent the Hellenization of the young men, which she
must have feared, like many other Christians of the day, was nothing other than the
corruption of evangelical simplicity, and the exposure to the corrupt world of pagan
religious sentiment and practice, then she perhaps arranged to moderate its effects.
The places arranged for the children's studies were all centers of Christian intellectual
and religious life: the first years, between 342 and 344, learning letters at the local
school under the Grammaticus at Nazianzus,[3] and soon afterwards with her brother
Amphilokios on his estate at Ikonium, learning further advancement in writing and
style, in the company of his tutor, companion, and servant Carterios. The latter was
implicitly trusted by the family as a devoted Christian and, like Gregory, adopted the
life of philosopher-monk when their travels were over.[4] His uncle Amphilokios was
practicing law in the city, and could probably offer a level of instruction finer than any
other local rhetorician. His own son, Amphilokios the Younger, later to become an
ascetical bishop and close ally of Gregory's, was as yet merely four years old.

At this period it is possible that Gregory's sister Gorgonia, then about sixteen years
of age, was already installed in the Ikonian estate of her husband Alypios. The mar-
riageable age for girls would allow such a possibility, although Alypios would
undoubtedly have been older and advanced some way in his military career when they
were married. At the house of Amphilokios Gregory also met his cousin Theodosia, an
intelligent and enterprising character who was destined to marry into one of the highest circles of Constantinopolitan society, and later to effect Gregory's life and career in
the most dramatic fashion by calling him to Byzantium in his mature years.[5]

After their preliminary work the boys were sent on to lodgings in Cappadocian
Caesarea where they could attend the local school of grammar and rhetoric.[6] The
provincial town had a reputation for learning unsurpassed in the whole of the
Cappadocian province. It was here that Gregory and Caesarios perhaps made the
acquaintance of Basil,[7] a rich young Christian from Caesarea; itself, an unremark-
able meeting but one that was to flower into an important friendship when much
later they met up again, for higher studies in Greece.

After Cappadocian Caesarea came the time for the young men to travel further
abroad. Caesarea Maritima was selected as the school to which they should go.[8]
This was arguably because it was the closest thing in the fourth century to a Christian

2. Ep. 58, PG 37 113, 116; cf. also Ep. 56, PG 37.112.
3. Orat. 7.6, PG 35.761
4. Possibly as an assistant priest in Nazianzus.
5. As outlined in chapter 5 following.
6. Orat. 43.13, PG 36.512; also Gregory Presbyter. *Vita Gregorii*, PG 35.248.
7. Gregory's account of their meeting in Athens suggests he already knew Basil.
8. Orat. 7.6, PG 35.761.

university town.[9] The national saint-hero of Cappadocia, Gregory Thaumaturgos, had studied there with the great Origen, and the city had the advantages of proximity by land and sea for the province. In the third century Origen had labored there to institute the finest Christian library currently in existence, and his labors had been sustained by a succession of Christian scholar theologians, Pamphilos the martyr, and then the notable historian of the Church Eusebios, bishop of the city until 339.

In the time that Gregory, Caesarios, and Carterios lodged in Caesarea, that is throughout 347 and 348, the ecclesiastical and theological conflicts over Arianism were raging fast and furious in the Church, and Caesarea was a center of theological activity and policymaking. The successor to Eusebios as bishop of Caesarea, the scholarly but indecisive Akakios whose rule over the church was to last from 341 to 365, had been deposed in 343 by the Council of Sardica which had vindicated Athanasios at the expense of outraging many of the Eastern bishops. Akakios' theological career, an intelligent man steeped in the works of Origen who was at a loss over the christological issues involved in the Arian conflict, thus adopting several positions within Arianism as well as periods when he reverted to Nicene orthodoxy, must have been characteristic of many other Oriental bishops, of even less personal culture, who found the confusion at the very heart of Christian tradition immensely unsettling. Gregory was to make his first encounter with the theological and political realities of Arianism at this time. One of the key intellectual factors in the problem was the way in which some of the Arian party laid claim to the memory and heritage of Origen to justify their insight that Christ qua-Logos being inferior to the Father's glory could not, therefore, be absolute, a term which denied any inferiority, and so could not be God. This pressing of Origen's vast literary and theological legacy into ever tighter syllogistical theologies in the fourth century was a tendency that would outrage Gregory when he came into his own maturity. It is possible (considering the extensive knowledge he has of Origen, and the extent to which he venerated him later in life) that he first made use of Origen's Christian library at Caesarea. From his earliest years he regarded him as the greatest mind in Christian history, but was conscious of how he was a source of appeal for two contrary sides in the debate defining the nature of the authentic theological tradition of Christianity.

His fellow student in rhetoric at this time was another Christian young man, the even more devoted Origenist Euzoios.[10] The latter was to give his allegiance to the Arianizing party, and when he was eventually elected bishop of Caesarea in succession to Akakios, he renovated and restored Origen's library in a gesture that was at once symbolic of his intellectual discipleship and his vision of the "true" tradition of Christian theology—the subordinationist presuppositions of the third-century Christology which Origen represented.

9. Cf. J. McGuckin, "Caesarea Maritima as Origen Knew it," *Origeniana Quinta*, R.J. Daly (ed.) (Louvain, 1992), pp 3-25.
10. Cf. Jerome, *De Viris Illustribus* 113, PL 23.707.

Adolescent dialogue between Euzoios and Gregory, who shared so much in common and yet were poles apart in their theologies later in life, may have sharpened one another's awareness of the critical questions at an early stage. This time at Caesarea introduced Gregory to theological riches he had not hitherto dreamed of, and a system for interpreting the scriptures he would adopt and refine. Origen himself had come to biblical study from the background of professing a career as Grammarian and teacher of rhetoric. He called for the Christian scholar to adopt a life of retired solitude, and personal asceticism. His work was suffused with a spirit of mystical insight. His vision of Christianity was one in which he attempted to harmonize biblical revelation and Hellenistic philosophical culture through an intellectual eclecticism guided and inspired by a highly personal Logos-mysticism.[11]

In Origen, Gregory had found an early hero whom he could emulate and who provided many paradigms for his own life and thought,[12] but equally presented the young man with a very vivid example of how the Christian tradition, in relation to absolutely central matters of its intellectual and spiritual life (questions so basic and apparently simple as to whether it believed in the divinity of Jesus or not), was far from the assured and solid matter his mother had suggested to him when throughout his early years she had instilled in him the duty of defending his faith against a welter of external seductions. Now, in the Arian crisis, and in particular the role Origenism played in it, he came face to face with a full-scale battle at high intellectual level, as to the very identity of that faith he had been given in his childhood. The "Origenists" such as Eusebios and Akakios of Caesarea represented themselves as the intellectuals of the day, fighting against the twin fronts of rationalism and obscurantism: what they portrayed as the obscurantist piety of the Egyptians led by Athanasios, and the rationalist reductionism of such as Eusebios of Nicomedia or the radical Arians of the generation of Aetios and Eunomios (to be the main Arian opposition to Gregory Nazianzen in his maturity).

From the perspective of the Athanasian party this intellectual commonality of Origenists were regarded simply as "soft Arians," those who regarded the Son of

11. He has been classed as a Middle Platonist, but it would be more to the point to regard him, a student with Plotinus of their common teacher Ammonios Saccas, as one of the early and original developers of the Neo-Platonist tradition, and thus one of the reasons why the argument between the Christians and Hellenists (such as Porphyry and later Julian) continued into the next two generations as to whether "Neoplatonism" (an entirely modern description) is a movement external or internal to the Christian tradition proper. The standoff between Gregory and Julian in the Fourth Century is another act in a longstanding argument. Origen had already laid the foundations for a synthesis of Christianity and philosophy based on his Logos-mysticism. Gregory was to adopt that and take the argument more thoroughly than Origen into the literary and cultural arena that was at the forefront of the Fourth century debate about the future of the Hellenistic heritage.

12. Moreschini (1979); H. Crouzel, *Origène et la connaissance mystique* (Paris, 1961).

God as "like" the divine Father[13] but not "substantially similar to"[14] and even less "substantially the same"[15] as God. Much of their theological tradition, however, was familiar to the Cappadocian Church, because of the way that their own prized theologian, Gregory Thaumaturgos, had already mediated a Gospel tradition in Origenist style.[16] If the leading hierarchs of the day were so openly in conflict about central aspects of the Christian tradition it must have come home to Gregory, even in this youthful visit to Christian Caesarea, that much thinking was needed to find his way, like Theseos, through the labyrinth that faced him.

In Caesarea Gregory may have first heard of Cyril of Jerusalem, who in 347 was at the height of his fame as presbyter-theologian at the church of the Holy Cross at the site of Calvary, delivering the *Catechetical Lectures* which were to give him an assured place in the canon of Christian classics. In the *Catechetical Lectures* there is no trace of the Homoousion doctrine, and although this would not necessarily be expected in such literature at this time it is clear that Cyril's own theological progress took him along a wide range of allegiances. In his early days, under the metropolitan authority of Akakios he was more publicly aligned with the so-called "Arianizing tendency" than would later be the case. In his later years he was among those whom Athanasios regarded as substantially his: "brothers who mean what we mean, and

13. Known, consequently, as the Homoian party, the Greek term for "similar," a vague catch-all description, and at first attracting a broad Church.

14. Known as the Homoiousian party; from the Greek "like in substance or essence" to something. The central problem over this school was that Origen had already argued that, strictly speaking, it is rather reductionist to think of the supreme Godhead as "a substance" among other substances. More correctly he is beyond substance. Many more educated hierarchs, especially those of the Origenian tradition, found the term "substance" unusable in any form for such reasons. Homoiousios was, however, used generally as a more "substantive" theological affirmation of the Son's closeness to the divine Father, and his own divine status. Many Cappadocian hierarchs belonged to this grouping, and much of Basil and Gregory's time was to be spent in trying to move them towards the full Homoousian position.

15. Known as the Homoousians: from the Greek "same essence." Gregory and Basil, following Athanasios and the Nicene Council, were dedicated to this party, and ultimately responsible for its eventual triumph and emergence as the "Orthodoxy" of Christian theological tradition. It had an ambivalence in the term that allowed a normal usage: "same stuff as," and a particularly strong usage "exactly identical thing as," if one may try to bring out subtleties in a few brush strokes. Constantine the Great had proposed it in the former sense as a catch-all phrase, thus similar to the later Homoiousian intentions, but Athanasios had strongly argued that the preservation of Christian monotheism depended on the attribution of a single and identical essence to the Godhead: an essence which the Son, therefore, had, "exactly the same as" the Father. The logic of this great defense of the Nicene doctrine of Christ had brought Christian theology, at the time of Gregory's youth and Athanasios' failing years, to a critical point which needed to clarify what differences between the divine persons could be logically held if such sameness was to be affirmed so categorically. This, in short, was the pressing question to which Gregory's Trinitarian theology was later posed as the answer.

16. Consequently the Homoian and Homoiousian parties had a wide adherence among the Cappadocian Church.

only differ about the word."[17] But even if Athanasios was willing to claim him for the cause, never did Cyril agree to the utility of the term Homoousios, and many Nicenes, both at the time and afterwards, regarded his true allegiance as doubtful.[18] In Gregory's later life he was to regard Cyril as an ally in their mutual support of Meletios of Antioch, and a theologian and orator worthy of note. There are, for example, clear echoes of Cyril's works in Gregory's *Theological Orations,* delivered in Byzantium after 379.[19] There is no doubt that already in his youth he was taking a careful interest in the ecclesiastical life of the city he was visiting. He certainly found much to admire in its Bishop, the more clearly Arian sympathist Akakios, and obviously regarded him as a paragon of rhetorical culture, describing him as: "the foremost orator among the bishops of his day."[20]

His enthusiastic estimate was not tempered in later years as he came to recognize him as one of the leading lights of the Arianizing movement, and any hostility he has towards him subsequently as a theological opponent is "covered" by his obvious respect for him as a rhetorician. He obviously spent a lot of his time in Caesarea in 347 admiring the episcopal orations in the city church.

Gregory was soon to make up his mind as to which tradition he would defend but this exposure to a wide range of opinion from his earliest days of theological and philosophical study led to an unusual breadth of insight. He was to make a synthesis and carefully qualified mixture of schools and opinions. He endorsed, but moderated Origen's theological system; and allied himself with, but significantly developed, the theology of the Nicene party. As a result he was politically identified with the Nicene party, but possessed of a subtle and complex resolution of the crisis that went far beyond what the opposing sides of his early years could as yet envisage. Both he, and Basil (who adopted a similar approach though less revolutionary than that of Gregory, partly because Basil had not seen so much of Origen's systematic intent) were to be regarded at first with no little suspicion by the Athanasian party, and the Roman Church which was so strongly allied with Alexandrian theological interests in this period. Basil's later appeals to Athanasios and the papacy were met with some coolness, and Gregory's own magnificent defense of Athanasios was neither asked for nor possible to refuse, since it was given as an epitaph for the great man once dead. Its theological judgments should not be taken as a perfect representation of what Athanasios thought he was doing with his life, rather as a very finely crafted interpretation of the "Athanasian intent" by Gregory. Gregory's hermeneutics, however, were extremely sophisticated and consciously designed to argue that what he, Gregory, was

---

17. Athanasios, *De Synodis* 41.
18. Cf. R. Gregg. "Cyril of Jerusalem and the Arians," in *Arianism. Historical and Theological Reassessments* (ed., idem) (Cambridge, MA, 1985), 85-109.
19. Especially in Orat. 28, PG 36.25f, paralleling themes in Cyril's *Catechetical Lectures* 6 and 9. Cf. Bernardi (1968), pp. 184-185; Norris (1991), pp. 109, 119-121, 123 and 126.
20. Orat. 21.21, PG 35.1105.

currently preaching in Constantinople in 381 was synonymous with Athanasian doctrine in terms of spiritual pedigree, if not in terms of fidelity to the letter. It was a bold claim that not everybody recognized, not least because part of Gregory's avowed aim was to supply the intellectual infrastructure where he thought Athanasios' logic had not taken him far enough. The text will merit a closer scrutiny in due course. The larger process also merits careful consideration as part of the inner mechanism of the patristic sense of the transmission of Christian tradition across generations.

So, it was in Caesarea Maritima that Gregory began to sharpen his theological culture in the midst of the most intense controversy Christianity had ever known. His period of reflective maturation was a long one, and his judgments were delivered after he had seen and heard much from all sides of the argument, including the opponents of Christianity from outside the Church who set the internal debate into larger contexts of logical consistency, cultural continuity, philosophical coherence, and aesthetic refinement—all of which concerned Gregory passionately, and most of which passed over the heads of the average Christian hierarch of the fourth century, men who (Gregory was later to complain loud and often) were pontificating in a debate without having had any intellectual formation worth speaking of.

Apart from frequenting the Christian library at Caesarea (which was possessed of a great range of theological treatises comprising Christianity's past intellectual tradition as well as a full range of texts relating to the wider intellectual culture of a liberal school of the day, such as philosophy, literature, astronomy and ethics)[21] Gregory was already attracted to what was to become a consuming passion: rhetorical and literary study. He found in Caesarea a leading proponent of rhetoric in the style of late Second Sophistic: the professor Thespesios. Jerome also knew him as one of the leading rhetors of the day[22] and even though he has little love for the Arian Euzoios he mentions Thespesios as the teacher of both him and Gregory and he remembers Euzoios with some respect for his literary culture and his restoration of the great library at Caesarea.

Gregory's description of Thespesios, on the other hand, seems to imply he was merely a low step on the way to higher studies in Athens, and he calls him simply my "Grammaticus," the teacher of first steps in literary analysis; though without question Thespesios did more than conjugate and parse. He was in all likelihood a rhetor in the tradition of Second Sophistic, and to that extent involved with philosophical and metaphysical enquiry. When Gregory later composed his epitaph he gives away

---

21. The range of Origen's curriculum is described by Gregory Thaumaturgos in the rhetorical presentation he delivered at Caesarea, in Origen's presence, in 245 to mark the end of his period of study, *Letter of Thanksgiving to Origen*; cf. W.C. Metcalfe (ed.), *Gregory Thaumaturgus: Origen the Teacher* (London, 1907) (2nd ed. retitled: *Address to Origen* [London, 1920]).

22. Cf. Jerome, *De Vir. Ill.* 113, PL 23.707.

the extent to which Thespesios was concerned with hermeneutical questions, and the excellence with which he pursued his literary analyses. But there is a detachment here that is noticeable. Perhaps Gregory did not care to be too closely associated with a teacher who had to be shared with a leading Arian of his day. Nonetheless Thespesios was surely more than the simple and reductionist designation "Grammaticus" might connote. And this in turn might suggest that from the beginning of his period of higher studies Gregory was initiated to understand the scope and range of rhetoric to include matters of philosophical concern, not merely the sterile exercises of the literary dilettante. In pursuing rhetoric with teachers who were well aware of the power of the hermeneutical tool they were placing at the disposal of their charges, Gregory was ideally positioned to advance his reflections on the inner meaning of texts and contexts, and the correct manner of analyzing and exposing the weaknesses of discordant intellectual theses.

He was to be one of the first of many Christians who had been educated before him in forensic rhetoric who would systematically apply the results to the theological arena at a level deeper than surface stylization (with the possible exception of Tertullian in the West, who although he knew and used the power of rhetoric in his theological analysis had little idea that the insights of classical culture and the Christian religion could, or ought to be, synthesized).[23]

Often Gregory speaks of "rhetoric" in an apparently disparaging way, characterizing it as superficial decoration and verbosity.[24] At such times he is, if one looks closely, merely using a carefully crafted rhetorical device to persuade his audience to lay aside their resistance to the craft he is employing to convince them of his argument's merit. This apparent disparagement is, in fact, a stock motif of the rhetorician, propounding an argument to the effect that: "though many others use stylistic brilliance to disguise lack of substance, my own stylistic restraint argues for substantial profundity of argument." Later, when he heard that Gregory Nyssa had apparently turned away from a dedicated Christian career to try for a chair in secular rhetoric, he was disparaging in the extreme,[25] though being careful not mention the same temptation had been his in Athens. But here, it was either Macrina or Basil who had probably asked him to intercede and Gregory, typically, warns his younger namesake of the dangers of rhetoric in a beautifully crafted epistle[26] which can only have been designed to demonstrate to the young man that a Christian career did not spell the end of such literary aspirations as he currently cherished. He refuted Gregory's argument: "Have I not been a Christian while acting as a rhetor?" not in the absolute, but in the particular. That is, he does not disagree with the principle of the

---

23. "What has Athens to do with Jerusalem?" he once asked in a famous rhetorical question, expecting the populist Christian answer, "nothing much." *De Praescriptione Haereticorum* 7.
24. Cf. Fleury (1930), pp. 89-90.
25. Ep. 11, PG 37.41-44; Gallay (1964), pp. 16-18.
26. In a short text he makes no less than four explicit citations of Euripides and Hesiod.

possible reconciliation of the two things, which is very much his own aspiration, he simply argues particularly and explicitly: "No my friend you have not been." It is a clever riposte, for he suggests the younger man has not found the measure either of his Christianity, or his rhetorical skill. His remarks chastising Gregory Nyssa, therefore, must be understood in the context of the latter's tentative abandonment of a Christian career in rhetoric (in the ordained ministry) in favor of a secular profession, and Gregory is clearly writing only to call him back to rhetorical service, but this time "for the good of the sacerdotal order, and for the good of all Christians."[27] The question was not whether or not he should be a rhetor, but where.

Despite his remarks, and allowing for the fact that a generally more positive attitude is manifested in his private correspondence than in his official Christian discourses, even so his habitual attitude is one that sees rhetoric as inseparable from the philosophical quest. Gregory is not only a rhetorician through and through, he sees his role in philosophical terms which mark him as a practitioner in Second Sophistic style:[28] someone who has resisted Plato's distinction between rhetorics and the quest for truth. Thespesios was certainly someone Gregory regarded as one of the most eminent literary practitioners of his day. But when he heard of his death many years later he composed an epitaph that sets out to praise him while subtly subordinating his stature to that of Prohaeresios, his teacher in Athens, whom he explicitly calls "a Sophist": a philosopher in contrast to a Grammaticus.[29] Of course this also reflects the fact that Gregory studied only for a very short time in the school at Caesarea Maritima, at an age when his first mentor might not have thought him ready to embrace philosophical speculations of a very high order, but it is primarily a device to signal to the reader that wherever else he had been, his "real studies" began once he had arrived in Athens, and Athens alone.

He similarly disparages his time in Alexandria,[30] but this was not only from a similar desire to heighten his Athenian pedigree, but also because in 382, when he wrote his autobiographical poem, the memory of how the Alexandrian clergy had so recently attacked him still rankled. Gregory was more than aware that some circles in Constantinople regarded a "Cappadocian" rhetor as a contradiction in terms,[31] and partly from personal desire, and partly from apologetic needs, he diminishes the significance of his other centers of study in order to focus attention on Athens.

By describing Thespesios as Grammaticus Gregory wishes to signal that it was he who taught him the principles of literary criticism and symbolic exegesis. This makes him significant at least as the teacher of the fundamentals of Gregory's craft of

27. Ep. 11.11, PG 37.44.
28. Guignet (1911); Ruether (1969); Norden (1909) II, p. 562.
29. *Epitaphion* 5, PG 38.13.
30. Cf. Gallay (1943), p. 34f.
31. Ps. Lucian (*Epigram* 43) had already set the tone of much that would follow: "Can a Cappadocian speak intelligently? Can a tortoise fly?"

rhetoric. It was evidently from Thespesios that Gregory began to feel at home in the Attic Greek of which he can be a master when he chooses:

> What grief, what grief; for even you are dead Thespesios.
> The envy of the fates has brought you to your tomb;

> Yet no tomb can rob you of your deathless fame.
> How much you savored your tender words.
> Now your shade cries out in Attic forms:
> Who is there now sustains the glory of my craft?[32]

The last "rhetorical question" was surely meant to suggest the answer—Gregory himself as the living heir and testament to his teacher's greatness. In his time with Thespesios the overpowering love of Hellenic culture took root in Gregory. He would have initiated here his profound knowledge of the works of Homer. The extent of that knowledge is shown when, in his last years, he is able to compose hymns and poems fluently in archaic style. The imagery of Homer is naturally, almost instinctively, brought out, as we shall see shortly, in the way he even interprets his life's progress, and the advancement of his understanding of religious destiny, in the form of Homeric symbolism.

The time at Caesarea Maritima was brought to an end partly by the desire of his brother Caesarios to advance his own studies in the science of medicine. For that, there was no other city that offered so much as Egyptian Alexandria, where dissection of corpses had first begun, and whose medical schools excelled internationally. From Caesarea in Palestine it was a relatively short and easy journey by sea to the great capital. Gregory himself, though not as interested in medicine as his brother, who already possibly wished to adopt the profession of Physician, could be well satisfied at Alexandria. It still boasted the greatest library of the ancient world, and was also noted for its Christian school of theology. At the time Gregory was there Didymos the Blind, the leading Origenist scholar of his generation, was teaching in the theological school under the Bishop Athanasios, the most noted of all the Nicene theologians.

While in Alexandria, in the latter part of 348, Gregory may have heard Didymos' expositions of the scripture. His symbolic exegesis of the Christian scriptures became a paradigm for Gregory's own subsequent approach to the mysterious exegesis of scripture as the unfolding of hidden symbols.[33] Although Gregory tempers this highly allegorical form of "Alexandrian" exegesis, he was influenced by the twofold stimulus of devotion to Origen's system and his own studies in literary hermeneutics to the extent that he habitually employs the text as symbol, whereas for such as Basil, in his later theological works, the symbolic reading of the text is often set aside in favor of a more "literalist" reading in support of immediate ethical, doctrinal, and philosophical positions.[34]

32. *Epitaphion* 4, PG 38.12.
33. Cf. Weiss (1872); Donders (1921); Capelle (1929).
34. Basil's *Hexaemeron* is one such example (ET, NPNF series 2., vol. 8).

Didymos' spiritual anthropology had already moved beyond that of Athanasios in positing the soul of man as a critically important bridge between a twofold human nature poised uncertainly between its substrates of spirit and flesh. The notion of the inner dynamic of the "composited" human being called to a constant transcendence of self is something that Gregory develops considerably.[35] In his relation of Christology and the notion of the salvation of the human being this concept of the transformation of the soul is extremely important for him, and in this aspect of his work he antici-pated the classical Christian solution in Christology and soteriology which Cyril of Alexandria was later to systematize fifty years after him. Didymos' theology of the Holy Spirit was to prove an extremely important linkage between the theology of the Alexandrian school as represented by Athanasios the Bishop in his *Letters to Serapion,* and the Cappadocian theology represented by Basil and the two Gregories.

In Didymos, Gregory found an Origenist who reversed the thesis of Eusebios and Akakios of Caesarea that the Origenian system necessitated the rejection of the Homoousian position, and who elaborated Origen's concept of the soul of Jesus to rework it in an acceptable form for fourth-century Christianity. Both aspects of Didymos' synthesis were to be remembered by Gregory in the theology of his mature years.

At the time of this stay in Alexandria Athanasios himself was in residence in his see, having returned in 346 after his second exile, newly vindicated by the Synod of Serdica three years previously, to enjoy a ten-year period of the possession of his city. It cannot be doubted that Gregory here made his first encounters with the theology of the Nicene party, in the sense of a detailed knowledge of the arguments behind the credal controversies. The Arian crisis was still in full flight and Athanasios tow-ered internationally as the living symbol of the Nicene cause. His writings were assuming the status of Christian classics, and it is possibly at this period in Alexan-dria that Gregory came to know a range of his works, such as his early writings on the Incarnation of Christ. Athanasios' concept of the incarnation of a perfectly divine Logos as the only sure way to secure the concept of redemption of the whole human race, collectively caught up into the divine life, or deified in God's hominization, was an idea that struck deep roots in Gregory's mind, becoming a definitive substrate of his thought. Gregory regarded Athanasios with immense respect, and presents his life in an idealized form when he delivered a panegyrical oration many years later in Byzantium in 380.[36] But for all his praises there is little sense in this Oration of any personal involvement in the Bishop's entourage. At times there are some confused elisions of facts in his hero's story. We are led to sur-mise that Gregory's real knowledge of Athanasios came to him by reading, at a dis-tance, and later in his own theological career, most probably at Nazianzus or Seleukia where he made a serious and systematic study of Christian theology.

35. Gilbert (1994); Ellverson (1981).
36. Orat. 21, PG 35.1081f.

While in Alexandria Gregory probably joined with Caesarios in making preliminary studies in medicine. Some skill as a physician was regarded then as an essential
attribute of a gentleman's education. The educated élite would often be the only
source of medical knowledge for their estate workers and the local inhabitants of
their region. The medical curriculum not only encompassed practical issues but was
also interested in dream diagnosis, such as the priests of Aesculapios practiced, and
concerned with more extended philosophical enquiries into the condition or
"nature" of man. This kind of general anthropological speculation can be seen evidenced in the works of such Christian gentlemen-scholars as Lactantius[37] and
Nemesios of Emesa.[38] Gregory of Nyssa's work *De Opificio Hominis*[39] similarly
shows the results of much physiological research. Gregory was undoubtedly a fragile
character, and was very conscious of it. At times he fell back on illness as a welcome
let-out from moments of crisis.[40] Even when he was perfectly vigorous he likes to
portray himself as barely able to drag along.[41] He says, a few years before his death,
that his body was "debilitated,"[42] and by this stage his health certainly seems to have
been a genuine trial to him, although in earlier and more optimistic days the worst
physical troubles he is able to call to mind, to elicit the reader's sympathy, are the
occasions when he accidentally scratched his eye on a rose thorn in his garden, and
another time when he suffered a bronchial infection.[43] In the time after his parents'
death he grew increasingly "fragile," though even then he was capable of immense
bursts of energetic work such as the eighteen months he spent at Constantinople
delivering a grueling series of lectures immediately after coming out from a "retirement on the grounds of ill health" at Seleukia. During his time at the fraught council
in 381, however, he was "grateful," he tells his readers, for the nervous prolapses he
suffered which saved him from the angry wrangling. In his final years he was greatly
depressed by long-drawn-out illnesses from which he tried to find relief by visits to
the hot spa at Xanxaris in Cappadocia.

He remarks in his *Panegyric on Basil* [44] that the latter was also in fragile health
and used his time at Athens to advance his medical skills so that he could treat

37. In his *Divine Institutes* and the *De Opificio Hominis*: "On The Workmanship That is Man,"
ET by M.F. McDonald, in FOTC vols. 49 and 54 (Washington, 1964 and 1965); cf. P.A.
Roots, "The Workmanship of God and Lactantius," CQ 37, 1987, pp. 466-486.
38. *On The Nature of Man* shows a wide reading in philosophy, physiology and psychology. ET,
W. Telfer, *Library of Christian Classics* vol. 4 (London, 1955), pp. 224-453.
39. PG 44.125-256.
40. "Fortunately illness came to my rescue," he says in relation to a time in Constantinople when
decisive action was called for on his part. Cf. *De Vita Sua*, v. 1745, PG 37.1151. After his parents' death in 374 he took to his bed convinced his own last hour had come. Cf. Ep. 64, PG
37.125-128; Gallay (1964), pp. 83-84.
41. Cf. *De Vita Sua*, vv. 1336-1340, PG 37.1121; *De Vita Sua*, 1920, PG 37.1163.
42. (*Soma luthen*) Carm. 2.1.92. (verse 8), PG 37.1447; *Compendium Ipsius Vitae*, PG 37.1447.
43. *De Rebus Suis*, Carm. 2.1.1, vv. 327-334, PG 37.994-995.
44. Orat. 43.23, PG 36.528.

himself and others. Gregory says explicitly that Basil extended his reflections from the practical into advanced "theoretical studies" about the human condition. Basil certainly put his medical knowledge to advantage later when he founded important hospices in Cappadocian Caesarea, a project in which Gregory was involved with him in the early stages of its design. Typically less practical than Basil, the main effect of Gregory's studies emerges in his anthropological reflections on the fragile mixture that composes man from a "union of opposites." It gives to his anthropology a philosophical dynamism which he puts to good advantage in creating his doctrine of salvation.[45] It is very probable that he continued and developed his studies in medicine at Athens, attending alongside Basil, for there is certainly a specific element in his references that argues he did not pick up his knowledge merely in the form of commonplaces.[46]

Whatever joys the city had for him, and Alexandria is the only place in the whole account of his life where Gregory gives even the slightest hint of having had a wild time,[47] there were other drawbacks. The winds blowing the sands of Egypt over the city reminded its inhabitants that for all its aspirations to be a Greek metropolis, it was still an island in a Demotic Egyptian sea. The city life was notoriously violent, and the memory of two Cappadocians who had not long ago been responsible for the persecution of the great Athanasios, George the Arian bishop who took over the see until murdered by the mob, and Philagrios the iron-fisted city Prefect, perhaps made it a place where it was wiser to disguise one's Cappadocian ancestry.

More than this, other voices were calling. Gregory's eyes were set on the pinnacle of any literary or philosophical quest in that era, and that could only be Athens, the true heart of Hellenic civilization:

> The fame that accompanies letters was all that engaged me.
> East and West combined to procure that for me,
> and above all, Athens, the glory of Greece.[48]

As Caesarios had settled in well to his medical studies, Gregory made his preparations to leave. The family tutor Carterios would accompany him. He decided he would not overwinter in Egypt, but found in the November of 348[49] that the sailing season had already come to a close. He decided to risk the journey when he discovered a ship ready to sail for Aegina and Piraeus that belonged to acquaintances of his family.

45. Cf. Ellverson (1981), Mathieu (1982).
46. Keenan (1941).
47. "The usual tendency of youthful spirits I did experience; a certain readiness to be swayed by chaotic impulses, just like a spirited colt rearing for the race—I had been getting a smattering of letters at the time in Alexandria." *De Vita Sua*, vv. 121-124, 128-129, PG 37.1038. What gentlemanly reserve there is here, so different from Augustine's sensational confessions, but probably less of a story to tell anyway.
48. *De Rebus Suis*, vv. 96-97, PG 37.977.
49. Cf. *De Vita Sua*, vv. 125-126, PG 37.1038; Jungck (1974), p. 157 explains the date in more detail on the basis of the astronomical reference to Taurus' tail.

Up to the point of Alexandria, the study program had followed a path which Gregory's mother, though she might not be wholly in favor, could hardly have objected to, since all the cities so far included (the two Caesareas and Alexandria) had large Christian contingents. When Gregory broke that pattern to go to Athens, the city of cities for rhetorical study, but a place known universally for its devotion to the gods of antiquity and regarded in the Christian world as even excelling Rome in its devotion to pagan cults, it is interesting to detect signs of a guilt complex emerging in Gregory that is to have decisive effects on the future man. It is not only the youthful high spirits he seems to confess to in Alexandria which is at stake here, but more significantly the desire to embrace Hellas for all its culture and beauty, and perhaps an uncertainty how that left him placed in relation to its underlying metaphysic and all that this meant in his mother's mindset: frivolous and demonic paganism.

Gregory seems to be conscious that perhaps for the first time ever he is deliberately moving against her will, and out of her ambit. The journey to Greece was more than he had envisaged when first he arranged his passage. It was to be a veritable Odyssey from which he could not return the same. The voices of his female sirens sang loud in his ears but our young Odysseos had his face set on returning home to Achaia, and though tormented by them his ship continued on its way. As with Odysseos, another form of shipwreck lay before him.

He describes how his ship sailed from Alexandria's harbor, past the Pharos and across the open sea, while he looked behind, musing on a time in his life when he was more than ready to devote himself to the new quest for culture and beauty that so possessed him. He had reviewed other possible avenues, as he tells us,[50] such as marriage, the management of his father's estates, or an independent career in politics, but they held little attraction for him:

> Not for me the labor
> of trying to embrace the onrush of the river,
> picking up shadows in my hands,
> or feeling for the mist.
> Such are the generations of mortal men;
> such is prosperity;
> all as fragile as the wake a ship leaves behind,
> perceptible for a while,
> then fizzling into nothingness.

Such philosophical thoughts of self-dedication to culture from the twenty-year-old Gregory were to be qualified by other massive forces that were already gathering overhead, to scare him, quite literally, out of his wits. It was to be shock to the system that like many other such occasions cannot be shrugged off subsequently, but calls out for a thorough realignment of one's life. For it to happen at his age amounted to

---

50. *De Rebus Suis*, vv. 63-90, PG 37.974-976.

no less than a "conversion" experience. In this case the road to Damascus was the sea route to Rhodes.

For twenty days and nights on that journey a great storm raged across the Mediterranean. Gregory's sheltered upbringing had not prepared him for the trauma. He spent the entire time shaking, huddled into the recess of the ship's prow, in terror for his life: "prostrate, crying out to Almighty God in supplication":[51]

His two accounts of that storm,[52] especially the longer version in the autobiographical poem, are rightly famous as pieces of literature in their own right, and have often been excerpted since. This is in line with an ancient tradition, old before Gregory, for the composition of a "storm at sea" episode in Homeric style was a set exercise of the rhetorical schools of the day, and several of his contemporaries have also left good examples of the genre.[53] As soon as he arrived at Athens he probably set about composing the first draft of this narrative that was to be polished and edited thirty-three years later. Nevertheless, despite its crafted character and the fact that we know from the outset that Gregory is striving for the greatest effect in his descriptions, something of the genuine sense of his terror at the time comes across starkly:

> The waves foamed all around the ship
> towering up like mountainous crags on every side.
> Water flooded in on us.
> All the rigging shook and whistled
> in the lashing blasts of wind.
> The heavens grew black with storm clouds
> lit up by cracks of lightning
> and great thunder crashes on all sides.[54]

He repeats this description to similar effect in the *De Vita Sua*[55] and then goes on to add further details in a more intimate personal reflection on the way the incident proved a cardinal point in his life. Poor Gregory, huddled in the covered prow, was lamenting all his secular aspirations of so shortly before, filled with terror at the thought of dying unbaptized. He characterizes the crew as in fear of their lives:

> A confused and heartrending cry rose up:
> sailors, helmsmen, officers and passengers alike,
> all called out as one to Christ,
> even they who had not formerly acknowledged God.[56]

But by his own admission, his own terror was so vast and all-encompassing that

51. *De Rebus Suis*, vv. 313-315, PG 37.993-994.
52. *De Rebus Suis*, vv. 307-321, PG 37.993-994; *De Vita Sua*, vv. 121-209, PG 37.1038-1039.
53. Quintus Smyrnaeus, *Post Homerica*, "The Return From Troy," Trypanis (1971), p. 355; Musaeus, *Hero and Leander*, "Leander's Death," Trypanis (1971), pp. 356-358.
54. *De Rebus Suis*, vv. 314-319, PG 37.994. Cf. M. Kertsch, "Zum motiv des Blitzes in der griechischen Literatur des Kaiserzeit," WS, 13, 1979, 166-174.
55. *De Vita Sua*, vv. 129-139.
56. *De Vita Sua*, vv. 139-142.

even when the storm abated, and the others regained their confidence, it was Gregory that everyone found they still needed to calm:

> I could not stop sending up great shouts,
> Stretching out my hands to God.
> My shouts were even louder than the pounding of the waves.
> I lay prostrate and prone, my garments torn,
> And though it seems beyond belief,
> Every word is true,
> For they all forgot their private fears
> And these righteous sailors on a sea of woes[57]
> Then joined their prayers to mine,
> To give me solace in my grief.[58]

Apart from shouting to God at the top of his voice, one suspects he must have called on mother a few times too, for as things were calming down and his companions were trying to console him, a servant boy from his entourage told him that in the darkest hour he had thought he had seen, as if in a dream, Gregory's mother Nonna walking to the ship and dragging it single-handed to the shore, to answer her son's urgent need. In this she is characterized remarkably like Pallas Athene coming to the rescue of Odysseos her client, and some of the parallelism is underlined in other parts of the narrative, although specific elements from the Gospel story of Jesus and the disciples in the storm-tossed boat are also at play[59] in a typically Gregorian synthesis.

By the time of his Father's *Funeral Oration,* thirty-six years later, the story has become part of the family folklore, and amplified by a prescient dream his parents had[60] during the very crisis. In the *Funeral Oration* he tells his audience that his mother's thaumaturgic intervention had gained common credence onboard the ship after the story was made known, and even that he himself received a spiritual intimation of his mother's spiritual involvement, shortly after the occasion itself, when still onboard the ship: "This was also revealed to me in a salutary sleep, which at last I experienced after the storm had died down a little."[61]

These last developments seem largely retrospective, attracted in by the self characterization as Odysseos and the Homeric assonances this encourages. Nonna, on this occasion, is like Penelope, visited by the goddess Athene in her dreams and anxious to intercede for her son (Telemachos) in danger on the sea.[62]

---

57. The image of the turbulent sea as an analogy for human life subject to endless vicissitudes, and longing for the stability of the eternal, is a constant refrain for Gregory. Cf. Guignet (1911), pp. 144-145; Lorenz (1979); and R. Freise, "Zur Metaphorik der Seefahrt in den Gedichten Gregors von Nazianz," pp. 159-163 in Mossay (1983).

58. *De Vita Sua*, vv. 167-174, PG 37.1041.

59. Mk 6:47-51; Mk 4:37-41.

60. The mother really, for she is the only one that features significantly.

61. Orat. 18.31, PG 35.1025.

62. Cf. *Odyssey* 4.790-840.

In the two accounts of the storm in the long poems his mother is not mentioned at all. There is, however, an interesting psychological indication that Gregory found her propelled to the foreground of his terrorized consciousness when his dreams for rhetorical glory seemed all but doomed by a premature death, for a phrase he has particularly associated with her sprang to his lips instinctively when he described the sailors making common cry to God: "What a suitable teacher fear is."[63]

In all three accounts, the climactic purpose of the dramatic narrative is to demonstrate what Gregory did at the height of his fear. And this was to make a bargain with God. He describes his prayer in a stylized form that transmutes it into a veritable liturgical and biblical canon of supplications,[64] but the point is quite clear—if he survived to see Athens he would take the warning to heart and complete the dedication of his life to Christ initiated by his mother long beforehand, when he was an infant, by dedicating *himself* to God and that, I think, can only be read as meaning he would seek baptism as a young man, and all the ecclesiastical discipline consequent on that decision:

> Despairing of everything here below
> I raised my eyes to You, my life, my breath, my light,
> My strength, my sole salvation,
> Source of my terror and affliction,
> But even so my gentle healer
> Who always weaves good things into disasters...
> I said, I am Yours, Lord,
> From times past, and even now,
> Accept me once again[65]
> The child of your honored servants
> A gift of earth and sea,
> Dedicated by the prayers of my mother
> And because of these extraordinary terrors;
> Thus I shall live for You.[66]

Such a dedicatory vow could not be gainsaid. It would have a serious effect on tempering the dreams he was nurturing for a rhetorical career. The result of his vow, he tells us, indicates why his mother's figure does not feature much in the poetic versions of the story, for the vow is presented as having a dramatic and immediate effect. The offering is heard, and accepted:

> These things I said, and
> The winds grew calm again,
> The sea fell still and

63. *De Vita Sua*, v. 143, PG 37.1039.; cf. ibid., v. 67, PG 37.1034.
64. *De Vita Sua*, vv. 186-193, PG 37.1042-1044.
65. A second dedication, as it were, following the way his mother dedicated him at his infant dedication as a catechumen (unbaptized child of a Christian household).
66. *De Vita Sua*, vv. 182-185; ibid., vv. 194-198, PG 37.1042-1043.

> The ship sailed straight on its course—
> All this the result of my prayer.[67]

From terrorized and quivering mass in the ship's prow, Gregory thus assumed heroic proportions, as the real savior of the vessel. In the composition of this narrative Gregory has spoken much about his "double salvation"; rescue from drowning, and also salvation from the fate of the unbaptized dead. He attributes this double salvation as something the crew also experience,[68] but at this point the seams of his literary editing begin to show.

It is clear that he has gone to some pains to break his narrative into two distinct sections, the one climaxing at the height of the storm when Phoenician sailors tie up alongside them for extra stability, reprovisioning the ship at the same time,[69] and the other, rather weakly introduced by the phrase:

> The sea continued to be much disturbed,
> and we were in trouble for many days to come... [70]

which leads up to the story of the crew coming to despair even of God's help, until Gregory's prayer delivers them, with the power of a new Jonah[71] or a new and courageous Paul[72] who like Gregory was caught in a storm for several weeks[73] until he received an angelic vision to assure him of his companions' safety and his own destiny to "appear before Caesar" to preach the Gospel in all his eloquence: the task and destiny for which God had saved him from the waves. The subtextual Pauline parallels are evidently very suitable, since Gregory is editing the story just after his career in Christian rhetoric had received its highest accolade when he preached before "Caesar" Theodosius in the Church of the Apostles in Byzantium, only a year before.

But this Christianizing symbolism does not explain his need, against the narrative's obvious inner dynamic, to divide the storm sequence into two distinct episodes. For this we need look no further than Homer in his description of Odysseos' several trials at sea. The eponymous hero, crafty and consummate in his rhetoric,[74] is thwarted in his hope to return to Greece by the anger of the sea-god. Twice he is beaten by wrecking waves,[75] and twice rescued by tutelary goddesses, first by the nymph Ino, of the lineage of Aphrodite goddess of love, who gives the hero her veil,

---

67. *De Vita Sua*, vv. 202-204, PG 37.1043.
68. *De Vita Sua*, v. 207, PG 37.1044.
69. *De Vita Sua*, vv. 150-157, PG 37.1040.
70. *De Vita Sua*, vv. 158-159, PG 37.1040-1041.
71. Cf. Jn 1:16.
72. The writer of Acts similarly begins his story of Paul's ill-fated journey by ship with the same indication Gregory uses, to the effect that it was past the safe date for sailing. Cf. *De Vita Sua*, vv. 125-127, and Acts 27:9-10.
73. Cf. Acts 27:20: "For many days both sun and stars were invisible, and the storm raged unabated, until at last we gave up any hope of surviving."
74. "Naught he looked, but when he sent forth that mighty voice from out his breast, and words like wintry snowflakes fell, no longer then could mortal man contend with Odysseos." *Iliad* 3.218.
75. *Odyssey* 5.290-437.

and subsequently by the goddess of Wisdom, Athene, Odysseos' divine protectress throughout life. The two figures of the immortals, implicitly present in this form of textual parallelism, are the more interesting when one reads on in the *De Vita Sua* to find the subsequent narrative about his stay in Athens almost oddly reticent about his experiences there. He says only that he will: "let others recount the story,"[76] before going on to tell the reader copious details anyway, but details focused externally on his relationship with Basil. The device, keeping silence in the face of a mystery,[77] is significant in signaling to the reader not the peripherality of the experience but its importance despite the writer's inability to encapsulate it in words.

When one reads his other versions of the stay in Athens it is clear that something is being left out of the narrative at this point; something which is important to him, yet which he chooses to hint at by this pregnant silence rather than expound explicitly in the poem. Perhaps the intended destination of the *De Vita Sua* accounts for the omission, given that it was written from the outset as a public apologia for his time in Constantinople, and in it he seeks to explain the basis of his judgments in rational terms against a hostile audience who regarded him as too readily swayed by feelings and affections than a man in a high position ought to be. In other accounts which were written more intimately, with less of an eye on public circulation, he gives more explicitly formed versions of an extremely important event which transpired: his vision of two immortals, an epiphanic experience which is the "seal" of his earlier dedication to God at sea. The vow at sea, in a sense, merely provides the occasion and preparation for this vision experience which he sets as the real locus of his consecration to divine service.

The two immortals who speak to him in Athens are the Christian counterparts of Athene and Aphrodite: Wisdom and Chastity.[78] To this extent, even when he has excised the event from his narrative version given in the *De Vita Sua*, it is clear that it is still at the back of his mind, as a cardinal episode, in the way he structures his text. If it is the case that he first wrote the poem years previously, it is conceivable that he only excised the vision narrative late in 382 when he came to edit and finalize the form of the complete work. The remaining signs within the text, of the Homeric parallelism of the two immortals, would suggest that the story originally did play a part in the *De Vita Sua* too. It certainly is still visible in the poem *De Rebus Suis*, and more explicitly described in the long autobiographical poem of "Lament on my soul."[79] To which we shall turn in a moment.

76. *De Vita Sua*, v. 210, PG 37.1044.
77. So named from the devotee's refusal to divulge the secret of initiation (*muein*).
78. He also plays on the symbolism of the two immortals Demeter and Persephone when he develops on the vision in other poems, apart from the context of the sea-storm; something we shall discuss subsequently.
79. See *De Rebus Suis*, Carm. 2.1.1, PG 37.969f, lines 195-210; *Carmen Lugubre*. 45, PG 37.1370-1371, vv. 251-262.

After the storm had blown out, the ship passed Rhodes and came to Aegina, the home port for the crew. When he had sufficiently recovered, Gregory passed on the final lap to Piraeus and Athens. He undoubtedly half suffered, half enjoyed, the student initiation rituals which it had long been the custom to inflict on "freshers" newly arrived for study. Gangs of students would tout for more recruits for their favorite professors,[80] and would seek new companions in the student lodgings.

One of the rituals was to harangue the newcomer in a group, half of them being kind and favorable, and the others making the most bloodcurdling threats. Gregory played his part, and after the final visit to the public baths in Athens the new student was duly declared "one of the club." When he heard that Basil was coming to the city to study he made it clear to all and sundry that from what he knew of his character he would not be at all amused at these ceremonies. The fact that he persuaded everyone to agree with his plan to give a special dispensation to Basil suggests that already he had found his niche and was a popular member of the student society. He forgets himself only a moment later in his narrative of these students days, (given in his memorial Oration for Basil)[81] when he lets slip that he himself was host one evening when Basil was harangued at just such an "initiation," a heated debate with Christian Armenians at which Gregory first took sides against Basil, then in the traditional *volte face*, spoke for him,[82] but his point in recounting that story is to express some resentment against Armenians in general, and probably the Arian Eudoxios of Germanicia, and the "Pneumatomachian" Eustathios of Sebaste in particular. The latter was Basil's early mentor who, by the time of the Basil's death was no longer any friend to the circle of Basil's family and disciples before whom Gregory was then preaching. Even so, Gregory's obvious courtesy and hospitality to the very serious young man[83] he had once met in school at Caesarean Cappadocia touched a chord with Basil and was the beginning of one of the most longstanding, famous, and stormy friendships in Christian history.[84] In the years they were to spend together in Athens they met many of the famous and great, not only Julian the future Augustus, but figures such as the Cappadocian Sophronios who was to become Prefect of Constantinople and Master of Offices in the imperial administration,[85] or Julian the Praeses of Phrygia,[86] or the two fellow students Eustochios and Stagirios who were later to become professors of rhetoric,[87] and

---

80. Thus earning discounts on their own studies.
81. Orat. 43, 15-17, PG 36.513-520.
82. Orat. 43.17, PG 36.517-520. In other words, some form of initiation ritual *was* arranged; but it was reserved as a Christian occasion with Gregory playing a large part.
83. Orat. 43.23: "Who was ever so serious and venerable even before his hairs were gray?"
84. "Thus was rekindled, no longer a spark but a manifest and conspicuous blaze of friendship." Orat. 43.17, PG 36.520.
85. Cf. Gregory's Letters 21-22, 29, 37, 39, 93 and 135; cf. Hauser-Meury (1960), pp. 156-157.
86. Cf. Hauser-Meury (1960), p. 110. Julian was the recipient of *Letters* 67-69, and *Oration* 19, PG 35.1044-1064.
87. Epp. 187-192, PG 37.308f; Gallay (1967), pp. 78-84. The three old rhetors ended in a massive dispute over who should educate Gregory's great-nephew Nicobulos. Gregory, in *Letter* 192,

others like them in the upper ranks of civic life, figures who appear in the patronage letters of Gregory later in life, and represented that circle of mutual regard between whom recommendations and favors were passed in a web of relationships that formed the substructure of political organization in the Roman dominions.

It cannot be doubted that Gregory sought out baptism during this time in Athens, as the fulfillment of the vow he had made.[88] It was unusual then for one so young to offer himself for such consecration, unless life-threatening illness intervened. Gregory knew that the decision to seek baptism at that time was tantamount to a radical commitment to Christian discipline. And yet he had just arrived in Athens, which remained for him the goal of all his highest aspirations for knowledge and culture. The tension generated in his mind between the demands of academic study and the unknown requirements of "giving himself to Christ" was soon to be hastened on to a kind of resolution by another terrifying event, an earthquake in Greece[89] which he recounts as if it were a warning to him from God not to delay any further. The decisive moment of "conversion" is then represented as resolved in the form of a dream, this time his own dream which marks out his claim to have emerged as a spiritual initiate in his own right.

Basil was soon induced to join Gregory and Carterios in their lodgings, and a few others who formed a small society of Christians, probably the Cappadocian and Armenian circle of friends, who combined a regime of Christian religious observance, allied with higher studies in rhetoric and philosophy. Basil was one of the leading spirits of the group, and although Gregory tries to describe it as a serious ascetical community, in his later *Funeral Oration* for Basil,[90] it was more likely that

tells Stagirios to calm down and postpones the lessons because he cannot reconcile Eustochios to the arrangement.

88. Gregory the Presbyter's (7th c.) *Vita Gregorii* notwithstanding (PG 35.257), which sets the baptism, without foundational evidence of any kind, on his return to Cappadocia. Baronius had already dissented from such a presupposition and suspected Gregory was baptized in Athens, though not seeing any textual allusion to it. Tillemont followed Gregory the Presbyter. Cf. Benoit (1973) fn. 2, pp. 47-48; Gallay (1943), p. 67. Clémencet (cf. PG 35.173A) also suspected that Gregory must have been baptized, to account for his ascetical endeavors at Arianzum, thinking that Gregory the Elder would have baptized him when he returned home. But this does not take into account the evident fact that Gorgonia was not baptized even at the time of her final illness, nor Caesarios until he received "clinicus" baptism on his deathbed; nor that Gregory the Elder can hardly be credited with encouraging his son's ascetical leanings. If Gregory the Elder had baptized him, the bishop could have controlled his son's Christian lifestyle more than if he had been presented with a *fait accompli* which Gregory ascribed to a fulfillment of a vow taken earlier.

89. *De Rebus Suis*, vv. 322-326: "When all the foundations of spacious Greece were shaken, and there seemed to be no hiding place from disaster, how fearful I was because my soul was still uninitiated in heavenly rites, for lack of the salvific cleansing that brings to mortal men the grace and illumination of the Spirit." PG 37.994.

90. And so, for centuries, causing puzzlement about Basil's ascetical "conversion" in Cappadocia which Gregory Nyssa (in the *Life of Macrina*) ascribed so much to his sister's influence which

such an ascetical tone was predominantly the manner in which the newly baptized
Gregory viewed it, whereas the other Christian young men (Basil among them) were
more seriously interested in future political careers.[91] Tillemont drew up a list of that
circle of Cappadocian friends[92] and, as we have already noted, several of them did
indeed form later a circle of influential Christian politicians in Cappadocia. Even
though Gregory and Basil's families expressed their political power through the chan-
nel of the Church rather than directly in imperial administration, it is still clear that
subsequent social and political eminence was something expected by all the group,
Gregory included, and a dedication to ascesis notwithstanding. Basil soon found
Athenian student life very dissatisfying.[93] He may have already wanted to satisfy his
curiosity about what he had heard about Christian Egypt and journey out to study the
eremitical and "philosophic" movement associated with Antony and actively propagated by Bishop Athanasios.[94] He was to make such a journey a few years later when
he came under Eustathios' ascetical influence and then, with all the dedication of a
new convert, regarded it as the sole true pattern of monastic life, much to Gregory's
distress. For the moment Gregory had influence enough to persuade him that he was
still insufficiently initiated to understand the value of his studies, and he appears to
have been convinced,[95] though Athens, for Basil, was never the golden dream it was
for Gregory, and Gregory's recollections of Basil in the time he shared with him as a
student tend to overemphasize Basil's attraction to asceticism. This is partly because
Gregory wishes to make an encomium of the great man and point up his lifelong consistency, but is partly also for apologetic reasons, to underline to Basil's family that he
(Gregory) had taken the lead in initiating Basil into the ascetical life from their time in
Athens (and thus answer the criticism that he had not been a loyal enough follower of
Basil) and also to describe Basil's ascetical career while simultaneously deleting one of
its main causes—bishop Eustathios of Sebaste. For the Cappadocian Nicene party the
latter had become a non-person through his theological opinions on the Holy Spirit,
and the difficulties his monastic zealots had caused for the bishops in many of the
Cappadocian churches—including Gregory's father's.

The curriculum of the schools of Athens at that period has been described by
several of the leading sophists of the age, especially Eunapios and Libanios.[96] But

        had to work hard to turn aside his political ambitions (or more accurately redirect them into
        Church politics). Cf. PG 36.521-524.
91. The dissonance between Gregory's Basil as drawn in the *Funeral Oration,* and the Basil that
        emerges from more purely "Basilian" sources was already noted by Gallay (1943), p. 67, and
        has recently been more elaborated by Rousseau in his critical biography of Basil (1994).
92. *Mémoires pour servir à l'histoire ecclésiastique,* vol. 9, p. 18.
93. Orat. 43.18, PG 36.520.
94. Athanasios' *Vita Antonii* had been published only a few years earlier, and achieved great liter-
        ary success.
95. Orat. 43.18.
96. Cf. Capes (1877), p. 66f; Kennedy (1983), chs. 3-4; and Athanassiadi (1992).

even if their records had not survived, in literary terms it could be deduced from the scintillating mosaic of authors that survives in the writings of Gregory, making him unarguably one of the most widely read men of his time, a fact which is not diminished in significance if it is argued that many collections of "selected works" formed the staple of reading in several schools in an age when the written word was still expensive to produce and maintain,[97] for Gregory's allusions are quite evidently deeply embedded in his context of argument and form the pattern of his entire mentality in a way that is never the case for one who merely adds citations for show. His literary culture is wide and it has not stifled his creative thought processes, but forms a constellation against which and through which he articulates what he has to think and say in his own right as a Christian theologian.

The explicit references in Gregory's writings to the classical authors are wide ranging and impressive.[98] Anaxilas, Apollonios of Rhodes, Aratos and other poets of the Palatine anthology, Aristophanes, Aristotle, Callimachos, Demosthenes, Diogenes Laertios, Evagoras, Heraclitus, Herodotos, Hesiod, Homer, Isocrates, Lucian, Lysias, Philo, Phocylides, Pindar, Plato, Plutarch, Sappho, Simonides, Socrates, Theocritos, Theognis, and Thucydides. There are, moreover, a host of implicit allusions and resonances lying deeper than the surface, particularly to Homer. At times other more arcane sources glimmer through, such as an Apollonine oracle,[99] and the religious speculation of the Neo-Platonists that partially influences his Trinitarian theology, and understanding of religious insight. All the time there is the constantly flowing stream of biblical consciousness that spreads over and around the whole, acting as the Christian counterpart to Hellenistic oracular wisdom, and serving as the binding agent for his system.[100] It is far more than merely the constant biblical awareness that one might expect of an educated fourth-century hierarch.[101] He prided himself in that biblical knowledge as well as in his sure knowledge of the classics.[102]

In terms of philosophical influence he was, much in the tradition of Origen, a pragmatic eclectic; giving pride of place to biblical revelation and the sense of an inherited Christian tradition (both seen through the perspective of a Platonically influenced metaphysic), but combining in a particularly visible manner, the

97. Meehan (1987), p. 8, sets the context well when he says: "It is likely, of course, that a great deal of reading was done in anthologies or private collections of passages for comparison made by individual sophists; but even by contemporary standards Gregory must have been unusually learned."
98. Cf. Fleury (1930), p. 76f; for a more extended survey, cf. sections 4-6 of the Thematic Index to the Bibliography at the end of this present work.
99. Recognized by Cameron (1969).
100. Cf. Section 7f of the Thematic Index to the Bibliography. See also F. Young, *Biblical Exegesis and the Formation of Christian Culture* (Cambridge, 1997).
101. For the extent of his biblical allusions, and the way they are so frequently melded with classical allusion, cf. Sykes (1982).
102. Cf. Wyss (1983), p. 793f and sections 4-6 in the Thematic Index to the Bibliography.

Aristotelian categories (used to such effect, for example, in the *Five Theological Orations*),[103] Neo-Platonic resonances, and definite traces of Cynic and Stoic elements in his thinking:[104] such as can be discerned also in the great Origen. The sum of philosophical influences, in fact, mirrors those of his greatest theological mentor. And while the metaphysical sweep of Origen's speculative mind is broader and greater than that of Gregory, the capacity to synthesize and relate, discriminate and combine, a variety of ideas and theses is no less apparent in Gregory than Origen. This was to be his greatest contribution to the history of Christian ideas: his synthetic ingenuity.

At Athens in the period Gregory and Basil lived there, many of the leading minds, Christian or Hellenist, shared common principles laid down for them by Origen and Plotinus, who had fought one another for the memory of their common teacher and for the right to be seen as the authentic interpreters of the "New Platonism" of Ammonios: whether this was to be a Christian or a purely Hellenistic phenomenon.[105] Origen's position had been much weakened since his death by the tawdry way in which his genius had been received by the majority of Christians, but Plotinus and Porphyry had advanced the work. So much so that it was, as it were, common orthodoxy in the mid-fourth century (at least among Platonists, Neo-Pythagoreans, and Stoics) that the highest form of philosophical insight was the visionary experience of God. Maximus, Julian's Neo-Platonic teacher, was famed for his communication with the world of the daemons, and the range of his thaumaturgic powers.[106] This kind of contact with the supernatural world was commonly attributed to Julian himself as an expected attribute of his function as "sophos" or wise man. Himerios, one of Gregory's main teachers in Athens, persuaded Julian to approach the Eleusinian Mysteries for initiation,[107] and was persuaded by Julian to be himself initiated into the Mithraic mysteries. These stages of initiation were, of course, often assimilated at this stage by sophist intellectuals to become symbols of the Neo-Platonic ascent of the soul to noetic union with God, such as that experience attributed by Porphyry to Plotinus, the great Neoplatonic teacher-saint.[108] At Ephesus in 351 Julian had already been initiated into the Neo-Platonic mysteries by Maximus,[109] and the first stages of Mithraism, and he was subsequently to undergo initiation into the higher Mithraic mysteries,[110] and the mysteries of the Great

103. Orats. 27-31 delivered in Constantinople between 380 and 381 to set out a complete apologia of how he saw Nicene systematic theology to be defensible.
104. Cf. Asmus (1894); Kertsch (1976).
105. Cf. P.F. Beatrice, "Porphyry's Judgment on Origen," in *Origeniana Quinta*, ed. R.J. Daly, (Leuven, 1992), pp. 351-367.
106. Cf. Eunapios, *Lives of the Philosophers* 7.2.6-11; ibid., 6.9.3-7; Giangrande (1956).
107. Eunapios, *Lives of the Philosophers* 7.3.1; ibid., 7.3.6-7; cf. Athanassiadi (1992), p. 48.
108. Porphyry, *Vita Plotini*. Armstrong (1966).
109. Julian. Ep. 111; Athanassiadi (1992), pp. 37-43.
110. In Constantinople in 362, where he built his own private Mithraeum, and there acted as

Mother Cybele which Gregory took for the final act of his renunciation of the true "mysteries" of Christian baptism: "Through impious blood[111] he washed away the waters of baptism."[112]

Throughout his short time in Athens, Basil and Gregory were disgusted to see the way Julian courted the Iamblichean Neoplatonist Priscos, in his eagerness to learn more of the mystic rites that would his assist the intellectual purification and spiritual ascent to which he aspired. Gregory had already discerned where Julian's true allegiance lay,[113] and genuinely so, not merely from the wisdom of hindsight, for the temptation to enter into Hellenism's very soul was something that was troubling him too, and which he was wrestling with on the way to elaborating his theory, later to be so roundly castigated by Julian himself, that the essential form of Hellenic civilization was entirely separable from its accidental pagan religious sentiment. Both Gregory and Basil had cause to be anxious about the consequences, not only on the individual level of young Christians discovering that the ancestral faith was looked down upon in many intellectual quarters, and fearing for the survival of their own faith in the light of what was transpiring with Julian; but also on the wider stage, of what would happen to the Church if imperial patronage was withdrawn: fears that were entirely justified, but ultimately resolved by the Emperor's early death in Persia. "See what a mischief the Roman Imperium is nursing in its bowels"[114] was Gregory's famous remark on his royal Athenian contemporary.[115] This mysterious atmosphere of Julian's early experiments with the ancient rites of initiation (and Gregory's subtle apologetic) is masterfully captured by Cavafy in his poem "Julian at the Mysteries."[116] This was a world of discourse and religious expectation that affected Gregory too, though with a surer Christian foundation he found the whole aspect of Iamblichean theurgy nothing more (or less) than demonic influence. This

---

sponsor-initiator for his teacher the philosopher Maximus. Cf. Athanassiadi (1992), 37-41. Julian also invited Himerios to be initiated at the capital, and Himerios' speech delivered on the subject survives: Himerios. *Oration 7*. The text shall be noted shortly in connection with Gregory's form of an initiation account.

111. It is not clear whether he means the (very expensive) Taurobolium ritual, or merely a generic reference to animal sacrifice.

112. Orat. 4.52, PG 35.576.

113. He had accepted Maximus' invitation to commit himself to the gods of Hellenism from 351 onwards, though kept his own counsel about it.

114. Orat. 5.23, PG 35.694.

115. In this *Oration* (Orat. 5.23, PG 35.664-720) Gregory gives a famous and devastating caricature of Julian, depicting his ungainly appearance and hysterical cachinnations. It makes him appear an out-and-out neurotic, and was meant to, for by thus depicting his mental instability Gregory was casting dark aspersions on his right to claim spiritual wisdom as a philosopher. Cf. Bowersock (1978); Regali (1980).

116. "He found himself in the darkness / in the frightful depths of earth / in the company of unholy Greeks. / Bodiless figures appeared before him / haloed in radiant light. / The young Julian for a moment lost his nerve / and made the sign of the cross..." Cf. C.P. Cavafy, *Collected Poems*. ed. G. Savidis (London, 1984), p. 133; ibid., pp. 89, 91, 103, 108, for other parts of his "Julian Sequence."

did not prevent him from using the language-symbolism of Mystery Initiation to connote his own religion's approach to sacrament and commitment, a procedure which had already been sanctioned by the apostle Paul.[117] Such was the world of discourse that shapes the account of his most profound experience of "commitment," the initiation experience that was at once his Baptism and entrance into the mysteries of his ancestral religion, and his concomitant decision to embrace the solitary and celibate life—what he often sums up as Sophrosyne: holy simplicity becoming to the philosopher. There was no definite canonical requirement (except in parts of the Syrian Church still influenced by Encratism) for a young person entering on baptism to be committed to lifelong celibacy, but it was certainly expected of a serious philosopher, and implicitly looked to as a sign of the earnestness that made a young man go forward for baptism at such an early age. Years later when Gregory was delivering his teachings on the nature of baptism, in Constantinople,[118] he urges his hearers not to delay and explicitly reminds them that it does not demand subsequent celibacy. That he had to remind them is indicative.

If the professor of rhetoric that he shared with Julian, Himerios, had induced his royal pupil to go forward for the Eleusinian mystery initiation we might deduce as much for Gregory too. And more to the point that his other great mentor, the Christian professor Prohaeresios, offered him an alternative perspective on the mysteries, consolidating his own desire, vowed at sea, to offer himself for baptism if he survived.

Prohaeresios was the unrivalled "King of Rhetoric" in Athens.[119] Gregory gave him high honor, and not lightly done, in two short Epitaphion verses he composed[120] in which he bestows on Prohaeresios the "victor's palm" among all other sophists:

> Land of Athenians be proud no more.
> It is not right to vaunt your little flame
> before a burning sun,
> Or set another mortal man to match Prohaeresios in craft;
> He who once shook the world with his orations.[121]

Eunapios was still breathless with admiration for the old man when, thirteen years after Gregory's first encounter, he found Prohaeresios still, at eighty-seven, "possessed of a rhetorical power so great that he sustained his worn body by the

---

117. Cf. Eph 3:3-4 and 9; 1 Cor 2:7, et al. Cf. H.A.A. Kennedy, *St Paul and the Mystery Religions* (London, 1913).
118. Orats. 39-40, delivered in 381, PG 36.336-425.
119. Eunapios, *Lives of the Philosophers* 9.1.4; The Roman senate had dedicated a statue to him inscribed: "Rome, the Queen of all, to the King of Eloquence."
120. Printed as one in PG 38.13, *Epitaph* 5.
121. It is a stock rhetorical phrase for heroic power in oratory, but it is a nice fancy to imagine it may also be a witticism remembered from Gregory's lecture room in earthquake-prone Athens. Cf. *De Rebus Suis*, vv. 322-326, PG 37.994.

youthfulness of his soul."[122] He thereby seemed to embody the principle enunciated by Origen[123] and Athanasios[124] when they described how the inner spiritual vitality gives a proof of the ascetic-philosopher's authenticity, and already gives a foretaste of the transfigured life. Eunapios expresses this in the Hellenistic motif, going on to describe him as "an ageless and immortal being, a god who, unsummoned, had revealed himself to humanity."[125]

But for Prohaeresios, although his fame had made both Eunapios and Julian want to make him an honorary Hellenist in all ways (the one canonizing him as a pagan saint, the other making him the sole exception to his legislation banning Christians from the rhetorical profession),[126] it was not necessary to receive his directions from pagan intellectuals. He was quite sure of his religious foundations, and carried on Origen's tradition of finding no disparity between the works of the Logos and the highest aspirations of human culture, once refined and reclaimed by the Logos' own revelation. The sources of his inspirations and actions rose from a deeply and fervently held Christianity. The way in which he had combined his religion and his cultural achievements presented Gregory with a living image of all he wanted to be himself, and (critically for this period of his life) a definitive proof that religion and literature were not incompatible paths. A similar movement of men and ideas can be discerned in the West around Victorinus in Rome, and Simplicianus and Ambrose in Milan: a circle that was to be so influential on the young Augustine who also sought his vocation in the interstices between Neoplatonic philosophy and literature.[127]

It may also be the case that Prohaeresios' philosophically ascetical lifestyle also gave Gregory a paradigm for the kind of monastic and studious simplicity (the life of Sophrosyne) which he was later to favor[128] in his own understanding of the monastic state. Eunapios gives witness to the simplicity of Prohaeresios' lifestyle in Athens, telling us that his home and school:

122. Eunapios in his *Lives of the Philosophers*, which was designed as a collection of chief philosopher "saints" of the old religion, incongruously includes the Christian, for the simple reason that his admiration is so great he cannot bear to leave him out. He makes Prohaeresios a counterpart to the Hellenist Libanios.
123. Cf. Origen, *On Proverbs*, PG 13.24. "As long as I cried to God in doxology and was theologizing all day long, nothing in me ever grew old, but was subjected to constant renewal. But when I stopped saying what theology commanded me, I immediately became aged and the aging entered into my very bones and the parts that seemed to be the steadiest in me."
124. *De Incarnatione*, 3.4; *Vita Antonii*, 93 (ET, NPNF series 2, vol. 4).
125. Eunapios, *Lives of the Philosophers* 10.1.3-4; cf. also Libanius, Ep. 275.
126. He resigned anyway as a public protest against Julian's policy.
127. Cf. J. McGuckin, "The Enigma of Augustine's Conversion," *Clergy Review* 72, no. 8, Sept. 1986, pp. 315-325.
128. Being always less than enthusiastic about the wilder forms of Syrian and Egyptian monastic asceticism which so excited Basil at first.

was in a small and cheap house; but the place exhaled the fragrance of Hermes and the Muses, thus differing in nothing from a Temple.[129]

Athanassiadi[130] attributes this to the economic decline of fourth-century Athenian life, but I think this misses the point. The combination of an ascetic lifestyle as an essential accompaniment to the philosophic quest was a principle the early Church shared with the Neoplatonists. Prohaeresios' simplicity is certainly a result of his personal religious and intellectual mentality, in which he exactly mirrors Origen before him.[131] Gregory must have spent much time in this atmosphere of Christian simplicity, and despite the fact that he was always an aristocratic "monk," the quality of this simplicity of lifestyle always characterized Gregory too in his personal conduct and preferences. It cannot be doubted that Prohaeresios was a significant figure in the life of the Christian Church at Athens.

As at Alexandria with Pantaenos, Clement, Demetrios and Heraclas, or Jerusalem under bishop Alexander, or at Caesarea under Origen and Eusebios, so the Church at Athens had, over the previous generations, been long preparing inroads into the establishment and making its presence felt as a "schola" in its own right. Origen had visited the Athenian Church twice in his career, seeking books for his own library, as well as lecturing there. When Gregory says that only two roads were familiar to Basil and himself: "the first and more precious leading to our sacred buildings and the masters there,"[132] it could well be that he is referring to Prohaeresios' place in the official life of the Athenian Church, not as a cleric or preacher, but as part of the wider educational establishment that can already be witnessed as part of the formal Christian mission as early as the third century.[133]

Such was the intellectual and religious environment that contextualized Gregory's "conversion" narrative, as he gives it in his autobiographical writings. The notion of conversion as mystery initiation is much to the fore. His literary treatment of the event habitually pairs it with his story of his consecration by his mother when he was an infant, but the vision he recounts in his young manhood is the more significant, and the texts are worthy of close scrutiny.

Gallay[134] attributes this important visionary event to Gregory's childhood. He does so, by mistake, I think, apparently misrendering verses 267-268 of the poem *Carmen Lugubre*, the section in which Gregory recounts the event,[135] giving the lines

---

129. Eunapios, *Lives of the Philosophers* 9.1.4.

130. Athanassiadi (1981/1992).

131. The ascetical climate was part and parcel of the philosophical renewal going on from the early third century, the Middle Platonic revival to which Origen (and perhaps even Ammonios Saccas) already belonged as Christians. Cf. Eusebios, *Hist. Eccl.* 6.3; see also R. Berchman. (1984).

132. Orat. 43.21, PG 36.524.

133. See J. McGuckin, "Caesarea Maritima as Origen Knew It," *Origenian Quinta*, R.J. Daly, ed. (Leuven, 1992), pp. 3-25.

134. Gallay (1943), p. 28.

135. *Carmen Lugubre.* 2.1.45, vv. 229f, PG 37.1372.

only paraphrastically as: "the moment when his reason first began to distinguish clearly between good and evil."

In the wartime catholic context of the author's narrative, this seems to suggest "the age of reason" for a child, that is (traditionally) the time between seven and eight years of age. The verses he cites, however, have no hint of that meaning in the original Greek. The paraphrase is wholly out of context. Gregory's text in verses 267-268 actually refers quite specifically to the fact that years later, even now in his old age as he is recounting his vision, whenever his soul holds fast to the good, or whenever his "mind is master of the desires," then the recollection of his shining vision returns to encourage him in his ongoing duty of "stabilizing the virtues." The context here is not childhood at all, rather mature dedication to Christianity and the philosophic demands of virtue. Up to verse 228, the poem has certainly been talking of the formative and stabilizing influence his parents have had on him, but from verse 230 a new section begins (introduced by the conjunction *kai pote*), intent on describing his dream vision. This section culminates in the verses mentioned above (267-268) which signify that, as a man, the vision had the effect of bringing what his parents had initiated to its mature conclusion, an effect that has endured even into his old age. It is clear that Gregory sees this vision as a fundamental experience, a dramatic moment of conversion. It is a description of what he recalls as one of the most important formative influences of his psychic life. There is no doubt either, that he uses it to dissociate himself from his parents' consecration of himself as a child. This vision declares his own personal choices, his election, and consecration as a man. It is his coming of age. To mislocate the event as a phenomenon of his childhood is a large misreading of the evidence, and has accounted for many Gregorian commentators missing the significance of this narrative entirely.

As we have noticed earlier, the vision is passed over discreetly in the poem *De Vita Sua*,[136] yet represented, *in loco*, by the phrase: "I will leave to others the account of what transpired there."[137] This signals a modest reserve, not a disclaimer about his educational prowess while in Athens, but specifically about something to do with his spiritual state, as evidenced by the immediately qualifying phrase: "About how I walked in the fear of God."[138]

This it is which gives us our first clue to the experience that has been so passed over in silence. Gregory is, in fact, telling the attentive reader that he is deliberately "keeping silence" on it, or in precise terms "guarding the mystery" (*Muein*); for silence was imposed on the initiate as the only fit way to encompass a transcendent experience of the divine (and in both Christian liturgy, as well as in the rites of the Mystery Religions imposed as the highest moral duty on the newly initiated not to discuss the details of the initiation process or the sacred things heard and seen therein).[139]

136. Carm. 2.1.11, PG 37.1029f.
137. *De Vita Sua*, v. 212, PG 37.1044.
138. *De Vita Sua*, vv. 212-213, PG 37.1044.
139. For further elaboration of the theology and practice of the Mysteries, cf. Reitzenstein (1978).

The visionary and psychic aspects of the experience could only be hinted at. One such famous peripheral account is the reference to the Isis initiation given at the end of Apuleios of Madaura's *Metamorphoses of Lucius*.[140] At the end of a bawdy tale the narrator introduces his conversion story, (wherein his transformation back into a human being from the form of a donkey which had been imposed on him, is symbolic of his understanding the higher spiritual verities through the mercy of Isis). Similar motifs to Gregory, of the locking out of all uninitiated persons, the lighted tapers, the splendid vestments, the ineffable visions,[141] the sense of conversion of life, can be found throughout this section of the text. An excerpt from Apuleios' narrative should give the flavor:

> As evening approached a crowd of priests came flocking to me from all directions... then the chief priest gave orders for all uninitiated persons to depart, invested me in a new linen garment and led me by hand into the inner recesses of the sanctuary itself. I have no doubt, curious reader that you are eager to know what happened then. If I were allowed to tell you, and you were allowed to be told, you would soon hear everything...but I will record as much as I may lawfully record for the uninitiated, but only on condition that you believe it: I approached the very gates of death and set one foot on Proserpine's threshold, yet was permitted to return, rapt through all the elements. At midnight I saw the sun shining as if it were noon; I entered the presence of the gods of the underworld and the gods of the upper world, stood near and worshipped them. The solemn rites ended at dawn and I emerged from the sanctuary wearing... a most sacred and splendid costume... I remained for some days longer in the Temple sanctum enjoying the ineffable pleasure of contemplating the goddess's image, because I was bound to her by a debt of gratitude so large that I could never hope to pay it.[142]

The power of the experience, and the initiation proper, is left outside the story as such. It is essentially "agraptos": unwritable because incircumscribable. It is something of this which Gregory is evoking by his reserved silence in the *De Vita* account. Its significance, even in the *De Vita Sua* where he does not expand on the event *in loco*, is manifested by the way he culminates this massive poem with a final appeal to his heavenly vision as his one comfort left in life. It is more evidently so in the other accounts he gives of the vision: two brief allusions in the autobiographical poem *De Rebus Suis*,[143] and then a longer and splendid version set out at the highest level of crafted poetry. The latter version is found in the *Lament on the Disasters Affecting My Soul*,[144] and has been

140. Commonly known in Antiquity as "The Golden Ass." ET by R. Graves, *Apuleius: The Golden Ass* (London, 1950).
141. Both (as at the end of his narrative) concrete epiphany-visions of the image of the goddess in the shrine, and visions in dream form: "Not a single night did I pass, nor even doze off during the day, without some new vision of her," Graves (1950), p. 282 (*Metamorphoses of Lucius*, ch. 18).
142. Graves (1956), pp. 285-6; *Metamorphoses of Lucius*, ch. 18, passim.
143. Carm. 2.1.1, PG 37.969f; see ibid., vv. 194-204, 210-212; and again vv. 452-453. The texts will be discussed below.
144. *Carmen Lugubre*. Carm. 2.1.45, PG 37.1353f, see vv. 228-266, PG 37.1369-1372. The poem was written while Gregory's father was still alive (cf. ibid., vv. 216-218) possibly shortly after his

unjustly neglected as it is one of his finer writings. It has, however, been mauled in the various translations it has endured, and long unrecognized as one of the most interesting early Christian formulations of a theology of baptism as illumination and mystical marriage, in a form reminiscent of the great rites of Hellenistic initiation, weaving in themes gathered from the Eleusinian Mysteries and the Panathenaean festival, as well as rhetorical "set-pieces" he remembered from his time as a student of rhetoric in Athens.

That Gregory fundamentally connects the story of his vision with his baptism is evident in the *De Rebus Suis* from the way he introduces the scene with the keyword denoting the baptismal sacrament: *sphragis* or seal, and immediately qualifies it as a "seal so notably made manifest" (*anaphandon*), a term connoting epiphany[145] which is how it will be translated below to bring out the nuance. It is also the case that when giving two Orations (39-40) specifically devoted to the theology and significance of baptism, Gregory chooses the context of Mystery Initiation to introduce his theme. In Oration 39 he contrasts the Eleusinian, Mithraic, Dionysiac, and Memphite Mysteries,[146] as well as theurgic initiation (Neoplatonic),[147] with the Christian experience of baptismal illumination. His implied thesis here is that just as the Christian Gospel fulfils and advances on the purificatory rites of the old Jewish law, so does baptism, by enlightening and mystically advancing the devotee, fulfil all that the Mystery Religions promised but could not deliver since they were corrupted, defiled, and perverted by demonic influence.[148]

In the *De Rebus Suis* account he first opens his narrative by telling the story of his mother's dedication of him to God as a child. This pairing of these two events is a regular and significant factor. When, for example, in his last days he composed an epitaph for himself, a twelve-line synopsis of his entire life, beginning with his rank and ending with his persecution by other bishops, the two spiritual experiences he highlights out of it all are his mother's dedication of her infant, and his own vision of the immortals in Athens.[149]

own consecration as bishop, circa 372. Rufinus, in his preface to his translation of Gregory's Orations, gives a paraphrastic rendering of the vision, reflecting more of his own psychology than that of Gregory (cf. *Corpus Christianorum. Series Latina* 20. Turnhout, 1986, p. 255).

145. Carm. 2.1.1, vv. 452-453, PG 37.1003-1004.
146. For an overview, cf. A.H. Armstrong, *Classical Mediterranean Spirituality; Egyptian, Greek, Roman* (New York, 1986).
147. Orat. 39.4-6, PG 36.337-341.
148. Orat. 39.7, PG 36.341.
149. *Compendium Ipsius Vitae*, Carm. 2.1.92, vv. 3-6, PG 37.1447. "Why, O Christ my King, have you bound me in the nets of flesh? Why have you set me under the baneful cares of life? I was born of a god-revering father, and a mother of no small repute. Through her prayers I came into the light; for she prayed and dedicated me, her child, to God. A vision of the night instilled in me a burning love for virginity. This Christ did for me; but then I was buffeted by stormy seas, suffering rapacious hands, a debilitated body. I ran up against hostile shepherds, finding only treachery, and was deprived of my children. Now at last I am done with calamities. This has been the life of Gregory. Have it inscribed on stone."

After so beginning the story with the maternal dedication in the *De Rebus Suis*, he continues as follows:

> My tender soul began to be shaped
> in this new mould of holiness,
> But the seal was reserved by the will of Christ
> who so epiphanically conversed with me his servant.
> He bonded me in love to holy simplicity (Sophrosyne)
> and put a rein upon my flesh.
> He breathed into me a burning love
> for divine wisdom,
> And for the monastic life, the first fruits
> of the life to come.[150]

This follows a previous discussion of the same event earlier in the same poem:

> Long ago I cut myself off from this world.
> My soul was melded with radiant spirits of heaven,
> and my spiritual intellect carried me aloft,
> setting me down far from the flesh;
> thence it arose and took refuge
> in the innermost chambers of heaven.
> where the radiance of the Trinity shone around our eyes[151]
> brighter than any light I have ever known,
> enthroned on high and emitting ineffable and harmonious radiance,
> the principle of all those things that time shuts off from heaven.
> Then I died to the world, and the world died to me,[152]
> And I became like the living dead,
> as devoid of strength as a dreamer,
> but groaning under the yoke of the crass flesh,
> that which wise men have called the "darkness of the mind"
> And yet with the eyes of the mind made pure
> I shall gaze upon[153] the Truth itself;
> yet all this is still to be.[154]

Both this and the previous description in the same text sets Gregory's election of *Sophrosyne*[155] in terms reminiscent of Neoplatonic initiation—the transcendent *ecstasis* of the soul.

---

150. *De Rebus Suis*, 2.1.1, vv. 452-456. The key terms here, of epiphany, sophrosyne, and "burning love" for divine wisdom, are exactly paralleled in Carm. 2.1.45 as we shall shortly notice, when he makes it explicitly clear that he is talking about his vision in the night, PG 37.1003-1004.

151. Not so much a "royal we" as a reflection of the context of plurality as revealed in the other versions of the story—that two spirits spoke with him.

152. Cf. Gal 6:14.

153. Cf. Mt 5:8.

154. *De Rebus Suis*. Carm. 2.1.1, vv. 194-204, 210-212, PG 37.985-986

155. A term which is difficult to render, and which is here consistently translated as "holy simplicity." It is the ascetically withdrawn life necessary for one devoted to wisdom, and the common aspiration of Hellenistic philosopher and Christian monk alike which Gregory at the present instance is eliding (in a deliberate synthesis).

In part it is meant to evoke the Pauline texts describing the apostle's own rapture from the flesh[156] and his vision of the heavenly radiance of Christ who converts him, and thus leads him directly to his baptism,[157] and other Pauline resonances are set well forward in the text itself. But the overall tenor of the verses has been well and truly assimilated to the form of Neoplatonic mystery-experience. Synesios of Cyrene gives another example of similar style and content in his great poem describing Christ's entrance into the "innermost chambers" (*skenai*) of heaven, beyond the drag of time's current,[158] although Gregory is much more successful than Synesios in synthesizing the Neoplatonic influences with the core and tenor of the Christian message.

The real extent of his deliberate evocation of the language and experience of the Mysteries emerges all the more clearly in the long account of the "visionary dream" in the Hymn of Lament, which merits a fuller exposition. Once again, this critically formative spiritual experience of Gregory's is paired literarily with its "preparation," which is his mother's dedication of him as a child. That this act, done at the altar of his father's church in Nazianzus, was in all probability within the rite of enrolling the infant as a catechumen, we have already noticed. This makes the second part of the syzygy, the vision itself, stand out all the more in relief as symbol for the actual baptism. The relevant section of the text begins as follows:

> 191 God governs all men of good will
> but keeps the heights of his wisdom still hidden
> and opaque darkness lies between our race and God
> which few can ever penetrate[159]
>
> 195 with farseeing eyes, acutely discerning beyond this life:
> the pure who attain to pure wisdom,
> and yet to me Christ gave this outstanding honor.
> First of all in answering the secret prayers of a mother's heart
> he gave her me. Then from my parents
> received the gift returned; their child,
>
> 200 the finest thing of all that they possessed.
> Secondly he gave to me, in visions of the night,
> a divine and burning love for the life of wisdom.
> So hear the tale if you are godly souls

---

156. 2 Cor 12:1-4.
157. Acts 9:3-19.
158. Cf. J. McGuckin (ed. and tr.), *At The Lighting of the Lamps: Hymns From the Ancient Church* (Harrisburg, PA: 1997), pp. 40-45, 95-96. Synesios. *Hymn* 8.
159. A shared Neoplatonic and Christian theme. Gregory Nyssa and Pseudo-Denys elaborate it formally for Christian mystical theology (as in Gregory Nyssa's *Life of Moses,* for example) but for Gregory Nazianzen it is equally a central notion of the vision of God, and is usually set within a liturgical context: the mind's admission to the heavenly sanctum where the radiant presence of God is veiled from creaturely eyes, to protect them. Cf. McGuckin (1996).

<blockquote>
but all who have a profane mind

204   stay back, outside the doors, so as not to hear.[160]
</blockquote>

The last three lines of the above signal an explicitly liturgical context. In Christian practice the non-baptized catechumens had to leave the Church before the recitation of the creed and the celebration of the Eucharistic mysteries. So too, did all the non-initiates of the Hellenistic Mysteries have to remain outside so as not to hear (or see) the sacred things that cannot be heard by the uninitiated.[161] The motif of the "doors" in line 204, therefore, signals his account of the Mystery proper is to begin, that is the record of his vision as a young man in Athens.[162] The account then continues:

<blockquote>
229   "Then while I was asleep there came to me this dream

230   which drew me so sweetly to the incorruptible life.

There appeared to me two virgins dressed in shining robes,

standing by my side in brilliant light.

Both were matched alike in beauty and stature,

and both were adorned without that adornment which

women take for beauty.

235   No sapphires or gold adorned their necks.

They did not dress in diaphanous silken gowns

or drape their slender limbs in finest linen tunics;

they did not flash their eyes tinted with cosmetics.

240   They needed no invented artifice to entice men,

no potions to incite desire;

No dyed blonde hair was combed out over their backs

to sport and dance in the gentle breeze.

No, for fastened around their waist

was the most beautiful of vestments

hanging in folds down to their feet, their very ankles.

245   Above, a veil shrouded their heads,

their eyes were cast down to the ground.

How gracefully did their modest blush become them,

as far as I could make out beneath the veil.

Both kept a mysterious silence with sealed lips,

250   like a rosebud[163] cupping the dew in its calix.
</blockquote>

---

160. *Carmen Lugubre.* Carm. 2.1.45, vv. 191-204, PG 37.1367.

161. A principle of theological method he will put to great effect in preaching against the Neo-Arians; cf. Orat. 27.

162. Winslow (1979, p. 4) seems to have mistakenly referred this vision to Gregory's childhood, by eliding lines 204 and 205 in his reading without noticing that this section of the poem (vv. 205-228) amplifies and refers back to his "In the first place" of v. 198, whereas after v. 229 (beginning with "Kai Pote"—"and then") he amplifies and refers back to a second and different event to that of the childhood consecration that is his later visionary experience (vv. 229-276). He seems to have been misled here by Gallay (1943, p. 28), as discussed earlier.

163. The frequent use of the image of roses, especially as here in reference to young women, is one of the several influences of the poetry of Sappho on Gregory. Cf. Cataudella (1926).

> Seeing them, how great was my elation, and I said:
> How greatly they surpass all human kind.
> My soul went out to them, and they kissed me
> upon the lips in token of love as to a beloved son,
> 255 And when I asked who these women were,
> and whence they came,
> One answered: "I am Virginity; the other, Simplicity.
> We stand within the presence of Christ the Lord,
> rejoicing in the beauty of the heavenly choir of virgins.
> But come now, child, and meld
> 260 your mind with ours; merge your lighted flame[164] with ours,
> until we bear you up on high, transfigured in light,
> through the very Aether
> to stand in the radiance of the Immortal Trinity.'
> Saying this, they were borne through the Aether as I watched
> their departing flight. These things were all as a dream,
> 265 But long after, my heart would take delight
> in these beautiful appearances of the night,
> these shining images of incorruption,
> 267 And yet, their sacred discourse worked on my mind
> until discernment of good and ill became fixed and stable in my soul,
> 269 And the spiritual mind at last was master of my desires.

In verses 235-242, he indulges in a stock oratorical theme found in both Hellenistic and Christian sophists, against women's cosmetic adornment. He takes the idea to considerable length elsewhere[165] and will only be outdone in it later by Chrysostom, who learned his own craft from the rhetorician Libanios. But the appearance of the motif is not entirely out of place here; first as a graphic literary contrast with the solemn, almost severely hieratic simplicity of the two maidenly spirits he is about to describe, a contrast which heightens all the more the effect of the "kisses on the mouth" which these impart; but secondly, I think, as a specifically historical reminiscence which is psychologically pertinent to his general recollections of the occasion of his time of baptism in Athens and all its associated memories.

The natural fabrics of the silken gowns, clinging and diaphanous as he describes them and as they would be if worn outdoors, and the finest linen tunics draping the slender limbs of his Greek maidens, are not entirely explicable by

---

164. A lighted pine-torch: a common enough object but also significant as a ritual element in the mystery cults whose initiation ceremonies took place in darkness. The significance of the lights or tapers, as used in the Baptismal liturgy is also apposite, and has been pointed out by Szymusiak-Affholder (1971). Gregory is also evoking a Stoic conception of the Logos's bond with his thinking creatures: as reason to rational beings, or as fire to little flames. Gregory elsewhere uses the notion of three flames forming one as a symbol of the unity in diversity of the Trinity (e.g., Carm. 2.1.99, PG 37.1451-1452).

165. Cf. Queré (1968); Knecht (1972).

recourse to the obvious Freudian connotations, nor so merely by appeal to a Jung-ian canon to interpret the dream,[166] although the latter's understanding of the psy-chic force latent in the Anima figure (and its growth from the mother-son relationship) certainly gives many insights into the nature of Gregory's spiritual and psychological experience.[167]

These details may be more usefully contextualized, and more accurately applied as guides to Gregory's mentality, if one approaches them as idealized reminiscences of a particular occasion, namely the great Panathenaean festival held in honor of the patron goddess of wisdom—Athene Pallas. In this procession the noble families of the area vied for the honor of having their daughters process through the Agora, on the Sacred Way, to the virgin's shrine (the Parthenon) on the Acropolis. It was a mag-nificent and internationally famous occasion, and one in which the whole of Athe-nian civic life played a part, including the "university men," who were expected to provide suitable Homeric recitations and rhetorical displays for the occasion, some of them even to join the procession singing hymns to Athene/Wisdom immediately in front of the young women. The women in the sacred procession were forbidden by tradition to wear any clothes that had been dyed—hence, perhaps, the relevance of the silk and linen fabrics Gregory mentions which were not only luxury garments, suitable for the rich celebrating a major festival, but also "liturgically" correct for the Panathenaeum. The sight of the young girls processing in solemn state, with mod-estly downcast eyes, slightly self-conscious at the young men gathered from the schools and peering at them under their sacred veils,[168] all of this was an occasion capturing the quintessence of his youth, the quintessence of elegant Hellenism, the quintessence of style. It was an occasion which, old ascetic or not, he was not going to pass up if he had the chance to use it, and even edify by telling of it, once the structure of the narrative had been sufficiently Christianized in the recasting.

The indication that this is a story which he has elevated as the quintessential "form" of his "commitment" story is borne out by the manner in which the overall shape of this narrative is reminiscent of another orator's account of his dream vision of two female figures. In this case it concerns Lucian's story of how he chose his

166. Szymusiak-Affholder (1971) approaches the text from this perspective.
167. Cf. C.G. Jung, *Man and His Symbols* (New York, 1969; also see C.G. Jung (tr. R.C.F. Hull), *The Structure and Dynamics of the Psyche* (Princeton, 1975).
168. The image is used in reference to his spiritual visitors: *Carmen Lugubre*. Carm. 2.1.45, vv. 246-248, PG 37.1370. Here, the two female figures are acting as the liturgical attendants, the "sponsors" of his own admission to the heavenly choir of virgins (the choice he had made for the monastic/philosophic state). The liturgical-spirit imagery had already been Christianized long before Gregory. In Hebrews, for example, the angels are the "liturgical spirits" (Heb 1:14). Origen too had developed the theme in his theology, and it was to leave a decisive mark on Gregory's own preference for the liturgical matrix when discussing the question of the soul's vision of God. Cf. J. McGuckin, "The Vision of God in St Gregory Nazianzen," *Stud. Pat.* 32 (1996), 136-143.

career from a possible choice of statue carver (a family business) or Rhetor.[169] The two figures of Lucian's tale (an oration which he delivered back in his home town after leaving his full-time studies) represent possible choices. One has a beautiful form (Rhetoric) but the other is repellent and dusty. His choice is clear. It explains his commitment. The formal element of this narrative, as perhaps it does with Gregory himself, goes back to the custom of the schools of oratory in Athens of setting the students to think seriously of occupational futures,[170] and symbolically electing them in rhetorical compositions. Gregory's choice, in a rhetorically crafted dream narrative, just like Lucian's, is at root his defense of why he elected the life he did. In his case it was not Rhetoric as such, but *Sophrosyne*, and as this was not so much an occupation, rather a defense of why he would not elect one in the normal manner, Gregory has to elaborate his choice of commitment even more completely than the normal conventions as represented in Lucian.

In Gregory's account of the vision, two key words support the view that he has chosen to develop the story of his "commitment" in the intellectual context of initiation, and has partly done so from the perspective of the greatest of the Athenian rites, approached from a paradigmatic basis of Neoplatonist initiation theology, and then reapplied as an analogy of Christian baptism and his subsequent decision to adopt the celibate philosophical lifestyle that resulted from that initiation in Gregory's case.

Both these revealing keywords refer to the antique style of dress in which his spirits approach him. First of all, they are, we are told, "veiled" in the antique manner from head to waist. The word is immediately allusive of the veil of Ino, Aphrodite's nymph, with which she invests Odysseus to protect the hero; an image we have already seen at play in his narrative of the storm at sea which was the immediately preceding context for his arrival in Athens. The description of the veil is also a hieratic device, a detail supported by the liturgical manner in which they keep their eyes downcast.

The second key word is Gregory's description of the spirits' robe as a most beautiful "Peplos." Once again this was deliberately meant as an antique style of dress which draped down over the ankles. The Sacred *Peplos*, however, and especially one which was woven with the most beautiful embroideries that the skill of the Athenian women could manage, was an item especially associated with Athene's festival of the Panathenaeum. On the occasion of the sacred procession, a new *Peplos* for Athene was the chief object carried, set as the sail on the mast of a processional ship. As the chief focus of attention it moved in solemn state first to the temple of Eleusinian Ceres, and thence to the Parthenon, whose frieze records the event.

169. Lucian. "The Dream." (ET, P. Turner [1958], 23-29). Lucian's speech is close to that of Gregory's not from any mutual dependence but because both go back to a similar archetypal form: the "choice of best profession speech" as an exercise set by the rhetorical schools.

170. Gregory notes in Ep. 178 that he thinks this is an excellent custom. He was presented with choices of estate management, politics, or rhetoric.

The evocation of the ancient Mysteries through the antique dress of the *Peplos* opens up further resonances within Gregory of the Eleusinian initiation. Both great rites are here associated, I think, because they stand for the highest level of "aristo-cratic-philosophic" religiosity in the period. This we can gauge from Julian's desire to be publicly admitted into the Mysteries when he emerged from behind the veil of his Christianity.[171] Two female figures well indicate the overall context of Eleusinian initiation, as can be seen from a surviving full-scale marble frieze from the sacred precinct at Eleusis, now preserved in the Archaelogical Museum in Athens[172] where the goddesses Demeter and Persephone appear in a sacred epiphany before their young initiate "son" Demophon/Triptolemos.[173] Again, they are depicted as clad in the antique *Peplos*, though this time they are not veiled, standing on either side of the young man. In Gregory's account, twice the spirit-figures call him "son,"[174] sig-nifying "aspirant initiate." In the Eleusinian theological context the epiphany of Persephone to the Triptolemic initiate figure, is meant to symbolize the human being's passage from death and the darkness of Hades, to immortality and life: pre-cisely the central symbolic movements of the Christian theology of baptismal initia-tion. In this sense, Gregory, the initiate-son of the heavenly spirits, who is being divinized by the mystery of rebirth, stands between the virgin Agneia[175] and the fer-tile matron Demeter, who has elected to close off the abundance, make the very earth to fast, in the course of calling her daughter back from Hades into the light of life. It is a perfectly apposite classical allusion to what Gregory perceives to be the fertile and life-giving aspects of the Christian ascetic renunciation (*Sophrosyne*) which he is here announcing he has adopted as his high road into the mystery of life.

There are other textual indications which Gregory gives to his readers to signal the "philosophical" interpretation of his dream narrative in the style of a Mystery Initiation in the grand manner. It comes out not only in the generally hieratic con-text but specifically, as for example at v. 249, in his reference to their mysterious silence (muein): to keep the mystery, or swear the silence as the initiate must do,[176] and also in v. 267, where he sums up the words they addressed to him as their "mythos": this being the technical word for the sacred dogmas and initiations given to the Mystery initiate as one of the last stages of his admission ritual.

171. Gregory, by thus implicitly comparing Christian initiation with the greatest Hellenistic rituals is arguing that the Church is no less suitable as a bearer of the highest cultural aspirations of his age.

172. Image reproduced in U. Bianchi. "The Iconography of the Eleusinian Mysteries," in *The Greek Mysteries* (Leiden, 1976).

173. Triptolemos, the half-god, half-human, child of Demeter who tried to divinize himself by burning off his mortal part. A copy is in the Metropolitan Museum, New York.

174. *Uia, Teknos: Carmen Lugubre*. Carm. 2.1.45, vv. 254, 259, PG 37.1371.

175. Perhaps an evocation of Koré the virginal Persephone.

176. One of the reasons for his final motif (to justify his disclosure) when he says "these things were all as a dream," v. 264. But his epiphanic understanding of dreams is given positively and clearly in Orat. 18.12, PG 35.1000, where they are marks of the soul destined for salvation.

The heart of this extraordinarily well drafted poem is undoubtedly meant to be Gregory's own "admission" by the heavenly spirits into the heavenly choir of virgins (v. 258), and that is presented on two levels. In the first instance he is setting forward the experience as the essential "mythos" or sacred discourse that explains and interprets his decision to abandon the various professions he has so far considered at Athens, farming, politics, and rhetoric[177] and commit himself decisively to the philosophic life and the celibacy he sees necessitated by this. On the second level of the text he is following and expanding on Origen's theme,[178] also familiar to much Neoplatonic religious discourse though in another form, that the soul's destiny is loving union with the divine on a plane where the purification of its materiality is presumed to have been accomplished. The physical ascesis presupposed in the life of Sophrosyne which he elects, thus prepares him psychically for the ecstatic experience of union with the divine—a theme signified to his readers by the double motif of the erotic kisses of love and the vision of unbearable light; both of which, in this instance, are employed in an Origenist and Biblical mode of discourse.[179] The account coyly tries to reduce the deliberate erotic evocations of the passage, but such a contrast of ideas between the luxuriant[180] evocation of Chastity is quite deliberately chosen as a central dynamic of the text, and seen not only in the ambivalence of the use of the word "mixis" in verse 259, which I have rendered as "melding" yet which carries strong associations of sexual union, but also in the deliberate contrast between the descriptions of the gaudy women in verses 235-242, and the sober women whose kisses enrapture Gregory in verses 251-254. The latter, in the climactic part of the epiphany narrative, are pictured in the phrase:

> My soul went out to them, and they kissed me
> upon the lips in token of love as to a beloved son.[181]

The maternal themes are certainly there, but overlaid so much in the rhetorical complex of chaste-sensuality, that they are fundamentally reconfigured. Here, I think, Gregory intends his meaning to rise out of the initiation context: for the

---

177. Ep. 178, PG 37.289.

178. *Commentary on Canticles*, begun when Origen was at Athens.

179. The beloved's kisses as in Canticles, understood according to Origen's mystical interpretation of the noetic rapture of the soul by the Logos, and the unbearable radiance of the *Shekinah*, or light of God's glory, which is shrouded, for the approaching creaturely intellect, by the "dark cloud" separating the divine presence, as at Sinai, or in the Gospel account of the Transfiguration. Cf. J. McGuckin, "Origen on the Glory of God," *Stud. Pat.* 21, (Leuven, 1989), pp. 316-324; idem., *The Transfiguration of Christ in Scripture and Tradition* (New York, 1987). For Gregory's exegesis of *Canticles* see Capelle (1929).

180. Not least linguistically.

181. The evident sense is that of being kissed "as a beloved and elect": just as the welcoming of "Son" Triptolemos, in the Eleusinian context, indicates his admission, finally, into the ranks of the divine through initiation. For Gregory the close association of *Sophrosyne* (a life of ascetic chastity) and his baptismal initiation, would not have seemed far apart in many fourth-century Christian circles.

passage signals exactly his liberation from the world of Real-Mother, that is his spiritual (and psychological) dependence on Nonna's spiritual dominion, and his own final "coming of age" as spiritual man, fully formed in maturity:[182] one who is for himself, and through his own spiritual acuity, chosen and kissed as an elect of the company of the truly beautiful, the choir of immortals. This is Gregory's story of emergence from childhood to adulthood, in intellectual, psychological and religious terms. He stands, through this narrative, self-proclaimed, in his own right, as Christian spiritual Seer and Initiate.

Here, he passes out of, though of course not entirely free from, the visionary and dreaming world of his mother, and he is anxious to announce to the world that he has arrived on his own terms and in his own right as mystic and visionary; in short as the philosopher who is doubly, and thus entirely, qualified (by the double gold standard of intellectual training and personal religious experience) to hold forth as supreme authority: the earthly representative of God and the oracle of religious truth. This demand that both qualifications be met before a theologian can have the right to speak is one of the main arguments he will apply in his later career to attempt a *Praescriptio Haereticorum:* a move to strike Arians from the record in advance, as mere ill-trained "word-jugglers" who have no real experience of what they are supposed to be theorizing about, like poor rhetoric students murdering a graceful poem or oration in the way they declaim it.[183]

This principle of the essentially necessary union of intellectual training and personal religious ecstasy, or, put another way, releasing the significance of a logically constructed metaphysic[184] only in and through and by the crowning principle of direct personal religious experience—this principle for which he stands so strongly, is one of Gregory's most distinctive marks. It had certainly been elaborated in Christian discourse before him, and he shows his dependence on Origen in the way he weaves together philosophical arguments and scriptural demonstrations (especially from what he understands of Paul's ecstatic revelations) but the fine balancing of the two sides of the equation where logic and spiritual insight are mutually entwined, yet with the deciding voice given to the latter, is one of the distinctive emphases that announces him as the father of Byzantine theological style. We are at this point, as with many other aspects of the period of Gregory, poised between the world of Late Antiquity and the religious spirit of Christian Byzantium.

Gregory may have learned the tradition of associating philosophical insight, set in the context of the Mysteries, with the craft of rhetorical *ekphrasis* (something that is so noted in his narrative) from his Athenian teacher Himerios. The latter defined

---

182. Cf. 1 Cor 2:10-16, where Paul also allies epiphanic revelation to spiritual authority.
183. His greatest single *tour de force* on this theme is *Oration* 27 (cf. Orat. 27.3, PG 36.13-16), delivered in 380, which attempts to define the nature of theology and the theologian. It became a classic of Christian discourse. It will be the subject of scrutiny in chapter 5.
184. That is, in his case, all discourse about philosophy, anthropology, and Christian dogma.

the rhetorical craft along the lines of the poetic aspiration for religious insight, an approach to rhetoric as inspired religious discourse which Gregory explicitly commends in his *Oration* 27. Himerios' father-in-law was the Torch-Bearer[185] (a high Mystery-initiate's office) in the Eleusinian rites. The *Dadouchos* carried the torch in the Eleusinian processions to signify the quest of Demeter for Persephone. It was Himerios who was also called to Constantinople by Julian in 362 to be admitted to the Mysteries of Mithras-Helios, and in the surviving oration which he delivered subsequent to that occasion, Himerios explicitly connects the rhetorician's *ekphrasis* with the notion of the offering (intellectual sacrifice) that the initiate should bring to the god.[186] Gregory, in a real sense, is clearly Christianizing much of Himerios' presuppositions, and certainly adopts his teacher's views about the relation of letters and religious wisdom, as he would put it: Logoi in the service of the Logos.[187]

Such then, I think, has been Gregory's highly crafted account of his own baptism in Athens, refigured in terms of the rites of Mystery initiation, set as the highest level of social attainment and spiritual refinement, and demonstrating to the reader that Gregory's "monasticism" is not going to be of the "common order" of the many other unwashed solitaries that were beginning to be a regular feature of the early Christian movement. In the whole refiguring of this "baptismal account," needless to point out, there is not the slightest reference to, or even a hint of, a drop of water or a bishop, or a church. But by dint of hammering out this essentially apologetic narrative, he has demonstrated, not least to himself, that Christianity was neither socially, philosophically, or mystically inferior to the very best of anything Hellenism had to offer. That he is able so skillfully to put this message across, subverting the old forms to convey the claims of a new class of Christian intellectual, was an important development in the Church's educational and missionary strategy—its attempt to gain the high ground of civilized values and move in to the role of established religion of the Romans instead of occupying the peripheral place of a protesting sect.

The poetic versions of his mystical vision are designed to encapsulate his personal struggles in Athens, both before and after his baptism there, and they both explain and depict the result of his decision to commit himself to Christianity and follow the retired life of a Christian philosopher in preference to all the allurements and advantages a refined Hellenism seemed to offer men of his class. Both

---

185. Cf. *De Vita Sua*, v. 260, PG 37.1047.
186. "The sun of Mithras has purified our soul, and here we are re-united (thanks be to the gods) with a prince (Julian) who is a friend of the gods. Let us offer our oration to this prince, as well as to this city, just as if we were lighting a sacred torch, wearing Attic dress, as is prescribed for initiates, to carry our sheaves of wheat to Eleusis, our tokens of a civilized life. We, the initiates, should bring as our offering our eloquence, if (as I imagine) Apollo is also the Sun-god, and if eloquence is the daughter of Apollo. (Himerios Orat. 7. Fr. Tr. in Puech. 1930, pp. 12-13.)
187. Cf. *De Rebus Suis. Carm.* 2.1.1, vv. 97-102, PG 37.977; see also T. Camelot (1966).

personally and collectively they capture a key moment, not only a critical point in what Gregory sees as his conversion and initiation into the deepest levels of Christian experience, but also a social and apologetic movement of the highest order, what Florovsky (deliberately reversing Harnack's thesis and phrase) described as "the Christianization of Hellenism."[188] Here Gregory in this highly crafted rhetorical narrative of his conversion and initiation into "Christian mysteries" is quite consciously offering to his contemporary peers in class and culture a missionary outreach of the Church: comparable to that which Origen once attempted in establishing the Christian *schola* at Caesarea,[189] and which Clement had attempted in Alexandria before him.[190]

Dependent on all too brief cameos as we have been, it is pressing upon us to leave behind Gregory's decade spent in Athens and begin to consider how he tried to live out his experiences in the decidedly un-Arcadian world beyond the Academy. To lead us there we might resume the story of his relationship with Basil, and the emotional crisis that shook him when the latter, clearly having had enough of the people and the place, where he never seems to have been completely happy,[191] decided to move on to investigate the monastic lifestyle as evidenced by the rigorous ascetics of Egypt.

Gregory's stay in Athens had been stretched out as long as it possibly could be. There are a few indications that he was even offered some kind of post there if he had decided to stay on. Throughout his decade in Athens he appears to have been idyllically happy, and he betrays not the slightest hint of intending to return home. The strings that bound him, of course, were far from insignificant, especially on the financial level, for it was only his father's allowances that paid his Athenian bills. Gregory admits that almost from the very first Basil had found the city a little precious and disillusioning,[192] and had wanted to move on. Gregory had successfully

188. Cf. G. Florovsky, *Collected Works* vol. 2, *Christianity and Culture* (Belmont, MA, 1974).
189. Origen had already tried to make the Christian school at Caesarea serve for this missionary purpose, and the principle must have been recognized by one of its chief students, the apostle of Cappadocia, Gregory Thaumaturgos; cf. A. Knaube, "Das Anliegen der Schule des Origenes zu Caesarea," MTZ 18-19, 1967-1968, 182-203; also J.A. McGuckin, "Caesarea Maritima as Origen Knew It," *Origeniana Quinta*, ed. R.J. Daly (Leuven, 1992), pp. 15-21.
190. Especially in the design of his *Protreptikos*.
191. Despite Gregory's attempt to depict their common stay as a paradisial time together in his *Funeral Oration for Basil* (Orat. 43.19, PG 36.520-521). P. Rousseau's study of Basil (1994) has rightly argued the need for caution in relying on this Oration for interpreting Basil's motives (as opposed to what Gregory wanted them to be). Even so, the evidence of Gregory's own "conversion" via baptism already in Athens, casts a light on Basil's own experience of Christianity when he returns to Cappadocia, and suggests that the version of Basil's conversion inspired by Macrina and Gregory Nyssa (that makes a strong contrast between "secular" Athens and "religious" Cappadocia) may also have to be toned down for its own apologetic tendencies.
192. "An empty happiness." Orat. 43.18, PG 36.520.

persuaded him that he was only on the very threshold of his literary and philosophical studies, and so he had agreed to continue. Part of the attraction for him, and a reason for his continuing stay was perhaps the ascetical life he could pursue with Gregory, Carterios and Philagrios—a scholarly community maintaining a high profile for the Christian party in the city. Of its very nature, however, like all student associations, initially with strong internal bondings it was still a transient community, and however happy Gregory was in that lifestyle, it only took Basil's decision to leave to destroy his paradisial condition utterly. If such an envisaged context of intellectual Christian ascetic community gathered around Prohaeresios, with Gregory and Basil living communally, around the Athenian Church, is correct, then it relocates both Basil's and Gregory's concerns for the polity of monasticism in the Church to an earlier date and location than their respective returns to Cappadocian Caesarea.

In Athens, however, and probably for most of his life, Gregory suffered the unfortunate disability of loving his friend more than his friend loved him. He vaunts his friendship with Basil. He uses words to describe it that spring up from the emotionally affective depths of his heart—terms such as: love, fiery attachment, eternal bonds, a single soul in different bodies,[193] and others similar. He cannot bring himself to call it a mere friendship. It is: "A friendship, or to speak more exactly, a full harmony of heart and nature."[194]

Basil's vocabulary of friendship, on the other hand, is much more contained, dignified, and detached.[195] Gregory describes his feelings for Basil in generous and idealized forms. They are the new twins Orestes and Pylades,[196] or the Molionidae.[197] He depicts the relationship, at first, as one in which he is taking a directing and paternal care, although one senses that in the long term this aspect of the relation was more truly in the opposite mode. Gregory, for example, is alone able to soothe Basil's disillusionment and set him on the right track of intellectual development.[198] Again Gregory tells his readers that it was he who alone who could help Basil shine as a successful orator when on his own he was unable to fend off his Armenian opponents.[199] He tells us that their alliance in scholarship and the

---

193. Cf. *De Vita Sua*, v. 230, PG 37.1045.

194. Orat. 43.14, PG 36.513.

195. Cf. Treu (1961).

196. Orat. 43.22: the most famous pair of friends in classical legend.

197. Cf. *Iliad* 2.621; ibid., 11.750.

198. Orat. 43.18, PG 36.520.

199. Orat. 43.17, PG 36.520; A pointed remark in its context, in 382, when Gregory was delivering these remarks to Basil's own family and monastic circle. The reference to Armenians who are not to be trusted (Orat. 43.17, PG 36.517) particularly evokes the circle of Eustathios of Sebaste, who began as Basil's mentor, but with whom Basil had serious theological divisions in the end. It is an interesting speculation to wonder whether the Armenian students (if one may presume them to be Christian) who argue with Basil in the Athenian circle of Gregory, actually mark Basil's first contact with the circle of the disciples of Eustathios.

"philosophical life" caused the friendship to move from a spark to: "A flame that burned bright and high."[200]

He depicts the strength of the relationship as reciprocal, and carefully chooses the most significant words he can to evoke it: "It was thus we were wounded with love for one another."[201]

This equal mutuality is doubtless how he perceived it. He is also having, in the time he delivered his funeral panegyric, to offset criticism from Basil's circle that he had abandoned his friend both personally, politically, and theologically: and there was much in that criticism that needed to be disarmed. Even after the panegyric it seems that Gregory never regained the confidence of Basil's monastic circle which he had once enjoyed.[202] While it would be overstated to question Basil's affection for Gregory (though Basil was one who was all too willing to sacrifice personal ties and loyalties for a desired political goal and left behind him several ruined relationships) the fact remains that Gregory needed and relied on Basil far more than he on Gregory.

Basil's strength of character and purpose had filled an emotional void in Gregory's life. The former was a symbiosis of his father and mother in Gregory's eyes, masterful and spiritually sensitive at the same time. The young Gregory was awfully impressed and hopelessly infatuated. He insists on the depth of his love for Basil to such an extent that he sees it to be necessary to pre-empt his audience's suspicions of erotic involvement. For him, the chastity of their relationship heightened rather than moderated their love:

> Philosophy was the object of our zeal. We were all in all to one another, sharing the same roof, the same table, the same sentiments; our eyes fixed on the same goal, as our mutual love grew ever warmer and stronger. Carnal loves pass away, for they are based on that which passes away, like springtime flowers. A flame cannot survive when the fuel is all spent, but disappears along with whatever kindled it... but those loves which are pleasing to God, and chaste,[203] since they have a stable object, are thereby the more enduring... This is the law of higher love.[204]

At the end of the day, Gregory's philosophical "detachment" always failed before the openness and genuine warmth of his heart. He confesses as much to another colleague from the Athenian days after Caesarios died.[205] It is one of his most endearing "failings."

The first disillusionment of his too eager heart came on the day when Basil shocked him with the news that he was going, with or without Gregory, to study

200. Orat. 43.17, PG 36.520.
201. Orat. 43.17, PG 36.517; *ep allelois etrothemen.*
202. Cf. *De Rebus Suis,* vv. 607-619, PG 37.1015-1016; *De Vita Sua,* vv. 385-486, PG 37.1056-1062 is also consciously addressed to Basil's circle; written immediately after the *Funeral Oration* for Basil, it shows he still feels the need to justify himself before them.
203. Lit. in accordance with *Sophrosyne.*
204. Orat. 43.19, PG 36.520-521.
205. Ep. 30, *To Philagrios,* PG 37.65-68; Gallay (1964), pp. 37-38.

monastic life further afield. There were to be more disillusionments in the relationship to follow, more in the end than Gregory could endure, and indeed, as we have
already noticed, the whole series of the affectionate remembrances he catalogues
above are delivered as a funeral oration several years after his friend's death, and after
several years of bitter estrangement.[206] The speech is meant as a posthumous
reconciliation.

In the *Funeral Oration* Gregory puts the best face on matters relating to their Athenian breakup and he suggests that as they had both reached the end of their studies
they were mutually ready to set off together for home in Cappadocia, but he also gives
clear enough evidence in the same section that he knew quite well that Basil wanted
rid of him, and he could not cope with the pain of that knowledge, sensing and reacting to it as a betrayal on the deepest level. He tells how all their academic circle gathered round at the news of their mooted departure trying to prevent them:

> They were all crying out with pleadings all mixed up with threats and arguments, that
> whatever happened they would refuse to let us go. They said and did everything that
> might be expected from men who were overcome by grief.[207]

If Gregory was obviously and easily persuaded to give in to them, not so Basil.
He sensed a double opportunity to slip the leash and leave Gregory in the custody of
other friends. It might even have been the case that Gregory had prearranged the
demonstration, as he probably had the debate with the Armenians earlier in their
association, hoping thus to change Basil's mind again, and press him to stay on in
Athens. That was his miscalculation, and the hurt of it remained unhealed for
twenty six years, from 356 until he brings it up again as an accusation against his
dead friend, in the latter's own church, in 382:

> Here I shall be presumptuous and bring an accusation against myself and also, it may
> seem, against that holy and irreproachable soul. He, after explaining the pressing
> reason for his return, overcame their restraint, and they, although it was against their
> will, consented to his departure. But I was left behind in Athens, partly because I
> weakened before the entreaties of friends, for the truth must be told, but partly
> because of his betrayal, for he had been persuaded to forsake one who had not for-
> saken him, and to hand me over to those who were holding him there. It was a thing
> that before it happened I could never have believed possible. It was like cutting a
> body in two parts, with the resulting death of both parts, or like the separation of two
> oxen that have shared the same manger and yoke, bellowing pitifully for each other
> in distress at their separation.[208]

Basil, however, was not recorded as having bellowed with grief as he took ship
from Piraeus to Byzantium, eager to see the capital before returning home, where he
would practice rhetoric for a short time before setting off on a factfinding tour of the

---

206. A bitterness that is far from completely healed even at the time of his composition of the pane-
    gyric; cf. *De Vita Sua*, vv. 385-414, PG 37.1056-1058.
207. Orat. 43.24, PG 36.529.
208. Orat. 43.24, PG 36.529.

Egyptian monasteries.[209] In the *De Vita Sua* Gregory gives some interesting variants on the theme. Here his bitterness at the memory of Basil's betrayal is softened by the motif (not so visible at this point in the *Funeral Oration*) of his own pre-eminence in literature in comparison to his friend, and the deeper affection in which he was held by the Athenian circle. There is a sardonic dryness here that is not to the fore in the panegyric, and a witty indication that while his comrades could not bear to lose Gregory they were able, more or less, to bring themselves to say farewell to Gregory's friend. The detail of the pressing crowds is here referred only to Gregory himself, while in the panegyric it was referred to both men:

> Basil set forth his reasons for going and people were persuaded to yield only with great difficulty (but yield they did all the same)... Then suddenly I was encompassed by everyone, strangers, friends, students, and teachers. Affection drove them to such lengths that they mingled some pressure with their protestations and laments. They clung to me so tightly, insisting that they would not let go of me for any reason. It was not right, they said, that venerable Athens should lose one to whom they were prepared to concede by vote the primacy of letters. They prevailed on me in the end, for only an oak tree could withstand such a gale of laments and entreaties.[210]

Gregory continued to live in Athens, but the lights had gone out in Arcadia. In the *De Vita Sua* he says that he stayed on for a little while until attracted by the desire of living the philosophical life back home in Cappadocia, and supporting his aged parents (two noble motives that he elsewhere complained loudly enough were mutually incompatible);[211] but later in the *De Vita Sua* he gives a fleeting indication of his tortured state of mind at this time: "My brain was in a terrible whirl..."[212]

He says that a "short time" after Basil's departure he "stole away" from Athens like a thief in the night.[213] It was a dispiriting end to a golden dream, and his language brilliantly encapsulates the depression that overwhelmed him. In the funeral panegyric he is more ready to admit how empty the streets of Athens had become without his friend:

209. Influenced in his decision to turn to a different and more rigorous type of monasticism both by Macrina, his sister, who regarded the lifestyle he had been leading in Athens as irrelevant and thus characterized him as experiencing his "conversion" to the ascetic life only on his return to Caesarea (cf. Gregory Nyssa's *Life of Macrina*), and Eustathios of Sebaste (to whose monastic circle Macrina also probably belonged in some style) Eustathios was at this stage an important mentor for Basil, and inducted him into ecclesiastical life and politics. Gregory lamented the theological marks, Christological and pneumatological, which Eustathios left on Basil even after he had detached himself from Eustathios, and alienation had set in. Cf. Ep. 58, PG 37.113-117; Gallay (1964), pp.73-77.
210. *De Vita Sua*, vv. 245-259, PG 37.1046-1047.
211. *De Rebus Suis*, vv. 261-274, PG 37.1047-1048.
212. *De Vita Sua*, v. 280, PG 37.1049.
213. *De Vita Sua*, v. 264, PG 37.1047.

> My loss, however, was not of long duration, for I could not bear for long to be such a pitiable spectacle; could not bear to keep explaining to everyone the reasons for our separation.[214]

At the end of this version of the tale he does not slip away from his beloved city like a thief, to bring consolation to his aged parents, on the contrary he rears like Homer's young stallion ready for the charge. His spirits were restored, his eagerness uncontainable. What had happened to reanimate him?

> I could only stay in Athens a little while longer. My yearning made me like that horse in Homer. I snapped the harness of those restraining me, and racing over the plain I sped to join my companion. [215]

The image is an Homeric self-characterization of Gregory as Paris "no longer delaying in his lofty halls" but speeding to the side of "his noble brother Hector." The two are reunited in war, in Homer's story, and set off in harmony again to rally Troy, reconciled after Paris's reluctance for the fight had angered the brave Hector. If all this is a rhetorically coded message, as seems more than likely, then it is easy for "war" to read "monastic life," and perhaps Gregory's unwillingness to follow Basil's inclination for cenobitic monasticism on the more rigorous models he had encountered, was at the root of their separation and differences. It would seem to be the case that after Basil's tour of the Palestinian monasteries and anchoritic settlements had been concluded, news had reached Gregory in Athens that his friend had returned to Cappadocia and was expecting Gregory to join him in his monastic foundation at Annesoi. New hope rose within his lonely soul.

Gregory's bags were packed in a trice, and he was off on the long journey to Cappadocia, deliberately avoiding the sea route this time, and traveling by way of Constantinople, overland. If he had thought his problems would be solved once he met up with Basil again, and could combine monastic lifestyle with scholarly activities on their own estates, as befitting gentlemen, he was to be sorely disappointed. He had felt in his heart that he could hardly bear to exchange the freedom, the white stone and sun and olive groves of Athens for the dreary plains and mud-bogged villages of Cappadocia, but without being able to rely on Basil at his side, Athens was no longer bearable. Could Pontos, where Basil's monastery was, prove to be a new Arcadia? He probably set out in such hopes, but the gnawings of disquiet were always ready to stir whenever he thought, bitterly, of how he had been betrayed by his friend's evident eagerness to escape from him and his adoring attentions.

When Gregory left Athens his luggage, like that of many another traveler before him, was infinitely greater than on his arrival. Scholars departing for a provincial backwater took with them as many scrolls and texts as they could afford or carry. It might be a long time before they had the chance to purchase texts again in such variety and at such prices. He took home with him a decent library. In later life, several

---

214. Orat. 43.24.
215. Orat. 43.24, PG 36.529; cf. *Iliad* 6.506f.

of his letters to highly placed colleagues contain bibliographic requests or promises of literary volumes. He had some scruples about books. He was ready to lend whatever was legitimately his, but he drew the line at passing on manuscripts he had, but which he himself had borrowed, without reference to the owner. It was an honorable principle, and one which could save his bacon if a visitor spotted a tome in his collection that he did not wish to risk consigning to oblivion. After all, everything he possessed belonged, in the end, not to him but to the church he served. When one of his friends made an unpardonable request for his Homer, we find such a polite evasion:[134] and quite right too. But he still sent him his copy of Demosthenes.[135] He was a generous soul.

His intellectual baggage at the end of his Athenian studies was, however, far greater than merely volumes of literature and notes on rhetorical technique. He had studied at one of the greatest schools of antiquity for almost ten years. He had absorbed the whole gamut of literature, philosophy, ethics, and the liberal sciences. It had been brought home to him just how eclectic this intellectual world of Late Antiquity really was. In the domain of religion, to which he felt especially drawn, he saw at every turn the conflicting claims of religious systems that thrived on eclecticism, were ready to immerse themselves in an all-embracing universalism, and yet also claimed a distinctive voice within the choir of sirens that sang about human enlightenment and spiritual wisdom. This experience was within Gregory like a great sea, teeming with life beneath its surface. It was of inestimable importance for him as a Christian intellectual of the fourth century, for the fertile ambivalence of the Hellenistic myths of religious and philosophical truth made him face up to the massive problems facing his own religion in its claim for particularity alongside universality. Its specifically historical rootedness in the life and death of Jesus, sat ill at ease with its claims to be a universally relevant Logos-religion of the highest intellectual standing. Its claims for absolute allegiance jarred with the vague and open-ended spirit of the age, where religions were mixed and assorted, like personal adornments, to fashion a style. At a deeper level, Gregory's awareness of the rigors of logical process alongside his instinctive allegiance to the whispers of psychic inspiration, and the demands of transcendent revelation (all of which Christianity admitted as central authorities in its system) faced him with a particular dilemma that would reach critical proportions shortly, when he found his major intellectual opponents no longer outside the Church, but within it, and at the highest levels of the hierarchy. He found, along with many others in the Church of that period, that what had been thought to be a fairly basic and obvious thing, that sum of central truths which constituted the main line of Christian tradition, was in fact a highly controverted notion. Unlike many others within the debate, Gregory was possessed of an intellectual context that embraced extensive readings in Hellenistic religious

134. He is "not able to lay his hands on it." Ep. 31, *To Philagrios*, PG 37.68-69; Gallay (1964), pp. 38-39.
135. "I deliver it to you willingly, and from the heart." Ep. 31, PG 36.69; Gallay (1964), p. 39.

thought as well as Christian theology, and it was a precious resource to enable him to approach the issue and attempt a resolution.

Many of his contemporaries may have thought his long education a wasteful exercise, typical of a dilettante aristocrat. Christian history should be ever grateful for it, since it allowed him the intellectual space and culture to turn to face one of the most pressing and difficult questions of the age: what exactly was this "Christian Tradition" to which opposite parties were laying claim? What intellectual coherence did it have when one reviewed its historical development? In the long Cappadocian nights, as he began to turn his mind more and more to Church affairs, such were the issues that gripped him. At Athens his student colleagues had been united, as if it were in one great quest for the grail of a refined culture. He had seen how union could be brought about from disparity. "Sub Aege Pallas" was a principle not only theoretically delightful, but obviously capable of working in practice. What could be its Christian counterpart: to hold together a movement that was in imminent danger of collapsing internally, in an internecine bloodiness over essential matters of its self-definition? His mind was to turn, time and again, to the overriding harmonizing possibilities of the notion of a Christian culture, with the most refined and exact canons of taste to include or exclude, to recognize the true or exile the false. To exercise and apply such canons would require no less than a priesthood of the most exquisite sensibility and spiritual perception. The foundations of a great theory were about to be laid down. His first hopes to ground such a system in the real soil of the Church made him think of the ordinary, solid, orthodox and conservative bishops of his home province. Although imperially sponsored synods already had a poor record in achieving consensus, surely there were still numerous men of God who could speak and perceive the truth with a homely freshness and simplicity? bishops like his father, who for all their faults were straightforward and honest men, open to the inspirations of the deity, and thus able to read and interpret the essential tradition. Surely this was the case?

Poor Gregory. It did not take long, no more than a few encounters with the hierarchy of Cappadocia, to topple that pedestal of illusion. It did not shake his principle. It simply shook him, and was to shake him more and more as he was drawn, with ever vociferous protests, into the real, and rather dirty, world of ecclesiastical politics.

He had come home, like a reluctant bridegroom, and all too soon the honeymoon was over, and a dull and dour reality was advancing towards him menacingly.

3

POLITICS AND PRIESTHOOD
IN CAPPADOCIA

Ah, love, let us be true
To one another! for the world, which seems
To lie before us like a land of dreams,
So various, so beautiful, so new,
Hath really neither joy, nor love, nor light,
Nor certitude, nor peace, nor help from pain;
And we are here as on a darkling plain
Swept with confused alarms of struggle and flight,
Where ignorant armies clash by night.

Matthew Arnold

Doubtless fearing the complete curtailment of his freedom, Gregory made one last effort to extend his student travels, and took the long road back to Cappadocia, so that he could see the new capital of Constantinople, dedicated less than thirty years earlier, and already filled with splendid works of art from all over the ancient world. He must have traveled from Athens to Thessaloniki, and onwards through Thrace to Byzantium. His visit opened his eyes to sights which would become more familiar to him when he eventually moved to the capital, nearly twenty-five years later.

There, in a surprise meeting, he came across his brother Caesarios who was also making his way back home[1] and had come to the city by sea from Alexandria. Caesarios had already established the foundations of a reputation and was now exploring the opportunities that life in the capital might afford for an ambitious man to make his way through his skills as a physician upwards in political life. Gregory tells later that he had some difficulty in persuading Caesarios to abandon the city where he had already made political inroads with his career.[2] It was undoubtedly Gregory's family connections there[3] that assisted Caesarios' rapid rise, just as they would assist Gregory in later years when he came to the city as a missionary bishop. Gregory notes how reluctant Caesarios was to leave, and indeed the latter's residence back home must have been of a very short duration, for he was to make his life, after that point, in the imperial service. They traveled together on the endless trek to Cappadocia, weeks of travel on the royal Anatolian road East, until they came past

1.   An indication that Gregory the Elder had simultaneously cut the allowances to bring the errant children home to work.
2.   Orat. 7.8, PG 35.764.
3.   Cf. Bernardi, VChr. 38 (1984).

85

the great lake and soon saw the majestic peaks of the mountain that told them they were near the end of their journey.[4] It was a homecoming which Gregory was later to describe as mystical fulfilment of a mother's secret prayer.[5] The return to mother compensated, for a while, the hurt which Basil had given him with his all too obvious eagerness to flee from Athens. The scene of that reunion, when finally they reached their estates, with his mother running out through the vine blossoms to meet them, etched itself on his mind, and was to reappear again years later as one of no less than sixty-five epitaphs he composed about her after her death.[6] In this scene, as one might expect, there is no place for the junior sibling, and Caesarios is effectively elbowed out of the cameo in favor of the true "child of her breast,"[7] the real object of her love, a mother's boy who even in his thirties was jealous of his brother's presence and even when writing the poem when he was forty-five, cannot bring himself to share the passionate remembrance of that reunion with any other.

This return to the estate at Karbala, near Arianzum, must have been sometime around spring of the year 358. When his arrival in Cappadocia became public news he gave, at Nazianzus, the customary display of rhetoric that was expected of returning students, for the benefit of his local patrons who refused to be put off by Gregory's (equally customary) show of diffidence:

> When I arrived home I gave a display of eloquence to satisfy the inordinate demands of certain people who kept importuning me. It was, so to speak, a debt I owed to others. For myself I place no value on vapid applause, or those stupid and intricate conceits in which sophists delight whenever a crowd of youths gather round them... but for my friends I gave a performance.[8]

For a short time he gave lessons to a young man called Evagrios.[9] He seems to have been a good teacher—at least the father of the young man wrote warmly to thank him for his services. It is possible that his pupil was Evagrios Pontikos the Origenian savant and ascetical theologian, who mentions Gregory as one of his teachers, and who is traditionally associated with Gregory as part of his clerical entourage during his later stay in Constantinople.[10] If so, it underlines again how closely tied were the lines of connection between wealthy Christian families seeking mutual support, and the class of Christian intellectuals which grew out of this, to rise to pre-eminence in the latter half of the fourth century.

4. It is the same for a traveler today coming from Istanbul by road to Aksaray or Nevsehir in Cappadocia. The twin peaks of the Hasan Dagh announce the proximity of Nazianzus and Karbala.
5. Orat. 7.8, PG 35.764.
6. Carm. 2.2.71, PG 38.48.
7. That is, the only child she herself suckled.
8. De Vita Sua, vv. 265-274, PG 37.1048; see also Orat. 43.25, PG 36.529.
9. Greg. Ep.3, PG 37.24; Gallay (1964), pp. 2-3.
10. There is some confusion in this tradition, however, as we shall see in chapter 6.

At Athens, he hints,[11] they had offered him a professorship if he would stay. There is no doubt that Gregory's scholarship merited public recognition,[12] but his private means must also have been attractive, both to the Church and the schools of the city. And here lay the problem. The previous reference to the anonymous importuners of Cappadocia signifies, without question, his father (and probably Amphilokios his uncle), who wanted to take some of the reflected glory from his son's expensive education. Perhaps he was even hoping that he might follow in the steps of other notable members of the family, and their noble acquaintances, and enhance their public reputation by adopting the profession of rhetoric in the province, as prelude to some higher office. He was soon to be disappointed. His son had no intention of adopting the profession. Having lost his chance of a golden chair in Athens, a muddy schoolroom or courthouse in Cappadocia held no attractions whatsoever. The display before his family felt to him like the retrospective payment of a debt, not a way forward to his future. It must have left him profoundly dissatisfied, and acutely aware that he still faced the crisis of an unresolved future, little short of his thirtieth year.[13] The renewed experience of how powerful his father's persuasion was made Gregory realize with sharp clarity that he was truly back home in the provinces; and not supporting old and feeble parents, as in his fantasy of the flight from Athens, but once more firmly under the parental thumb of the redoubtable old man.

In his quest for alternative relationships in which to stabilize his personal identity Gregory had already turned his back on marriage or professional rhetoric, and sought to move in the as yet uncharted waters of Christian celibacy. Not for him the literal wilderness of the Egyptian monastic tradition. In his mind's eye he knew that he wanted to combine a gentlemanly solitude, in which he could study and contemplate, with a ready access to civilized society, as befitted his rank. His correspondence demonstrates just how much the intercourse with literate pagan and Christian intellectuals, socialites, and provincial aristocracy, was meat and drink to him through all his life. Such a typically Gregorian "synthesis" was, of course, a wholly new notion to his local community.[14] Both the monks of the area, and his family, regarded it as eccentric.

For a short while Gregory lived on his father's estates, but while he used their resources to finance his lifestyle, he dwelt in a separate building, possibly an outlying farm at the edge of the territory his family owned. This was a time of much soul

11. *De Vita Sua*, v. 257. PG 37.1047.
12. His "hint" does not commit him to making clear whether a prestigious paid post was in the offer, or merely a polite invitation to him to stay on in some didactic capacity.
13. A time of life more significant in that age of common premature death than would be the advent of middle age for someone today.
14. It would be more common as a Christian definition of the "perfect life" after Paulinus, Prudentius, Gregory the Great, and other aristocrats of the fifth century and afterwards had spread the religious idea of "Otium" more commonly in the Church's literature.

searching as he clarified to himself how he wanted his life to develop, and tried, with even greater difficulty, to explain it to others and bring them into agreement. There was time now for a visit to Basil in Pontus, living the monastic life there. Gregory had exchanged several letters with his friend, seeking his advice, and receiving in return descriptions of the monastic community Basil had made his own,[15] on his own property, since he had inherited on his father's death.

Gregory made at least one visit to his friend in Caesarea, including an extended stay at the monastic settlement at Annesoi.[16] He wanted to sound Basil's opinion as to his own future, and agreed to try out life at Annesoi to see if he could take up his friend's invitation to be a monk there. Gregory's dilemma lay in the fact that he was a pioneer in the style of Christian "monasticism" he wanted to espouse, and none of the available options suited him, which made advisers on all sides regard him as a difficult character.[17] Basil had discovered, or been discovered by, Eustathios of Sebaste, an important Armenian ascetic and philosopher-theologian. He had taken Basil on an extended tour of the eastern provinces in 356 to study how the ascetical life was lived in Egypt, Palestine and Syria. Basil was now posing as an expert on monastic life, and persuading Gregory to join him.

Gregory's family, unlike that of Basil which was now dominated by the ascetical Macrina, was a factor that counterpoised his religious tendency to ascetic with-drawal. The Church was Gregory's chosen path and the way in which he was deter-mined to differentiate his identity from his father, and yet the Church (in all that it meant locally and concretely) *was* his father. Gregory the Elder was not only the payer of all bills, he was the local bishop, theoretically superintendent of all local Christians, monks included. This situation of living in the interstices, a state

15. Macrina can claim the initiation of it, but Basil was the landowner, and increasingly set his own stamp on the kind of Christian community life in the men's group; for Macrina eventu-ally separated the organization of the respective camps.

16. The village of Annesoi has traditionally been located just to the west of the confluence of the rivers Iris and Lycus in Pontus, by the (modern) village of Sounisa. The monastic estate has been placed on the opposite bank of the Iris at the foot of Mt Heris Dagh. Cf. G. de Jeraphion, "Iboura-Gazioura?" Mélanges de la Faculté orientale. Université de Beyrouth. vol. 5. 1911, pp. 347-351. Recently George Huxley has argued in the *Analecta Bollandiana* that it was at the pre-historic site of Annisa, just outside Kayseri/Caesarea itself, making the "retirement" of Basil perhaps far less of a withdrawal from the local Church scene than has hitherto been imagined.

17. This type of "home-based" monasticism can claim direct continuity with the earliest pattern of ascetic withdrawal which was found in the early Church: the lifestyle of the Apotaktikos. This was, in subsequent centuries (already so by the time of Gregory's generation) completely over-shadowed by the new "norm" of cenobitic monasticism. Even when such later paradigms had been disseminated, however, there were other Christian aristocrats, apart from Gregory, such as Melania, and Paulinus of Nola, and Prudentius, who continued to represent the classical ideal of retreat (*otium*) as the epitome of the "perfect life." In Paulinus' Ep. 5.15, for example, he too des-ignates his country villa as his monastery, and in it lived the ascetic life, still as *Grand Seigneur*, with his wife and companions. The early ascetic years of Gregory the Great are comparable.

Gregory seems to have constitutionally preferred because of his many ambivalences, was one that could hardly continue for long while under the power of another. His customary introversion failed to analyse the politics of his condition realistically:

> However much I wanted to be involved with people I was seized by a still greater long-ing for the monastic life, which in my opinion was a question of interior dispositions, not of physical situation. For the sanctuary I had reverence... but from a distance.[18]

His last sentence echoed what was to become a traditional and sardonic piece of advice offered to Egyptian monks by their elders: "If you see a bishop approaching, flee from him faster than you would before a woman." The point being that a bishop could ruin a monk's life far more effectively than any other conceivable cause. But the advice was hardly apposite for Gregory, when the smoke from his father's house was visible over the fields, and the old man must have insistently kept asking him when he was going to start to do something with his life.

He openly admits that his interior life was greatly unsettled at this period, and he still had not resolved the issue of what relationship with Basil would be able to con-tinue in the new circumstances. He always wanted to depict that relation as one of equals, with perhaps the stress on his own wisdom and prudence guiding his more forceful friend. Needless to say, this was not how Basil read it. The reality was brought home to Gregory from every encounter, exchanges that were becoming more and more difficult to sustain. Letters that began with jovial affection ended, after several years, with frustration and bitterness on both sides. The reality that Gregory resisted was that Basil saw himself as the undisputed leader of anything in which he was involved, and in his relationship with Gregory was a constant source of instructions and demands which his friend found increasingly irritating and circum-scribing. He had fled from one overbearing father figure only to fall into the grip of another. He says as much later when he composed his autobiographical poem, only slightly apologetic for the fact that he had just preached a eulogy for the man he was now criticizing. In the public memorial, in the presence of Basil's friends and family, he had to be more circumspect. As it was, his speech on that occasion was a tentative reconciliation with a circle with whom he had once been intimately involved, and who felt he had neglected them in slighting Basil. In his private poem, he feels able to state the truth more bluntly:

> I should like to pass over the intervening matters in case I seem to be insulting the memory of a man whose eulogy I have so recently pronounced,[19] but he came [to visit], much to my regret, though for the sake of the story I shall tell of it. He was to prove another father to me, and a far more burdensome one. In the case of my real fa-ther, even though he tyrannized me, I have an obligation to shelter him. But no such duty applies in his case, where his friendship was an occasion of injury, not benefit.[20]

18. *De Vita Sua*, vv. 327-330, PG 37.1052.
19. Orat. 43, PG 36.493f, which Gregory preached at Caesarea on January 1, 382.
20. *De Vita Sua*, vv. 386-394, PG 37.1056; referring to Basil's visit to Nazianzus in 371.

In the early days of his return from Athens Gregory still felt that Annesoi might be an attractive way to escape the strictures of life near his father, but his experience of life in that community made him realize that his ideal position of floating free-lance between monastic settlements while living in retirement on his father's land, was not going to be tenable.

He was certainly attracted to, and impressed by, Basil's enthusiasm, just as he had been first intrigued by his friend's idyllic descriptions of life by the Iris river,[21] but the first-hand experience of the rigorous conditions seems to have shaken him. It may have been a family estate of Basil's own patrimony, but the form of monastic life lived there was modelled on the ascetics of Egyptian Scete, and the common life was serious and ascetically Spartan in its tone.[22] Basil had also taken his inspiration from the important mentor and adviser of his early years, Eustathios of Sebaste. The historian Sozomen gives an indication how much Basil's monasticism drew from Eustathios when he writes:

> It is said that Eustathios, who governed the churches of Sebaste in Armenia, founded a society of monks in Armenia, Paphlagonia, and Pontus, and became the author of a zealous discipline, both as to what meats were to be eaten or avoided, what garments were to be worn, and what customs and exact course of conduct were to be adopted. Some assert that he was the author of the Ascetic Treatises[23] commonly attributed to Basil of Cappadocia.[24]

Basil had fallen in with the energetic Homoiousian churchman Eustathios with all the enthusiasm of a man returned from Athens looking for a purpose and direc-tion that a small-town rhetorical career could not afford. When he returned to his family in Pontus, the ascetical Macrina had already established a community of ded-icated Christians on the estates at Annesoi and had drawn their mother Emmelia there. Basil's own writings, and those of Gregory Nazianzen depict this foundation as a feat of Basil's own origination. But this was hardly the full story. Gregory is party to a tendency, also witnessed in Basil's own large literary corpus, which more or less damns his sister to silence.[25] This is in stark contrast to Gregory of Nyssa, Basil's younger brother, who speaks more openly and wholeheartedly of Macrina's great influence on himself and on Basil at this period.[26] It is difficult to deduce the

21. Basil. Ep. 14.
22. Cf. S. Giet (1941b).
23. Of the ascetical corpus of Basil (ET, W. Clarke, *The Ascetical Works of St Basil* [London, 1925]) it has long been accepted that several of the traditionally ascribed treatises were inauthentic, and some confusion still holds generally to the history of the recension of Basil's Rules for monks. The *Moralia* and the *Small Asketikon* are writings that accurately depict Basil's monastic posi-tion between 358 and the early 360s; cf. J. Quasten, *Patrology* vol. 3 (Utrecht, 1975), pp. 211-214.
24. Sozomen. *Hist. Eccl.* 3.14.
25. The fine recent study of S. Elm (1994) sensitively re-contextualizes Macrina.
26. See Gregory Nyssa's *Life of Macrina*—where he depicts her as the Christian teacher of Basil himself.

motives for this relegation to silence in regard to Macrina. It may have simply been part of the patriarchal bias of ancient textuality: with Gregory Nazianzen affording the starring role to his friend Basil, on whose property the monastery at Annesoi technically was, and whose subsequent ascetical career he wished to elevate over that of his rivals, however close they may have been. But something else seems to have been operating, something precise and more substantive that gives rise to the quiet abandonment of the memory, if not exactly a "damnatio memoriae," of Macrina. There is an odd contrast with the versions of Basil's early return to Cappadocia and his "conversion" story as given between Gregory Nazianzen and Basil on the one hand, and Gregory Nyssa on the other. Family and mentors who transgressed in the eyes of the orators (in this case Basil and Gregory Nazianzen) were to be spared denunciation for the sake of family honor, but their lapses in regard to orthodoxy could, and did, call down other forms of judgment even from family members. This is something that we can see operating clearly in regard to Gregory's treatment of his father who later signs an unorthodox confession during Gregory's absence from Nazianzus. He does so, his son tells us, out of "innocent ignorance." It is, at best, a dubious distinction to have as one's defense. In the case of Basil and his relation to Macrina (and more openly with Eustathios of Sebaste) the bitterness that came into the once close relation was probably caused by a parting of the ways in theological allegiances.

The point of dispute may lie in the manner in which Macrina stayed faithful to Eustathios of Sebaste, even when Basil began to part company from his powerful mentor, a cooling of relations that finally grew into bitter acrimony in later years. Perhaps it was Macrina, who was already a dedicated ascetic following the patterns of Eustathios' particular views on monastic life,[27] that first introduced Basil to the charismatic philosopher ascetic, and whose discipleship was such that she applied Eustathios' views that monastic commitment took precedence over any familial or hierarchical allegiances. Both views were things that Basil and Gregory Nazianzen came to resist vigorously as undermining their episcopal authority. But with regard to Eustathios, it was the theological parting of the ways that was to be more decisive. Gregory Nyssa's *Life of Macrina* studiously does not allow the reader to enter into the more intimate theological landscape of Macrina's form of Christianity, for he keeps her interventions to the large scale of philosophic intimations on immortality. But if she followed Eustathios in her Christology and pneumatological doctrine, there would have been profound trouble on the home front too, for it was mainly on

27. That monasticism, for example, broke the social barriers between owners and slaves–who must now be freed. Macrina demonstrates (even in Gregory Nyssa's sanitized "Life") this aspect of aristocrats setting themselves to manual labor alongside former servants. Eustathian asceticism (as we can see from the condemnation it drew from the Synod of Gangra) also held a view that monasticism could develop freely and independently of the local hierarchies. Gregory Nazianzen had good cause to fear and resist this view (cf. Orat. 6, PG 35.721f). And once he was himself the leading local hierarch, Basil soon lost his enthusiasm for the concept of local monastics who could withstand their bishop. Gregory composed *Epitaph* 120 in Macrina's memory: PG 38.75.

the grounds of their increasing theological alienation on both counts that Basil's relationship with Eustathios foundered so severely after 374.

Eustathios' Christian theology (and by analogy that of Macrina) was acceptable to Basil in the early years. The Christology of the Homoiousians (Christ was substantively like God) was a broad enough Church to contain both men at this era, and Eustathios not only introduced Basil to the ascetical life, he also introduced him to the ecclesial stage as a young theologian of growing repute. In 356 the Synod of Ancyra where Eustathios played a significant role, alongside Bishop Basil of Ancyra, proclaimed Homoiousian doctrine as the best way forward towards an acceptable "orthodox" standard of Christological confession in the Eastern Churches, and Eustathios from that time began to use the services of Basil in the defense of that theology. Basil traveled with Eustathios and served as his secretary, learning the inner workings of Church politics from an old master. Soon Basil would be drawn into rhetorical battle with the Neo-Arians Aetios and Eunomios, who were to be strong opponents against whom he and Gregory Nazianzen would struggle for the rest of their lives. But by the time Basil himself emerged as a notable Christian leader in Cappadocia, Eustathios' theology and that of Basil had moved apart. Basil's thought developed more in line with Athanasios of Alexandria's influential synod of 362 when Athanasios had called for the reconciliation of efforts (and terms of reference) between the Homoiousians and the Homoousians in favor of the original Nicene homoousianism. This was a bold agenda which Gregory Nazianzen and Basil took up in their mature years, Gregory more passionately than Basil, but which Eustathios rejected, not only adhering to the early point of Homoiousian theology (which was to reject the dominance of Nicene thought and its claim to represent a universal orthodoxy) but, more to the point, resisting firmly and decisively the movement of the later Nicene party towards an explicated theology of the Holy Spirit—the roots of the Trinitarian theology that grew logically from Neo-Nicene thought about the co-equal deity of the Son and the Spirit of God. Basil always retained a certain "economy of words" on the question of pneumatology. It was to be Gregory Nazianzen's role in the Cappadocian dynamic to spell out the clearest Neo-Nicene theology of the divine Spirit of God, and the co-equality of the Trinity of divine persons that was the logical result of such a theology. Eustathios (though a strong opponent of Arian Christology) was vehemently opposed to this developing theology of the hypostatic Spirit, and so became "branded" as one of the leaders of the so-called Pneumatomachians[28] all of whom "fought against" this developing Pneumatology.

28. The Neo-Nicenes (chiefly Gregory) disparagingly called them "Spirit-Fighters," or those who perversely fought against divine inspiration by denying the co-equal deity of the Spirit. The designation "Pneumatomachian" apologetically began to roll in together all the enemies of the Neo-Nicene movement as Gregory had designed it, including the Homoiousians such as Eustathios, the party of Macedonios the former (homoian Arian) bishop of Constantinople, and especially the Neo Arians. Gregory was willing to "clarify" the lines of battle in this way, but the success of his strategy was also why he needed specifically to exempt Basil from such an Arian hereticization of those who did not confess the Homoousion of the Spirit. He did so by his device of the "economy" of Basil (see fn. 64 below).

At this juncture then, after 374 certainly, Eustathios passed from being mentor and spiritual father, to the paradoxical state of a significant and venerable figure now ranged with the worst of the enemies of the Neo-Nicene movement. From this time he is wiped from the record of Basil's "religious history." The strategy adopted by both Basil and Gregory Nazianzen (and thus the circle of theologians following them, including Gregory Nyssa) was to relegate Eustathios to a *damnatio memoriae*. It probably also wove in to the silence Macrina herself, though Gregory Nyssa's sense of immediate familial loyalty would not allow him so severe a stance as his brother. When Basil was dead he published his own encomium of Macrina, though even here she suffers from the retouching hand of a master orator who was himself now the leading light of the orthodox Neo-Nicene movement, and so cannot allow any trace of Pneumatomachianism to be associated in the record with any member of his circle. It was this encomium of Nyssa's that probably elicited the short epitaph[29] which Gregory Nazianzen wrote for her.

In any event, in this time of 362, such alienations lay still in the future. Gregory found his friend Basil's ascetically inclined estates a welcome enough relief when he fled from the pressures at Nazianzus. And yet, Basil's demands for a more rigorous and permanent commitment both surprised and disturbed Gregory; such a basic and egalitarian lifestyle, centered round physical labor, was not in harmony with his own inclinations or his own dreams for the future of Christian monastic life. Gregory was more interested in the theory,[30] the development of the intellectual and spiritual life in reflective solitude. He did not want his solitude peopled with eager groups of former serfs and aristocrats mingling together to plant root crops and dig wells and such like. Psychologically Gregory also seemed to need to have an escape route always near at hand which he felt could rescue him, honorably, from any difficult circumstance, just that type of mental disturbance which he regarded as inimical to his own conception of fostering the life of peaceful *theoria*. After his visit to Annesoi, he knew he could not possibly live there, and his parents again provided the excuse. They were old and infirm, to leave them would be contrary to Christian charity. With such arguments he was able to hold Basil at bay, though without ever really convincing him.[31]

The more Basil continued to expect Gregory to adopt this "proper" (by which he meant Egyptian/Syrian/Eustathian) pattern of monastic life the more Gregory took refuge in sardonic humor. He makes his dismay obvious in the most charming manner: one aristocrat writing to another. Basil kept up his invitations for a while but they produced only counter-requests from Gregory that Basil live his style of retired life at Arianzum,[32] and a ready stream of more elaborate jokes debunking

29. *Epitaph* 120, PG 38.75.
30. Cf. Kertsch (1974).
31. Greg. Ep. 1, PG 37.21; Gallay (1964), p. 1.
32. Greg. Ep. 2, PG 37.21-24; Gallay (1964,)), pp. 1-2. This was not so much a serious proposition as a way of refusing to be tied in, subserviently, to Basil's scheme.

Basil's seriousness. He writes to Basil with carefully elegant humor, designed at once to express his admiration and his total inability to adopt such a lifestyle, but without offending his friend's sensibilities:

> I see that you are pulling my leg (perhaps to draw me to yourself?), if I understand you aright, like people who dam streams in order to divert them into another channel. That is how your words appear to me. On my part I stand in admiration of your Pontos and its Pontic darkness; your place of abode—so worthy of an exile; the hills over your head and the desert underneath; the wild beasts that serve to test your faith; even your rathole of a house with its sonorous room titles like "Place of Contemplation" and "Monastery" and "School." What impressive forests of overgrown brush you have. Your precipitous mountains encircle you all, not so much as a crown, more like a prison. Your air comes in rationed doses, and the sun, which you long for so much, you can peer at like someone looking up a chimney.[33]

Gregory's next letter continued the debunking, once he found that Basil was taking it in good humor. He summed up his visit to Annesoi in the revealing phrase of "thank God mother intervened":

> Since you take my jokes in good part, I will send you the rest of them. I take Homer as my preface where he says: "Come now and change your tune, sing of the inner adornment,"[34] that is—your roofless and doorless hovel, your fireless and smokeless hearth, your walls of fire-dried clay to stop the mud dripping on us ceaselessly, condemned as we were to be like Tantalos, thirsting in the midst of waters. And what of that pitiable feast to which we were invited all the way from Cappadocia, only to find nothing to eat. And I had thought to come to the table of Alcinous, not to the poverty of the Lotus Eaters,[35] we poor young survivors of a wreck. I remember your loaves and the broth (well that was what you called it anyway). How could I ever forget them? My poor teeth, slipping on your hunks of crust, and then bracing themselves, ready to pull themselves out as if they were stuck fast in sucking clay. You yourself can raise these themes to a higher strain of threnody, since you have learned to speak so loftily through your experience of such suffering. As for me, if we had not been speedily rescued by that great benefactress of the poor—I mean your mother of course, who came just at the right moment, like a port in a storm—we should long ago have been corpses, and our "Pontic faith" more an object of pity than admiration.[36]

It would be easy to dismiss Gregory's objections as merely the refusal of an aristocrat to adopt poverty. It would also be easy to dismiss his incipient theories of monastic life (with mother and family near at hand, and safely under the shelter of an aristocratic establishment) as rather weak-kneed dilettantism in the face of Basil's radical monastic settlement. But this would be too facile a judgment. At stake was

33. Gregory Ep. 4, PG 37.24-25.
34. *Odyssey* 8.492.
35. Both images are from Homer. Alcinous was the king who provided Odysseos with unstinted hospitality after his shipwreck; the lotus eaters were crazed, and in this state of being out of their minds they grazed the land and were reduced to a pitiable state. Cf. *Odyssey* 9.84.
36. Ep. 5, PG 37.28-30.

not, essentially, a question of ascetical rigor. Gregory was of an ascetical tempera-
ment himself, but in moderation, preferring simplicity of lifestyle to the bold feats of
ascetic endurance in which some of the Egyptian and Syrian monks indulged. What
was really at question between Basil and Gregory's idea of the life of solitude was not
its ultimate point, rather its methods and proximate purpose.

The actualities of life at Annesoi centered round hard physical labor and the
chanting of the psalms[37]—a typical pattern of simple monasticism Basil saw at work
when he visited the Palestinian monasteries in 356. It was only considerably later,
and after relationships with Eustathios had cooled, that Basil's idea of monasticism
began to take a different line. After his ordination to the priesthood he began, in a
more focused way, to extend the principles of monastic organization into the corporate
structure of local Church affairs.[38] In contrast, what Gregory saw as the whole purpose and justification of the solitary life was that it afforded time for the highest level
of reflection, speculation, prayer and reading. It was this he wanted to do, not dig
irrigation systems or cultivate turnips, or even direct recalcitrant congregations.

The classic forms of Christian monasticism as they have come down to the present century are a combination of many diverse patterns and traditions. Gregory is
traditionally associated with Basil in the composition of the monastic "Rules,"[39] and
it is certain that the two friends exchanged ideas on monastic theory at a deeper
level, when they were together in Pontus in 360 and 361, than emerges from the
humorous correspondence that has survived. It is, however, somewhat ironical that
Gregory should be so associated with Basil (the "father" of eastern monks) in this
regard that his own ideas on monastic life were simply supposed by the majority of
commentators to be synonymous with those of his friend. Nothing could be further
from the truth. Gregory's presuppositions are those of a born aristocrat. The notion
of a rich and powerful family being at the center of the monastic community, and
protecting and fostering the wider family by the ties of religion bolstered by clan loyalties, is something certainly not unknown to the history of Christian monachism.
Monastics of the higher ranks did not renounce the ties of family and clan by entering religious life, but on the contrary ordered religious life in and through those
social bonds and obligations. This was a notably different concept to the more peas-
ant-orientated communities in Syria and Egypt, but that does not make it any the

---

37. Cf. Geoghegan (1945).
38. Cf. S. Giet (1941b).
39. Basil's first writing on the ascetical life is the *Moralia*, or *Ethica* (PG 31.700-869) a collection
    of 80 moral instructions with corresponding NT authorities. The so-called "Two Rules" can
    be found in PG 31.889-1052 and PG 31.1080-1305. The *Moralia* was, in all probability, written
    at Annesoi in the company of Gregory (cf. J. Gribomont, "Les Règles Morales de S. Basile et
    Le Nouveau Testament," SP II, TU 64 [Berlin, 1957], 416-426). The later monastic writings,
    as Gregory himself tells us (Orat. 43.29) were composed in the period of Basil's second retreat
    to Pontus, in 364, after his ordination, when relations with his Bishop Eusebios of
    Cappadocian Caesarea, were at a low ebb.

less authentic as a foundational archetype for Christian monachism, and it has some claim to be remembered as an important paradigm for much of what was to follow, certainly in Byzantium, but further afield as well. In Saxon England, for example, such a structure seemed the normal and sensible pattern for the early royal foundations. It was a standard pattern for many of the more important Byzantine foundations up to the end of the Imperial period.

Gregory's ideas may as yet have been unformed and unfinished, but he knew from an early stage what he wanted and what he wanted to avoid, and in many ways he was the real pioneer of an alternative form of monasticism that from the outset was culturally orientated,[40] and which would re-emerge more clearly in the city monasticism of Constantinople after the fifth century.

Evagrios Pontikos, who was later probably his associate and disciple in Constantinople, would take Gregory's ideas back full circle to Egypt after his own flight there, and although this scholar-monk was in his lifetime regarded with undisguised suspicion by many of the Coptic Egyptian ascetics among whom he lived, nevertheless his influence spread far afield in Syrian and Byzantine Christian letters, and ensured the survival of Gregory's initial concept of the hermit-scholar. What was at root between the different aspirations of Gregory and Basil for monastic lifestyle was already in evidence in Athens, when Gregory had tried to persuade Basil, unsuccessfully, to settle down in the scholarly Christian community he found around him. Basil's discovery of cenobitic monachism was one of the great and exciting events of his life. He depicts it as a kind of conversion experience.[41] Important to Basil in expressing this conversion, is as much what he felt he was turning from, as what he was turning to. In a late epistle Basil describes the period when he left Athens to seek wisdom in the desert monasteries:

> I had wasted so much time on follies, and spent nearly all my youth in vain labors, devoting myself to doctrines of a wisdom that God has rendered into foolishness.[42] But suddenly I woke up; as if from a deep sleep. I beheld the wonderful light of the Gospel truth... I shed a flood of tears over my wretched state, and prayed for a guide who might form me in the principles of righteousness.[43]

Gregory Nazianzen not for a moment, not even in his rhetorical flights and those moments when he castigates the "wisdom of the world" and the vanities of Hellenism, would ever describe the life of the mind as an allurement from which one had to turn to seek God along another road. In this he was truer than Basil to the legacy of the great Origen, who saw the intellectual quest of the human mind (or *Nous*) as fundamentally driven by its desire to rediscover union with the supreme

40. Gregory's ideas on monasticism have not, so far, been extensively studied apart from the pioneering essay on the theme by Plagnieux (1961).
41. And indeed it was surely the prelude and spur to his presentation for baptism soon after his return to Caesarea, *pace* Hanson (1988), p. 680; see rather Rousseau (1994), pp. 25, 61-92.
42. 1 Cor 1:20.
43. Basil. Ep. 223.2.

Wisdom of the Universe, the Logos who called to creatures to bond themselves with him through the refinement of the spiritual intellect.[44] Though Basil might agree with much of Gregory's theoretical system of Logos theology and clearly shared many common conceptions with him about ascetical theology in general,[45] nonetheless, in practical terms it is clear that the two men had different understandings of spirituality and monasticism alike. At the most concrete level where Basil saw physical labor as important in the monastic day, Gregory felt the place of study and reflection had been underestimated. The inquiring mind cannot perform its task at the most serious level while currently engaged in digging water channels for the community. A settlement trying to be self-sufficient in a basic economic and cultural way was also, in Gregory's perception, a *de facto* renunciation of the achievements of Hellenistic culture. For most of the Syrian or Egyptian hermits, for example, this was exactly the point of flight to the desert. For Gregory it was not such a renunciation of culture he sought at all, but the transformation of all that was good in human culture: the Christianization of Hellenism.

Asceticism has been until recently, perhaps, too easily seen in Christian history in terms of physical renunciations. What many critics of Gregory have failed to realize is the deep seriousness of his own intent and ascetical endeavor. He is not a figure reclining idly at home, but someone who wanted to follow the demands of intellect in a serious spiritual quest. The tools of his ascesis were books, enquiring conversation, and reflection in simple solitude. He is certainly an early and serious witness to the physical asceticism of vigils, and simplicity of lifestyle,[46] and in this followed the intellectual tradition of simplicity of lifestyle such as advocated by his intellectual hero Origen and his own Christian teacher Prohaeresios. Perhaps he sometimes "protests too much" about his ascetical rigors so as to offset the criticism of the Eustathian radical monastic groups in Cappadocia who demanded complete renunciation in monastic life—to the point of complete equality. To symbolize this the Eustathian communities forbade any social distinctions,[47] and certainly vetoed the slave-master relations. Gregory refuses to go this far. In his withdrawn solitude on the estates at Arianzum, when he was an old man, he certainly had the attendance of several family slaves[48] and it would be a normal presumption to imagine that it was so all his life. For him the ascetical life is understood still, primarily, in the older

---

44. Cf. Spidlik (1971); Bouyer (1963). Origen's dictum was that the soul must follow "wherever the Logos leads" (*Hopou Logos agei*).

45. Cf. Fellechner (1979).

46. See Sotiropoulos (1990).

47. Macrina's community at Annesoi represents interesting examples of such a social leveling, both in terms of rank and gender. See Elm (1994). There is no evidence to suggest Gregory agreed with this, and his extended doctrine of philanthropy and social compassion (which is highly admirable) is more of a Christian rehabilitation of Hellenistic social theory rather than the new modeling suggested by Eustathios.

48. Manumitted in his will.

philosophic form of intellectual abstraction from the daily round. Gregory is an aristocrat to his marrow, and follows Aristotle's presumption that the virtue of intellectual life is only possible for landowners who can support the necessary leisure for contemplative *theoria*. Such elitist ideas of antiquity sit uneasily on us today.

In the conflict that was operative in Gregory's time over who had the right to lead Christian communities—aristocrats, ascetics, local councils of elders, or civil servants—and partly visible in the tension introduced into local Church hierarchies in Cappadocia and Armenia by the radical Eustathian monastics who used asceticism as a way of modeling a new Christian social egalitarianism, Gregory's sympathies lay entirely with the idea that only "men of the best quality" (aristoi) should lead the Church. Admittedly, he modified the idea with the Christian admission that such an "aristocracy" must, of course, include spiritual attainment and discernment,[49] but his sympathies lay more with the hierarchs of the Council of Gangra[50] than with any nomadic groups of Christian radicals. And for all his closer involvement with the Eustathian circle, the same was more or less true for Basil as well. The asceticism of the men in the network of the Cappadocian Nicene movement is an ascesis of philanthropy, led firmly and energetically by a very wealthy élite who support one another closely and know how to use the corridors of power to their advantage.

To conclude that Gregory's asceticism was primarily a matter of the intellectual rigor and simplicity of the scholar is not to denigrate it. Even in contemporary Western society, where widest access to education is given a premium, advanced scholarship is an immensely costly and élitist business still. Those, both ancient and modern, who have never known the rigorous demands of such a focused intellectual lifestyle might more readily regard Basil's form of communitarian simplicity as archetypal for monks, or Eustathios' social leveling as more authentic,[51] but this would be to miss the chief point that Gregory was making despite all his aristocratic élitism. Such a life of dedicated reflection is not for all. It is meant for those who have the necessary intellectual sensitivity, and are ready to devote themselves to the painful asceticism of the life of theoria: a long and difficult road that customarily brings hardship, financial straightness, solitude, and simplicity in its train. Gregory

---

49. See Orat. 27, PG 36.12f.
50. The Council of Gangra probably met in 340 (its date is conflicted in the Church historians Socrates and Sozomen, but Sozomen agrees most with Basil. Ep. 288.13). (See T.D. Barnes, "The Date of the Council of Gangra," JTS 40 [1989], 121-124.) It tried to deal with the upheaval caused by radical ascetic groups allied with Eustathios. The conciliar canons condemned monastic separatism, and the radical social "leveling" advocated by the ascetics, and defended the rights of married Christians and a married priesthood. Eustathius was forced to accept its criticisms of his "zealotry."
51. One needs to remember that "social equality" even as envisaged by Eustathios was not the same as a modern might imagine. Eustathios was a vigorous and dynamic leader of monarchist tendencies. The world was not big enough to contain both him and Basil, and this (apart from theology) was at the root of much in their large falling out.

knew that, and suspected what cost his chosen lifestyle would involve. It was his great misfortune that those who have not experienced the pains of the intellectual pilgrimage have often tended to regard it as a "soft option." To hear Gregory trying to formulate his visions of "proper" monastic life sounded to his contemporaries as simple avoidance of responsibilities, and mere dalliance with the idea of asceticism while refusing to engage with it seriously as it was offered to him in the ready-made forms of Egyptian peasant monachism, or Armenian rigorism.

Gregory's understanding of the purpose of the retired life is crucial to his whole theological mind, resting as it does on the principle of the inspiration by God only of the refined mind and its divine uplift to an intuitive understanding of truth— *theologia*. At this period, Gregory's thoughts were forming quickly, and were to reach a maturity at Seleukia, the monastery at the shrine of St Thekla, to which he was later to retire in a pregnant and highly creative period immediately prior to his arrival as a theological teacher in Constantinople.[52]

Gregory's correspondence with Basil in this period was a very important part of his larger theological and ecclesiastical formation. Large events were taking place in the troubled waters of the international Christian scene. In 360 the army had proclaimed Julian the rival Augustus, and civil war seemed inevitable. It would be averted only by Constantius' death the following year. The Arian party had held, the year before Constantius died, a series of synods in Constantinople affirming Homoian Christology as the standard of orthodoxy, and the emperor had promised his wholehearted support in breaking the back of Nicene resistance. Among the bishops, Julian's elevation gave cause for rejoicing only to the radical Arians, for his tutor had belonged to that party and Aetios and Eunomios had already received indications of his favor and personal esteem. Almost as soon as they returned to Cappadocia Gregory and Basil realized how seriously they had to take the cause of articulating a new and solid basis for the rehabilitation of Nicene thought, and both had a vivid sense of how difficult that task would be, both intellectually, and politically.

In the winter of 361, after three years living in retirement on the family estates, Gregory's experiment in finding a new type of monasticism was, in his eyes, rudely shattered. His father insisted on his ordination to the priesthood. If his son was serious in refusing all other roads to social eminence, and religion was to be his life's course, then his father demanded that this should be publicly acknowledged in a way consonant with his son's social status: a priesthood of the new religion, which at that period was an office that was just coming into some kind of comparable social esteem with the priesthoods of the old gods.[53] The old man must also have been

52. This insight was to become central to his whole understanding of "theological method" as outlined in the first of the *Five Theological Orations* he delivered at Constantinople after 380 (Orat. 27), to which we shall return in more detail in chapter 5.
53. Cf. R. Garland. "Priests and Power in Classical Athens," pp. 75-91 in: M. Beard and J. North, *Pagan Priests* (London: 1990). Gregory's understanding of priests is a complex mix of Hellenistic

filled with forebodings at the worrying state of imperial politics. Constantius, the last of Constantine's children and the last of the line who could be expected to pursue his father's policy of favoring Christianity, was clearly coming to the end of his reign. In its final stages, the armed rebellion by Julian was fictionally resolved by the dying Emperor's device of formally proclaiming Julian as his true heir and son. Constantius died on November 3, 361, and on December 11 Julian entered Constantinople, glorifying the pious memory of the predecessor whom he hated with such venom, and determined to weaken the social and religious standing of Christianity in whatever way he could, as part of his reversal of what he saw as the fundamental decadence of the Constantinian dynasty.[54]

In the winter of that year, Gregory the Elder and his son knew well enough that less-favorable times were ahead, and it was unsettling. It was hardly the case that the old man pushed Gregory into an arduous work by ordaining him, but the symbolism was more important, and by forcing the issue of consecration he felt he had distanced his son permanently from the radical form of monasticism as it was evidenced around him in local monks who took their lead from Armenia and Pontus and were, as restless and dedicated enthusiasts for the Christian cause as they understood it, one of his greatest sources of difficulties in the maintenance of his role as religious Squirearch for the region. The church in Nazianzus, which the young Gregory was expected to serve, was one the family had built themselves for the townspeople, and his duties there amounted to standing in for his father. It was a clever move on his father's part. If Gregory had long refused to administer the farm estates on behalf of his father, pleading a dedication to the service of letters and the duties of religion, his father had called his bluff by passing over to him the administration of the Christian affairs of the whole region, and the liturgical duties of preaching, a practical employment of his rhetorical skills he had not deigned to exercise in the secular professions. Gregory's reaction to the proposal of ordination was little short of hysterical. He had little room to maneuver since his father had called his bluff on every front. He knew that priestly office was almost universally seen, at this period, as incompatible with monastic seclusion, and could recognize that once he had assumed the duties of regulating Christian life for the town, the many other managerial responsibilities his father was only too eager to

and biblical ideas, but it is clear enough that he saw the priestly "authority" of his office in terms that combined the various Hellenistic hieratic functions of magistracy, law-interpretation, sacrificial mediation, and manteia. Not only religiously, but socially, Gregory was working for the ousting of an old religious order and its replacement by a Christian alternative. In a more specifically Christian consciousness, he saw the priesthood as particularly characterized by the twin liturgical offices of the eucharistic offering, and the explanation of the word. His encomium of his father as priest in *Oration* 18.26, however, shows how he regarded the old man's imprecatory powers as a good way of keeping religious control over the local population.

54. For an excellent analysis of the wider context, cf. P. Athanassiadi-Fowden, *Julian and Hellenism* (Oxford, 1981 [reprinted London 1992 as: *Julian An Intellectual Biography*]). Cf. also G. Bowersock, *Julian the Apostate* (Cambridge, MA: 1978).

pass on to him, could not be long in coming after. Gregory's father was unable to appreciate his son's antipathy to the idea. In the actuality of their condition as country squires, surely his son could combine priestly office and status with his desire for a studious and quiet existence in the service of Christianity? Time was to prove him quite right. The oscillation of Gregory's life between times of public preaching and times of seclusion was a rhythm that suited him ideally, and brought out the best in his abilities.[55] Almost all his surviving Orations, containing the burden of his philosophical and dogmatic work, stem from his priestly ministry.

At the time, however, Gregory felt that his father's refusal to accept his excuses was an exercise of manipulative and naked power over him, tantamount to bullying. The deep waters of his relationship with the old man stirred again. In fact, his personal distress was such that it burned in his memory until the end of his life. It appeared to him that his father's obsession with the conventional proprieties of rank[56] had destroyed all hopes he had for a scholarly and retired lifestyle. And yet, there was something in Gregory's character in which he was more akin to his father than he would have cared, perhaps, to admit. Issues of rank did matter to him too. It is seen again, later, in the Sasima incident when he became a bishop. He again acted like a reluctant bridegroom, but then accepted the highest Christian office only to be wholly insulted by the paltry dignity of the see when he saw it in the light of day and deeply offended by what he surely took to be a studied offense from Basil.[57] Gregory certainly desired rank and status, and clearly, although he rarely reflects on it directly, needed the affluence his position gave him to fund and protect the lifestyle he so earnestly sought. But if he secretly wanted this public recognition, especially in Church circles, he still had enough of the innate sense of the born aristocrat to be supremely confident of the worth of his own person, and had some of the concomitant weakness of that self-assuredness in that he was not always able to see why rank should thereby have to involve him in the responsibility and duties of the office concerned.

On Christmas day 361[58] his father ordained him priest in the church at Nazianzus. The old man's delight that his son had finally, at thirty-one years of age, attained a formal rank in society, albeit solely by his own patronage in an obscure

55. Cf. Otis (1961); Spidlik (1971), p. 128f.
56. The contemporaries of Gregory's father, Amphilokios the Elder and Basil's own family, certainly acted as a closely bonded nexus of Christian aristocrats who were always very careful to advance one another's interests and one another's ecclesiastical careers, at every opportunity. Cf. Bernardi (1968), p. 103.
57. Cf. S. Giet (1941a).
58. Whether this was December 25 or January 6, at this period in Cappadocia, is not certain. Cf. Gallay (1943), p. 73, fn. 3. To state 361 presumes a feast on December 25. Baumstark (1902) thinks the December 25 feast was inaugurated at Caesarea by this period. He also presumes the December 25 custom was introduced at Constantinople by Gregory in 381, which seems unlikely judging from the suite of Orations he gave there (Orats. 38-40) celebrating the birth of Christ in the context of his baptism.

town, was perhaps enhanced by the knowledge that in the uncertain times ahead for Christian landowners, the tax exemption conferred by clerical status would be a very useful insurance policy. Gregory describes his own feelings at this period in several writings that range over many years, some near the event, others almost twenty five years later. They all witness to the violent mixed emotions of humiliation and anger at the way he felt his father had manhandled and outmaneuvered him. A crowning indignity was the invitation to his ordination issued to the local monks, whom Gregory the Elder felt might now be more tractable to his authority if he could present, for their obedience, a cleric who shared their ascetic spiritual philosophy.

Within days of the ordination, Gregory's suppressed passion burst its bounds. Without preaching his first sermon, which had been widely announced, he stormed out of Nazianzus to take refuge with Basil at Annesoi. Here he stayed for about two months. In the harsh Pontic winter his temper cooled. He had already made it clear to Basil that such a life was not feasible for him in the long term. In any case, Basil's advice had changed in an important respect. He was no longer pressing for Gregory to stay with him at Annesoi. After ordination a man was canonically bound to the obedience of his bishop and the service of his church, and Basil seems to have impressed on Gregory the fact that it was at Nazianzus that his duty now lay. It was a strange and typically convoluted reversal of direction for Gregory. Only the year before he had been stoutly resisting Basil's requests for him to adopt the ascetical life in Pontus, warding him off with excuses that he had to assist his father in his duties at Nazianzus. Now that those duties had been formalized, here he was back at Annesoi trying to elicit Basil's sympathies for what he portrayed as the blighting of his monastic aspirations.

If one accepts the tradition that Basil and Gregory cooperated in the formation of the first *Philocalia*[59] then this would have been the time when its composition was most likely, in the immediate aftermath of his ordination, rather than in the previous visits as described in Gregory's *Letters* 4-6. This edition of Origen represents the moderating tone that was already characterizing Gregory's theology. The selection filters out some of the more controversial aspects of Origen's doctrine such as the speculations on the pre-existence of souls, and the apparent subordinationism of his Christology. In the course of the Arian crisis several opponents of Athanasios had appealed to the authority of Origen to attack the Nicene Christological tradition. Origen, coming at the Christological problem from wholly different premises, actually

59. The *Philocalia* (of Origen) collates some of the principles of Origen's approach to the sacred texts in an attempt to offset growing criticism of their hero's orthodoxy on other, particularly Christological, points. Gregory describes it in a letter [Ep. 115.] to Theodosius of Tyana, to whom he sent a copy, as a "memorial of us and the holy Basil for the use of the learned." This *Philocalia* should not be confused with the [now] more famous *Philocalia* compiled by Nikodemos the Hagiorite (1749-1809) from the mystical writings of the fathers of the church (ET published by Faber and Faber, London, 1979+). Cf. Junod (1972), pp. 149-156.

offered much that both sides—those for and against the Nicene creed—could latch on to. For philosophical reasons of not wishing to attribute material substantiality to the Deity, Origen had, a generation in advance of the argument, frowned on the applicability of the terms *ousia* or *homoousion*,[60] and to that extent in the eyes of the Nicene party of the Fourth century his reputation was in growing danger of being tarnished by association with his Fourth century supporters such as Eusebios of Caesarea, even Arius himself. Gregory wished not only to reclaim Origen for the Nicene cause, but to demonstrate on a wider front why Origen's greatness had to endure in Christianity despite his occasional "lapses" from the standards of subsequent conciliar orthodoxy. He thought it more circumspect to set about this task by means of Origen's undisputed value as biblical interpreter. The *Philocalia* included several sections on the right manner of interpreting difficult biblical passages and their true dogmatic intent. It was at this time that Gregory obviously began to reflect for himself on the problems of correlating the biblical record and Christianity's tradition of philosophical theology on the nature of God and the Person of Christ. This work was to pay off in the mature writings of 381, his Orations in Constantinople where he presents his developed system in opposition to Arian theology, and which were to win him his reputation as one of the greatest successors of Athanasios. The presence of Origen, for him a benign and stimulating influence, was never far away from Gregory's thought. It was through Origen that Gregory was able to assess Athanasios' achievements in the history of doctrine and advance the work he began to its classical resolution later in the reign of Theodosius.

For the moment, working once more with his beloved Basil soothed the immediate crisis. The collation of Origen's texts is far more than a mere compendium. The selection stood, as it were, as a first general manual of theology for use by the clergy, an attempt to standardize doctrinal reflections across a wider range of clerical teachers than those few intellectuals who had hitherto achieved eminence in the schools. It was also a collection of texts that began to focus attention onto the mystical power of Origen's theological work. His speculative universality and the beauty of his ascetical doctrine made him a perennial favorite with subsequent Christian intellectuals, and in some ways Gregory has a right to be regarded as one of the earliest brokers of Origen as a "father of the mystical life."

In the most recent critical edition of the *Philocalia*,[61] Marguerite Harl has cast doubt on the reliability of the tradition of Gregory's editorship. It is, admittedly,

---

60. Cf. R.P.C. Hanson. "Did Origen Apply Homoousios to the Son?" in: *Epektasis, Mélanges Offerts à Cardinal Daniélou* (1972), pp. 293-304 (arguing that he did not); also Hanson (1988, pp. 60-70). Here he argues that there is hardly a real line of connection between the authentic teachings of Origen and Arius's system. This is certainly true, but in fourth-century Cappadocia not everyone who fell under the wider influence of questions Origen had initiated need be presumed to have read much of the original texts. Gregory had, and recognized his essential value.

61. Ed., M. Harl. *Philocalie d'Origène*, pp. 1-20. *Sources Chrétiennes*, vol. 302 (Paris, 1983).

possible to read Gregory's Ep. 115 without the necessary conclusion that Gregory was claiming editorial authorship, but on the other hand he would not have been likely to claim authorship for what was, after all, a work of collating and re-presenting the famous texts of his mentor. Moreover, the fact that Jerome too does not ascribe the composition of the Philocalia to him can be disregarded. Jerome was not only careless at times in listing the achievements of others, but he often censored out of his accounts evidence of which he disapproved, and he certainly came to disapprove of Origen, after having been a devoted admirer for many years. Jerome's economical silences allowed him to carry on anathematizing the name and work of Origen while using vast amounts, unacknowledged, of Origen's exegetical writings. If Jerome approved of Gregory, in the main, he certainly did not approve of Gregory's influential championing of the theologian whose name he had set himself the task of blackening. And if Jerome's influence carried the day in the West, it is perhaps due to the larger reputation of Gregory that Origen's memory and value has never been wholly abandoned in the East, despite the sixth-century conciliar condemnation of Origenism. The hand of Gregory can rightly be discerned in the *Philocalia* project, and it is partially revealing of the difference in spirit between the two friends; with Basil engaged at this time with thoughts on the precise and the particular aspects of the ascetical discipline as evidenced in his *Moralia*, and Gregory taken with enthusiasm for the wider intellectual and mystical culture represented by one of the greatest literary and religious geniuses that the Church had so far produced in its three centuries of existence; and in Gregory's time, its one and only philosopher of international stature.

This period of close discussion with Basil was important on another level—that of the politics of Christian theology as reflected in the realities of Church life in Cappadocia, and the eastern provinces generally, where the Arian crisis had for so long disrupted communion into a host of complicated factions, further complicated by personal animosities. The affairs of the Christians in the East were as a muddy pool and, as everyone sensed, far from settling, those waters were about to be deliberately raked again. It was to be one of the most effective anti-Christian moves that the hostile Julian made as Emperor to allow all the prominent exiled bishops to return to their sees (in many cases occupied by another of opposite theological persuasion) for thus he hoped to paralyze Christianity with internal dissensions while he set forward his plans to deconstruct the religion's previously favored status.

Basil and Gregory already had intelligence to share on this front. In 359, the year in which the new leader of the late Arian school, Aetios, had published his *Syntagmation*[62] and set the movement on a newly radicalized trajectory destined to call forth substantial treatises from Basil and Gregory in response, Basil had volunteered to

---

62. Cf. L.R. Wickham, "The Syntagmation of Aetius the Anomoea," JTS 19 (1968), pp. 532-569 (text and comm.); see also idem., "Aetius and the Doctrine of Divine Ingeneracy," SP 11 (1972), pp. 259-263; also Hanson (1988), pp. 598-636.

accompany Bishop Basil of Ancyra to a council held in Constantinople.[63] He had been brought there as a rhetorical "heavyweight" to help the delegation in their disputations with the Arian party who held preeminence. Akakios, favored by the Emperor Constantius, presided over the council which eventually produced an Arianizing, "Homoian" creed. This was intended definitively to supplant the Nicene creed with its "Homoousian" confession, which Constantius had abandoned as a basis for ecclesiastico-political harmony at that stage.[64]

The primary business of the council of 359 was to break the resistance of the pro-Nicene homoiousian party in the East, and politically a lot of old scores from the long-running and bitter dispute were settled with a vengeance on that occasion, to the detriment of the Homoiousians. Basil of Ancyra, Eustathios of Sebaste,[65] Macedonios of Constantinople[66] and Cyril of Jerusalem were all among the leading

63. Socrates, HE 2.42; Sozomen, HE 4.24.1-26.1; Philostorgius, HE 4.12 (64).
64. Although the detailed articulation of the very complex Arian crisis in all its various phases and schools is not within the scope of the present work, it is obviously central to the whole understanding of Gregory's life work to see why he so dedicated himself to the defense of a Neo-Nicene Homoousian position, and thus the essential outlines of the debate will be approached through the resolving lens of his mind. Several excellent general studies of the period exist such as Hanson (1988) and Kopecek (1979). The theological issues will be further analyzed in the discussion of Gregory's Orations in Constantinople 380-381, so here we will attempt to do no more than delineate the shape of the main dispute. The Homoian creed tried to establish Christian confessional union on the widest, vaguest, yet certainly pro-Arian basis by the statement that the Word of God was generically "like God." It implied an essential difference, which the various Nicene parties thought definitively denied the deity of the Word of God, and thus the divine status of Christ. Both major divisions of the opposition to the Arians (Homoiousians, and Homoousians—The Like-Substancers, and the Same-Substancers) wanted to specify the Word's relation to God as "substantive." The Athanasian school insisted on "sameness of essence" (*homoousios*) while the party of Basil of Ancyra and Eustathios of Sebaste preferred "likeness in essence" (*homoiousios*) to which school we presume Basil the Great had been initiated by his mentor Eustathios. (Gregory always glosses over the transition of Basil). Gregory, possibly from his earlier days in Alexandria, was more fully and wholeheartedly Homoousian in the Athanasian manner than was Basil at first, although the latter certainly moved much more to Athanasios and away from his early mentors Basil of Ancyra and Eustathios as his life developed. Even at the end, however, Basil held back from the position that a confession of the Homoousion of the Spirit was required. It was this confession that Gregory was able to attribute to him only after his death, and on the basis of the very weak argument that Basil held back from making it publicly and wholeheartedly only because of tact, (the so-called "economy" of St Basil). Basil's brother, Gregory of Nyssa, however, seems to have been party to blocking Gregory's plan to insert the doctrine of the Homoousion of the Spirit into the credal confession of Constantinople 1 in 381.
65. Two prominent patrons of Basil the Great at this early period, from whose positions he later distanced himself, especially when the latter denounced his own efforts to move the Cappadocian church from any vestige of the Homoiousian position, to a full and frank allegiance to Nicaea and its creed.
66. Who later was to give his name to the party resisting any moves to include the doctrine of the Divine Spirit into the debate on the nature of God, the so-called Macedonians, or Pneumatomachians as the Neo-Nicene party were to call them, disparagingly.

theological lights who were deposed by the Arian bishops, and exiled by decree of Constantius. The Arian Church historian Philostorgios says that on this occasion Basil the Great, then a young deacon, was roundly and humiliatingly beaten in debate when he locked horns with the radical Arian theologian Aetios and the latter's disciple, the logician Eunomios, the two most significant intellectual enemies of all Basil and Gregory stood for. The arena at Constantinople was certainly hostile, though whether or not Basil's debating skills were up to the mark at that time or not, it is difficult to judge fairly from the nature of the sources. In any case, Eunomios emerged from the council rewarded with an episcopal throne at Cyzikos, and Basil came away with the deep realization of the extent of the labors and practical endurance that of necessity lay ahead of him and his friends.[67]

All that his own family tradition had stood for was assayed and rejected by that Homoian council. In political terms the presentation of his party's position had been little short of disastrous. In the aftermath he began a long process of self-examination. His own grandmother had been the disciple of Cappadocia's native saint Gregory Thaumaturgos, who himself had advocated an embryonic form of the Homoiousian theology. The weight of this "traditional" Cappadocian theology pressed on Basil in a way in which it does not seem to have burdened Gregory. Basil was beginning the process of rethinking the lines of connection between Homoiousian thought and the full Nicene confession, and also beginning to realize the massive extent of the leadership responsibility that had fallen to his generation of associates. Gregory Nazianzen, for his part, was less in awe of Gregory Thaumaturgos' tradition and influence because of his own preference for Origen, who had been the Thaumaturg's own theological master when he was a young student in Caesarea. By going to the wider source, and with a bolder taste for speculative thought than Basil, Gregory was to approach the same problem from a different perspective.

When Basil and Gregory spent the winter of 361-362 locked up together in Pontus they assisted each other inestimably in clarifying their respective ways forward. In the spring of 362 Gregory was persuaded to return home by Basil. The intractable problem was how to come back without loss of face, but this was resolved for him by a turn of events which made his father utterly dependent on his skills as theologian and orator. Roles of dependency were reversed.

It was news of the severe difficulties his father had called down on upon his own head that brought Gregory back to Nazianzus, to take stock of the situation. The first three Orations of his corpus date from this period, although the second of those (*Explanation of My Flight to Pontus*) was to be extensively remodeled and amplified by Gregory in the aftermath of his retreat from Constantinople in 382, and therefore needs to be read with some caution for the chronology of the historical information

---

67. Further on the councils of this period see Lohr (1986); Hanson (1988).

it offers. The severe castigations of venal monks and clergy, for example, usually reflect the conditions of 382, when his view of the Church hierarchs was decidedly jaundiced, rather than those of 362. *Oration* 1 is like the Prodigal Son's wellrehearsed excuse[68] though perhaps less remorseful. He has prepared the ground for his first sermon in the very Church which he had so publicly fled.

His discourse was given after the Easter liturgies:

> Brethren let us forgive all offenses for the Resurrection's sake. Let us give one another pardon; I, for the noble tyranny which I have suffered (for now I can call it noble); and you (who exercised it) if you have had cause to criticize my reluctance.[69]

It is a brief but elegant oration that promises the people he will be a reformed character, a new life begun on the day of resurrection. Already he signals a theological style that encapsulates doctrines in memorable antitheses and antithetical balances that weave together biblical themes and rhetorical devices.[70] Such was to be the hallmark of all his great work. The climactic part of the discourse, however, is not so much Paschal theology, but the urgent reaffirmation of hierarchical authority.

He stresses his own position as natural heir to his father, and in reminding his people that his father built the church he implicitly lays claim to their allegiance to his priestly authority also.[71] The peroration of the speech gives an indication why this inaugural address sounded such a consistently somber note:

> This August Abraham...today brings to the Lord his willing sacrifice... You, for your part, must offer God and us your obedience... You know your shepherd well, and are known by him[72] so follow him when he calls you as your shepherd. Come openly through the gate of the sheepfold, not following a stranger climbing up into the fold like a robber and a traitor... who with deceitful and corrupt words would wrest the sheep from their true shepherd.[73]

The dire news that had brought Gregory hurrying home is obliquely witnessed here. His father's Church was actually in schism. As he preached his first sermon he could tell immediately the extent of the trouble. The numbers in the congregation had fallen alarmingly as some of the most respected and venerable figures in the local Church (the monks) had called for a boycott of bishop Gregory's Church on the grounds that he had lapsed into heresy.

This *First Oration* is, of course, something of a case of preaching to the converted, the loyal element who had continued to attend his father's liturgy. Basing himself on John 10, he characterizes his father's opponents as mere "hired men" who were leading

---

68. Lk 15:18-19.
69. Orat. 1.1, PG 35.396.
70. Cf. Orat. 1.4, PG 35.397.
71. Orat. 1.6, PG 35.400.
72. Cf. Jn 10:1-14.
73. Orat. 1.7, PG 35.400-401.

the flock to destruction. The image is piquant if we remind ourselves that most of those still in the Church must have depended on the bishop for their immediate livelihood, as farm laborers and the like, and were not ready to endanger their jobs for the subtleties of theology. By such a barely-disguised appeal to institutional order and social status Gregory may have secured the allegiance of the home front, but he knew he could not resolve the ecclesiological crisis by merely holding out against his more independent critics, and this gives an indication that in terms of the numbers involved and the authority of the dissidents, Gregory's Church was seriously divided.

The authority of the dissidents was based on other grounds, their right to spiritual preeminence as ascetics, and unable to contradict that platform baldly, he had to fall back on legal, institutionalized, natural inheritance. The charismatic power of the illuminated ascetic is, in fact, the theological argument which Gregory habitually employs to validate all authority in the Church. It was ironical that his opponents on this occasion had beaten him to it. In addition, knowing his father was in the wrong, but having to defend him anyway, left him with little room for legal rhetorical maneuver; for these early orations are nothing if not an exercise in casuistical pleading. The sense that his father was in the wrong comes out in the manner in which he does not denounce his opponents, the group of dissidents, collectively. Instead he chooses to concentrate on the apparent ringleader (a traitor, a robber, a deceitful stranger) who has taken charge of them. It is not their judgment that Gregory is attacking, for intellectually he seems to have shared their dismay at Gregory the Elder's behavior, it is their disloyalty in rejecting the spiritual leadership of his family. This is, of course, the typically Gregorian sentiment of the wounded heart, but (again typically) not really a sustainable logic.

If Gregory had made any statement when he fled from the church at Nazianzus it was surely that he refused to minister as priest to these ascetics. This being so, it is hardly surprising that they preferred to find a priest of their own spiritual and theological persuasion to minister to their communitarian needs, rather than rely on the old régime of Squire Gregory, no great lover of monks, who had just lost the one asset of his archaic community when his ascetically-minded son fled to Basil in Pontus to escape the old man's tyranny. In fact, by his flight, had not Gregory himself given the signal to the remaining ascetics of the region to break communion with the gruff bishop just as Gregory had done *de facto* by physically removing himself?

It has often been thought, generally on the presumption that his first orations after ordination betray no sign of schism, that the conflict in the church at Nazianzus began a year later (363). Bernardi[74] restricts it specifically to a few months in the course of 364, and understands Gregory's absence from his father's side, during which time the crisis evidently blew up, as the occasion of the visit the former

74. Bernardi (1968), PFLS 30, Part II, pp. 102-103.

made to Basil in the winter to spring of 363-364.[75] On this occasion Basil had sought Gregory's advice in healing the division that had arisen between himself and Bishop Eusebios of Caesarea[76] when the monks of that region, loyal to Basil in preference to Eusebios, were also threatening schism in the Church. Though ingeniously argued, this schema seems to telescope the events and issues unnecessarily severely. In the first place, the point of Basil asking Gregory's advice on a highly complicated issue of Church politics (not normally an issue on which Basil would respect Gregory's judgment) takes on particular relevance if Gregory was himself several stages down the road of resolving just such a crisis in his own church. Secondly, it is clear from a close reading of *Orations* 1 and 2 that the presumption that there is no sign of division in these early homilies is not sustainable. Gregory is, admittedly, speaking to his own congregation, and that means the loyal part which had physically gathered in the church to hear him, but he must have known that his message would be reported, and so is obliquely addressing the dissidents as well in an attempt to gain them back. The tenor of *Oration* 3 is a complaint to a group of especially significant Christians (surely the monks are meant) that they have acted too severely in the face of his flight to Pontus, and judged him too uncharitably. This is more than an attempt to justify his renunciation of priestly duties, it is rather a plea to reassert his standing in the affections of that élite community, one which is meant to serve as a prelude to the greater task of reconciliation that lay before him—persuading the ascetics to rejoin his father's communion by means of rejoining *his* communion. The latter theme is explicitly developed in *Oration* 6, which was probably delivered early in 364, after returning from his conversations with Basil. Moreover, the major step of ecclesiastical policy taken by his father (however disastrous it turned out) is more understandable as an independent decision taken of necessity when he thought his son had definitively renounced service alongside him for a monastic life far away. In short, when Gregory left Nazianzus in the winter of 361-362 both his family and the local monks must have regarded it as a permanent and definitive move.

The preliminary Orations are, of course, concerned with his own personal rehabilitation, as presbyter of the Nazianzen church, above and beyond the larger problem of Church order, but this is so closely bound up with the wider problem that they cannot be separated, because he knew that his urgent task of resolving the complex doctrinal conflicts would be impossible without an acknowledged status within the Church hierarchy. He was aware that his behavior was tantamount to a canonical rejection of ordination within the very week of receiving it. He had not only

75. Cf. Orat. 43.28, PG 36.533-536.
76. Bernardi (1968) pp. 102-103, also suggests that the occasion of the Nazianzen monks' renunciation of Gregory the Elder was his signing of a "heretical creed"—not the homoian creed of Rimini, as is generally supposed, but the creed promulgated by the Emperor Jovian's entourage, passing through Cappadocia late in 363.

weakened his claims to office[77] but had caused animosity towards him in the ranks of the local monks. If we may rightly interpret the opening words of *Oration* 3.1 as hinting that it was even the monks who had sponsored and petitioned for his elevation, then his sudden flight would have offended them as much as it did his father, for he had clearly preferred the community of Basil to that of his self-styled brethren at home.

His *Third Oration*, a masterpiece of bridge-building, was designed for them specifically,[78] and here[79] he uses vividly affectionate language (love scorned, the stings of love, the sufferings of the neglected heart) in a bid to regain their affections. This itself is once more employed as a prelude to a serious attempt to broker a theological reconciliation and settlement. This, his first draft of a conciliation, amounted to a demand that they demonstrate the proof of their affection for him first by being reconciled, and then by renouncing all theological arguments and leaving it entirely up to him to negotiate a settlement, confident in his orthodoxy and ability.[80] This was a hopeful attempt, but one that failed. If the monks were unsure of Gregory's stability, they did not doubt his theological orthodoxy; but equally they were certain of his father's lapse, and were not going to be persuaded to forget it so easily.

One final indication that the schism ought to be dated to 362 rather than later, is that *Orations* 4 and 5, Gregory's *Invectives Against Julian*, were composed during the time of the schism.[81] The appeal for reconciliation within that considerable work follows the tenor of *Oration* 3, and is best understood as reference to a conflict[82] that

77. In ancient theology ordained office was not seen as an inalienable character or proprium of an individual but an office that had to be exercised within due canonical forms or risk being voided and nullified.

78. It was probably sent to them, rather than preached before them in church (Orat. 3.1 passim, PG 35.517f) as a response to their demands for a fuller indication of his own mind, and his proposals for reconciliation.

79. Orat 3.5, PG 35.521.

80. Orat 3.7, PG 35.524. "Hold fast to the faith you received and in which you were brought up, by which you are saved and hope to save others... consider righteousness as not to speak of God too much, but to remain quiet for the most part... leave the more accurate search into these questions to those who are stewards of the word." This is a variation, as it were, of the larger argument he was to use against the Arian theologians in Constantinople 381, as seen in the *Five Theological Orations* (27-31), esp. 27-28, where he defines who has the right to theologize. There, he denies it to those who merely hold the office of teachers, and demands it be reserved to those who are "spiritually sensitive" teachers. It is the old issue of who holds superior authority in Christianity the *Didaskalos*, the Prophet, or the Hierarch. Gregory, allowing for the amount of occasional rhetoric he uses in the course of disputes, consistently follows Origen's opinion that the higher authority belongs to the Didaskalos who relies on prophetic insight to validate his teaching, and that this ability and quality is, in the end, the only legitimate justification (for hierarchs too) of the holding of any authoritative office within Christianity. Cf. McGuckin (1985).

81. Cf. Orat. 4.10, PG 35.540; Orat. 4.37, PG 35.564.

82. Gregory is appealing to the dangerous times coming upon them in Julian's reign, as a motive for reconciliation locally.

has been dragging on throughout that year (363) and which was not destined to be settled until early in the following year, a duration of eighteen months or so in total. When Gregory found out the root of the problem he knew his only hope of reconciling the monks was to argue that his father had no real knowledge of the theological positions he had seemed to be adopting.

This amounted to the curious case that the only perceived way to defend his father's right to continue to rule over the church as bishop was to argue that he was theologically incompetent. It was largely due to the son's skills in legal pleading and his genuinely affectionate personal interventions between the monks and his family that he was able to carry off such an implausible argument to such good effect, even though the monks, in the interim period, appear to have persuaded another unspecified hierarch[83] to ordain some of their number. This canonical act signaled their renunciation of Gregory the Elder's authority,[84] but may also have been a power play, planned in advance, to ensure their representation in the governing counsels of the local Church—a move in monastic circles that can be witnessed across Cappadocia and elsewhere in the Church of this era.

Part of the reconciliation process was the forced acknowledgement by the two Gregories of the legitimacy of the new clergy. The argument excusing the old man on the grounds of incompetence, once accepted, was tantamount to acknowledging the younger Gregory as the primary preacher, or theologos, for the Church, a task which the Elder Gregory was certainly willing to relinquish to him. All this was to mean that Gregory's very first priestly ministry was an experience that was to stand him in good stead to act as a synthesizing theological midwife, in a Church divided beyond the point of its own wit and imagination to find methods of reconciliation, compromise, and unity wherever possible. It would be a synopsis of his life's great work when, for a brief moment, he held the center of the world's stage at Constantinople and his counsels became part of the international construct of Christianity's universal consciousness. With force he had had it brought home to him that:

> The direction of human beings, the most variable and multifaceted of all the creatures, seems to me, without question, to be the art of arts and the science of sciences.[85]

Given, then, that the crisis of his local Church was precipitated by his father in the winter of 361-362, the traditional supposition that he had signed the Homoian creed of Rimini (360) at the same time as his metropolitan archbishop, appears dubious. Apart from the chronological issues, the whole theological tenor of Gregory's family, not just the younger Gregory himself, but his mother and the wider circle of friends such as Basil's and Amphilokios' families, was set against the kind of identification with the Arian sympathizers which a Rimini signature would have meant. To accept the argument that the old man was indeed so theologically

83. Eustathios of Sebaste perhaps?
84. Cf. Orat. 6.9, PG 35.732.
85. Orat. 2.16, PG 35.425.

incompetent as not to know the difference between an orthodox and an Arian confession, is to take too literally the narrow context of argument in which this rhetorical ploy was gleefully applied by his triumphant son, who, for a change, had the old man in a corner instead of being there himself. Gregory the Elder cannot be set in the same camp as Dianios of Caesarea who had signed the Rimini creed, to the great (and publicized) disgust of Basil.

Similarly, Bernardi's interesting suggestion that Gregory's father had signed the Homoiousian creed of Jovian[86] on the occasion the court moved through Cappadocia from Antioch to Constantinople in the late winter of 363, though theologically it is more closely aligned with the ancestral position of the households of Christian families such as those of Nonna and Basil's parents, again does not seem to fit with the chronology, for it is clear from Gregory's expectation that the monks should have been in church to hear his *First Oration*, that matters were all harmony and light in December 361, and in complete disarray by April 362.

Whatever the text was which Gregory the Elder signed (and it was perhaps only a local form of agreement—not necessarily a synodical confession), it was probably heretical by omission—in line with the current tendency of Constantius' late ecclesial policy, to achieve a large measure of consensus by the vaguest terms possible (such as Christ being "like the Father according to the scriptures" which was the line taken at Rimini. Perhaps it was an even vaguer form of agreement that Gregory the Elder signed to establish his continuing allegiance to the ecclesial discipline of Dianios that caused the Nicene ascetics to rise in revolt. It is also my suspicion that the flight of Gregory from Nazianzus had itself also contributed to precipitating the schism with the monks, as Gregory the Elder showed little sympathy for their expanding claims to a voice in the affairs of the Church. Since they envisaged themselves as the cutting edge of the defense of Nicene orthodoxy[87] in the fraught times when Homoianism was being pressured upon the Churches of Cappadocia by imperial policy, then his old fashioned and apparently crude understanding of the affairs of the Church (the possibility of disagreement with Dianios in theology while maintaining "diplomatic" relations with him as Metropolitan) seemed to them to be irresponsible and unrealistic. To defend the Nicene cause they separated themselves from the old man by withdrawal of their confidence. It is clear enough, even though Gregory applies this as a primary excuse for his father, that the ins and outs of theology were not his *forte*. His perspective was an intensely local one; the monks, on the other hand (like the younger Gregory), held an international viewpoint, one that grew out of their more extensive range of ecclesiastical contacts in the ascetical movement.

86. Bernardi (1968), PFLS 30, Part II, p. 103.
87. Probably Homoiousian—which is why the Christological aspect of Gregory's reply to them is so vague, and also why he regarded the schism as a bad move, doctrinally, both on the part of his father, and on the part of the local ascetics; to both of whom he more or less made the demand that henceforth they should leave the theology to him.

The episode brought home to the younger Gregory how pressing was the need to clarify the authentic Christian tradition: what it was and how it was to be discerned. This need to identify the correct theological method of the Church was crucial in his day (and not only his time) when scriptural exegesis in the course of the Arian controversy had proven so variable and capable of so many internal contradictions, and when conciliar process had served more to divide than to unite. To Gregory, his family and friends, and not least the local monks, their concept of authentic tradition meant their ancestral faith. This Cappadocian tradition, seen to be epitomized in Gregory Thaumaturgos, the disciple of Origen, was (in the main) thought to be represented by Nicaea but not simply reducible to Nicaea. The local schism at Nazianzus had demonstrated, however, just how difficult it was to articulate the mind of Nicene orthodoxy in any clear and simple fashion; a simplicity that could be transferred from the salons of theologians to the comparative rusticity of provincial bishops and clergy, and thence reduced and reproduced in appropriate catechesis and homiletic.[88]

Even the doughty Athanasios had come to realize the complexity of the task of holding together a common international ecclesial commitment to the "mind" of Nicaea without reducing that ecclesial mind (the substrate of that "mystery" of tradition to which Athanasios was appealing[89] and which he was consistently arguing Nicaea represented, and thus from which it gained its authority) merely to the terms of the council of 325. Without ever denigrating the formulae of Nicaea (although these were more the policy of Hosius of Cordoba than the invention of Athanasios), especially its central focus on the consubstantiality of the Logos and the Father (the doctrine of the Homoousion), Athanasios actually preferred, until later in his life, to employ other theological formulations than the Homoousion to express the Son's relation to God. His own favorite conceptions were identity of nature, or equality of power, as better suited to express the biblical sense of the divine status of the Son as a dynamic relation not merely a static dignity. In his later works, however, realizing the symbolic need to find a highly visible rallying point in a sea of factions, he returned to the active promulgation of the Nicene Homoousion as a test of faith. Yet, by this stage, he was more ready to accept the political necessity of drawing a new line in the sand: between, on the one side, those who would accept the council of Nicaea, albeit with a desire to clarify more of the implications in the light of their own Church's understandings of theology (and Cappadocia was a special case in point here), and on the other side those who wished to cast aside Nicaea either as a fundamentally flawed doctrine, or one which could never hope to achieve the status of the commonly agreed faith of the Church universal. In his abiding hostility to the

---

88. The Constantinopolitan Orations show Gregory was very conscious of the need for both approaches. His Orations offer high theological speculation alongside simple catechetical "synopse" of faith in the Trinity.

89. Cf. McGuckin (1998).

latter factions, and in the light of his long trials in the defense of his orthodoxy, Athanasios was more ready in his later years to make common cause with the former parties and, thus, their young thinkers. Men like Basil and Gregory, were ideally placed to serve as mediators in the argument.

In the new political circumstances of 362, and symbolized in his convening of the Synod of Alexandria that year, Athanasios had realized that the mind of Christianity had to be clarified beyond the terms of the Nicene Creed alone, and he sought for a conception of orthodox faith in the full deity of Christ which would tolerate other expressions and other perspectives in the common cause of uniting against Arian reductionism and rationalist method. This synod represented the initiation of a new phase in theological debate. It might be called the beginning of the Neo-Nicene movement that culminated in the work of the Cappadocians, and the articulation of the refined Christian doctrine of the co-equal Trinity.

Gregory and his circle of friends were faced with the important task of rising to Athanasios' challenge—and explaining how their Church's traditional insistence on the Son of God's role of service (what many have called the subordinationist trend of the Cappadocian tradition, its Homoiousianism)[90] could be correlated with the implications for the co-equality of the divine persons inherent in Athanasios' interpretation of Nicaea.[91] Of all the younger Cappadocians it was Gregory Nazianzen who went furthest in pressing the radical implications of the Son's equality with God. This can be represented most graphically in his bold insistence that not only the doctrine of the consubstantiality of the Son should be reaffirmed at the Council of Constantinople in 381, but even that of the Spirit:[92] something that the other conciliar fathers, Gregory Nyssa among them, shied away from—much to the disgust of our Gregory, as he will make clear in his late poems.

This story, and the complex theological arguments it involves, is better reserved for the following chapter which recounts Gregory's journey to Byzantium, when he marshaled his arguments against the Arians, and produced the mature theological

90. In older text-books this was often referred to (unhelpfully) as "Semi-Arianism."
91. After the Synod of Ancyra in 358, the Homoiousian party in Cappadocia had certainly advanced towards an ultimate reconciliation with the Athanasian Nicenes, insofar as the former had proclaimed their acceptance of the creed of Nicaea, still arguing, however, that their Homoiousian tradition was the best development and clarification of some of Nicaea's central paradoxes and obscurities.
92. Although this had been part of the grounds for reconciliation published at the Synod of Alexandria in 362, that meeting had offered no theological context or rationale for its extending of the Homoousion doctrine in a Trinitarian direction, and no theological comment on the manner in which co-equality could be reconciled with the biblical sense of the Father's commissioning of the Son and sending of the Spirit. The deep-rooted Christian understanding of this essential dynamic in the life of God was undermined by the doctrine of co-equality, and a new intellectual basis was called for—one that Gregory attempted to supply, and to which we shall turn our attention in chapter 5.

orations that won him an international reputation in his own lifetime, and an enduring place among the classics of theology ever after. For the moment, let us resume our account of his increasing involvement, after the schism of Nazianzus, in the day-to-day affairs of the Cappadocian Church, and thence with larger Christian politics on the international front. It was largely this experience (an increasingly bitter disillusionment with bishops being the main element within it), that brought Gregory, in his own turn, to something like the personal experience of Athanasios, and which underlined for him the impossibility of reliance on the common mind of local bishops for the discovery of the common mind of the Church: its substantial doctrinal and spiritual tradition. This was a hard lesson to learn, but once it had been brought home to him he grasped the urgency with which he had to theologize on the way in which the Church, across generations, is able to recognize itself, and preserve and pass on its authentic tradition. This central insight which Gregory was to elaborate, began to grow in the dark soil of ecclesiastical politics: how the Christian offices to which he aspired were, once gained, not what he thought they would be. His typically nervous and fraught ascent through the ranks of the clergy, therefore, is more than a mere record of his personal career, it is a symbol of his disillusionment with the actualities of the Church of his day and how this disillusionment forced him back into a deeper ecclesiological analysis than might otherwise have been possible.

At the end of that year, 362, Gregory wrote anxiously to his brother Caesarios asking him to resign from Julian's service at court.[93] The local Church, he says, was scandalized at the idea of a bishop's son accepting the patronage of one who was by now known to be an avowed enemy of Christianity, promoting only those who shared his enthusiasm for a turning back to classical values. Caesarios' service in the court of the "Apostate" emperor must have been further grounds for the local dissident monks at Nazianzus in justifying their rejection of their bishop's authority. Gregory wrote to his brother that he is ashamed for him, and hints at the amount of criticism his behavior has already attracted to his family. The hints, and the anxiety, may well have been based on more solid intelligence than Gregory would have admitted to his parents who had begged him to plead with his brother. If, as seems feasible,[94] the character over whom Gregory draws a discreet veil in his later *Fourth*

93. Ep. 7, PG 37.32-33; Gallay (1964), pp. 8-10.
94. In Gregory's *Funeral Oration for Caesarios* he uses a phrase reminiscent of the earlier event, describing Caesarios being able to stand against Julian by his use of the sign of the Cross. Orat. 7.12, PG 35.769. Gregory sets Caesarios' rebuttal of Julian, in the *Funeral Oration*, in the context of a formal trial scene. But this is largely for literary reasons, and because he wants to draw the closest possible parallels between Caesarios' actions and those of a martyr-confessor. The actuality of the event—an informal banquet where Julian's displeasure was roused because he caught sight of Caesarios making the sign of the Cross, is a far more likely occasion that gave him the alarm and caused his withdrawal from court, and his duties as a physician, at the very time of the preparations for the Persian campaign, which he also thus abandons.

Oration, Against Julian[95] is none other than his brother (who narrated all the internal court gossip to him) then Caesarios was indeed playing with fire. He was trying to hold on to his position at court despite the sea-change he knew was taking place, and managed a politician's ambivalence well until one day he was exposed.

The story, as Gregory tells it, concerns a group of courtiers at dinner with Julian who drew hostile attention their way by signing themselves with the cross, a Christian replacement of the normal Hellenistic invocation of the gods at the time in the banquet when the wine was brought in. Julian asked them how they could continue to confess Christ after explicitly denying him, to which they protested innocence of any known denial of their faith. The Emperor replied to them that this was precisely the meaning of the act of offering incense at the beginning of meals.[96] Gregory narrates the story as if they were, one and all, seized with horror at the thought that they could ever have so unwittingly compromised their faith, and has his characters running through the streets reaffirming their Christian dedication and their renunciation of the Emperor's inducements or threats. The essence of the tale is, thus, economic compromise, exposure, and flight. By any standards, however, this was a fine line between pursuit of a career and a readiness to compromise one's religion, as Gregory had already hinted might be the case for his brother in *Letter* 7. If the edifying tale in *Oration* 4 is meant to be a rehabilitation of any who could be seen to have compromised themselves at court, then the final clause of his letter, written earlier, shows a sharper sense of political realities, appealing to Caesarios' instinct for self-preservation, when it cleverly indicates that real political danger may not be much further away from him than the ever-present spiritual dangers he is currently being warned about; a danger so great that he ought to flee the court. If not, Gregory tells him, only one of two possible outcomes would be inevitable:

> You will either remain an authentic Christian and be counted in the ranks of Christians which (the Emperor) so despises and then will receive only that which is unworthy of you and your hopes, or you will scheme for honors and come to grief in the very things which are most important: damaged by the smoke if not by the fire itself.[97]

95. Orat. 4.84, PG 35.609-612; critical text by J. Bernardi. *Discours 4-5 Contre Julien*, SC 309 (Paris, 1983). ET, C.W. King, *Julian The Emperor* (London, 1888).
96. The emperor surrounded his imperial standard with images of the gods and also used this to encourage soldiers to affirm their old religious duties. On paydays, soldiers who offered incense to the divine images for the emperor, were rewarded with a bonus. Gregory says that some Christian soldiers thus bartered their faith for a paltry award. It was an easy method to identify those who would accept his new religious policy and cut themselves off from the powerful Christian lobby. In the context of the court and army it was probably the need for security that determined this policy of Julian's rather than religious fervor in propagandizing, nevertheless Gregory fixes his attention, as usual, on the religious and symbolic aspects of what Julian does.
97. Ep. 7.9-10, PG 37.33; Gallay (1964), p. 10.

The Emperor Julian's policy of hostility to the Christian cause had already begun to express itself in edicts disabling certain rights, such as tax exemptions, and the more famous prohibition of any Christian holding the office of teacher.[98]

The ideology of such a rescript went further than the obvious reversal of previous policies favoring Christians under the Constantinian dynasty, it broadcast Julian's low opinion of the intellectual respectability of Christian belief and teaching per se. For Julian, if Christians could not subscribe to belief in the very gods of Hellas who inspired the myths that in turn inspired the great arts of Hellenistic culture and philosophy, then they were merely uncomprehending hypocrites who attempted to fasten as parasites on a great cultural achievement and claim it in pretence as their own. His key argument in this regard is that a culture cannot be divorced from its religious inspiration without being fatally compromised, and terminally damaged. In this he was perfectly correct in his theory, but not ready or willing to accept Christianity's claim, seemingly premature in the fourth century, to be able to offer a new inspiration for a new imperium and a new society. For Julian, Christianity had had its chance and failed. All that he felt most hostile to in the Constantinian dynasty (not least the carnage inflicted on his nearest family) he laid at the door of the influence of the Christian religion, which he saw as elevating the doctrine of forgiveness to dangerous heights.

In the rescript forbidding Christians to teach letters,[99] Gregory recognized himself as an object of Julian's scorn. It set him to establish what the nature of Christian culture might be, and how the Church could escape the intellectual's mockery as a religion of the ignorant, eclectically picking up scraps of doctrines and intellectual positions as it careered from one crisis in its history to another; a position on its historical development which seemed self-evident to its hostile critics of that period.

Brief though Julian's effect was on the Church, and on Gregory in particular, the serious questions he raised went straight to the heart of the matter and raised Gregory's level of thinking beyond the internal ecclesiastical politics of many of his contemporaries. One of the immediate results of Julian's proscriptions was that Gregory determined to compose classroom rhetorical texts for independent use by Christian

98. *Edictum de Professoribus*, given (probably) from Ancyra on June 17, 362: "It is dishonest to think one thing and teach another. No professor, therefore, who does not believe in the gods must expound the ancient writers. Christians may go their churches and expound Matthew and Luke there. Children are, however, free to attend what schools they please."

99. Julian specifically exempted his former teacher at Athens, the Christian professor Prohaeresios, from the terms of the decree. The latter snubbed him by refusing to take advantage of any privilege Julian offered. There were few other Christian thinkers Julian seems to have had much respect for. He did envy his old tutor's library (bishop George of Cappadocia—the Arian intruder into Athanasios' see) and sequestered it after his murder in 361. He counted the Arian bishop Aetios among his friends (Julian. Ep. 31) and, of course, knew Basil and Gregory. He generally seems to have regarded Christianity as a fideist religion for the low-class and ignorant.

students. His verse renderings of the Gospels[100] are probably the first fruits of that activity, but his sense of the importance of providing a body of didactic material for Christian training took root at that period and determined more or less every major work that he subsequently composed. It was this governing insight that led him, at the end of his life, to select and edit his letters as examples of epistolary art,[101] but more importantly to arrange a collection of Orations which effectively cover the major needs of preaching by a Christian hierarch; examples, that is, of how to approach the fundamental duties of Christian leadership: encomia, consolations, doctrinal instructions, missionary apologetic, political intervention, and invective. The sum total of the Forty-Five Orations covers the whole gamut, and this was the reason he selected and edited them before his death—a deliberate intent to offer a theological manual for the use of the Church's intellectuals and episcopal leaders, and one which was doubtless present in his mind from his early career. There is no doubt of his deep attachment to the sentiment that the Church leadership needed such instruction, and his remarks on the moral and intellectual quality of contemporary bishops are generally scathing[102] in the extreme. The whole corpus of Gregory's work, therefore, was in a real sense shaped and focused by Julian's brief but portentous challenge.

Caesarios tried to hold on at court for as long as he could, but in a quip he later related to his brother, and which Gregory used in Caesarios' funeral service (again to distance his brother from any compromise that might have been suspected of him as once having served that Emperor),[103] Julian signified that he and his brother had been marked down as Christian intellectuals. It was a phrase Gregory was to recount often, so that it came to have the status of a "famous" family boast:

100. Cf. Carm. 1.1.12-28, PG 37.472-507.
101. Cf. Epp. 51-54, PG 37.105-109; Gallay (1964), pp. 66-70.
102. As, for example, in Carm. 2.1.12, PG 37.1166f, *De se ipso et episcopis:* "For me there is one thing above all that one has to beware of—a bad bishop. Do not be overawed by the dignity of the throne, for all have the dignity but not all have the grace. Set aside the sheep's clothing, watch out for the wolf." (Carm. 2.1.12, vv. 35-38); ibid., vv. 334f: "They are wretched folk, abominable and miserable monsters, ambiguous with regard to their faith, whose rule is opportunism rather than God's law...stunted growths, flatterers of women, disseminators of seductive venom, lions among poor folk and craven before the mighty. At every table they make fine parasites..." This poem, which shall be discussed later, also sets out a program for reform. It is partly an acerbic reaction on Gregory's part to his recent treatment at the council of Constantinople in 381 (cf. McGuckin, "Autobiography as Apologia in St Gregory Nazianzen," *Studia Patristica* [Leuven: 2001]), but on a more sustained level it epitomizes much of his life-long desire to reform the episcopate, and set out the terms of a solid foundation of the Church's intellectual tradition. This intent shaped his own literary work from an early stage.
103. There are several indications throughout his funeral oration for Caesarios that some at least, in the audience, nurtured suspicions about the politician's authenticity as a Christian, particularly his record under Julian. Cf. Orat. 7.13, PG 35.769: "Surely you were not fearful that something unworthy of Caesarios' zeal might befall him? Be of good heart, for the victory is Christ's who conquers the world."

On that same occasion [Julian] uttered his famous cry in the hearing of all: "O fortunate father, O unfortunate sons." For he deemed it proper to honor me also with association in dishonor, since he had known our learning and piety at Athens.[104]

When Caesarios returned to Nazianzus, and confirmed the family's worst fears about the extent of the Emperor's anti-Christian policies, Gregory decided to begin his *Invectives* (*Orations* 4-5), his most overtly political work, and two pieces in imitation of the classics of Greek political oratory.

These Orations were literary exercises, probably never delivered at anything more than an informal reading. They have attracted criticism for the unwaveringly hostile tone they adopt to Julian, and the unbelievably idealized picture they draw of Constantius his predecessor. The sharp contrasts of character between the two Emperors derive from the structure of Invective, as part and parcel of the genre. An Invective in the Hellenistic tradition did not call for balanced assessment. Julian is a bad thing in the same way, and for the same reason, as Constantius is a good thing: in Gregory's text this is simply because of their respective attitudes to Christ and his Church.[105] For one nothing can be forgiven, for the other all is forgiven. On other occasions Gregory demonstrates a less-than-enthusiastic attitude to Constantius,[106] but his opinion of Julian remained constantly disdainful. He hated his policies, he despised his resurrection of ancient religiosity, he disliked his character—even, he tells us, from the time he met him in Athens.

Commentators such as Quasten have gone too far in concluding that the personal animosity Gregory has towards Julian make his *Invectives* wholly unreliable for factual information.[107] They need to be used cautiously but, allowing for stock rhetorical license in the denunciations, they should not be dismissed out of hand. Caesarios was an undoubted firsthand source of much that was happening in the court, and other members of the family held property in the capital, and enjoyed senatorial rank.[108] The extent of Julian's physical actions against Christians have definitely been exaggerated, on occasions simply to give scope for learned references to other orators and poets describing carnage.[109] The tale of the atrocities, even when he tells it in its most lurid details (slaughter of virgins, executions and exiles, torture

---

104. Orat. 7.13, PG 35.772.
105. Orat. 4.20; 4.31; 4.33, PG 35.548f.
106. If one reads the signs in the Invectives subtly enough, one can see the fine distinction Gregory makes about Constantius personally, where contrasting the two emperors he argues that the one is of the best "of stock," the other is of the worst. This indicates his contrast is really between the Constantinian dynasty and the Julianic policy of reversing one of the latter's chief characters: the favoring of the Church.
107. "Hate and anger so predominate in them that their historical value is almost nil." J. Quasten, *Patrology*, vol. 3 (Utrecht, 1975), p. 242.
108. Bernardi (1984).
109. Cf. Orat. 4.92, PG 35.624, where Homer has the Phrygian river denouncing Achilles for the number of corpses thrown into it (*Iliad* 214).

of clerics, to force them to surrender Church property[110] still has creeping into it, despite itself, Gregory's truer sense that this was nothing like the ferocity of earlier persecutions against the Church. At times he even criticizes Julian for the half-hearted effort which is all he can muster, calling his persecution typically mean-spirited and unable to match the full-blooded and virile persecutions of other imperial enemies of Christ who came before him.[111]

Julian's own letters reveal a different perspective, a more moderate picture in some senses, but one that certainly is inspired by an implacable spirit of opposition to the Christian movement.[112] Gregory's account of the execution of Bishop Mark of Arethusa, for destroying a pagan temple, is substantially accurate. His death is praised in glowing terms, as Gregory composes his martyr's oration. Like Constantius, Mark's allegiance to Christ, and his martyr's death seem to carry all before them. He is allowed a large latitude of theological economy. Gregory describes Mark as "an out-standing man," a great orator, and a man of pure life, one grown old as a fount of wise doctrine. Nowhere, in this text, would one guess that here he was talking about a lead-ing Arian bishop; a Homoian theologian and thus an enemy of all that Gregory stood for in his own religious understanding.[113] In the face of enemies from without, even the chasm between Arian and Nicene could be overcome in a moment.

The supposedly "hysterical" tone of Gregory in the *Invectives* has been much exag-gerated. In fact their Greek is sublime, and the series of unrelenting condemnations, basic to the classical form of the Invective but tedious to the modern reader, is often alle-viated by sardonic humor and wonderfully vivid stories. The latter, always to the detri-ment of Julian, may indeed have all the hallmarks of Christian street gossip, but they are nonetheless worthy of retelling, especially the story of Julian's encounter with the epiph-anies of the pagan gods in a subterranean initiation ceremony which he ruined by instinctively protecting himself from malign influence by the sign of the cross; a child-hood habit he could not shake in times of crisis. The episode is wonderfully recreated by

110. Cf. Orat. 4.64, PG 35.585; Orat. 4.86, PG 35.613-616; Orat. 4.87, PG 35.616.
111. Cf. Orat. 4.61, PG 35.584.
112. *Letters of Julian*, F.C. Hertlein (ed.), 2 vols.(Leipzig 1873, 1876); cf. Ep. 7 *To Artabius:* "The Galileans must not be killed or beaten unjustly, but worshippers of the gods must be encour-aged in all ways." He was not setting out to be vindictive, but if his path was crossed his for-giveness would not be forthcoming: "I have ordered the Galileans not to be ill-treated, but the Arians of Edessa have attacked the Valentinians. I order, therefore, the money of the church to be divided among the soldiers and the estate to be added to the treasury." Despite his apparent objectivity, one ought to remember that he did purge the court of Constantius severely and vindictively, after his arrival in the capital in 361. When the citizens of Alexandria murdered George, the Arian bishop, he simply rebuked them. This leaves open the question of what Julian's position on the active disestablishment of Christianity would have been had he returned successful from the Persian campaign.
113. Cf. Orat. 4.88-89, PG 35.616-620. Mark was a signatory of the main Arian creeds. Baronius and the Benedictine editors of Gregory are so puzzled over the meaning of his laudatory remarks that they (wrongly) presume Gregory has mistaken identities (PG 35.616, n. 71).

Cavafy.[114] If the event did not happen, one feels it surely "ought to have." Such rhetorical crafting of common gossip is a mark of a superb level of apologetic skill.

In those passages where Gregory deconstructs the poetic and mythological basis of Hellenistic religions, he proves himself the equal of any Christian apologist before him.[115] All the usual rationalist reductionism which Christianity applied to Hellenistic religion is there; the normal ridiculing of the myths, all expressed with a fine rhetorical verve that is often missing in the Latin apologists who traversed the same ground. But in his (equally traditional) attacks on the moral looseness of the old religions there is, in Gregory, a new and sharper sense of the social direction of Christ's religion. This is a religious philosophy, he argues, which is capable of synthesizing old and new.[116] To Julian's intellectual disparagements he simply replies that the Church has no need to apologize. It can stand by its record and its achievements over the last generation since imperial toleration, and point to its works—its monasteries, hospices, its philanthropy and its wide-scale efforts in teaching morality and monotheism to the masses.[117] His argument rises from apologia to a ringing challenge and counterattack: the theology of the Hellenes is bankrupt, their religion false. Could ever such a religious system raise up a human soul from materialism to true contemplation? Never, he protests.[118]

This twofold description of Christianity as a society of loving *philanthropia*[119] that catches up humans into an ascent to union with God, is the peroration which culminates the Invective: Christians will overcome their enemies by love and patience. This is nothing other than the process of living out their destined deification (*theosis*), and it is no less than God's design for their spiritual elevation to mystical union, a destiny that cannot be frustrated no matter how earthly powers may rage.[120]

To sustain this thesis is, paradoxically, why he so unrelentingly assassinates the character of Julian—philosopher, priest, and mystic as the latter wanted himself to be seen. This is, perhaps, not due to an inconsistent lack of balance or charity in Gregory's case, although many commentators have approached the matter in this way, rather a direct result of his own commitment to the doctrine of *philanthropia*. The Invective is thus related primarily to a central theological thesis of the text. It is not gratuitous insult added for its own sake. As Gregory sees it, if the Emperor's claim to have rescued *Pietas* from the perfidious hands of Christians is correct, then

---

114. Orat. 4.55, PG 35.577-580; cf. "Julian at the Mysteries," C.P. Cavafy, *Collected Poems*. ET, E. Sheeley and P. Sherrard (London, 1984), p. 133.
115. Cf. Orat. 4.115-116, PG 35.653-656; Orat. 4.118, PG 35.657; Orat. 4.120.
116. Orat. 4.110, PG 35.648.
117. Orat. 4.111, PG 35.648.
118. Orat. 4.117, PG 35.656.
119. It is typical of Gregory (both as a man and as a theologian) to define the essence of Christianity as mutual love (Orat. 4.123, PG 35.661-664).
120. Orat. 4.124, PG 35.664.

the Church's entire foundational impulse of social love must have been rejected also. For Gregory, if Julian claims to have personified the rescue of *Pietas* in his own sacred person, then it is legitimate to argue that the merits of the respective doctrines of *Pietas* could be assessed by relation to the persons who embody it. Since Gregory reduces the whole impetus of Hellenistic cult to demonic influence, he sees everything Julian does (whether or not he is aware of it) as directly motivated by demonic forces. This, in the simplest terms, is why Julian is nothing other, and nothing more, than a bogeyman for Gregory.

Julian's physical attributes, which Gregory so famously exaggerates and caricatures, his ungainliness and nervous, high-spirited laughing, are subtly suggested as signs of his unnatural and demonic possession, and certainly as proofs that his claim to be a philosopher is all show.[121] His other attitudes are examined to test his "philosophic" integrity, and Gregory sums up his perceived character as fundamentally hypocritical, insofar as he had evidently abandoned his protestation of Christian religion as soon as he had assumed supreme power, thus demonstrating his falsity even as a Christian.[122] The accusation, although true, is somewhat severe given Julian's fraught history, often living in terror of his life under the savage sons of Constantine. What Gregory means to highlight, however, is the element of inconstancy of psyche in Julian (all too explicable in modern psychological terms given his childhood traumata), but which was, in the ancient estimate, incompatible with the wisdom and personal calm seen to be the necessary corollary of philosophic advancement.

The modern estimate may well be that given his personal history it is a wonder that Julian was not pathologically deranged. It was, of course, Gregory's estimate that he was. Gregory sees the madness of his tyranny as a double proof: first that he is no true philosopher, secondly that he had successfully invoked one too many demons in his incantations, and that this demonic possession, the great sickness envisaged in the New Testament narratives, was the real root of his incomprehensible and hostile behavior to the Church. This thesis Gregory demonstrates in a traditional manner, by admitting Julian's celebrated *thaumata*, but ascribing them all to a demonic, not a "divine," agency.[123]

Julian was a devotee of theurgy. The quest for signs and wonders was part and parcel of the philosophic synthesis of wisdom and religion which this form of late Platonism aimed for.[124] Gregory too aimed for a synthesis of philosophy's highest

121. The famous caricature is shown to have some basis in reality (like a cartoonist's cruel but truthful eye) as can be seen by the intended flattering contemporary portraits of the Hellenistic orators Claudius Mamertinus, *Panegyric* 6.4, and Ammianus Marcellinus, 25.4.22. See Bowersock (1978), pp. 12-13.

122. Orat. 4.52, PG 35.576.

123. Orat. 4.53, PG 35.577f.

124. Cf. Eunapios, *Lives of the Sophists* [*Vita Maximi*], ed. Boissonade, 2 vols. (Paris, 1822), pp. 48-51. Maximus was the philosopher-theurgist who initiated Julian and inspired his whole program of religious policy.

aspirations and the vision of the face of God. Both men shared a vision of wisdom that defined it as, essentially, a religious experience. Gregory, however, saw Julian's alliance of philosophy with theurgy as a fundamental betrayal of rationality, and thus a denial of the philosophical vocation. Gregory did not deny Julian's effectiveness in theurgy, but by relegating it to the world of deceitful demonic whisperings, he suggested that the Emperor's insights belonged to that demi-monde of supernatural suggestions designed to lead astray the soul from the true vision of God. For Gregory, demonic possession destroyed the soul's union with the divine Logos: that union which Gregory defines as the true goal and purpose of that logos (rational spirit) in the human being which ever seeks for understanding through clear and graceful discourse (*logos*). This turning away from philosophy's serious quest for the divine, Gregory argues, is revealed in Julian's last great levity and fraud, his self-divinization.[125] It is something that Gregory sees as the ultimate contradiction of the Emperor's statement that he too sought religious truth through reflective insight, and thus the definitive disproving of any claim that he should be regarded as a philosopher.

In an interesting passage Gregory considers Julian's *Edict on the Professors,* which forbade Christians to teach rhetoric. He considers the relationship between words or discourses (*logoi*) and the Word of God (*Logos*). Here again in this passage the essential relation between culture and religion is provided, for Gregory, by philanthropy. Here he argues that discourse (human logos), which covers all aspects of societal association, from basic communications to the heights of gracious rhetoric, is the root and foundation of all civilized society. This bonding of mankind by means of discourse, gives to the latter its religious quality:

> Human speech does not belong to those who invented it,[126] rather is it the possession of all who participate in it, or any other art. The Creative Word, the Demiurge, gave to various people the gift of discovering or instituting a variety of arts, but he set each one of the arts in the midst of all, for whoever wanted to make use of them, that they should form a common bond of philanthropy, to make our human lot so much better.[127]

It is this belief which explains why, if Julian's policy of "Renovatio" was allowed to go unchallenged, Gregory believed that society would soon return to the kind of savage and hostile *mores* that were all too frequently celebrated in the pages of Hellenistic literature which so often recounted the savagery and immorality of the gods and their unthinking devotees.[128] This also explains why Gregory genuinely thought the Julianic proscription of Christian letters to be the real crux of the argument. In this he was quite right, and held the longer view, not swayed by those who felt the

---

125. Orat. 4.59, PG 35.581
126. Answering Julian's claim that Greek letters belonged, inalienably to the Hellenes, not the Christians
127. Orat. 4.106, PG 35.641.
128. Orat. 4.116-118, PG 35.653-657.

loss of financial or political privilege to be the worst aspect of the new dynasty's anti-Christian policy.

It is certainly this aspect of Julian's scheme which he assails with greatest relish:

> How did it ever come into your mind, most idiotic and intemperate man, to seek to deprive Christians of their words (*logoi*)?[129]

Gregory takes an obvious delight in arguing the obvious illogicality of such a policy, and in parodying its proposer as being no great thinker. His point is that, whatever Julian says, civilization is not the invention of the Hellenes alone. He turns Julian's contempt of the Christian system back on his own head when he accuses the Emperor of sheer folly in condemning Christianity for its rustic simplicity and preference for belief over reasoned argument, while at the same time embracing Pythagorean fideism and theurgic superstition with an all-encompassing credulity.[130]

If Gregory is ready to defy Julian, he is clear that he will make his stand on religious grounds, for the proscription of Christian discourse and the civilization that flows from it are, for him, the fundamentals of Julian's attack against the Church's destiny to preach the Kingdom of God on earth. His defense of rhetoric is not the defense of a luxury for a few wealthy élite, it is a matter of the very substance of the Church's divine mission, and for him that vocation, which he sensed as his own, was worth dying for:

> I am ready to abandon all other things, quite willingly; riches, noble status, good reputations, power, and all such earthly concerns that are, all of them, like illusory dreams. But I will cling to the Word (*logos*) alone.[131]

Because of his unusually pugnacious tone in the *Invectives*[132] Gregory has often attracted criticism for posing as an armchair warrior. This, of course, is something which might be leveled at Demosthenes himself the greatest exponent of the genre. Words are one thing, fearless political behavior another. Gregory is certainly no man of war, nothing like Basil who a few years later was to withstand the boorish Valens to his face. But then again, that famous encounter needed Gregory to paint it in words, and it has become so famous only because of those words. If Gregory is an armchair warrior, it is only just to conclude that this is not the same as being a supine coward. Words are the main political service an orator may rightly be called on to supply, and to underestimate the importance of dissident literature, even when it seeks to protect itself, is misguided.

Gregory's passionate tone, in evidence throughout his Invectives, indicates clearly enough that at least at the time of beginning this work he felt himself and his church to be in a crisis of immense proportions. That this crisis passed into being merely a

---

129. Orat. 4.102, PG 35.636.
130. Orat. 4.102, PG 35.636-637.
131. A deliberate pun relating the Divine Word (*Logos*) and rhetoric (*logos*) by which Gregory is enabled to defend the proclamation of the Gospel, and confess his Christian allegiance. The Logos inspires his logos since it is in the service of God's philanthropy.
132. Though a standard "tone" for any Hellenistic Invective.

"Damnatio Memoriae" of the fallen Julian should not blind the critic to the fact that late in 362 matters looked very different indeed, and Gregory was determined not to go down quietly. Gregory's reading of events was sober and realistic. While the emperor was on the Persian campaign he was busy composing his last work, the *Adversos Christianos*,[133] and that signaled his attack on the "Galileans" would be resumed with vigor had he returned successful from the field.

It was Julian's premature death in the Orient that made the *Invectives* turn into a triumphant vindication of God's judgment of the wicked. In their present shape the *Orations* thus mirror the *Book of Maccabees*,[134] which has shaped their style and content as much as the *Philippics* of Demosthenes, whose oratory Gregory consciously attempts to emulate. At the time he wrote the *Invectives* Gregory was also engaged in the composition of *Oration* 15, which is a commentary on the Maccabean account of the death of the persecutors, and a large section of *Oration* 4 is comprised of a sustained biblical account of God's unfailing support of his persecuted faithful.[135] When he began to compose the work Gregory had little idea that within the year his enemy would have fallen in battle, and consequently he expected a far more radical disestablishment of Christianity to be enforced after the Emperor's return. He may well have feared a genuine threat to his own safety, gauged from Caesarios' own experiences. In this context, his original motive behind the *Invectives* is given most clearly in his exclamation:

> But how many such (calamities) did he cause? Who, I ask, will give me the learning and eloquence of a Thucydides or an Herodotus that I may pass down the remembrance of the wickedness of this man to coming ages, and carve the history of this present age as if on a column of shame?[136]

He was committing to paper a denunciation of the tyrant while there was still time, and had his eye more to the future record than the present, fearful for what appeared to him as possibly the permanent end of Christian influence in the highest power. Gregory certainly had his firsthand sources, for what transpired on the Persian campaign, and it is an overreaction to dismiss him as so biased that his historical worth is nil. Hostile he certainly is, but that does not make his political analysis naive. The most telling detail, perhaps, of all that Gregory records is the fundamental reason why Julian's strategy turned into disaster.

That downwards spiral arguably began with the emperor's extraordinary burning of his own fleet at anchorage on the Tigris river. Gregory records[137] that Julian

---

133. Or—*Contra Galilaeos:* It can be largely reconstituted from the allusions to it in Cyril of Alexandria's *Contra Julianum*.
134. As does the similar denunciation of the persecuting Emperors by the Latin writer Lactantius, a servant of Constantine the Great: *De Mortibus Persecutorum*. It was for both writers the combination of the classical rhetorical model of Invective with the theology of judgment contained in 2 Maccabees which accounts for the harsh tone of the respective works.
135. Orat. 4.18-19, PG 35.545-548.
136. Orat. 4.92, PG 35.624.
137. Orat. 5.11-12, PG 35.677.

had been duped by a double agent promising to lead him North by a quick land route, to join the Roman reinforcement armies, and having burned the fleet to save it from enemy hands he then found, to his dismay, that the promised guide had disappeared[138], leaving him with his back to the great river and soon to face the army of Shapur II. Libanios in the funeral oration for Julian attempted to defend the emperor's logic for this[139] and makes no allusion to the intelligence disaster which had misled the Roman strategists. He says, testing our credibility, that the ships were burned because the river current was too fast for further progress upstream, and so that Julian could stop lazy soldiers from sleeping on the decks. But the later Roman historians Festus and Ammianus Marcellinus do give credence [140] to the Christian report that Gregory first announces.

When Gregory first began writing his *Invectives*, then, he was concerned to account for God's strange providence: arguing that his mercy is unfailing but his just decrees difficult to interpret.[141] Using Amos 5:8 as his text, Gregory calls for calm resignation and trust that God will vindicate his people however dark events may seem.[142] This initial attitude was altered by news of Julian's death on June 26, 363, a calamity for Roman arms which shifted the perspective radically, and was interpreted as a wholly positive outcome by Gregory and most of his contemporary Christian ecclesiastical peer group.[143]

At the same time that he was drafting his *Invectives* Gregory delivered an Oration[144] to his Christian congregation at Nazianzus, to prepare them for oncoming trials. He hoped to make the threat of persecution a cause for re-uniting his divided flock and so, for the subject of his discourse, he chose to dwell on that paradigm of biblical martyrdom and heroism: the Maccabees. Like most of his other treatments of scriptural themes, Gregory was identifying his own time with that prefigured in the scriptural revelation, and consequently seeking to divine a meaning and a program of behavior from the scrutiny of the sacred text. The occasion afforded to him was August 1, 362, the liturgical feast day of the Maccabean martyrs.[145]

At the time Gregory delivered this Oration, Julian was making his progress from Constantinople to Antioch, and was quite possibly known to be in the region of

---

138. Cf. Ephrem Syrus, *Hymn Against Julian* 3.15: "So his idols and his demons were confounded by a mere trick."
139. Libanios. Orat. 18.255.
140. Festus Brev. 28; Ammianus Marcellinus 24.7.5. Cf. G.W. Bowersock (1978), pp. 114-115.
141. Orat. 4.54, PG 35.577.
142. Orat. 4.12, PG 35.541-544.
143. If Libanius was right (he claimed intelligence from a Syrian source years later) the spear that fatally wounded Julian may have been thrown by a Christian in a planned assassination with the aim of installing the Christian commander Jovianus. Cf. Bowersock (1978), 117.
144. Orat. 15, PG 35.912-933.
145. Sinko (1907) Bernardi (1968), pp. 101-102. See H Leclercq, DACL 1, 2 (1907), cols. 2375-2379, and ibid., 10.1 (1931), cols. 724-727 for the cult of the Maccabees at Antioch.

Nazianzus. Gregory retells the story of the Maccabean martyrdoms as if they were a prophecy of the fate he saw lying ahead for himself and his circle. The whole form of the Oration mimics that of a Stoic Diatribe[146] and of all Gregory's works is the one that is most formally dependent, a sign that it is an early composition. The Maccabean scriptural text tells of the faithful old man, Eleazar, who is punished by the persecuting and wicked king Antiochus Epiphanes.[147] The symbolism is quite obvious throughout Gregory's preaching. King Antiochus has reappeared as Julian, a new defender of the false gods of Hellenism attacking the new people of the covenant, the Christians. The old Eleazar, steadfast and courageous, represents his father the bishop.[148] To make the identification more "smooth" Gregory takes some license and transforms Eleazar into an old priest, and the seven brothers thus become "seven disciples"[149] when he elides the adjacent biblical story of the seven brothers and their faithful mother. He is thereby enabled to identify the courageous mother with Nonna who:

> Encouraged them all in their ancestral tongue. Filled with noble conviction she reinforced her womanly argument with manly courage.[150]

It follows then that the seven brothers, by analogy, represent Gregory's circle in Nazianzus and the local region. He calls himself, explicitly, the "elder brother." Bernardi identifies the seven as collectively and generically representing the faithful of the church at Nazianzus[151] but perhaps a closer literary and theological circle was in Gregory's mind when he crafted the narrative? Not all Christians needed to fear Julian, only the literate, the vociferous, and the wealthy of the leading classes, those in other words, who coincided with the bright circle of young Christian talent which Gregory saw as gathered around his own leadership: that is, himself, Caesarios, his cousin Amphilokios, Basil, Gregory Nyssa, and their two brothers Peter and Naucratios.

Perhaps these are the "seven disciples" he has in mind; and as the elder ordained rhetor among Eleazar's "priestly" sons he can legitimately claim the leadership of that circle from Basil—though only for a short while to come. The benefit of such an identification would be to realign his own family (and it is necessary to recall that not only his father, but also Caesarios had been the subject of much critical gossip on the part of the ascetics in the local church) with the ascetical circle of Basil, and insofar as the latter still commanded respect among the Nazianzen ascetics, thereby

---

146. Cf. Sinko (1907), pp. 1-29. Sinko identified the Stoic model as the *Oration on the Dominion of Reason*. It was greatly admired by Jerome. *De Vir. Ill.* 117.
147. 2 Macc 6:18-7:42.
148. Thereby Gregory rehabilitates any collapse of reputation on his father's part—for the constancy of the martyr's confession was widely regarded in the church of this era as sufficient in itself to cover a multitude of offenses—doctrinal lapses included.
149. *Orat.* 15, PG 35.921, 925C.
150. 2 Macc 7:21.
151. Bernardi (1968), p. 102.

to strengthen the case for his family's rehabilitation by such an association. Thus, by three implicit arguments in the *Maccabean Oration* (that his father has atoned for any apparent lapse by his readiness to face martyrdom with constancy, that he himself has assumed the active leadership of Church affairs to ensure no further lapses will occur, and that he can call upon Basil's ascetical circle to support him in this demand he is making for ecclesial unity and loyalty) Gregory strives for an end to the schism in a time of crisis. His arguments began to work, though the fruit would not be immediately visible for some months to come.

The Oration, finishing as it does with a resounding call to all the members of the church—priests, mothers, or young men—to stand firm in this time of crisis and complete their verbal testimony for Christ with the proof of decisive action, must have put fresh heart into Gregory. He made a rousing statement in this oration: "Whatever you threaten against us: we are ready to endure more![152]

And then he made a further gallant gesture, to seal the words he had just preached (with relative impunity) in church, for he addressed the Provincial Governor directly. Thinking, as he possibly did, that his life was in real danger from the approaching Emperor,[153] the letter which he wrote to the Governor[154] at this time witnesses his determination not "to go down quietly" to the likes of Julian. If his *Invectives* were designed (not least by virtue of their sustained brilliant Greek oratory) to make nonsense of Julian's claim that the Christians were a boorish lot who held to an ignorant religion, then his letter to Candidianos, the Praeses of Cappadocia,[155] sets out to be a public declaration to the authorities that he is a notable Christian intellectual. Far from signaling any readiness to compromise he invites the Governor himself to become a Christian.[156] It is a typically amusing and sardonic touch from Gregory, hopefully reliant though he may well have been on his sense that the aristocratic and literary bonds of civilized communion which he knew he shared with his correspondent would rule out anything so barbarous as an "applied" religious persecution.

The letter is an encomium in praise of a just magistrate, and in it Gregory speaks of how he has turned from the public profession of oratory into a new kind of silence. The irony is, as is usually the case with Gregory, that his turning to silence is an ambivalent reference to the *Edictum de Professoribus* (as well as to his ascetical renunciation of an oratorical career) and in, and by, this brilliantly polished letter of self-recommendation he makes a mockery of that imperial policy to the very politician expected to enforce it on the local level—whom Gregory knows has more

152. Orat. 15.6, PG 35.921.
153. Not least because of the recent alarmed withdrawal of Caesarios from court.
154. The text designates him as Archon. Tillemont identified him as the Praeses of Cappadocia, a pagan litterateur whom Gregory respected. Cf. Hauser-Meury (1960), pp. 51-52.
155. Ep. 10, PG 37.36-41; Gallay (1964), pp. 13-16.
156. Ep. 10.15, PG 37.41; Gallay (1964), p. 16.

intelligence than to think it could ever be enforced. He appeals to Candidianos' natural sense of justice and his patriotism, so that he will not ally himself with the "time-servers of the present moment" but will (despite his Hellenic religion) recognize his true friends and those who have the true interests of the state at heart.[157] Given the events which would soon happen in regard to Julian, this little piece is an interesting political gambit on the part of Gregory, underlining for the Praeses what he must have known all too well, that the time of the power of the Christians was certainly not over, and they would remember their friends (and enemies) when this brief rain cloud had passed overhead.

Only one *frisson* is known to have touched the Nazianzus community directly in regard to Julian's anti-Christian policy, and even then it was incidental in character, but Gregory makes a vivid symbol out of it. In the course of his encomium of his father in the *Funeral Oration*[158] Gregory mentions how a troop of imperial archers passed through the town and demanded their church. He describes how his father resisted their officer to such effect that, even though possessed of a troop of soldiers to back up his intent, he thought better than to press his demands and made a tactical retreat. The rhetorical point of the story is to demonstrate how good a pastor and how courageous a man was Gregory the Elder who refused to bow to the demands of a tyrannical apostate emperor who was sequestrating Christian churches. The historical verité of the episode certainly represents the character of Gregory the Elder who thus gave his son valuable political lessons in the actualities of power, but the wider context outside the funeral panegyric was most likely nothing to do with Julian's religious policy, except tangentially. It was rather connected with the Persian campaign when troops were being amassed on the Eastern border and Nazianzus, a town on the main route towards Persia from the capital, experienced an increase of military demands on its local resources. The attempt to sequestrate the church "by the order of the emperor" is technically correct but not really a direct order from Julian to seize the church at Nazianzus, rather an exercise of the local commander's general imperial rescript to demand shelter and supplies from any towns en route to his station. The order to take the church was probably his own idea to temporarily requisition the church building to house his company of archers overnight; certainly a sign that the local commander was a pagan not a Christian, and perhaps an indication too that he knew enough of the emperor's attitude to Christians to know that his studied insult to the local Christians could only gain him favor with his commander in chief. The mistake was to underestimate the strength of the local Christian community and the militia it could muster. Accordingly, the plan backfired to such an extent that the old bishop, acting as Christian high priest defending the

---

157. "Though you are Hellene by religion and serve the current dynasty and its policies, nevertheless you do not serve it like many other of the current sycophants, but as a friend of the good and the great-souled." Ep. 10.13, PG 37.40; Gallay (1964), pp. 15-16.

158. Orat. 18.32, PG 35.1025-1028.

"temple," as well as chief local magistrate defending his town's honor, could send the company and its commander packing. Such incidents as this supply of transit troops were common enough not to merit particular mention, this episode alone was enshrined because it related to the church building and so formed the single basis when (by suitable rhetorical license) Gregory the Elder could be said to have withstood Julian's religious policy in the face of imperial arms and so gained the rank of "confessor of the faith" which his son so earnestly wished to restore to him in the repair of his posthumous reputation. For Gregory, the episode becomes a happy memory of the local prestige that surrounded his father in the aftermath, and was thereafter transmuted by him rhetorically into a standing joke against an emperor who: "first took leave of God, and then took leave of his senses."[159]

Julian's death in the campaign against the Sassanids, on June 26, 363, disaster though it was for Roman arms and the security of the state, lifted a cloud from the horizons of the prominent Christian intelligentsia. All thoughts of a wide-scale religious oppression of the Christian movement receded rapidly. The time of his rule had seen a renewed turmoil in the churches as the various forms of Arian thought and their Nicene and Homoiousian opposition, had been mixed together in a volatile way, with exiles returning home, and numerous disputes both individual and synodical taking place. With Julian, no longer did a Christian emperor (Constantius) attempt to foster an approved form of orthodoxy. When he had, both the Homoousian Nicenes and the extreme Arian parties had been equally handicapped. Under Julian, the disarray among the Churches of the East was looked upon by a hostile Basileus with scornful amusement. His dream that the Christians might self-destruct in their mutual hatreds and inability to adhere to a commonly accepted substance of belief seemed to him (and others) to be a real possibility. Now that he was dead, and news of the elevation of Jovian trickled back to the provinces, the Christians felt relief and vindication, for Jovian was known as a Christian himself. He gave clear indications that the Nicene party could expect favor, when he received Athanasios kindly at Edessa. The full extent of his humiliating treaty with the Persian King Shapur II did not overshadow this reputation, although the Syrian and Armenian Christians felt the impact strongly, as Rome had to abandon Nisibis,[160] part of the Empire since the time of Diocletian. Even so, Jovian was a savior. The Syrian Christians celebrated him even long afterwards in their romance literature.[161] An accident on the way back to the capital at Constantinople, nevertheless, removed him quickly from the scene. He expired at Dadastana, on February 17, 364. The

159. Orat. 18.32, PG 35.1025B

160. Ephrem the Syrian (306-373) speaks of the loss of the city where he served as a deacon and hymnographer, and of the large refugee movement to Edessa. On the terms of Jovian's negotiation all the Christian population of Nisibis had to vacate the city. Ephrem wrote a cycle of "77 Hymns on Nisibis." He had seen the body of Julian on its catafalque as he himself left Nisibis as a refugee.

161. Wordsworth in DCB vol. 3 (1882), pp. 461-465.

story circulated that he had died of "overheating" in his apartments, which might well have been carbon monoxide poisoning from a brazier, though it may also have been a euphemism to cover the fact that he choked in his sleep after a heavy bout of eating and drinking. He was rapidly replaced with another Christian career soldier, Valentinian, who assumed the purple and subsequently stabilized the northern borders of the empire. He was a broadly tolerant Nicene Christian, and that stance marked the general religious policy of the western provinces in his subsequent administration. Shortly after his accession, and against the advice of his political advisors, he appointed his considerably less talented brother Valens as his co-emperor ruling the eastern provinces. Valens was an adherent of Arian Christianity, and was to have a marked effect on the fortunes of the eastern Christian Churches until his own death on the battlefield, in the disaster of Adrianople, when he fell before the Gothic tribes in 378.

In the church at Nazianzus, as 362 moved into the new year, Gregory was still experiencing the damage to the Nicene cause that a schism of monks could effect. Despite his best efforts, the dissidents could not be induced to return, and it had proved to be an unnecessary burden in what Gregory saw as a time in which active steps had to be taken against the Arian propaganda. Basil had been working effectively against the Arian movement in the forms of the Homoian theologians as well as the dialectical radicals Aetios and Eunomios. His rise in the circle of Eustathios of Sebaste had resulted in his more and more frequent absences from his "retired" ascetical life in Annesoi. In 362, after the wealthy layman Eusebios had been elected to the metropolitan see of Caesarea in place of the malleable Dianios, Basil took the opportunity to enter the ranks of the local clergy. He consulted Gregory by letter[162] who encouraged him to regularize his position in the Church leadership since the "times" demanded it and "many tongues of heretics are busy against us."[163] The move is part of the same wider trend that can be observed in the Nazianzen schism—when monastics pressured the local churches by the paradoxical move from withdrawn ascesis (the raison d'être of the monastic state) into public service as the ordained town-clergy. It is a policy identified with Eustathios of Sebaste whose disciple Basil had been.

Dianios, the former bishop of Caesarea, had earlier signed a Homoian confession of faith, issued by the emperor for subscription in Cappadocia after the council of Rimini, and Basil had then organized the noisy disaffection of the local monks. Only on Dianios' deathbed had a reconciliation been effected. Now with Basil's installation as a priest among the clergy of the theologically incompetent Eusebios, a person who had to be hurriedly baptized before he could be consecrated a bishop, he was effectively making a bid to seize hold of the chief see of Cappadocia for the Nicene cause. Within a very short time trouble resulted. Basil was far from being universally liked among the local hierarchs, or among the older clergy of the see.

---

162. Basil's original is lost, only the reply survives.
163. Ep. 8.4, PG 37.36.

By the end of 363, the relations between Basil and bishop Eusebios had reached their nadir. Basil's political, rhetorical, and theological ability had become abundantly obvious. Gregory Nazianzen tries to explain the whole grounds of the disagreement between Basil and Eusebios on the grounds of the bishop's jealousy of the younger and more able man, but his diplomatic silence covers over a good deal of active machination on Basil's part.

The latter's alliance with bishop Eustathios of Sebaste, and his active participation in several of the main synods of the preceding years, when even as a deacon he had locked horns with the chief theologians of the Neo-Arian party, and thereby identified himself publicly as one of the leading defenders of the Nicene cause, had all given him a security of ecclesial standing which made him less than patient with his local, and uninspiring, superior. The large monastic following Basil now commanded, and perhaps also the political reputation of the wealth of Basil's family which was already expected to have a suitable "outlay" in the local region,[164] all proved to be volatile elements in the local tension with Eusebios. The monastics seem to have been agitating against the bishop, indicating that any disrespect to Basil would be taken as a slight to them. Basil's leadership in this cannot be doubted, even if he could not legitimately break communion with Eusebios who as yet had given no grounds for any theological protest against his administration. Basil's need to break out of the impasse was becoming urgent.

Gregory Nazianzen soon received a letter asking for advice, and support. The Elder Gregory was one of the oldest, wealthiest, and most respected bishops of the province, and his political weight counted, as was abundantly evident in the way Basil was so anxious to gain his suffrage in the later period when he was to seek the episcopal throne of Caesarea himself in the face of concerted opposition. When he received Basil's request for help Gregory saw the way towards a mutually beneficial solution. If he brokered a reconciliation between the Caesarean ascetics and their hierarch, as the official representative of his father, then in turn he could command the support of Basil's monastic contacts to bring the Nazianzen dissidents back into line. Gregory set out for Caesarea at the end of 363 and seeing the situation at first hand counseled Basil to make a tactical withdrawal to his estates at Annesoi. Gregory himself made a short stay at Annesoi and, while here, probably showed Basil the text of his *Invectives Against Julian*, for when he was to publish them he added to the end of the *Second Invective* a tribute to Basil's collaboration.[165] The tone of this is buoyant and positive. The *Invectives* not only

164. He had adopted the ascetical life (as a monk) and thus renounced personal wealth, but had now re-entered public life as the city's deacon, then priest and spokesman. The townspeople had more or less elected Eusebios as their bishop because of his great wealth, their expectation from Basil must have been similar. Indeed, Basil would soon determine to build a large philanthropic settlement outside Caesarea. It is probably the ruins of this settlement which now lie as the foundations of contemporary Kayseri in Turkey, though precious little remains can be seen (even in the museum) from this era.

165. "This is what Basil and Gregory offer you, the adversaries and enemies of all your policy...men celebrated throughout Greece." Orat. 5.39, PG 35.716.

denounced the now fallen emperor Julian, they served as public declarations of loyalty to the imperial successor, and at this time the Nicene party must have been secretly delighted at the manner in which the circle of Aetios and Eunomios had been favored under Julian. It was now a liability for them politically. They sensed, and rightly so, that the Neo-Arians' moment of glory had definitively passed. The reception of Athanasios by Jovian was to open the door for the flourishing of all that the Neo-Nicene movement desired to achieve. The time for a reconciliation with Eusebios would be a little way off, in the meantime Gregory certainly promised his offices as an ambassador. When he returned to his local church he had Basil's support entirely, and his own minor schism was quickly brought to an end. Some time in the early part of 364 he preached, with the local monks once again present in the Nazianzen church, an oration celebrating the restoration of peace.[166] His affectionate terms of reference to the local ascetics demonstrate his expectation that they will accept him as both their theological leader, and the local leader of their ascetic brotherhood. On their part, they retained the priest who had been ordained to serve them in the time when they had separated themselves from Gregory the Elder.[167] Face had been saved all round.

Possibly while he had stayed at Annesoi, Macrina expressed her desire for him to intervene and turn her brother Gregory Nyssa away from the rhetorical career he had decided to follow.[168] As she had been with Basil, Macrina was a powerful influence in arguing that the ascetical life and the affairs of the Church demanded the renunciation of secular politics. Perhaps at this time can be dated his letter to Gregory where he advises the young man that his rhetorical gifts can be best used in the service of the Church. The letter is similar in tone to the one he sent to Caesarios[169] calling him back from Julian's court. Like his own letter to Candidianos the Praeses of Cappadocia, it is a cleverly written display of his oratory, showing the younger Gregory his superiority in the art, and how the Christian life was not incompatible with the highest exercise of those skills they both valued so highly. It may not have been exactly what Macrina intended, but it served its purpose as far as Gregory was concerned, for a few years later Basil was able to induct his younger brother into Christian political life as his subordinate bishop in Nyssa, and from his role as an episcopal rhetor grew some of the most brilliant Christian writing of the period.

More or less at the same time, probably soon after hearing the news of Julian's fall and Jovian's elevation to the throne, Gregory wrote a letter to his cousin Amphilokios[170] who by then had finished his rhetorical studies and assumed a government

---

166. Orat. 6, PG 35.721f.
167. Cf. Orat. 6.9, PG 35.732.
168. He does not mention her by name, but refers to the familial bonds that bind Christian ascetics as his inspiration to write. Ep. 11.2, PG 37.41; Gallay (1964), pp. 16-17.
169. Ep. 7, PG 37.32-33; Gallay (1964), pp. 8-9.
170. The son of his maternal uncle Amphilokios who had served as his earliest tutor.

post. He gives an indication of how much the clan interrelation mattered, and not merely the familial ties but those of religion, class, and education: something that his letters consistently reveal.[171] This time he wants Amphilokios to restore the tax benefits[172] for one of his immediate clergy, an important privilege that Julian's hostility had threatened to end. Such relief from tax was a significant benefit, and if the clergy were wealthy local magnates, as was the case with the families of Gregory, Amphilokios, and Basil, then clerical status was a very significant way of bolstering and maintaining the clan wealth and thus, by extension, the political power of leading groups of Christian families. Later, when Basil as metropolitan of Caesarea needed bishops to support his cause, he would immediately turn to the clan of family and friends and consecrate his brothers, as well as Gregory Nazianzen and this same Amphilokios,[173] to episcopal sees around him.

At about this time, his cousins Helladios and Eulalios bought a property to which they also could retire to live in philosophic retirement. Years later Gregory would ensure that Eulalios inherited the episcopal direction (and possession) of the church at Nazianzus. Soon after buying their estate, they had trouble with the hostile encroachments of neighbors, and Gregory came immediately to their defense, writing appeals on their behalf to two magistrates in Cappadocia, Caesarios and Lollianos. To Caesarios[174] he makes it clear that their "family rank" as well as the "quality of the manner of life they have chosen" will make his intercession hardly necessary.[175] Lollianos appears to have been one of his circle of friends from youth, and he wrote to welcome him back into local affairs, asking him to be a good neighbor to his cousins and again recommending the "pinnacle of philosophy" which his cousins were striving after.[176] Both magistrates were probably Christian, and in these brief letters we gain another indication of the important and mutually advancing cross-connections between highly placed members of the Christian ascendancy in Cappadocia.

In the meanwhile, during 364, Gregory Nazianzen bided his time until bishop Eusebios' anger cooled, and with an exchange of letters he could negotiate Basil's return to favor, and an active role in the politics of the Church at Caesarea. Basil would use his time in retirement at Annesoi during 364 to good advantage in composing an extended attack on the theology of Eunomios the Neo-Arian whom he

---

171. See Kopecek (1973), Van Dam (1986), and White (1992).
172. Instituted as a Christian benefit in the Constantinian dynasty and discontinued under Julian. In 365 he again asked Amphilokios to come and act as defense lawyer for a case brought against his niece Alypiana's husband, Nicobulos. Ep. 13, PG 37.45; Gallay (1964), pp. 20-21.
173. After having exercised a legal rhetorical career, he "retired" to solitude in 370 spending some years as a subsistence farmer and hermit before becoming an active member, as bishop of Ikonium after 372, of the Neo-Nicene theological circle.
174. Not Caesarios his brother, but a resident magistrate in the legal circuit where his cousins had raised their lawsuit.
175. Ep. 14.6, PG 37.48; Gallay (1964), p. 22.
176. Ep. 15, PG 37.48-49; Gallay (1964), pp. 22-23.

had recognized as the leading intellectual in opposition to his Nicene circle. The intellectual war with Eunomios was to dominate most of the important theological work the group produced, even after Basil's death, when his brother Gregory Nyssa continued the attack after Eunomios had written a refutation of Basil's first treatise. When Gregory Nazianzen came to Constantinople in 379, Eunomios was still the leading Arian intellectual in the city, and his *Theological Orations* are explicitly designed as his own "Contra Eunomium." He makes less explicit reference to Eunomios than Basil, but this was because he was fairly sure in that later period that Eunomios' circle was more or less a spent force, and Gregory was more concerned to present in the form of these Orations a memorable, succinct, and above all clear statement of orthodox Nicene belief which could attract wide agreement.

In 364, however, the turbulent affairs of state seemed to have been resolved enough to secure the immediate security of the Cappadocian province. Within that tense political climate the Christian churches in Cappadocia played out their affairs. In the previous five years a stream of synods had been taking place in the eastern provinces, trying to stabilize the Christian doctrinal tradition in relation to Christology. The ebb and flow of these synods marks the tidal fortunes of the variety of forms which Arianism took in the latter part of that century in which it had first come to prominence in Alexandria, and then moved internationally to be the single largest crisis of coherence Christianity had yet faced.

Constantine's religious policy, anxious to secure peace in the Christian Churches after his conquest of the eastern provinces and his emergence as supreme ruler of the empire in 324, had produced the credal statement of Nicaea as a rebuttal of the main tendencies of the Arian movement. In his later years, however, Constantine, and his son and successor Constantius, progressively sought after a new statement of faith as an alternative to that of Nicaea. The Western Church provinces, usually in alliance with the then regnant western emperor, were firmly committed to the Nicene standard. This professed that the Logos, the divine Son of God, was "of the same substance" or Homoousios, with the Father. The creed, in explaining what this newly introduced technical philosophical term meant, used the surrounding nexus of images: "God from God, light from light, true God from true God." At Nicaea, in 325, this was meant, and was largely clear enough in its intent and effect, to state a high Christology, in other words to argue that the Logos was indeed divine in the fullest and deepest sense of what that signified. Most Christians of the era were prepared to affirm that as a synopsis of their belief, though some of the more philosophically trained theologians held widely differing interpretations of how the divine Word could be conceived as being "God" if one still committed the Christian religion to a firm belief in the Unicity of the divine being.

Moreover, many bishops, even among those who signed the Nicene creed,[177] were unhappy with the intrusion of philosophical and non-scriptural words like

177. Many original signatories later joined synods that radically qualified the Nicene creed.

Homoousios—consubstantial, into the heartland of credal statements of the faith, and wished instead to retain the older tradition of using only scriptural passages, or traditional liturgical confessions, as authoritative definitions of Christian belief. The scriptural and liturgical language (such as—the "Word is the Image of the Unseen God,"[178] or the poetic image of the light issuing from light)[179] was openended, suggestive, and applied fertile linguistic imagery in a way that was evidently polyvalent. Many of those bishops who supported the idea of the "true" divinity of the Son preferred this more open and less syllogistic method of articulating the faith and, accordingly, among them a wide palette of Christological coloration could be expected.

Others were pressing the need for a more rigorously logical statement of Christian belief, as the Church entered into an international arena and had more and more to defend its doctrine and religious system before an articulate and refined world of religious philosophers. Origen had, in the third century, set the terms of the agenda here, and it was largely his Christological system, in all its manifold aspects, that the variety of theological schools in the eastern fourth-century Church were taking as their starting point. The Alexandrian tradition, represented even at the time of Nicaea by Athanasios, laid stress on that part of Origen's system which argued for the eternal status of the divine Logos who issued from the Father before time, and thus was with God from everlasting to everlasting. The various "non-Nicene" schools laid stress on that part of Origen's system that argued for the absolute unicity of God the Father, whose being transcended all others, the Word of God included. From this perspective, although the Word was divine, it was not divine in the absolute and unconditioned sense in which the supreme originative Godhead, the Father, could be spoken of as divine. Origenians of this tradition could confess the Word as "god from God" while at the same time denying that the sense of divinity being used was "consubstantial," that is absolutely the same meaning of "God" in each case. One could belong to this broad church either as a member of the Homoiousian party (the Son was "substantively" like the godhead but not the same as God, though related to God essentially), or as an adherent of the Homoian faction (the Son was like God—a very wide range of possible meanings admissible in this regard—but not comparable to God in any essentialist term. The Homoiousian thinkers, although generally uncomfortable with the essentialist positions the Nicene theologians adopted[180] were obviously closer in theological tenor to the Nicenes than to most other factions. There was a widely sensed understanding

178. Col 1:15.
179. A longstanding Christian image to be used with great effect by Gregory Nazianzen in his Trinitarian doctrine; cf. McGuckin (1994).
180. And some groups here were even more uncomfortable with the implications that the Nicene homoousion theology brought in its train—such as the elaboration of a theology of a consubstantial Triune God (the Neo-Nicene movement).

that to insist on the removal of the Son of God's "essential" term of relation to the Godhead was to move radically towards a merely honorific sense of deity for the Christ. There was another, smaller, section of thinkers, though one that was highly dynamic in terms of the intellectual and political agitation it brought to bear in the Church politics of the period, which decided that the way Christian vocabulary had evolved in the Nicene aftermath was fundamentally misguided. This party suspected any attempt to "divinize" the Christ except in an honorific sense, and certainly regarded essentialist theology in regard to divine relations as a dead end. The whole vocabulary of the Nicene Homoousion and the compromise term of Homoiousion were wholly misguided, for them. To this extent their affections lay clearly within the Arian camp, but their method of pressing the terms of theology that were in use among the various parties was so de-constructive in its tendency that they were regarded with disfavor by all sides among the antagonists, and they chose their party's catchword (*Anhomoios*) deliberately to bear-bait all the three opposite factions, Homoousian, Homoiousian and Homoian. For them the Son of God was simply and absolutely different in essence to the supreme Godhead. This difference was the only way one could properly theologize about the transcendence of God—in fact that was entirely what the whole point of affirming divine transcendence was all about—that nothing else was remotely like it in its simple unicity. This radical and highly skilled group of debaters, trained in Aristotelian logic and using syllogistic method as their preferred mode of discourse, were the so-called Anhomoians,[181] chief among them Aetios[182] and Eunomios. They have come to be called the Neo-Arian movement,[183] and they occupied the opposite pole to the Neo-Nicene party led by Athanasios (after the Synod of Alexandria in 362) and more so by the Cappadocian circle around Gregory and Basil. In between were a large number of convinced Homoians and Homoiousians, and an even larger group of the bewildered, or (as Gregory often accused the episcopate)[184] those who were merely political timer-servers, watching to see which faction gained imperial favor.

Throughout the fourth century this large morass of Christological arguments, later to be known collectively, from the viewpoint of their Nicene opponents, as "Arianism," was a complex problematic tearing at Christian unity in the Eastern provinces. It had, by the middle of the fourth century, produced a bewildering array of factions, and a large body of bishops who were only aligned to any given movement in so far as they were pressed by local or imperial pressure. As this changed, so did they, and therefore, among the factions and faction leaders we ought to imagine a large number of fluctuating bishops and Church congregations who held to a

---

181. The word, a negation of Homoian, means "Unlike party."
182. Who had a reputation as a saintly thaumaturg (though needless to say not for the Cappadocian Nicenes), whose devoted disciple Eunomios was.
183. Cf. Kopecek (1979).
184. Cf. Carm. 2.1.12, *De se ipso et de episcopis,* PG 37.1166-1227, esp. lines 330-340.

traditional faith but were often unsure how their faith corresponded with the theological parties that were presently claiming to speak for them.

The religious policy of the court of Constantius had been to continue that of his father, supporting the broad church of those who favored a sense of the divine status of the Christ of God, but were not willing to accept the Nicene doctrine of the Homoousion, which increasingly, after the time of Nicaea in 325, had been interpreted (especially by the Athanasian party and the West which supported him) to connote the equality in essence and power of the Father and the Word, to such an extent that Homoousion was taken to mean "identity" of essence or being.[185]

Gregory had much time in Athens to refine his theological mind, and declared himself publicly for the Nicene cause, allied to the monastic party near to Nazianzus.[186] But it was soon clear to him from the fracas the monks had already caused at Nazianzus, that he could not allow the monastics to determine the theology of the Church. This was to be done in the episcopal preaching, and in the case of Gregory, after his presbyteral ordination, that meant by his preaching. Even in his eirenical welcome home to the dissident monastics, and his heartfelt assurances to them that he was truly "one of them,"[187] he cannot help dropping hints as to how much he disapproves of their behavior,[188] and

185. Athanasios preferred "identity of essence" (*tautotes tes ousias*) to the Nicene formula but thought the Nicene creed had better chance of success in rallying a larger international agreement in the body politic of the Church.

186. If these were, as is likely, a party related to Eustathios of Sebaste, then they held a form of Nicene theology which was limited compared to the later career of Athanasios of Alexandria, who is Gregory's intellectual hero, and to whom he dedicates a large encomium in Constantinople in later years, holding him up to the capital as his model of orthodoxy. Gregory was steering a new course for all concerned in his locality. It will later be referred to as Neo-Nicene theology which stresses the absolute nature of the Son's deity, and insists on the co-equal Trinity of divine persons.

187. He has to explain how, of course, he no longer owns the riches he "had of old," and now possesses only the "ministry of the word." After his description of the monks as unkempt and impoverished (Orat. 6.2, PG 35.721-724) it is an interesting argument that he makes. His monasticism, of course, was very different to theirs. He is "dispossessed" only in the sense that his property, since he is a consecrated Christian priest, is now (arguably) that of the church. In his last will and testament he can still disburse a large fortune, but there says that he does so to direct most of it to the church. He does have an argument—but it is stretching it to think he convinced the local monks that he was really just like them. It is worth remembering that not all forms of monasticism in church history (especially not in the Byzantine era) were wholly dedicated to the notion of personal "non-possession" as fundamental to the monastic state. After his retirement in 381 he addresses a prayer to Christ where, significantly, he identifies himself as the "needy rich man" in the parable of Dives and Lazarus (Lk 16:22-24). Cf. Carm. *De Rebus Suis*, PG 37.969f, esp. v. 580.

188. He celebrates the angelic state of the monastic life in glowing terms as the opening section of his oration, and then turns, quite pointedly, to discuss examples from the created world (since God alone has no dissension in his nature) of how dissension arises. He considers the peace-seeking angels (Orat. 6.12, PG 35.737), but goes on to tell how it was the arrogance of angels which itself began dissension and the woes of creation (Orat. 6.13, PG 35.737-740). In this way he cleverly pricks the pretensions of those living the "angelic life" even as he praises them for it. Moderation (not monastic zeal) is his real message in this text.

suggesting in the nicest possible terms that they had better not fall out of line again, since it was only his father's eirenical moderation that led him to exercise the exemplary patience of a good shepherd so that none of his (errant) flock would be lost.[189] Not only does he make his father out to be Christlike[190] he also reminds them subliminally how Christ taught that "thieves" would set out to make the sheep wander away from the true shepherd[191] and also points up, while expanding on his father's Christlike "moderation," the fact that the bishop held magisterial power in the whole region, a power that included the right of judicial punishment. It was to be Gregory's consistent belief that political enforcement of religious conformity was counter-productive. When he had the opportunities to exercise physical persuasion, as here, and as later in the time when Theodosius entered his capital, he never resorted to it. It was one of his noblest features, yet it made him, at the same time, appear as weak and eccentric in the company of other leading fourth-century bishops and ultimately led to his political downfall and dismissal from his office as imperial bishop.

These early years of Christian priestly life in Cappadocia, during which time Gregory exercised himself in ascetical withdrawal in the hillside estate of Arianzum, and preached regularly in the church at Nazianzus, must have been a period of ongoing study of theology, as well as study of the varieties of ecclesiastical factions that comprised the wider "communion" of the other churches around him. The search for consensus in doctrine and liturgical praxis among such a local network of churches had always been the preferred Christian method of elaborating the Church's collective (oecumenical) mind, and although Gregory formulates his theology apologetically in several instances, he is by natural habit a seeker and builder of consensus, a constant devotee of the "middle way." This character is certainly marked in his Christology. His Trinitarian doctrine is more boldly and originally elaborated and comes mainly from his more mature years[192] when he is ready to press the logical conclusions of his lifelong thought and sees others holding back.

In the death of Julian and the nascent policy of Jovian, Gregory felt supremely confident. The settlement of the schism at his own church encouraged him to positive

---

189. Orat. 6.21, PG 35.749.
190. The Good Shepherd of Jn 10:11 (he cites Jn 17:12 to the same end).
191. Jn 10:1-10.
192. Orat. 6 which he addressed to the monks to celebrate their return to communion notably, and strangely, does not have Christology to the fore. In his text he praises the monastic condition (Orat. 6.2, PG 35.723-724) and generally asserts doctrinal agreement on all sides (even though the dispute had probably been over Christological differences), concluding with a Trinitarian encomium (Orat. 6.22, PG 35.749-752). The place of this Trinitarian confession within the *Oration*, however, makes me suspect that it has been added later, after his stay in Constantinople, when he prepared all his early Orations for publication in retirement. If one were to remove it from the end of the text a perfectly sensible end to Orat. 6 would be provided by the reference to his father as a good shepherd who, through his moderation, has not lost any of his flock (Orat. 6.21, PG 35.749). So, theological ideas in the original version of Orat. 6 are glossed over, perhaps deliberately, in the cause of achieving a wide consensus.

thoughts. Even news of Jovian's death probably did not prove too disturbing. The army had moved quickly to ensure another Christian soldier filled the vacuum of power. As yet he could not see what difficulties the new emperor would bring for them, since Valentinian had been acclaimed by the troops and, like Jovian, was known as a supporter of the Nicene cause. Valentinian left to make his capital in the West, which needed a strong defense against the increasing problem of the migration of Germanic tribes pressing against the border of the Danube River. He was soon to nominate a ruler of the Orient against the advice of his council. It was his brother Valens whom he raised to the rank of Augustus of the East. In his theological policy, Valens would prove to be a supporter of the Homoian cause, and from 365 onwards this began to become abundantly clear to Gregory and Basil. Valens was a determined foe of the Nicene Homoousians, but was handicapped in his capacity to move against them violently or extensively in public by the manner in which his brother, and senior Augustus, was himself a Nicene. Exiles or select dispossessions of sees were means which lay readily at his disposal, and his preference for the Homoian religious policy became clear when he renewed the sentence of exile, for a fifth time, against Athanasios of Alexandria in 365.

In that same year, news was reported in Caesarea that the emperor was to make a progress eastwards, aimed at enforcing his ecclesiastical policy, bringing with him an entourage of court bishops who could suitably pose as a synod to unseat those who resisted his wishes. Caesarea was a strategically important metropolitan center lying in the middle of his path. Eusebios, faced with the prospect of having to make an account of his non-existent theology before the emperor and the court's traveling synod, was in a panic. Basil and his monastic circle, supposedly his secretariat and church rhetoricians, were in self-imposed exile in Pontus, and the still festering ill will between the factions made Eusebios determined to leave him there.[193] Desperate for some skilled theological assistance the metropolitan wrote to "the most learned Gregory"[194] in Nazianzus asking him to come, to advise and speak for the Caesarean synod during the emperor's visit.

Gregory summed up the bishop's character with some real insight. He began his letter of reply[195] appealing to bluff common sense and a desire to cut through any sophistic pretence. Such was his way of disarming a man who knew his need to rely on educated sophists yet resented them immensely. In his opening words Gregory paints himself as a plain speaker, conscious of the honor which Eusebios has done to invite him as an expert in Church matters, and thereby able to exercise that boldness of speech (*parrhesia*) which the professional adviser must apply for the benefit of his

193. Gregory provides a synopsis of the affair in Orat. 43.28, PG 36.533-536.
194. "Logiotaton Gregorion." Ep. 17.1, PG 37.51; Gallay (1964), p. 25. Eusebios' letter is not extant but Gregory reminds him of his very words with dry irony when Eusebios rejected the advice he had so urgently asked of him.
195. Ep. 16, PG 37.49-52; Gallay (1964), pp. 23-24.

noble client.[196] He then seizes his opportunity. He would love to assist but he is obliged to speak to the truth:

> I am unable to bear the affront you have offered, and continue to offer, to my most honorable brother Basil, whom I have elected from the beginning as my soul mate in terms of life, of thought, and his most exalted philosophy, and do so to the present. And nothing has unsettled my judgment as to his character.[197]

He goes on to tell Eusebios that to give him the honor of speaking as the main theological expert in Caesarea while simultaneously banning Basil was like patting someone on the head while cuffing their neck.[198] Even so, his professional advice and help has been asked, he will give it:

> This is what you should do...if you treat this man with the attention you once had for him, you will receive his attentions in return. And then, we too will follow in train, as surely as a shadow follows after a body; for I am of little account but more than ready for anything that leads to peace.[199]

His eirenical intercession for Basil called down a storm upon his head. Eusebios wrote him a letter in reply making it clear that he thought his "boldness" quite impertinent. This was where Gregory's aristocratic upbringing came into its own. Though he was a pacific and sensitive person by character, he was far from being cowed by bluster or cant. He wrote another letter, a model of restraint, though pressing his earlier point frankly, that is if Eusebios applied for his advice then he ought to take it, and not as from an inferior either (albeit as a priest writing to a bishop) but as one gentleman to another. The sweetened pill comes at the end:

> I did not write to you with any intent to insult you. I wrote in the capacity of a spiritual and philosophical person, and in the manner I should have done, even if it causes trouble to the "most learned Gregory." Though you bear a high dignity, you ought to allow us some boldness and legitimate freedom. And so, be more kindly disposed to us. On the other hand if you regard my letter as coming from a lackey who has no place looking you in the face, then we shall bear the blows without tears—or would this too be held against us? But such an attitude is surely far removed from anything that would characterize Your Reverence, for it is the mark of a high-minded man to accept the liberties of friends rather than the sycophancies of the malignant.[200]

196. He was playing on Eusebios' sensibilities at the same time, for "boldness of speech" was an expected characteristic of the town bishop speaking before the powerful and mighty of the land, and it was just this prospect of having to make an account of himself before the emperor which had so put Eusebios into a panic. For episcopal *"parrhesia"* see Carm. 2.1.12, *De seipso et de episcopis*, vv. 762-775; cf. Meehan (1987), pp. 72-73.

197. In such words he made it clear that Eusebios was largely at fault in the alienation that had occurred in Caesarea. His judgment would, perhaps, not be so sure about Basil's innocence when a similar alienation later affected him more personally.

198. Ep. 16.6, PG 37.49; Gallay (1964), p. 24.

199. Ep. 16.7, PG 37.49; Gallay (1964), p. 24.

200. Ep. 17, PG 37.52; Gallay (1964), p. 25. Gregory came to know him from working alongside him in Caesarea and retrospectively called him (even before the hostile audience of Basil's

The Caesarean bishop was in a tight place, and could hardly bluster any more without making himself out to be an idiot, but his dignity could be saved by one more strategy, and he seems to have applied it. Unamused, he summoned Gregory once again, apparently appealing to his canonical right to summon a priest to a synod. Gregory assented to the call, assuring him that he certainly did not, as the bishop suspected (and had accused him in his latest letter), hold any ill will against him.[201] He was more than ready to come. He made an allusion to the "wild beasts" ranged against the Church, thus referring to the anticipated "Games" he suspected they would have to engage in the forthcoming contest with the emperor's entourage. He is, in fact, very buoyant about the whole thing, even saying that he will bring with him a contingent of local young men to cheer on with suitable "unction" his sophistic athletics. It is as clear a reference, without spelling it out, that he is ready to bring a large enough claque of able-bodied retainers to persuade the imperial entourage that a polite attitude to their Cappadocian hosts would be the best policy all round. Eusebios had received his first piece of strategic political advice from the gentle and retiring Gregory. It obviously was to pay off, given that if every Cappadocian hierarch loyal to Eusebios did as advised, the local reception for the emperor would be suitably "awe-inspiring," and assure Eusebios of retaining his episcopal seat—as it did, in fact.

Once he was settled in his temporary position as chief ecclesiastical adviser to Eusebios in the Cappadocian capital, he continued, loyally, to work for Basil's reha-bilitation. It eventually paid off. Both Eusebios and Basil were each waiting for apol-ogies from the other. Gregory seems to have told them that the necessary letters were en route from each one, and that each one ought now to pre-empt the other's "first move" by writing kindly and sending it off while the other's letter was still in transit. His letter to this effect to Basil[202] ends by suggesting that he should come in person to Annesoi to bring him back to Caesarea, because the theological discussions already being prepared needed the urgent assistance of someone skilled in negotia-tions such as the Old Testament hero Beseleel.[203] His strategies of mollification pro-duced the desired result and Belseleel returned[204] in the company of his devoted Ooliab[205] to lead the preparations for the impending synodical examination of the Caesarean Church to be presided over by Valens' agents in Caesarea in 365.[206]

monastic disciples) "A man of no ignoble quality, and quite remarkable in his piety." Orat. 43.28, PG 36.533.

201. Always the master of subtlety he selected the word "smallness of soul" in his official reply to Eusebios. Ep. 18, PG 37.52; Gallay (1964), pp. 25-26.

202. Ep. 19, PG 37.53; Gallay (1964), pp. 26-27.

203. A reference to Ex 31:2-3 and 35:30-31.

204. Cf. Orat. 43.31, PG 36.540.

205. The companion and adviser to Belseleel in the OT story.

206. Following Gallay (1943), p. 85, and Maran in PG 29, pp. xli-xlii, though Tillemont placed Valens' visit in 366. It was a pressuring visit to set in place his own ecclesiastical policy—

Honor had been saved on all sides, as Basil could represent Gregory's personal journey to Pontus as an official delegation from the bishop of Caesarea asking him to
return, and Eusebios could represent Gregory's trip as a visit to a friend to make him
see the error of his ways. When Gregory and Basil returned to Caesarea, they were
ready for the oratorical contest.

The outcome, as Gregory describes it in Basil's funeral encomium, is rhetorically
built up as a great victory for the cause of orthodoxy. The entourage of Valens, with
a dedicated group of Arian theologian-rhetors in tow, probably had little difficulty
in making their progress alongside the emperor and deposing local bishops who
resisted them, on the grounds of theological incompetency.[207] Valens had already
ordered the re-imposition of the sentences of exile on those Nicene bishops Julian
had allowed to return to their sees, especially Athanasios who had to go into exile
again in the winter of 365-366, before Valens realized he could not sustain the sentence. So, it was already clear in the first year of his reign that he would be no friend
to the Nicenes. According to Gregory, when the delegation came to Caesarea they
met their match for the first time, for Basil:

> proved himself to be a solid wall and bulwark, an axe shattering the rock, a fire among
> thorn bushes, as the divine scripture says,[208] effortlessly burning up those paltry sticks
> who so disgraced the concept of the Godhead...[209]

> And for the first time[210] they had to retreat without accomplishing their intended
> aims; wretches as they were, experiencing wretched shame and defeat.[211]

The "investigations" which Valens instituted took the form of public disputations wherein the winners of the rhetorical contests in the churches were rewarded
with ecclesial offices[212] or cash donations. It was this very public success which probably confirmed both for Gregory and Basil, that their future lay undoubtedly in the
public administration of Church life. Basil had been inclining this way from years
before; the apparently seamless combination of rhetorical skills in defense of theological verities probably led Gregory to think more positively of a public church

though one that basically continued that of Constantius after the Julianic interruption, and
restored the pro-Christian, pro-Arian status quo.
207. Gregory suggests this was a common enough scenario in Orat. 43.31, PG 36.537.
208. Cf. Jer 1:18; Jer 23:29; Ps 117:12.
209. Orat. 43.32, PG 36.540.
210. He was tactfully reminding Basil's family that the last time Basil met with Arians in theological debate he was beaten (360) and Eunomios was rewarded with an episcopal see from which
to propagandize radical Arianism. This time (with himself as leading orator in the disputes—the learned Barnabas at Paul's side (Orat. 43.32, PG 36.540) they were successful. It is
a mirror-reflection of the story he has just told them about their time as students in Athens
when Basil was fighting with the Armenians but only conquered when Gregory rhetorically
came to his assistance.
211. Orat. 43.32, PG 36.540.
212. By this means Valens could populate sees with adherents of the imperial policy.

career, and might have been a major influence when he was later pressured to accept episcopal office, a step that the little voice in the back of his mind continued to whisper to him was a fatal move.

The Arian rhetors were disappointed on this occasion and Valens had no cause to depose the successful Eusebios whose rhetoricians, Basil and Gregory, had performed so well, and whose own local political and financial weight was perfectly satisfactory to the emperor. This was a period of close and fraternal collaboration between Basil and Gregory. He probably stayed in Caesarea for a little while longer. He had responded to the bishop's invitation to serve among the clergy there and had distinguished himself, but he allows Basil the lead in the church's affairs. Years later when he recalls how energetic Basil had been in those days, he describes him as the veritable bishop of Caesarea in all but name.[213] The time he spent working with Basil, acting as an Aaron to his friend Moses,[214] and facilitating the latter's genius for activity with his own genius in oratorical display perhaps led him to think that his own church career might in future develop along such a path of equal and fraternal collaboration. One of the causes for the great bitterness that overshadowed their friendship in later years was Basil's refusal to allow Gregory to work beside him in Caesarea after he became the archbishop there in 370. For Basil at least, two swans was one too many in the Caesarean home pond.

In those years, under the presidency of Eusebios, who highly regarded Gregory, the collaborations in church affairs were heady and exciting. Things seemed to be full of potential for the Nicene cause, even though Valens' policy was not in their favor. The great Nicene figurehead, Athanasios, had been allowed to return to his see in Alexandria in 366, and would retain it now until his death. In the following year, 367, the charismatic and highly skilled leader of the radical Arian party, Aetios, would also die in Constantinople, leaving his disciple Eunomios to serve as the whetstone to all the Neo-Nicene movement. After Aetios' death the movement was deprived of a figure who, in popular estimation fuelled by a hagiographical campaign, was a wonder-working healer and holy man. Eunomios, who did not have the same common touch, though he inherited his teacher's skill in advanced dialectic, remained in the capital, and was a thorn in the side there even of the Homoian Arians who, accordingly, began to sideline him and his work.

Gregory was to specialize in attacking the whole Arian cause by describing its logical outcomes as everything Eunomios represented. By this means he castigated Arianism without ever attacking, frontally, the leading political representatives of the Arian cause who more often oscillated between forms of Homoianism and Homoiousianism, both parties which found the Anomianism of Aetios and

---

213. Orat. 43.33, PG 36.540-541.
214. This use in Orat. 43 of the images of himself as Aaron or Barnabas, to Basil's Moses or Paul, is a subtle way of insinuating his own superior learnedness while still allowing Basil's political leadership.

Eunomios to be offensive. To lump in the Homoians as if they were the same thing as the Anomoians,[215] was a clever rhetorical strategy that has since often been taken as a literal map of the theological world of the fourth century. It was not, though the Gregorian argument selling that position was obviously very effective.

In 366 the newly re-energized clerical leadership at Caesarea sketched out a philanthropic program that would start to see the light of day in 368. It was designed to provide medical care and housing for the large number of lepers who milled on the outskirts of the local capital, living desperately, and frequently lawlessly, on handouts and anything else they could turn their energies to. Gregory began to plan a great Oration which, like many a travelling rhetor before him, could be taken on the rounds for the purposes of raising money. The Oration as it now stands is probably a refined and polished form of that initially preached, but there is no reason to think that it is substantially other than the discourse Gregory delivered as his part in the philanthropic enterprise. It has often been thought that the oration was only delivered once, and so Gregory's part in the overall strategy of the program has been diminished by a large degree. Gregory himself is largely responsible for shrinking his own role in this enterprise, because he describes it with characteristic generosity and modesty in the funeral panegyric for his friend, as a work of philanthropy for which Basil's memory should live in history. The fact is, however, it was in origin an enterprise of the administration of Eusebios, to which Basil's money (and that of Eusebios) contributed, as also did the imperial treasury, as authorized by Valens who was to endow the project generously. In this wider context the proper contribution of Gregory to the "Basiliad,"[216] ought to be re-estimated. The project was hindered in its early stages by a great famine that hit Cappadocia in 368, and was to be extensively developed later in the time of Basil as archbishop of the city, when he would not allow Gregory any further collaboration with his administration. So it was that it became predominantly associated with Basil's name only.

Oration 14, "On Love for the Poor" is probably (in substance) the discourse which was designed in 366 and 367[217] as the church's official money-raiser for the Caesarean Leprosarium whose building started in 368[218] and, if so, was surely delivered in several

215. Etymological opposites.
216. So the complex outside Caesarea was to be called. Cf. D. *Constantelos, Byzantine Philanthropy and Social Welfare* (New Jersey, 1968), pp. 68-69, 154-158, 260-261.
217. It was the year the leader of the Neo-Arian party, Aetios, died at Constantinople. His disciple Eunomios buried him with great honors and circulated a hagiography about him depicting him as a great theologian as well as a thaumaturgical healer. Eunomios continued to reside at Constantinople and was to be one of the chief intellectual targets for Gregory's preaching campaign in the city later in 380.
218. It is wholly unnecessary (as well as extremely unlikely) to think of it as delivered for the occasion of the dedication of the Basiliad in 372—as was first mooted by the ninth century scholiast Basilius Exiguus, whose ideas were adopted by the Benedictine editors of Gregory and so made their way into *Patrologia Graeca*. Gregory explicitly says in this Oration that the

places perhaps, one might surmise, even in the capital itself, to solicit imperial sup-port. Gregory's friend, Sophronios,[219] after having exercised a successful legal career in Cappadocia had in this same period of 366 or 367[220] risen to high office in the city, probably occupying the rank of Master of Offices in Constantinople within the secretariat of the Urban Prefect, the higher office to which he would himself succeed in 369. Gregory's social vision, therefore, is not free-floating, but grounded in the actualities of having powerful friends and relations[221] at the highest level of the state who could advance his schemes. When he writes to Sophronios,[222] to ask him to take his niece's husband into political service alongside him he offers to make a suitable return. This favor is to be the "only thing he can offer," his orations, but in the course of making this amiable remark he makes it clear that if Sophronios is associated with those orations he will achieve a lasting fame. This might be no more than a sophistic nicety: Sophronios will live in the (epistolary) text of Gregory, cele-brated there for his magnanimity. But it may well be much more significant than this; for at the time Gregory writes to Sophronios in the capital he is circulating his *Oration On Love For The Poor*. It is the first of his large-scale politically focused works, and it is perhaps this very text which he indicates he will send to Sophronios as a gift in return for his patronage of Nicobulos. If this is so, then the promise that if Sophronios associates himself with Gregory's orations he will achieve lasting fame, is perhaps an invitation for the Imperial Master of Offices to identify his social policy with Christian philanthropy in the manner Gregory is sketching out. It casts a direct light on the manner in which Gregory was a skilled and energetic political operator, something which readers of his letters have always sensed, even though the general "icon" of him (taken largely from his poetic persona as an old and sick man) has tended to depict him (very misleadingly) as fussy, and unworldly, and slightly ineffective.[223]

lepers have to roam the streets without shelter. Sinko (1917) I, pp. 121-122 envisages its delivery in Caesarea, again without evidence. Gallay (1943), p. 87 surmises whether it was a hos-pice-project of Gregory's designed for Nazianzus.

219. The recipient of Gregory's *Letters* 21, 22, 29 and 37; and of Basil's *Letters* 32, 76 and 96.

220. Ammianus Marcellinus indicates that he was Notarios in 365 (Amm. Mar. 26.7.2; cf. Gallay [1964], p. 29, fn. 1), and as Gregory's later letters celebrate his further advance, this missive probably marks his recent promotion to the staff of the Urban Prefect.

221. Some of Gregory's large extended family, were already resident in the capital and occupied sena-torial rank, cf. Bernardi (*Nouvelles perspectives*, 1984). Ep. 21 shows Gregory himself advancing the political placement of those close to him, and so, long before he arrived in the capital as bishop-spokesman for the Nicene cause he probably had a network of political support.

222. His Ep. 21, petitions for his adopted son Nicobulos (the husband of his niece Alypiana, and father of his grand-nephew Nicobulos who was to be his heir and literary executor) to be admitted to Sophronios' side in the bureau of the Master of Offices.

223. Newman's poem about him is a typical example: "Peace-loving man of humble heart and true/what dost thou here? /...Thou could'st a city raise, but could'st not rule." J.H. Newman, *Verses on Various Occasions* (London, 1896) (St Gregory Nazianzen), pp. 110-111.

In a manner which is markedly different to his *Funeral Oration* for Basil, Oration 14 never once refers to the church's concern for the support of the poor in the context of any work of Basil's. Nor does it mention Caesarea. This does not necessarily imply either that the oration was not delivered in Caesarea, where most commentators have localized it, nor does it argue against a view that it originated there, but it does suggest that its scope was considerably larger than Caesarea. It was, I think, always conceived as a general fund raiser, that also served as an important discourse setting out the terms for the Christian imperium's policy of *philanthropia*. As such it is an keynote piece of political oratory, as well as a decisive theological essay in which Gregory sets out his mind on the social altruism that characterizes the inner spirit of the religion of Christ. It was something that he was, perhaps, willing to lend to Basil's particular cause of the Caesarean project, but something from the outset which he designed on a larger scale for his own work as Christian philanthropist and Bishop-*Philoptochos*.[224]

After Basil had been elected to the see of Caesarea in 371, Eustathios of Sebaste would send him a contingent of ascetics from his own diocese to assist in the administration of the charitable institutions, and these were working by Basil's side with a distinctly different set of theological ideas to those we can presume for Gregory.[225] Their presence ensured that the Basiliad would develop along distinct lines such as Eustathios had already achieved in Sebaste. It is not admissible, however, to read the influence of Eustathios so closely into Gregory's mind and intentions, and this is why *Oration* 14 ought, perhaps, to be read more discretely apart from the context of the Basil's program at Caesarea than it traditionally has been.

The Gregorian oration begins with a clear appeal for generosity. The hearers are cleverly disarmed from that instinctive closure-response to a financial appeal, however meritorious, in the first sentence when he addresses them with the easy good humor that emanates from a wealthy man asking the townspeople for funds:

> My brothers and fellow indigents (we are each one of us, after all, poor folk in so far as we stand in need of God's grace, even if some of us seem to have more than others)... do not receive this oration on love for the poor in any pinched or tightfisted way, but with great magnanimity, so that you may lay up treasure in heaven.[226]

Most ancient rhetorical displays were professional entertainment events of a high order and, if delivered in front of an imperial or aristocratic patron as well as

---

224. That is—"friend of the poor." Peter Brown's study, *Power and Persuasion in Late Antiquity* (1992), demonstrates how fourth-century bishops rose to social prominence precisely as "lovers of the poor." Their authority rested on the creation of a new class of popular political support. Gregory is combining models of authority quite creatively (Classical Rhetor, Christian Ascetic, and Hellenistic Philanthropist), when he offers himself as both a political orator speaking on behalf of his region (as he does so on occasion for his city—for example Orat. 19) and as a bishop speaking on behalf of his Church.

225. They were, from what one might suppose from their leader, homoiousianist and anti-Trinitarian.

226. Orat. 14.1, PG 35.857-860.

the civic audience, would be treated by the orator as worthy of a high payment, much like the appearance of an internationally known musician today would naturally command a high fee. Gregory is making it clear from the start that this oration is intended to be a money raiser. He gave it on the occasion of the gatherings of large crowds, when church festivals were celebrated, or special theatrical or athletic performances had been arranged. Then the towns and cities were crowded. The occasion was perfect, for it was on just such occasions that the most wretched of the poor also thronged the town gates[227] begging for alms, and asserting their right to appear in public because of the Christian religious festival which ought to exclude none of the suffering. This re-presentation of themselves in public, after having been forced normally to eke out an existence exiled to the wildernesses, set the "problem" of the poor in a new light which Gregory wished his audience to consider.

He plays his audience like a musician. Having begun by making them smile, he turns their thoughts to "beautiful things," searching out what is the good (*to kalon*), and reviewing a whole series of lifestyles that would be pleasing to God. From this series of beautiful things (*ta kala*) he turns their thoughts to the round of problems that beset them in daily life. He lists the usual "horrors" of civilized existence: the burdens that the tax agents inflicted on honest folk, the harshness of magistrates, the ferocity of brigands, and the insatiable greed of thieves. He then goes on to extend his list to make the audience consider the wider range of those in society who are deserving of pity: widows and orphans, exiles, slaves suffering under harsh overlords, those who have been ruined by shipwreck.[228] But having enumerated all these causes for compassion, he turns to focus on what is, for him, the supreme example of the abject wretchedness of a class of people who were forced into silence and invisibility—the lepers. So it is that within a few minutes from the commencement of his oration he has his audience laughing, elevated with noble thoughts, and (literally) weeping where they stood, for the pity of it all.

The opening section of his speech appears at first sight as oddly positioned, for in it he discourses on the monastic state of seclusion and solitude, and discusses it among a series of "beautiful" lifestyles. It is, however, not too far from his intended master-theme if we consider that he is beginning his oration on poverty and beneficence with two important and necessary foundational arguments.

The first is an answer to Julian's witty attack against the Christian claim that their religion excelled over his return to the ancient gods, because Christianity had a love for the poor and a philanthropic purpose based upon the image of the poor man of Nazareth who inculcated a poor and simple lifestyle as a blessed good. Julian had been well aware of this powerful attraction of Christian philanthropy, and had tried to instruct the priesthood of his newly endowed temples to have some care for the poor as a visible part of their religious program. As well as this, however, he had

227. Orat. 14.13, PG 35.873.
228. Orat. 14.6, PG 35.864-865.

tried to dent the gong of Christian philanthropic philosophy at Edessa, before his military collapse in Persia, by making a mockery of the Christian communities there which were in legal conflict. A Valentinian Gnostic congregation was in dispute over property and ownership rights with an Arian congregation, and Julian dispossessed the Valentinians to the benefit of the imperial treasury, with the remark that he had thus hastened the way for them to their chief theological goal, since he had made them "blessed" by impoverishing them.[229] It was a funny and memorable dictum, with a lot of serious philosophical point behind it, and thus one which set into sharp relief the need for the ascendant Christians to articulate just how could a religion which elevated poverty as a blessed state rationally seek to control massive fiscal resources, through state subsidies and church ownership, in order to alleviate poverty—which it supposedly canonized as a blessed and godly thing.[230]

The second reason, I think, that Gregory opens by discussing the way in which Christianity prioritizes the quest for poor simplicity is because he is not only addressing external critics but (at this instance) internal doubters—the monks. The clergy at Caesarea (and Basil presses this point later in his development of the Basiliad's medical program) probably intended the complex to be staffed by Christian "religious," and therefore Gregory has to spend some time explaining why the ascetics, dedicated in principle to abstraction from the whirl of social activity, ought now to turn their attention towards the resolution of the social problematic. After so many centuries of having witnessed monastics directing the cutting edge of the church's involvement in works of mercy it may seem to us almost a matter of course that religious should be so involved. In Gregory's time, however, many would have regarded any social effort as absolutely contrary to the fundamental purpose of the monastic vocation, and so he gives attention to redefining the monastic state in terms of his favorite conception of the "middle way"[231] between reflective withdrawal and social engagement. In this he becomes the veritable founding father of what might be called Byzantine "city-monachism," especially after the fifth century when the capital became the real hub of monastic developments and both male and female ascetics were used to staff the philanthropic institutions there.[232] In this, his impact on the

229. "Blessed are the poor," Lk 6:20.
230. As opposed to the common Hellenistic understanding of indigency as a curse from the gods, for example, which would have been a direct and easy theological rationalization of why some were impoverished or sick, and others were wealthy and well. Gregory notes in the oration how closely the two go together, and thus how control of a fiscal program largely determines the health of a community.
231. "In short, contemplation is a beautiful thing; action is a beautiful thing. The first lifts us from our present life, allows us to pass into the holy of holies, and initiates our mind into what is truly akin to it. The second receives Christ himself and ministers to Him, proving the quality of its love by its works." Orat. 14.4, PG 35.864.
232. Cf. D. Constantelos, *Byzantine Philanthropy and Social Welfare* (New Jersey, 1968); G. Dagron, *Naissance d'une capitale: Constantinople et ses institutions de 330 à 451* (Paris, 1974).

shaping of monasticism must be seen as equaling that of Basil. The latter had an influence on subsequent ages chiefly through his ascetical writings (some of them apocry-
phally attributed), whereas Gregory impacted the larger Christian world through his
institutional polity which became standard reading since his collected works were studiously scrutinized in the Byzantine schools for centuries after him.[233]

To work for the benefit of the poor and suffering, he tells his listeners, is to serve
Christ in the *eikon*[234] of the suffering, and has the highest authority commending it
as the primary Christian obligation:

> If we place any reliance on Paul, or on Christ himself, then we shall take love as the
> first and greatest of the commandments, the summation of the law and prophets
> and, accordingly, take love for the poor as the highest pinnacle of charity... for
> "mercy and truth walk before our God"[235] and nothing more than this befits a God
> who "prefers mercy to justice," and in no other way whatsoever can God be served
> religiously except through mercy.[236]

This argument enters the world of classical political rhetoric through Gregory's
text. It is not, however, an idea that is any part of the Hellenistic canon of "givens"[237]
and it is Gregory's concern to translate this Gospel perspective into culturally and
politically recognizable discourse.

The Oration turns often around the theme of the divine image (*eikon*) which is
in the human person, and how compassionate generosity (*philanthropia*) mirrors in
the one who has compassion for the poor, the divine mercy shown to the world. In
Gregory's argument this not only merits the grace of God for the giver, but also con-
firms the benefactor in his or her ontological status as a mirror, or icon, of God the
supreme Lover of Humankind (*Philanthropos*). Charitable compassion, therefore,
becomes constitutive of true humanity, and true humanity is discovered in the mind

---

233. Cf. Noret (1983); The same appears to have been true even in the medieval west. Cf. P.O.
Kristeller and F.E. Cranz. (edd.), *Catalogus Translationum et Commentariorum: Medieval and
Renaissance Latin Translations and Commentaries*, vol. 2 (Washington, 1972), pp. 43-192 (sec-
tion by A.C. Way), as noted by D.M. Meehan, FOTC 75, p. 16, n. 21.

234. He often applies the biblical concept of the human person as the "image of God" (*eikona*)
within this oration, to argue that even a disfigured, sick, and impoverished human being is no
less the essential image of God (a divine sacrament) and a co-equal in humanity to the wealthy
and well. By this means he argues theologically that the poor are essentially "deserving" of
assistance, not relatively as an object of the exercise of accidental philanthropy, but because
intrinsically, even though paradoxically, they represent the presence of God within a fragile
world, and thus call out to the Christians around them to alleviate their pain in the measure
and capacity of their own assimilation to the God who gives mercy as the supreme Philanthropos. Cf. Orat. 14.5, PG 35.864.

235. Ps 88:15 LXX.

236. Orat. 14.5, PG 35.864.

237. "The idea that the poor, the sick and the old, ought to be helped because they were there, and
even God's creatures, is not 'classical.'" J.H.W. Liebeschuetz, *Continuity and Change in
Roman Religion* (Oxford, 1979), p. 187.

of this Christian philosopher, not by fatalistically accepting the limitations and fragility of human nature but in seeking to transcend them. The definition of what it is to be a human being is given its starting point in love, and projected to the ascentive point of mystical communion with God. What Gregory is offering, therefore, is more than a new social policy, it is a fundamentally renewed anthropology based upon the Christian doctrine of the incarnation, when image and archetype were reconciled in the hominisation of God as a poor man. He adds one more element to his philosophical premises: the nature of the human condition is a problematic mixture of clay and divine destiny. Humans have within themselves propensities to a heavenly life, and also to the misery of a return to dust and dissolution of being. When a human life shows proper "measure" the material fallibility of others who are in physical need must be met by those who are more materially well endowed. This "measuring balance" in the material domain reflects that inner spiritual and intellectual balance that should constitute the true human being, one who uses the mixed condition of their anthropological state[238] as a dynamic of progress.

In this doctrine of "balance" Gregory is applying standard categories of Hellenistic ethics, albeit in a new context. The balance of what the classical world understood as the supreme virtue of moderation, is here transformed into a specifically Christian meditation using a double axis of thought: the theological relation of a fragile creature to the divinity which offers existence, and the societal relation of the individual as image of God, towards other fellow creatures whose iconic status is endangered because of their pressing material needs. For Gregory, the balance is fundamentally one within the ontology of a person who (unlike material creatures such as animals, or spiritual beings such as angels) is uniquely poised between two disparate conditions (materiality and spirituality) and who is given a destiny to apply that ontological tension to the end of an ascent to God, a progressive spiritualization that seeks stability, even though the earthly environment often does not permit it to be realized.[239] So far this has been a fairly standard patristic application of the doctrine of the divine image in the human being, adopted and adapted from Origen of Alexandria his great mentor. Where Gregory extends the analogy, however, is in the social domain. Those around us in society who are most obviously demonstrative of "lack of due measure" are the poor and suffering. The imbalance of their material and physical condition, be it destitution or chronic illness, threatens their very capacity to transcend their human condition in the cause of rising to divine vision through the fabric of their earthly experiences. This, for Gregory, is a cause of imbalance in the whole rationale of the Church as elect

238. The human *krama* (synthesis) of the divine image mixed with clay. Orat. 14.7, PG 35.865.
239. The suffering character of this bipolar human ontology is a favorite theme of Gregory's. The human being aspires to ontological stability but can never find it in this earthly condition, cf. Carm. 1.2.33, vv. 85-88, PG 37.934; Carm. 82.1, vv. 3-5, PG 37.1025. For more on the theme, cf. Gilbert (1994), Ellverson (1981).

society. This is why such an imbalance in the very "Image of God" calls out to those who have the benefits of material "measure," that is wealth and health, to aid those who are in need. In short, Gregory has applied the doctrine of the image of God for a vitally important ethical end. In this he prefigured the way John Chrysostom would dynamically connect theology and ethics in his episcopal preaching. Both rhetors, will use the marked antithesis between wealthy and poor in the world of late antiquity to make this point of the "seeking of balance," and both will skillfully apply the antithesis in their rhetorical structures, where the textual contrasts between excess and penury is used to great effect for pathos and for stirring calls to action.[240]

Gregory, as Bernard Coulie has effectively demonstrated in a long study devoted to the subject,[241] had spent a long time in his career reflecting on the moral value of wealth. This is hardly surprising when we consider his personal situation as the son of a very wealthy, landowning, bishop who wished to follow the ascetical life but could never extricate himself from civic and ecclesiastical responsibility. His *Oration* 14 rises from, and represents, his wider consideration of wealth as part of the divine economy of salvation. In his mind the only proper approach to the possession of wealth is one that accepts its extreme conditionality. No one can claim an absolute right to property since all humanity is given everything by the providence of a generous God. All things, the possession of life itself, but especially material goods, can only be held in temporary stewardship by human beings.[242] It is, however, the current distribution of material wealth which is particularly problematic in any generation, for some have more than they need, while others go without basic necessities. Gregory sees this inequity among humans, again in the light of Origen's doctrine of creation's primal fall from spiritual equality, as something which is the particular mark of sin.[243] In the original creation, and again in the ultimate plan of God for the restoration of creatures, such inequality is not envisaged as part of the Kingdom.[244] Those who seek to remove it, therefore, by redistributing their wealth in benefactions to the indigent, are sharing in God's work of salvation[245] and making some movement, however conditional and limited, to that equality of status (*isotés*), a life lived in communion rather than under dominance, that marks the plan of God for the world. He comes, at the end, to a startling yet illuminating conclusion—only almsgiving can restore to a human being that condition of freedom that humanity

240. Cf. Coulie (1985) 153f. For Gregory's generic predilection for antitheses, cf. Guignet (1911b), pp. 95-96.
241. Coulie (1985). See esp. pp. 171-177.
242. Orat. 14.22-24, 29, PG 35.885f.
243. He regards slavery as the result and mark of sin also. Orat. 14.25, PG 35.892.
244. Cf. Orat. 14.25, PG 35.889-892; Orat. 32.22, PG 36.200. Echoing the Apostolic Constitutions, he says: "Blush with shame you who withhold what belongs to someone else. Imitate the equitableness of God, and then no one will be poor." Orat. 14.24, PG 35.889.
245. Almsgiving mimics God's providence as a small sacrament of it. Orat. 14.25, PG 35.889.

lost in the ancient fall from grace, since it renders us liberal in the image of God, rather than cramped in cupidity which is the mark of oppression.[246]

The hideous condition of leprosy Gregory takes as a starting point for a harrowing reflection on the fragility of the human condition. It exemplifies for him one of the clearest instances of the fundamental philosophical question: why are we alive at all? His point is that suffering makes philosophers of us all by facing us with the meaninglessness of an existence that is frustrated in its fundamental design for transcendence and liberation.[247] The image of the leper stands, of course, as the supreme example of the loss of "balance" in the human condition: a loss of wealth, status and even the very image of human form. Gregory's point, both philosophically and theologically, is that if the case can be made for the leper as an icon of God, it can be made even more easily for the whole list of other indigents he enumerated earlier.

Taking the condition of the leper in late antiquity, Gregory begins to play on the affectivities of his hearers. Here, Gregory explains, are the most wretched of all human beings. They have lost all nobility of birth, and claim of kinship, and rank in society. Even the kindest person in society regards them as non-persons:

> Who is there even among the most gracious and humane of men who does not habitually show himself hostile and inhumane to the leper? This is the only case where we forget this is someone who is flesh like us, and must bear the same fragile body we have.[248]

He presses the same point shortly after in a moving evocation of how the mother of a leper laments the suffering of her child:

> What lamentation will she raise when she sees her son before her very eyes like a living corpse. O wretched son, she will say, of a tragic mother, stolen away from me by this disease. O pitiful child; son I can no longer recognize. You who must now live among wild animals in deserts and craggy mountains, with only rocks as your shelter; nevermore to see mankind except for the most holy among them... With cries such as this she pours out fountains of tears.[249]

He is expecting similar tears from his audience, and after enumerating some other shocking things about the condition of the leper he probably achieved his result. He is struck by certain telling details, such as how an evil brigand can expect more compassion from society than them,[250] or how the lepers define a "merciful man" not as someone who gives them relief but as one who does not drive them away with blows,[251] or how strangely it moves him that when someone does show them a small kindness they receive it with gratitude, rather than with outrage for the neglect they have suffered,[252] or how the greatest of all their indignities may be that

246. Orat. 14.26, PG 35.892.
247. Orat. 14.6, PG 35.865.
248. Orat. 14.10, PG 35.869.
249. Orat. 14.11, PG 35.872.
250. Orat. 14.11, PG 35.872.
251. Orat. 14.12, PG 35.873.
252. Orat. 14.12, PG 35.872.

all who help them take them for idiots because "they can only give thanks through their eyes since their lips are no longer visible."[253]

> I have said these things to help you change your minds. What has all this vast unending misery of humankind got to do with this festival you may ask? I suppose I had better stop developing the theme of tragedy, for otherwise I shall spoil the fun by moving all to tears; though some grieving may be better for you, perhaps, than what you'll go to see on stage, and a few tears will be more worthy than the dirty jokes you'll share.[254]

Having established, by the elicited sympathy of his audience, that the leper is indeed a human being deserving of recognition, he concludes his arguments by demanding that Christians take a stand. Disciples of the merciful Christ, who spent his time healing the sick to show the proper way to respond to suffering, must renounce all inhumanity to the sick.[255] Moreover, the amount of money dishonorably wasted on luxuries such as perfumes, foreign wines, and household slaves, is an excess that ought to be redirected to merciful ends.[256] He makes his appeal:

> Why do we do these things my friends and brothers? Why are we so sick in soul like this? For it is indeed a sickness, far worse than any bodily ill...Why do we not rush to help while we still have time?...Why do we sit and feast while our brothers are in such distress? God forbid I should enjoy such superabundance, when the likes of these have nothing at all.[257]

The suffering of the poor shall be a constant reminder, he says, of how fragile and precarious is all human life. It is like a ship's wake frothing into nothingness, or the figures of a child's game in the sand.[258] He wants them to remember this when they see the suffering rather than casting them away into social oblivion. Life can only be given its meaning through making it a journey towards God, and this avoidance of luxury is a critical aspect of keeping spiritually alive to the demands of being the divine image, and recognizing the image of God in others.[259] Those who understand this are truly wise, and by their almsgiving they "steal from the devil," discovering in the process, that God will see all that is done, and will never be outdone in generosity:

> So dedicate a little to God, from whom you received so much. Even, give Him everything, for he gave you all that you have. You will never be able to surpass God's generosity to you, not if you gave away every single thing you owned, even selling yourself into the bargain.[260]

Support for the poor, Gregory teaches, is a duty for all. It can be fulfilled in great scale or in small scale depending on the differing capacities of each one. Those who

253. Orat. 14.16, PG 35.877.
254. Orat. 14.13, PG 35.873.
255. Orat. 14.14-15, PG 35.876.
256. Orat. 14.16-17, PG 35.877.
257. Orat. 14.18, PG 35.880.
258. Orat. 14.19, PG 35.881.
259. Orat. 14.20, PG 35.884.
260. Orat. 14.22, PG 35.885.

have been given much from God are expected to be correspondingly generous. But no one is able to plead an incapacity for generosity. Those who have little should supply basic medicines for the suffering. Even if this is beyond them, they should supply love and even the testimony of tears of sympathy: "for even commiseration is a great help in misery."[261] He shows some illuminating insights into the psychology of his audience when he urges them not to be like the characters in the parable who "passed by on the other side of the road" out of fear of becoming involved. "Let the fear of God, he says, conquer the inertia of your desire for ease."[262]

This royal road of charity is, for Gregory, the surest form of ascent to the divine. It replaces all Socratic knowledge as the basis of true ethic:

> And therefore, Know thyself! Know from what source comes all that you possess, all your breathing, your knowing and your wisdom. And this is the greatest of all—to know God, to hope for the Kingdom of heaven, the same honor as the angels, and the vision of glory. For now we see that we are the children of God, and co-heirs of Christ, only as if in a mirror, in dark reflections, but then we shall see more clearly and more purely.[263] And, if I may put it a little more daringly, we shall see that we have even been deified.[264]

His constantly reiterated advice to hold nothing in life as secure was to come home to him in an unexpected way in October of that very year, 368, through reports of a natural disaster.[265] Bithynia, the province of Asia Minor, southeast of Constantinople, had suffered a massive earthquake. The news increased his anxieties tenfold, for it was the station where his beloved brother Caesarios held his current post as provincial treasurer in the imperial tax service, based in the city of Nicaea. In 368 many parts of the city were demolished. Gregory found out that Caesarios had survived a close encounter with death. The building in which he had been living had collapsed, and he had emerged with merely a few scratches. To Gregory it seemed like a miracle of God's deliverance. He sent messengers from the estate at Karbala to congratulate his brother on a wondrous escape, asking him to come back home, telling him to bear his sufferings with magnanimity: "Since those who suffer are close to God, as Peter so admirably says, somewhere."[266] Basil also wrote to Caesarios at this time,[267] certainly on Gregory's urging, and both the clerical friends tried to convince the young man to renounce political service in favor of a life of retirement dedicated to Christ and the Church. It was a ploy that Gregory had tried

---

261. Orat. 14.28, PG 35.896.
262. Orat. 14.27, PG 35.893.
263. Alluding to 1 Cor 13:12.
264. Orat. 14.23, PG 35.888.
265. See Gregory's Orat. 7.15, PG 35.773; and Socrates' *Ecclesiastical History* 1.4.11.
266. This is one of a few indications that Gregory possessed, or had close knowledge of, the apocryphal text the "Preaching of Peter" (*Kerygma Petrou*). Cf. Demoen (1991); Greg. Ep. 20, PG 37.53-56; Gallay (1964), pp. 28-29.
267. Basil, Ep. 26, PG 32.301.

on his brother earlier, when Julian had begun to look unfavorably on Christians at the court. It had failed then. Would it work a second time when the shock of mortality had impacted so dramatically upon him?

Basil applies the argument that his avoidance of death was so miraculous it was a sure sign that God had intended to preserve him for a second kind of life. Basil certainly had plans that could include using this vigorous and politically astute friend in the service of the Christian cause, and Gregory on his part was hopeful that the family might be able to claim Caesarios back at Nazianzus. Perhaps there were some self-referent motives at play here, for if Caesarios returned home the whole burden of assisting his father in the management of the estate would be passed over to the able younger son. But Gregory's warm relation to his brother also suggests that he genuinely looked forward to the possible return of a much loved sibling. It was not to be.

To a stunned family the messengers brought the latest news, that having escaped the earthquake, Caesarios had gone down before the wave of deadly plague that came in its aftermath. Only his ashes would be brought back to his home town. To mark the occasion Gregory prepared a suitable funeral oration and made ready the family tomb near the Nazianzus Church.[268] The Oration is now generally entitled: "On His Brother: St Caesarios,"[269] and the title immediately gives an account of the long-term success this piece of funeral oratory had: for in it Gregory strangely metamorphosises the happy-go-lucky Caesarios into a model and ascetical Christian. He canonizes a brother whom only a few years before the local Church had been ready to censure because of his allegiance to the service of Julian. On that occasion Gregory had written anxiously to him that he was becoming a cause of scandal to the whole locality. Now under the immediate impact of his death, all his virtues are celebrated. It is, perhaps, a natural instinct of a kindly soul preaching a eulogy of lament for a beloved brother, to focus so decidedly on the model aspects of his character. The prior tradition of Greek funeral oratory also had a long tradition of using a stock repertoire of epideictic images. The Greek rhetorician Menander, a century before Gregory, had composed a guide to the composition of funeral orations which allows us to gain an idea of how formally structured they were.[270] In his *Oration for Caesarios* Gregory is also (consciously or not) advancing the very genre of Christian funeral oratory, to make the retelling of the life

---

268. It had been prepared as the tomb of his father and mother, and was hastily made over to Caesarios. Orat. 7.24, PG 35.788.
269. Orat. 7 (ET, L.P. McCauley. FOC vol. 22, 1953), PG 35.756-788.
270. For a good review of classical Greek attitudes to funeral orations, see McCauley (tr.), "*Funeral Orations*," FOC 22 (Washington, 1953), pp. viii-xiii. Menander advises that a typical *Epitaphios Logos* should have the following three elements: An *Exordium* that introduces the subject; the *Encomium* that praises the dead person together with a lament for their loss. This focuses on the history of the deceased, their natural endowments, education and career. The moral character they showed in success or adversity is focused on, as an example for the hearers, and points of comparison are drawn with other famous heroes. The oration closes with a Final Exhortation and Prayer to the gods.

into a modeling of archetypal Christian virtues for the benefit of the Church audience. His own structure models all the classical forms and stylistic devices.[271] A notable difference, however, is the restraint which his Christian faith imposes on the Hellenistic style of lament for the dead. The bitterness of lamentation is reined in, and a far more serene sense of confidence in the mercy of God and the hope of an afterlife is brought to the forefront. This text was to have a great influence, for centuries to come, on the Christianizing of the themes of classical death-oratory. Gregory and his younger friend and colleague Gregory Nyssa were the leading Christian rhetoricians who would develop this form of oratory. In the West Ambrose would follow their example and, in so doing, transmitted the classical form in a new medium that would be greatly copied in the history of Christian preaching.

In his opening remarks Gregory tells his listeners that a Christian discourse will hold back from the usual Greek exaggeration of the virtues of the deceased.[272] Even so it is still odd to see Caesarios so lauded as a saint.[273] As further news was brought back to Nazianzus about the state of financial affairs attendant on Caesarios' decease, the furore about the young man did not abate with his death. Creditors began demanding redress, claiming that Caesarios had left behind him massive debts unpaid.

Gregory was to make counterclaims that his brother's so called creditors were in fact parasites who had robbed the dead man's household. The case was to go to judgment and would drag on interminably, it seemed to him. Whether or not this was an initial intent of Gregory when composing this funeral oration, it certainly became relevant in the following year, when the legal case to exonerate Caesarios and protect his estate was being assembled; because the only way in which the deceased could be made to speak in court in his own defense was for Gregory to offer the text of the funeral panegyric as evidence of Caesarios' good standing and uprightness of character. There is, therefore, a very important legal aspect to the composition of this piece, and if it was not operative from the outset, this certainly became an issue during the time the Oration was being edited subsequently. It was, in short, important to present Caesarios in the best of all possible lights, as a model character, not only for the benefit and general edification of the local congregation, but especially for the close scrutiny of the courts who would soon receive this liturgical testimony, carrying the weight of the church behind it, as part of a large and controversial legal dossier about fraud, posthumous debts, and property rights.

271. *Exordium,* Orat. 7.1; *Encomium,* Orat. 7.2-23; *Final Exhortation and Prayer,* Orat. 7.24.
272. "We shall not bestow immoderate and unmerited praise." Orat. 7.1, PG 35.756.
273. All of Gregory's family entered the Christian calendar, as saints, as a result of his oratory. Caesarios' feast day was celebrated on February 25, Gregory the Elder's on January 1, Nonna's on August 5, and Gorgonia's on December 9. Gregory enjoyed two days, January 25 and January 30. The Latin Church removed the day to May 9 which it also posited as his birthday. Cf. Cox (ET of Ullmann), 1851, p. 135.

Gregory begins by distancing himself from the "falsity" of a rhetorician who uses a funeral for mere display of craft. He seems to be disarming the hostile opinion of some in his audience in advance, at the same time as rebuking those who wanted to hear a good address simply for the pleasure of it. His opening words: "My dear friends, brethren, fathers..."[274] indicate that the local clergy were certainly present and it is the gathering of the monks in the congregation who have probably called out this initial "self-defense," for he goes on to explain that the practice of his oratorical craft, a last gift to his beloved brother, is still in accordance with his "philosophy," a term that by this period had already become a code word for monastic asceticism. He had certainly intended the funeral speech to be a memorable occasion, standing in for the funeral games, libations, funerary portraits, and food offerings which their familial Christian tradition disallowed. His text even expresses the hope that "it will remain to be kept by future generations" as "a far better image than any picture of our beloved."[275]

The discourse develops its first argument by a public testimony to the high standing of Caesarios' parents, the bishop and his virtuous wife; and this in order to canonize his brother, as it were, by association. He senses, surely, he has a long way to go to convince the locals that Caesarios could fit the stern ascetical canons for Christian sanctity. He almost challenges the doubters with the proposition that to raise an eyebrow over the dead politician is to cast aspersions on the whole family:

> I have not mentioned these things in order to preach their praises, nor am I unaware that one could dedicate an entire oration and hardly begin to sound out their worth. I did so in order to show that in terms of virtue Caesarios was indebted to such parents. And surely this can be no matter of wonder to you, and hardly beyond your belief, if the son born of such laudable stock showed himself worthy too?[276]

He moves on quickly after this to lay out the "unarguable" character marks of Caesarios: his intellectual achievements in medicinal and astronomical studies in Alexandria, and his meteoric rise in the political life of the capital.[277] He apologizes to his congregation that Caesarios could not be persuaded to exemplify the quiet ascetical life at home, even though the family pressed him to remain in Nazianzus.[278] His heart was set on a political career in Constantinople. At this juncture Gregory makes an innovative claim. Up to this point in Christian history, saints had been recognized only from the ranks of martyrs. In Gregory's generation the monastic ascetics were making claims to exemplify the status of living saints and, along with that, assuming the role of paradigms and guardians of Christian

---

274. Orat. 7.1, PG 35.756.
275. Orat. 7.16, PG 35.773-776.
276. Orat. 7.5, PG 35.760.
277. Orat. 7.6-8, PG 35.761-764.
278. Orat. 7.9, PG 35.765. "For the least place with God is a better and more sublime condition than having even the first place with an earthly emperor."

tradition—an authoritative role that Church hierarchs were not willing to relinquish so easily. In Gregory's time, therefore, the categories of sainthood were of primary significance. Monastics as well as hierarchs were being included in the category of the saint-guide.[279] Gregory's own characterization of himself as dedicated to God by his double standing as both ascetic and hierarch exemplifies the manner in which the consideration of sanctity was an integral aspect of the claim for the right to stand as the authoritative leader of the Christians in the region. To have a member of the family who was less than enthusiastic about the local Church and the ascetical life was a liability not merely for Caesarios' posthumous reputation but more significantly for the standing of Gregory's family, who continued, through the offices of himself and his father as local hierarchs, to guide the Church of the region.[280] In order to secure a hallowed place for Caesarios within this picture of his family as god-graced saints, Gregory stretched the canons of sanctity to include the argument that Caesarios' political career was tantamount to an ascetical life, since the young man lived interiorly, and did not seek after the glory, but was actually "living for God" all the time.[281] It was an extraordinarily innovative argument for its time, though it was soon destined to become a standard ascetical argument addressed to "those in the world," and (through the way in which Gregory the Great, the later Roman Pope would launch the same idea in his *Pastoral Rule*) would dominate the Christian imagination for centuries ahead.[282]

Gregory, in the following sections of this oration, turns back to consider his brother's career in Julian's court. This had been a cause of much local criticism at the time, and Gregory had to write to him, begging him to distance himself from an emperor increasingly becoming hostile to the Christian cause. When Caesarios finally returned home, Gregory does not clarify whether it was a dismissal from the court, or because Julian was passing through Cappadocia on his way to the Persian campaign. In any case, for the purposes of the *Funeral Oration* the return home is offered as a dismissal by the emperor because Caesarios' Christian faith could not be

---

279. Gregory's Oration (21), *In Praise of Athanasios*, is a prime example of this movement of elevating cardinal and significant hierarchs of the past as "patristic" exemplars for future generations. See also Elm (1999) and eadem (2000).

280. For a wider consideration see P. Brown, *Society and the Holy in Late Antiquity* (Berkeley, 1982); also idem., "The Rise and Function of the Holy Man in Late Antiquity," *Journal of Roman Studies*, vol. 61 (1971), pp. 80-101. For a more particular consideration see N. McLynn (1998a).

281. Orat. 7.9, PG 35.765. "We know this for certain, that this indeed was Caesarios' attitude."

282. Pope Gregory codified for the medieval west the concept of the two states of life: the perfect life of ascetical contemplation and the lesser, though admirable, active life in the world. Gregory (of Nazianzus) was to elevate the principle of "moderation" in the spiritual life that argued it was the inner disposition not the outward condition that "made the man." His theory was partly a justification of his own decision to follow the ascetical life on his own estates, with his own servants, in Cappadocia, but it was widely adopted later in Byzantium to justify city monachism that grew up there vigorously from the fifth century onwards.

overcome.[283] It is by this device that Gregory even associates Caesarios with the status and honor due to confessors of the faith:

> So it was that he lived in retirement during those evil times in accordance with his Christian duty that urges us, when the times require it, to brave dangers for the sake of truth, and never to betray the faith from cowardice; but also, when possible, never to provoke those dangers either.[284]

To that he adds the final argument of a heavenly sign,[285] telling his hearers how Caesarios had been miraculously preserved, one of the only, or at least one of the very few, imperial agents to have survived the great earthquake at Nicaea. Gregory offers this as a sign of God's special providence for his brother.[286] He tells his audience that in his exchange of letters afterwards, when he (and Basil) called to him to make a second life dedicated to the service of God, Caesarios had indicated that he would indeed follow such a path in the future. At this moment, Gregory says, illness carried him away. The miraculous preservation was a "testimony to his righteousness," the fatal illness a "mark of his common humanity."[287] So it was that the city-loving and brilliant politician was, after all, really a dedicated ascetic, even though he did not have time to manifest his change of heart to the public. Gregory apostrophises, as if in Caesarios' own voice, and scornfully casts aside the delights of fine living: costly robes, perfumes, games and celebrations. The oratory almost carries us away with the idea of Caesarios having ascetically renounced all these things, until we remember that he has cast them aside only because: "his beautiful body lies hid under this bitter stone."[288]

When he speaks of how his brother's ashes were brought back to Nazianzus, Gregory describes the scene almost as if it were a triumphant return of relics, to the martyr shrine in Nazianzus:

> But now noble Caesarios has been kept safe for us, a noble dust, a praiseworthy death; sent back with hymns upon hymns, escorted to the shrine of the martyrs there to be honored by the hands of his parents.[289]

Accordingly, Caesarios will not merely look upon the choirs of angels, he will join in with them, will be radiant with the light of the Great King, and will even send back to those on earth a reflection of this radiance.[290] It is Gregory himself, who can testify to this new glorious status by a revelatory dream he has had of his brother, beautiful and radiant after death.[291] His implication is more than that Caesarios' deathbed

283. Orat. 7.13, PG 35.772.
284. Orat. 7.14, PG 35.772; cf. Mt 10:23.
285. "Another of the *thaumata* [wonders] associated with him." Orat. 7.15, PG 35.
286. Orat. 7.15, PG 35.773.
287. Orat. 7.15, PG 35.773.
288. Orat. 7.16, PG 35.776.
289. Orat. 7.15, PG 35.773.
290. Orat. 7.17, PG 35.776.
291. Orat. 7.21, PG 35.784.

baptism has transfigured him into heavenly glory,[292] for such were the characteristics of heavenly intercession which had hitherto been reserved to the great martyrs alone.[293] This aspect of the claim for sanctity will subsequently be expanded by Gregory in the coming years to embrace his whole family; father, mother and elder sister Gorgonia. It is not so much a self-referent presumption, as more a specific claim that his family exemplifies the true standard of Christian behavior and is thus graced by the charisms of Christ, as is fitting for a family God has chosen to lead the local Church. By controlling the developing notion of the charismatic "holy man" in the mid-fourth century, Gregory is appropriating the idea and the powerful symbolism it commanded, and then subsuming it within his other claim (based on much older Roman and Christian legal bases) to stand as the local Christian leader, by virtue of his father's dominion over the locality as senior magistrate, landowner, and priest-bishop.

Having given his brother the formal farewell, he turns to his rhetorical conclusion and offers his hearers the traditional "Consolation." The normal Hellenistic fatalism here seems to be replaced, at first, by a suitably Old Testament fatalism, a world-weariness to which Gregory often returned (and often with the same images) in his more "philosophic" moments:

> Brethren, such is our life, whose present existence is so evanescent. Such is the game we mortals play. We do not exist; then we are born; then once born we slide again into dissolution. We are a fleeting dream,[294] a phantasm that cannot be grasped, the flight of a bird passing over the sky, a ship which leaves no trace upon the sea.[295] We are but dust and mists, like the morning dew,[296] or the flower that springs up in a moment, and withers[297] just as soon.[298]

In his conclusion, Gregory goes on to rehearse the usual Hellenistic motifs of funeral consolation: the dead man is deprived of so many joys, but he is also spared the griefs of life, and so forth. It is in this context that we find the first fleeting reference made to Caesarios' wealth and his all-important inheritance intentions.[299] Gregory announces to the Church that Caesarios has left his money for charitable purposes. It is the nearest equivalent we have (and probably all that the family could muster too in the chaos of the manner of his unexpected death) of "registering a will."

This telling detail was to become something of great moment soon afterwards, when the family was embroiled in serious disputes over the inheritance. The story was then forwarded to the law courts of the capital, that Caesarios was the rightful

292. On the hasty (*clinicus*) baptism of his brother see Orat. 7.15, PG 35.773.
293. Cf. McGuckin (1993).
294. Job 20:8.
295. Wis 5:10, 12.
296. Hos 13:3.
297. Is 40:6-7.
298. Orat. 7.19, PG 35.777.
299. "He will not inherit property perhaps, but he leaves behind the best of all heirs, such as he personally desired—and thus he leaves this world bearing all his wealth before him." Orat. 7.20, PG 35.781.

owner of all his capital assets at the time of death, and that he had bequeathed his property on his deathbed "to the poor," but that his household servants had mistaken his intentions and distributed assets indiscriminately before the creditors had been satisfied. Who "the poor" were, whom Caesarios is supposed to have really meant, is never quite specified in Gregory's texts, and it may well be a code for bequeathing his wealth "to the Church"; which if it was the Church of Nazianzus, a charitable and tax-exempted body whose concern it was to administer goods for the poor generically, was tantamount to leaving all his wealth to his family, but with the family not having to pay any tax on the gift. Convoluted the argument may be, but it also has to be remembered that while Caesarios may have been caught unprepared by his sudden death, he was, after all, the leading imperial tax agent of Bithynia, and it was well known as a sinecure that could vastly enrich its officeholders as well as provide them with an intimate knowledge of every tax loophole possible.

Gregory's public testimony in the funeral speech, that this was indeed the testamentary intent of Caesarios' will, is known otherwise only from Basil's *Letter 32*[300] which shows Basil in his role as an advocate for the cause of Gregory's family. Here, Basil writes to Sophronios[301] (a mutual old friend to whom Gregory had written on several occasions),[302] adding support to a legal appeal Gregory had evidently sent on for redress in the capital. By this stage the extent of the claims on Caesarios' estate had become patently clear and Gregory was anxious they might prove the ruin of the family. Not only was the legacy negligible in itself (so he had argued to Basil and got Basil to repeat in his own evidence), the portable goods had seemingly been distributed by Caesarios' household servants on the grounds that the dying man had instructed money to be spent on the poor as a final almsgiving. Though this beneficence to the poor was held up for admiration in the funeral speech, it is clear from the other accounts in Gregory's letters, and from what Basil repeats in his own letter to Sophronios, that the family held Caesarios' Bithynian servants in contempt for the manner in which they botched the arrangements[303] by taking their master so literally that they simply gave away all Caesarios had, without investigation of the full legal implications. As more and more demands from creditors further afield began

---

300. Which also represents intelligence Basil could only have received from Gregory. Basil is careful enough to state: "It is declared that Caesarios said on his deathbed..." Basil. Ep. 32 (NPNF series 2, vol. 8).

301. Master of Offices in Constantinople and (after 369) Urban Prefect. Sophronios had risen in Valens' favor by informing him of the usurpation of Procopios at Constantinople, when the former was in Caesarea in 365. (Amm. Marc. 25.9). Basil also writes Ep. 33 at the same time to Abourgios, another official, and asks him to intercede to the same effect with the Imperial Treasurer. In Ep. 33, he argues that it is an intolerable burden to Gregory as an unworldly ascetic to be so dragged into the limelight by this affair.

302. Cf. Greg. Epp. 21-22, 29 and 37.

303. As Basil puts it with all the social scorn of Late Antique nobility: "His property was in the hands of slaves, and of men of no better character than slaves." Ep. 32.

to pour in, Gregory's anxiety increased to the extent that he wished simply to abandon all the estate to the Imperial Treasury.[304]

Once this route was taken[305] the family could no longer lay claim to much, unless the imperial tax office gave them an unlikely benefaction, but the important thing was that creditors could not longer pursue the estate at Nazianzus for anything. All matters of claims still outstanding would have to be submitted to the tax authorities in the capital, no longer to the family. It is to this end Basil appeals to Sophronios for "consideration" to be given to Gregory by the *Comes Thesaurorum*, the imperial capital's chief tax inspector. He cites, to Sophronios, Gregory's wish to cede the remainder of the estate as a ready proof of their common friend's disinterestedness; though it was, of course, a major financial relief Gregory was seeking.

Gregory himself composed a careful appeal to Sophronios,[306] informing him of the death of his colleague and friend Caesarios, and representing him as having been betrayed and robbed by all who were with him in Nicaea. Into this category fall both household servants and the mass of creditors indiscriminately. He describes them as parasites who left the dead man in shabby funeral clothes without hardly bothering to give him a "little myrrh, if even that." He argues in this studied personal appeal that he is not so interested in the money that was feloniously alienated from Caesarios, as much as he is determined to put an end to the dishonor that has been done to his family. He couches the letter to Sophronios in classical terms of shame and redress. If Sophronios was "the first among his brother's true friends" he will surely wish to avenge the wrongs done to him, for "Caesarios seems to me to have had no friends at all, though he once believed he had many." It is this abandonment by false friends which for Gregory is the "most insupportable aspect of the shame of it all." The rhetoric, however, is clearly calling for more than Basil anticipated. Gregory is here urging Sophronios to take vengeance in the name of his dead friend. He concludes not by asking for any abandonment of the estate to the Treasury, but rather by being "content to accept whatever help you can give us, in whatever way it seems best to your prudent judgment." Judging from the laudatory letters Gregory subsequently wrote on other matters to Sophronios,[307] we have every ground for

---

304. "No one is so ignorant of Gregory as to have unworthy suspicion of his giving an inexact account of the circumstances because he is fond of money. We have not to go far to find a proof of his liberality. What is left of the property he gladly abandons to the Treasury, so that the property may be kept there, and the Treasurer may give answer to those who attack it and demand their proofs, for we (bishops) are not adapted for such business." (Basil, Ep. 32).

305. There is no indication that it was done, only that Basil tells us Gregory was "willing" to abandon the estate to the Treasury if the Treasury would protect them by henceforth assessing all claims against them. Having expressed this willingness, however, Basil expects that Sophronios the Master of Offices will give personal "consideration" to Gregory's plight.

306. Ep. 29, PG 37.64-65; Gallay (1964), pp. 36-37.

307. Two letters from this same time send on young scholars for service in the household of Sophronios. Cf. Epp. 37 and 39, PG 37.77, 80-81; Gallay (1964), pp. 46-49.

thinking that the Master of Offices intervened for the family to decisive and very positive effect. The contrast between the Gregory of *Letter 29 to Sophronios*, someone who appeals as one powerful lord to another in terms of honor and kinship redress, and the Gregory who is depicted in Basil's *Letter 33 to Abourgios* as the incompetent and unworldly man of letters, could not be more markedly different.

At about this same period he received news from his old friend Philagrios, a Christian student with him at Athens, in the form of a letter offering him condolences on the loss of Caesarios. Philagrios was himself suffering from a disease that progressively weakened him, took away his eyesight, then his mobility, and finally proved fatal. Gregory saw in his languishing contemporary an image of the common fragility of humankind, and spent several letters[308] offering philosophical condolences.[309] He began by confessing to his friend in private what he felt was inappropriate in his public orations: that Caesarios' death had left his efforts at philosophical detachment in tatters:

> I no longer have my Caesarios! I have to tell you, even if such feeling is inappropriate for a philosopher, that I find myself treasuring all that once was his. Whenever I come across something associated with him, something that brings him to mind, I find myself clasping it in my arms and covering it with kisses. For a moment it even seems to me that I can see him again, be with him, talk with him once more.[310]

This moving confession of his private grief is reflected in the more tragic tone of lamentation to which he gives vent in the poems which equally, like this letter, were not meant for public edification. In several epitaph verses he composed for Caesarios his shock at the "unjust loss" expresses the bewilderment of having the youngest member of the family die first.[311] The overwhelming grief of his father also seems to have affected him, for he devotes several poems to the lamentations he must have heard from the old man, to the effect that the tomb destined for him had been taken by his youngest child,[312] and how the grief had taken away his own desire to live on.

If the old man was reduced to bewildered silence, the younger Gregory's feelings were shaped and articulated by his poetry. He returns in private, as so often, to his favorite image of roses, borrowed from his much loved poetess, Sappho:

> Caesarios has flown from this life,
> Like a rose falling from the bush,
> or the tear of dew dropping from a petal.[313]

---

308. And composed several poems to celebrate his friend's courage in the face of adversity; cf. *Epigrams* 4-9, PG 38.84-86.
309. Epp. 31-36, PG 37.68-77;. Gallay (1964), pp. 38-46. Written most likely over the course of a few years, the correspondence was begun (with *Letter* 30) shortly after Caesarios' death.
310. Ep. 30, PG 37.65; Gallay (1964), pp. 37-38.
311. "Unjust tomb ...what kind of justice is this?" Epitaph 6, PG 38.14.
312. *Epitaph* 10, PG 38.16. "What manner of justice this? O King of mortals how did you permit such a thing?"
313. *Epitaph* 19, PG 38.20.

Called upon to give meaning to sufferings through the craft of his discourse he found himself challenged by Philagrios' example. As they exchanged letters of consolation it became clear that his friend's illness was terminal. Gregory paid him a visit and later recounts what it had meant to him when he had exhausted his stock of philosophical advice on the subject of bearing one's trials with patient endurance, and Philagrios, in response, had risen from his bed to pray, making the hairs on Gregory's neck stand up:

> I have been thinking back to the visit I made at our last meeting in my dear town of Mataza[314] (for I will call and regard as mine everything of yours). I think back to that philosophic attitude which you so truly demonstrated to me. Even to recall it still makes me shiver. I was expounding for you Psalm 72, since you had demanded I should, and there was no denying you... and I tried to relate it as best I could to the philosophical elucidation of your suffering in the light of our own teachings, and those of the outsiders.[315] I knew, of course, that I was speaking to you, a most learned man, someone who carried the Spirit and was under the spur of suffering—for nothing reveals more to us than pain, and so my speech developed. And you, even as I spoke, as if readying for a race, lifted your hands to heaven and turning East as you supposed (for you were no longer able to see) you cried out: "Father I give thanks to you who made and who correct those you have chosen as your own, to work good for them despite themselves; to cleanse the interior by means of the exterior; and to make us pass through adversities to the blessed goal, for reasons you alone can understand." ...So it was, that from being your teacher I was turned into your student.[316]

Gregory never quite recovered from the grief that would pile in on him in these few years. He grew increasingly lonely.[317] He would later look back and call the death of Caesarios "my inheritance of sorrow."[318] He described the loss in terms of losing a massive oak tree that had sheltered him all his life.[319] Nothing would ever be the same afterwards.[320]

The hammer blows of misfortune were to continue with a relentless rhythm. The old man, whom he feared would slip away from life under the force of his grief at losing his youngest son, was distracted by other family sorrows. In close succession came the loss of his cousin Euphemios for whom Gregory had a deep regard,[321] possibly from the time when they were fellow pupils in the days when he studied grammar at the home of his uncle Amphilokios. The twenty-year-old Euphemios

---

314. A Cappadocian provincial town; cf. Ramsay (1890), p. 307.
315. Hellenistic philosophy.
316. Ep. 34, PG 37.76; Gallay (1964), p. 45.
317. A noted aspect is the extraordinary amount of "epitaph verses" he begins to compose from this time onwards, for the increasingly large number of his dead relatives and friends. See also Coman (1938 [b]).
318. *De Rebus Suis*, vv. 187-190, PG 37.984; *De Vita Sua*, v. 374, PG 37.1055.
319. *De Rebus Suis*, v. 187, PG 37.984.
320. *Epitaph* 19, PG 38.20.
321. To judge from the nine *Epitaphia* verses he composed for him, PG 38.24-29. *Epitaphia* 28-36.

died suddenly in the course of the preparations of his own wedding celebrations.[322] Gregory's sister, Gorgonia, also contracted a strange disease and was herself dead within the following year, 369 or 370 at the latest, followed soon afterwards by her husband Alypios whose company Gregory had always enjoyed. It seemed to him that the angel of death was passing over his whole clan, leaving him feeling isolated as the sole survivor in the company of very aged parents.[323] Gregory once more pronounced a large-scale *Funeral Oration*,[324] this time in the Cappadocian Church of Bishop Faustinos at Ikonium from which Gorgonia was buried. He told of the ascetical life of his sister, and the wonders she had received from God in terms of healings. She dreamed in advance, he tells his audience, of the very day of her impending death, and was prepared for it by baptism.[325] As with his oration for Caesarios, he celebrates those classical virtues expected in the Greek funeral oration, but powerfully refashions the whole impetus of the eulogy into a Christian celebration of the sanctity of the deceased. So, Gorgonia appears in the usual characterizations of ideal wife and dutiful daughter, but emerges more powerfully and more sharply delineated (both in Gregory's text as well as perhaps in the new sociopolitical conditions afforded to Christian ascetic women in the fourth century) as a Christian holy woman. That Gregory had already imported the categories of martyr-canonization into his brother's funeral eulogy was one thing, but to do it for Gorgonia who was a married woman with three children, was a radical innovation. His achievement in presenting this wealthy *matrona* as an impoverished ascetic is quite extraordinary. Even slight details that give away her great social standing, such as her financial support of large numbers of local indigents, or the case when her private carriage turned over on the highway and injured her, are recast as raw material for her sanctification.[326] "Her female nature overcame that of man in the common struggle for salvation."[327] We are, once more, almost carried away by the force of the words, to attribute to her the virtues of monastic virginity:

> Consider her chastity preserved after baptism, and her soul espoused to Christ in that pure bridal chamber of her body.[328]

Except that we remember she was baptized on her deathbed only, and wonder at how Gregory so transfigures the edifying Christian aspects of her life (as he says he

---

322. *Epitaph* 29, PG 38.25; "Envy came as a too-eager guest to the feast." *Epitaph* 33, PG 38.27.
323. "I have been preserved to deliver funeral orations for my brother and my sister," he says at the conclusion of *Oration* 8, "whether anyone will pay me a like honor now that you [Gorgonia] are gone I am unable to tell." (PG 35.816).
324. Orat. 8, PG 35.789f.
325. Orat. 8.19-20, PG 35.812. Gregory sees nothing unusual in this correlation of an active ascetical life as Christian with the fact that she still delayed baptism until her deathbed; in fact in Orat. 8.20 he even suggests that Baptism in her case was like an afterthought.
326. Orat. 8.15, PG 35.808.
327. Orat. 8.14, PG 35.806.
328. Orat. 8.14, PG 35.806.

will in his introduction)[329] while "passing over in silence what ought to be passed over." Both as wealthy woman and Christian ascetic Gorgonia cannot quite escape the typecasting of Late Antique rhetoric. She died, with the family at her bedside,[330] as bishop Faustinos leaned over to catch her last words. He told Gregory they were the verses of the Psalm:[331]

> I shall lie down in peace and take my sleep,
> for you alone Lord have established me in hope.

This simple thing, more than all the other "signs" he has been recounting seems to have moved Gregory the most:

> How blessed are those who can indeed take their repose with words such as these ...for this is indeed what you chanted O most gracious woman, and how well it fitted you.[332]

After the family had returned home to Nazianzus, sometime around this same period, Gregory returned his epistolary debt to Basil[333] by writing, certainly at Basil's request, a stern letter to Basil's brother, his young friend Gregory (of Nyssa).[334] It is one of those small letters which can have an extraordinarily great effect on a person's history and, in this case, on the history of world literature. For the young rhetorician looked to Gregory Nazianzen as a consummate artist, a model of what he himself wanted to become and retained a deep personal affection for him all his life. He had tried to resist his family's ascetical inclinations[335] and wanted to adopt a political rhetorical career. With two massive forces on either side of him, Basil and Macrina, he had little chance and was reined back in. The request from Basil's family of a letter from Gregory of Nazianzus to assure him that his duty lay with Christian rhetoric in the service of the Church, not a career as a Christian rhetor which he had been arguing for, was the final tipping of the balance. Christian theology would have been immeasurably impoverished for the loss of Gregory of Nyssa's contribution, and it was very important for him at this stage to hear, from the pen of someone he admired as a greater scholar than himself, that it was the title of "Christian" that was more noble than that of "Rhetorician." Gregory apologizes in the text for leaning heavily on his younger friend[336] but underlines, on two occasions, the danger the young Gregory runs of losing his friendship permanently if he turns his back on his Christian obligations.[337] His words found their mark, and the

---

329. Orat. 8.1, PG 35.792.
330. Bernardi (1995), p. 137, thinks the oration was pronounced as an anniversary memorial speech, making it possible for Gregory not to have been present at the time of death; but he specifically tells us his mother Nonna was present at the deathbed, and given her age it is unlikely she would not have been accompanied for an event that was anticipated in advance.
331. LXX Ps 4:9. Orat. 8.22, PG 35.816.
332. Orat. 8.22, PG 35.816.
333. Basil's Ep. 26 which he had requested his friend write to Caesarios.
334. Ep. 11, PG 37.341; Gallay (1964), pp. 16-17.
335. He did so to the extent that he married, Theosevia.
336. "Forgive me if I upbraid you so for the sake of friendship." Ep. 11.11, PG 37.44; Gallay (1964), p. 18.
337. Ep. 11.9 and 11.12; PG 37.44. Gallay (1964), p. 18, using the appropriately double image from

younger Gregory was further "sealed" in his Christian vocation when a few years later in 372, his brother was to consecrate him as his suffragan bishop in Nyssa.

This letter shows the way in which Basil wished to gather his family around him and consolidate their status as a significant Christian power in the land. It is comparable to the manner in which Gregory's family had already done much to advance their own claim to be one of the leading Christian families of the region. Unlike Basil's family mythology, Gregory could not lay claim to a great-grandmother who was a disciple of the Cappadocian national saint, Gregory Thaumaturgos. But his *Funeral Orations* for Caesarios and Gorgonia, and later for his own father (a convert to the Christian religion), demonstrate a considered "apologetic" to advance himself, his immediate family, and his wider kin-group to a prominent and exemplarist role in the affairs of the Church. An alliance with Basil's family is part and parcel of that enterprise. Having secured Basil's brother Gregory for the cause, he would soon secure his cousin Amphilokios, and could rely on his other relatives Helladios and Eulalios[338] who had independently demonstrated ascetic tendencies.

It was to be yet another death in Cappadocia that would put all these Christian networkings on high alert. This time the funeral ceremonies would be dominated not so much by grief, but by energetic political machinations, for in the summer of 370[339] bishop Eusebios of Caesarea, the metropolitan see of Cappadocia, had died in Basil's arms. His was an important office, both politically as well as economically, and one that could determine the received theological orthodoxy of the whole region. Basil's plans, as he arranged for the funeral of his local bishop, kept still a secret within his own immediate circle in the episcopal residence, were to have a dramatic effect on the Christian careers of all that expansive network of friends and kin. Basil decided it was time to call in favors on a larger scale than anything that had been attempted before. It was to have momentous effect on the life of Gregory, and in ways completely beyond anything that he could ever have imagined at the time.

Pythagoras and the Resurrection of Lazarus to show how relationships can become "dead" or be "raised to life" depending how the young disciple behaves.
338. Cf. Hauser-Meury (1960), pp. 70, and 96.
339. Tillemont, *Mémoires* 9, pp. 657-658.

4

Bishop of Sasima

"That utterly dreadful, pokey little hole"

And so the choice must be again,
But the last choice is still the same;
And the awe passes wonder then,
And a hush falls for all acclaim.
And God has taken a flower of gold
And broken it, and used therefrom
the mystic link to bind and hold
Spirit to matter till death come.

Robert Frost

Basil had determined to make an all-out effort to secure the post as the new Archbishop of Caesarea. Hitherto his whole public self-identification as a Christian had been in monastic terms of ascetical withdrawal. How could it now be possible for a dedicated "ascetic" to take on the office of city bishop? It seemed to many to be tantamount to abandoning his earlier renunciation of a life in civic politics. How could he now turn to an ecclesiastical career in the public domain based upon his wealth and rhetorical skills? For the wider adherents of Christianity in the late Constantinian age, an even more worrisome question, perhaps, was how could such zealots as the monk-ascetics claim the proper direction of the civic and metropolitanate Church of the majority of Cappadocian Christians? Basil had some difficulty in changing his monastic-reclusive self-definition that had hitherto served him well[1] and, very much aware that he was not universally loved, or even much wanted in the ranks of the hierarchs, was very conscious that he needed all the assistance he could summon to ensure his success. He expected, almost as a right, that the two Gregories in Nazianzus could be counted on in his support.

---

1. Basil's *Letter* 223 (NPNF, series 2, vol. 8), *Against Eustathios,* represents the changing priorities in his own life story. He skims over his early experiences of monasticism, after Athens, and uses them to show that he knew about the ascetic life before, and independently of, Eustathios. He tells his readers that his friends had tried to separate him from Eustathios' influence (one suspects Gregory Nazianzen is meant in this number as Basil appeals to his authority in Ep. 223.5 to offset Eustathios' accusations of unorthodoxy) but he had only seen through his mentor late in life. He begins his period of "awakening" with the words: "Once I had been called to preside over the Church..." (Ep. 223.3). In this way Basil describes how he had found, in his political ascent to the episcopacy, the ultimate vocational goal he had been seeking. Nevertheless, the combination of monastic lifestyle and episcopate were still, generally, seen as incompatible ways of life in ascetical Christian understanding outside of the Eustathian circles, and Basil has some explaining to do as he changed his direction to seek the episcopal election.

Years later in his funeral oration for Basil, Gregory Nazianzen described, in the presence of Basil's own family and monastic disciples who could, presumably, check his version, the problems that led up to Basil's election. He puts the best face on everything, but admits that Eusebios of Caesarea the old bishop "suffered a natural antipathy towards him."[2] One of the results of this was the readiness of Basil's monastic admirers to cause dissension in the Caesarean Church.[3] On that occasion Eusebios had required the services of Gregory's fine mediation skills to bring Basil back to join with Gregory in the rhetorical contest with Valens' theologians. Gregory uses the story in his funeral encomium to throw a heroic light on Basil's priestly virtues, but it is reasonable to expect that many still remained in Caesarea who resented the threats of schism that the ascetics of Basil's circle were willing to wield to ensure the elevation of their candidate. The support of such a dedicated group of ascetic disciples could, to any outside eyes, look very much like a claque of "inexperienced hotheads," as Gregory hinted to him in a letter of advice about the controversy caused by his election.[4]

Now that the episcopal office was vacant, the same group was agitating again, this time with the full encouragement of their leader who had no intention of retiring a second time to the Pontic wilderness in the cause of peace. In his five years as the right hand of Eusebios, Basil had initiated a series of ecclesiastical reforms: of the liturgy, and of monastic regulation. It was, however, his work organizing the philanthropic institutions of the Church that brought him widespread popular fame, and his use of his personal fortune, alongside the money of Eusebios and the official church funds, to alleviate a famine in 369[5] remained very much alive in the memories of the poor of the region.

Drawn up against him, it seems, Basil had the

foremost men of the region, and those of the most vile character in the city government who had ranged themselves alongside them.[6]

McCauley interprets this passage[7] to mean that the local bishops were hostile, as indeed many of them were, but the text in Basil's *Funeral Oration* bears a more obvious meaning in reference to the imperial authorities, who obviously had marked the theological opinions of these Nicene intellectuals, at least from the engagement during the official visit of 365, and were not willing for people so opposed to Valens' Church politic to assume charge of such an important metropolis. The men of "vile character," as Gregory describes them, are paired alongside the imperial officials in his text, and surely means the local nobles who either were not ready to alienate their

2. Orat. 43.28, PG 36.533.
3. "They considered separation and revolt from the great and undivided body of the church, taking off with them a not inconsiderable number of the people."
4. Greg. Ep. 45.2.
5. Orat. 43.34-36, PG 36.541-545.
6. Orat. 43.37, PG 36.545.
7. FOTC 22 (1953, 1968), p. 59.

political overlord, or did not want to see Basil's influence increased any further, in case it could injure their own or their town's standing in the good graces of the government. To have any real hope of election as the new archbishop of Caesarea demanded, therefore, that Basil should play to the full his local popular support, but should also strengthen his standing in the counsels of the bishops who would be gathering in the city for the local elective synod. The metropolitanate of Caesarea at this time had fifty suffragan bishops under its governance[8] and the meeting was certainly going to be a conflicted one.

If Basil's recent efforts in distributing relief during the famine of 369[9] constituted the solid base of his local political support at the popular level, he still needed episcopal rhetors to articulate his merits in the synod, to offset criticism from the local curial officials who stood against him, and the Caesarean suffragans who did not like him. This larger episcopal support was exactly what he counted on from his friend Gregory; that he would speak for the cause of Basil on behalf of his father, one of the oldest (hence most senior) and most respected bishops of the local region. Speaking on behalf of the elder Gregory would allow Gregory access to the business of the episcopal synod itself.

As Gregory tells the story, after hearing the news of the death of Eusebios, his father was not inclined to travel for the synod, as they had no idea that Basil had determined to seek election, and his advanced years and recent bereavements had left him frail and depressed. As far as the younger Gregory knew, he and Basil had allied themselves in the spiritual cause of studiously avoiding ecclesiastical posts for the end of scholarly retirement. It came as a great shock to him when he finally discovered, through what he regarded as a deceit of Basil's, that his friend's encouraging ascetical words had to all appearances been forgotten, and his "spiritual affinity" with Gregory existed more in Gregory's mind than in any life-plan of Basil. Ironically, he mused on Basil's momentous decision to seek ecclesiastical office years afterwards:

> Whatever happened to our agreement about spurning the world so as to live a life together in the service of God? Whatever happened to the dedication of our literary skills to the Wisdom of the Word alone? All is scattered, cast down upon the ground.[10]

As soon as Eusebios had been laid to rest, in September of 370, Basil laid his plans, and one of them involved bringing Gregory back to Caesarea, where his eirenical political work in the Church must have gained him considerable favor among the majority. Sensing his colleague's probable reaction, Basil did not reveal the circumstances of the vacant see, but asked his friend to come and visit him as he was engaged in a struggle to the death. Whether or not he put it, in a blatant lie, that he was near to death, or whether he just led on Gregory to mistake his references to ecclesiastical troubles for those of his health, be it as it may. Gregory fell for it

8. *De Vita Sua*, v. 447, PG 37.1060.
9. Gregory relates it as one of Basil's great achievements as a priest. Orat. 43.34-36.
10. *De Vita Sua*, vv. 479-482, PG 37.1062.

completely, and in tears made his way post haste to Caesarea. It was while he was on the road that he began to notice how many other bishops were also traveling to the same destination, and a brief conversation in transit revealed all. He returned home in a fury and sent off a scathing letter:

> Do not be put out if I seem to tell you something that appears odd, or that you might not have heard before. You seem to me to have the reputation of a steady, reliable and strong-minded man. But I see in some of your decisions and actions more signs of naivete than prudence. When someone is devoid of trickery they are also slow to suspect it in another; which is exactly the present issue. You summoned us to the metropolis at the very time a council had been called for the selection of a new bishop, and your excuses were very fitting and persuasive, for you pretended that you were sick, even to the point of your last breath, and said you wished to see us once more to say your farewells. I cannot tell what your motives were in this, or what you thought my presence would achieve. So I set out, of course, deeply distressed by the whole business, for what could there be, as far as I am concerned, more sublime than your life, or more grievous than your departure from this world? I shed rivers of tears, and lamented to the point that for the first time I could hardly be called "philosophic" any longer. What, of all that pertains to funeral rites, was there that I left undone? But when I saw the numbers of bishops hastening to town I stopped short. I was astounded that you could not, in the first place, comprehend how to behave, and had not guarded yourself against the tongues of those who delight in calumniating the most upright. Secondly I was amazed you did not think that what was suitable for me was good enough for you, though from the very first God had associated us so closely together, such that we had all things in common, sharing the same belief, the same life. Thirdly—and I must say this too—I wondered if you thought promotions of this kind were more appropriate for those who were more pious, or for those who could command more power or appeal more to the crowd? So it was I heaved my ship around and came home. If you share my mind, determine to flee from this present tumult and from all evil suspicions. I shall come to visit your Reverence when matters have been decided, when it is the proper time. Then indeed I shall address you with even heavier reproaches.[11]

One wonders, reading this, if Gregory was outraged because Basil had deliberately sought the throne without any regard for his own claims? Gregory many times protests that he did not seek office, either that of a professor of rhetoric, or a priest, or eventually that of a bishop; but on as many occasions he tells his readers that the Athenians were ready to vote him a position in rhetoric, that his congregation demanded him as a priest, and that he was indeed the rightful bishop (of Constantinople). At times it is difficult to decide whether the constant stated desire to live in seclusion and quietness is genuine, or a rhetorical ploy to elicit the acclamation and affirmation of his hearers. To have sought for those plaudits, to have maneuvered for political position in the open forum through the crass political machinations of the

11. Ep. 40, PG 37.81-84; Gallay (1964), pp. 49-50.

day, was certainly for Gregory a vulgarism to which he would never stoop, but the principle of "acclamation" was, as we have seen, a classical rhetorical device he had learned from his teachers in Athens, and it was also a traditional practice of the Church when it came to episcopal selection. By acclamation, it was thought, the most venerable Christian would be charismatically acclaimed by the congregation as a whole, in a unity of spiritual wisdom, and thereby would be clearly designated as the Spirit's true candidate destined to assume the leadership of a Church. This is something that he seems to hold to idealistically, though with another part of his mind he is well enough aware that acclamation in the local context is far from the ideal of "spiritual recognition" to which he is appealing. If Gregory was agreeable to the claims of Basil to have some right to be recognized as "among the most pious" of the contenders, is it the case that he is also presuming (rightly or wrongly) that he might himself have some grounds for thinking his name could, and indeed might be, set forward in the Caesarean synod as a possible candidate?[12]

Perhaps this is why he is so shocked by Basil's self-promotions, and scandalized that his friend never once considered his own claims, whereas he himself was seeking to be scrupulously detached from the deliberations until the "best man had been chosen." Such idealistic sentiments are typical of him later in his time in Constantinople when he so signally fails to appreciate the whole range of political dirty tricks his opponents are ready and willing to play. It is certain, however, that after his most successful activity serving under Eusebios, and reconciling the alienated Basil to the local hierarchy, Gregory could have reasonably counted on some support in the Caesarean election. If, that is, the other contender had played the game in a "gentlemanly" way and not advanced his own cause so energetically.

Once Gregory knew that Basil had thrust him aside and was making a strong bid for his own interests, he soon came back to earth, and persuaded his father that the defense of Basil's candidacy was necessary for the preservation of the Nicene cause. He was already known as the author of a substantial treatise "Against Eunomios" and this made him attractive to a large doctrinal constituency, not only the Nicene homoousians, but a whole range of homoiousian and even homoian hierarchs who regarded the Neo-Arians as a bridge too far, and welcomed Basil's attack on them. As for his possible election to a see that had influence over the whole civil diocese of Pontus[13] the local Cappadocian hierarchs could not all be counted on for seeing in Basil the philosopher of their choice. Basil's episcopal support needed to come from farther afield, and Gregory helped to organize it:

> It was inevitable that the Holy Spirit should triumph, and this victory was indeed decisively won, for He raised up for Basil's consecration men from distant regions who

---

12. Fialon, *Étude historique et littéraire sur S. Basile* (Paris: 1865), p. 85; and Fleury (1930), p. 216. both considered this aspect, though it has not commanded subsequent attention.
13. Cf. Tillemont, *Mémoires* 9, p. 101.

were famous for their piety and zeal, and among them our new patriarch Abraham. I speak of course about my father.[14]

Here he chiefly means Meletios of Antioch[15] who advocated Basil's cause, and Eusebios of Samosata, the immensely charismatic Nicene heavyweight who from an early date had recognized the great worth of Basil and Gregory as defenders of the cause. But, in this text from Basil's *Funeral Oration*, he prioritizes his own family, to underscore for his audience his own role in the elevation of Basil to the throne. This is undoubtedly because his apparent vacillations had been noted unkindly by the circle of Basil's ascetical disciples (who were present for this *Funeral Oration*), and he needed to rehabilitate his standing among them.

Gregory wrote to Eusebios,[16] using his father's name at the head of the letter[17] to make it a formal canonical appeal of a Cappadocian Church, so that Eusebios' presence at the synod would be justified. The deacon Eustathios from the Nazianzus Church carried it to him in person. It was a hard journey, more than three hundred mountainous miles from Samosata to Caesarea, and in late autumn, but Eusebios saw the implications for the Nicene cause and came at the summons to support Basil. It would have taken at least a month to alert him of the need and accomplish his presence. This telling detail was not lost on Gregory.

And so he composed another two encyclicals, in his father's name, addressed to the synod gathering in Caesarea, acknowledging their canonical letter to the elder Gregory which informed him of the impending meeting but apparently in terms that took it for granted that because of his age he would not be in attendance to register his vote. At first he berated them for lack of respect to his seniority. He claimed they had deliberately kept him in the dark about the circumstances attendant on the election.[18] It was kind of them to inform him of the proceedings, he said with caustic irony, but they had omitted the important details of when the meeting would open. By this letter, Gregory signified that he would be able to raise canonical charges against them if they dared to proceed without the old bishop in attendance. Even in the next letter he sent[19] he made it clear that the old man was still unsure of whether or not he would be able to attend in person. By this means Gregory had secured the vital delays necessary to bring in outside assistance. The synod could not proceed safely without representation from the see of Nazianzus once its bishop had accused other colleagues of attempting to shut him out, and so he slowed them down in their

14. Orat. 43.37, PG 36.545.
15. Soon to be banished a third time (second time by Valens) in 371.
16. An ally of Meletios and leading pro-Nicene political activist. He too was involved in the policy of securing pro-Nicene bishops in sees, to counteract the imperial policy. Gregory held him in high esteem, and apologized to him later for not joining in wholeheartedly "until slightly later" with the selection process of Basil. Ep. 44.7, PG 37.93; Gallay (1964), p. 57.
17. Ep. 42, PG 37.88; Gallay (1964), pp. 53-54.
18. Ep. 43, PG 37.89; Gallay (1964).
19. Ep. 41, PG 37.84-85; Gallay (1964), pp. 51-53.

deliberations until Eusebios of Samosata could arrive. In his second letter the younger Gregory included a strong recommendation for Basil; registering his father's vote in advance to influence the discussions even before he arrived.[20]

The elder Gregory's scribe, the ghostwriter son, now touched ever so lightly on the fact that there were indeed others who were worthy of the post, though Basil was their chosen candidate. With what exquisite acid he etched his testimonial for his friend, acknowledging that he was the "best of those who were willing to stand":

> I am but an insignificant shepherd presiding over a tiny flock, the least of the servants of the Spirit. But grace is not restricted or circumscribed by geography, and thus let freedom of speech be afforded even to little ones... You are deliberating a matter of no ordinary importance... for our subject is the Church for which Christ suffered... I believe there is among you more than one who would be worthy of the highest rank, as befits the greatness of your city, and because it has been governed in times past by such eminent bishops. Nevertheless, among those you hold worthy of consideration there is one before whom I can prefer no one else. I mean our son the god-beloved priest Basil. I take God as my witness that here is a man whose life and doctrine are pure. He is the only one qualified (or at least the best available one) in both respects to stand against these prevailing times and the propaganda of the heretics.[21]

The attempt to win the episcopal vote by force of arguments at the Caesarean synod was a difficult task indeed, and needed a presence on the ground. Having delayed the start of the synod as much as he could, the old man had no choice but to make his way to the metropolis for the election, and so made provisions for the journey to meet Eusebios there. He summoned his carriage and climbed into it more dead than alive. Gregory himself, still refused to take part. It would be to his immense astonishment some weeks later that his father returned from the fray, triumphant in Basil's election, and jumping down from his carriage like a man restored to life.

> Though he was weakened by length of years, and brought low by disease, almost to the point of expiring, he braved the journey to bring the assistance of his vote, relying on the help of the Holy Spirit. In short, he was placed in his carriage like a corpse onto a bier, but came back home in the vigor of youth, head held high, eyes shining brightly.[22]

All the old man's despairing grief over Caesarios had been assuaged by the pleasures of engaging once more in a good fight. He was filled with new hopes, and his hopes, for better or worse, were now revolving around his son Gregory, as the sole surviving scion of the family, now perhaps to be established alongside the successful

20. He touched with humor on one of the main reasons advanced publicly against Basil's candidacy, one that skirted personal and doctrinal reservations people may have held—his "weakness of health," and he reminded them that in this instance they were looking for a doctor not an athlete.
21. Ep. 41, PG 37.85; Gallay (1964), pp. 52-53.
22. Orat. 43.37, PG 36.545-548.

and resourceful Basil who was, after all (had he not heard it many times?) his son's dearest friend and religious soulmate.

The resentment of that party of bishops who did not welcome Basil's election would remain a problem within Basil's diocese for years to come. Gregory tells us that it stemmed from smoldering resentments that sprung up in this time of the controversial selection process.[23] He also says that some of this ill-will grew out of matters of doctrinal disagreement, though he is very vague in what he means by this; seemingly using the idea only as part of his ultimate rhetorical strategy to present the rise of Basil as a victory for the Nicene cause, a "righteous" explanation of affairs that he adopted subsequently to make a positive value out of Basil's decision to bid for the throne. Basil's elevation was a move Gregory must have known would involve him in a far greater public role in the future than he perhaps wished for. His own ideal, hitherto, had been to fight for the Nicene cause only through words and local influences, and remain as hidden as he could in the cold weather of the Arian ascendancy, when little promotion could be expected from the court for a Nicene as dedicated and as public as himself, who had so often expressed himself theologically with far less circumspection than Basil. With Basil's election as archbishop, Gregory must have realized immediately that both their roles in publicly disputing with Arian teachers would be elevated to a far higher profile than even when Basil had attended synods as a companion of Eustathios and engaged in debate directly with Eunomios. Gregory was well aware that if he was unable to resist the canonically legitimate demands of Eusebios of Caesarea, when the latter had called him to speak as Church theologian in the metropolis, he would be far less able to resist the demands of such an archbishop as Basil.

That the younger Gregory played his part successfully enough in this enterprise, to the extent of writing his father's speech that carried many of the local bishops with it, and certainly by securing the charismatic presence of Eusebios of Samosata, undoubtedly indebted Basil to his family, but Gregory's initial censorious reaction to Basil's "ambition" had earned him the deep resentment of his colleague, and was the beginning of the bitterness that overshadowed all their remaining years. Basil regarded Gregory's reluctance as a betrayal and his friend's refusal to attend the synod as a slight to his honor, and would soon avenge that slight with one of his own. It is beyond doubt, however, that the elder Gregory had accepted the grateful thanks of the young Basil at his enthronement ceremony in much more than a symbolic sense, and must then have secured from Basil what he thought was the right of his own son—more public acknowledgment in the Church. A deal had been struck, and it is more than likely that the younger Gregory was still unaware of the terms. The payout would be made later in the form of Basil inviting his son for a ceremonial visit to the Caesarean Church.

23. Orat. 43.58. "They had not completely laid aside the resentment they felt at his election." PG 36.572.

It is clear enough, however, that the younger Gregory was not so willing to cooperate in the deal that his father had apparently made. When Basil did invite him to Caesarea, possibly in the early part of the year 371, to discuss some form of official post in the Caesarean clergy Gregory makes no bones about having turned down Basil's offer of an episcopal throne, and turned down the other offer of a position as leading priestly adviser to Basil. As far as he was concerned, honor had been saved on all sides. "Far from blaming me for this, Basil quite properly applauded my action."[24]

But the letters surviving from the time of the election, which were exchanged privately between himself and Basil, give a different picture. They do not support the smooth view of the affair which Gregory sets out to Basil's circle in the *Funeral Oration*. In the latter text, Gregory attributes his unwillingness to come and congratulate Basil in Caesarea, and then his belated arrival whereon he refused any offer of collaborative work, as merely his scrupulous desire to avoid the suspicions of "favoritism." Such an explanation is, once again, an attempt to put the best face on matters to Basil's family and friends, years later when the distance of the events allowed such smoothing. The more likely explanation of Gregory's reluctance in the immediate aftermath of the election is that Gregory had become, and with good reason, highly circumspect now that his friend had assumed real ecclesiastical power, and his natural ebullience was now beginning to be bolstered by canonical force. In a letter Gregory wrote shortly after Basil's election[25] he sends his congratulations, "for the candle has now been placed in the candlestick" and professes (three times no less) that he was glad to hear the news:

> I was glad to hear it. I confess so. And why should I not be glad seeing that the commonwealth of the Church lay in such a parlous state, and needed your guidance? Even so, I did not run to you straightway and I still shall not run to you, not even if you ask me to do so. In the first place I wish to guard your reputation so that you do not seem to be surrounding yourself with partisans, under the influence of who knows what stupid ambition, as your detractors might say. Secondly, I need time to re-establish myself in calmness, free of all ill sentiment.[26] So when will you come, perhaps you ask me? And how long will you hold back? Until God instructs me to leave, is the answer.

If Gregory was playing his old tactic of staying as far away as he could, however, and even when pressed to visit his new Archbishop in Caesarea had thought he had escaped by pleading reasons of conscience why he could not serve as a collaborator, the old man his father was not so ready to let Basil off the hook of his obligations. Basil recognized another slight in the way Gregory was lying low, and wrote to him complaining that as far as Gregory was concerned his "affairs" seemed no better than "grape-gleanings."[27]

24. Orat. 43.39, PG 36.549.
25. Ep. 45, PG 37.93; Gallay (1964), p. 58.
26. Exactly what, he does not specify, whether it is the envy of outsiders, as he has just been speaking of, or the bad feelings he still nurtures inside himself. The master orator is never ambivalent in his meanings without reason.
27. The detritus of the grape harvest that was not even fit for crushing into wine.

This now lost letter produced a splutter of outraged justification on Gregory's part[28] that this was hardly the case. How could Basil have possibly thought so? How could the paper have accepted such outrageous words from his pen?

This letter has traditionally been taken as evidence for the deep love Gregory continued to hold for Basil, and in this vein the reader is meant to take the rhetorical praises at face value. This is, however, even for Gregory who can lard his text with hyperbole at any excuse, something approaching the gilding of a lily. Is the excessive praise meant as an irony, pointing to the division that had come between them on the basis of Basil's desire to "elevate" himself above his friend? It is precisely this claiming of superior status that Gregory time after time refuses to admit in regard to Basil, and in texts that were more private than Basil's funeral encomium he confesses it explicitly:

> I do not know if it was more the fault of my sins
> which have often galled me bitterly...
> or whether the blame lies with you, best of men,
> for the arrogance that came to you with the throne.
> In other affairs, in our common scholarship for example,
> you would not have regarded yourself as so superior.
> In earlier times you did not hold such a view, dear friend.[29]

If Gregory's first letter declining attendance at the "wedding feast" was recognized by Basil to be a slight, the second letter, full of high-sounding praises, if read with an eye to the ironical,[30] instead of being taken literally as a profession of love (which of course in many ways it still is, though of love offended) might be a reaffirmation of that slight, explaining its reasons more clearly. In this case the hyperbolic praises can be read as an ironic way of referring to how great a man Basil has now become; so much so that his former friends have to resort to the flattering language of the obsequious courtier.

Basil had apparently accused him of no longer holding him in admiration, and of disdaining his friendship:

> Your words to me almost call forth a tragic declamation in reply. Do you not know me that well? Do you not know yourself? You who are the eye of the universe, its very voice, the pealing trumpet, the royal palace[31] of eloquence! Are your affairs a matter of small account for Gregory? But what other object of admiration could there be left on the face of the earth if Gregory did not admire you? There can only be one springtime among the seasons, one Sun among the stars, one heaven that encompasses all things, and one voice that bears all before it: only yours![32]

28. Ep. 46, PG 37.96; Gallay (1964), pp. 59-60.
29. *De Vita Sua*, vv. 395-402, PG 37.1056-1057.
30. Gregory's reference to Basil's letter as almost moving him to write "a tragedy" is a clue not to take the whole thing too literally, so too the reference at the end of the letter to the "rules of eloquence governing laudatory remarks."
31. Making a pun on his name, Basil.
32. Ep. 46, PG 37.96; Gallay (1964), p. 59.

All these rhetorical excesses, in my opinion, amount to an allusion to that old dictum that one pond cannot contain two male swans, and Gregory in this letter is piling it on thickly. The text, far from being used, as it has been for centuries, as evidence of the deep bond between the two men, is actually the first evidence we have of the major split that was to come between them, predating even the Sasima incident which was soon to follow, and perhaps explaining this too. His text finishes with an ebullient disdain for his old friend's new claims of supremacy:

> Are you annoyed because I continue to act as a philosopher?[33] Allow me to insist that this, and this alone, is more "elevated" than your words.[34]

Here he plays Basil's old trick that he himself had used in the past to keep Eusebios of Caesarea at arm's length by insisting that the vocation of monastic seclusion was to a large degree independent of episcopal interference. In his own continuing philosophical life, Gregory is implying, he remains free as his own man. They were brave words that he could not quite sustain but they were, in all likelihood, his real sentiments in the immediate aftermath of Basil's ascension to power. It also signaled that Gregory at least, continued to see the influence of the monastic circle as more detached from the ambit of episcopal governance than Basil had presumed. Perhaps Basil would not be able to command the allegiance of the ascetics as easily as he had done before his episcopal vocation intervened? There is an incident a few years later when it seems that monastic dissidents against Basil's rule thought Gregory was a suitable authority to whom they could send their appeal, and it is one of the causes for another flaring up of resentment between the two former friends, as we shall see.[35]

Gregory had put his foot down, insisting that he would stay where he was until God gave him leave to go. The command actually came in a rather more direct and peremptory fashion, with his father surely giving him his marching orders for Caesarea. But when his son returned, having wriggled out of accepting any post under Basil's dominion, the old man was forced to play another card. He would not let Basil escape from his obligation to him for services rendered in the Caesarean election. It is the old man's pressurizing insistence, undoubtedly, that is responsible for Basil insisting that Gregory the younger should assume an episcopal see, despite his own first instinct not to. The changing of Gregory's mind in regard to episcopal ordination should not be ascribed simply to Gregory's vacillatory character as several commentators have suggested. It came about by Basil and his father representing to him that a new crisis had arisen that called for his services. This much was true, but

33. Applying freedom of speech (*parrhesia*) before great men, and also continuing to live in retirement (unlike Basil who has abandoned that vocation so publicly).
34. Ep. 46, PG 37.96; Gallay (1964), p. 60. The phrase is difficult to render. I take it to mean that he resists the persuasions of Basil (king of eloquence he may be, etc.) on the grounds of having a higher calling, one that allows him not to be overawed by the "elevation" of Basil as archbishop.
35. Greg. Epp. 58-59, PG 37.113-120; Gallay (1964), pp. 73-77.

not the whole truth, and in the aftermath Gregory felt, once again, that he had been tyrannized and betrayed. His "elevation" to episcopal rank, he came to regard as a further deceit of Basil's, and far from overcoming the alienation that had begun to set in between them, it made the rupture final, still not healed by the time of Basil's death in 379, and still smarting when he posthumously delivered his former friend's funeral encomium three years after that in 382.[36] This was the Sasima affair, and it seems to me that Gregory always wondered after it, and was never quite sure, whether Basil had deliberately sought to dishonor him by this ordination.[37]

Basil and Gregory had already made themselves known publicly as the leading Nicene opposition to imperial orthodoxy as Valens was imposing it, not least in the time of the visitation of the Caesarean Church when Eusebios was bishop. Now, as news came back to them of Valens' continuing determination to secure doctrinal agreement in the East around the broad terms of the Homoian Arian formula, Basil was perhaps anxious to make Gregory stand beside him again. The news was highly alarming for the Nicene party. Gregory had been able to boast to Eusebios in 365 that a good strong detachment of Cappadocian youth would be enough to send the imperial entourage packing. Things had changed over the last five years. The report that came to them at this time gave good grounds for anxiety. The emperor Valens himself had been making a progress through the East, and this time appointing his own candidates in episcopal sees and enforcing political exile on opponents. As he moved through Bithynia some of the leading clerical resistance to his broad Arianizing strategy, totaling eighty in number, had been collected together on a ship which had mysteriously caught fire at sea. All were lost. Few believed it was anything other than a "planned accident." Gregory castigates Valens at this time in some of the harshest words he uses for imperial tyrants:

> That Christ-fighting emperor, and tyrant over the faith, came at us once more with an even greater wickedness and a more fierce assault, aware that he had to contend with a stronger opposition...

> While his first crimes were notorious, his later efforts directed against us were even more notable. What should I speak of first? Of the exiles? the flights we undertook? the legal deprivation of our goods? the plots both open and secretive? of the inducements offered when occasion allowed, or the violence when the blandishment of words did not suffice? Some who professed the orthodox faith, our faith, were cast out from the churches, while others were intruded in their place, men who accepted the wicked doctrine of the emperor, who sought after certification of their impiety, and composed

36. There is an emotional appeal to Basil who sat in the Church to hear Gregory's funeral oration for his father (Orat. 18) in 374, reminding him how much affection he held for him, but still passing rapidly over the events of his election to Caesarea as "best left to silence," and accusing Basil and his father openly of tyranny in regard to his own episcopal ordination. The reference clearly angered Basil, as Gregory mentions. Orat. 18.35, 37, PG 35.1032 and 1036.

37. Further on the subject see Giet (1941a); an account which sets out to put the best of all possible light on Basil.

even greater impieties.[38] Priests were set on fire in the midst of the ocean. Evil warlords no longer turned their attention to conquering the Persians, or subduing the Scythians or casting out some other barbarian nation, but carried their war to the Church, dancing on the altars, defiling the bloodless sacrifices with the blood of their human victims, even making mockery of the modesty of the virgins. And to what end? So that the patriarch Jacob might be driven out and Esau[39] (hateful even before his birth) could be intruded.[40]

As part of his overall attempt to revive the faltering Church policy of the late dynasty of Constantius, Valens determined another attempt would be made to scrutinize the credal professions of the Cappadocian churches in the course of his imperial progress through the province between 371 and 372. The fate of the Bithynian clergy who had been burned to death had sobered the Nicenes. This level of punitive action was arising now from a supposedly Christian emperor. The theological strategy the emperor applied was the usual one of insisting that local hierarchs signed their assent to the Homoian creed of Rimini as elaborated at the synod of Constantinople in 360.[41] If there was resistance the penalties this time would be of the order of exile or worse. The two Cappadocian friends would be temporarily reconciled over this common danger. Realizing the trouble which would be facing Basil, it is to his credit, and noteworthy, that Gregory did not take refuge in retreat, but courageously came forward again to assist the new archbishop of Caesarea, as once he and Basil had assisted Eusebios.

His father knew that he too, as bishop of Nazianzus, had now been marked down publicly as a Nicene propagandist; probably from the fact that he had defended Basil's cause so vigorously in the episcopal selection, alongside Eusebios of Samosata. Gregory the younger does not give much detail but refers generically to his father's defiance of Valens' threats at this time, and tells how the old man encouraged him to take up the fight alongside Basil who could not avoid being at the forefront as Archbishop and still surrounded by so many enemies in the local and international church. Gregory tells the story, addressing Basil who sat in the audience at his father's memorial liturgy, reminding his friend of the last time they had

38. He refers to the attempt to make homoian doctrine a standard for the East by forcing the episcopate to sign the Creed of Rimini, and also to the writings of the Neo-Arians Aetios and Eunomios. Aetios had been George of Cappadocia's deacon in Alexandria, and Eunomios was his own leading opponent in Constantinople in 380, and an enemy of Basil's family.
39. Gregory prioritizes in his general account of Valens' persecuting efforts the several exiles of Athanasios from Alexandria (only the last of which took place under Valens' order in the winter of 365-366), and the intrusion of the Arian George of Cappadocia which had taken place in 356 (his murder occurred in 361). Gregory sees Athanasios as the greatest of all the Nicene advocates and, accordingly, regards George as the worst of the Arians: their "right hand" as he calls him in the festal oration he later dedicated to Athanasios (Orat. 21).
40. Orat. 43.44-46, PG 36.553-557.
41. Convened by Constantius in 359, and even affirming the Nicene creed, but later manipulated by the Arian party to represent Eudoxios' theology of the Son's likeness to the Father (not "substantial identity with" as in the Nicene clausulae), and his radical subordination to God.

worked together in harmony and hope. He uses the image of the old bishop as if in the vigor of his youth when he let loose his hunting dogs in the field:

> What zeal he showed in the fight against the heretics when they came against us, because of the emperor's wickedness, intent on reducing us also to their power, adding even us to the list of those others whom they had almost completely beaten down. Here again he offered us no small service, both in his own person, and through our mediation as it were, for he cheered us on, loosing us like thoroughbred hounds against those wild beasts, and by this means exercising us in righteousness.[42]

Two events came closely together at this period. The first was Valens' visit to Caesarea en route to winter quarters in Syria, which happened at Epiphany 372.[43] The other was the emperor's decree, again early in 372[44] which divided the civil boundaries of Cappadocia. Gregory's own elevation as a bishop enlisted to serve alongside Basil emerges directly from both events.

In response to the impending visit of the emperor, Gregory seems to have once again moved to the Caesarean Church to offer his services in debate. It is a parallel to the role he fulfilled with such success in the time of the last imperial scrutiny of the Church in 365. I suspect that he acquitted himself so well on this second occasion when he was working directly on Basil's staff as priest rhetorician, that Basil thought he would be able to use him in a regular capacity as an administrative ally, overestimating Gregory's capacities. While he was a first class rhetorician serving with a capable man of action, he would never be so successful when expected to combine brilliant words with decisive political rule, as would be demonstrated several more times in his life. Gregory has described the events of the visit of Valens as part of his funeral panegyric of Basil, and here he has given Basil the central role. The story is so charged and luminous that it has remained for centuries one of the most memorable "icons" of Basil's life story. Valens sent as part of the advance guard a contingent of officers who commandeered the normal duties of the local Curia. When they scrutinized Basil's doctrine they found him to be a part of the alien Nicene party. The chief investigating officer was Modestus, the Prefect of the East. He summoned Basil for an arraignment soon after he arrived in Caesarea and refused at first to recognize him as a bishop,[45] probably indicating the emperor's initial intention to depose him.

The Prefect "roared like a lion" but Basil was like a martyr unflinching in his trial, as Gregory paints him. He was accused of "not honoring the religion of the emperor," and answered that if he followed the Arian tradition he would be guilty of worshiping a creature. Gregory depicts Basil before Modestus' tribunal as if he were a martyr from the old times confessing his faith before a persecuting pagan magistrate. The more the official "seethes and rages" the more Basil replies with calmness

42. Orat. 18.37, PG 35.1036.
43. Orat. 43.52, PG 36.561.
44. Cf. Hauser-Meury (1960), fn. 47, pp. 41-42.
45. Orat. 43.48, PG 36.557-560.

and superior dignity, as Christ did to the servant of the High Priest when he too was under the duress of arrest.[46] Basil is threatened with punishments for his insolence: confiscation, exile, torture, even death. All of these things lay within the power of the prefect, but Basil enjoyed the bold freedom of a confessor. The famous encounter deserves a retelling:

> "None of these things can hurt me," Basil replied. "How can that be true?" said the Prefect. Basil said to him: "It is because confiscation holds no threat for a man who owns nothing unless you want to have these few threadbare rags, and a few books which represent my whole substance. As for exile I do not know the meaning of it since no place can confine me, nor do I have any place that I can call my own,[47] either where I live now or anywhere else where I might be exiled. All belongs to God and I am merely a passing guest enjoying his hospitality. As for torture how can I suffer that since I barely have a body any longer? Unless you mean the right to inflict the first stroke, of course, for this alone is in your power. But death would be a welcome friend as far as I am concerned for it would send me to God, and for him alone I live, and order my existence, and for him I have died to the most part, and towards I him I have long been hurrying."[48] The Prefect was struck with amazement.[49] He said, "No man to this day has ever spoken to me like this, with such boldness."[50] "Perhaps you have never met a bishop before?" said Basil.[51]

Gregory notes that after this "trial" encounter the Prefect dismissed him, but not with the same threats, "but now with some degree of respect and deference."[52] Rousseau is certainly right in postulating that if Valens' first decision had been to remove recalcitrant Nicenes along his way, he realized after hearing the report of Modestus, that here in this city was a man of some nobility whose services they could use,[53] Nicene or not. Indeed, afterwards Valens confirmed him in office, supported his charitable building work in the Basiliad project,[54] and gave to him supervisory duties in the Church of Armenia, a sensitive political commission which he fulfilled

---

46. Jn 18:19-23.
47. Another depiction of Basil's Christ-like detachment. Cf. Mt 8:20.
48. Gregory here characterizes Basil as a new Paul in a composite of references: cf. Gal 6:14; Col 3:3; Acts 17:28; Phil 1:23.
49. Like Pilate before Christ's confession. Cf. Jn 19:8-10 (Gregory applies the image explicitly in Orat. 43.56); or the crowds in the face of Christ's miracles in the Gospels. The theme of amazement (*thauma*) relates to the epiphany of a divine charism, and is here being used by Gregory to depict Basil as a new holy man, full of divine grace and manifesting this in an epiphany. Connected with this is the manner in which Gregory depicts Basil as a new Elijah. When Valens and the prefect stand against him, they both fall under the judgment of God: the emperor loses a son (Orat. 43.54); and the prefect has to call on the holy man to deliver him from illness (Orat. 43.55).
50. Gregory depicts Basil as being the supreme example of a bishop exercising *parrhesia*.
51. Orat. 43.49-50, PG 36.560-561.
52. Orat. 43.51, PG 36.561.
53. Cf. Rousseau (1994), p. 174.
54. Theodoret, HE 4.16.

to the court's satisfaction.[55] Gregory's account of the conflict focuses on one meeting with the imperial prefect, though Gregory of Nyssa suggests there were two.[56] One of these might have occurred on another occasion, though it is clear that Nyssa is referring to the same incident as our Gregory in his main account. Gregory himself suggests, however, that the trial with Modestus was not the only clash that took place on this visit, and before Valens himself had taken residence in the city. He also speaks of an occasion, whose connection with the imperial visit of 372 is not very clear, when Basil was on the point of being sent into exile, and the emperor's son fell ill. Basil was among those who were summoned to attend to pray for him,[57] which suggests Valens was in the local region rather than at court in the capital, or in Caesarea itself.

In terms of the visit at Epiphany 372, Gregory refers to another protagonist, apart from Modestus, a court eunuch and high official called Demosthenes, whom he and Basil took great delight in disparaging.[58] The eunuch is nicknamed by Gregory "the cook Nabuzardan," since he was the head of the imperial household: and thus to the Cappadocian wits merely the "chief cook and bottlewasher" of the wicked king Nebuchadnezzar,[59] who was very "lacking" in key regards as far as they were concerned. He thus combines classical Roman disparagement of the eunuch with caustic rhetorical ridicule of his opponent's arguments. Later, in his rhetorical attacks on the Neo-Arians in Constantinople, he will return again to this Aristotelian idea that men of low social rank (however high they have risen) cannot possibly represent the truth since they have not that essential nobility of mind which "freedom"[60] confers. Noticeable in all the apologetic attacks of the Cappadocians on the Neo-Arians is this element of a landed aristocracy indignant in the face of a new class of socially-ascendant radical thinkers.[61] Demosthenes was, in fact, one of the leading

55. Cf. van Dam (1986). See also Rousseau (1994), ch. 8. passim.
56. Gregory of Nyssa, *Contra Eunomium* 1.119-146, ed., W. Jaeger, 1, pp. 62-67.
57. Gregory says he would have recovered too if Valens had not preferred the prayers of Arian bishops in his entourage. He still attributes a "partial" recovery to the boy, as soon as Basil prays for him. This probably took place at another occasion to the visit of 372 (Orat. 43.54, PG 36.564-565).
58. Basil, not generally renowned for his humor, seems to have borrowed Gregory's joke when he averted to a grammatical mistake Demosthenes had made in the course of his arguments: "An illiterate Demosthenes! Best leave theology to us and return to your soups!" (Theodoret, HE 4.16).
59. Cf. 2 Kgs 25:8. He was the commander who despoiled Jerusalem, defiled the temple, and carried off Judah into exile. Gregory knows that he is a leading Arian propagandist and so depicts him in this biblical code. The connection of Nabuzardan with the real Demosthenes is given by Gregory of Nyssa in his *Con. Eunomium* 1.139; cf. Rousseau (1994), pp. 351-353 for a good discussion of the actual order of the events of this period—which are probably telescoped in the texts, but possibly began with an appearance of Basil before Modestus two years previously.
60. Meaning the longstanding "possession of land" in Greek terms.
61. We shall return to the implications of the "social context" of the theology in the following chapter, when we review how Gregory engaged in apologetic with the Eunomian party in the capital.

theoreticians in the imperial entourage who argued the Arian theological cause as the party made its way eastwards; but as far as Gregory is concerned:

> Though he threatened us with his cook's knives, we soon sent him scurrying back to his kitchen fires.[62]

But Demosthenes did not forget his enemies so quickly, and would later avenge himself by securing the deposition of Gregory from the see of Nyssa on the grounds of financial mismanagement. He would remain a leading defender of the Arian cause. On this occasion he seems to have met his match in debate. The Cappadocian clergy acquitted themselves with honor and Valens, when he entered the city for the celebration of the feast of Epiphany presumably received a report from Modestus that caused him: "to start showing some philanthropy towards us. Indeed it was the beginning of our restoration."[63]

It is interesting how Gregory's account wholly cuts out the presence of the Arian bishops who were in attendance on Valens, and were undoubtedly part of the advance party who tested their ideas against the local hierarchs on the course of their progress eastwards. Euippios the Arian was one of that number and probably the leader of the party.[64] Gregory carefully describes only how the emperor attended Church when Basil was celebrating the liturgy, presumably when he too was present. The emperor, as custom dictated, brought forward the offerings to the clergy in the course of the Eucharist. Gregory tactfully masks the question that his orthodox readers might well want to raise: why did Basil not refuse communion with this notorious Arian? Instead he diverts his readers by telling the story emphasizing how Valens was so weakened by the sight of a new Samuel,[65] Basil, like an unshakeable pillar at the altar,[66] that his eyes grew dim and he felt dizzy: "a fact unnoticed by most of those present," as Gregory says, who is probably the "reader of the signs" in this case as one of the celebrating priests. But Valens is unable to hide his discomfiture, and when he approached the altar with the offerings "still uncertain whether Basil would receive them" he almost falls, "until one of those on the altar lent him a supporting hand."[67] It is a wonderfully vivid story, keeping the listener in a state of suspense to the end, and used by Gregory to demonstrate how God punishes heretical kings. The outcome was, of course, already determined long before Valens made his appearance in church. Gregory's suspenseful version of the tale is a most clever device of distracting our attention from the obvious facts that both Basil and Gregory felt happy enough on the occasion to enter into communion with Valens, an

62. Orat. 43.47, PG 36.557.
63. Orat. 43.53, PG 36.564.
64. Cf. Basil Epp. 68, 128 and 251. NPNF vol. 8, pp. 165, 197, and 291.
65. 1 Kgs 19:20. Orat. 43.52, PG 36.561.
66. Sozomen, HE 6.16.7, repeats Gregory's point that the sight of the liturgy as celebrated by Basil greatly impressed Valens.
67. Orat. 43.52, PG 36.561-564.

heretical Arian, at their liturgy. If they accepted his offerings they certainly admitted him into the sanctuary (the imperial liturgical prerogative) where Gregory depicts him as listening to the divine discourse of Basil. Knowing he has let the cat out of the bag in some respects, Gregory then puts the blame squarely onto Valens: since he had entered into communion with the orthodox he should have retained his happy state,[68] though as everyone knows he soon declined from that state of grace, incurring the wrath of God once again when his infant son Galates subsequently fell prey to a fatal illness that not even the prayers of Basil could avert for long.[69] Gregory demonstrates some real sympathy for Valens in his grief over the young prince, comparing him to the humbled sinner David who poured out his prayers as never before. But in the end his account is concerned primarily with the depiction of Valens' as the Saul who falls from grace, contrasted with Basil as the Samuel who stands firm, and so he concludes with a moral on the way in which heterodoxy defeats the whole purpose of prayer: "If only he had not mingled salt water with fresh," Gregory says, and had not invited Arian bishops alongside Basil to his son's bedside, God would have perhaps heard those prayers.[70]

The young prince died soon after he was baptized. The hapless emperor would have other sorrows to bear before his wretched end, burned to death by Gothic insurgents on the fields of Adrianople in a few years' time. For the Cappadocian Nicenes, all told the visit had gone off better than anyone could have dared hope, but it had been a close shave. Valens' officers had brought with them papers necessary for all the exiles of recalcitrant bishops. But after the encounter Basil received marks of high esteem and confidence, and Gregory (though he does not tell the reader) most likely received some measure of reward for his own successful appearance as a rhetor before the emperor. Not long after this, and it is surely not coincidental, his brother Caesarios received a high appointment from Valens, as imperial Treasurer in Bithynia.[71] Most of the tracks of this patronage have been deliberately covered over in the dust because of Valens' theological stance, and Gregory's usual custom of "passing over in silence" whatever is not fitting, as he puts it,[72] but it seems obvious that Basil and Gregory benefitted from the emperor's recognition of their worth as leading provincial clerics. They were not only spared deposition but gained some measure of imperial patronage, and some breathing space for a while.

---

68. Orat. 43.53, PG 36.564. "In a sort of a way he entered into ecclesial standing with us again and came behind the altar veil."
69. Orat. 43.54, PG 36.564-565.
70. Orat. 43.54, PG 36.565. The point is taken up by a number of other Nicene historians following Gregory's lead—the child's recovery was attributable to Basil's prayers, his subsequent death was attributable to his (Arian) baptism: Theodoret, HE 4.16; Sozomen, HE 6.17; Socrates, HE 4.26.
71. Orat. 7.15, PG 35.773.
72. Cf. Orat. 8.1, PG 35.792. "We shall give praise where it is merited, and pass over in silence those things that deserve silence."

In regard to the imperial division of the boundaries which was promulgated early in 372, the problems arising from this came largely in the aftermath of Valens' departure when local bishops who had little love for Basil saw it as a means of reducing his sphere of influence, though it was originally a fiscal and political move that was not primarily related to any ecclesiastical strategy in its conception.[73] Anthimos of Tyana quickly made a move to declare his own see the ecclesiastical capital of the new province of Cappadocia Secunda. Caesarea and Tyana were the only two possible contenders for metropolitan status, and the principle of the civic capital of the region assuming the status of the ecclesiastical capital seemed a logical enough one to follow, though it was by no means as yet the "natural" conclusion it would later become in Christian Byzantine practice. Anthimos, therefore, was making a definite play for the advancement of his own city, by refusing ecclesiastical allegiance to Basil.

Gregory suggests on occasions that there was a theological motive behind all of this, and perhaps Basil had so represented it to him at the outset. But his long-term view seems to drop the religious significance of this dispute, and when it was settled he entered into reasonably smooth relations with Anthimos, as did Basil himself once the initial row subsided. At that time the accusations of heresy were quietly dropped by both sides. Gregory claims that Anthimos had at first justified his refusal to send supportive taxes to the metropolitan at Caesarea on the grounds that it was not righteous to fund heretics. If this was indeed his position, and Anthimos attracted a large body of support among those bishops who were theologically hostile to the Nicene cause, then the division of boundaries allowed for a new drawing up of the map of theological influence, and one in which the ascendancy of Basil and his Nicene monks would be set back. This, of course, would seem to put Anthimos in the ranks of the Arian party, which it makes it very unclear why Gregory and Basil later enter into relatively friendly relations with him.[74]

The likely explanation of this puzzle which has long been a subject of notice,[75] is that the theological lines were at this period, sufficiently fluid in the provinces as to allow all but the Nicene Homoousianians, and the Neo-Arian party of Anomoians, to blend in and out of shades of opinion, seeking the kind of consensus of broad agreement the imperial policy was looking for. If relations had already been exacerbated by other things, such as a political opportunity for civic advancement, it would have made sense for Anthimos to play a theological card accusing Basil of "extremism" in terms of his homoousian beliefs, so that he could be ousted by the emperor, and

73. The emperor had initially selected Podandus to be the new metropolitanate of Cappadocia Secunda (Basil, Ep. 74), whose bishop had no known theological difference with Basil. It was Basil's letters of protest that probably caused the second thought of Tyana as the alternative metropolitanate. His strenuous defense of Caesarea's civic rights could only have increased his popular standing in his town.

74. Cf. Basil, Ep. 210.5. NPNF vol. 8, p. 250.

75. See Cox (1851) (ET of Ullmann), p. 121, n.1.

Anthimos himself could emerge as the leading hierarch of Cappadocia. Such a view would explain Gregory's later conclusion that the incidents of religious conflict over the division of the ecclesiastical boundaries were at bottom a sham:

> Souls were set forward as the reason for all this, but the real motivation was love of power. Though I hesitate to confess it, it is rents and taxes that shamefully drive on the whole world.[76]

In his *Funeral Oration* for Basil, however, Gregory is constantly aware that he is speaking to Basil's immediate circle, whose own collective memory of the incidents was not necessarily that of Gregory himself. To this audience he repeats the party line that the division of boundaries was yet another attack on the orthodoxy of their great leader. But even here[77] he says that Anthimos' ascription of heterodoxy to Basil was something the man did as often as he wished to make a capital gain:

> As a result of this dispute the churches were reduced to an even worse state of affairs and rent into factions and parties...

> What really set [Anthimos] into a fury was to see the taxes from Taurus passing on to Basil in front of his eyes. He had set his heart on collecting the offerings from the shrine of St Orestes[78]...What specious reasons he set forward, pretending that spiritual children, and care of souls, and the teachings of the faith were his concerns. Such things were facile inventions and merely masked his real venality; so too was his argument that tribute should not be rendered to heretics. Anyone who fell into the category of his enemies he labeled a heretic.[79]

Basil fought from the outset to have this policy of division reversed, representing his city, somewhat histrionically, as if it had overnight fallen into ruin and decay.[80] One of his ideas to reverse his loss of ecclesiastical support, and to counter the negative effect of the number of his suffragans on whom he still felt he could not rely, was to expand that base of suffragan bishops on whom he could rely implicitly. If, in the process, he elevated some towns to the status of new episcopal sees that refused to admit Anthimos' larger claims to act as Metropolitan of Cappadocia Secunda, so much the better. Gregory passes off this policy of emergency ordinations as the leading idea Basil had for restoring peace to the Church and extending its missionary affectiveness, though it was at best a holding action, and one that caused as much friction within the Nicene camp as it did without:

> The holy man of God [Basil], truly now a metropolitan of the heavenly Jerusalem...turned this dissension in the churches into a happy cause of their increase, for he

---

76. *De Vita Sua*, vv. 460-463, PG 37.1061.
77. Orat. 43.58, PG 36.572.
78. A *Martyrion* chapel and site of pilgrimage at the foot of Mt Taurus.
79. Orat. 43.58, PG 36.572. One suspects the last reference is a whimsical reminiscence of the hot temper tantrums that had passed between Anthimos and Gregory himself both at Sasima and when he had returned, afterwards, to Nazianzus, and started the process of reconciliation with this leading hierarch of his immediate region.
80. Basil, *Letters* 74-76. NPNF vol. 8, pp. 168ff.

settled this disaster in the most happy way possible by creating many more bishops for the country.[81]

This would be a political decision that would impact Gregory's life dramatically. Gregory introduces it at Basil's memorial liturgy with words that show his own pain has not been erased by the ten years that have passed, and which demonstrate quite clearly that his own conduct at that time caused Basil permanently to alter his view of his friend. Because of what transpired here, Gregory would no longer be one of the trusted inner circle of Basil's confidants afterwards, and this caused him more pain, perhaps, than anything else in his life apart from the death of his brother. He suggests, (although here he is setting out to win back the sympathy of his audience and thus to regain the good favor of Basil's Cappadocian circle to whose ambit he was returning permanently after 381) that the loss of Basil's trust was a fundamental cause of his own loss of self-esteem and his consequent inability to succeed in the public life of the Church.[82]

> I have to say that in this plan of his[83] I was merely an afterthought. While in regard to everything else about this man I stand in awe, more so than I can express, on this subject I cannot give any praise (I admit my feeling about the affair and it is not as if it is unknown to many here), for he became estranged towards me and lost faith in me, and time has not effaced the sorrow of it.[84]

Basil, knowing that the division of his province had further disrupted his restless suffragans (many of whom were seeking an opportunity to dissociate from his administration), called in as many old loyalties as he could think of. He would ordain Gregory's cousin, Amphilokios in the following year 373 for the province of Lycoania, but turned to his own immediate family, ordaining his younger brother Gregory as bishop of Nyssa, and conspiring with Gregory's father to make sure that his son would be installed as bishop of Sasima.[85]

Gregory's response to the whole affair of his consecration to Sasima has, over the centuries, provided fodder for interpretations of him as a vacillating dilettante. The image needs some cautious reassessment. Rousseau continues the old trend in a recent work on Basil, somewhat unjustly describing the incident as superlatively demonstrative of Gregory's "capacity for muddled thinking."[86] Gregory's response, however, is a classic and perfectly understandable reaction when one considers all

---

81. Orat. 43.59, PG 36.572-573. This is expressed so positively because Gregory of Nyssa is surely present for the Oration, who was one of those new bishops so created at the time; but it has to have been spoken with some degree of irony, given the way he describes his own part in this plan of Basil's as an absolute disaster.
82. He is speaking from the context of his recent expulsion from Constantinople.
83. His consecration to Sasima.
84. Orat. 43.59, PG 36.573.
85. Now Tirhan/Hasankoy. There is a ruined nineteenth-century Orthodox church and a few ancient fragments around it. It is still a desolate crossroads.
86. Rousseau (1994), p. 235.

the elements involved. If he made a fatal mistake it was to be once again led by his father's insistence to trust in Basil's explanations of the necessity of assuming this public duty for the defense of the Church; an office which he did not particularly want, though a rank which he (rightly) felt ought to be his within Christian circles. When he discovered he had been embroiled in a plan that had little to do with the defense of the Church, and everything to do with the defense of Basil's honor at the cost of his own, the Hellene aristocrat in Gregory responded perfectly normally.

Basil wrote to Gregory lamenting the dreadful attacks that were being made on him by this division of boundaries. The representation of Valens' bureaucratic moves as part of the wider theological drive against the Nicenes sufficiently impressed itself on Gregory to elicit an offer to come to Caesarea and stand by Basil's side as a sure ally among false friends. Basil seems to have replied that he did not need Gregory's presence again, but would come to Nazianzus himself for business.[87] In a mood of optimism and good humor Gregory wrote to his cousin Amphilokios, ostensibly to ask for vegetables for the feast on Basil's arrival, but mainly to encourage him in his newly chosen life of seclusion as an ascetic.[88] After Basil's arrival in Nazianzus, consulting with Gregory the Elder, he had little difficulty in persuading him that his son was needed in the defense of the Church against an Arianizing emperor who was now threatening the "whole collapse" of Cappadocia.[89] The episcopal elevation would also satisfy the old man's desire to see his son advanced through the Church in civic and political circles once more and perhaps weaned away from the ambit of the "zealot" monks for whom he had little regard. The combined influence of the two, against Gregory's better judgment, proved irresistible. His appearance as a bishop would allow him full access to the councils and debates which would be critically necessary for any work alongside Basil striving to keep his seat in Caesarea, and from which his presence could be proscribed by even a small complaint from the least of the suffragan bishops who were hostile. Priests, deacons, and monks had no automatic right to join the deliberations of the hierarchs. Gregory had to work, if he really wished to work alongside Basil, as a bishop among bishops. I suspect that it was something like this nexus of arguments which was used to sway Gregory. The idea that he might actually have to dwell in the see may not have really been stressed. That would come later after the excitement of the imperial visit had died down, and practical realities clouded the ideal picture. It was, in my estimation, the offer of Sasima as if it was a coadjutant episcopal post alongside Basil in Caesarea as the Church orator (a kind of sharing of the throne of the metropolitan see) that induced Gregory to accept the charge. And it was precisely when he found

87. Cf. *De Vita Sua*, vv. 386-390 (and ibid., vv. 386-525 for the whole Sasima adventure), PG 37.1056.
88. Epp. 25-27, PG 37.60-61; Gallay (1964), pp. 33-34.
89. Such is Basil's overview of affairs in his *Letters* 74-76, and in his general report to supportive foreign bishops on the state of Cappadocian Christianity.

out that Basil had no intention of allowing him to stay in the capital alongside him but actually expected him to take up more or less permanent residence in Sasima, that the scales dropped from his eyes.

Canonically, the metropolitan archbishop's command to a priest to assume an episcopal office, in concord with the agreement of the local bishop who had charge of that priest's ministry, and allied with the local acclaim of the Christian people and city Curia, (which would have followed Gregory the Elder's directions), all left Gregory with little real choice. It was either ordination or flight. He had tried flight once before, after his priestly ordination, but was not able to sustain a self-imposed exile then. Now, the assumption of episcopal duties at Sasima might not be so bad after all. It was a town he must have known in advance. It cannot have been the case that his visit to claim the town as its new bishop was the first time he had set eyes on it, a visit which then made him realize what was in store for him, for Sasima was a place he must have passed through innumerable times before. It was a major staging post, the cross-road division of three important land routes through Cappadocia, and it lay only thirty two miles from his own town.[90] His frequent and disparaging references to the miserable nature of the place could have been uttered by anyone about his own town of Nazianzus, or indeed about most of the small settlements of Cappadocia, over which he can be patriotically defensive elsewhere when he wants to be. The castigation of Sasima needs to be contextualized very particularly, for in the *De Vita Sua* he is consciously addressing the population of Constantinople after his loss of the most prestigious see in the Roman world, and deliberately offsetting the specific charge that the Egyptian bishops had raised against him—that he was already "wedded to" Sasima as its legitimate bishop. It is his constant intention in this long, late autobiographical poem to represent to an aristocratic audience at the capital that he was not really the bishop of Sasima at all, and that the whole thing had only been a crack-brained provincial dispute over borders, pennies, and donkeys.

At the time these events were taking place, however, whatever his misgivings[91] might have been, the ordination proceeded. Gregory consistently describes it as a "forced" ordination. Most commentators have taken him metaphorically in this regard, seeing the tyranny as that of strong-minded individuals (his father and Basil) persuading him, though most reluctant, to be advanced to the episcopate. There is much in this that rings true, for though Gregory did not particularly see himself occupying the day-to-day practicalities of an episcopal function, he certainly sees himself in terms of "rank" at the highest level in the Church, and is half attracted to the office of Christian bishop as it was emerging in the fourth century as an open acknowledgment of his status, but also more than half repelled by the idea of having to be associated with the other types who composed the body of Christian leaders.

90. Cf. Ramsay (1890), p. 293. It was the junction of the roads from Tyana, Archelais and Mokissos.
91. "I had bent my neck, not my will." *De Vita Sua*, v. 487, PG 37.1063.

These aristocratic feelings of dismay and disgust at the type of demagogue who had taken over the office of bishop in his day, are given full vent when he commits his pain to paper after his ejection from Constantinople,[92] but they are sentiments increasingly close to him from his earliest experiences of Cappadocian Church politics, and closely related to the more bitter personal experiences of trying to initiate his own episcopal career in Sasima.

The other side of his frequent references to a forced ordination ought not to be entirely subsumed into the allegorical, because he tells us elsewhere, almost incidentally, that his father was entirely in agreement with the principle of compulsory ordinations. Gregory the elder had participated in the forcible consecration of Eusebios of Caesarea,[93] even when the military were required to hold down the candidate who was shouting out his resistance. When the imperial authorities subsequently heard an appeal from several of the bishops involved in that consecration for its annulment on the grounds of compulsion (in their case meaning of the bishops by the towns-people) the elder Gregory refused to allow the invalidity of the process. In his own case, then, knowing what his father was capable of, and indeed what he had already done in regard to ordinations, Gregory probably decided to save his own dignity. If physical force was not actually used in his own consecration, he was aware that it would have been if he proved recalcitrant.

He exercises his resistance in the only way he felt safe—by defiant words even in his submission. The office of bishop was supposed to call forth two supreme charisms from the candidate so elevated: the first was mystagogy, where the new bishop would preside over the Church rites and definitively represent pure doctrine,[94] the second was *parrhesia*, or boldness of speech, where the new bishop would have to speak up on behalf of his congregation and city in the face of the powerful, without fear of the consequences. Gregory wittily applies this principle of episcopal *parrhesia* in his first episcopal sermon—and criticizes the two powerful men who have just consecrated him: Basil and his father.

Bernardi has set the order of the appearance of the first episcopal orations as: 10 followed by 9.[95] He sees *Oration* 10 as preached before the episcopal ordination and 9 coming a few days later when Gregory addressed his father and Basil who were both

---

92. Cf. McGuckin, "Autobiography as Apologia," *Studia Patristica* (2001).
93. And seems to approve of, supporting his father's role in this other tyrannical consecration, and using his father's absolute refusal to admit there was anything wrong in it, as evidence of his noble-mindedness. Cf. Orat. 18.33, PG 35.1028-1029.
94. This is why, for the first time, Gregory becomes publicly specific in regard to his theological teachings in his episcopal orations, and immediately boldly announces himself (through his orations' doxologies) as a defender of the full deity of the Son and of the Spirit, and thereby an opponent to a range of famous theologians such as the obvious Arians Eudoxios and Eunomios, but also Eustathios of Sebaste (with whom Basil did not break ranks until two years later and only because Eustathios attacked him first).
95. Bernardi (1968), pp. 113-116.

present in the church. This order seems problematic to me, for Orat. 10.4 clearly supposes his consecration had already taken place, and while *Oration* 10 can be read as certainly addressed to Basil and his father, nothing in it makes us presume that Basil was in the church to hear it. It could as easily have been sent on as a token of reconciliation afterwards. For these reasons I suspect that the traditional order assumed by the Benedictine editors is the correct one, with *Oration* 9 being the homily delivered the day after his ordination, and 10 the homily delivered when he returned after his panicked retreat. *Oration* 11 comes somewhere less determinately in the middle. It has been suspected by Weijenborg that *Oration* 11 is inauthentic[96] but his arguments against this particular piece are met by everything that Bernardi had already demonstrated fourteen years previously, that although the oration is a "false one" in that it is a composite piece put together in the editor's studio,[97] it is still authentically Gregorian in terms of style and content. It is welded together from parts of different orations he gave, most likely from this same period we are considering. *Oration* 11 begins with an address to Gregory of Nyssa, and halfway through mutates into a homily at a great festival in honor of the martyrs. *Oration* 12 finishes this series of early episcopal addresses showing us that he has returned home to Nazianzus after a recent period of self-imposed exile.

I think the original sequence, therefore, was *Oration* 9, followed by *Oration* 11 in its second part (the homily on the martyrs' feast, which I think might have been from the shrine of St Orestes[98] to which Basil had taken him on his first "public appearance" as a bishop). *Orations* 10 and 11, part 1, come after this. *Oration* 10 is a speech of apologetic for his flight to the local congregation at Nazianzus where he mainly appeals for the consideration and allegiance of the monks of the region as being a monk at heart forced into episcopal service unwillingly. It is comparable in purpose to the *Apologia After his Flight* when he became a priest, but written with infinitely more poise and assurance. *Oration* 11, part 1, is a writing-up of an address delivered when Gregory of Nyssa came to try to reconcile Gregory to Basil when Gregory had returned home after his most recent "flight."[99] Finally comes *Oration* 12, where Gregory himself tries to initiate a reconciliation after he had agreed to be based as bishop in his father's church at Nazianzus, part of the eirenical settlement he reached with the triangle of involved bishops, Anthimos of Tyana, his father, and Basil. This nexus of texts does not make entirely clear the order of events immediately related to his ordination, although those events themselves are relatively clear, especially when one consider the amplifying details provided in the autobiographic poetry,[100] and the *Funeral Oration* for Basil.

96. Weijenborg (1982).
97. More likely that of Nicobulos his great-nephew and first editor than Gregory himself.
98. If it comes from the period after his ordination it might also reflect the pilgrimage shrine in Seleukia where he took refuge, but it is less likely as it makes no reference at all to Thekla.
99. Gallay sees *Oration* 11 all of a piece and sets it in the context of a martyr festival at Nazianzus. Gallay (1943), p. 115.
100. *De Vita Sua*, vv. 439-485, PG 37.1059-1062. Orat. 43.58-59, PG 36.569-573.

Gregory's episcopal ordination took place, most likely, in the great Church at Nazianzus which his father had built from his own fortune. It was a beautiful octagonal building with a double-storied row of colonnades and outside statuary in surrounding porticoes; one of the biggest churches in the region[101] with an adjacent *martyrion* shrine. The ordination rite involved the other bishops laying hands on him before the altar and anointing his head with chrism as a sign of the "unction of the Spirit." Then he was divested of his old clothes and dressed in new high priestly vestments of a linen tunic and the miter of the high priest, before being led around the sanctuary of the church by the bishops, and brought to sit alongside Basil on thrones set around the altar. At this point the newly consecrated gave a short symbol of his faith.[102] Gregory repeats all these elements in *Oration* 10.[103] His profession of faith makes it clear that he defends the incarnation of God and Man in Jesus, who "anointed the humanity with godhead" and thereby reconciled the world "by making the two natures as one." Jesus is "our God and Lord." The Spirit of God has "set us in this present ministry," but interestingly he goes no further in describing the status of the Spirit or any theological character associated with the Spirit, beyond the most basic traditional ascription of its "sanctificatory" role. It is the last example in Gregory of that "spiritual economy" in episcopal preaching, for which he will later blame Basil. His subsequent episcopal orations soon afterwards show him making the plunge and ascribing full divine status to the Spirit of God in the doxologies that conclude his own preaching. It was this pneumatological clause that was now emerging as the distinctive mark of the high Nicene homoousian party, before which Gregory was making a bid to be recognized as an intellectual leader (and perhaps to Basil's increasing annoyance, "the" intellectual leader).

The text of *Oration* 9 refers to his ambivalence over the ordination, but it also demonstrates clearly enough that he accepted the episcopal charge with a forwardlooking sense of responsibility, and conscious that he had been publicly elevated. He says he feels overwhelmed by the anointing of the Spirit, and laments more than rejoices.[104] But he goes on to justify this attitude in terms of great figures of the scriptures who had also received the Spirit of God, and had been raised up as prophets or kings. He is conscious of having been admitted into the ranks of the prophetic teachers of the ways of God by virtue of his anointing, but fears in case he should decline from his status, as Saul did who fell from grace.[105] He fears for himself, for human nature is mutable and vacillatory, a common theme of his "philosophy."[106] He summarizes his condition in a brilliantly memorable image: he senses the new duties to which the Spirit of God has anointed him

---

101. Cf. Orat. 18.39, PG 35.1037.
102. The elements have remained standard in the Eastern Church ordination rituals for centuries.
103. Orat. 10.4, PG 35.829-832.
104. Orat. 9.1, PG 35.820.
105. Orat. 9.2, PG 35.821.
106. Orat. 9.2, PG 35.821; cf. Ellverson (1981).

and feels like a child looking out on a lightning storm, at once terrified and fascinated by the beauty, elated yet quivering.[107] The obligation to take charge over a flock constitutes the shepherd as the governor of a real people who will require strong leadership.[108] He appeals for help to the two bishops who have elevated him, Basil and his father, that they would assist him in learning the scope of his new duties.[109] Resuming his image of the terrifying storm he uses *parrhesia*[110] to tell them the truth which he feels and already fears, that he needs support, because: "we lie in the midst of the tempest and are cast in every direction by the force of the waves."[111] He tells Basil, face to face, that though he might have been "beaten down."[112] even so he was never "persuaded" of the advisability of accepting this episcopal charge, only forced into it,[113] a strange, compulsive, thing which had never before been part of their relationship as friends. The present times of stormy seas are largely caused by the "stupidity of the bishops who surround us."[114] He needs his mentors to teach him the art of shepherding, and that includes, as he can already tell and pointedly refers to, the necessary "arts of war."[115]

His discussions with Basil before the ordination must, therefore, have already focused on the problems that were brewing with Anthimos of Tyana. Basil wanted Gregory to occupy a see dividing the two rival metropolitanates that could command the roads, and so act as a filter for any tribute or official intelligence that was passing down the highway. He determined to take him to see the problem at first hand and probably immediately afterwards intended to install Gregory in his new city. First they would attend the martyr festival at the shrine of St Orestes to give Gregory his public epiphany as the latest sign of Basil's continuing archiepiscopal jurisdiction. Being the first year that the boundary division was in force, Basil was determined to act as if his rival had no rights at all. To take Gregory in his entourage to appoint him to Sasima, and to attend the festival (and claim his rights to tithes from the offerings there) was a deliberate provocation to Anthimos and the latter was forced into a showdown in his own city. The shrine of St Orestes was a popular *martyrion* that drew large pilgrim crowds for the festival and fair. It was situated at foot of Mount Taurus, adjacent to the city of Tyana. If *Oration* 11, part 2 is from this period, it is possibly the Oration that Gregory delivered on the occasion of the festival itself. It is a generic speech on the correct religious way of

---

107. Orat. 9.3, PG 35.821.
108. Orat. 9.3, PG 35.824.
109. Orat. 9.4, PG 35.824.
110. "I pray you to take what I am now saying in a 'philosophical manner'." Orat. 9.4, PG 35.824.
111. Orat. 9.4, PG 35.824.
112. Orat. 9.4, PG 35.824. "You have me under your hands. I who once was unvanquished am now overcome."
113. Orat. 9.5, PG 35.825.
114. Orat. 9.6, PG 35.825.
115. "Battles to be undertaken for the safety of the flock." Orat. 9.5, PG 35.825.

observing feasts, and not allowing oneself to be overcome by the secular revels. His theme is that "purification" is more in order than good eating.[116] It could not have been a popular message, and maybe it was aimed sideways at Anthimos, whom elsewhere[117] he describes as a grasping character. He appeals here, however, not to the sympathy of the crowds at all, but once again to the monks present for the festival,[118] on whom he knew he could count for support. Basil must have brought with him a monastic contingent from Caesarea to give substance to his assertion of rights, and the local ascetics from the Nazianzus region can also be presumed to have been in attendance.

Gregory moves on at the end of this oration to declare boldly, for the first time as a bishop, the neo-Nicene agenda, that those who "war against the Spirit"[119] are those pseudo-Christs mentioned in the scripture[120] who would deceive the Church at the last times. They are worse than the enemies of the Church who "make war from the outside" (the hostile authorities). His ultimate point is that the martyrs represent a purer faith, being closer to the nascent source of the tradition and those who imitate them are, by implication, themselves closer to the pure sources of Christ's doctrine.[121] It is an out and out claim that the monastic party of Neo-Nicenes in attendance with him, who affirm the deity of the Holy Spirit, are the true arbiters of the Christian faith. This is an extraordinary claim in its context, given that Basil was beside him, who was still trying to keep in association with Eustathios of Sebaste whose own theology was dead set against this. Perhaps Gregory was intending to embarrass Basil into an open and public statement of this faith by his strong suggestion in public that just as the ancient martyrs were called upon to confess their belief in Christ without fear of the consequences, even if this meant death, so too people of the present day ought to confess their belief in the Spirit of God openly and courageously. If this contextualization of his meaning is correct, it is the first example of Gregory pressurizing Basil to make explicit his pneumatology, a trend that can thus be observed from the very beginning of Gregory's episcopal ministry, and something that will continue to grow in volume. Basil would not be induced to publish his views on the subject until 375, two years after his breach with Eustathios.[122] This gathering of a core of strong-minded neo-Nicene monastics around him is a strategy that can be discerned from the outset of Gregory's episcopate. Soon he will use it to pressurize Basil even more,

116. Orat. 11.5, PG 35.837.
117. Orat. 43.58, PG 36.572.
118. So his address to them as "brothers" who have to ensure the fitting observance of the day. Orat. 11.6, PG 35.840.
119. He is one of those who makes up the designation of the anti-Trinitarians as "Pneumatomachians" or Spirit-fighters. Orat. 11.6, PG 35.840.
120. Mk 13:22; 1 Jn 2:19-20; 1 Jn 4:1-3; 2 Pet 2:1-3.
121. Orat. 11.6, PG 35.840.
122. In the *Treatise On the Holy Spirit*; and Epp. 223, 224, 226, 244, all from circa 375.

coming at him in terms of his pneumatology and voicing the concerns of the monks, in the guise of their favored episcopal patron. As Basil had done to Eusebios of Caesarea, Gregory now begins to do to Basil, and this too goes along way to explain the bitterness of their falling out.

The ascetic entourage in attendance at the St Orestes' fair shows that Gregory and Basil did not come unprepared. But this was home ground for Anthimos. He did not need to rely on ascetics to defend his interest as he could summon a large array of interested parties to defend the new claims of his city, since he was spear-heading its potential bid for civic independence from Caesarea. So, after the festival was over, the real war broke out. Basil sequestered the usual tithes for the Arch-bishop, and was leading off the train of mules when Anthimos sent after him a much larger group, a "gang of thugs" as Gregory describes them.[123] After an undignified scuffle, in which Basil and Gregory's party were trounced, the mules bearing the col-lections were taken back to Tyana, and Basil was shown who was the effective ruler of the Christian churches of Cappadocia Secunda. The intention to install Gregory at Sasima was deferred for another day, and Gregory seems to have made his way back to Nazianzus disgusted by the whole event, but with instructions from Basil to take the town of Sasima at an early opportunity and thwart Anthimos' pretensions from that station.

It is probable that Gregory never once entered Sasima as its bishop, though he already knew it well enough to caricature the town in the most disparaging terms. This was many years later, in a poem that was meant to prove to a legally-minded audience in the capital that he had never really been formally installed (anywhere, he claimed unconvincingly) as a canonical bishop. But his seething venom against the place, still sharp after ten years, seems to suggest that its officials were ranged more on the side of Anthimos than him. He has no love at all for the:

> Utterly dreadful, pokey little hole; a paltry horse-stop on the main road where it splits into three on its way through Cappadocia; a place wholly devoid of water, vegetation, or the company of gentlemen.[124] All dust, and noise, and wagons, weepings and lam-entations, magistrates, implements of torture and leg irons,[125] a population consisting only of foreigners and migrants. This was my Church of Sasima![126]

His concluding words to the tirade, show the radical loss of mutual esteem that happened between him and Basil after this point. It is a rupture he masks in his

123. Orat. 43.58, PG 36.572.
124. *Eleutheroi. De Vita Sua*, v. 441, PG 37.1059.
125. Sardonically implying that the population was servile, and that the place was so dreadful no one would have willingly stayed there without the threat of torture. It is a caustic joke against the town, and ought not to be taken as an accurate description. It did, however, induce Eusebios of Samosata, to whom Gregory complained, and to whom he must have sent a simi-lar "tragic" report, to write to Basil in wonder that he could have been so insensitive as to send Gregory there.
126. *De Vita Sua*, vv. 439-446, PG 37.1059-1060.

Funeral Oration for Basil, but it comes out clearly enough in his autobiographical poem:

> And this was the gift of one who had more than fifty suffragan bishops under his juris-
> diction. I was overwhelmed by his generosity.[127]

It was easy enough for Anthimos to frustrate Basil's attempt to take the mules
with the tribute from the feast of St Orestes but once Gregory was installed at
Sasima, the argument could be carried out, like a war of attrition on the scene itself.
To prevent Basil gaining the upper hand, Anthimos immediately sent his own candidate in as bishop of the neighboring village of Limnai.[128] As Gregory wrote to Basil
at Easter 372:

> I will keep you in the picture by letting you read the letter Anthimos sent to me when
> he occupied Limnai, in spite of our protestations and warnings. In it he insults us and
> rails at us, as if he were composing a victory chant over our defeat.[129]

Gregory says to Basil in this letter that he was willing to make an effort to defend
Sasima. He does not say how much of an effort it would be beyond the level of a
minatory epistle. Once Anthimos had established his agents in the next village,
Gregory knew that he would be risking a large street fight if he took possession of
the town,[130] and considering the way Basil himself had been sent packing only weeks
earlier, he rightly foresaw it was a fight that he would surely lose. In any case, as
Limnai was the next settlement northeast of Sasima on the road to Caesarea, any
gain to be had in diverting supplies to Basil that came through his town, would certainly be lost a few miles further down the road to the metropolis, where Anthimos'
servants could dispossess any caravan quite easily. In the face of growing rumors and
gossip about the falling out of the local leading families (the intrusive aspect of fame
Gregory could never bear) he seems to have disappeared for a retreat into the mountains.[131] The route he took was possibly by sea, for he turns up in the mountain villages of Pamphylia,[132] hundreds of miles to the west, and a sea route from the Cilician
coast, south of Nazianzus would have afforded the quickest and most convenient
mode of travel. If he did go this way, he certainly passed by the monastic retreat of St
Thekla at Seleukia, near to the coast. It was the monastery and martyr shrine which
he would soon choose as his more permanent place of retreat when his parents died
not long after; and this might be the time when he first made the acquaintance of
the community there. How long he was gone from home is not certain, but when he

---

127. *De Vita Sua*, vv. 447-448, PG 37.1060.
128. Gallay (1943), p. 116. Ramsay (1890), p. 294, first posited that the reading "limnon" in Gregory's letter 50, where he tells of the episode, did not refer generically to the outskirts (or even
less likely the surrounding marshes) but to a specific place called Limnai. Ramsay notes how
in the late nineteeth century the Greeks of the area still called it Limna (Turkish—Goljik).
129. Ep. 50, PG 37.104. Gallay (1964,), pp. 65-66.
130. *De Vita Sua*, v. 455, PG 37.1060.
131. *De Vita Sua*, vv. 490-491, PG 37.1063. "Once again I fled and ran off like a thief into the
mountains alone, to find there that life I loved so much, my true delight."
132. Ep. 28, PG 37.61-64; Gallay (1964), p. 35.

did make his way back he turned criticisms of his "flight" to his own advantage, by once again appealing to the concept of "retirement" in mountain seclusion as perfectly proper behavior—for a monk.[133] It is a small detail, but one that shows Gregory in an interesting new light. It demonstrates how far he had matured politically since his priestly ordination, and the flight that was consequent upon it; and it also shows that he was consciously deciding to base his episcopal rank on the allegiance of the ascetics who remained loyal to him, rather than on the civic loyalties that a *Curia* and *polis* could be expected to show toward their local bishop; at best a tentative political base. In regard to the population of Sasima he knew he had little to gain from them. As to the monks, he emerged from his retreat in the mountains with a new sense of purpose. He would be a bishop-ascetic, and his Church would be the zealous gathered around his leadership. The way in which he configured this, however, was worlds apart from Eustathios' ideas of ascetic-bishop, and retained in Gregory's case all the attendant advantages of a landed aristocrat using the power base of his own *Chora*, his own estates and indentured labor. The idea, if not already in his head, would soon be put to him by his father. Why could he not continue in episcopal rank from the basis of his own estates? All that was needed was to secure synodical agreement.

In later years he presents to the audience of the capital, the fact that his return to public ecclesiastical life was merely his dutiful response to an aged parent: a "last request" as it were, from a dying father, as he laid his feeble hands upon his son's beard,[134] a solemn request which no child had the right to refuse:

> I was, however, not even good at my flight. For though I can stand all things, there is one thing I cannot bear, and that is the anger of my father. First of all he agitated to have me installed at Sasima and then, when he failed to secure this, he determined the second best thing would be that I should not remain devoid of rank, but should rather assist him as his suffragan.[135]

At first, Anthimos was triumphant at his victory, but he also wanted to restore relations with the family of the Gregories at Nazianzus. The younger Gregory does not admit to it in his letters, but the political negotiations of his father were surely important here, and the old man seems to have been willing enough to enter into dialogue with Anthimos as the new *de facto* leader of the local Cappadocian churches.

So it was that Gregory came home again. As time passed in the spring of 372 and he

---

133. Orat. 10.1, PG 35.828. "I had desired to leave all political business behind so that I could enjoy a certain inactivity and philosophize by myself in retreat (hesychia), holding private colloquy between myself and the Spirit. I conducted my soul like Elias on Carmel, or John in the desert; like the heavenly life of those others who gain so much from this manner of philosophy." By appealing to these paradigms he places himself firmly in the category of monastic hesychast, for whom flight into solitude was a central ecclesiastical "right" not a failing to be criticized.

134. *De Vita Sua*, v. 500, PG 37.1063.

135. *De Vita Sua*, vv. 492-498, PG 37.1063.

still had not taken possession of his appointed town, Basil's letters began to arrive, increasingly annoyed at his inactivity, and accusing him of feebleness. This was a level of war in which he could more easily engage with chance of success, and his replies to Basil[136] meet his friend's aggression with robust outrage of his own. Basil called him an "ignorant fool, a rascal, a faithless friend."[137] Gregory asks why the insults when all he had done was recognize Basil's deceit that had been operating in his regard all the time:

> One thing I can see clearly enough. I have been played for a fool. Perhaps it is somewhat late in the day, but at least I have woken up to it.[138]

The letter protests that he had done Basil no wrong whatsoever. The latter need not expect any apology to be forthcoming. It was Basil's elevation to the episcopal throne that seemed to have gone to his head, and had he not made it clear from the outset that he had no intention of being a bully-boy to advance Basil's personal interests:

> I am sick of hearing complaints about the way you have been behaving, and sick of having to defend our position before those who know only too well our past and our present circumstances. What is the most ridiculous, or rather the most tragic, part of this whole affair, is the manner in which I have been cast at one and the same time as villain and victim... The more kindly disposed accuse you of having treated me with scorn and disdain, saying that you have thrown us aside as soon as we had served our purposes in your regard, like a cheap and common tool, or like the scaffolding for arches that one constructs which has no further use once the building is complete. But forget what these people are saying, for no one can ever prevent the exercise of free speech. For your part, just renounce (you owe it to me) these empty hopes that seem to make you happy which you have fixed in opposition to your critics, those who are saying that you have deliberately scorned us under the pretext of honor, as if you were a straw man well fitted for such behavior.[139] I shall open my heart to you just as it is. I want you to leave off your anger towards me. I am going to remind you of what I cried out to you in my first distress.[140] For I was not carried away by anger that day, or overcome by the occasion to the point of not knowing what I was saying. I told you then that I would not procure arms; that I would not study military tactics; when I had resisted this even when the times seemed to indicate it was more pressing[141] when all the world was armed and mad for war. You ought to know how unfit the weak are for service.[142] I am not going to stand up

---

136. Epp. 48-50, PG 37.97-104; Gallay (1964), pp. 61-66.
137. Ep. 48, PG 37.97; Gallay (1964), p. 61.
138. Ep. 48, PG 37.97; Gallay (1964), p. 61.
139. We have here a representation of the discussions that had been taking place between Anthimos and Gregory's father. Basil has clearly got wind of reconciliation processes already underfoot in Cappadocia Secunda, and is pressurizing Gregory to remain loyal, but this letter is already part of the process of brokering the reconciliation between Basil and Anthimos, and the sacrifice of Sasima was a price Gregory was all too willing to pay.
140. When he was forced to accept episcopal ordination.
141. Under Julian's persecution of the Christians.
142. An ironic reference to the fact that Basil (who had persistent bad health) was no better than he in masquerading as a strong man, and had himself been trounced by Anthimos.

against Anthimos the Bellicose... make war on him yourself if that is what you want. As for me just give me peace and quiet above all else. Why should I do battle for sucking-pigs and poultry, when they are not even mine to start with? Just carry on like a strong man, a virile warrior, drag all down before your glory like rivers pull in streams regardless of any claims of friendship or that intimacy which derives from virtue or righteousness. Don't have any worries about the kind of impression you are creating while you behave this way, as if you alone were a spiritual being. As for us, we have gained a great advantage from knowing you; never again to trust in "friends" and never again to prefer anything to God.[143]

His conclusion is withering. It did not seem to dent Basil's anger, drawing out only a further accusation that he was lazy and did nothing. In a dignified, and very short, rejoinder,[144] Gregory admits that "inactivity"[145] has been his lifelong study. He is making a play on the notions of laziness and monastic detachment, since the latter defines itself by withdrawal from the affairs[146] of the world. If only Basil had a similar love for "inactivity," he says, the Church would be better off by never learning the path of turning to armed conflict to settle its internal disputes.

If Gregory was offended when he saw what Sasima was really about, there are grounds to think that his father too was indignant at the way Basil had repaid his debt of honor by appointing his son to this insignificant town that could not even be regarded as something within Basil's own gift; a paltry response when the latter had received decisive assistance from his family in the recent election struggle. What was at stake here was more than ruffled feathers and the "muddle" of an over-sensitive soul; it struck at the root of the whole concept of honor and shame in Greek mutual relations. Basil had not only sinned against friendship, he had sinned against family honor and that demanded redress. The Gregories appear to have sent off a letter of complaint from Nazianzus to Eusebios of Samosata, the old bishop's colleague in arms at the Caesarean election, and one of the few senior mentors that Basil still looked up to with some awe and respect. Eusebios was asked to remonstrate with Basil exactly on this point of offering an episcopal see to Gregory which was so beneath his dignity. He appears to have raised the complaint critically, and Basil's reply to Eusebios survives, in which he pleads innocence and suggests that his intention had originally been to give Gregory an important office (in the immediate aftermath of his own election perhaps) but that this had "proved impossible" (because of Gregory's own intransigence when he at first refused to visit and then turned down the offer of a post in the Caesarean clergy). His argument settles down to the point that since no possible church could be worthy of Gregory, Sasima will have to do. I suspect it is written with some degree of ironic disdain, and in part it seems deliberately to allude to the open letter Gregory the Elder sent to the electoral college

143. Ep. 48, PG 37.97-100; Gallay (1964), p. 62.
144. Ep. 49, PG 37.101; Gallay (1964), pp. 63-64.
145. *Apraxia*: the doing of nothing in particular.
146. *Praxeis*.

gathered in Caesarea after the death of the former archbishop. In this letter, crafted by Gregory the younger, which formed the basis of the constraints and complaints Basil felt the family in Nazianzus held against him, they had argued that "grace is not circumscribed by geography"[147] or, in other words, the smallness of the see does not diminish the dignity of the bishop holding it. Basil is taking them at their word, and implying that he fulfilled his obligations to the old bishop who had helped him in the same spirit in which they had assisted him (less than wholeheartedly in his estimate). Since the letter still expects Gregory to assume the duties of his new office, it must date from a time shortly after the consecration:

> I too was anxious that our brother Gregory should have the government of a Church commensurate with his own abilities; and that would have been the whole Church under the Sun gathered into one place. But as this is impossible let him be a bishop, not deriving dignity from his see, but conferring dignity on his see by himself. For it is the part of a really great man not only to be sufficient for great things, but by his own influence to make small things great.[148]

In *Letter* 50, the last of the series Gregory sent to Basil regarding the conflict after his ordination. He lets it be known clearly that negotiations have already been carried on with Anthimos. Basil seems to have found out anyway and accused Gregory the peacemaker of being a traitor to the cause. He once again tries to occupy the middle ground as reconciler:

> The most noble Anthimos did come to us with several of his bishops, either to visit my father (as was the apparent reason) or for trying out a strategy.[149]

Gregory depicts Anthimos as alternating between pleading and bullying, writing as if he was Basil's confidant and spy in the whole process. Gregory heroically resists the blandishments of the meeting (a de facto synod of bishops held in Nazianzus of all places, though he will not describe it as such even though Basil knows it was so, and he was certainly chagrined not to be invited to it).[150] Gregory even stands against the synod so that he is accused of "Basilism." But however much he bends over trying to soothe his friend, it is abundantly clear that Gregory writes Letter 50 on behalf of, and as a direct result of, the local synod at Nazianzus at which the two Gregories reached agreement with Anthimos, that Sasima would be abandoned as a useless base for a new bishopric, and Gregory the younger would retain episcopal dignity though serving alongside his father in their own familial Church at Nazianzus. Try as he may, Gregory cannot mask the fact that this agreement was effectively secured without reference to Basil at all. He presents his letter to Basil as the beginnings of an eirenical seeking of resolution of the conflict. He offers to show Basil the letter Anthimos had written to him just after he had been consecrated,

147. Greg. Ep. 41, PG 37.85; Gallay (1964), pp. 52-53.
148. Basil, Ep. 98. NPNF vol. 8, p. 182.
149. Greg. Ep. 50, PG 37.101; Gallay (1964), p. 64.
150. Cf. Basil, Ep. 98. NPNF vol. 8, p. 182.

where he insulted him with all manner of bluster. Is this not sufficient proof that Gregory could never prefer Anthimos in friendship to his old friend Basil? He senses, perhaps, that Basil is far from being convinced, and ends his essay in reconciliation with just sufficient bluster and disdain of his own to make it clear that he is not merely speaking for himself, but is indeed writing on behalf of a larger synod:

> In any case, if you have too much pride and pretentiousness, and still want to talk down to us like a metropolitan archbishop to a bishop of a little village, or even to a bishop without a see at all, know that we too have some hauteur with which to stand against you. It is something anyone can do. Perhaps it is the best course to take.[151]

In due time the dust would settle. The ecclesiastical relations calmed down. Gregory of Nyssa came to Nazianzus to try and heal the breach that had come between the two families, and was received with customary warmness by his elder friend.[152] But one thing would never change: Basil would never again trust him as an ally in Church politics. The breach, to that extent, was permanent and hurtful. Gregory's problem was like that of many another sensitive soul: he cared for Basil far more than Basil cared for him. Despite the resumption of apparently friendly relations, and despite the constant claims that they both represented "one party" in doctrine, Gregory sensed from this time onwards that he no longer had a place in the counsels of the friend from whom he had once expected so much. It was a grief that would never leave him, and like most instances of deepest hurt in humans, was a grief that ever afterwards would alternate between sorrow and anger.

By the winter of 372, he was certainly back in Nazianzus, at the side of his father, and to the common agreement of the local hierarchs, if not to Basil's mind, installed as the canonical co-adjutor there. Gregory makes a point of telling his readers that he made it clear to Anthimos of Tyana that he would serve in this capacity only as long as his father was alive. The acceptance of a bishop's throne as co-adjutor to another incumbent he, at least, regarded as not being a permanent canonical commitment.[153] The local hierarchs of the region would disagree with him when his father's death left him in sole charge of a Church on his own property which they could not staff without his permission. Moreover, he makes the point that he only accepted the episcopal charge at Nazianzus to an audience in Constantinople, as part of his legal defense after 381, that he had not accepted the episcopacy of the capital illegitimately as the Egyptian and Roman churches had then argued. In the *De Vita Sua* he was actually making the legal case that Constantinople was the first time he had ever been appointed to an episcopal see canonically. This was a refined

---

151. Greg. Ep. 50, PG 37.104; Gallay (1964), p. 66.
152. Orat. 11.1-3, PG 35.832-836.
153. *De Vita Sua*, vv. 521-525. "I considered to myself that there could be no harm in acceding to my father's desire in regard to the bishop's throne. 'This can not hold me down unwillingly,' I said to myself, 'and there is no proclamation or contract to restrain me.'" The use of the rhetorical soliloquy here may explain why no one else in the Cappadocian hierarchy was aware that his intentions to occupy the see were so temporary.

argument to make. It may have been just about defensible in a court of law, but to all local observers the case that he had never been bishop of Sasima, and had never been bishop of Nazianzus, strained common credibility.

Between winter of 372 and spring of 373 Gregory preached the first of his four episcopal orations in his home Church.[154] *Oration* 12, which can be considered his first formal address as a bishop within his own cathedral Church, is nothing less than a sensation dressed in drab clothes. It announced an entirely new policy of theological openness, being in large part a program statement meant to summon the loyalty of the Nicene monks of the area to his leadership. It begins with an invocation of the Holy Spirit of God. The bishop in the ancient Church had always been understood as the foremost initiate and mystagogue of the community. The Bishop was chosen as the utterer of the *Anaphora*, the sacred prayer of the Church gathered together at the altar of God. As the Church had socially advanced, the office of bishop had assumed more and more administrative powers to the point where the "spiritual aspect" was being overshadowed. Gregory makes a critical reference to this as all too well exemplified in his own case being elevated to Sasima and effectively dropped into a war:

> I suppose that most will think we are undertaking this office from material motives, in spite of all my spiritual professions. This is because the majority [of bishops] have made a great business out of the office, something fit for warlords, and yielding a most wonderful life of leisure, even if a man may rule over a more slender flock than this, and one that renders more sorrows than joys.[155]

He returns to the older model of the bishop as the instrument of the Holy Spirit. His opening peroration sets the theme, and in so doing lays the basis for the explicit development of the theology of the Spirit which he wishes to announce loud and clear in his address. He is the Mystagogue. Now is the time to speak out:

> I opened my mouth and drew in the Spirit.[156] To that Spirit I dedicate my entirety, and my very self: all my deeds, my discourse, my contemplation and my silence. Only let him have me, and lead me and move me—hand, mind, and voice. Take them wherever he wishes, wherever is right, and stop them moving wherever is unfitting. I am the divine instrument, a rational instrument, tuned and played by that master musician the Spirit. Yesterday he worked a silence in me. My philosophy was not to speak. Today he plays the instrument of my mind—let the word be heard. My philosophy shall be to speak. I am not so talkative as to desire to speak when he is moved to silence, or so taciturn and stupid as to "set a watch before my lips"[157] when it is time to speak out. I shall open and close the door of my self to that Supreme Mind, to the Word, and to the Spirit, who are all of one nature and Godhead.[158]

154. Orats. 12-13, and 16-17.
155. Orat. 12.3, PG 35.845.
156. LXX Ps 118:131.
157. Ps 140:3.
158. Orat. 12.1, PG 35.844.

He addresses words of respect to his father, comparing him to the High Priest Aaron, who grew more godly as he grew older, and graciously offers his assistant ministry as a work in the shadow of one who needs only physical assistance, since he remains spiritually alive,[159] but in paragraph four he turns to his primary audience, the monastics gathered in the Nazianzus Church:

> My brothers, my friends, I have suffered compulsion. If I did not ask for it before, I ask for your assistance now. I suffered the tyranny of my father's old age and, if I can put it mildly, the tyranny of my friend's[160] graciousness. So each one of you come to my help if you can. Reach out your hand to me.[161]

He goes on to reaffirm his own monastic vocation, but one that is destined by God's calling to be worked out in a "middle state." This was to become a classic of Byzantine monastic theory: the middle state of the person withdrawn into the inner life, who also serves the larger body of the Church as faithfully as possible. One part of him desires:

> mountains and desert retreats, and quietness of soul and body so that the mind can retire into itself, withdrawing its powers from the sensible world so as to be wholly purified and hold communion with God, and to be brilliantly illuminated by the flashing radiance of the Spirit, with nothing earthly or cloudy mixing in with that divine light until we come to the very source of that radiance.[162]

The other part of him senses that he is called:

> To publish abroad the divine radiance, and bring to God a people for his own possession, a holy nation, a royal priesthood.[163]

And so, with the assistance of the ascetics, he will test his new vocation as ascetic bishop. In his inner life he will speak out the intimations that the Spirit gives him for the direction of the Church. His point is made nowhere more clearly than in the long doxology which forms the end of his oration. Normally this is a small finial to a discourse. In Gregory's text it becomes the point to which the whole speech has been moving. By giving the final doxology such prominence he shows the method he has learned from Athanasios[164]—that the full understanding of Christian pneumatology is given only in the praxis of worship. As such, it can be expounded best by the Mystagogue, the bishop in the act of praying, or in delivering extempore discourse. The doxology to end the oration reverberates around the octagonal Church as the first time a Christian hierarch had ever stated the issue publicly in the "inspired preaching" of the ecclesia. This is the time for speech, and his speech is that the Spirit is consubstantially God, and that this is the time to lay aside all equivocations.[165]

---

159. Orat. 12.2-3, PG 35.844-845.
160. Basil of Caesarea.
161. Orat. 12.4, PG 35.845-848.
162. Orat. 12.4, PG 35.848.
163. Titus 2:14; 1 Pet 2:9.
164. *Letter to Serapion*, PG 26.529f.
165. It is a long way from Athanasios himself, in 364, when he set out the catholic faith to the emperor Jovian, insisting that the belief in the "consubstantiality of the Father and Son"

Such is my speech to you men.[166] It is uttered in all simplicity and good will, for it is the inner secret[167] of my mind. And may whatever will be for our mutual benefit, as the Spirit guides all our affairs, be that which shall win the day (for once again my discourse comes back to the same point). To Him I have given my self even as my head was anointed with the oil of perfection; in the Almighty Father, and in the Only Begotten Word, and in the Holy Spirit who also is God. For how long shall we keep hiding the lamp under the bushel-measure? or begrudge others his perfect Godhead? when it is surely necessary to set it out on the lampstand so as to illuminate all the churches, and every soul, and indeed the whole fullness of the wide world; no more by metaphors; no more by intellectual shadow play; let us speak out quite openly now. For this indeed is the most perfect exposition of Theology for those who have been accounted worthy of this grace in the same Christ Jesus Our Lord. To him be glory, honor and dominion, unto the ages. Amen.[168]

The new bishop had begun from day one with the fearless *parrhesia* expected of his office. But where Basil had accused him of pusillanimity because he could not exercise sufficiently warlike *parrhesia* at Sasima, Gregory now turns the tables, and accuses him of theological pusillanimity because he could still not bear to break with Eustathios of Sebaste, and still courted his circle of Homoiousians who thought the doctrine of the consubstantiality of the Son and the Father a bridge too far, and regarded the consubstantiality of the Spirit with both as that extreme logical end which proved the nonsensical nature of the whole Neo-Nicene position. Gregory's attribution of the full consubstantial deity of the Spirit, in the most unsensational way in this Oration, must have come across to his hearers in the Church like a startling thunderclap. Apart from anything else it was clearly meant for Basil's ears. If it did not elicit a response soon, Gregory was determined to provoke one.

The spring of that year 373 proved especially bitter in Cappadocia. The extraordinary cold weather caught the vines as they were in bud and ruined the blossom and thus the fruit for that year.[169] Gregory who was busy in completing the plaza surrounding wall of his church at Nazianzus had later that year to beg wine from an

---

ought to be joined with a belief that the Holy Spirit "was not foreign to the Father," but all had to be "conglorified" in the Trinity. Cf. Athanasios. *Ep. ad Jovianum* 4, PG 26.817-820.

166. He specifically addresses "men" [*andres*] only. I think it is another indication that the ascetics are his primary audience.

167. *Mysterion*. The play of words connotes that the inner secret of his spirituality is in fact the indwelling mystery of the Divine Spirit. He picks up the trinitarian motif he has previously applied: the mind is hidden in the secret mystery, and uttered by the word. So Gregory, as mystagogue of the Divine Trinity, manifests from his exterior image the inner trinitarian structure of the enlightened Christian.

168. Orat. 12.6, PG 35.849.

169. Ep. 57, PG 37.112. Gallay (1964), p. 72. Gallay (1943), p. 122 sets *Oration* 16 in the previous year, taking the rhetorical motifs of Gregory's reluctance to speak in front of his father as indications that he had just been ordained a bishop and was insecure of his task.

aristocratic woman, Thekla,[170] so that he can offer it to his stone-layers. The weather continued to prove erratic and one disaster seemed to come hard on the heels of another in his locality. Following on the failure of the vines, a sickness decimated the livestock of his congregation, and when their hopes were resting on the grain crop, a prolonged drought thinned the new growth. Then a heavy storm of hail in April or May flattened the ripening crops in the field and ruined the harvest. In the early summer his people were facing financial disaster, and by autumn famine had arrived instead of festivals. To crown it all the imperial tax inspectors refused to allow them any remit of duties. The people sent the agents packing with threats, but were soon cowed by the Prefect's threat in return to burn Nazianzus to the ground for insurrection.

Gregory the elder was dismayed, and tired, and overwhelmed by the scale of the troubles. His theology had run out of answers. Why would God so castigate the flock? Before a whole town of frightened and ruined farmers the old man felt unequal to the task and seems to have resigned his episcopal charge, asking his son to take over the whole duties of the Church.[171] He lapsed into a dark silence. Gregory's oratorical skills had never before been so pressed. He spoke to the people using an abundance of agricultural imagery.[172] But, as is customary in Gregory's early orations, he goes on in the first place to address words of encouragement to the old bishop enthroned in the assembly. His wise words, Gregory says, coming from a simple, though full, heart, are worth more than those of his younger son and disciple. Fair words are not as solid as those simple truths that rise out of a long life lived in faithfulness. "By such words a crew of fishermen caught the entire world in the mesh of their Gospel net."[173]

Gregory begins by asking his congregation to choose between understanding the events that have happened to them as a natural disaster without explanation, or as an act of God, which is itself difficult to understand if God is merciful and benevolent. The world may be just as it is and there is no need to invoke a governing meaning to events. Such, he says, is the doctrine of "those who are stupid sophists, and themselves are carried through a random life by the disorderly spirit of darkness."[174] Or, alternatively, the world may indeed be under the governing providence of God. The latter case is the belief of his people, but if they are indeed under the care of God

---

170. Cf. Hauser-Meury (1960), p. 159. The Thekla I and II of Hauser-Meury (ibid., pp. 158-159) are probably the same person, the wife of the priest Sacerdos with whom Gregory was connected (Epp. 222, 361), and probably distinct from this aristocratic patroness.

171. Orat. 16.4. "I who was your disciple, then a shepherd, and now the chief shepherd." PG 35.937. It can, of course, just mean his episcopal status, but it does seem to me to indicate he has taken over the governance of the Church by the fact of having to make this important oration in the face of civic disaster and his father's "resignation." The old man would be dead within the year.

172. Orat. 16.1, PG 35.936.

173. Orat. 16.2, PG 35.936C.

174. Orat. 16.5, PG 35.940.

why do events such as these natural disasters happen? He turns to the scriptures for an answer and draws a parallel between the sufferings of the town and the plagues visited on Egypt. God, has been punishing them for their laxity. It is their lives which have been "disordered" and have called forth the "disorders" of the seasons which are normally constituted by the divine providence to serve all human needs. Even so, God has spared them many of the plagues which he once visited on the wicked Egyptians, sending them only three: a plague on the livestock, followed by a drought, and then a plague of the hail. Three signs God had sent them and they had not recognized that they were being visited by a divine Judgment.[175] The people are to repent, recognize their submission to God and reform their lives.

In taking this argument of an Old Testament biblical theodicy, Gregory is apparently anxious to set himself against a common response that has already taken hold of the imagination of the town, one that must have been inured in them from time immemorial: that these disasters are the lot of mankind, and the only proper "philosophic" response is to "endure it."[176] Gregory, as ever, takes a more subtle middle ground. If one considers the case of the visitation of sufferings on the wicked, the issue is clear cut. It is difficult in the case of the visitation of sorrow on the just, the Christian people. If in these circumstances one scorns adversity, he says, one runs the risk of being unable to recognize the signs God sends for the correction of our manners. If one falls craven before every visitation, one loses the character necessary to address God and cry out for mercy. The proper response is to be found midway between craven abject despair, and hardened endurance of all that befalls us. If one acts as Pharaoh in the time of plague, God will increase our sorrow all the more because of the obdurate blindness. If one despairs (he is addressing his father obliquely here) one loses the capacity to invoke the mercy of a God who is only sending troubles for our correction and improvement, and is ever ready to hear us in the day of trouble. No complaint that we are really innocent bearers of a punishment we have not merited will really stand the light of scrutiny, certainly not in the context of the final Day of Judgment when the thoughts of all will be tested by God himself.[177]

Gregory calls upon the whole Church to acknowledge their failings in having disordered the harmonious form of the world by their sins:

> We have conducted ourselves in ways unbecoming to the calling and the Gospel of your Christ, and of his holy sufferings and his kenosis for our sakes. We have become a reproach to The Beloved. All have sinned, priests and people together... We have cut short your mercies and kindness and our sins have closed off the depths of the compassion of our God.[178]

175. Orat. 16.9, PG 35.945.
176. Orat. 16.5, PG 35.940-941.
177. Orat. 16.8-9, PG 35.944-945.
178. Orat. 16.12, PG 35.949.

He then begins a long psalm-like prayer of intercession to God. Even if the people have sinned, and been punished for their infidelity:

> Even so we are your people, your inheritance, and so correct us, but not in anger in case you bring us to nothing and make us a thing of contempt to those around us.[179]

His last words show that his preliminary reading for this discourse had been based in the Book of Jeremiah when the prophet was told the meaning of the sufferings of Israel. In that case the prophet was instructed not to intercede for the nation,[180] but Gregory knows, through his own exercise of episcopal prophecy which he consistently envisages through his own identifying assimilation into the narrative,[181] when the scriptural paradigm applies and when it does not, for he goes on from here to the end of the Oration to mount an extensive priestly invocation for God to have mercy and lift the sufferings of his faithful:

> With these words I call upon God's mercy and if it were possible to turn aside his anger with burnt offerings and sacrifices,[182] I would not even have spared these. You my people, imitate your trembling priest. Beloved children do as we do. Share at one and the same time the correction God sends, and also his loving kindness. Guard your soul in tears and avert his anger by amending your lives. I charge you along with the blessed prophet Joel: to sanctify a fast and call a solemn assembly[183]...I know what God requires of us, that we should enter his house in sackcloth and lamentation, day and night between the narthex and the altar.[184]

A modern reader might look upon such a theological response as excessively unworldly, and perhaps typical of an aristocrat blaming his people's sins for their sufferings in time of famine. But it does not do justice to the preacher. Gregory is not merely offering a theoretical theology in this time of crisis but emerges as a man of action, and a worthy local leader with a clear eye on the social problems he must also direct and repair. He began in his speech by solidly identifying himself with his people, and instigating a solemn time of fast and prayer of intercession. So much was

---

179. Orat. 16.12, PG 35.952; cf. Jer 10:24.

180. Jer 11:14.

181. He sees himself and those around him as characters in the ongoing drama of the biblical story of salvation. This typical Gregorian style of biblical exegesis is not merely a rhetorical trope, but also a deliberate exercise on his part of "inspired reading" of the text, and its application to contemporary events. To this extent he sees the task of discerning the text's connection to life as a mode of prophetic hermeneutic, and as it is the bishops' chief prerogative to interpret the scriptures in Church, this becomes the primary mode the Christian bishop has of exercising the prophetic charism in the contemporary age.

182. These are Old Testament allusions, but the non-Christian inhabitants of the area still had this as a traditional spiritual consolation for averting times of disaster which was denied the Christians, but may have tempted them on occasions such as this. The forbidding of animal sacrifice in the legislation of Constantine the Great was not necessarily widely observed in the provinces at this period.

183. Joel 2:15.

184. Orat. 16.13, PG 35.952.

his primary duty as a priest but he turns at the end of his discourse to remind all his hearers that: "it is a terrible thing to fall into the hands of the living God, and fearful is his countenance to those who do evil."[185] The fast and prayers are meant to open his community's hearts in repentance to God, and to root out the practices abhorrent to the divine justice. Gregory enumerates them using the language of the prophets Isaiah, Amos, Zechariah, and Habbakuk:[186] the amassing of land that deprives the neighbor, the refusing of charitable first-fruits from the harvests, the neglect of the support of widows and orphans, the "defiling of the land" by usury and interest.[187] His final words are an excoriation of the sellers of grain, who have raised the local prices and tried to make a market gain in the face of the misery around them. These are the "new worshippers of Baal, Astarte, and that abomination Chemosh."[188] The rich who only care for their garments and jewels, their slaves and animals, are compared to the leech whose hunger can never be satisfied however much blood it gorges.[189] The rulers who sit on thrones and are unmoved in their pride "take no account of God and forget that they rule their subjects as fellow servants,[190] being themselves just as much in need of God's compassion."[191] Gregory makes it clear that the rich ought to bear the burden of delivering the people from the present troubles though so far they have not given much cause for hope:

> reclining on their ivory beds, of which the prophet Amos rightly complains... though they ought to have had compassion on those who had faced disaster before they had to face it, like the fir tree lamenting the fall of the cedar,[192] for by such mercy they could have found mercy. Let them be instructed by their neighbors' punishment and let them be instructed by sight of the sufferings of others to change their own ways.[193]

In his final words, the orator graciously turns back to his father, and delivers all the "discourse" back into his own mouth, lifting him up, as it were, from his paralysis and giving him the charge to act as bishop of the flock and chief local magistrate once more, telling him to command his people to share their bread with those who are hungry, and offer shelter to the homeless. Then he and Gregory can stand together and offer the eucharistic sacrifice in the church for the averting of any further trouble.

> For God knows well how to respect the white hairs of a father making intercession for his children. Intercede for us... beg for bodily sustenance, yet plead for the food of the angels that comes down from on high. In this way you will make God be our God

185. Orat. 13.16, PG 35.956; Heb 10:31.
186. Orat. 13.17, PG 35.957.
187. Orat. 13.18, PG 35.957-960.
188. Orat. 13.19, PG 35.960; 1 Kgs 11:33.
189. Prov 30:15.
190. I.e. of God.
191. Orat. 13.19, PG 35.961.
192. Zech 11:2.
193. Orat. 13.19, PG 35.961.

again, you will conciliate heaven... and our land shall yield its fruit once more.[194] The dust of our fields will yield again the fruit of a short day, and our own dust, our mortal frames, shall yield a fruit that abides for ever.[195]

It is an extraordinary discourse, full of biblical erudition in a way that shows the profundity of his scriptural reading, and his immersion in the story of the salvation of the elect people. Gregory has seen his own life and that of all his contemporaries as another living-through the whole story of salvation. It is not merely in times of trouble that he applies this ongoing biblical typology, for it is a constant aspect of his thinking, and probably that one chief characteristic that later made Jerome describe Gregory as his supreme teacher of exegesis, even though of all the fourth century fathers Gregory left the least amount of explicit biblical commentary. Its conclusion, as he took up his old and bewildered father and led him into the sanctuary to begin the solemn intercessions for the town is truly a touching spectacle. The bewilderment of the old man, of course, has to be contextualized in the beginning of his terminal decline. He was already in his late nineties and would not last another year. The image of Gregory, a mature man already "old" for that era at forty-four leading the gruff and dominant paterfamilias by the hand like a child marks a full circle in several ways. It recalls, for me, those lines of the Irish Nobel laureate about his own father:

> My father worked with a horse plough...
> I stumbled in his hobnailed wake,
> Fell sometimes on the polished sod;
> Sometimes he rode me on his back
> Dipping and rising to his plod...
> All I ever did was follow
> In his broad shadow round the farm.
>
> I was a nuisance, tripping, falling,
> Yapping always. But today
> It is my father who keeps stumbling
> Behind me, and will not go away.[196]

This moment, above most others, is perhaps the time of Gregory's maturing as a man, as bishop, and as Christian social and theological leader. That liberating social program of relief he sets out as necessary for the time of recovery after famine surely gives the lie to that common and clichéd picture of Gregory as an ineffectual muddler. Yet, knowing that the powers concerned were not even there to hear him, he set his hand to compose a formal address to the imperial authorities who had responded to the people's sufferings in so callous a manner.

Oration 17 partly represents the text which he offered for the political salvation of his town, for their resistance of the taxes in the time of famine had called down on

194. Ps 67:6.
195. Orat. 13.20, PG 35.961-964 passim.
196. Seamus Heaney, "The Follower," *Selected Poems 1966-1987* (New York: 1991), p. 8.

their heads the threat of military action.[197] Never before had he had to act so urgently as a local bishop standing in defense of his people before the mighty of the world. The text is formed of several parts, and has probably been edited together at a later date. The first section is an exegesis of Old Testament texts based round Jeremiah,[198] this moves on to a general *paranesis*,[199] exhorting the townspeople to bear up under their troubles, and then becomes a more philosophically based essay on the nature of trials, that itself turns into a formal appeal to the Provincial Governor on behalf of his town.[200]

The sections are generally connected by the idea of the correct manner of bearing suffering, but it is clear enough that there were probably two discourses later made into one. The break seems to occur at *Oration* 17.8, where he directly addresses the "Dynastai" and "Archontes." It is possible that imperial representatives were in his Church to hear the whole discourse, but it is more likely, and a more efficient form of directing his appeal, that he had sent on his text to the Governor privately as a legal supplication. The response to it was in general favorable, as the former *Praeses* Julian[201] was sent to reallocate the tax imposts for Nazianzus soon afterwards, and he was a notable Cappadocian Christian who had studied with Gregory in Athens, worshipped in Gregory's own Church, and was very well-disposed to him.

In its parenetical section the Oration resumes many of the ideas of his previous *Oration on his Father's Silence*. The world is changeable and the affairs of human beings even more so. Only God is an unchanging power who rules the world by certain fixed tenets of his Providence. These rules can be understood by the wise[202] who must use the enigmas of scripture to assist their exegesis of reality. The fundamental truth is that God uses the distresses of humans to educate and reform them spiritually.[203] God is near to them, he tells his people, but they have to submit to their earthly rulers for such political order is part of the providential scheme for the common good. Their submission, however, is not to be absolute dependence. Their obedience calls out to the imperial powers to act in accordance with providential laws themselves:

> Let us submit to God, and after that to those others who bear power on this earth. We submit to God for all manner of reasons. Let us submit to the authorities out of brotherly love, and let us submit to the princes for the sake of good social order, so that it will

197. Jacob Billius had surmised they had instigated a riot. The Benedictine editors think *Oration* 17 does not suggest the trouble was so dire. Cf. PG 35.964 (*Monitum in Orationem* 17).
198. "Of all the prophets the one most ready to feel compassion for his people," he says. Orat. 17.1, PG 35.965. Almost a quarter of the whole discourse is given over to exegetical reflections, PG 35.964-969.
199. Orat. 17.4, PG 35.969.
200. Cf. Bernardi (1968), pp. 121-124. Bernardi sees the final addressee, the most senior official, as the Governor of Cappadocia Secunda.
201. Former *Praeses* of Phrygia. *Peraequator Tributorum* in Bithynia and Galatia in 373.
202. Orat. 17.4-6, PG 35.969-973.
203. Orat. 17.5, PG 35.972. "Only those are wise, who allow their trials to instruct them."

facilitate their kinder behavior to us, for it would be a grave and dangerous thing to exhaust their clemency.[204]

Having appealed to their consciences to leave off their suicidal political protests, he ends by simply commanding them as their bishop to be peaceful.[205] It was only by establishing the peace that he knew his intervention with the Governor would be able to pay off, and he probably sent this Oration on to the imperial office as well as what would follow, to give evidence that his town was now observing the law. It is probably this joining of texts that led to the different parts being edited together as a single whole.

The appeal to the Governor is another example of episcopal *parrhesia*: the appeal to the powerful on behalf of the needy. He begins by reminding the imperial agents of political realities. The Empire is Christian, its agents must obey Christian moral laws. This is not merely a generic piety; he wants their attention. He, as well as they, know its subtext: that Gregory will certainly prosecute them at the capital on the grounds of moral dereliction if they oppress his people beyond proper order:

> You bear power alongside Christ. Your administration is under Him. From Him you received the power of the sword, not so that you should use it, only that you should threaten it. Its blade is to be kept clean, like a sacred offering to the one who gave it to you. You are like an icon of God, but you also stand in dominion over icons of God...Stand in solidarity with God, not with the prince of this world,[206] with the God who is kind, not with the bitter tyrant.[207]

Gregory then reminds the Governor that he too is a Christian.[208] He supposes that he has doubtless heard of the story of the sacrifice of Abraham who was called upon to offer up his only Son:

> We do not ask anything like this from you. All we ask is that you would show us some philanthropy, a gift which is pleasing to God beyond all other things... Mingle leniency with terror; temper your threats with room for hope.[209]

Gregory tells him the story of the unforgiving debtor in the Gospel parable. Life is not long, he says, and soon there will be an account before God; remember that the Lord was angry beyond measure at the man who had proved so hard of heart.

> What do you say to all of this? Surely we have taken you captive by these words of ours,

---

204. Orat. 17.6, PG 35.972-973.
205. Orat. 17.7, PG 35.973D.
206. An ambivalent meaning. The prince of this world is a biblical designation of Satan, to which Gregory certainly refers, but the earthly prince is also indicative of the emperor, fear of whom has been outweighing, in Gregory's opinion, the natural feelings of humanity which the local powers ought to have had for his people.
207. Orat. 17.9, PG 35.976.
208. He seems to have grown up in the region of Nazianzus and knew Gregory's father, for Gregory alludes to him as "disciple of the great pastor" (Orat. 17.8, PG 35.976) and calls upon his "father's white hairs" (Orat. 17.12, PG 35.980) as another reason he ought to have leniency.
209. Orat. 17.10, PG 35.977.

you who have so often confessed yourself to be in love with oratory? O Best of all Archons, add now to your reputation and prove most lenient too.[210]

Gregory ends with an unusually vivid piece (he calls it an audacious idea) where he offers to the Governor the merits of his priestly Eucharist sacrifice in the Church as a gift to him in return for his leniency, a gift no less than "Christ himself, his self-emptying, and the sufferings of the impassible one." If the Governor has pity, he promises him, affairs in his life will be blessed by God and go well for him, and his judgment in the next life will be made lenient in return.[211] The appeal worked well. A review of the whole regional debt was set in process by the imperial authorities and the officer appointed for a review in the course of the following year was an old friend of the family. Much could be expected. He had performed extraordinary service for his town, and for the Church at large he had boldly signaled a public adherence to the "Neo-Nicene" policy of full trinitarian confession. Many were beginning to look to him as a man of substance. He did not know it at the time, but in this very month, May 3, 373, Athanasios of Alexandria had died in Alexandria. In many senses it was Gregory who picked up the fallen mantle, and one of the key figures who noticed this, and in turn passed it on to Meletios of Antioch in terms of high commendation, was Eusebios of Samosata, who had taken note of the young man. It cannot be doubted but that these two old and leading stalwarts of the Nicene cause promoted his affairs after his episcopal consecration, and both were concerned that he should have a greater platform than Sasima in Cappadocia from which to work for the Church universal.

Gregory's *Oration* 13 dates from autumn of the same year, 373,[212] and reveals him back in an ebullient mood. He had been one of the consecrators of a new bishop for the town of Doara in Cappadocia Secunda.[213] It is highly probable that Anthimos was there[214] though perhaps not his father whose powers were more and more failing in that year, his hundredth. Basil had already agreed to the inevitable and sent a letter to the city of Tyana suing for peace.[215] Tyana was, then, already the recognized canonical center for Cappadocia Secunda and this ordination must have been conducted under the aegis of the local bishops. The new bishop of Doara has often been thought to be Eulalios, his cousin[216] whom Gregory would later install as bishop of

---

210. Orat. 17.12, PG 35.980.
211. Orat. 17.13, PG 35.981.
212. It is closely connected with his *Letter* 58 which comes from mid-September, the feast of St Eupsychios of Caesarea.
213. Now Kulluce; about 15 km on the road South from Karbala/Guzelyurt, past Arianzum/ Sivrihisar.
214. Gallay (1943) thinks it is a consecration done on behalf of Basil, and so without either his or Anthimos' knowledge or presence. This to me seems an incredible supposition, and without any canonical precedent. It also belies the large gathering of clergy that are in evidence in the symposium following the consecration.
215. Basil, Ep. 97. NPNF vol. 8, pp. 181-182.
216. The recipient of three letters from Gregory (Epp. 116-117, 158); cf. Hauser-Meury (1960), p. 70

Nazianzus in the years after the Council of Constantinople, somewhere around 383, when he decided to make his "final" retirement. This identification, however, rests upon a misreading of the Oration title, as Gallay has observed.[217] *Oration* 13 does not celebrate the election of Eulalios to Doara, rather it is a homily given on the occasion of an election to Doara, and "edited by Eulalios the bishop." The name of the candidate is, thus, unknown.

Tillemont deduced from the large number of references to "warlike struggles" in the course of the Oration that the previously incumbent bishop of Doara had been forcibly ejected.[218] If this is so, the installation should be contextualized as an act of the Nicene party ensuring the new bishop would be an orthodox. Gregory refers to the Church as being "storm-tossed" and its "people scattered into the desert."[219] His intervention at Doara, he says, has been to "overthrow heretics."[220] This makes it clear that Anthimos was not an Arian in persuasion, even if Gregory did call him an "Amalek" on the occasion of his own earlier prevention from occupying Sasima. The occupying of the Church had not gone off without incident. Gregory refers to one of the clergy of the place, still loyal to the ousted bishop, who had physically assaulted him as they made their entrance. He addresses him directly in the course of the Oration, describing him as one of the rebellious priests that stood against Moses and Aaron, a "son of Dathan and Abiram."[221] His words indicate that this man too, like his former bishop, was to be deposed and rejected.[222] Gregory clearly felt confident in exercising a legally validated magisterial decision for this appointment. He could not have been working alone.

Gregory's invitation to pronounce the discourse for the ordination was a celebration of the peace that had been restored in Cappadocia Secunda, and Gregory seems here to be in all harmony with Anthimos. One phrase of his discourse may have been added later to the written version of the text he sent on to Basil, or it might have been spoken on the occasion, but Basil was certainly not present, and Gregory is anxious that his action as a consecrating bishop in this event should not be taken as a slight to the rights of that "holy and honorable man" the Metropolitan of the great city (Caesarea); which of course it was, and gave, in and of itself, the clearest indication that Gregory no longer regarded himself as canonically subordinate to Basil.[223]

Once again he underlines the fundament of the Trinitarian theology which he

(who is mistaken about letters 111 and 118); cf. Gallay (1967) (fn. 5 to p. 6 as listed on p. 150). Bernardi (1968) continues the misidentifications.
217. Gallay (1943), p. 123, n. 3.
218. Tillemont, *Mémoires*, vol. 9, p. 394.
219. Orat. 13.2, PG 35.853B.
220. Orat. 13.2, PG 35.853C.
221. Num 16.
222. Orat. 13.3, PG 35.856. The harsh language of exclusion from Israel and "alienation from the grace of God" suggests the priest was an Arian.
223. Gregory mentions a "large synod" was with him (Ep. 58). It must have been of Anthimos' clergy.

proposes to the new episcopal candidate as the standard of the faith he must protect and sustain in his new Church. It does not matter, he says, how many make war against them, or vainly bark like the dogs they are; such trials are merely the prelude for the glory of the Kingdom, and Gregory is no longer going to worry about threats of war. The new bishop must now make his stand too:

> Teach [your people] to worship God the Father, God the Son, and God the Holy Spirit; three in hypostasis, one in glory and effulgence.[224]

He presided over a gathering of monastics, some of whom had been coming over to his side from Basil. His clarity of Nicene homoousianism and his bold theologization of the Trinity had attracted a following among the ascetics, and some of the brethren present for the festival at his Church criticized Basil's "economy" of speech, contrasting it unfavorably with Gregory's *parrhesia*. Gregory took the occasion to write a letter putting some pressure on Basil to make a move more in favor of the decisive doctrine of the Spirit's deity. The text has for centuries been taken in patristic florilegia to demonstrate the generic point of Gregory's subordination in all respects to Basil's theology. Read in its particular context, that exegesis is wildly amiss. Gregory lays on the compliments thick and fast precisely because he knows the letter will raise a storm. Basil knows very well, that he is being pushed, and that Gregory is hiding behind the convention of rebuking someone else who dared to criticize Basil, while all the while he is mounting the criticism himself.

Gregory tells Basil that he has always held him[225] as his "guide of life" and his "teacher of dogma."

> The greatest joy of my life has been friendship and closeness with you, but what I now write to you, I write with no joy in my heart. I write it nonetheless. Do not be angry with me, or else I too shall be very angry if I think that you do not accept what I say and write as motivated by my affection. Many people are accusing us of not being strong in the faith. They are people who regard themselves as in communion with our affairs, and rightly so.[226]

A banquet was being held, which represented a large number of the "communion" of Gregory and Basil. It might well have been the feast after the consecration of the new bishop of Doara. On that occasion, and after his own oration when he returned to Nazianzus, Gregory had openly preached the deity of the Spirit. One of those present for the meal was a young monk. While the majority of the symposium[227] fell to praising the "synonymity of philosophy" that Gregory and Basil showed, this character "with all the fire of a young man" took exception violently. He decried the orthodoxy of Basil, claiming that he had just left the celebration of the Caesarean martyr

---

224. Orat. 13.4, PG 35.856.
225. The past tense is highly indicative, and never sufficiently recognized by commentators who abuse this letter to evidence that Gregory was totally dependent on Basil for this theology.
226. Ep. 58, PG 37.113; Gallay (1964), p. 74.
227. "The wine had not yet been brought in," Gregory says. Ep. 58.4, PG 37.113; Gallay (1964), p. 74.

Eupsychios where Basil preached.[228] Neither Basil nor Gregory, he maintained, were deserving of the praises of the company: "The one betrays the faith by what he says, the other is an accomplice in this betrayal by what he allows."[229] Gregory tells his friend that he gave the young man a good rebuke for his temerity.[230] But the young man pointed out that while Basil's preaching on the Father and the Son was perfectly orthodox, he made only obscure references to the Spirit. Gregory, on the other hand had clearly said the Spirit was God. To the young man Basil's speech seemed like "one of those discourses that, like water, bypasses rock and tries to hollow out sand." The young man went on (as Gregory says with a blow-by-blow narrative that is unusually, and deliberately, vivid) to remind Gregory of his own image of the "Lamp needing to be placed on the lampstand," and compared Basil to a man who was still trying to hide it under the bed:

> Basil does not proclaim the truth openly. He drowns our ears more with politics than righteousness, masking his duplicity by his oratorical power.[231]

Gregory tells Basil that he defended him before the young man, on the grounds that he was able to speak openly because he lived in a small out-of-the-way place, whereas Basil had charge of a large city and was in the spotlight, "with heretics trying to catch any word out his mouth that would allow him to be expelled." Gregory argued Basil's case, he says, insisting that one of the last surviving Nicene leaders must not be allowed to be overthrown because of this economy of teaching, when all knew that he had a correct faith in the divine status of the Spirit of God. But he goes on immediately to tell Basil that he was drowned out by the protests of all who surrounded him, and as he has just described them a few moments previously as a "large synod," he is making a telling point. The protests against this kind of "economical caution" rejected it as "ridiculous and old-fashioned." If Gregory held to it (in point of fact it was Basil who sustained it, and it is merely Gregory's way of sweetening the pill of complaint), then it was a mark of his cowardice, nothing more. "Far better to protect your people by the truth than weaken them through such a so-called economy." Gregory ends the letter saying that he was "very vexed" with Basil's critics, and disingenuously tried to lead out Basil on the subject by pleading ignorance of what he ought to do for the future, though he is clearly, already, the leading theologian of the area who is advancing the cause of the full deity of the Spirit, and ready to make open war on the subject, confident that he has the backing of energetic young monks, such as the one he ostensibly "rebuked." If we doubt Gregory's readiness to risk his position for the doctrine of the Trinity, we need only recall to what extent he alone among the

228. The feast was held on September 7.
229. It sounds suspiciously like the monk criticized Basil alone, and Gregory softens the harshness of the charge by deliberately associating himself in with it for Basil's sake. It is a rhetorical device of "association in correction" he uses elsewhere. Gregory's orthodoxy is not questioned, it is his association with Basil that is the trouble.
230. Again calling him a new Dathan and Abiram, as he did his violent critic in Orat. 13.
231. Ep. 58.8, PG 37.116; Gallay (1964), p. 75.

Cappadocian writers is the chief architect of the neo-Nicene doctrine of Trinity, advanced in his Constantinopolitan orations (but already declared as early as 372), and how willing he was to risk the anger of the factions of the city when he went there in 379, and suffered lawsuits and stonings for his preachings.

The letter's ending is a typically Gregorian "innocent challenge" to Basil:

> For your part, O divine and sacred head, tell us how far we ought to go in regard to the theology of the Spirit; what terminology ought to be adopted, and how far prudent economy ought to be involved. I need this knowledge for the next time I meet with critics; for if I, who know you and your affairs far better than anyone else, and have often given you full assurances of where I stand, and have received them in return from you, am still in the dark here, then I must be the most stupid and miserable of men.[232]

Gregory's letter was carried to Caesarea by the priest-monk Hellenios.[233] Basil, who knew every turn of Gregory's rhetorical meanings as well as he knew the streets of Caesarea, knew exactly what was going on, and he reacted with an anger that seems in his text to have been coldly and wearily suppressed. He is certain he has done nothing to offend Gregory, but is amazed that his "best friend among the brethren at Nazianzus"[234] should have been so ready to listen to his detractor. The latter is described as being the "leader of brethren," and seems to be some kind of monastic higumen near Caesarea, now disaffected with Basil's leadership. Basil asks Gregory to come to Caesarea and: "place yourself at the head of our party" from that base. Gregory's very appearance in Caesarea, Basil says, will have the effect of stopping the slanders against him, and the "facts will show who are your true disciples and who are really recidivists, and the cowardly betrayers of the truth." At the same time as he advises this, Basil evidently has little expectation that Gregory will do it, and so ends his reply by suggesting that for his part he will demonstrate his fidelity to the Church soon enough perhaps, in deeds not words, by an exile which he is expecting to happen any day. If Gregory is proposing to him a local synod of the Church to discuss the matter in hand, he will assent to it. If not, he has no intention of making himself clear on anything, to anybody.[235]

All in all, it is a masterly rhetorical avoidance of the main subject in hand, still "drowning the ears" of his audience by the consummate rhetoric. Basil would continue to avoid explicating his pneumatology even until 375 when he felt it necessary to signal his complete departure from the ranks of Eustathios of Sebaste, and then composed his *Treatise On The Holy Spirit*. Even so, throughout this classical exposition of fourth-century Christian pneumatology, it is still notable that he never calls the Spirit God outright, and certainly never affirms the Spirit's consubstantiality with the Father and the Son. Even when he decided to put his position clearly in a

---

232. Ep. 58.15, PG 37.117; Gallay (1964), pp. 76-77.
233. Cf. Hauser-Meury (1960), p. 97.
234. Thereby indicating that a monastic community had accumulated there around Gregory.
235. Basil, Ep. 71. NPNF vol. 8, p. 167.

text, it seems, Basil did not hold to the same pneumatology as his friend in Nazianzus, and only Gregory's claim that Basil after all really did hold the same doctrine as himself has been taken by the common tradition to make us believe so.

Gregory's inner state of mind is revealed to us most intriguingly in this time of his emerging political independence. It comes across in a highly personal reflection, the first of his long poems of lamentation, entitled *Poem of Lament Over the Calamities Affecting his Soul*[236] which he composed at the end of 373.[237] It is, perhaps, dominated by the knowledge that his father is near death,[238] and his thoughts turn to the insecurities of what this will mean for his future, since the care of his aged parents had been a primary factor in keeping him at Nazianzus for so long. His mind is yearning for the quiet and retired life he had envisaged for himself in his early years after returning from Athens. He recalls with regret the "shining visions" he once enjoyed as signs of grace from God[239] which first initiated him to the ascetical life of virginity. Now he mourns over the state of his soul, "like a father over his dead son, or a wife mourning the loss of her spouse." His involvement in the "mire" of human affairs has seduced him, he says, from "preserving the true mysteries of God."[240] He feels lost in the eternal struggle between the ascent to light in Christ, and the allurements of material things which obscure the mind and cloud decisive action for virtue.[241] "So many cares toss and turn in this heart," he says, that he feels as if Christ has abandoned him since he has adulterated "the spouse" of his soul, with all the political affairs he has undertaken to the detriment of his earlier and fervent monastic dedication.[242]

He longs for his soul not to be "dragged along in the dust any more," but once again "to take wings of flight."[243] He gives an interesting sidelight on what has already[244] been popularized as the ascetic practices distinctive to monks when he lists their spiritual exercises.[245] some load themselves with chains, or eat ashes in their bread, while others water their drink with tears; some stand immobile like trees for long periods of prayer, some refuse to speak at all except in psalm recitation, and yet others grow their hair long as a sign of Nazirite dedication, or keep their eyes

236. *Carmen Lugubre.* 2.1.45, PG 37.1353-1378. It can be found in English translation in Peter Gilbert (1994), cf. pp. 40-48.
237. Gallay (1943), p. 122. Gallay set it in 372 in the context of his grief over the Sasima incident. The more likely context is his massive involvement in civic affairs in the aftermath of the local famine.
238. *Carmen Lugubre.* 2.1.45, v. 217, shows his father is still alive, PG 37.1368.
239. *Carmen Lugubre.* 2.1.45, vv. 19-26, and 227-266, PG 37.1355f.
240. *Carmen Lugubre.* 2.1.45, v. 35, PG 37.1356.
241. *Carmen Lugubre.* 2.1.45, vv. 71-88, PG 37.1358-1359.
242. *Carmen Lugubre.* 2.1.45, vv. 37-44, PG 37.1356.
243. *Carmen Lugubre.* 2.1.45, vv. 117-120, PG 37.1361-1362.
244. And will soon be more widely publicized by the transmission of collections such as the *Sayings of the Desert Fathers*, or the *Lausiac History* of Palladios.
245. *Carmen Lugubre.* 2.1.45, vv. 147-160, PG 37.1364.

fixed on the ground and their thoughts only on God. He feels he has slipped away from this lifestyle of "spiritual flight," and offers instead a rare glimpse into his own spiritual practices. He looks at the joys of others around him who have married and found happiness in their wives and children; those who enjoy life at the baths, or in their gardens, with their retainers making a great show as they go about town. He specifically mentions the local rhetors, "pompous on their high podia."[246] He, on the contrary, has become an object of local ridicule for his lifestyle:

> I have set a guard upon my stomach, and consume my spirit with grief, shedding streams of tears through nights of vigils, and bending worn knees to the Lord. I wear the wretched vestment of one who mourns[247]...Dead to this life I only preserve a meager breath upon the earth. I flee from cities and the company of men. My conversation is with beasts in rocky places, where in solitude, apart from all others, I inhabit a miserable and stony little dwelling.[248] I own one coat, no shoes, have no hearth. I live only on hope.[249] I am an object of ridicule to worldly men. My bed is of straw, my blankets are rough sackcloth, my floor is beaten earth watered by my tears.[250]

His personal ascesis may not be as spectacular as that of the Egyptian monks he has mentioned previously, he implies, but he still retains some claim to be "monastic" even in the midst of his civic duties as local bishop, and his chief right to that state he sees as the time when his soul did indeed fly in the presence of divine visitors, and was initiated into mystical union with the choir of immortals. He goes on to tell the story of how he was dedicated to virginity after his vision of the two female immortals,[251] an important passage which we have earlier discussed in relation to the rhetoric of classical mystery-initiation.

This category of visionary experience is notably lacking from the whole range of the desert monastic literature. If a monk in that tradition sees visions, he is usually cautioned. For Gregory it has become the supreme category of authentification.[252] After him, the concept of the luminous vision will take center stage in Byzantine mystical understanding. Gregory serves as the most important of all midwives for this tradition in Greek Christian thought.

The *Poem of Lament* ends with thoughts of impending death, and yet, like the psalms of Lamentation in the Old Testament, which he has obviously used as

---

246. *Carmen Lugubre.* 2.1.45, vv. 130-138, PG 37.1362-1363.

247. More than a generic reference this suggests that tattered clothes were already commonly regarded as the "monastic habit." Gregory has left aside the clothes that signify his curial rank and adopted this kind of clothing. He will mention again in his late autobiographical poem that the Constantinopolitan aristocracy did not approve of his shabby dress when he was there as their bishop.

248. It suggests that he still has as his private quarters the estate's hill station at Karbala.

249. That is on the charity of the donations of his father, owning nothing personally.

250. *Carmen Lugubre.* 2.1.45, vv. 125-128, 139-146, PG 37.1362-1363.

251. *Carmen Lugubre.* 2.1.45, vv. 227-266, PG 37.1369-1372.

252. Cf. McGuckin (1996).

models, such an end is enlivened with sentiments of trust, of hope, and recovery.[253] He asks Christ to:

> Deliver my old gray head and grant me a merciful end as once you so clearly loved me, and led me forward to the highest and best realities. Deliver me from envious and bitter cares, into the safe haven of your Kingdom where I may ever praise you in the company of the immortal lights.[254]

By late 373, when he wrote his offended letter to Gregory, Basil had been very worried that he would face exile, and with good cause. Demosthenes, who had attacked them in Caesarea on the occasion of Valens' last visit, had opened up a new front in his war against the pro-Nicene theologians. Now that Athanasios was dead, and Meletios of Antioch in exile, he secured the exile of other prominent Nicenes in the course of 374. Among his victims were Gregory of Nyssa, whom he managed to have dismissed from his Church on the grounds of financial mismanagement, and Eusebios of Samosata, who was a venerable pillar of the party.

Gregory does not seem to have been threatened. The happy outcome of his correspondence with the Governor who so admired his oratory let him know he had nothing to fear and much to hope for. At the end of 374, the Imperial Tax Administrator Julian began to set in force a substantial review of the tax liabilities of the Nazianzus region. As Gregory had hoped, he showed particular favor to his own homeland. Gregory wrote to him, as to an old friend from student days, anxious that Julian would not let his falling out with another of Gregory's relatives, Nicobulos, spoil their own easy relations.[255] In the letter he asked for, and apparently received, a great benefit for his clergy and local monks, achieving for them dispensation from taxation.[256] Julian invited him to come to his villa so that they could settle the accounts together. He declined to go, pleading the fact that he had to seek medical help in Tyana. So he sent *Letter* 68 instead. The complete correspondence between them shows that all his aspirations were fulfilled. Not only did the clergy receive exemption, but the townspeople seem to have been afforded a large measure of abandonment of back tax debt.[257] Julian, however, demanded a more

---

253. Some commentators, have found his later poems of lamentation depressed (which they are in part) and despairing—which they certainly are not. He is well aware of the structure of the biblical Psalms of Lamentation, and from bitter complaints poured out directly to God, he consistently ends with resignation and hope. His darkest expressions of hopelessness are meant as prayers for assistance. It is a wholly misplaced reading to see them as evidence of his loss of spiritual direction, as much as it would be to read Hopkins' late "Terrible Sonnets" as evidence of the latter's apostasy, rather than the testimonies of enduring fidelity that they are. There is a good discussion of the opinion of scholars (Misch, Rapisarda, Coman, Villemain) over the melancholia of the poetry in Gilbert (1994), pp. 7-16.

254. *Carmen Lugubre.* 2.1.45, vv. 343-349, PG 37.1377-1378.

255. Ep. 67, PG 37.132; Gallay (1964), p. 87.

256. "Other towns allow this to the ministers of the altar. It would be a cause of shame if you, a close friend did not afford this to those who live and work with me." Ep. 67.2.

257. Epp. 67-69. "There is one who knows the great extent of all your gifts and rebates, and that is God, the supreme remitter of debts." Ep. 69, PG 37.133; Gallay (1964), p. 89.

particular payment from Gregory than his promise "to offer sacrifice" on his behalf.[258] He came to Nazianzus, probably in late 374 or early 375, and demanded Gregory declaim an oration dedicated to him. This survives as *Oration* 19. It makes several opportunistic references to the wintertime census when Jesus was born (suggesting it emanates from a time near Christmas)[259] and compares Julian's recent tax census to the other liberal and happy events of that time that saw the birth of the Word of God and the beginnings of salvation for the human race. His Oration gets off to a slow start. Gregory says he has had to be compelled into giving it, most unwillingly, as he has been much occupied recently by thoughts of retirement and has preferred to slip into silence, desiring to "lie hidden in Christ."[260] He is referring to the time he has spent in solitude at Arianzum, composing his song of lament. Julian has "tyrannized him out of love"[261] by demanding this Oration as a debt of honor. It is, of all Gregory's surviving Orations, the one which has the least spark about it, and Gregory apologizes at the end, for what he, at least, senses as its deficiencies.[262] He goes on in the early sections to praise the life of retirement and virginity as always preferring the life of quiet to an involvement in the world's affairs that brings trouble in its train so often.[263] The speech as a whole turns much around the issues of gratitude of "the whole choir of priests" and the townspeople for Julian's leniency in remitting a large amount of their debt.[264] In his preaching, before the whole town gathered for the local festival of martyrs,[265] he seems to be returning a favor to the authorities by insisting once again that his people observe good political behavior in future. The shepherds are to be obeyed by the sheep, not vice versa,[266] and in future must "render to Caesar what belongs to Caesar."[267] It is perhaps the first time that the text had been applied to Christian imperial tax policy. Afterwards it will become a favorite quotation of the Byzantine civil service, and can even be found set in mosaic on the floor of the tax office in Byzantine Caesarea Palestina.[268] He also insists that the principle of good order means that laypeople (possibly referring to the monks)

258. Another reference to Eucharist as *sacrificium*, comparable to Orat. 17.12, PG 35.980.

259. Orat. 19.12-13, PG 35.1057-1060. Bernardi does not agree the Christmas references give any indication of the season of origin: Bernardi (1968), p. 132, but they are too developed *in situ* to be merely occasions for a parallel between the census of Quirinus and Julian's recent benefactions. Gallay attributes it to Christmas 374. Gallay (1943), p. 128.

260. Orat. 19.1, PG 35.1045.

261. Orat. 19.1, PG 35.1044.

262. Orat. 19.17, PG 35.1064.

263. Orat. 19.7, PG 35.1052. Bernardi (1968), p. 133 sees in his reference to the two states of life— virginal and married, a further reference to the tax situation. The poor who would suffer if the debts had not been remitted were the monks who drew their subsistence from the tithes of local Christian landowners.

264. Orat. 19.16, PG 35.1061-1064.

265. Orat. 19.5, PG 35.1048.

266. Orat. 19.10, PG 35.1053C.

267. Orat. 19.11, PG 35.1056.

268. Cf. K.G. Holum, *King Herod's Dream: Caesarea on the Sea* (New York, 1988); McGuckin (1992).

must not try to lead their bishops in matters of doctrine.[269] To silence their pressures he seems to have adopted his prior strategy of silence.[270] Gregory puts his finger on a possible cause of the earlier civic unrest when he insists, quoting the authority of the ascetic John the Baptist, that "soldiers are to be content with their allotment of pay."[271]

This was his last oration pronounced in the Church at Nazianzus for several years to come. It clearly follows in the immediate aftermath of his father's death.[272] Consequent on the loss of the old man he was greatly depressed, and was also left exposed in terms of his canonical position. The more he exercised the functions of bishop in the local Church, the more he would be committed to retaining the charge of the community. His period of mourning, as well as his desire not to exercise the pastoral charge of episcopal preaching, were two of the main motives behind the retreat into silence which he refers to in *Oration* 19. The crisis with the imperial authorities, however, had forced his hand. He had to exercise his skills as rhetor for the civic good. Now that the crisis was over, and he had served his community more than well, he felt he wished to retire permanently.

Gregory's father was almost a hundred years old when he died and had served as a Christian priest for forty-five years—as Gregory says, almost as long as the average human life at that time.[273] The *Funeral Oration* he offered in his father's memory is a magnificent example of Greek oratory, and one of the most interesting sources of our knowledge of Gregory's life and times. Ullmann justly described it in the following terms:

> Stone and brass would by this time have been broken in pieces and crumbled away, or have been trampled underfoot without respect by the barbarians of those parts; but this oration will be read and admired as long as Greek literature remains.[274]

The death occurred in late spring 374,[275] after a lingering illness in the previous year. A constant thread in the praises of the old bishop is the "simplicity and sincerity" of his manners. He received a Church that had only one predecessor before him (Leontios who is described as an old-time rustic)[276] but had left behind a splendid Church building which would be his own monument.[277] His father is in this same

---

269. Orat. 19.10, PG 35.1053. "Dedicate your words to the Word, live simply and righteously, and take care that your doctrine does not become the cause of your ruin."
270. The motive of presenting himself as a leading "monk" as well as leading theologian-bishop is clearly discernible in the *Carmen Lugubre* (Carm. 2.1.45) he wrote at this time.
271. Orat. 19.11, PG 35.1056.
272. Orat. 19 is the first of Gregory's Orations where he does not make an explicit reference to the old bishop's presence.
273. Orat. 18.38, PG 35.1036. He himself was 45.
274. Ullmann, *Gregory of Nazianzus*. ET, G.V. Cox (1851), p. 147.
275. The date is determined by Ep. 63, written for his cousin Amphilokios who had in the winter of 373/374 become bishop of Ikonium. Cf. Gallay (1943), p. 124, n. 6.
276. Orat. 18.12, 16, PG 35.1000, 1004.
277. Orat. 18.39, PG 35.1037.

mold "a simple and godlike soul."[278] His like will not be found again in the present age of dissemblers and unworthy leaders. It is partly a lament on the state of the times, the ending of the glory days of the Constantinian era, as he sees them, but also a perspicacious comment on the shape of things to be, for Gregory knows that the selection of bishops is passing definitively into the hands of the ascetics of the Christian community, and the days of the old landowning gentry who rose to episcopal office because of their civic standing, are becoming a thing of the past in the provinces. He applauds the process that will soon see the episcopacy drawn solely from the ranks of the monks.[279]

Basil the Great came to Nazianzus to hear Gregory preach the memorial oration, and had to sit in patience and hear yet again several references to Gregory's displeasure at his actions over Sasima,[280] and how the old man had been largely responsible for Basil's own elevation into the episcopate.[281] In Basil's presence he defends his rejection of Sasima by saying he had been inducted into Nazianzus instead.[282] He even seems to throw a few lightly disguised insults his friend's way, all the time covering the rocks with his customary velvet glove of praise.[283] The present version of the text has clearly been refined into a literary masterpiece from that original extempore version, in the course of which Gregory invited Basil also to offer an extempore speech, which has not survived.[284] Gregory focuses attention away from his father's lapse from orthodoxy in the early years of his own priesthood, describing it as a schism caused by "overzealous" elements in the locality[285] and emphasizes, instead, his father's efforts at opposing heresy in the time of Valens, when he encouraged Gregory and Basil to debate with the Arian theologians at Caesarea.[286] As Bernardi points out, this retrospective reference suggests the final edition of the text post-dates the fall of Valens, and thus was one of the many literary activities of Gregory's time in retirement after the Council of 381.

278. Orat. 18.26, PG 35.1016.
279. Orat. 18.35, PG 35.1032.
280. "One thing I have to blame in both of you, and do not be angry at my frankness in speaking…
    for you seized me and handed me over to this treacherous market place of souls." Orat. 18.37,
    PG 35.1036.
281. Orat. 18.35-36. 1032-1033.
282. Orat. 18.40, PG 35.1040. Addressing his father's tomb he says: "Excuse me for the people I left
    and the people whom I accepted for your sake." It is one of the few times he will admit to the
    canonical transfer in public, but on this occasion it served his purpose to defend himself
    against any claims of Basil. The opening words ask Basil pointedly: "Why have you come: to
    superintend us, or to seek your bishop? We no longer exist; but for the most part have
    departed with him." Orat. 18.2, PG 35.985-988.
283. The praises of Basil in Orat. 18.35, PG 35.1032, end with a reference to a diplomatic silence over
    "what needs to be forgotten." Here Gregory uses the image of a river flowing over rocks, the
    same he had used in his letter attacking Basil for pusillanimity in his theological teachings which
    had then called down Basil's fury on his head. Cf. Ep. 58.7, PG 37.116; Gallay (1964), p. 75.
284. Orat. 18.3, PG 35.988-989; cf. Bernardi (1968), p. 125, fn. 185; Gallay (1943).
285. Orat. 18.18, PG 35.1005.
286. Orat. 18.16; Orat. 18.37, PG 35.1005, 1033-1036.

Very shortly after his father's death, his mother Nonna also died. He never dedicated a funeral oration to her memory, though he probably expanded the sections of *Oration* 18 which refer to her, as in the final version they represent a short panegyric of Nonna too. Words failed him on that loss. He spent much time in his remaining years, however, sketching out epitaphial miniatures for her. They amount to the extraordinary number of thirty six distinct tomb-verses.[287] Nonna had come to the Church at Nazianzus for prayer, and had died there suddenly. Gregory says that at her death a lament shall rise forth from the poor, the orphans and the widows of the region whom she so assiduously supported in her lifetime.[288] The fact that she was "taken up by God from before the very altar as a pure oblation" as she was in the very act of prayer is taken by Gregory as a great sign of her election.[289] She at least had been able "to take wing back to God."[290] Once again, and for the last time, he calls her a Sarah, unable to bear separation from the bosom of her Abraham, to whom she has willingly flown.[291] The simplest of all his tomb verses sums it up succinctly:

> Nonna daughter of Philtatios.
> Where did she die? In the temple.
> How did it happen? While praying.
> When so? In advanced age.
> Then what a beautiful life and what a holy end.[292]

Gregory seems to have fallen into a prolonged state of depressed ill health after the death of his parents. He retreated into his quarters at Arianzum and began strenuous efforts to disentangle himself from the episcopal charge of Nazianzus. In that year 374, Eusebios of Samosata was passing nearby on his way into exile in Thrace,[293] and Gregory writes after him, apologizing for being too ill when he was near Nazianzus to come over to greet him. He says he was so ill that he could not move from his bed, and thought he too was going to expire. Gregory asks him to remember him. This first letter was meant as a testimony to Eusebios' stature as a confessor suffering exile for the faith. His second letter was crafted as a gracious consolation for exile, which Eusebios took with him on his journey to Thrace, sending him his own letters of benediction in thanks. The short "consolatio" was a tangible memento of Gregory, and (in line with Gregory's final request in *Letter* 66 that Eusebios should not forget him in their mutual troubles) was probably one of the reasons why Eusebios and Meletios of Antioch did indeed call him to mind at a crucial time when they were discussing the affairs of the capital in 379 at their synod to settle the affair of the schism in Antioch, and were also wondering where

287. *Epitaphia.* Carm. 2.2.66-102, PG 38.44-63.
288. Carm. 2.2.67, PG 38.45.
289. Carm. 2.2.69, PG 38.47; Carm. 2.2.73, PG 38.49; Carm. 2.2.78, PG 38.51-52.
290. Carm. 2.2.79, PG 38.52.
291. Carm. 2.2.90, PG 38.56.
292. Carm. 2.2.99, PG 38.60.
293. Theodoret, HE 1.4; Greg. Epp. 64-66, PG 37.125-132; Gallay (1964), pp. 83-86.

they could find a Nicene orator to represent the cause in Constantinople after Valens' death.

Try as he might, however, Gregory could not get Anthimos to hear his claim that he had never intended his ordination to Nazianzus to be a permanent one. Gregory's idea that his episcopal ordination was merely temporary, and terminated with his father's death had no canonical precedent at a time when an episcopal ordination was commonly regarded as a "marriage" to the local Church. The more he appealed to have a new candidate established for the Church, the more the surrounding hierarchs turned a deaf ear. He was anxious too over increasing criticisms that he was too "proud" to assume the duties of a small country Church.[294] These, as with the accusations to the same effect over Sasima, he more or less shrugs off, telling us that it was not duties in a big city he wanted he wanted, merely a release from all public works. But there is also a sense, though he guards it in a veil of words as if he is sheltering someone, that his chief problems after his father's death came from a specific circle of Nicene zealots. These he seems to identify as Apollinarists[295] who were all too eager to grasp the episcopal throne at Nazianzus if Gregory did not want it. They would have done so in the name of Nicene orthodoxy, and at this period could still have claimed the mantle of orthodoxy, but were increasingly being regarded as an enemy within the camp by the leading Nicene protagonists of the East who gave allegiance to Meletios. The more they were pressed on every side, by Arian denunciations as Sabellianists, and by Syrian-Nicene criticisms over their "mindless" christology,[296] the more they tried to reinforce their school by "accumulating" vacant episcopal sees, in imitation of the strategy Meletios himself had initiated for defending the Nicene cause. One band of Apollinarist Nicenes certainly had its eyes set on Nazianzus, and made a bid to seize that Church when it became clear that Gregory was not intending to resume duties there after his retirement from Constantinople. One his first activities in the aftermath of the council of 381, was to instruct his priest Cledonios to have them ejected. There is, however, a great deal in this latter story that is left unsaid, and I suspect that among the contending Apollinarist clergy were people known to him that he still wished to shelter, even though he would no longer patronize them. Gregory knew these Apollinarists were in the region even at the time he left Nazianzus in 375, and it may well be that his typically frustrating ambivalence, when he set off on his travels, as to whether he would ever come back to act as bishop in his own Church, was partly intended to frustrate their candidacy.

In the end, as on so many other occasions when he came to a brick wall in his life, he just had enough one day and turned to the open road. He slipped away quietly, without announcing his plans to anyone, least of all Basil,[297] and set off on new

---

294. *Complaint on His own Calamities*, Carm. 2.1.19, v. 71-74, PG 37.1277.
295. *Complaint on His own Calamities*, Carm. 2.1.19, vv. 61-74, PG 37.1276-1277.
296. It was a joke, reproduced often by Gregory, that their doctrine that the Word of God did not require a human mind when he assumed the body—was indeed a "brainless" position to adopt.
297. Cf. Basil, Ep. 217, PG 32.793.

adventures to the coast at Seleukia. His priests would administer the Church at Nazianzus. That made it clear to all he was no longer there. The fact that his priests were administering the Church made it equally clear to all that he was still bishop there if anyone should come calling. It was one more of those logical conundrums he liked to puzzle over in Seleukia, which would later come out in his *Theological Orations*,[298] analogous to receiving a voice mail that confidently tells the caller: "There is no one here. Please leave a message." It hit just the right tone of meaningless ambivalence to cover his tracks for a decent time.

298. Orats. 27-31.

5

AN INVITATION TO BYZANTIUM

That is no country for old men...

A tattered coat upon a stick, unless
Soul clap its hands and sing, and louder sing
For every tatter in its mortal dress,
An agèd man is but a paltry thing,
Nor is there singing school but studying
Monuments of its own magnificence;
And therefore I have sailed the seas and come
To the holy city of Byzantium.

Yeats

Gregory calls this place of retreat the "Parthenona"[1] of Thekla in Seleukia.[2] This suggests to me that this was an organized convent dedicated to the memory of Thekla.[3] Most previous commentators have taken this to be the great pilgrimage site at the coast near Isaurian Seleukia, about 130 miles southwest of Nazianzus. It was the metropolitan church in Isauria, which Egeria would visit later and of which would leave a description. Moreschini[4] has recently suggested it was Seleukia-Ctesiphon by the river Tigris to which he was referring, though there is absolutely no reason to connect Gregory with travel in such a region; and Hanson thought it was Seleukia in Cilicia.[5] Norris[6] noted that there was, apart from the tomb and pilgrimage site of Thecla at Isauria, a large basilica dedicated to her in Seleukia near Antioch in Syria. It

1. House of the virgin—or house of virgins.
2. *De Vita Sua*, vv. 547-549, PG 37.1067.
3. One of the legendary early saints of Cappadocia. She was believed to have come from Ikonium, and to have been an apostolic companion of St Paul. An early apocrypha survives: *The Acts of Thecla*. The connection with Ikonium, may explain why Gregory can expect hospitality in the Seleukian monastery as, apart from his own status as Cappadocian bishop and philanthropist, his sister Gorgonia had been a patroness of ascetics from her base in Ikonium, and his uncle Amphilokios' family were also prominent Christian philanthropists there. His cousin Theodosia (originally from Ikonium) was the family member who invited him to come from Seleukia and take up residence in one of her villas in the capital. His cousin, Amphilokios, was bishop there after 373, ordained by Basil but not dependent on Basil's patronage.
4. Moreschini. *I cinque Discorsi Teologici* (Rome, 1986), p. 11.
5. Hanson (1988), pp. 702-703. He offers no reasons for this, which seems to have been a simple mistake of geography on his part. The same thing is reproduced in White (1996), p. xvi. fn. 16. Silifke is near Tarsus of Cilicia, but within the provincial boundary of Isauria. Cf. F. Van der Meer and C. Mohrmann, *Atlas of the Early Christian World* (1958) (map 16.a).
6. Norris (1991), p. 8, n. 43.

is possible that Gregory traveled to Antioch, but all his known connections tie in with the site in Isauria. The Antiochene shrine of Thekla was actually at Seleukia-Pieria, and was by no means as famous as the tombal site nearer to Cappadocia. The bishop of Isauria, Hilarios, was a friend of his who later witnessed the signing of his will.[7] The more obvious meaning of Gregory's reference, presuming as it does that the place is famous for Thecla's memory, seems to me to be the tombal pilgrimage site of Seleukia in Isauria. One thing is clear, the bishops of the Antiochene metropolitan, Meletios, were soon aware that Gregory was there. This can be accounted for quite easily, for Isaurian Seleukia was only a hundred miles from Antioch by sea, and the bishops who were Nicenes in the larger surrounding region were predominantly partisans of Meletios.

Bernardi is not sure what kind of life Gregory lived there, in common, or alone, but offers as his hypothesis that it was a convent that sheltered him for more than four years. Gallay, however, did not think the word *parthenona* meant that he entered any kind of specific place at all, interpreting it to mean simply a poetic way of saying he retired to the home town of the Virgin Thekla. But Thekla's home town was actually Ikonium according to the apocrypha. I am of the opinion that the word *parthenona*, in its context here, does suggest a formal community of virgins (an ascetic community was certainly operative on this site as we know from later evidence) and that Gregory was associated in some way with them. Gregory the Presbyter, in his sixth-century *Vita*, gives the information that Gregory retired to a "healing center," and was looked after in his time of ill health. It is impossible to know what information he used as his source for this, or whether it is an abstracted speculation (he offers many suchlike) gleaned from general truths of Gregory's life.[8] If it was a convent to which Gregory retired, and it was operative as a healing site, it fits what is known of the monastic center at Isaurian Seleukia. It has been thought most unlikely that a man should be so associated with a convent, but such a supposition is unnecessary. Gregory was an ascetic bishop, and though he was himself very hostile to the notion of mixed sex celibate communities,[9] the concept of being attached to a convent where the ascetics took some care of him does not involve us in imagining him living in the community in any way at all. Female eastern monasteries, from the outset, and even to the present, had regular arrangements for the care and reception of clergy visitors and family. The abbess at Macrina's monastery entertained Gregory of Nyssa who visited his dying sister, as he tells us in the *Vita Macrinae*, and also

---

7. *Testamentum*, PG 37.396.
8. Gregory was ill immediately before his arrival here, as he tells Eusebios of Samosata, apologizing for being unable to meet him in 374 when the former was exiled. He also wrote to Gregory of Nyssa apologizing for missing Basil's funeral in 379, on the grounds of ill health. This does not tell us he was an invalid all the rest of the time, of course, but his health took another turn for the worse in the capital in 381, and troubled him throughout the ten years of his last retirement: so there are grounds for thinking he needed the solicitations of a supportive "healing" community.
9. Cf. *Epigram* 12, PG 38.28. ET, McGuckin (1986, 1989), p. 19.

informs us that though the women's monastery was by then wholly separate in its organization and remit from the men's quarters, the two sites were still near one another and mutually supportive. Gregory, one might suppose, took up residence at Seleukia near the convent and was possibly looked after by ascetics there who were skilled in medicinal arts, as well as by his own servants whom he doubtless brought with him.

Seleukia also served him as a center of theological research. It was a city that had witnessed the earlier attempt under Constantius to provide a standard of international Christian orthodoxy on the terms of the twin synods of Rimini and Seleukia in 359. At Seleukia the Homoiousian party of Eustathios of Sebaste had overcome the Nicene Homoousians and the Arian Homoian and Anhomoian parties alike, but the emperor had subsequently refused to endorse the Homoiousian agenda, favoring instead the Homoian theology of Akakios of Caesarea, which had been published at Rimini.[10] It was, therefore, a city with a notable theological past. Whether in the monastery or the bishop's archives, the records seem to have been kept there of many contemporary Christian writings. It is clear enough that Gregory made some personal researches here, for the results are abundantly apparent in his later orations. His preaching in the capital city in a few years' time shows someone who has prepared his case very well indeed.

Gregory stayed in Seleukia from the Easter of 375 onwards. He heard the news that the new emperor Gratian had assumed power in the West. Like his predecessor, he too was a Nicene supporter, but his early legislation allowed toleration of the religious status quo, in deference to Valens' Homoian policy in the East, and Gregory expected little change from the intelligence of his elevation to power.

In the latter years of Gregory's time in Seleukia, his attention was drawn by someone to the unsavory aspects of Apollinarism. It was possibly Diodore of Tarsus, the chief disciple of Meletios. Diodore, who would come as a bishop near Seleukia in 378,[11] had taken a particularly intense dislike to Apollinaris and was set on reversing the tendencies of the latter's christology. Gregory would study the case and also seems to have become aware of the work of Diodore himself. He says little at the time in regard to either theologian. Both were known to be supporters of the Nicene creed, and he was in no hurry to add further divisions to the general cause he had supported for so long. And yet, it is equally clear, when he does make a public statement after the Theodosian endorsement of Nicene orthodoxy in 381, that he regards Apollinaris and Diodore as two "extremes" which any sensible mind would avoid studiously. The attack on Apollinarism was something mounted by the Meletian party as part and parcel of their strategy in this period to reposition the

10. Cf. Hanson (1988), pp. 371-380.
11. Diodore, who had been leading the Antiochene Church in the absence of the exiled Meletios, was set in place at Tarsus immediately after the death of Valens, as part of the strategy to seize significant sees again, the chief way the Nicene party in the East redrew its lines of battle after 378.

Nicene cause, and distance it from the "old-style" early Alexandrian theologians. In the early days Athanasios himself had favored Apollinaris bishop of Laodicea, for his strongly anti-Arian apologetics, and his monist Christology which so positively argued for the deity of Jesus. In his later years, however, many of Athanasios' closest theological allies warned him of associating with Apollinaris. Apollinarist monism seemed to most observers one of the dead weights preventing the Nicene party from coalescing into a wider Church freed of its internal factions. The other dead weight was Marcellus of Ancyra. Both these early supporters of Athanasios, had been slowly but surely abandoned by the old Nicene stalwart, and by this period, several years after Athanasios' death, had become as lambs to the slaughter. The Nicene party, to make headway against its enemies, had to sacrifice Apollinaris and Marcellus as two examples of "Sabellianist" thinkers, the ancient heresy which had nothing to do with either of them at all, but which conveniently synopsized their objectionable tendencies as reducing the separateness of the divine persons into an ill-considered theological monism. Gregory calls the position "Judaising" or "Sabellianising" and in this shows his allegiance to the wider circle of the Nicenes around Meletios. After 381, however, he would more publicly make a stand against what he saw as a dangerous counter-tendency emerging in the circle gathered around Diodore of Tarsus. This was a school that would have some famous disciples: Theodore Mopsuestia, Nestorius of Constantinople and Theodoret of Cyr, and its christological dualism would produce enough problems of its own in another generation, though that is another story, and a very large story, in itself.[12]

Gregory had intended his stay in Seleukia to deliver him from the demands of the Cappadocian hierarchs that he should take over the direction of his father's church at Nazianzus. It was their opinion that he had been synodically assigned this church after he had agreed not to take up residence in Sasima in defiance of the new metropolitanate of Cappadocia Secunda. Gregory's version of the story is that he had only decided to accept his father's offer of episcopal rank alongside him,[13] as his co-adjutor bishop, for as long as the old man was alive. Once his father died, he felt no commitment to the town at all.

The matter was massively complicated, however, by the fact that the church was his own private property, and the hierarchs were not entirely free to appoint another bishop, nor had Gregory given any sign that he had abdicated the property (something which he certainly had not, as he would demonstrate by retiring back to Nazianzus as a bishop after the Council of 381). Gregory makes the unlikely argument that the local Cappadocian hierarchs had misunderstood the terms of his appointment to Nazianzus, a settlement Anthimos, his father, and himself had worked out with the agreement of the local Cappadocian synod. He says that after

12. Cf. J. McGuckin, *St Cyril of Alexandria and the Christological Controversy* (Leiden, 1994); idem., *On the Unity of Christ* (Crestwood, NY: 1995).
13. He omits to mention the role Anthimos played, or the local synod with him.

his parents' death that he "was in no manner committed to the church entrusted to me,"[14] but does admit that he had been the episcopal administrator of Nazianzus,[15] and then makes the unbelievable statement that he was "simply like a stranger there," who had begged the local bishops to appoint a replacement. This they would not do, and instead urged him to carry on with his responsibilities, demanding that as bishop he should now be ready to conduct the necessary baptismal services for the local region.[16] They wanted him to take an oath of allegiance to his see. This, the nearest thing we have in the fourth century to a formal contract of appointment to the episcopate, was the one thing Gregory held out against. No oath had been requested for his co-adjutorial appointment to Nazianzus (and whatever he had promised for Sasima must have been dispensed by agreement with Anthimos and the synod) so now that he was being pressed to such a contract he refused and decamped for Seleukia. This left the Cappadocian hierarchs in a quandary, and in fact the situation could not be regularized until Gregory returned to Cappadocia after his retirement seven years later and arranged with Anthimos' successor, Theodore of Tyana, to have his own cousin Eulalios set in as the new owner-incumbent of his own church. By going to Seleukia Gregory simply hoped that the Cappadocian clergy would get tired of hounding him.[17] His belief that if he left the region, he *de facto* left their communion, is an interesting indication that at several times in his life Gregory uses Church law to his own advantage; sometimes holding to it scrupulously, and at other times impatiently dismissing it as something that can hardly be expected to apply to a gentleman of his means and stature. In his attitude to canon, as well as to civil, law, Gregory remained first and foremost an aristocrat of the old order.

If the Cappadocian bishops seem to have left him alone, the new local clergy of Seleukia did not, and this was the beginning of his new set of problems. He seems to have enjoyed his scholarly retirement for some time[18] before he was pestered yet again by clerical colleagues. The start of the troubles was certainly the great disaster of Adrianople.

Valens died on August 9, 378.[19] He had taken a largely superior Roman army to suppress the rioting Goths, who had been allowed to settle in the Empire a few years previously, and whose refugee administration had been incompetently handled. Faced with a choice between starvation or military annihilation, the Goths overcame

14. *De Vita Sua*, vv. 529-530, PG 37.1065-1066. Here he means Sasima.
15. "For a short time I admit I did look after my father's Church, like a stranger looking after someone else's property." *De Vita Sua*, vv. 533-537, PG 37.1066.
16. Once he did this, as bishop in his own right for the Pascha baptisms of 375, everyone knew he would have been permanently "assigned" to Nazianzus. *De Vita Sua*, v. 535, PG 37.1066
17. *De Vita Sua*, vv. 549-551, PG 37.1067. It is an odd set of reasons to justify a certainly dubious canonical behavior.
18. "I spent some considerable time there ... but then found myself up against problems again." *De Vita Sua*, vv. 551-552, PG 37.1067
19. Socrates, HE 1.4; Sozomen, HE 1.6.40; Theodoret, HE 1.4.36.

a numerically superior force. In the aftermath of the first major losses in the fighting, Valens withdrew to a villa in the local countryside that served as his headquarters. There he was discovered by a Gothic war party who set fire to the house, killing the emperor and the leading generals, and thereby forcing the Romans to sue for a humiliating peace.

The massive loss to Roman military security (a time when the eastern empire might well have fallen permanently) passed over without the collapse of the capital city. The Goths migrated south, where they would eventually be defeated by Theodosius out of his campaign headquarters at Thessaloniki. The military disaster proved to be a critically significant advantage to the Nicene supporters in the East, however, for the new Augustus would be appointed from the West, from an old Spanish Christian family.

Theodosius became co-emperor and Augustus of the East on January 19, 379. His was an emergency elevation. His father had been executed by Valentinian on suspicions of plotting the throne, and at the news of the Gothic disaster at Adrianople, the Emperor Gratian, knowing he was a highly able general, and also perhaps desiring to move him out of the western provinces, proclaimed him Augustus of the East. The family of Theodosius, were traditional Nicenes.[20] In August of 379 Gratian and Theodosius conjointly issued an edict suppressing all heresies "under the terms of divine as well as imperial law." At the same time, from Milan, Gratian revoked the edict of toleration he had issued earlier in that same year from Sirmium.[21] Palanque and Liebschuetz[22] see in this move the unmistakable influence of bishop Ambrose of Milan, but it is clearly also a firm commitment of Theodosius himself, well aware that the chaos of Valens' policy of hit and miss encouragement of the various factions of the Eastern Church had proved completely ineffectual. Gratian and Theodosius simply determined to enforce the orthodox theology of the West in both parts of the empire. This signaled that the Nicene party would now be in favor. It indicated that those in communion with the theology of Rome and Alexandria could expect to be in the imperial favor. The influence of Meletios of Antioch and Eusebios of Samosata, the two senior Nicene protagonists of the Eastern Church, and that of Basil of Caesarea, would not be negligible, as they had already proven themselves as martyr-confessors for the Nicene cause, but the "pro-westerners" would have the edge, as Athanasios had never offered Meletios his support over the crisis of the succession[23] in Antioch, always suspecting him because of

20. Sozomen, HE 7.4.
21. *Cod. Theod.* 16.5.5; Socrates, HE 5.2; 7.1.
22. J.R. Palanque, *S. Ambroise et l'empire romain* (Paris: 1933), pp. 64-67, 71; Liebschuetz (1990), p. 157.
23. Athanasios refused to admit the legitimacy of his episcopal ordination as he had been pro-posed, and consecrated, by Arians, and then immediately broke with them advancing a pro-Nicene theology. He tried to meet with Meletios later when passing through Antioch, but Meletios did not want to be seen to be too closely associated with him, and refused to receive him, confirming Athanasios' worst suspicions of his orthodoxy.

his early years in the Arian camp. Despite Basil's desire to win over Athanasios, some of that suspicion also attached in the minds of the Alexandrians to Basil too, Homoiousian as he had been; though after 364, when Athanasios had passed through the East after seeing Jovian, he gained a higher estimate of Basil as a man of substance. In this new western ascendancy, Gregory was the one whose background was perfectly "clean." And from the very outset of his episcopal career he had declared himself for Nicaea in all its fullness, and for the trinitarian faith in its most radical form. From this time onwards his politics also develop in a strongly "pro-western" direction. It is something that gets him into the limelight very quickly, but also causes his downfall, as we shall see.

The fact that Theodosius sided so strongly with Nicene orthodoxy from the outset of his reign showed that he was willing to take a calculated risk on the loyalty of his new capital at Byzantium, which was completely Arian in persuasion, the center of the Homoian movement. Theodosius consulted about the religious situation in the East and was apprized of the "map of theological loyalties" centered on the four places where Nicene orthodoxy could still be said to be strongly represented—Alexandria where Peter had succeeded to Athanasios, Cappadocia around Basil's party, Antioch and Meletios' party, and finally Illyricum and the pro-western bishops in the ascendancy there.[24] Sadly, the two leading factions on that map, the Alexandrian clergy, and the clergy gathered round the leadership of Meletios of Antioch, were bitterly divided among themselves to the point of almost complete animosity, for the Alexandrians continued the policy of Athanasios, and refused to admit the legitimacy of Meletios as archbishop of Antioch, favoring and fostering his (uncanonical) rival Paulinus. The latter was an intruder into the see, directing a minority Nicene faction, who had been consecrated by Lucifer of Cagliari, a loose cannon of a western bishop, whose loyalty to the Nicene cause had inspired him to set in place an alternative to (what he thought to be) the duplicitous ex-Arian Meletios. This uncanonical choice was fixed, as far as the West was concerned, and the bishops of Rome, Illyricum and Alexandria were as firmly set against the legitimacy of Meletios' claims, as the rest of the eastern party of the orthodox Nicenes at this period, was drawn up behind him.

Almost as soon as they heard of the news of Valens' death in 378,[25] the Nicene party began to work in the open once more. The prominent exiles started to return, chief among them Meletios and Eusebios of Samosata. Meletios' senior disciple who had been holding charge of affairs in Antioch during his last exile, the priest-monk Diodore, was sent to be bishop of Tarsus to the east of the province, near Seleukia. Communication was had with Basil at Caesarea, then in his final illness, and he seems to have reminded them of the merits of Gregory, his old friend, now in

---

24. Cf. Liebschuetz (1990), p. 158; Sozomen, HE 7.4; Basil, Epp. 91 and 204, show how strongly Illyricum was attached to the Nicene cause.
25. A fuller study of the whole issue can be found in Snee (1981) and (1985).

self-imposed exile at the shrine of Thekla.[26] If this is so, it would have been one of his last actions, and an indication that whatever the personal hostilities clouding the later years of their uneven friendship, both Basil and Gregory constantly recognized one another's theological worth. In the spring of 379 Gregory was weighed down by the news of Basil's death, and the fact that he had not had time to make up with him over their large falling out over Sasima. He wrote a letter of consolation to Gregory of Nyssa, apologizing for not attending the funeral.[27] His ill health had not permitted it. It was a consolation to him, when he finally turned up to preach the promised memorial sermon in Caesarea in 381, that he could recall how Basil had some hand in his appointment to the capital city, by approving the idea of Gregory's invitation when it had been proposed to him.[28]

In the mid to late summer of 379 Meletios, acting to end the schism in his own city once and for all, and also with an eye to bringing together the whole party of pro-Nicene theologians in the East, called a large synod of one hundred and fifty bishops, to meet at Antioch in the autumn of 379.[29] Its primary agenda was to settle the internal conflict over the rightful succession of the episcopate in the city. Its wider goal was to bring to an end the greater Arian "schism" in the East.[30] Eusebios of Samosata, and Gregory of Nyssa were in attendance at the side of Meletios. This council was in substance identical with the synod that opened later in Constantinople in 381. The latter at first had more or less all the same adherents, and was probably intended as a more solemnly sanctioned rerun of that earlier Antiochene synod, to give it a more powerful status in resolving the eastern schism. It was only when the council of 381 came to a critical impasse after Meletios' death, and Gregory proved unable to negotiate a new settlement to Theodosius' satisfaction, that the emperor decided to break the deadlock by summoning a wider representation from Egypt and Illyricum. Up to the point of the arrival of the Egyptian and Illyrian bishops, the synod of 381 still bore all the marks of the hand of Meletios. His death, in the very midst of the deliberations was a disaster as far as the Antiochene bishops (and Gregory) were concerned, for Pope Damasus of Rome was determined to work through both of the new episcopal contingents to dismantle whatever he could of Meletios' plans, Gregory's appointment included.

It seems most likely that it was the synod of Antioch which sent off an urgent summons for Gregory to come to Constantinople and mount a serious theological

26. Gregory says that Basil had "approved" of his appointment to Constantinople. Orat. 43.2, PG 36.497.
27. Ep. 76, PG 37.140-141; Gallay (1964), pp. 93-94.
28. Proposed to him, I think, by Eusebios of Samosata, not Gregory himself. Orat. 43.2, PG 36.497.
29. A.M. Ritter, *Das Konzil von Konstantinopel und sein Symbol* (Göttingen: 1965); Hanson (1988), p. 716.
30. Cf. Hanson (1988), pp. 803-804. Hanson is mistaken when he says (p. 804) that Theodosius "had not yet openly declared his hand" before the council started. He does not take into account the edict of August 3 issued from Milan (cf. Liebschuetz [1990], p. 157).

campaign to win over the local populace. Gregory makes it clear, more than once, that he was invited to the capital by corporate synodical decree, and did not go there on his own initiative.[31] These pro-Nicene Meletian hierarchs particularly wanted Gregory to speak about the dangers of the Apollinarist christology.[32] When he did come to the capital, it is interesting that he did not follow their instructions. The more he had studied, the more he knew that there were indeed many serious problems with an Apollinarist christology. He also became increasingly alarmed, from his reading of those Meletian anti-Apollinarists (especially Diodore of Tarsus the leading light of the younger element of the party), that the opposite view being propagated among the Syrian clergy was even worse. In retrospect, when he describes this aspect of the christological controversy, he pairs Apollinarists and "anonymous" teachers of the "Two Sons" theory[33] as two extreme examples of "wicked thinking."

The imaginative concept of having Gregory lead a preaching campaign in the capital[34] was an idea that was perhaps encouraged by Basil, but can also be ascribed to both Meletios and Eusebios of Samosata who had long been patrons of Gregory and aware of his record in Cappadocia. The idea of Gregory's mission was also encouraged by leading politicians in the capital, who were well aware of the change in religious policy that Theodosius would inaugurate publicly soon enough, and were anxious to disarm the potential troubles which his proclamation of Nicene faith could cause him.[35] This political dimension was visible from the time of the

31. Cf. *De Vita Sua*, v. 596. "At the invitation of many shepherds and their flocks I came to assist the congregation and help defend the word." PG 37.1070; see also *De seipso et de episcopis*, Carm. 2.1.12, vv. 81-82, PG 37.1172. In these poems his apologia is based on this fact of his synodical invitation: those who had once so eagerly courted him (the party around Meletios) were the very ones who so loudly abandoned him after Meletios' death. These (and their leader Diodore) he regards with only a little less rancour than the Egyptians. The historian Socrates also attests that a large body of bishops summoned Gregory to Constantinople. HE 1.5.6.
32. Gregory tells us that this was the primary reason he was invited at *De Vita Sua*, vv. 609ff, PG 37.1071.
33. This certainly means Diodore. Cf. *De Vita Sua*, vv. 632-651, PG 37.1072-1074; and see McGuckin, "Autobiography as Apologia" (2001). He describes his theology a "wickedness" and calls for him to be "banished from the discussion" (ibid., v. 646). White (1996), p. 59, n. 61, mistakenly supposes this to be a reference to Paul of Samosata. This hostility to Diodore and his (later) condemnation of Apollinaris positions Gregory, most interestingly, as someone who cannot really be described as either "Antiochene" or "Alexandrian" in his christological tradition. He is very close to the position of Athanasios as outlined in his *Letter to Epictetos*, but also has a strong sense of the importance of the psychology of Jesus from his intimate knowledge of Origen's soteriology.
34. It is a strategy (mounting a campaign of orations) which can be seen again in Constantinople when later both Chrysostom and Nestorius came there as reformer-bishops. Like Gregory, both of these orators fell foul of the Alexandrian clergy.
35. Cf. *De Vita Sua*, vv. 607-608. "And so I came, not on my own initiative, but summoned by powerful men to defend the word." PG 37.1071.

early news of the elevation of Theodosius, though no Roman emperor before him had ever dared so much and in so short a time to reform the religion of his future populace.[36] Gregory's arrival in the city, therefore, was no hare-brained individual scheme, but a deliberate and sponsored political movement on behalf of the Nicene party, and with the blessing of those political forces in the capital who expected to be part of the new power-élite. The hostile reception to Gregory as Nicene preacher in the city, as well as his charmed ability to continue in spite of the opposition can be explained on the basis of his known sponsors and protectors, as much as the policies he adopted.

Bernardi[37] has pointed out that one of the agents advancing Gregory's invitation to Constantinople was his cousin Theodosia. She was his maternal cousin, the sister of Amphilokios who was now returning to his see at Ikonium, from which he had been ejected by Valens' agent Modestus. Now that Modestus' suppression of the Nicenes had run out of steam, the Nicene party of aristocrats in Constantinople made common cause with the Meletian Nicene bishops and encouraged their hopes for redress in the future. Theodosia was very well informed of the Nicene cause through her contacts with her brother Amphilokios and with Gregory himself. She is undoubtedly one of those who recommends Gregory's name at court in the time before Theodosius arrived at the capital. She had married the senator Ablabios, the grandson of Constantine's Praetorian Prefect, one of the grandest "old" families of the new capital.[38]

So it was that Gregory agreed to represent the Nicene cause in the city, and preach a "theological campaign there" to inform the population (and more particularly the leading intellectual power brokers who governed city politics) what was the faith that they had to "adapt to" now that a new master was coming to them as their political savior. Theodosius would show his hand openly in August of 379 when he withdrew legal toleration for heresies,[39] and even more so on February 27, 380 when, from his campaign headquarters, he instructed the Constantinopolitans to follow the faith of "Peter of Alexandria and Damasus of Rome," that is the Nicene belief. These edicts were the fulfilment of all that the Nicene party had hoped for after the death of Valens, and certainly no more than the logical confirmation of all they had expected after hearing of the accession of Theodosius. This was, then, the political

36. Cf. Liebschuetz (1990), p. 157.
37. Bernardi (1984a).
38. Their son Seleukos would become Praetorian Prefect of Africa in 412-415, the couple also brought up the orphaned sister of Ablabios, Olympias, who as widow of the Prefect of Constantinople Nebridios, would be a leading patron of John Chrysostom (though see McLynn [1998] for a different perspective). Olympias was 18 when Gregory came to the capital. Cf. Bernardi (1984a); idem. (1995), pp. 177-179. Gregory dedicates his Carm. 2.2.6 to Olympias, PG 37.1542-1550. Chrysostom wrote 16 letters to her: ed. A.M. Malingrey, SC vol. 13 (Paris, 1968).
39. *Cod. Theod.* 16.5.5. Issued at Milan on August 3, 379 (Liebschuetz [1990], p. 157).

scenario that Gregory had already seen initiated, which induced him to accept the commission to come to Constantinople. The extent of the hostility of the residents was something that still caught him unprepared.

Gregory said farewell to his retreat in Seleukia. It was the only time he had actually practiced that retirement from all the commitments of public life that he had so often said was all he desired. He says he stayed there "quite a long time"[40] but in fact it was little more than three years. We know what his feelings were on his departure from two poems he wrote on the journey to Constantinople,[41] in which he is oscillating between anxiety at the size of the task ahead of him, and great hopes for what it might produce. One of his prayers on the journey calls on Christ to help him fulfil the role of Moses crossing the Red Sea. Another asks that he may be led, again like Moses, by a pillar of fire to fulfil his task. But once he has fulfilled his duty he says he wants to be able to "return once more to the dear friends and companions I have known." He was very well aware that he had been called on to produce his greatest performance ever. This invitation to exercise his skills as a rhetor (which he himself knew were sublime), was a very flattering public acknowledgment by the chief synod of eastern Nicenes, that he was the leading orthodox rhetor then alive. More than this, they wanted him to play on the greatest stage of the Eastern world, for the benefit of the Church universal. Yet in retrospect all he says about the end of his stay in Seleukia is:

> I found myself up against misfortunes once again. I realized that I had gained none of the advantages I had hoped for, only more of the very problems I had fled from.[42]

But this is a hindsight colored by his bitter experiences at the council of 381. All that can be said of his time in scholarly seclusion at Seleukia is that he indeed lived a most retired life, and seems to have been very happy in it. It is a quite extraordinary thing to realize that if he had not been called out in this way onto the stage of Constantinople, his greatest work, which lay still ahead of him in a remarkable, brief, and intensely bright, period of his life, would never have seen the light of day. From that short stay in Constantinople resulted twenty-two out of a total of forty-four orations in his genuine corpus.[43] It is an extraordinary proportion, and demonstrates the pressure he was under while in the capital as well as his skill in extemporization, and the usefulness of his studies at Seleukia. If it had not been for his summons to the city Gregory might only have been known to us from his body of poetry, with some of the most vivid historical autobiographical pieces deleted from that corpus too. Gregory may well have hated Constantinople, in the aftermath of his time there, with all

---

40. *De Vita Sua*, v. 551 (*ou brachys chronos*), PG 37.1067.
41. Carm. 1.1.36, PG 37.518-520; and Carm. 2.1.3, PG 37.1020-1021; cf. Gallay (1943), p. 136.
42. *De Vita Sua*, vv. 552-555, PG 37.1067.
43. Orat. 35 is spurious; cf. Masson (1984). *Oration* 45 is extensively interpolated (cf. Trisoglio 1965), but *Oration* 11 is the result of two Orations of Gregory combined editorially: so even with the removal of 35 it could be said he still retains 45 Orations.

his heart, and may indeed have greatly lamented ever having been so stupid as to place his trust in synods of bishops, but the fact is that sager counsels from Meletios, Basil, and Eusebios of Samosata, had prevailed. They knew what he was capable of, and though his work there seemed a disaster both to his contemporaries, and certainly to Gregory in the immediate aftermath, in fact it was a universal intellectual triumph, for it formed the architecture of Latin and Greek Christian orthodoxy for the centuries to come; centuries outside his own immediate purview.

Since he obeyed the synodical invitation, it follows Gregory can only have taken up residence in the capital in the autumn of 379, and this in turn leads us to shift the dating of some of the Constantinopolitan Orations, as previously established by the main commentators.[44] Most of these have presumed that he arrived in Constantinople early in 379,[45] and more or less underestimated the import of his claim that he was summoned by a "large number of bishops"[46] which is without doubt the hundred and fifty of Meletios' assembly in Antioch. The result of this new adjustment of the dating of his arrival is that the Orations he preached in the capital are even more compressed than has been previously thought.

The Arians were so much in the majority in this city, and had held the churches for the previous forty years, that their school was simply equated with standard orthodoxy there, and the arrival of Gregory was soon noised abroad as yet another extreme hierarch from the Cappadocian provinces[47] seeking to make a name for himself. The Constantinopolitan clergy did not recognize his existence. They would allow him no access to the churches or their Bema-pulpits. At first, they felt not the slightest threat from his presence[48] and the local population did not care about him either, though they were theologically hostile (from the beginning to the end) to all he represented, and singularly unimpressed by his claims to be "aristocratic." They had all the inbuilt racist xenophobia of the era that made them think that anyone born outside the city walls was *untermensch*. In particular they regarded the Cappadocian dialect as immensely funny in an orator. The improbable idea of such a

---

44. Sinko (1917, 1923); Gallay (1943); Bernardi (1968); Gallay (1943, pp. 132-211) sets the Orations delivered between spring 379 and summer 381 in this order: 22, 32, 25, 41, 24, 38-40, 26, 34, 23, 20, 27-31, 37, 42.

45. Gallay (1943), p. 136, presumes it was early in 379 on the basis of "general opinion." His case does not take account of the synodical command, and attempts to hang the chronology of Constantinopolitan orations around a commencement at Easter, April 379. The Easter preaching, however, which attracted much hostility from the local inhabitants, was of the following year, when Gregory's plans were becoming more well known, and when leading figures were signalling their new allegiance to Theodosius by joining the Nicene ranks at the Anastasia.

46. *De Vita Sua*, v. 595-596, PG 37.1079.

47. Eunomios the Anhomoian Arian was well known in the city as a Cappadocian.

48. And with good reason. Even when Theodosius entered his capital with troops, his first act was to offer Demophilos continuance on the episcopal throne if he would sign the creed of Nicaea (which he would not); only then did he offer the vacancy to Gregory.

provincial practicing the craft of words was a standing joke in the capital, and Gregory was more than once the butt of the mockery.

On his part, his aristocratic distaste for the *hoi polloi* and his constant demands that the great unwashed had no right whatsoever to practice theological speculation, made him singularly inappropriate as an orator to catch the hearts of a wide and popular capital audience. This, of course, was never his intent. He was there merely to signal to the most powerful classes, how it was that they could slowly shift allegiance without loss of face or intellectual credibility. His was a ministry aimed at demonstrating, through the most refined demonstration of rhetorical skill he could muster, that the Nicene cause which had hitherto been languishing as a repressed sect in the East, had a right to command their allegiance: not merely out of political necessity, but also because on its own terms, it could stand up both intellectually, and culturally, as the true "Religio Romanorum."

Only when it became more and more clear that he was serving as an advance guard for the unpopular moves Theodosius was making to disestablish the Arian cause, did the anger of the clergy and people became more focused on Gregory personally, that is in the course of 380. But at first he was more of an oddity, and it is interesting to see him respond to the way in which this larger audience would give him no hearing except that which he could claim by force of eloquence alone. His strategy was intriguing. Asked to preach against the Apollinarists by the Antiochene synod, he stayed off the subject carefully, and instead sketched out a whole history of the Nicene cause. He decided he would attack the extreme Arian party, the Neo-Arian school of Aetios and Eunomios, whose faction had already been penalized at the capital. Eunomios was a figure of great dislike to the resident Arian Bishop Demophilos, and to base his arguments on the premiss that Demophilos and Eunomios represented one and the same thing was a clever pleading of a case of "damnation by association."[49] His words would soon be carried to their target, and Eunomios himself came back to the capital at Chalcedon with three other leading episcopal supporters to meet these criticisms with a robust counterattack later in 380.[50]

Gregory was offered a splendid villa for his residence in the city. It was the property of his cousin Theodosia.[51] He immediately dedicated part of it as a Church, calling it, in prophetic symbolism, the church of Anastasia. The greatest of the city churches had traditionally been dedicated to abstract verities in this way rather than to particular saints: Hagia Sophia was an evocation of "Divine Wisdom"; the

---

49. Demophilos was, like Valens, a Homoian; Eunomios was Anhomoian: its logical opposite. To equate them was a humorous rhetorical strategy with a serious point.
50. See Kopecek (1979), pp. 494-497.
51. Gregory compares it to the gift of hospitality the Sunamite woman gave to the prophet Elijah, which was also a coded reference to the initiation of the "resurrection" he brought to the city. Cf. 2 Kgs 4:8; Orat. 26.17, PG 35.1249.

neighboring Hagia Eirene was "Sacred Peace." The church of the Holy Apostles was an exception, but this was in origin more of a mausoleum for Constantine, than a standard city church.[52] By choosing his title Gregory signified "church of Resurrection" since he intended to bring back to life the faith that had lain dead in the city for more than forty years,[53] since the last Nicene bishop of Constantinople, Paulus, had been sent off to die in mysterious circumstances in exile in Armenia.[54]

In later years, perhaps beginning with extensions made by Nektarios Gregory's immediate successor, the Anastasia church was built up into a larger complex favored by the diplomatic classes of the city. By homonymity, it attracted there the relics of the martyr unmercenary St Anastasia Pharmakolytria, and afterwards became increasingly confused with her as the patronal saint, which she was not. From this church the relics of St Anastasia were taken to Rome in the time of Gregory the Great and her cult developed greatly there to the extent that western hagiographies metamorphosized her ever after as an indigenous Roman matron.

The exact site of the Anastasia remains unsure. The Byzantine chroniclers locate the original villa-church at the junction of the Mese and the Long Portico of Maurianos which ran off from the Mese down to the Golden Horn. This would put the building very much in the center of the city, in the region between the Forum Tauri and the Column of Constantine, between modern Beyazit and Cemberlitas on the Istanbul city tramline. There was from the outset, however, some confusion between Gregory's church of Anastasia and a small church the Novatians occupied in the city also called by that name. The latter reverted to orthodox use, and this was possibly the one that Nektarios possessed and redeveloped.[55] A recent archaeological report has suggested that Gregory's Anastasia church might be found more towards the Marmara coast, as the foundations of the Mosque of Sokollu Mehmet Pasha, 100 meters south of the Hippodrome, which can be found more or less halfway on a walk between the furthest limit of the Hippodrome (away from Hagia Sophia), and the church which Justinian later constructed for the other millionaires who lived beside him nearer the sea, the beautiful architectural jewel of Saints Sergius and

52. These are the only four churches in the city in which Gregory is known to have served, though the Council of 381 moved from church to church in the course of its meetings, not settling on any particular building for its several gatherings.
53. Gregory characterises the city, before his arrival, as in a pitiable state of religious death *De Vita Sua*, vv. 584-586, PG 37.1069.
54. Theodosius, perhaps on Gregory's recommendation, would later ensure that the bones of Paulus would be brought back in ceremony to the capital, and placed as the bones of a martyr in the very Church which Macedonios the Arian leader had used as his "home" parish. It was as striking a symbol as he could make of the complete routing of the Pneumatomachian party on their home front. Cf. Liebschuetz (1990), p. 164; Dagron (1974), pp. 422f; and on the Church building, Janin (1969), pp. 377-378.
55. Since the bishop that supplied Nektarios' profession of faith when he was consecrated bishop of Constantinople was himself a Novatian, something that suggests more than a passing connection. Cf. Liebschuetz (1990), p. 163; Socrates, HE 5.8; Sozomen, HE 7.8.

Bacchus.[56] Whether it was by the Column of Constantine or between the Hippodrome and the Marmara shore, the Anastasia was evidently in a very high class part of town. Like Justinian's church later, the Anastasia was meant for the gentry. The whole area was a center of intellectuals and senatorial aristocrats, and one of the most expensive pieces of real estate in fourth-century Constantinople.

Gregory probably consecrated only one room off the central courtyard of the villa, and used the courtyard itself as the assembly room for his audience, an open-air narthex, as it were, that could be canvassed over in case of rain. He would thus have been able to preach to a fairly large gathering from the loggia of his own church and living quarters, and could use the ambivalence of preaching in church and at the same time outside church to his advantage, thus addressing an audience that was wider than that "inner community" that was his eucharistic congregation. The latter body of Nicene communicants he admits to having been a very small remnant indeed[57] and a group that was very circumspect and anxious in a hostile environment.[58] He tells us in a poem describing a dream he later had about his beloved Anastasia church[59] that people pressed round to hear him, and the women and children gathered in the gallery, which was possibly the raised porticoes around the courtyard.[60]

The new preacher's first orations are exercises in self definition, and focus on the state of the Nicene party. This, in the autumn of 379, meant broadcasting news of the recent Antiochene synod as the achievement of a peaceful settlement to internal strife among the Nicene believers in the East. It was also a way for Gregory to present his credentials to the population as the "official" Nicene spokesman.

Oration 20 probably represents the "substance" of his first "lecture." It has an odd title given later: "On Dogma and the Installation of Bishops."[61] The discourse, however, has nothing specifically to do with installing bishops; except that Gregory is setting out to his early audience of the converted few what his policy will be in the approaching theological catechesis. In later years he has possibly set this oration in his complete corpus as general example of how a bishop should "take charge" of his city and ensure that he, and he alone, is the authoritative theological orator. In the final

---

56. Now commonly known as Little Aya Sofia. For photographs see Mathews (1976). The Mosque of Mehmet Sokullu Pasha (16th c.) is in a walled complex which contains an Islamic day-school, and is located on the hill below the Hippodrome, in an area of decaying Ottoman buildings. The best view of the whole area is from the roof of the Arcadia hotel by the modern lawcourts.

57. *De Vita Sua*, vv. 587-589, PG 37.1069.

58. Orat. 26.17, PG 35.1249.

59. Carm. 2.1.16, PG 37.1254-1261.

60. Bernardi (1965), p. 184 thinks he might have had wooden galleries specially constructed inside the reception hall.

61. Gallay (1943), p. 186, suggested it was a corruption of an original title: "An Exposition of Dogma on the Occasion of a Reception of Bishops." *Katastasis* had been used in this sense by Herodotos. Cf. Mossay, SC 270 (1980), pp. 47-48.

editing of his complete works he chose to elevate as an exemplary model (a synopsis of theological preaching), the gist of the inaugural homily he gave, on taking up his new church in what soon became his own episcopal see.[62] The shorter manuscript title is "First Oration on Theology" which correctly signals its close relation to the *Five Theological Orations* (27-31) which he would give in the following year, of which the first three elaborate more fully the themes announced here. The text is consistently critical of the extent to which theological discussion is a common occupation of everyone in the city. For Gregory this is a scandal. The exposition of theological dogma is, like a sacrament, something that should be reserved for the church, and a mystery that is part of the *proprium* of the ordained bishop, his peculiar priestly "office." This is a theme he developed several times when his small community at Nazianzus was in conflict. It was another matter to try to impose it at the capital, where religious philosophy was not at all seen to be the sole prerogative of the bishop, and the love for exhibitions of public speaking rivaled the attractions of the hippodrome for the intelligentsia. Nothing seemed more normal to the Constantinopolitans than including the leading religious issues of the day in the matters for public debate. Gregory has to be contextualized in his argument, of course, for in returning to this constant motif of his city orations, that true theology is a matter of "simple economy" of words, he is elaborating this point in public with extensive, and highly elaborate, words. What he is really advocating is two things: first that he ought to be listened to as an authoritative voice; and second that Christian theology ought to reduce its speculative side which has brought such religious divisions in the course of the last generation, and don once more the sober dress of "simple discourse." It is an appeal to settle the great problems of his generation in traditionalist terms. This *apophatic* turning away from speech is not merely a gimmick with Gregory, for it is constitutive of his whole mental and spiritual approach; but equally it is not a straightforwardly "simple" appeal either, for as he develops his episcopal dogma in the course of the next eighteen months, especially his doctrine of the consubstantiality of the Holy Spirit in *Oration* 31, he certainly emerges as the least traditionalist theologian the Constantinopolitans have ever heard, and his homely "simplicities" are massively complex theology wrapped in the most carefully crafted rhetoric possible.

The *Oration* has been shown by Sinko[63] to be a composite edition from pieces of *Orations* 2, 6 and 23.[64] Because of its pastiche nature Gallay thought it belonged to the year 381 and stood midway in the series of the *Five Theological Orations* (27-31). The use of the early *Orations* 2 and 6, however, and the very general nature of his argument seem to suggest it was a piece of extemporization[65] and something of a first draft for

---

62. Though he had not envisaged it as such, at the time.
63. Sinko (1917), pp. 11-12.
64. For details, cf. Gallay (1943), p. 183-186.
65. As Sinko suspected it was.

the more specific theological lectures that were to follow,[66] its purpose being merely to give the broadest "thumbnail sketch" of who this new orator was, and what party he represented. The parallelism of themes, however, does not demonstrate its chronological dependence on the Orations of 381, as much its appeal to common notes from which the whole sheaf of Constantinopolitan orations devolve, and the extent to which Gregory later edited all his corpus for publication after his retirement.

The Oration denounces orators before him who have passed off mere verbiage as wisdom. Gregory, by contrast, will enter deep inside himself to seek for true philosophy. He will try to teach them like a philosopher who has overcome the domination of the senses, someone who has already had experience in trying to escape the boundaries of sense perception, to speak with God Himself; such a solitary can then emerge to reflect on divine realities "without the contamination of the erroneous impressions of this lower world."[67] His imagery is based on an appeal to the Moses archetype, where the prophet, on Sinai, receives a luminous revelation of God, and conveys it to the elect people as the basic constitution of the covenant.[68] Gregory laments that this radiance cannot be sustained for long: the fragile duality of human nature means it has a propensity to fall down to lower realities all too soon—but for the moment Gregory is making a loud claim to prophetic and luminous vision to inaugurate his teaching.

Though he is to offer a series of rhetorical discourses, he builds his first claim for authoritative hearing on the nature of his inspired vision of God, gained through long ascetic purification. Anyone else who assays the heights of the mountain of theology is making a very dangerous ascent. This is evidenced by the dangers attendant when Moses received the luminous vision on Sinai, and all, even Aaron and the priests, had to stay a safe distance away.[69] The mass of people can no more do theology than the common man can safely touch the Ark of the Covenant. To do so recklessly is fatal.[70] The practice of theology, therefore, is a priestly activity, just like entering the veil of the holies, or approaching the altar of the temple. It is sacrilegious for it to be done in a secular way or by those not properly chosen, and even the chosen High Priest of Israel had to purify himself rigorously when he entered the *Sanctum*, just as Gregory does when he discourses about God.[71] Having explained the qualifications needed of a theologian who, in short, needs to be an ascetically experienced bishop, Gregory announces that the rest of his oration will serve to "give a synopsis" of correct doctrine about God:

66. Especially Orats. 28 and 29 which attack Eunomios more directly.
67. Orat. 20.1, PG 35.1065.
68. An image which will be central to Gregory of Nyssa's later treatise, *The Life of Moses*.
69. Orat. 20.2, PG 35.1068.
70. Orat. 20.3, PG 35.1068. Using the image of Oza struck dead because he touched the Ark but was not a priest: 1 Chron 13:9-10; cf. Josephus. Ant. 7.4.2.
71. Orat. 20.4, PG 35.1069.

So it is that we worship the Father, The Son, and the Holy Spirit. We observe the individual distinctions[72] while numbering the Godhead as One. We are careful not confound the three into one, so that we might not fall ill with the Sabellian virus. Nor do we divide the Godhead into three different realities, in case we suffer from the Arian madness...We occupy the middle ground, observing the correct boundaries of righteousness.[73]

His general résumé is at once very clear and simple, easily memorable for non-specialists, and yet also a clear appeal to the classic high ground of Hellenic philosophical wisdom: the Golden Mean.

One extreme to be avoided is the party of those Christians who are terrified of falling into polytheism and so only admit only one *hypostasis* in God, with all the names being simple synonyms of this single reality.[74] The other extreme is "that mad hypothesis so rightly associated with the name of Arius"[75] which sees the three names as "alien and unlike essences, separated from one another, without principle or order, almost like anti-gods."[76] By his code words "Sabellians and Arians," he knows exactly who he is attacking: and so do his audience: the party of Marcellus of Ancyra on the one hand, and the followers of Eunomios on the other. He ironically praises the first party for their insistence on the rights of the Father. They have so specialized in the theology of Fatherhood, however, that they have deprived the Church of the hypostatic existence of a Son of God, and so have killed the very notion of "paternity" by their zeal in its defense. He recognizes the Arians as specialists in the conception of the Son. But they too have so strenuously maintained that he is an inferior Son, not comparable to the Father, that they have made him out to be an alien essence, and by this means have killed off the very meaning of Sonship.[77] Gregory very wittily caricatures his leading opponents as over-fussy connoisseurs who have killed their hothouse orchids by too much attention. His own "middle way" will be understandable to the masses, practicable, and prove its veracity accordingly. The doctrine of the Trinity is then set out with great clarity:

In short we must hold that there is One God, and we must confess that there are three *hypostases* (or three *prosopa* if you wish) each one with its own characteristics.[78]

Gregory explains that the Son and Spirit are in the Unity of God not primarily by virtue of "dynamic power" as the ancient Apologists and Marcellus had argued[79]

72. *Idiotetas.*
73. Orat. 20.5, PG 35.1072.
74. Orat. 20.6, PG 35.1072.
75. Gregory uses the name as etymologically associated with "madness": cf. Orat. 2.37, PG 35.445; Orat. 25.8, PG 35.1209; Orat. 43.30, PG 36.537.
76. Orat. 20.6, PG 35.1072.
77. Orat. 20.6, PG 35.1072.
78. Orat. 20.6, PG 35.1072.
79. The Son and Spirit emerging from the original divine unity for the purposes of creation, and being absorbed back again once these purposes would have been completed at the eschaton—a theory from the primitive Logos theologians that the party of Marcellus of Ancyra had revived.

or by "conformity of will" as the Arians had posited;[80] rather the unity came about as the direct logical result of both Son and Spirit having the self-same, direct, and single cause, the Father Himself. This idea of the single causality in the divine essence is his critical foundation of trinitarian philosophy, but we shall return to it later, for Gregory leaves the notion of Trinity at this point to focus primarily on the relations of the Father and the Son—the critical factor at issue in the Arian and Marcellan theologies alike.

Our proponent of "simple discourse" now goes on to offer those dense and pithy syllogisms the Byzantines so loved.[81] He is, in fact, offering them the very "salon theology" he has earlier criticized them for wanting, just to show them he can do it. The hypostatic "characteristics" follow from the fundament of the unity in the single cause of the Father. They are that: the Father is the "One Without Beginning" and also "The Beginning." The Son is "Not Without Beginning" but is "Partly Without Beginning," and is also "The Beginning of All." The solution to the conundrums is that the Father is the Beginning[82] since he is the Beginner. He whom he begins is the Son, and this is why the Son is like the Father (the caused result of the supreme direct First Cause), and yet unlike the Father because the Father has no beginning whereas the Son has the Father as his beginning. But since the Father has no beginning, he begins his Son without a beginning too, since all he does is without beginning; and thus the Son begins in a timeless way, that is without beginning. Accordingly the Son too is partly characterized by being "without beginning." And as such he is like his Father in two respects: first by being begun from this primal cause (Only Son from The Father, caused from a single, indivisible First Principle, implying a sameness of nature) and then by sharing in this capacity of being "beginningless" that is eternal. In a complex cascade of witty syllogisms Gregory has thus defined the Son as "like his Father"; "unlike his Father," and "co-essential with his Father"—a *tour de force* which has hung out to dry the programs of the Homoian Arians, the Anhomoian Arians, and the Nicenes alike, and invited whoever in his audience felt attached to any of these parties now to accept him as their pedagogue and guide, leading them to a resolution in the truth. He has wittily shown that this old simple bishop from the provinces, is nobody's fool.

He ends the Oration by turning to the key issue for the Anhomoian argument: if the Son was engendered,[83] he must be secondary to the Father, and must be inferior, and so cannot be considered as divine in the full sense of that term. Gregory answers by insisting that generation in terms of the deity is beyond the range of human

---

80. Taking this as the basis for the "unity" of Father and Son being nominal not essential.
81. Orat. 20.7-8, PG 35.1073-1076.
82. The opening words of the Fourth Gospel.
83. The Anhomoians argued that the supreme definition of deity was *Agennnesia*: the State of being Unbegotten. Since the Son was, by definition, "the Begotten," it followed he was *de facto* not "Supreme God."

words that apply when material generation is considered. The logical necessities of a temporally conditioned "birth" cannot be said to apply to the divinity. To speak at this highest level of *theologia* is like looking at the sun, a hazardous enterprise that can only be sustained for a short time without risk of blindness.[84] A theologian can properly say only that the Son is from the Father timelessly, and entirely co-equal to the Father except in the sole matter of causal relation. To say anything more is inappropriate, he insists, just as looking too long at the sun is reckless. If his argument is not convincing (and he surely senses dissatisfaction at this point) and his audience insist on "more answers" in regard to the "Generation" of the Son and the "Procession" of the Spirit[85] then he will first ask them some answers to simpler questions concerned with the material world; which they ought to know more surely and more immediately. If they can get these answers right, he suggests, then he will provide answers on the theological issues. He asks them to consider the relation of the soul to the body. How is it that a human being who is fragile dust can also be the image of God? Or how can intellectual perception be located in the flesh and yet range beyond it and transcend its scope? How do the heavens rotate? What is the system of the movement of the stars? He knows these questions will be enough to silence anyone in his audience. Even as "material concerns" within the scope of human science, they are mysteries beyond the wit of a few syllogisms to answer. So it is with the even greater mysteries of theology. They ought to be left alone for the moment, he concludes.[86] In the meantime all should strive to become theologians—by purifying the inner eye. Only in this way will the collective spiritual perception of Christians be strengthened to receive the vision of theological realities. Then his audience shall be like Paul who was caught up into heaven to see beyond present limitations.[87] But that vision will be in Christ, he says, a vision of the light of the Trinity and it shall be for another age, beyond this present material one.

The next speech he delivered in the autumn of his first year in Constantinople was *Oration* 22. This is the piece where he certainly refers to the recent attempts to bring settlement to Antioch, though it was a solution that would not be formally achieved (and then only in part) until the council of 381. *Orations* 23 and 24 have a particular bond with *Oration* 6 which he wrote "On Peace" when he returned to his father's side after the schism at Nazianzus in 362. The ancient editors traditionally numbered them together as the *Three Eirenika*,[88] discourses concerned with the settlement of community divisions. There has been much speculation on the exact chronological sequence of these lectures,[89] but it seems to me that *Orations* 22 and 23

84. Orat. 20.10, PG 35.1077.
85. Orat. 20.11, PG 35.1077.
86. Orat. 20.12, PG 35.1080.
87. 2 Cor 12:1-4.
88. Three "Pacific" Orations; cf. Mossay, SC 207 (1980), pp. 194, 260. Orat. 22 is the *Third Eirenika*, Orat. 23 being the Second, and Orat. 6 the First.
89. Elias of Crete from the eighth century argued that Orats. 6 and 23 were given in Nazianzus in

are definitely related to Constantinople,[90] though not to the same set of community problems: with 22 referring to the wider divisions of the international eastern Nicene party, especially the history of the Antiochene schism,[91] and 23 relating to his own particular headaches over a divided Nicene congregation at Constantinople.

Oration 22 is a general call for peace[92] among those who are right minded. Gregory depicts himself as a man seeking peace with the same eagerness as those biblical heroes who had once been alienated; Jacob and Joseph, or David and Absalom.[93] His context is clearly a reference to the recent attempt to resolve the schism between Meletios and Paulinus, the two rival Nicene contenders for the great see of Antioch. Meletios had, in his old age, sponsored an eirenical deal that he would occupy the throne until his death and then it should pass to the other contender, Paulinus, until his death when a new election should take place. In the interim Paulinus would be a kind of honorary "parallel-bishop" alongside Meletios. This (uncanonical) policy was much disliked by the younger partisans of Meletios, and would be thrown over by them when Meletios did in fact die unexpectedly in the capital in 381, though Gregory tried to make it law, and came to grief over his attempt. In this discourse he offers the symbolic "agreement" at Antioch as a sign of great hope for the future of the Nicene movement. The Church, he says has been divided to the scandal of all. Christianity is a philosophy that is based on evangelical charity, yet it has been unable to sustain its own internal communion, to the amusement of its numerous enemies outside[94] and the great weakening of its political effectiveness.[95] The barbarian invasions, he says, which have so devastated the empire have not done so much harm to Roman affairs than the long drawn out internal divisions in the Church.[96] The Church has lost respect, and endangered its hopes to be "a great people and a glorious nation" as

the early years of his priesthood, 362, and this became the standard Byzantine belief, largely based on the reference in Orat. 23.5. to the scene of a "father sitting once more alongside his son." The dating we take for 23 makes it follow 22 by six months, appearing early in 380. The "father and son" refers, as we shall see, to Meletios and Paulinus of Antioch sharing the episcopal throne, not to Gregory and his own father in former times at Nazianzus.

90. Mossay, in the recent critical edition of Orat. 23 (SC 207 [1960], pp. 274-275), wished to reverse the trend of most modern scholarship in regard to Orat. 23. and relocate it to Nazianzus in 362. Gallay (1943) is right, I think, in seeing this as one of the early pieces Gregory gave in the capital, though thinking he came there in the early spring he brings this forward by nine months. As he came only after the autumn council of Antioch, and refers to the resolution achieved there, the text can only have been delivered in the winter of 379.

91. Seen already by Tillemont, *Mémoires* 9, p. 436.

92. A Protreptik Oration in its genre; cf. Mossay, SC 270 (1960).

93. Orat. 22.1, PG 35.1132. The second image is an ambivalent one considering the fate of Absalom.

94. Orat. 22.4, PG 35.1136.

95. Orat. 22.9, PG 35.1141.

96. Orat. 22.2, PG 35.1133. Already by late 379 the realisation that the Goths would not march on the capital must have given everyone a breathing space, and news of Theodosius' successful campaign against the barbarians in Thessalonike would confirm Gregory's judgment. In any case, it is a striking political image to apply.

once in times past.[97] Gregory is making his position absolutely clear. What he is doing in his office as Christian orator in the capital in this year after the disaster of Adrianople, is offering the one way forward for the political and religious reestablishment of Roman security. It will consist in one thing: the adoption of a unity of belief among the Christians of the East (and by implication a unification with the Christians of the West who have just rescued Byzantium from the fire). If East and West reunite, which he posits as the only hope for the continuance of Rome, it can only be on the basis of the Nicene faith. And this he will now elaborate to his audience.

Excessive speculation is one of the things, Gregory argues, that brought about the lamentable state of internal weakness that has now been exposed in disaster. What ought to be discussed and what ought now to be abandoned shall be set out simply.[98] The essential matter of the Christian faith is summed up in the Nicene Trinitarian confession:

> The one and only definition of righteousness is to adore the Father, the Son, and Holy Spirit, the one single power and Godhead in the three; and not to worship the single Godhead too much, or too little.[99]

This alone is the golden mean between Sabellian "synairesis" and Arian "diairesis," those who teach Christian dogma to excess on either side of the question of divine unity. This quest for peace is the only reason, he tells his listeners, that he has agreed to occupy this teacher's chair, which has already been the occasion of "conflict and envy."[100] This final appeal for concord cleverly sets the Arian doctrine of God as one "extreme" pole beside the "Sabellian." He has therefore offered his listeners, knowing the majority of the court in the city were Homoian Arians, the prospect not of a reversal of their beliefs, that is a reversion to the Nicene Homoousianism they had hitherto regarded as an "extreme sect," but rather a small readjustment of their position. They do not have to make a *volte face* to the Nicene faith, for the opposing extreme to them is presented by the Marcellan party. The Nicenes, in fact, are closer to them than they had ever hitherto believed. His eirenic policy of easy reconciliation was indeed sustained by the administration when Theodosius finally took possession of his capital. The emperor then certainly proscribed the Arian system and prosecuted its leading protagonists, but the large mass of homoian laity, and the multitude of Arian bishops who were willing to realign with him, were folded back within the ecclesiastical structures with remarkably little problem. Arian ordinations, and even Arian baptisms[101] were accepted with eager economy by the incoming Nicenes.

97. Orat. 22.2, PG 35.1133.
98. Orat. 22.11, PG 35.1144.
99. Orat. 22.12, PG 35.1144.
100. Orat. 22.14, PG 35.1148.
101. Which were hardly "Trinitarian" in the eyes of the Nicenes.

Those who stubbornly turn away from "peace," however, will be fighting against God. Gregory ends his speech by repeating that the movement to peaceful reconciliation is a divine commandment, and those who insist on retaining the "extremist" views will be resisting the God who has determined to establish concord once again. This last statement is a not too veiled indication that the Arians who insist on spurning the Nicene faith, will not only be resisting God's desire for mutual reconciliation, they will be resisting the restoration of the Roman ascendancy. The implication cannot have been lost on his hearers that such "resisters" will be exposed as heretics and traitors by the agent of God's peace—the Emperor Theodosius, who was now on his way to Thessaloniki to crush the Gothic armies in the field, and soon to enter his capital with the motto engraved on his coins: "Reparatio Reipublicae." Such a politico-theological diagnosis must have sharply focused the attention of Gregory's audience as he gave his blessing and left the podium that day. Attendance at his future lectures would start to increase.

On October 2, 379,[102] Gregory gave an oration to mark the festival of St Cyprian, one of the main patronal-saints for a section of his Nicene congregation at the Anastasia. He would perform the same service in the following May, for the other Nicene element of the Anastasia who looked to Athanasios of Alexandria as the leading "saint of Nicaea," and indeed Gregory's sermon the following year actually constitutes one of the first "canonization" hagiographies of the great Alexandrian theologian. Gregory invests more into that later sermon. The panegyric for Cyprian, *Oration* 24, is something of a disaster. He clearly has very little idea who the saint was. He had been taking a few days holiday in the countryside with a female benefactress[103] and was informed that the feast of Cyprian was a specially important one[104] for some of his new congregation. He came back to Constantinople hurriedly "as a loving father would" and cobbled together something as best he could.[105] The resultant festival oration is a gaudy cocktail that confusedly mingles elements of Cyprian of Carthage with Cyprian of Antioch.[106] The sober North African confessor is transmuted into the wondrous magician of Antioch who is converted by equally wondrous signs after having failed to seduce a Christian virgin by selling his soul to the devil. And after this remarkable conversion he becomes a leading confessor of Christian orthodoxy and a

---

102. The liturgical feast of Cyprian of Antioch in the later Constantinopolitan Synaxarion. The feast of Cyprian of Carthage was celebrated in the West on September 14, but at this stage was not observed in the East. Cyprian of Antioch and Justine were celebrated in the West on September 26.

103. "A woman who also loves the martyrs." Orat. 24.1, PG 35.1172.

104. Orat. 24.1, PG 35.1172.

105. Considered in that light the speech is an interesting example of extemporisation written straight down, and is the clearest example surviving of Gregory's renowned ability in extempore preaching—though usually he had better preparation.

106. Delehaye observed that Prudentius makes the same mistake in *Peristephanon* 13; cf. Gallay (1943), pp. 151-152.

martyr under Decius.[107] Gregory says that his relics have been recently "rediscovered" to underline the extent that his life is a model for all to follow, since he spent his time fighting against the worst heretics of his day: Sabellian and Arian opponents of the Trinity.[108]

The hagiographer Delehaye called this oration "one of the oddest works Gregory has left behind."[109] The history, such as it is, simply subordinates the figure of Cyprian to a symbol of trinitarian orthodoxy. Gregory has no awareness of anything Cyprian of Carthage actually wrote, mentioning only that he "produced several works." He is especially interested in the figure of Justine, the woman the magician Cyprian tried to seduce by magic potions. He plays this romance for all it is worth, and his text retains signs of its extemporized delivery, for as he goes on unraveling the lurid adventure, he sees his audience are hanging on every word:

> What? Are you caught up in my tale? I can see you can hardly wait for the rest of it. Are you worried about what will happen to this young girl and the man she loves? Are you afraid that their affair might turn out badly for them both in the end? Ah, don't be worried. In this case love showed itself a good servant of the faith.[110]

It is possible that in this focus on the strong woman of faith in Justine, we have an indication that the festival of the saints, rotating around the cult of relics, was a factor particularly related to aristocratic female practice in fourth-century Constantinopolitan society. In the following century we can see this clearly at work in the circle around Pulcheria. On that occasion Nestorius attacked the female aristocrats' involvement in cathedral services, because it was an arena where they exercised considerable theological as well as social patronage, for the benefit of his enemies. His attempt to forbid these women's religious meetings proved singularly unhappy for Nestorius, as I have outlined elsewhere.[111] I think that Gregory's sermon on the feast of Saints Cyprian and Justine, is perhaps an indication that the cult of the saints and transferral of relics was a continuation of the ancient practice of martyrial feasts at the tomb, relocated into the capital and now presided over by powerful aristocratic women. The Anastasia Church is itself a prime example of powerful female patronage, and three of those leading women are known to us from Gregory's references, all of them closely associated with his own family: Theodosia, Olympias, and Thecla.[112]

107. Cyprian of Carthage was martyred under Valerian.
108. The anachronisms are not as important as making the martyr a symbolic patron of Gregory's present theological enterprise. Orat. 24.13, PG 35.1185.
109. H. Delehaye, "Cyprien d'Antioche et Cyprien de Carthage," *Analecta Bollandiana* 39, 1921. 314-322.
110. Orat. 24.11, PG 35.1181.
111. "Nestorius and the Political Factions of Fifth Century Byzantium: Factors in his Downfall, in The Church of the East: Life and Thought," eds., J.F. Coakley and K. Parry, *Bulletin of the John Rylands University Library* (Special Issue), vol. 78.3 (1996), pp. 7-21.
112. See Bernardi (1968), p. 161-164; Mossay, SC 284 (1981), pp. 28-29; Hauser-Meury (1960), pp. 167, 158, and 136.

To the end of his first year in the capital, winter of 379, also belongs *Oration* 32. This is a fuller form of his argument in *Oration* 22, from the winter of 379, and reflects both the greater degree of hostility that he sees gathering against him, and in particular internal dissensions among the Nicenes of the capital. His last words in *Oration* 32 had asked the martyr saint Cyprian to accept the homage of his words and offer him, in return, the grace of protection from "those cruel wolves who prowl around me hunting words and phrases."[113] *Oration* 32 gives further evidence that his presence was beginning to attract hostile attention.

It was thought by Tillemont[114] that the size of the audience and the hostility of the hearers reflected a condition when Theodosius had expelled the Arians from the churches of Constantinople, that is in January 381; but Gregory's references to himself in the exordium as "a little poor pastor," which echoes his self-description in *Oration* 24,[115] suggests more the context of his early discourses in the city. The Anastasia is filled with a large crowd to hear him this time, and it is natural that he extends the range of his message to encompass all the city "young and old, magistrates, and monks." The general argument is once again that peace must be pursued because of the nature of the times. Here he refers to a conflict between Paul and Apollos. It is a reference to the "schism of Corinth" that Paul refers to when the Church was divided into three hostile factions, around the three apostles Kephas, Paul and Apollos.[116] The same thing appears in the Poem *De Vita Sua* where he gives us some more explicit information that:

> Straightway[117] a terrible rivalry broke out among my own faithful. One section wanted to drag me to the side of Paul, the others to the side of Apollos. But neither of them was made incarnate or poured out their blood for us, so why should we name ourselves after such men and not rather after our Savior?[118]

Gregory was glad that his Church was now much fuller than when he first began his series of lectures, but the Nicene party which had rallied around him was starting to give him as many problems as the hostile Arians. This oration is aimed at his own

---

113. Orat. 24.19, PG 35.1193.
114. *Mémoires*, vol. 9, p. 464. Tillemont noted that Gregory spoke to a full church, and appealed to the magistrates, and monks and young and old to give up their "vain ambitions." (Orat. 32.1, PG 36.173; Orat. 32.33, PG 36.212). The vain ambitions referred to in the text, however, are not aspirations of his opponents to hold on to their Arian creed, but general references for all his hearers that they should desist from theologising. See also Gallay (1943), pp. 143-146, who attributes the Oration to late 379.
115. Orat. 24.1, PG 35.1172.
116. 1 Cor 3:6.
117. The conjunction "epeita" at *De Vita Sua*, v. 679, which introduces the internal dissension does not necessarily indicate a chronological line for the events he narrates. It is his usual way of introducing new sections of his narrative in this poem, and the numerous events of the stay from autumn 379 to May 381 are clearly set where they will get the best effect, not in a strict historical sequence, though the general order is clear enough.
118. *De Vita Sua*, vv. 679-683, PG 37.1076.

people. The schism between Paul and Apollos, which features so prominently in it, is a coded reference to Meletios and Paulinus at Antioch. At the synod in 379 Meletios had already sketched out a settlement of the bitter dispute that had long set the Eastern Nicenes at one another's throats, in terms of the plan to have a joint presidency with the throne finally going to whoever survived the other. This was not a popular idea with any of the partisans,[119] and the Antiochene Nicenes who had been surprisingly gathered together for the first time in years in the communion of Gregory's Anastasia soon made their bitter differences public. Gregory was very anxious, as he tells in the *De Vita Sua*, that this "infant in swaddling clothes" of the newly constituted Nicene party at Constantinople might be destroyed by internal dissension even before it got a chance to establish itself.[120] He was also aware that the "wolves" were gathering to attack him, that is the Arian theologians making their counter-arguments ready, and the other "enemies outside" who would be all too happy to see the Christians collapse.[121] He had to settle the dispute quickly, and *Orations* 32 and 23 which come from the same period, were his response. As in *Oration* 22, Gregory is concerned that the Nicene partisans should lay aside their internal fighting because the Church is at a new crossroads. They need to take the wider picture and see how the massive divisions caused by heresies (Apollinarism, Marcellianism, Sabellianism, Photinianism, Macedonianism and Arianism are the examples which he elevates)[122] are not of the same order as schisms around the episcopal succession at Antioch. He appeals once again for common rapprochement around the simplest profession of the Nicene Trinitarian faith.[123] He insists they should hear him out and not "storm out" of the building prematurely[124] because of an intemperate zeal which is not as admirable, or as beneficial to the Church, as they might think. Anything beyond this "golden mean"[125] is a path for fools. Gregory concludes with a long and beautiful section extolling the wonderful way nature demonstrates the divine plan revolving around order and harmony.[126] The order of the universe is the hallmark of the creative Word of God and is his command for the Church which is his body. Gregory demands obedience as the leader of the Church. Those who subvert his teaching thereby stand against Christ who appointed that only a few should teach and the majority listen.[127]

---

119. And was more or less abandoned at the council of 381 because hostility to Paulinus made it impossible for him to assume the leadership of the Nicene majority in the shoes of Meletios.
120. *De Vita Sua*, vv. 690-695, PG 37.1077. The idea of an honorary joint episcopate was uncanonical and hardly meant as a serious long-term solution.
121. Orat. 32.4, PG 36.177.
122. Orat. 32.5, PG 36.180.
123. Orat. 32.5, PG 36.180.
124. Orat. 32.2, PG 36.176.
125. Orat. 32.6, PG 36.180-181.
126. Orat. 32, PG 36.7-13, PG 36.181-189.
127. Orat. 32.12, PG 36.188; and Orat. 32.32, PG 36.209-212.

Returning to a main theme of his doctrine he tells again how God is "supreme light" and can only be approached through the laborious purification of the Nous until it too is made radiant.[128] Even when possessed of divine revelation the inspired person ought to observe moderation in theological discourse; the basic foundation of trinitarian orthodoxy should suffice for all.[129] The time of bitter disputes must now end. People have been engaging in hostile debate as if they were enemies. There is no need for such behavior. Even if we disagree with one another, Gregory says, we must treat the other with charitable care,[130] imitating the gentleness of the Christ. All of his audience, whatever age or class they represent, should lay aside their excessive desire to be theological disputants and commit themselves instead to "approach God through the quality of their lives" not their arguments.

Gregory probably managed to contain his community, at least until the following year when other factions broke out and almost led him to despair of having a solid Nicene party in place before the Emperor's arrival. But it was most likely the growing hostility of the Arians (the Homoian clergy who were the majority in the capital, and the Anhomoian intellectuals who had heard he had opened a campaign and came to dispute with him) that rallied his Nicene faithful around him. He complained to them that they did not appreciate how much he was suffering from Arian attacks, and it seems to have sobered them a little.[131] His attempt to make them submit to the authority of divinely-appointed bishops allowed him to take the lead in making a single and coherent theological case for the Nicene faith, which he was to set out in the *Theological Orations* later that year. To that extent he had success in controlling them. But he had also intended his eirenical speech to move the Anastasia community somewhere towards a resolution of the Antiochene schism. The fact that the unpopular settlement put forward at the synod of 379 was ultimately to be rejected by the bishops of the Antiochene metropolitanate would prick the bubble of his argument here that bishops could be safely left in charge. The even greater recalcitrance of the hierarchs who gathered around him in 381 pulled the whole pack of cards down on his head again, for by that time he was the president of the council of Constantinople, not merely trying to settle a small and cantankerous congregation. His peacemaking efforts that had just about

128. Orat. 32.15, PG 36.192.
129. Orat. 32.21, PG 36.197-200.
130. Orat. 32.30, PG 36.208-209.
131. Orat. 32.14, PG 36.189; He also says in the *De Vita Sua*, vv. 660-664, PG 37.1074-1075. "People are drawn towards those who suffer, and so it proved with the people's attitude to their shepherd and leader at that time, who received their pity as a champion being hurtfully wounded." White (1996) refers this to Demophilos receiving the pity of his city (after he was exiled in 381) but the line appears in a section about the troubles that attended Gregory's first months in the city, and by that stage Demophilos hardly knew of his existence, and was certainly not threatened by Gregory's presence. I think Gregory is here referring to himself, gaining sympathy (from the Nicenes) the more the (Arian) population turned against him.

carried the day now, were not listened to a second time, when old scores could be settled definitively.

Gregory tells us that at first the Arian clergy were content to laugh at the old man from the sticks of Cappadocia, who dressed in rags and had a tiny congregation.[132] But the spring of 380 changed the mood of the Arian bishops and clergy in the capital and made them realize that Gregory was far from being someone they could dismiss as a crank. What sobered them was Theodosius' promulgation of a decree on February 28 of that year, from Thessaloniki where he had just been baptized into the Nicene community, indicating that his loyal subjects should henceforth observe the faith as taught by Damasus of Rome, and Peter of Alexandria; that is the Nicene confession. From that moment onwards Gregory's community felt endangered. The Emperor was a long way off, and still fighting the Goths. The outcome was still unsure until the end of that year gave him a decisive victory, and in any case his own survival was not assured. He had only received baptism at Thessaloniki, thinking that his last hour had come from a fever contracted during the campaign. The time from Easter to autumn was one where Gregory and his community felt particularly exposed.

Things came to a head when Pascha came round. It was the first time he had celebrated the great feast at the Anastasia. It was the traditional time for baptizing candidates. It is known that Eunomios the neo-Arian certainly insisted on the rebaptism of any Christians who had not been baptized by members of his clergy. Gregory criticized him for the practice, but also makes it clear in his own writings that an Arian baptism, delivered by those who do not profess the divinity of the three fold name in which they baptize, is more like a funeral ceremony than a life-giving initiation.[133] It is certain that when the large mass of the city's Christians started to come over to the Nicene cause after the arrival of Theodosius and the ejection of Arian clergy from the churches, re-baptisms and re-ordinations were not demanded as a policy of admission. It seems, however, that the baptisms Gregory planned to celebrate in the city had a very symbolic force in 380. In the first place they indicated that he scorned the position of Demophilos, the incumbent bishop. The canons stated that the bishop alone had the right to conduct ordinations and baptisms. By admitting baptismal candidates Gregory was declaring publicly that as far as he was concerned there was no current bishop in Constantinople other than himself. Secondly, to offer the opportunity of baptism at this juncture, was a dramatic way of signaling through symbols the message he was already preaching to the

132. Orat. 33.7-9, PG 36.224-225.
133. The Arian baptismal service possibly baptized "into the death of Christ" rather than into the threefold name. Such was the historian Socrates' claim (HE 5.24). It is this ritual which is witnessed in the Arian compilation of the *Apostolic Constitutions* (3.17.1-4; 5.7.30; 7.40-44; ed. M. Metzger, SC vol. 329, pp. 158, 238; and SC vol. 336, pp. 96-104). If Gregory knows this, it would give point to his reference to their (non-trinitarian) ritual as a "sepulchral" achievement.

aristocracy, that this was a good time to change allegiances in advance of the Emperor's arrival. Even if we suppose Gregory had only one or two highly placed baptismal candidates for this ceremony, it would still serve the propaganda purpose. This was something that was a provocation for the clergy of Demophilos.

A concerted attack was made on the Anastasia. The Easter Vigil services had already begun when a crowd of monks and nuns from the city together with assorted troublemakers forced their way into the house Church. They let fly a hail of stones. Gregory ruefully says it was the only "banquet" he received while he was there, indicating how Demophilos had frozen him out socially.[134] The *De Vita Sua* makes light of the incident, saying that he will not criticize his attackers for their missiles, only for their terrible aim. The incident impressed itself on him, nonetheless, and appears as a *leitmotiv* of the troubles he braved in the city. It features in four other poems apart from the *De Vita Sua*: "On Himself and the Bishops,"[135] "On Himself After his Return from Constantinople,"[136] "On Himself,"[137] and the "Poem to Christ."[138] It is also the subject of discussion in the more informative letter[139] he wrote to Theodore of Tyana, the new Metropolitan of Cappadocia Secunda. The violence can also be seen in his references in *Orations* 33 and 23 which came shortly after the affair, and in *Oration* 41[140] which compares it to his share in Christ's passion.

In the letter to Theodore he informs the bishop that he was engaged in the rites of initiation when his community was attacked. Theodore, had expressed outrage over the way in which Gregory had been treated. Gregory advises against responding to the incident, cautioning patience, in case all that he has worked to achieve in the city might be lost in a moment. In the poem *On Himself and the Bishops* which he composed after he had retired from the capital in 381 or 382, he makes passing mention of his "stonings" in a series of complaints on the violence of the Arians, and again argues that forgiveness is the proper response. Once more the incident is put to humorous effect. In the face of being stoned, Gregory says, he had the "courage of a Lion." Whereas now, faced with the duplicity of bishops, he is reduced to a quivering mass.[141]

The attack on his community during the Easter rituals succeeded in completely wrecking their celebrations. The altar was smashed and the liturgical vessels overturned. Gregory told bishop Theodore that he was caught standing between the baptismal candidates and those throwing stones, "and had no other protection than

134. "I will pass over that 'feast of stones' I was offered." *De Vita Sua*, vv. 655-657, PG 37.1075.
135. Carm. 2.1.12, v. 103, PG 37.1173.
136. Carm. 2.1.15, v. 11, PG 37.1251.
137. Carm. 2.1.30, v. 125, PG 37.1295.
138. Carm. 2.1.33, v. 12, PG 37.1306.
139. Ep. 77, PG 37.141-145; Gallay (1964), pp. 95-98.
140. Orat. 41.5, PG 36.436.
141. Carm. 2.1.12, v. 32-35, PG 37.1168-1169.

my prayers."[142] Someone called Paul or Plautos was the organizer, but nothing else is known of the character.[143] He is very anxious to divert the bishop's angered insistence that his attackers ought to be prosecuted, telling him in reply that it would be very bad for the Nicene cause if they were seen to prefer strict justice to charity, for a prosecution would inevitably mean they would be taking issue against the poor and the monastics, whose loyalty they could perhaps more easily gain by kindness. In fact to add insult to outrage, it was Gregory who soon found himself summoned to appear before a city magistrate to give an account of himself. He says, in the *De Vita Sua*, that he was dragged to the courthouse as if he was a murderer. He gives no indication in his writings that any of his party committed violence on the night of the attack, but it might be suspected, and someone in bishop Demophilos' party clearly thought they had a legal case against him. This legal attack might be set to the door of the patrician Demosthenes, his old enemy from the time of Valens' visitation of the Church at Caesarea in 372. Demosthenes was one of the leading orchestrators of the former emperor's campaign to discredit the Nicene party, and presumably remained a firm ally of his Homoian bishop Demophilos in his last months of power. Gregory had caricatured Demosthenes as Nabuzardan, the chief eunuch of the wicked king, when he had first encountered him.[144] When Gregory looked back on his enemies in the city, apart from the bishops whom he felt had betrayed him, he selects for special mention one other particular class of foe: the "plotting eunuchs."[145] This might be an allusion to Demosthenes orchestrating the resistance to Gregory's activities in the capital. Gregory describes himself in the hostile courtroom like a martyr of old, facing persecuting authorities "who stared at me with proud and supercilious glances."[146]

He was happy in the knowledge that he had acquitted himself well in the court, though a little bemused that he was there at all: "Imagine—me who had never done anything wrong in my life, nor even thought about it."[147] The speech in his defense, turning on the fact that the violence was not of his making, but inflicted on him by Arian agitators was to be used again in *Orations* 33 and 23, immediately following the Easter fracas. They reproduce substantial parts of his legal case. The magistrate, described as a mere timeserver by Gregory[148] was too wise to the background of the events to be manipulated into any hostile decision, and Gregory was soon allowed to resume his affairs. Yet it was one of his low points. At this time another old friend, Philagrios, wrote to him from Cappadocia asking him how it was all going. He received a grim reply:

142. Ep. 77.3, PG 37.141; Gallay (1964), p. 95.
143. Ep. 77.16, PG 37.145; Gallay (1964), p. 98.
144. Orat. 43.47, PG 36.557; see also Gregory of Nyssa, *Con. Eunomium* 1.139.
145. *De Vita Sua*, vv. 1425-1431, PG 37.1127-1128.
146. *De Vita Sua*, v. 669, PG 37.1075.
147. *De Vita Sua*, vv. 671-672, PG 37.1075.
148. *De Vita Sua*, v. 670, PG 37.1075.

What a dreadful state of affairs. I no longer have Basil; no longer have Caesarios; my brother in spirit and my brother in the flesh. I can cry out with David.[149] My father and mother have abandoned me! My body is sick. Old age droops over my head. Cares overwhelm me. My troubles mount up. My friends prove faithless. The Church is shepherdless. The Good is extinguished. Evil goes about brazenly. It is like navigating by night; no light to be seen; Christ asleep in the boat.[150] What else can possibly happen? There is only one release from my troubles, and that is death. But to judge from what is going on round here the afterlife might be even more to worry about.[151]

He had his head in his hands. His eirenic policy, his determination to forgive and his refusal to allow his own party to take a more robust stand was already gathering criticism even from his supporters. He tells a dubious Theodore that Jesus rebuked those who called down fire on the heads of his critics and, while Peter used a sword to attack Malchus, it was Jesus who reversed the violent deed by healing the man.[152] The voices within his camp who demanded greater security, however, would soon carry the day by enlisting a strong body of Egyptian sailors to protect them. One result of his refusal to press charges was manifested to him shortly afterwards (it is the only success he can think of for his critics, and so he makes it into a cameo episode in the *De Vita Sua*).[153] A young man, shabbily dressed,[154] came into his apartment with a crowd of other well-wishers at a time when he was ill in bed. When the others were making ready to go, the young man (whom he thought was part of their entourage) fell by his bedside weeping inconsolably. Gregory, typically, started weeping with him, without knowing why, and after all the tears it finally emerged that the man had intended to assassinate him. He was suitably sobered:

> I was shocked to hear this, but managed to say something to absolve his crime: May God save you. It is nothing special that I should be kind to you, my assassin, since I too have been saved. Your rashness has made you mine. Henceforward look to how you can be a credit to God and to myself.[155]

He says this incident of liberality impressed his critics considerably. It was quickly noised around the city and the general animosity towards him began to subside.[156]

Oration 33 belongs to the late spring of 380,[157] and takes up the challenge of

149. Ps 26:10.
150. Mt 8:24.
151. Ep. 80, PG 37.153; Gallay (1964), p. 103. The PG text gives it as "To Eudoxios."
152. Ep. 77.10, PG 37.144; Gallay (1964), p. 96; Lk 9:54f; Lk 22:50-51.
153. *De Vita Sua*, vv. 1441-1474, PG 37.1129.
154. Gregory says in Ep. 77, that the party who attacked him at Easter were drawn from the poor.
155. *De Vita Sua*, vv. 1466-1471, PG 37.1130-1131.
156. *De Vita Sua*, vv. 1472-1474, PG 37.1131.
157. Gallay (1943), p. 145, set it in 379, but he saw Gregory coming to the capital early in that year. As he came only after the autumn synod of Antioch, he does not have the time to offer many orations in 379. Tillemont and the Benedictine editors located it in 380; *Mémoires*, vol. 9, p. 463, and PG 36.213-214.

answering the hostility shown to his congregation during the recent celebration of Pascha. There is an indication in his opening remarks that the discourse was delivered at this specific time, for he defiantly asks his Arian opponents "What imperial decree have we been guilty of ignoring and fighting against?" He means of course, that his slate is clean, but they will have much to answer for in due course. The words have special significance in the aftermath of his failed prosecution, and also of Theodosius' decree of February 28 calling the Constantinopolitans to the Nicene trinitarian faith held at Rome and Alexandria. Gregory mentions that he has been the subject of an assassination attempt, but has forgiven the assassin;[158] and that he has been like the proto-martyr Stephen (subject to stoning), but like him has prayed to Jesus to forgive his persecutors their sin,[159] all of which clearly puts this Oration after the tumultuous events of the Pascha rioting.

The attacks of the Arians had, as Gregory laments, clearly taken a more concrete form as the import of the new emperor's arrival made them take the Cappadocian bishop more seriously than they had at first. In the apologetic war that was raging between the camps, cartoons of doctrines were more important than precision. Just as Gregory had at first made it out that the Nicene faith was very simple and homely, fit for all to understand, without excessive subtleties, so the Arian clergy made it clear in their own turn that his doctrine was no more, or less, than polytheism. The teaching that there were three who were equally God, they argued, meant in anybody's mathematics that he was propagating a tri-theist heresy.[160] It was this frontal attack which made him realize that he could not get away with his homely appeals for "simple confessions," and so he started sketching out the full version of the portfolio of *Theological Orations*[161] which, historically, marked the high water mark of the Nicene party's trinitarian theology; going much further in their exposition than either Athanasios or Basil before him.

In *Oration* 33, Gregory begins to answer the charges his "worldly enemies" have raised against him, mocking his poverty and the smallness of his congregation.[162] His

---

158. Orat. 33.5, PG 36.221. The forgiveness of an assassin is also recounted in the *De Vita Sua*, vv. 1441-1474. There it is located in the aftermath of Gregory's installation in the church of the Holy Apostles, but it sits loosely in the chronological narrative of the *De Vita Sua* (he introduces the story as a generic example of his pastoral care and policy of charity at v. 1441) and so I think the episode is connected more with the earlier part of the year before Theodosius' arrival, that is the events following the Easter riot of 380. The "assassin" was probably one of those who had attacked him in his Church and now repented of it.

159. Orat. 33.13, PG 36.232

160. *De Vita Sua*, vv. 654-655, PG 37.1074. "The city was seething with anger against us thinking I had introduce many gods instead of the One—hardly surprising since they had been taught in such a way that they were completely unable to recognize orthodox doctrine as to how trinity could become unity and unity trinity once more, both understood as divine."

161. Orats. 27-31, delivered in summer-autumn of 380.

162. The same apologetic is seen in *De Vita Sua*, vv. 696-727, PG 37.1077-1079; again set in the context of a formal legal defense speech.

retort is that pebbles vastly exceed the number of precious stones lying around, but the latter are the more notable and significant.[163] He addresses Demophilos, *in absentia*, who certainly regarded his preaching in the Anastasia as an insult to his own office and dignity, and he gives the reply that his scorn for Gregory is misplaced, and his threats of violence unnecessary. He too has an equal episcopal dignity and will exercise *parrhesia* when it is necessary to correct him.[164] Sections three to five of the Oration bring into the open Gregory's concern about the growing rancor from the Arian clergy at Constantinople, and he takes the personal criticisms he has received (that he is a rustic, from an insignificant village, poorly dressed, an old-fashioned idiot and so on) and uses them to launch a legal testimony to the whole series of "Arian atrocities" that he can recall from recent times, up to the attacks made against Peter of Alexandria in his Church, and the murder of his old mentor Eusebios of Samosata.[165] In this strategy he is partly reversing the Homoian and Anhomoian attempts to gain the high ground of hagiography,[166] and partly making it clear to his hearers that he has gathered evidence. The history of the Arians is presented as a constant recourse to pugnacious repression. It is Gregory who evidences a different spirit: clinging to the apostolic simplicity that delights in obscurity and poverty, and refusing to treat his enemies as they have treated him.[167] Yet, by virtue of rehearsing the evidence so clearly, he is also saying: pacific he may be; an easy mark he is not. If there is further trouble, Gregory is implying, the data has been gathered for what would certainly prove to be a successful counter-prosecution—when the emperor comes.

It is notable that after this Oration, there is no further threat or occasion of personal violence against Gregory. He tells his audience that narrow though his sheepfold may be, and free though it may be from "wolves," he is expecting a time not too far off when it shall be vast number indeed, and even some of those who are presently wolves might be found as shepherds in it.[168] The message could not have been clearer. His main opposition is the Homoian clergy assembled around Demophilos. If they want to keep their jobs they had better start showing some cooperation soon.

163. Another witty allusion I think to the stoning of his congregation at Easter.

164. Orat. 33.1, PG 36.216.

165. Killed by an Arian woman who dropped a tile on his head from the rooftops in the town of Dolica (Theodoret, HE 5.4). After the conclusion of the Synod of Antioch in 379 Eusebius was engaged in ordaining as many pro-Nicene bishops in the East as he could, on his journey home. Akakios at Beroea, Theodotos at Cyrrhos, Eulogios at Edessa, and Maris at Dolica were among his consecrations, all of whom attended at Constantinople in 381.

166. Brennecke (1988) has demonstrated the significance of homoian hagiography. The same strategy is, of course, highly visible in Gregory's hagiographies of Basil, and Athanasios, and (not least) himself; cf. McLynn (1998a). It called out Gregory of Nyssa's urgent hagiographical works for Basil's reputation in answer to Eunomios, and also his *Vita Macrinae*. Eunomios was making great claims for the sanctity of Aetio, the fomer leader of the Anhomoian party, and describing him as a thaumaturg while Gregory was in the capital.

167. Orat. 33.6-12, PG 36.221 229.

168. Orat. 33.15, PG 36.233.

His doctrine is summed up as the denunciation of all previous heresies (Gnosticism, Marcionism, Montanism, Manicheism, Novatianism, Sabellianism, Arianism, and Photinianism). He makes no mention whatsoever of Apollinaris or Marcellus of Ancyra. In contrast to all these errors:

> We worship the Father, the Son, and the Holy Spirit, One Godhead: God the Father, God the Son and (Let this not distress you!) God the Holy Spirit. One single nature in three proprieties, intelligences, perfections, and individual subsistences. They are distinguishable by enumeration, but not divided in deity.[169]

Gregory ends by a last reference to the scandal of the attack on his Church during the Easter rites. If only those who now oppose him, he says, would recognize this teaching. Because, without the faith in the divinity of the three Persons, who are invoked over the initiates, how can Arian baptisms ever be anything more than "funeral rituals" that take living people down into the waters and bring them back up as dead souls in the sight of God?[170]

Oration 23 was delivered at more or less the same time, in the aftermath of Easter 380. He insists he has to speak out in case silence should be taken for acquiescence, although he is still barely able to deliver any oration because of his state of health.[171] Gregory again refers to the settlement of internal divisions of the Nicene community. He speaks of having being stoned by an angry crowd,[172] and having his judgment criticized, things he will accept gladly as an imitation of the sufferings of Christ, and which will (like the Passion of Jesus) build up the church. Bernardi has suggested that, as it is more or less entirely addressed to his attackers and critics, whereas his normal orations constantly refer to his present congregation, it was most likely a piece designed for publication rather than a preached oration.[173] It is, in my opinion, mainly a re-use of the legal defense he presented in court after the Easter fracas. This piece takes its starting point by holding up the "charity" in Gregory's community as a rebuke to the criticisms and mockeries of his enemies. It seems as if he is conscious of having established sufficient harmony in the disparate Nicene factions around him to allow him to go once more on the offensive.[174] Nothing in the internal dissensions of his own community, he says, has had a theological root, merely a dispute about "organizational" matters,[175] again referring to the Antiochene schism,[176] which he refers to in terms of a "father of noble soul,

---

169. Orat. 33.16, PG 36.236.
170. Orat. 33.17, PG 36.236-237. Eunomios' ritual baptized his candidates "into the death of Christ," rather than into the threefold name.
171. Orat. 23.6, PG 35.1157.
172. Orat. 23.5, PG 35.1157.
173. Bernardi (1968), p. 166.
174. Orat. 23.1, PG 35.1152.
175. Orat. 23.3, PG 35.1153.
176. It could be taken as a reference to the turmoil introduce in the community of the Anastasia after Maximus' attempt to secure ordination, but I think it is the dissensions of Orat. 22 that are being referred to.

and a son now submissive sitting side by side in good accord.[177] The substance of the discourse[178] is given over to presenting a more complete version of the synopsis of Trinitarian doctrine he has been setting out to date. He calls it

> A brief synopsis of doctrine not dialectic; given not in imitation of Aristotle, but of the fishermen,[179] not craftily, but spiritually; not as if I was in the market place, but as if I was in Church.[180]

His synopsis sets out the agenda which will be expanded later in the *Theological Orations* he was already drafting out. He attacks two theological positions: (a) the Son and Spirit are without cause (*agenetos*); and (b) they are caused by the Father as something other (*hetera*) to Him. His position again stands as the golden mean between them: the Son and Spirit cannot be described as Agennetos if this means without principle. The fact that they have the Father as their principle (*arche*) is the root of all that is meant by their divinity. Equally, however, they cannot be regarded as having a cause or origin that is different to them.[181] This dialectic sets aside the basic Anhomoian arguments, which would have been as distasteful to his Homoian audience as they were to his Nicene party, and is intended to gain a sympathetic hearing from the Homoians whom this Oration is primarily addressing. He goes on to explain that his opponents have not understood properly the manner in which the Nicenes apply the concept of principle and causality to the Son and Spirit. It is something other than what is meant by God's origination of the created order. When it refers to the Father's divine "generation" of the Only Son, and the mystical "procession" of the Spirit, in other words when it is used in precise theological terms rather than economic terms, the causality indicates the manner in which the Father relates his being to the other two persons. It thus connotes the equality of the persons: a sameness of nature and order (since there is no priority in the timeless God) and of divine honor:

> They constitute one single reality, in the distinctions; and distinct realities in their unity, however paradoxical it is to put it like this. They are no less worthy of glory in their mutuality, than when considered and perceived in their individuality: a perfect Trinity constituted of three perfect ones.[182]

Again he applies the simplest level of synopsis: his doctrine of the trinity is the golden mean. The other two "extremes" are Judaic monism, and Hellenistic

---

177. This has led some to see the Oration belonging to 362 when Gregory returned to sit alongside his father, at the end of the local schism there. But the issue is clearly a "sharing of thrones" held up as a notable restoration of accord. This certainly refers to two bishops (which is inapplicable in 362) and must mean the peculiar (and short-lived) canonical settlement of the Synod of Antioch in 379 when Meletios would be the senior incumbent and Paulinus would "sit alongside him" with right to inherit after Meletios' death.

178. Orat. 23.7-13, PG 35.1157-1165.

179. Viz. Apostles.

180. Orat. 23.13, PG 35.1165.

181. Orat. 23.7, PG 35.1160.

182. Orat. 23.8, PG 35.1160.

polytheism.[183] The trinity as he teaches it is not a plurality of divine beings. It cannot be conceived as a mathematical extension:

> Many, indeed beyond imagination, are the plural objects that could be mathematically listed; but when we talk about a union (syllepsis) of equalities, of the same honor, that are bound together in harmony and natural unity, this cannot be dissected by numerical differentiation.[184]

The science of reciprocal relations,[185] he tells his audience, forms part of the rationale of his discourse, but only part, for discoursing about the inner life of the triune God is also a matter of divine revelation reserved for those beings who have been purified, to whom God will reveal the truth now and in the age to come.[186] As for material analogies, the consideration of the intimate relation of spiritual awareness and rational reflection within the same person can stand as an example; though all ideas fall short as nothing can approach the reality of the absolute transcendent divinity: "If even to think about these realities constitutes bliss, imagine what the presence must be like."[187]

He is abundantly aware that this offering of such a synopsis of the trinity doctrine will not satisfy his critics. In fact, as an "introduction" to trinitarian theology it raises more questions than it really answers, though perhaps that was its intent, for his short speech serves the purpose of setting out the basics of what it was he was teaching (the consubstantial equality of the three persons in the indivisible deity of the Father's causality) and of refuting the general claim of his critics that he was a simple tritheist. Gregory ends with a rhetorical denunciation of those who will not listen to his words and looks forward to future debate, when he can crush the "scorpions and dragons"[188] through the apostolic charism given to him. This is certainly an ebullient reference to what he intends to be a stepping up of his public campaign against Arian intellectuals who are resisting him. This was a time when he was gathering his notes for an extended series of Discourses in the late summer, numbers 27-31, which were subsequently entitled the *Five Theological Orations*. These are the quintessence of his theological work, and the most important texts in Christian history for establishing the cardinal doctrine of the Trinity. Several of the informed regarded them as an important rhetorical showdown between two schools of thought that had been in conflict over the high ground of Christian identity for the whole of the previous generation. The churches of Rome and Alexandria were taking notice of what was happening in the capital, and the bishops of the eastern sees gathered around Meletios at Antioch were hoping for a sterling performance. Jerome traveled to hear Gregory preach, and

---

183. Cf. Athanasios, Ep. 1, *To Serapion*, 28.
184. Orat. 23.9, PG 35.1161.
185. *Pros allela skeseos.*
186. As in Orats. 20.12, 39.9, and 40.5-6.
187. Orat. 23.11, PG 35.1164.
188. Ps 90:13; Is 59:5; Lk 10:19.

was probably there for the *Theological Orations*. On the basis of that brief encounter he ever afterwards called Gregory, " my teacher in exegesis."[189]

Gregory had been in correspondence with Peter of Alexandria as soon as he had entered the capital. There can be no doubt about this, but no trace of the correspondence has been allowed to remain in his collected letters. His bile after 381 was so great that he could not bear even the thought had he had allowed himself to be taken in by "Egyptians." There are only traces left to suggest what was the gist of the correspondence he had, but it was certainly substantive. He remarks offhand that Peter of Alexandria had a pen nib as forked as his tongue, and seemed to like writing contradictory letters.[190] The heart of the matter is contained in the words:

> You who understand these things explain this conundrum for me (for I need a clever person to deliver me from my incomprehension): how was it that Peter, that leader of pastors personally installed me only a short time before,[191] by his letters, which are very clear and unambiguous, as the texts themselves show, and even honored me by sending insignia of office? Was this a case of someone switching the deer[192] for the virgin? What a confusion needing an interpreter! Of all the wretched scenes played upon life's stage has anything more melodramatic than this ever been seen?[193]

The letters from Alexandria must have come to him with a present of a more practical kind than the regalia of an archbishop, and that was extra manpower. It was the beginning of the season of the grain ships coming to Constantinople, each one full of Egyptian sailors, some of whom had been specifically instructed to put themselves at the service of Gregory and attend his services in the Anastasia church. He was delighted when they first started to come, itinerant congregation though they would prove. And he was even more delighted when another Egyptian Nicene philosopher came to offer his services; a striking figure with long blonde curled hair and a philosopher's robe, carrying the staff of a Cynic sophist. It was Maximus whom Gregory regarded as a port in a storm. His labors could now be shared with another appreciative sophist. Gregory fell upon Maximus too avidly, and too quickly, grateful for his moral support:

> Who else, apart from Maximus, so shared my house, my table, my teachings, my counsels, my friendship? And no wonder, for he was a mighty dog,[194] barking at all those who thought evilly, and applauding my speeches enthusiastically.[195]

189. Ep. 50.1; Ep. 52. 8; *De Vir. Ill.* 117; *In Isaiam* 3.
190. *De Vita Sua*, vv. 1015-1016, PG 37.1099.
191. Before the Maximus incident, when he supported the pretensions of Maximus for the throne of Constantinople.
192. In Euripides' *Iphigenia in Tauris* 28, the virgin Iphigenia is about to be sacrificed, when at the last moment the goddess Artemis switched a sacrificial deer. Gregory obviously thinks it is a dreadfully unbelievable ending.
193. *De Vita Sua*, vv. 856-867, PG 37.1088.
194. A pun on his profession as a Cynic deconstructionist thinker.
195. *De Vita Sua*, vv. 810-814, PG 37.1085.

He determined that celebratory Orations would be in order.[196] He composed one for the feast of May 2, 380, the commemoration of Athanasios, great defender of the Nicene creed and most famous of the hierarchs of Alexandria. It was for the benefit of his newly arrived Egyptian faithful, and as strong a statement as he could make that it was his congregation at the Anastasia that now exemplified the imperial command in the edict *Cunctos Populos*, that the faith of Peter of Alexandria must henceforth be regarded as the norm for the *Religio Romanorum*.

Oration 21 is the memorial sermon for Athanasios and it marks a new sense of confidence in Gregory's teaching. He says that he will no longer follow a discreet method, trying to appeal to those who have less sense of orthodoxy than himself but will bravely state the full trinitarian truth, just as Athanasios did in the midst of so many struggles and oppressions.[197] The phrasing here certainly suggests that the recent attacks on his church have convinced him that he might as well be stoned for the full version of his theology as the "economic" synopses he has so far been offering out of his hopes for reconciling the Arian clergy.[198] He had Demophilos in mind, rather than Eunomios or his party, because he specifically argues that a bishop cannot be an "intruder" into another's see if the incumbent is not orthodox.[199] He uses the life story of Athanasios to demonstrate the point in relation to the appointment of George of Cappadocia as his "replacement" bishop. Who was the legitimate hierarch of Alexandria in this case? One paid imperial eunuchs to protect him,[200] but suffered a terrible fall when the emperor's protection was removed as God struck him down in his wickedness.[201] The other taught the simple truth and was raised up high by God to claim back his city in a triumph.[202] The pointed parallel between Demophilos and Gregory cannot have escaped anyone. He is suggesting, subtextually, that the fall of the last "wicked emperor" Valens will precede the overthrow of this new "George of Cappadocia." The point was especially relevant to the Egyptian sailors who were present in the church, since it was an Alexandrian mob which had beaten the unfortunate George to an unrecognizable state, and tied him under a camel that dragged him to his death in the streets. Demophilos' spies in the congregation would undoubtedly have apprized him of this lightly veiled threat to meet further violence with violence.

The panegyric depicts Athanasios as the model Christian, and ideal ruler.[203] It is a

196. The idea came at a similar time, as Orat. 25 shows, for the praises of Athanasios are resumed in Orat. 25.11, PG 35.1213.
197. Orat. 21.34, PG 35.1124.
198. "I will no longer take heed of my own fears, looking to the opinions of men less sound than myself, for I have done this until I am tired of it, and have gained nothing but injury." Orat. 21.34, PG 35.1124.
199. Orat. 21.8, PG 35.1089.
200. Orat. 21.21, PG 35.1105.
201. Orat. 21.26, PG 35.1112.
202. Orat. 21.27-31, PG 35.1113f.
203. Orat. 21.20, PG 35.1104.

canonization text that recounts many of the details of his life, some of them given to him personally by his childhood friend Philagrios, who was in the city of Alexandria to witness the triumphal return of Athanasios after the death of Julian.[204] Gregory is very reserved in regard to any particular writings of Athanasios, mentioning only in generic terms the *Life of Antony,* and the confession of faith which he offered Jovian; something that Gregory takes to be paradigmatic of the common faith articulated between the orthodox of the eastern and western parts of the empire. He offers a brief history of Arianism in the oration, and sets it in a cameo of the fight between Athanasios and "that monster," George of Cappadocia.[205] He describes the Christian world as in a dreadful state of confusion, divided into three parties,[206] when bishops had become "brutish" and were ignorant of the law of God.[207] Only a few brave teachers of the truth escaped the common fate of oppression and exiles,[208] and others who escaped without compromising at that time only did so because of their relative insignificance.[209] The majority gave in to political pressure to conform. How can such leaders be excused, he says, when even in secular law ignorance is not accepted as a justification? The reference to the brave few who survived and those who were "too insignificant" to attract attention evidently sets himself alongside Basil as one of those teachers who in the time of Athanasios' life were consistently teaching orthodox doctrine. The inability of the large majority of time-servers to plead excuse, shows that he was progressively abandoning his earlier estimates that the Arian clergy could be brought over *en masse* when the emperor came. His political sense, now in his second year at the capital, was telling him that "exiles" were inevitable.

In doctrinal terms *Oration* 21 is not particularly detailed. It opens with a passage that was to have great resonance among the Byzantine mystics of later centuries, when it evokes the approach to communion with God as a mystery of noetic light,[210] but then it moves on to become a general history of the eastern Arian crisis, with particular reference to the imperial or Homoian party, under Demophilos. Predictably it labels Arius as the source of all the troubles of the last generation in Church History, and accuses his successors of extending his "wickedness" about the Son into a wickedness over the Trinity, thereby pointing the finger at Macedonios, Demophilos' predecessor at Constantinople. Gregory prioritizes Athanasios' *Letter to Jovian* as a cardinal moment in the turning back of the wave of Arianism in the Eastern Church, just as he singles out the council of Seleukia/Constantinople (359

204. Orat. 21.27-28, PG 35.1113-1116.
205. Orat. 21.14-16, and passim to ch. 27, PG 35.1096-1100.
206. Orat. 21.33, PG 35.1121. He means Homoousians, Homoiousians, and Homoians.
207. Orat. 21.24, PG 35.1109.
208. Orat. 21.23, PG 35.1108.
209. Orat. 21.24, PG 35.1109.
210. Orat. 21.1, PG 35.1084. Gregory Christianises Plato, repeating this text in Orat. 28.30, PG 36.69. It became frequently alluded to in later Byzantine mysticism.

and 360) as the lowest trough of decline, when heterodoxy was ushered in through the vague Christological phrase: "Like in all things according to the scriptures': the central Homoian Arian confession."[211] And yet, in positive terms Gregory himself is not especially forthcoming in this oration, even though he says he is tired with an eirenic economy, and has determined to speak plainly. He still uses the old synopsis of trinitarian faith as a golden mean between Sabellianism and other "mutilators," describing Athanasios as one who "happily preserved the unity, and religiously taught the trinity; not confounding the three persons in the unity, or dividing the substance among the three persons, but staying in the bounds of righteousness and avoiding excessive inclination or resistance to either side."[212] Later he suggests that it was a particular mark of Athanasios' greatness that he not only represented an orthodox doctrine of the deity of the Son, but even preserved the theology of the Holy Spirit, at a time when "to be only slightly impious meant that one had an orthodox enough reputation."[213]

The Oration's concluding words suggest that the clarification is to come soon enough. It is here that he specifically declares his readiness to speak out openly, and wants to clear away any confusion that might remain among his Nicene party over the issue of the different trinitarian terminology that has in past times been favored by the Latins and the Nicene Greeks. In an interesting passage, he says that the Latin tongue has a "threadbare vocabulary" and a certain "poverty of technical terms" that has caused much confusion in the past; but the terms hypostasis or prosopon must no longer be read as referring to the Latin sense of substantia.[214] The old confusions, he says, "would be laughable if their results had not been so pitiable." He is referring to the very important efforts at reconciliation that Athanasios sponsored, after the Synod of Alexandria in 362, which were designed to reach a common accord in regard to political cooperation and terminological agreement among all pro-Nicenes of good will in the East and West. Gregory ends by portraying himself as a new Athanasios, come to bring this work of reconciliation to a final resolution. This, he says, was the supreme achievement that was "worth all his banishments and flights, and more profitable than labors and teachings that many writers have developed over a long period."[215] His final prayer identifies himself with the saint in heaven:

211. Orat. 21.22, PG 35.1107; cf. Hanson (1988), pp. 371-180.
212. Orat. 21.13, PG 35.1096.
213. A tactful way of criticising the Homoiousian party that had not advanced a clear enough doctrine of the Spirit's deity in the life-time of Athanasios. Its ranks at one time included a lot of "Nicene" stalwarts, not least Eustathios of Sebaste, and Basil. Orat. 21.33, PG 35.1121.
214. Orat. 21.35, PG 35.1124-1125. The Greek word *hypostasis*, was used to refer to the plurality of persons in the Godhead, but etymologically it was a synonym for the Latin word *Substantia*, used to refer to the principle of unity in the Godhead. Those who did not appreciate the precise context of the various arguments were ripe for major linguistic misunderstandings. One wonders if this allusion to the poverty of Latin is a humorous acknowledgement of Jerome's presence?
215. Orat. 21.36, PG 35.1125.

Cast down on us, from above, your auspicious gaze, and lead this people in its perfect worship of the perfect Trinity, the Father, Son, and Holy Spirit whom we contemplate and adore. If my lot is to be a peaceful one, assist me in this pastoral charge. But if I must pass through strife, confirm me or else take me alongside you and your companions (though I ask for much) in the very presence of Christ Himself, Our Lord, to whom be all glory honor and power, for evermore. Amen.[216]

Even though the *Oration for Athanasios* is long and detailed, then, it is interesting that Gregory reserves the open defense of the Trinity he promises for another time. He was surely preparing the sheaf of Orations, 27-31, that would be dedicated to the issue in the later summer months. The presence of a church with strong Egyptian sailors around him, has given Gregory new heart for the fight. So far all is sunshine. His image of Alexandria is of a bastion of the faith. Soon his descriptions will be vitriolic. Still confident in Peter of Alexandria's acknowledgment of his work, however, he dedicated another Oration to the presence of the Egyptians in the Anastasia.

Gallay,[217] following Tillemont, sees *Oration 34* as coming after the affair over Maximus' pretended consecration, when Gregory was trying to effect a reconciliation with the Egyptian sailors who had sponsored his rival pretender. Bernardi has subsequently repeated this dating.[218] The evidence does not support such a view. The earlier commentators[219] had it right when they set the oration as coming before the Maximus affair, at the very beginning of the season when the grain ships started to come from Alexandria to the capital; a fact Gregory mentions specifically on several occasions.[220] The reference which Gallay sees to be an offering of the hand of friendship after a recent alienation,[221] I think is more a repeated reference to something he mentioned in the immediately previous oration in honor of Athanasios,[222] that he, a Cappadocian, will repair the damage inflicted on the honor and faith of Alexandria by his shameful namesake Gregory of Cappadocia, and the even-worse George of Cappadocia, the Arian bishops who had intruded into Athanasios' see. It is otiose to set *Oration 34* in the latter part of 380, for after the Maximus fiasco, it was clear to Gregory that no further assistance was forthcoming from Egypt or the sailors (who were now evidently taking new instructions from their hierarchs), and there was certainly no need to broker a reconciliation with Maximus himself as he had fled to Thessaloniki, and then to Alexandria and finally Aquileia to prosecute his case there. Gregory's pressing need, after this humiliating affair, was not to

216. Orat. 21.37, PG 35.1128.
217. Gallay (1943), p. 172.
218. Bernardi (1968), p. 179. Bernardi simply accepts Gallay's argument.
219. Beginning with Elias of Crete in the ninth century.
220. See, for example, Orat. 34.1, PG 36.242; Orat. 34.7, PG 36.248.
221. "I hold out to you the hand of friendship and will cast aside an ancient injury by a new-found friendship." Orat. 34.6, PG 36.245.
222. Orat. 21.15-16, PG 35.1097-1100. Orat. 34.3, PG 36.244, takes up again the praises of Athanasios from Orat. 21 and compares Peter of Alexandria to his great predecessor.

reconcile with Egyptians, who remained his opponents and bitterly resisted him even at the council of 381, but to reconcile with Constantinopolitan aristocrats who thought he had seriously damaged his credibility by the lack of judgment he had shown. It is this latter exercise in rehabilitation that he is still pursuing as late as 382 when he composed the *De Vita Sua*, and by that stage he has not a good word to say about Alexandria, or it current episcopal leadership.

Oration 34, therefore, comes in the middle of May 380, when the Egyptian contingent has started to become a regular part of the Anastasia congregation. It is designed to show Gregory as a "good Alexandrian," and he lards the praises on the audience as "descendants of these great men" who taught orthodoxy.[223] After these opening plaudits he says that his "brief exposition" of theology will be immediately recognizable to the Egyptians, since they too are orthodox, just as people can immediately recognize soldiers of their own camp. Sections 8-15 of the Oration begin to present another synopsis of his doctrine. This is the clearest of the several summations he has been offering so far. The main distinction that has to be observed is the one between Dominion and Servitude. The side of dominion belongs to God. To servitude belongs all the creatures. God is the Lord. The divine name strictly excludes any attribution of creaturehood, though the divine name:

> Consists in three supremely great realities; in the Cause, in the Demiurge, and in the Perfecter. I speak of course about the Father, the Son and the Holy Spirit.[224]

Once again they are not to be confounded into one reality, which is the heresy of Sabellius, or differentiated so strongly that they fall out of the common nature, which is the heresy of Arius. This is the simplest form of the central doctrine constituting orthodoxy: that the name of God is inalienable, but it is a trinitarian name, and all three persons are equally divine. After a very brief rehearsal of the previous heresies concerning the relations of the Father and Son,[225] Gregory takes it as read that the orthodox are now in complete agreement as to the divine status of the Logos. On this basis he begins a new level of argument. The titles of the Son, he argues, clearly connote divine power. The demons flee at the sound. The Son and the Spirit, he then tells his audience, have the same glory (as God).[226] The logical connection of the insight is provided by the biblical text on which he is basing himself. To deny the divine power of the Spirit would be to disgrace the whole Godhead. Gregory says it is the same as that blasphemy which is warned against by Christ himself, when the Pharisees attacked his own title to divine status by refusing to believe his name had the power to cast out demons.

223. Orat. 34.4, PG 36.244. After their involvement in the underhand consecration of Maximus Gregory blasted them as: "ape-shaped, dog-like demons of Egypt; a despicable and venal crew." *De Vita Sua*, v. 840, PG 37.1087
224. Orat. 34.8, PG 36.249.
225. Orat. 34.9-10, PG 36.249f.
226. *Homotimia*, Orat. 34.11, PG 36.252.

It is an allusion to the New Testament text that warns that whoever blasphemes against the Holy Sprit will commit an unforgivable sin,[227] and here the blasphemy against the Spirit is taken to be the denial of the Son's divinity. By this dense exegetical argument Gregory advances the central idea that the Son and Spirit are as one in divine power and divine title. His last argument repeats the theology Athanasios advanced in the *Letters to Serapion,* and Basil in his *De Spiritu Sancto,* that the liturgical practice of the Church demonstrated the theology of the divinity of the Spirit. If one is agreed that baptism in the Spirit divinizes, Gregory says, how can the Spirit be anything other than divine?[228] Only God can divinize others. To have it otherwise, means that the illumination of baptism becomes darkened, and instead of being a transition to divinized life, it becomes a "sepulchral rite," an argument he advanced in *Oration* 33, to insinuate that those who deny the deity of the Spirit thereby lapse from the ranks of true Christians. His final demonstration on the deity of the Spirit is once again taken from an exegetical base when he points to how the Word of God teaches that the Spirit has the same status as himself when he calls the Spirit: "that other Paraclete whom the Father shall send."[229]

Gregory is using a tightly wrought catena of biblical evidence when he sets out the argument for the Spirit's deity. He says that "the essential point of my doctrine"[230] is that the orthodox should give glory to God as the Cherubim do, that is crying out to the Single Holy One, in the threefold cry of the Trisagion: "Holy, Holy, Holy." The cherubim, who veil the "First Essence" with their wings, ceaselessly cry out the trinitarian truth they have seen with their superior spiritual intelligence, so as to reveal it to earthly creatures whose perception is more crass. Similarly, those who have been especially inspired by God, have also seen this truth of the Trinity. He notes that David, the prophet king, said: "In your light we shall see light"[231] which Gregory explains to mean that we shall recognize the divine reality of the Son only in the grace of the Holy Spirit. Again, John, the apostolic Son of Thunder, in his magisterial doctrine, has also taught the unity of the essence of God"[232] along with the distinction of persons.[233] The great hierophant of the trinity is also Paul, the apostle who was caught up into the Third Heaven and saw ineffable realities.[234] His doxologies,[235] like those of the

227. Mt 12:25-32.
228. Orat. 34.13, PG 36.252.
229. Jn 14:16.
230. Orat. 34.13, PG 36.253.
231. Ps 35:10.
232. Jn 10:30. "I and the Father are One Reality."
233. He is cited as teaching the hypostatic existence of the Word, alongside the Father, in Jn 1:1; and indicating the co-equality of the Spirit and the Son in Jn 14:16. Orat. 34.13, PG 36.253.
234. Orat. 34.15, PG 36.253-256.
235. Gregory cites Paul's carelessness in differentiating the "order of persons" when making a doxology to be evidence of how he knew the truth of the "equality of the divine nature." Orat. 34.15, PG 36.256.

Cherubim, evidence the single godhead, as well as the three *hypostases*, in their various forms.[236] In this short exposition Gregory has taken Athanasios' primitive liturgical argument for the deity of the Spirit, and advanced it in a particularly personal way: that the higher liturgical sense is not simply given from the forms of the praxis of the Church on earth (for example that it illumines believers by initiating them into the threefold divine name), but even more so from the higher and fullest sense of the Church's liturgy, when it celebrates the radiant truth in the heavenly choir of the angels; a liturgical concept of the entrance of the initiates into the holy of holies.[237] Only those of great soul have been permitted, while still on earth, to glimpse the truth lying behind the veil of the inner sanctum, the veil constituted by the wings of the Cherubim. David, John and Paul, are among the initiates. So too, he implies, are Athanasios and himself. They too speak as the inspired saints, and he invites his audience to recognize that their trinitarian doctrine is as one. In fact, Gregory's trinitarian doctrine is far more advanced than that of Athanasios, and he would have more difficulty than he thought in convincing the whole Nicene party that it was the correct way forward for the Church at large. The more he departed from the traditional Alexandrian theology, the less hold he had on the Egyptians of his congregation who were of the opinion that Gregory was no more (or no less) than the representative of Peter of Alexandria in this city. It was a view of affairs Gregory himself certainly did not share. Maximus, with the vantage of his closeness to Gregory and an apparently complete acceptance into his counsels, noted the growing fault line between Gregory's theological agenda and ecclesiastical intentions and those of his own bishop in Alexandria. He seems to have been a teller of tales from an early stage, and there were regular ships to keep Peter apprized of everything that was happening.

Gregory pressed forward with this unfolding theology of the Spirit. His next oration, on the great feast of June 9 that year, develops it even further. Pascha had been a disaster because of the Arian attack, but now he had the Egyptian sailors he knew he would be safe. A few hecklers certainly attended, and protested about his pneumatology. It would be very interesting to know if these were Arian visitors who demanded a debate (there were certainly Arian theologians present at his Theological Orations later in the summer) or members of his own Nicene congregation who were anxious at the way he was extending the doctrine of the Homoousion to the Spirit as well as the Son, something that had not been articulated before by any other Nicene theologian. Whoever they were, he felt confident enough to steamroller them:

> You want to present me with your objections? Well, I want to carry on with my Oration! ...Today we shall teach. Tomorrow we may mince words.[238]

236. He scrutinizes the different forms of doxology in 1 Cor 12:6, 11; Rom 8:9-11; 1 Cor 8:6; and Rom 11:36. They become a patristic "topos" of trinitarian evidence ever afterwards.
237. The liturgical matrix is very important in Gregory's theology; cf. McGuckin (1996).
238. Orat. 41.10, PG 36.441-444.

I have the suspicion that the hecklers were actually members of his own party. Not the Egyptians but the collection of monks from the Antiochene metropolitanate who were still pulled by the tradition of Eustathios of Sebaste, and who shied away from the confession of the full deity of the Spirit. It certainly seems as if he is addressing monks in particular in chapter eight of the discourse and hoping that his words will lead them to "follow him."[239] If this is so, the fractures in his own Nicene congregation at the Anastasia, which Gregory so confidently said were behind them in his previous orations, were obviously still capable of yawning open at times of stress. He could not fully rely on either the Antiochenes or the Alexandrians around him; and that left hardly anyone else.

The Feast of Pentecost was his great occasion for setting out more of the pneumatology. It was *par excellence* the Feast of the Spirit. He begins by contrasting the manner in which the Jews and the Hellenes observe feasts, the one "in the letter," the other "in the body."[240] Christians, he implies, observe the golden mean; their festal celebration is "in the Spirit." The point of this is partly to remind his listeners of the antithesis that has been the basis of all his previous synopses: the doctrine of trinity which Gregory maintains is to be envisaged as the mean between Jewish monism and Hellenic polytheism. It is also a reminder of the matrix of liturgical theology he sketched out in his previous discourse. Gregory, as inspired preacher at the liturgical festival of Pentecost, shall manifest to his hearers a sermon that is inspired by that very Spirit he celebrates.[241] There is a long section following, based largely on Origen,[242] which starts considering the significance of the number seven in relation to the festival.[243] It is not until section six that he turns to the pneumatology specifically.

The Spirit, he says, is no angelic servant,[244] for if he were he would be a creature.[245] This calls an end to an old tradition of angelic-pneumatology[246] that had been lingering on even in the new formulations of the Homoiousian and Homoian theologians. Those who reduce the Spirit to the ranks of creatures pour hybris on God, and are the "worst of the worst." They are like rebellious slaves. They are traitors to the supreme sovereign power. By contrast those who believe that the Spirit is

239. Orat. 41.8, PG 36.440-441.
240. Orat. 41.1, PG 36.429.
241. "The Spirit assists me and provides my discourse." Orat. 41.5, PG 36.436.
242. The notion of the eighth day as transcendent perfection (Orat. 41.2) comes from Origen. In *Lev. hom.* 8.4, SC vol. 287, p. 22; and the number symbolism as a whole is definitely Origenian. Gregory's reference to a theologian who is "careful" about the bodily stature of Christ is surely a nod to Origen also. Orat. 41.5, PG 36.436.
243. Seven, the perfect number, is squared to make the Feast of the Fiftieth day. Orat. 41.2.
244. Doulos. Such as the angels of God, directed to assist humankind. Orat. 41.5, PG 36.437.
245. Athanasios. *Letter to Serapion* 1.1.10-11; Didymos the Blind, *De Trinitate* 2.
246. Cf. J. McGuckin. "Spirit Christology: Lactantius and His Sources." *Heythrop Journal* 24, 1983, pp. 141-148; J. Barbel, *Christos Angelos* (Bonn, 1941).

God are themselves "radiantly divinized in their minds," "they are sublime."[247] It is no accident that he thus categorizes his Arian opponents, who have no pneumatology beyond the angelic, as traitors to the "sovereign power." Their doctrine is not merely an offence to God, he implies, it is hybris before the Emperor, whose edict of February they are continuing to defy. Since they are "like the deaf who could not hear the thunder," or the blind who could not see the bright light, Gregory once more says he shall reserve his full instruction on the Spirit for later, and rest content with merely presenting them with a few words to initiate them into the nature of the Spirit. The happy vagueness of believing the Spirit stands somewhere between the angels and the divine rank is an illusion Gregory is determined to scatter. There is no logical middle ground between creature and Creator. It is an absolute gap. Whoever denies the Spirit is God, thereby simply categorizes the Spirit as a creature, and such a theology is inspired by a spirit quite opposite to the holiness of God.[248]

The Spirit is timeless, eternal, and always in communion with the Father and the Son:

> The Spirit is part of nothing else, but has eternally allowed all to take part in it. It brings to perfection, needing no perfecting; fills all things, needing no completion; sanctifies, needing no sanctification. It deifies others though is not deified itself. It is eternally the same in the communion of those to whom it is united. It is invisible, timeless, boundless, unalterable. It is beyond quality or quantity, exterior form, or tangible reality. It is self-moving, ever in progress, powerful in itself, and all powerful, though all refers to the First Cause; which just as it sends forth all that is of the Only Begotten Son, so it does for all that is of the Spirit.[249]

In this passage Gregory gathers together all the "attributes" or rather the characteristic roles of the Spirit, and concludes:

> It is through the Spirit that the Father is known, and the Son is glorified, and from them alone that it too is known. They are one harmony,[250] one adoration and worship and power, and perfection, and sanctification. What need is there to say more? All that belongs to the Father belongs also to the Son, (except only for the character of being ungenerated). So too, all that belongs to the Son, belongs to the Spirit (except only for the character of being begotten). And these characters do not define the essence, in my opinion, but are themselves defined in relation to the essence.[251]

At that point he refuses to pause and listen to the objections of his audience, which have certainly come to him in the form of noisy protests. To interrupt his discourse and debate, he says, would be to bring shame to the feast: "Today we teach doctrine: tomorrow we can mince words... Today we celebrate mysteries, tomorrow you can

247. Orat. 41.6, PG 36.437.
248. Orat. 41.7, PG 36.437.
249. Orat. 41.9, PG 36.441.
250. *Syntaxis*: a constitution, a joining together, or the common modality of a music.
251. Orat. 41.9, PG 36.441.

have your pantomime."[252] Rolling over his hecklers he continues to sketch out how the Spirit has illuminated the angels first, then the prophets, and finally the apostles and disciples. He notes specifically that the Spirit did not illuminate Christ, it accompanied him in his earthly ministry as an "equal in honor."[253] The threefold activity is important to Gregory and something that he develops even more explicitly in *Oration* 31 when he gives his most expansive theology of the Spirit. It is something that he has learned from his long reflections on Origen, though in the form it emerges it is a *proprium* of Gregory's theology and must have appeared very startling to his hearers. He argues that the Spirit manifested its revelatory work in a triadic pattern, and in a threefold *kairos*.[254] The illumination it gave as its economy of revelation was first manifested in Christ's ministry before the Passion, then in the time between the resurrection and the ascension, and finally in the supreme moment when it descended as tongues of fire on the apostles at the Feast of Pentecost. This is Pentecost today.

He makes that reference for a far greater effect than merely the stating of the obvious calendrical point. The three stages of revelation, he says, are progressively perfected. The illumination which the Spirit gives to the apostles "today" at Pentecost, is greater in its profundity than that which he gave them during Christ's earthy ministry, when they were often at a loss in understanding Christ's mind. His strong implication is that the illumination of "today" is the perfect unfolding of the truth.[255] The new "apostolic" hierophant of the last age is thus Gregory himself. His doctrine is implicitly compared to the last age of revelation.[256] This threefold pattern of progressive revelation is taken further, soon afterwards, in *Oration* 31, but this is certainly its prototypal thesis, suggesting that the present-day initiates of the Spirit (particularly Gregory the hierophant speaking once again about the Spirit at this new Pentecost) are more radiant in their understanding than men of ancient days. The thrust of the argument is comparable to the incident where Jesus spoke about the Spirit in the synagogue and concluded: "This text is being fulfilled even as you listen to it."[257] It is a passage Gregory alludes to explicitly,[258] as he ends the discourse by commenting on the long chain of biblical texts which collectively present the Christian pneumatology. Among all this data, he points particularly to the association of the Spirit alongside the Son in the act of the creation of the world, using as

---

252. Orat. 41.10, PG 36.444.
253. *Isotimos.* Orat. 41.11, PG 36.444.
254. An evangelical word signifying a moment of history that is particularly significant for the divine revelation.
255. "The first manifestation was obscure; the second more expressive, and that of the present even more perfect." Orat. 41.11. PG 36.444.
256. The perfect "eight" that comes after the "Pentecostal" seven times seven, as in Orat. 41.2, PG 36.432.
257. Lk 4:18-21. Based on Is 61:1.
258. Orat. 41.13, PG 36.445.

his basis Ps 32.6: "By the Word of the Lord the heavens were made. By the Spirit of his mouth, all their power."[259]

He ends his speech with an exegesis of the events of the first Christian Pentecost, saying that he prefers that interpretation of the sign of the numerous languages that the crowd heard, which refers it to the apostles' manner of speaking, rather than the crowd's manner of hearing. In other words the miracle of the many nations hearing "their own language" occurred because the Spirit made each one of the apostles speak in a variety of foreign tongues, thus overcoming the ancient curse of Babel.[260] He takes it as a symbol for his own work, and ends with an anti-Arian doxology that leaves no doubt about the co-equality of the three persons:

> This is enough for this Oration. Now we shall celebrate the feast; today bodily but soon, hereafter, entirely spiritually. Then we shall know all about this more clearly and more purely in the Word himself, who is our God and Lord, Jesus Christ. On that day we shall keep the true feast in the joy of those who are saved. With Him be glory and honor to the Father, with the Holy Spirit. Now and to the Ages of Ages. Amen.[261]

What the reaction of the Antiochene and the Alexandrian bishops was to the news that would have been brought to them by their numerous agents about Gregory's policy, is not known. It is clear that already by mid-380 Gregory has set his course for nothing less than the proclamation of the consubstantiality of the three divine persons. To call the Spirit God, and to profess the Homoousion in his respect as much as the Son's, was his fixed intent. What is known, however, is that when the bishops from both Antioch and Alexandria assembled for the council in the following year, the creed that finally emerged steered clear of ascribing either the Homoousion to the Spirit, or the clear and unambiguous title "God." It remained in the safe ambiguities of the ascription of Basil's *Homotimia*: the Spirit is associated in harmony of glory and worship along with the Father and Son. To that extent the hecklers he faced that June evening, in the room where he was giving his discourse before they all moved on to the festive Symposium, seem not to have been carried along with him. Doubts about him were certainly being raised at Alexandria, and for that we can suspect Maximus, beginning to report that he was not fully in command of the situation.

Gregory's several references in *Oration* 41 to Origenian theories, and matters of detailed textual interpretation, suggest he was increasingly conscious of having some skilled theologians in the room with him. Maximus appears to have been supplemented by others. The presence of Jerome might explain it, but it is perhaps also an indication of the arrival of the young Origenist philosopher whose future career as a monastic theologian would put him in the highest ranks of patristic fame: Evagrios of Pontike. He had been associated with Basil and ordained reader by him, and later

259. Orat. 41.14, PG 36.448.
260. Orat. 41.15-17, PG 36.449-452.
261. Orat. 41.18, PG 36.452.

says himself that he was Gregory's disciple.[262] If he was in Constantinople in this period, it may well indicate the correctness of the disputed tradition[263] that Gregory ordained Evagrios as his deacon at the Anastasia. After Gregory's departure from the city, Evagrios had a brief spell as a famous city preacher himself, before falling into serious (amatory) trouble and having to flee for his life to Palestine. There he found Melania, and it was she who directed him to the Egyptian desert at Scete, where he wrote his works on Christian asceticism, and remade himself in exile.[264]

With skilled help, then, Gregory completed the dossier of Orations he had been working on for several months. These would represent his full doctrinal exposition, and were intended to be given in close succession to each other, and as the context sometimes indicates, probably allowed for subsequent debate. There were certainly Eunomian (Anhomoian) theologians, as well as Homoian clergy of Demophilos in attendance at these orations, and Gregory knew that he was expected to give the performance of his life. In the subsequent history of the ancient Church, these five Orations were never surpassed for their trinitarian doctrine and were, in fact, adopted as the ultimate statement of Trinitarian orthodoxy despite what the conciliar creed of 381 had to say. It is a providential irony that the creed, which was itself a clear and explicit rebuke of Gregory's boldness in teaching the consubstantiality of the Spirit, has come in the subsequent history of theology to be so strictly interpreted in terms of Gregory's Orations. He may have felt he lost the day when he made his way back to Cappadocia in the latter part of the following year. He could hardly have envisaged the manner in which his work would become established as the foundations of Christian orthodoxy. He could hardly win an attentive audience on the occasion, so restless were his critics when he preached. For centuries after him, this sheaf of Orations became the chief trinitarian curriculum of all the Eastern schools, and of almost as great importance to the West after Rufinus translated them into Latin.

He probably began preaching this last and focused aspect of his instructional campaign in July of 380, and continued through to late August. This would suggest

---

262. In *Praktikos* 100, he ends with an appeal to the: "prayers and intercessions of the righteous Gregory who planted me." This indicates a time shortly after Gregory's death. Cf. J.E. Bamberger, *Evagrius Ponticus: The Praktikos and Chapters on Prayer* (Kalamazoo, 1981), p. 42.

263. Socrates (HE 4.23) and Sozomen (HE 6.30) state that Gregory ordained him a deacon and took him as his attendant to Constantinople. But this perhaps confuses him with Gregory's own deacon Evagrios, whom he had brought with him from the church at Nazianzus. This Nazianzen Evagrios is mentioned in the *Last Testament* of Gregory and receives a legacy. Palladios, in contrast (*Lausiac History*, c. 86), states that Evagrios of Pontos was ordained deacon by Gregory of Nyssa who took him to Constantinople only in 381, and left him there as an adviser to Nektarios, Gregory's inexperienced successor. It is possible that Gregory of Nazianzen's *Letter* 3, PG 37.24, Gallay (1964), pp. 2-3, might be in relation to Evagrios of Pontos, studying rhetoric with him in 359.

264. Cf. McGuckin, *Aliens and Citizens of Elsewhere* (2000).

that they were evening lectures. Jerome, who was there for their delivery and possibly assisted in their preparation, retrospectively describes these Orations as two "books"; something which Bernardi takes[265] as a sure sign that they were designed from the outset as a coherent body of work: a "treatise composed of separate chapters rather than a collection of sermons."[266] The place of *Oration* 28 is not so solid as the others in terms of the manuscript tradition for the *Theological Orations* as a whole. Sinko[267] showed how at some stage (which he posited as the time when the collection was being prepared for publication) *Oration* 28 was set in place, slightly disrupting the flow between 27 and 29 which once immediately followed it. We shall treat them coherently and collectively here, conscious that they have all recently been the subject of a detailed and excellent commentary.[268] *Oration* 28 covers some of the same ground as 27 and it is easy to see why Gregory decided to amplify his Prelude, in *Oration* 27, with this other discourse on the Father.

If we rely on Jerome, the original form of the works would have been first a dialogue against Eunomios on the status of the Son of God, and secondly a defense of the Holy Spirit, against Eunomios[269] and (presumably) the Pneumatomachians.[270] That is, Book I would have amounted to *Orations* 27, and 29-30, with Book II comprised of *Oration* 31. In their final form, the "Five Theologicals" bear a triadic structure: On Theology or the perception of God (27 and 28); On the Relation of the Son to the Father (29-30); and On the Person and Status of the Holy Spirit (31). They gained the title "Theologicals" from the Byzantines, since they referred to the inner life of God (Theologia) as distinct from doctrine about soteriology, for example, which was classified as Economia. They are also, by extension, the reason Gregory himself was described, after the fifth century, as "The Theologian" *par excellence*.[271]

265. Bernardi (1968), pp. 181-182.
266. Bernardi (1968), p. 182.
267. Sinko (1917), pp. 11-12; cf. Gallay (1943), pp. 182-183.
268. Norris (1991).
269. Mason (1899), Barbel (1963) and Norris (1985b, 1991) are all in agreement that *Oration* 31 specifically addresses an Anti-Eunomian agenda.
270. Eunomios, of course, refused to allow the deity of the Spirit but, as *Oration* 41 evidenced, even Gregory's larger pro-Nicene party had an element in it that resisted his pneumatology, and his critical audience, he knows, is larger than the Eunomians on this point. This is why *Oration* 31 is more eirenic in parts than, say, *Oration* 27 which is attacking Eunomios personally.
271. Weijenborg (1973) is the sole voice calling for their partial ascription to Maximus the philosopher, who is also symbiotically transmuted into Evagrios Pontike in his thesis. His argument has gained no scholarly following. The manuscript tradition refutes such a view. The claims that internal arguments suggest another hand are equally not sustainable, as has been well demonstrated by Norris (1985a). I think, however, that Gregory certainly used the services of Maximus and possibly Evagrios when composing these works, something that accounts for the denser apologetic, and more elaborate citation of opponents' texts, though the overall product both in terms of style and theology bears all his own hallmarks.

The opening Oration of the series makes a reprise of a common theme he has sustained in almost all his Constantinopolitan lectures:[272] that theology, properly understood, is not a fit subject for common gossip, but rather a mystical ritual initiation that demands the attitudes of reverence and preparatory purification:

> Discussion of theology is not a matter for anyone, only for those who have been tested and have solid foundations in learning and, more important, have undergone, or are in process of it, purification of body and soul. It is as dangerous a thing for someone to lay hold of pure things who is not pure himself, as it is for weak eyes to look at the sun's radiance.[273]

Gregory contrasts this sacral attitude that is in harmony with the apostolic recommendation for succinct theological teaching (a "short and final account")[274] with the "babblers" and "technologians of words" which St Paul called "verbal strife," and Gregory describes as "elaborate verbiage."[275] He gives a passage caricaturing the amount of theological debate that is taking place in the city, which has since often been overused[276] to portray the Byzantines as collectively obsessed with discussing the finer points of trinitarian theology; in their homes and even on their way to the theater. It was meant as a caricature, but reflects the method of the Eunomian party in sidestepping the disapproval of the incumbent bishop Demophilos by specifically addressing the aristocratic salons of Byzantium, and proposing theological issues to them in a syllogistic format. This was a preferred method of their approach, and the tactic of appealing to the lay aristocracy was increasingly necessary since the Nicene and the Homoian hierarchs respectively had, by the late fourth century, progressively disabled their ability to preach in the churches. Gregory disapproves both of this appeal to a lay audience, and the logical reduction of a theological agenda. He himself, of course, is addressing an important aristocratic audience just the same, and uses an argument which he knows will strike home to his class-conscious audience. He casts the Eunomian method as a low-born entertainment, like sham wrestling:

> They have undermined every path to true religion except this one only, the setting and solving of logical problems presented to them. They are like the promoters of wrestling matches in the theaters—you know the type, not those where the rules of the sport are followed, and one party wins a victory, but the kind where the performers put on a show to give a dazzling visual spectacle before those who are ignorant of the game and thus compel their applause.[277]

This rhetorical attack takes up what he knows of the social origins of Eunomios and Aetios his master, who rose from modest backgrounds and trades[278] to become

---

272. Further on this see Tsichlis (1981).
273. Orat. 27.3, PG 36.13-16.
274. Rom 9:28; Is 10:23.
275. Orat. 27.1, PG 36.11.
276. Along with Gregory of Nyssa's parallel humorous remarks which he borrowed from Gregory Nazianzen, in his *De Deitate Filii et Spiritus Sancti*, PG 46.557.
277. Orat. 27.2, PG 36.13.
278. Eunomios was originally a serf from Cappadocia and Aetios was an itinerant tinsmith for a time.

Christian logicians and rhetoricians who attracted, for a while, considerable imperial patronage. Gregory, as well as Basil and Gregory of Nyssa in their treatises *Contra Eunomium*, frequently apply this social "critique" of the Neo–Arian school describing it as "servile."[279] This may well be little more than the ingrained disdain of families who were from several generations of the landed gentry, reacting to the smart set who had attacked them violently and seemed to have done well out of it.[280] Eunomios had taken issue with Basil since the time when they first engaged in personal debate at the synod of Constantinople in 360 when Eunomios was rewarded for his performance with episcopal ordination and Basil seems to have been shouted down. Much of Gregory Nazianzen's specific focus of attack in these remarks is directed against Eunomios himself, and he was well aware how Eunomios' *Second Apology* had continued the posthumous vilification of Basil, a slur on the honor of close kin that neither he nor Gregory of Nyssa would allow to stand. When Gregory of Nyssa came to the capital in 381, Gregory arranged immediately that he should give a public reading of his newly composed *Contra Eunomium*, and Jerome gave an account of the event.[281] This too was designed to repair Basil's honor. Eunomios was the brightest of all the neo-Arian logicians after Aetios, and certainly the cleverest in terms of spreading the message to a wider audience. He was the foil that drew out the best theological work from all three of the Cappadocian fathers.

There is perhaps more to Gregory's social disdain than mere prejudice, however. Eunomios prided himself on his Aristotelian logical method, and Gregory (always ready for the amusing ironical reply) is here firing back at him, in the form of invective, Aristotle's own rule that the those who are of the serf class cannot possibly engage in philosophy since only the leisured landowning classes can possibly practice "true virtue."[282] In addition, the device of classing Eunomios as a huckster attempts to wean away his last reserve of political support, the aristocratic intellectuals of the capital who still valued him for his writings, and allowed him to retain his residence at Chalcedon, where he was precisely at the moment Gregory was issuing this attack against him. A last point that might be kept in mind is also instructive.

279. Gregory of Nyssa, whose anger at Eunomios was at once more personal and bitter, makes the class attack on the Neo-Arians even more passionately. If Basil is a "plodding farmer," Gregory says, Eunomios is a "Singing Master" (*Contr. Eunom.* 1.4, NPNF vol. 5 [1890], p. 37). He implies Aetios was runaway serf and mocks his time as a tinker, accusing him of having once been branded as a thief (*Contr. Eunom.* 1.6, NPNF vol. 5, pp. 39-40). Theodoret, like the Cappadocians, calls him a "technologue." *Haereticarum fabularum compendium* 4.3, PG 83.420. Gregory Nazianzen calls Eunomios the head of "a revolutionary factory for profanities" (Orat. 27.9, PG 36.24) again implying he has a servile approach to life.

280. Caesar Gallus donated a large estate on Lesbos to him, which was confirmed by Julian, and retained until he died.

281. Jerome, *De Vir. Ill.* 128.

282. Aristotle argued: "No one who leads the life of a worker or laborer can practice virtue" and as such he concluded that only the rich and leisured should be citizens. For a fuller discussion of ancient attitudes to class and wealth, cf. P. Veyne (ed.), *A History of Private Life* vol. 1, p. 119f.

Both Aetios and Eunomios, from their low origins, had worked for everything they had achieved. Their fathers, in this sense, had contributed nothing to their social eminence. In contrast the fathers of Gregory and Basil had made them what they were by passing on a considerable inheritance. It is interesting to see how the first party implicitly understands the biblical references to Son and Father as hard and fast descriptors of the way things are in reality between sons and fathers: that is, in their estimation, a massive disparity of power and status. Thus, in God, the Father is Supreme, the Son is inferior. The Neo-Arians make their stand on this image, not considering, very much, that it owes more to the Roman notions of *patria potestas* than to any New Testament conception of the Father-Son relation which denotes, in the main, love, common purpose, and communion. By contrast, Gregory, who had lived so long in the shadow of a very demanding father, sensed instinctively that a son was by no means necessarily inferior to the parent who begot him. Similarly, he and the other Cappadocians, habitually use the scriptural Father-Son analogy to connote equality of being and communion of relation: the very opposites of the common Roman understanding of the semantics of fathers and sons. It is a curious notion, but here their very social privilege perhaps allowed them to be more radical in deconstructing the terms of a socially rooted analogy than their more proletarian opponents. In the ancient landed class, it seems, sons clearly felt themselves to be of the same rank as fathers. In the proletarian classes the older Roman ideas of awesome and forbidding paternal power distanced sons from their "seniors." This is partly why it fell to the Cappadocians to be the theorists of the Son's equality with God the Father.

Theology, Gregory insists, cannot be conducted as a salon exercise, in the way people might arrange their small talk around popular songs, the races, food or sex.[283] It has to be listened to carefully, in contemplative quiet as the psalmist instructed,[284] and by people "for whom it is a serious undertaking." Though we ought to remember God in prayer at all times, he says, there are certain things that are best left out of our theological scrutinies.[285] Like all things, human life has proper seasons and boundaries. Theology itself is sometimes appropriate and sometimes not, just as it would be "inappropriate for a man to dress as a woman," or to "laugh uproariously at a funeral."[286] Even the pagan devotees, who "worship demons" (he means the adherents of the Mystery Cults) "would rather die than disclose certain words to the uninitiated," Gregory calls on the Christians to be "no less reverent than them" and even if they cannot settle their disagreements, at least agree to conduct the

283. Orat. 27.3, PG 36.16.
284. Orat. 27.3, citing Ps 46:10.
285. Orat. 27.4, PG 36.16.
286. An ancient textual variant had "geometria" instead of "gelo ametria." It puzzled Maximus the Confessor immensely why Gregory had used the image of people doing geometry at funerals. *Ambigua.* PG 91.1212-1213; cf. Norris (1991), pp. 90-91.

theological debate with dignity and restraint,[287] for pagan audiences cannot help hearing the Christians argue about "generation" and "non-generation" in their own limited understanding of what this means in relation to the births of gods, and such knowledge is like a betrayal of the mysteries, making it very difficult to catechise them at a later stage. It is interesting to see from this reference, how much his thought on the "mysteries" and on the proper way to initiate has been determined by a Christian liturgical matrix. For Gregory theology is intimately rooted in the life of prayer and sacramental initiation, a point which he has sustained in several of his earlier discourses, and does not tire of repeating here. His last point to bring his exordium to an end is to ask why are people so fond of theological debate but not so eager to fast, or observe vigils, or tame their tempers and passions?

So far, this has basically been that appeal to "simplicity of doctrine," that had led Eunomios to castigate Basil as a "plodding farmer." Gregory is not willing to suffer the same barb. He begins now to set his argument in that syllogistic form he has just been arguing is inimical to the consideration of theology. He does this to show that he can work in that style of rhetoric just as well as Eunomios, and also, subtly, to indicate that the method is very good for some things, namely, deconstruction, but not good for positive systematics.

To demonstrate his point, he uses the method to parallel the argument he has just been making: how theology is better served by silent reflection. The series of dialogic questions he poses in *Oration* 27.8 lead up to the one solitary agreement he admits between himself and the Arians: that there are legitimate "various ways" to engage in debate. And yet, they have been very critical of Gregory's way of doing theology, describing it as "poverty" of thought. He has wittily concluded that even in regard to their one area of agreement they have parted ways because of his opponents' logical inconsistency.[288] Returning to an invective aimed at weakening their social contacts in the imperial court, he says will allow them their claim to be theological experts and initiates, like Elijah, or Paul, or Moses, but he then pulls the carpet from under them again with the sardonic question: if they have achieved such heights of theology why is it they have addressed themselves in so servile a way to flattering eunuchs?[289] The scorn of the Roman nobleman for the class of eunuch is typically manifested here, but he is also making the telling political point, that Eunomianism is irredeemably connected with the eunuchs of the court of Valens. If there ever was a class ready for being purged, consequent to the entry to the capital of a new war-like and victorious, and Nicene, emperor, it was these. To be associated with the Eunomians, Gregory is implying, is to be painted in unpatriotic colors, and his

---

287. Orat. 27.5, PG 36.17.
288. Orat. 27.8, PG 36.21.
289. "Why have you set up this revolutionary factory for profanities, exploiting the silliness of the weediest and most effeminate specimens of the male sex, softening them even further by your flattery." Orat. 27.9, PG 36.24.

audience of non-eunuch aristocrats, all with an eye to continuing their influence at the seat of imperial power, would not fail to grasp the implications.

He finishes this very robust start to his lecture series with another joke. He has consistently attacked the Neo-Arians in this discourse for their verbiage, but now suggests they should hold forth on other topics, not theology, where their dialectic skills would better serve the cause of research. His first and preferred choice for suitable subjects would be "Pythagorean Silence." He was referring to the tradition that Pythagorean candidates for initiation had to observe a five-year novitiate of completely taciturn obedience.[290] The image of the Neo-Arians sitting in such a philosophic silence is meant to raise a laugh. So too the recommendation they should investigate the meaning of "Orphic beans." But he concludes, in all seriousness, by suggesting that the Christian Tradition has many areas where further research would be useful.[291] In matters of the Economy there is much scope for debate; his point is that this is not so in the most sacred domain of theology proper, where reason cannot attain to what God only gives by revelation:

> In such questions [of the Economy] to hit the target is commendable, but to miss it would not be dangerous. But as to God in Himself, the knowledge we have in this life will be small indeed, though soon after it may perhaps be perfected; in Jesus Christ Our Lord, to whom be glory unto the ages.[292]

This ending with "theology proper" has led him in a natural editorial progression subsequently to insert *Oration* 28 into this part of the published series. It deals with the nature of God, and is meant to clarify what Gregory sees as the basic character of theology, its negative and partial character, what his opponents had claimed was his "poverty" of doctrine.

Aetios and Eunomios had argued in very provocative ways that God was entirely "knowable" because all one needed to know for a true theological understanding was that Ingenerateness (Agennesia) was the supreme quality of God. Since this was a simple idea, it could be apprehended fully by everyone concerned. In this sense all had a "complete knowledge of God" and anyone who argued (as the Cappadocians did) that God was obscure, or difficult to know, or only partly revealed, was merely being obscurantist, and not taking the revelatory force of the scriptures seriously. For the Neo-Arians, the scriptural words connoted realities. There was a direct correspondence between the analogy of scripture and the fact it demonstrated. If the biblical text described God as "Father." It clearly meant he was different to a "Son." Sons are not the same as fathers; one is begotten, the other originates. This means that God the Father is the supreme Originator. All that is originated from Him is ontologically dependent. Since the Son originates from the Father, he too is ontologically dependent

---

290. Norris (1991), p. 98.
291. He lists: missionary apologetics, the nature of the universe or the soul, or the economy of salvation. Orat. 27.10, PG 36.24-25.
292. Orat. 27.10, PG 36.25.

and subordinate and cannot be called God in anything like the same sense that the Father is God. For them, Agennesia: that state of not being subject to production, is the sole characteristic of the deity. It is uniquely proper to the Father. The Son, whose very scriptural title indicates his state of Gennesia, or filial origination, is of a different kind of being to God. Between the Son and the Father, in terms of being or essence, there can only be a strict difference (Anhomoia),[293] though in terms of will or obedience harmony or closeness could be posited.

The simple claim for a complete knowledge of God, of course belied the complexity of the full Neo-Arian position[294] but it was a propaganda coup that caused difficulties to the Nicene party precisely because it invited full lay participation in the theological debate, governed only by the terms of logical assessment of scriptural texts. In contrast, Gregory is highly ambivalent and particular in his understanding of how scriptural designations apply. Sometimes he sees them as revealing acts, other times as being merely analogies and poetic descriptors. This was a difficult ambivalence to maintain when one was considering how they were applicable in terms of the central "doctrines" of Christianity. The long Arian crisis had littered the field with the same scriptural proof texts being offered by Nicene and anti-Nicene theologians to signify different and opposing conclusions. Similarly, a doctrine that regarded the vision of God as merely partly revealed in the present age, even to the most diligent scrutiny of purified souls, seemed to set the scriptural proofs into an even dimmer light and make theology into an elitist and closed-door affair. What was offered as a doctrine of mystical darkness by the Cappadocian Nicenes, was taken as a *refugium obscuritatis* by their Neo-Arian opponents. Gregory knew that he had to expand on his *Via Negativa* to God, to win the propaganda war over Eunomios. This is why he added Oration 28 to the series, as a digest of his fundamental positions on the issue of generation.

He is eager, he says in his opening words, to teach more about the trinity, but he is not going to reduce it to easy descriptors. His subject is:

> That single radiance of the single Godhead, personally distinct in a way that unites, and united together in a way that keeps its distinctions: which is a paradox.[295]

The argument starts from a symbolical exegesis of the Sinai theophany.[296] He is ready to climb the sacred mountain, like Moses approaching the divine presence, but expects that there he too shall find the obscuring cloud. Those who would come with him must be like the priestly Aaron. If so, they can stand beside him, though outside the cloud. Others who have been less sanctified and purified must imitate

---

293. "God could never come into contact with generation so as to communicate his own nature to something generated, and he must escape all comparison or association with that which is generated." Eunomios, *1st Apology* 9; cf. Hanson (1988), p. 622.

294. Cf. Hanson (1988), pp. 598-636.

295. Orat. 28.1, PG 36.25-28.

296. Ex 19-20, Ex 24.

the Israel of old and stay further back for it is dangerous.[297] Gregory will tell them what he saw, like the new Moses: it was merely the "hind-parts" of God, and this partial vision he achieved even when he was, "detached from matter and material things and had withdrawn as far as possible into myself."[298] Gregory thus lays heavy stress on the extreme difficulty of theological perception and the path to it of revelatory gift (as well as claiming high prophetic status). This was in contrast to his opponents who had taught the opposite: that God's nature was a coherent and easily graspable concept, and could be approached, by anyone, through simple logical process.

Gregory describes himself, like Moses on Sinai, hidden in the crevice of a rock to see the "hind parts of God." The rock that shelters him is the incarnation of the Word. From this basis he is able to peer at the theophany, and he finds that; "This is not that First and Primal Nature, apprehended only to itself as Trinity, as it abides within the first veil and is hidden by the Cherubim," but rather the "majesty or glory of God manifested among the ranks of creatures."[299] Gregory has turned from the Sinai matrix to the concept of the Shekinah of the divine presence hovering invisibly in the sanctum of the Temple. He is setting out as the foundation of his theology that God cannot be known in the Trinitarian relations, and only known with great difficulty in the revelation of the effects of his presence in the created orders. The "revelations" that God has left for creatures are like the "effects of the sun on water." It is a carefully chosen and very graphic image: something at once scintillating and yet distorted. The sun reflecting off the surface of the Bosphorus is dazzling, even though diffused. It is certainly a true image of the sun, but only a fool would mistake it for the sun itself. To look at the sun, however, causes blindness. He is insisting, therefore, on a basic and primordial distinction between Theology, and Economy. Theology proper, the knowledge of God in Himself, is impossible for all creatures, even for the most elect among those who have been given the grace of revelation,[300] or for the highest ranks of the angelicals. And having made this cardinal point he pointedly says: "And so let us begin again."

Gregory discusses the revelations of God in the created world, as something that the human mind can grasp in part. He wants to establish the point, however, that the issue of "*What* God is, cannot be confused with the fact *That* he is."[301] To be able to make some "theological" statements about God, is a far different matter from claiming a comprehension of his being. The argument then leads on into a discussion of whether God is a bodily thing or not. The conclusion is commonly agreed, he says,[302]

297. Orat. 28.2, PG 36.28.
298. Orat. 28.3, PG 36.29.
299. Orat. 28.3, PG 36.29.
300. Such as Paul, elevated to the Third Heaven, or Moses.
301. Orat. 28.5, PG 36.32.
302. Orat. 28.9, PG 36.36. "No inspired teacher has ever asserted such an idea. The verdict of our sheepfold stands against it."

that God is bodiless. But if this is so, Gregory asks, then why have the Neo-Arians made such a fuss of the term "Ingenerate," as if this were the only thing to say about God's Supreme Nature, when in fact it is a minor aspect of the vocabulary of the Economy referring to his revelation to the world, and one that takes its start from an image of physical procreation, which his audience has just agreed is particularly unfitting to a non-corporeal God. In this syllogism he has struck in the very heart of the neo-Arian systematic, and he twists the logical knife as he withdraws the blade: for he adds on the little remark that even if they do say Ingenerateness summates all theological discourse, they have in fact said nothing about God, since their central term is a negation; a privation of something, rather than an affirmation of what is properly characteristic.[303]

All this is now presented as merely "a long digression" to demonstrate his point more forcibly that God "is incomprehensible to the human mind, and of an unimaginably glorious grandeur."[304] It follows, then, that the knowledge of God which others think they can demonstrate so facilely, is not so easily grasped. Gregory compares it to the attempt to overtake our shadow, or the ambition of a fish to walk on dry land. The everlasting desire for God is always present in the created being, always driving it on to seek, but the bodily condition is like that ever-present cloud on Sinai, separating off the direct presence of God from all that is flesh:

> Sight cannot attain its object without the medium of light and the intervening space. Fish cannot swim outside water, and no more can corporeal beings commune incorporeally with ideal realities.[305]

The restless desire to find God which Gregory sees as innate to the human condition has led many people to try to exceed their natural limits. This has either resulted in grief (the deification of material things and the collapse of any theology into idolatry) or the illumination of the few who have used philosophy to discern the loveliness of the creator from the beauty of the creation.[306] But as for knowing God in himself, that is his "nature and essence" as opposed to discerning the traces of the revelations he has left about himself in the creation (Theology as opposed to Economy), then the task is impossible. It may be possible to have a direct knowledge of God, in the Next Age, Gregory thinks, when he presumes a radical transfiguration of the human condition will have occurred, and "we shall know even as we are known."[307] But as for the present it cannot be, we must remain content "with a slight glimmer, a small beam from the Great Light."[308]

If people object that in the ancient tradition certain elect were described as

303. Orat. 28.9, PG 36.36-37.
304. Orat. 28.11, PG 36.40.
305. Orat. 28.12, PG 36.41.
306. Orat. 28.13-16, PG 36.41-48.
307. 1 Cor 13:12.
308. Orat. 28.17, PG 36.48.

having a vision of God, Gregory says, this does not contradict his argument.[309] Even the great patriarchs such as Abraham or Jacob, and the prophets such as Ezekiel or Isaiah, the one who saw the Shekinah leave the Temple, the other who saw the Glory of God and the seraphim in the Temple,[310] did not see God in his own nature: "None could boast that they had taken in the nature, the total vision of God." Paul was caught up to the Third Heaven, something Gregory consistently regards, in the manner of Origen, as a revelation of the divinity which far surpasses anything that was narrated in any other part of the scriptures; but even then he calls the noetic vision of God which he received merely "puzzling reflections"[311] and confesses that: "We know only partially. We prophesy, only partially."[312]

Gregory has made his point. The Eunomian claim to facilitate theology by logical syllogism, is a dead end. Its method encourages arrogance and dismissiveness, and its final result is doomed to failure, like those "idolaters" who cannot direct their desire for God properly, and so end up grasping at something which is not God, and deifying matter. He is implying that if the Arian method is so intrinsically wrong, the fact that it concludes that Christ is not divine, should not come as such a surprise. As he has said on several occasions earlier, to theologize demands the purification and enlightenment of the Spirit, and those who do not confess the divinity of the Spirit are clearly not capable of being spiritually inspired teachers. He seems conscious, however, that he has in some way left his audience disappointed. Does this "poverty" of the orthodox faith not in some way fail to satisfy? Is it not less exciting than the speculations of the Arians which have caused such a stir in the salons of the intelligentsia?

I think it is for such reasons, not wishing to leave the propaganda field to the Eunomians, that Gregory now offers an extended section on cosmological speculations. It has been called his *Poem of Creation*.[313] It covers the very material which he suggested at the end of *Oration* 27 could be profitably researched by speculative questioning. And so, he asks a series of very beautifully crafted questions about the wonders of the natural world. Who can understand the glories of the embryonic process,[314] the mysteries of animal behavior,[315] the condition of plants,[316] the wonders of the great sea,[317] or the patterns of the seasons?[318] All these things lie within the rage and grasp of Aristotelian scientific method, and yet every one of them, in

---

309. Orat. 28.18-19, PG 36.49.
310. Ezek 1:4-28; Is 6:1-8.
311. 1 Cor 13:12.
312. 2 Cor 13:2-3; Orat. 28.20, PG 36.52.
313. By Paul Gallay, SC vol. 250 (1978), p. 42.
314. Orat. 28.22, PG 36.56.
315. Orat. 28.23-25, PG 36.57-61.
316. Orat. 28.26, PG 36.61-64.
317. Orat. 28.27, PG 36.64-65.
318. Orat. 28.28, PG 36.65-68.

Gregory's estimation, exceeds the limits of human science, and causes wonderment. If even cosmological science can so lead us to the dawning of awe, his argument is that we must learn our lessons about theology. The very beauty and learnedness of his commentary is meant to give the lie to any suggestion that Gregory advocates this turning away from Eunomian scientific method because he is not as bright or as capable as his opponents. What is at issue is the very relation of faith to reason, and in a passage which was to become the mother of the entire medieval constructs of systematic theology, Gregory is one of the first to explicate the classical Christian position. He invites those of his audience who have been able to follow his cosmological arguments to come with him now and consider some "heavenly" questions. The manner in which they do this will demonstrate his point even more substantively:

> If by thought you have passed through the air with me and considered all that it involves, now come with me and reach out to heaven and things celestial. Now faith rather than reason shall lead us on, at least it will if you have come to realize the feebleness of reason even in matters that touch you; and have gained enough reason to know the limits of reason. If so, you will no longer be wholly earthbound, trapped in earthly thinking, ignorant even of your very ignorance.[319]

His consideration of "heavenly" things turns around three of the higher speculations of Origen:[320] the movement of the spheres, the motion particularly of the sun and moon, and the natures of the angels.[321] It is the last which captures his imagination most. To consider the angels is like passing through the initial veil of the temple,[322] leaving sensory things behind to consider the world of the incorporeals, for such he thinks the angels to be "or at least very near it." But what can a corporeal mind make of the nature of the angels? He cites the biblical descriptions which connote their incorporeality: fire and wind,[323] but notes that these things are merely corporeal analogies that cannot contain the notion of bodiless existence and immaterial intelligence; "things which apply also to the Primal being of God":

> How dizzy we become (take note of it) with this theme, and we can get no further than the stage of being aware of the existence of Angels and Archangels, Thrones, Dominions, Principalities, Powers,[324] Radiant Lights, Ascents, Intellectual Powers or Minds,[325] Beings of pure and unalloyed nature. Stable, and almost incapable of change to the worse, they dance the circle around God the First Cause. How can we properly sing of them in words? He makes each one shine with a brilliance particular to their nature's rank. So powerfully are they impressed and shaped with God's own beauty that they in

319. Orat. 28.28, PG 36.68.
320. Cf. A.B. Scott, *Origen and the Life of the Stars* (Oxford: 1991).
321. Orat. 28.29-3, PG 36.68-72.
322. Ex 26.31.
323. Heb 1:7; Ps 104:4.
324. Angelic titles given in Rom 8:38; 1 Thess 4:16; Col 1:16.
325. Gregory predates Dionysios the Areopagite (his *Celestial Hierarchy*) by almost a century in extending the biblical taxonomy of angels into a perfection of Nine Orders. This passage is a major authority for Greek and Latin medieval celestial cosmologies.

turn become secondary lights, able to transmit light to others, from the superabundant largesse of the First Light.[326]

He knows he has ended on a high note. His religious vision and the sheer beauty of his rhetoric in this culmination to *Oration* 28 must have left his audience spellbound. Apart from the great beauty of his cosmological speculations, he has just given a new theory of the Nine Orders of Angels (that so excited the Byzantines when Dionysios the Areopagite later reformulated it) at the same time as telling them that no ascent to the divine presence is possible through logical process. He has demonstrated his refined craft as rhetorician, and shown the results of a theological method that is biblically founded at every step, yet elevates the principles of purified reflection and utter dependence on an inspired revelation that takes guidance from the "great lights" of the previous tradition.[327] It is a masterful performance: demonstrating that his "poverty" of doctrine is abundantly rich, and that he is no "plodding farmer" as the Eunomians had raised in mockery against them. He tells his listeners that even if they remain "unsatisfied," he has fulfilled his task well enough, for the lack of satisfaction about God is the quintessential human condition. As his last word he hammers home the main point once again:

> We have been engaged in a struggle to show that even to contemplate the Second Natures[328] is too much for our minds to carry. Much more so is it in regard to the First and Single Nature, not to say the All Transcendent.[329]

The *Third Theological Oration* is even denser and more complicated to follow. Gregory is raising the stakes noticeably from his earlier speeches which were content to offer summatic synopses of faith. In *Oration* 29 Gregory turns to consider the communion of the Son and the Father. The relationship had been posited metaphysically as that of Progenitor and Generated by the Arians. Since *Agennesia*, or Non-Generatedness was their supreme definition of deity, it followed that the Son was not God in the way the Father was. He may be intimately related to the Supreme Deity, as the chief of the spiritual orders produced by God, but in terms of his "nature" he is of a wholly different order from the Father.[330] This is the background context to Gregory's defense of the Nicene, Athanasian, Christology in *Oration* 29. He commences

---

326. Orat. 28.30, PG 36.72.

327. It is clear that Christian Tradition, for Gregory, is not merely or mainly a formal matter of received doctrines, but a charismatic matter, a question of the selection and enlightenment of particular saints, whose lives determine the shape of the preached kerygma.

328. Gregory defined the angels as the First Creation, the heavens and earth as the Second Creation, and the human race as the Third Creation. In rank of being he describes God as: the First Being. Angels as Second being, and Humans as Third being, often implying (like Origen) that it may be the human destiny to be transfigured after life into a higher stasis of angelic glory—metamorphosis into Second Being.

329. Orat. 28.30, PG 36.72.

330. Aetios disliked being called an Anhomoian as he recognized well enough that it was being used as a hostile propaganda by his Nicene and Homoian opponents alike. He preferred the term Heterousiast: the Son is of a different nature to the Father.

the discussion by setting out the proper technical terms, but does so from the outset in a way diametrically opposed to the Neo-Arian premises, and one that goes further than Athanasios, for the relation of the Son to the Father, according to Gregory, can only be conceived in a trinitarian context:

> We hold in honor the principle of divine monarchy, but not as envisaged as the sovereignty of a solitary person…but that single dominion which is produced by the same glorious nature, complete harmony of will, and identity of action, together with the convergence of all its constituents to Oneness (something that is impossible for a created nature) so that even if number can be ascribed, the essence cannot be divided at all. And so, Unity, from the beginning[331] moved to Duality, and found its rest in Trinity. This is what we mean by Father, Son and Holy Spirit. The Father is "Begetter" and "Sender-Out"[332] (impassibly, timelessly and incorporeally). The Son is the "Begotten," and the Holy Spirit the "One Sent."[333]

These, then, are the proper terms of the discussion. Gregory suggests the terms Unbegotten, Begotten, and Procession, should be used, as all three concepts are biblically founded.[334] From that point onwards he takes up the central theses of the Arians, and presents a logical answer to them, "somewhat unwillingly, I admit, for light talk and verbal swordfights are not agreeable to men of faith."[335] He sets out his case in relation to ten chief points to which he has reduced the Arian theology, answering each one in turn.

The first problem is the question of the eternity of the Son. The Arians from the beginning had used the party slogan: "There was when he was not," to argue that the Son's generation from the Father meant that he was secondary to God, both in terms of sequence, for whatever came from one thing had to follow it, and in terms of status, for if he "came after" he cannot have eternally existed which is the divine prerogative. Gregory follows more or less the argument of Athanasios in his *Contra Arianos* to argue that the Son and Spirit come into being when the Father does, that is timelessly. But he moves on to a more precise argument of the later fourth century when he considers the Eunomian objection that if the Nicenes say that the Son was coeternal with the Father, they are ascribing to the Son the unique character of being Ingenerate. Gregory states his case: that Ingeneracy and coeternity are separate conceptions. The Son is from the Father, certainly, but not after him. The Father is the Cause but as he timelessly causes the Son priority cannot be involved in the process since it is a time-bound notion. It is a subtle thought. Order is not the same as sequence. He says it is also the characteristic of the person, not the nature as such, and so cannot be used as an argument one way or the other to make statements

---

331. *Ap' Arches*, echoing the Johannine Prologue: Jn 1:1.
332. *Proboleus*.
333. Orat. 29.2, PG 36.76.
334. The image of Father and Son in numerous parts of the Gospels; and the concept of the Spirit as "procession" from the Father in Jn 15:26.
335. Orat. 29.21, PG 36.101.

about how Generation logically demonstrates a non-divine status.[336] He suggests an example of a simultaneous cause and effect (or as near to it as he could conceive in the time-bound order of things): the Sun and the radiance it emits.

The second Arian thesis was that if the Son is begotten by the Father, it must mean he is subject to change. Gregory answers that this can only be seen as a logical necessity if we define the divine process of generation in corporeal terms, which he has previously shown to be illogical and inappropriate. For the Arians, the Son was produced from God as the first born of the creation. The Arians were collectively not as crude as this syllogism would suggest, that is they did not so much insist that the Son was a creature, as wish to state the difference between the Supreme deity and the divine agents of salvation: the Son and the Angels. They highly honored the Son of God as a divine being, but understood, generally, that his divine status was achieved through a moral assimilation to his Maker. It was a "moral" sense of god-head that the Arian Church ascribed to the Word in its worship. Gregory seizes on this and presses their insight to its limit. Again he is following Athanasios in the *Contra Arianos.* The denial of a complete sense of deity is tantamount to denying the Son's deity altogether. No member of the Arian community would be happy to be put in this position. Gregory can allow no median case, however, as the concept of divinity is not an issue that allows degrees. He ends the second argument by suggesting that the Arian ideas about generation are hopelessly immured in corporeal examples.

> Can you not understand that he who had a unique birth in the flesh (do you know of anyone else who has a virginal mother?) similarly had a unique spiritual generation? The One whose Being is very different to ours has a different manner of begetting also.[337]

The third point raised against the Nicenes was that the Generation of the Son is a concept that automatically introduces the sense of a beginning to his existence. Gregory answers this rapidly by saying that one ought to confess that he was begotten "from the beginning." He uses the concept of Beginning (*Arche*) here in his regular fashion of alluding to John 1.1, and therefore means that the Word, or Son, begins his existence in the beginning that has no beginning, and thus his generatedness is an eternal Sonship.[338] The Arian argument has no force, he argues, when the Son is considered as both spiritually incorporeal and ontologically eternal.

336. This is why in Orat. 29.2 he criticizes Plato for describing the divine generation as "an over-flowing bowl." Such an image, Gregory argues, suggests the process is (a) compulsory, and (b) a scission of nature, or a natural process. He wants to insist that the Father's generation of the Son is (a) entirely free, and (b) does not proceed from a natural basis (the *ousia* or divine essence) but from his personal relation "His fatherhood" which thus refers the generative process to one of the *hypostases* of the deity not the *ousia.* By this means ingeneracy or generation is not constitutive of the divine Being (*Ousia*) but refers to the manners in which the divine persons (*hypostases*) personally express the selfsame Godhead.

337. Orat. 29.4, PG 36.77-80.

338. Orat. 29.5, PG 36.80.

The fourth Arian syllogism was that the Son could only have been generated unwillingly or willingly. It could not have been done unwillingly (for who could have compelled God?) and so must have been done willingly. Their conclusion is that the Son must therefore be a product of the divine will. That is, the Son comes forth from the Father's will, not from the Father's essence, and so the image of Sonship cannot be used in the way the Nicenes have applied it, to connote the substantive identity of parent and child in the kinship of the Homoousion. Gregory turns first to a rhetorical joke to answer the charge. Like many another orator he asks questions about the "paternity" of his antagonists. Were their fathers free or compulsive when they decided to beget them, he asks? No one forced them, and nature cannot be said to demand procreation, as the example of celibates can prove. No, their parents freely chose to beget them. (His joke lies in the implied query, like a raised eyebrow, whether it was a wise choice). But this does not mean that they are "sons of the will" of their fathers. It would make no sense to conclude that. A child is the child of the person, the parent, who begets them. Just so, the Son is not to be designated as a child of the will of God, but a child of the divine Father, considered as a person. Even God's creation which proceeds from his will, is not sensibly understood as a "child of God's will." In terms of this latter analogy Gregory's argument starts to slip a little, for his opponents were arguing precisely that the terms child and product were interchangeable, and that both the Son and the Created order shared the common factor of being different forms of "products" of the will of God and as such morally (volitionally), not substantively, related to the divine being. He senses it has faltered, because he draws the discussion to a close with the rather flat argument that pressing this analogy simply does not work in relation to God, and he ends by musing whether, in the case of God, volition and generation are not the same thing, or whether generation connotes a higher reality?[339] Gregory falls back on another restatement of his themes from the previous Oration: no one can really explain the processes of human generation let alone divine generation. His opponents ought to honor the Father's generation of the Son by the silence that should accompany mystical rites. Even the angels cannot understand the manner of the divine generation. It is known only to the Father and the Son, beyond that the cloud of theophany coves it from view.[340]

The fifth Arian proposition is stated in the syllogism: the concept of begetting a son demands that the Son must have been either in existence or out of existence. That is, positing an act of generation logically calls the generated one into being. If he comes into being, "there was a time when he was not," and if he does not come into being what logical sense is it to describe him as generated at all? Gregory does not spend a great deal of time on this one. He calls it a logical drivel, something that only applies if the concept of generation is not also defined as timeless. If it is a

339. Orat. 29.6, PG 36.80-81.
340. Orat. 29.8, PG 36.84.

timeless generation, the issue of priority does not apply, as he has argued earlier. The neatness of the syllogism has caught his eye, however, and so he decides to use another in return. "I am now telling a lie," he says, and asks his audience whether this is a true statement or not. If it is true, it is false. If it is false it conveys the truth. But common sense knows that it cannot be right and wrong simultaneously. In other words the Arian syllogisms are like that too, amusingly clever, but theologically specious.[341]

The sixth proposition is particularly that of Eunomios. The notions of Unbegotten, and Begotten are by no means the same. The Son and the Father, therefore, cannot be the same thing.[342] Gregory agrees that this follows, but only if one first defines Godhead as supremely characterized by the concept of Ingeneracy. If to be God means to be ingenerate, it would follow that the Son, as generated from the Father, would not be divine. The logical flaw, however, lies in the definition of deity on the basis of ingeneracy. If they had argued that Uncreated and Created cannot be the same thing Gregory would have agreed with them, but Generator and Generated are not mutually exclusive in the way the former concepts are. They are terms that refer to relations, and the relation between the Father and Son implies a sameness of essence passed on through the generative relationship. Intelligence and Lack of Intelligence can both be predicated of the same thing—a human being. "They do not distinguish separate beings for they merely describe different qualities." What he means here, is that the terms Ungenerated and Generated, as relational, are to be referred to the *hypostases* not the divine *ousia*.[343] As a negative term, the Unbegotten cannot, as the Arians wish to make it, define the divine nature, since it only tells the hearer what God is not, and cannot approach what God is, which would alone make it serve as a definition of his nature *qua tale*.[344] Gregory concludes his answer to this key Eunomian argument by turning it round on itself. Far from signifying diminution or an inferior status the Son's generation from God, if one understands theology aright, is a positing of the very reason why the Son is divine and glorious. Even in his generatedness (Gregory prefers begottenness) the Son partakes of the Father's ingeneracy, since he is the Son of such a Father:

> If it is so great a thing for the Father to be Ungenerated, consider that it is no less a thing for the Son to be Begotten of such a Father. Not only does he share the glory of the Unoriginate, since he is of the Unoriginate, but he also has the added glory of his Generation, a thing surely great and majestic in the eyes of all who are not altogether of a crassly servile and materialistic mentality.[345]

341. Orat. 29.9, PG 36.84-85.
342. The Eunomian position was actually that the Son was unlike the Father in essence, or "of a different essence."
343. Orat. 29.10, PG 36.85-88.
344. Orat. 29.11, PG 36.88.
345. Orat. 29.11, PG 36.89.

The seventh Arian argument was that if the Nicene premise that the Son's generation is an eternal one, is taken seriously, then it follows that the generation is still in the
course of taking place. It must be in the continuous present. If that is the case it cannot
be a perfect generation, one that has been "perfected" by its closure. If the generation of
the Son is eternal, therefore, it must be imperfect and cannot be divine. Gregory answers
this by denying the logical force of the analogy. He offers the example of the creation of
the angelical beings, or human souls, as two cases in point where things are given a
beginning from God but will not have an end. Both existences are immortal. Life forms,
therefore, cannot be circumscribed in every case by the limits of commencement and
completion, and to posit this in terms of the divine generation of the Son is to make the
Son's birth paralleled with the lowest of all life forms, a crass form of materialism he consistently charges the Arians with.[346] He ends this section by suggesting, once again, that
Arians only call the Son divine by a loose use of words, their real intention, he suggests,
is to strip the Son of his deity by their ideas.[347] He is aware that they positively object to
being "caricatured" like this, but insists, nonetheless, that this is the real force of all their
theology, and to protest his diagnosis is more evidence of illogicality on the part of these
logicians. They are *Theo-machians:* fighters against the Godhead.[348]

The eighth point of Arian objections is raised in one of the densest parts of the
Theological Orations[349] and has been criticized by Meijering,[350] unjustly in my opinion,[351] as an instance where Gregory's logic is inconsistent.[352] I think it is rather a case
where his text has not been properly exegeted. The Greek is very compacted, but the
argument about models of causation, can resolve to the following. The Nicenes
teach that the proper meaning of the biblical text, "The Father is greater than the
Son," connotes the manner in which the Father is the Cause (*Aitios*) of the Son.[353]

346. Orat. 29.13, PG 36.89.
347. Orat. 29.13, PG 36.92.
348. Orat. 29.14, PG 36.93.
349. Orat. 29.15, PG 36.93.
350. Meijering (1973).
351. For a fuller consideration see McGuckin (1994).
352. Meijering thinks Gregory sometimes ascribes divine being to the Father's causality, but some-
     times considers it as a generic class of being common to all three persons. Gregory consistently
     sees the divine being as the Father's own being, which he personally communicates to the
     hypostases of the Son and Spirit. He certainly does not regard it as a generic class. When he
     considers the issue of a generic class in this section he is taking an argument from the created
     order to make a secondary point, not attributing this doctrine to the trinity. It is an idea which
     Gregory of Nyssa introduces in his treatise to Ablabios, and it is often used in Western theolo-
     gians as a model of the trinity, but it is never sustained in Gregory of Nazianzus, who regards
     it as logically defective. The causal power of the Father is the single *Arche* and *Aitios* of the
     Godhead for him, and this single sustained theory is borne out in numerous passages with
     abundant clarity, and was received (as the particular doctrine of Gregory) in the Greek theo-
     logical tradition with equal clarity.
353. Gregory also follows the Alexandrian exegetical custom of interpreting such texts as referring
     to the earthly economy of incarnation. So, the text would refer to how the Father is greater

The Arians take that admission of causality to be a clear indication that the one is greater "in nature" to the other. This, Gregory says, is a logical mistake, which has originated by the Arians extrapolating from the individual to the generic. They have done this by adding on (illegitimately) the concept of greater "in nature" to the notion of "greater by causality." It would be like someone who set forward the statement "X is a dead man" and they were to translate it as "Mankind is dead."[354] Gregory's point here is not to describe the divine being using the concept of a generic class inhabited by different individual exemplars (something he constantly avoids as a mistake of trinitarian theology) simply to use the generic argument to illustrate the class of logical mistake the Arians have committed in this exegesis of the Johannine text. The word "greater" in the biblical phrase cannot be presumed to be an absolute referent. It is a specific indicator of the manner in which the Father is greater than the Son. The ultimate question still remains, for Gregory, "what manner" is this? He concludes that the text simply does not say. It is illicit to presume, as the Arians do by simply interpolating into their reading the words "greater by nature"; and the more correct answer is given by the Nicene exegesis, "greater as cause."

The Gregorian doctrine of causality is fundamentally important to him. He does not develop on it here, but will do so soon afterwards. The Causation is synonymous with the Father's dynamic communication of the divine nature to the Son, in the act of generating the Son hypostatically. This means that the Father's greatness is particularly and properly the fact that he is the source and origin of the selfsame divine being which he communicates to the Son and Spirit. However, the fact that the Son and Spirit have no other being except that which is the Father's, means that they cannot be defined as inferior in divinity to their cause. They all have one and the same single nature, that of the Father, and by virtue of that fact are one God, and co-equal. The causality, therefore, is not attributable to the Divine Nature, as such, it must be referred to the relation of the hypostases. This is why Gregory uses the analogous idea of the class and the specific individual (the dead man and the death of humanity). The Arian mistake is a basic one of misplaced logical referent. Anyone prepared to speak about trinitarian theology must be aware of two basic laws: the one is to know when one is making statements about Theology, or about Economy (to know when scriptural texts refer to the Incarnation or the Trinity for example); and the other is to know what applies to the divine Nature (collectively to all persons) or to the *Hypostases* (the distinct persons in the Triad). Gregory's argument, though dense, is attacking his opponents on several grounds simultaneously: that they are bad exegetes because they have committed eisegesis; that they are bad logicians, because they have made a beginner's level mistake in their process; and that

> than the Son who has assumed lowly human form. Here, however, he admits the text also has a reference to theology proper, not merely economy, and exegetes it to explain how "greater' does not necessarily mean "superior."

354. Orat. 29.15, PG 36.93.

they are bad theologians because they do not know the simplest distinctions between Theology and Economy, Hypostasis and Nature. Two things are abundantly clear: firstly that far from being a dense passage because Gregory does not know what he is talking about, this is compact and convoluted because Gregory wants to show up his enemies on their home ground of logical process; and secondly, whatever else he is doing, Gregory is certainly not implying that one can approach the theology of Trinity using the image of three individuals inhabiting the same class. This is an exegesis of Gregory which is wholly, and always, false and is basically an illegitimate interpolation of later western theological process into a system that is very differently inspired.[355]

The ninth Arian syllogism is that the name Father must refer either to an essence or an action. If one accepts that it designates essence then it proves that the Son is of a different essence, since the name is different. If it refers to an action (a doing or a making) then the name signifies that the Son must have been made, and so is a product of the divine energy, just as the creation is, and as such cannot be the Uncreated God. Gregory likes the style of this argument, and says that it would have been "very impressive," if only the two terms had been as mutually exclusive as the shapers of the syllogism were pretending. For Gregory they are not, and so one slips out of the polarities easily. The name Father, he says, does not primarily connote an essence, or a dynamic action. It connotes a relationship. The peculiar force of the word "father" also specifies the terms of what that relation involves, and Gregory says that it evokes a commonality of essence, such as that which exists between any father and any son that comes from a father. This is why the concept of God's Fatherhood is used by the Nicenes to demonstrate the doctrine of the Homoousion: that the Father and Son are consubstantial, the distinctive christological statement of the Nicene Creed.[356]

This brings him to his tenth and last of the Arian objections. It is a coherent examination of the biblical prooftexts that have been used by his opponents to argue that scripture implies the Son is not God. He examines a veritable catena of texts that have been the subject of dispute for over fifty years; starting first with the catena of Nicene texts that are used to demonstrate the co-equality of deity of the

355. The case is further argued in McGuckin (1994). One of the chief differences between Gregory's conception of the Father as single Dynamic Cause of both persons (as opposed to the later western doctrine of the Spirit's double procession from the Son and the Father (the *Filioque* clause) or the classic western theory of three persons inhabiting the same abstract class of nature) is that Gregory's model preserves the ancient vitality of the early Church's understanding of the Trinity as single coherent process of the unfolding life of the Father. The "threefoldness" is thus the principle of unity as much as of differentiation, for it is the expression of the Father's single being. The preference for a model of abstract class to which three particulars belonged, on the contrary, reduces the Trinity (God) to an abstraction rather than a living person, and inevitably diminishes the sense of the Trinity as the inner dynamic of the unity of being of all the Cosmos as it is drawn into salvation and life.

356. Orat. 29.16, PG 36.100.

persons,[357] and then moving on to consider the catena the Ari
argue the opposite, a list that concludes with the many reference:
limitations of Jesus that can be abstracted from the New Testar
arguments, Gregory says, a simple solution can be found: a universal law of christological exegesis. They must all be contextualized in the doctrine of the incarnation.
He does not refer to the doctrine of the two natures, which would be standardized
only after Chalcedon in 451, but something more carefully delineated: the divine
nature which is above all earthly limitations (the Godhead of the Word) and the
"compounded reality"[359] which is the incarnated Christ, "the Word who emptied
himself to become man." The doctrine of *kenosis*, therefore, explains why scripture
at one and the same time ascribes divine and human characteristics to the same
person. The point is that the correct interpreter "must know what belongs to his
nature, and what belongs to God's economy of salvation."[360] He ends as he began,
characterizing the Arian opposition as incompetents who do not know the difference between *theologia* and *economia*. He senses he has supplied a decent and sustained exercise in the "logics of theology," it is certainly one of the most
intellectually demanding orations of his corpus, and yet he concludes his lecture by
saying that he has adopted this style and method only with regrets, pushed to it
because of his apologetic situation. Even so, his audience ought not to think that
such an approach is the best for understanding the things of God. It is "long-winded
controversy," and such language, he implies "voids the power of the cross'; alluding
to Paul's criticism of the "wisdom of this world" which God has made foolish.[361] In
contrast: "It is Faith alone that is the fulfilment of reason."[362] He prays that his
opponents will be "reconciled to God and cease suppressing the Spirit,"[363] but even

---

357. In Orat. 29.17, PG 36.96; Jn 1:1; LXX Ps 109:3; Is 41:4; Jn 1:18; Jn 14:6; Jn 8:12; 1 Cor 1:24;
Heb 1:3; Wis 7:26; Jn 6:27; Gen 19:24; Ps 45:7; Rev 1:8.

358. In Orat. 29.18, PG 36.97; Jn 20:17; Jn 14:28; Prov 8:22; Acts 2:36; Jn 10:36; Phil 2:7-8; Jn 18:9;
Heb 5:8; Jn 15:10; Jn 5:36; Jn 5:19; Jn 12:49; Jn 8:15-16; Mk 10:40; Jn 8:28; Mt 24:36; Lk 2:52;
Mt 8:24; Mt 4:2; Jn 4:6; Jn 11:35; Lk 22:44; 1 Cor 15:28.

359. *To syntheton.* Both Cyril of Alexandria (cf. J. McGuckin, trans., *On the Unity of Christ,* SVS
Press, 1995) and John Damascene (*De Fide Orthodoxa*) take up this aspect of the unity of the
incarnate reality most successfully. The Chalcedonian settlement stressed the "duality of
natures" as a corrective to Diodore and Nestorius' doctrines, but though Gregory is hostile to
Diodore, he clearly feels that two-nature language is not the only way to mount the orthodox
christological response. Gregory was to be an important source for both Cyril and Nestorius
in the fifth century christological debates. Cf. McGuckin (1994). See also Norris (1969),
Tsames (1969b), Wesche (1984) and Winslow (1979).

360. Orat. 29.18, PG 36.97.

361. 1 Cor 1:17.

362. Orat. 29.21, PG 36.104. An insight which lies at the heart of the way Gregory prioritizes the
gift of revealed mystery over the scope of natural deduction. Norris (1991) rightly sees this as a
cardinal point in Gregory's method and elevated it as his title for what is today the standard
critical commentary on the *Theological Orations.*

363. Citing 2 Cor 5:20 (1 Thess 5:19).

they continue to resist, Gregory himself will: "guard the Trinity in our safe keeping, for only in this way can we be saved."[364]

The Fourth of the *Theological Orations* was given soon afterwards, and is once again dedicated to the notion of the Son's relation to the Father. This too is structured on a ten-point basis. This time he takes ten major arguments from the scriptures that the Arians enlisted against the deity of the Son, and systematically gives a more precise exegesis of them. It seems, then, that *Orations* 29 and 30 were composed originally as one treatise that Gregory intended for publication, and which he divided into two sections suitable for rhetorical declamation. The ending of *Oration* 29, with brief surveys of the lists of biblical proof texts appropriate to the argument, is taken up again in *Oration* 30, at a much more careful pace.[365] The whole work is based upon exegetical premises rather than on logical syllogisms. He gives an extensive answer to the central Arian proof text of Proverbs 8:22, "The Lord made me (Wisdom) as the beginning of his works."[366] Gregory raises an interesting range of exegetical questions. Should not the reader wonder about the theological value of any theological wisdom in Solomon because of his later lapse into idolatry, something which demonstrates he was not fully a man of God? Gregory decides to give him the benefit of the doubt, but by this strategic question he has moved the prooftext away from commanding any central position in Christian theological tradition. Moreover it is not an unambiguous text, Gregory says, because of the way in which begetting and generation (birthing and making) are used so closely together in sense. This was the very reason it had been argued over so passionately throughout the previous generation. The Nicenes took it to refer to the pre-existent Wisdom and demanded that the phrase "created me" should be read only in the sense of begetting, thus making a strong metaphysical distinction between begetting and making in the case of the eternal Son.

Gregory (like the Arians) is simply not impressed by this exegetical process, or the grammatical theory on which it stands. He is not prepared to allow this single text, whatever its source, to determine the entire tradition, which comes from a whole series of "inspired visions." But if Solomon himself can slip, so too can the orthodox fathers before him. "I adopt none of their exegetical approaches," Gregory calmly says, and goes on to interpret the Proverbs text as clearly teaching the creation of Wisdom. This, he then adds, refers to the creation of Wisdom in a context of earthly economy, earthly history of salvation, and thus signifies the embodiment of the Wisdom of God in the incarnation of Christ. The phrase "created me" indicates the birth in flesh, not the pre-existent generation of Wisdom from the Father before all time. If it was a text that meant to refer to the generation of the Son, why do

---

364. Orat. 29.21, PG 36.104.
365. It partially overlaps with the list in *Oration* 29, but also introduces a range of further proof texts used by his opponents.
366. Orat. 30.2, PG 36.105.

commentators insist on its semantic meaning as a "creation" verb. One cannot have it both ways, if one insists on literary exactness in scriptural exegesis (as his Eunomian rival most certainly did).[367] He thus gives a most elegant and original exegesis based on the generic principle he announced at the end of *Oration* 29: the statements referring to the Son which are kenotic and humble, all refer to his incarnate condition. Those which are lofty refer to his eternal status as divine Son of God.[368]

As Gregory continues the series of the ten key texts he reveals an exegetical imagination which is distinctively original and highly personal. It is a great pity that he was never lured into composing a full-scale biblical commentary. His treatment of the last words of Jesus on the cross, "My God my God why have you forsaken me?"[369] argues that they do not indicate anything of the mind of Christ considered either as God or as the man-God. They speak out, at the great moment of his act of salvation for the world, the entire plight of the human race alienated from the divinity. They cry out to the Father the plea for the human race to be restored to God's favor, a plea that the Father cannot resist for it is the very act of the cosmic redemption of the race. Gregory says the intelligent reader ought to continue to read the rest of Psalm 21 (22) in context and there will fully learn, from the ending, that the psalm all throughout has been collectively uttered for the "ingathering" of Israel in a triumphant ending where the speaker's children will serve the Lord from generation to generation.

The same honesty of interpretation is demonstrated in his tenth case, when he treats the difficult logion of Mark 13:32: "No one except the Father knows the last day or hour, not even the Son himself." Gregory first applies the generic principle of his christological exegesis concluding that, as God, the Son knows the last hour but, as man, he professes ignorance. But sensing that while this is a suitably "reverent" explanation, it might not necessarily be a convincing or satisfactory one, he goes on to discuss it further, suggesting that it can be better handled if one approaches it as a demonstration that all of the knowledge that the divine Son possesses is none other than the knowledge which is the Father's. There is but one knowing, one loving, one willing in the divine Trinity, as all flows from the supreme First Cause who is the Father. This being so, the Son deliberately confesses ignorance at this point, not merely to silence his disciples' questions about something that exceeded their right to know, but because he also wanted to give a theological teaching, indicating that the origins and ending of the universe were something that could only be known by the

367. In other words, if the word means "making" there is no inherent reason to regard Prov 8:22 as a text referring to "Sonship." To go on to weld the ideas of Making to those of Sonship, and conclude that the making of Wisdom is synonymous with the making of the Son is a careless eisegesis, contradicting the Arian premise that scriptural words precisely and particularly delineate revelatory facts.

368. This is restated as the supreme exegetical principle of the passages relating to the Son at the conclusion in Orat. 30.21, PG 36.133.

369. LXX Ps 21:1; Mt 27:46.

Mind of the First Cause. Since that was his own Mind he was not excluded from it, but it was, nonetheless in Him from the First Cause, the Father Alone.[370] The "difficult" text is, therefore, interpreted as having three motivations: to instruct the disciples that they cannot hope to know the ways of God, to show them his own Kenosis as a man, and to show them what is proper to God (that the Knowledge in the Son is the same as that in the Father, not different from it, since it is the very knowing of the Father). In other words, the last theological revelation which Gregory is now mediating as the mystical interpreter of the text, is that the Son lives the Life of the First Cause. The Father alone is God, and this is precisely why the Son is God too, and why the Spirit is God, as they both have his life as from the First Cause. They do not mimic the life of God, they are the life of God, and also God's Knowledge, and Love, and whatever else can be said. Their relation to the Divine Cause is at once the reason why all three persons are God, and why there is only One God.

The careful context of the grammatician is abundantly in evidence in Gregory the exegete, but so too the insight of the poet and the grace of a mystical and far-seeing mind. The whole oration continues to cut through the Arian claim that they alone represent the obvious meaning of the texts as "honest exegetes," and he reaches the conclusion that their greatest failing lies not in their cumulative pile of exegetical mistakes, rather in the whole premise of their exegetical philosophy, that they could by the simple application of logic, lay bare the complete meaning of the sacred revelation in a commentary that "summed up the whole." Perhaps this is why Gregory himself refused to write a full-scale work of biblical commentary, though he had ten years to do so in retirement if he had wished. The task, as he sees it, is dangerous in the claim for "mastery" of the text which it represents. And the reason is that:

> The noblest theological interpreter among us is not the one who has mastered the text completely, since our earthly limitations do not allow us to see the whole. It is rather the one who is able to conceive of God a little more substantively than his predecessor, and gather into himself more of the Image or shadow of the Truth, or whatever else we may call it.[371]

The fifth and last of the *Theological Orations*, number 31, came in swift succession, and resumes (in greater depth) the terms and issues of *Oration* 41 which he delivered at Pentecost in the preceding June. It is dedicated to the exposition of his pneumatology. He knows, from the beginning, that here he may have some opposition from his own Nicene community, and the opening words attempt to divert it. Gregory has presented the synopsis of true faith in the divine Son of God, a theology that: "cannot be stoned, for he passes unharmed through the midst of his enemies."[372] By taking this line he intends to remind his audience how he too has had to

370. Orat. 30.15. PG 36.124.
371. Orat. 30.17, PG 36.125.
372. Jn 8:59, Lk 4:30.

suffer stoning for his orthodoxy, all because he taught the deity of the Son. This, when he raised it in *Oration* 23 served to rally his party to his side. He probably hopes it will do so again. Now, he says, he is to speak about the Spirit of God: "and there is something that is even more than usually difficult in the theology of the Spirit."[373] Even people who are "sound as far as their theology of the Son is concerned," go astray on this point, complaining that Gregory is "introducing a strange, unscriptural, new God."[374] His opening remarks suggest that in this oration he is not so much worried about the Neo-Arians, as about that large indeterminate party of "Pneumatomachians." There would be a contingent of thirty-six bishops at the council of 381 who were agreeable to a broadly Nicene Christology but stoutly resisted this theology of the Spirit, and most of them continued to do so until the point when they abandoned the council. These have all subsequently been labeled Pneumatomachians in a catch-all designation that is not very useful (except as an apologetic term) precisely because of its historical imprecision. Some of those who fought against the Homoousion pneumatology were certainly of Arian persuasion, since the Arians had resisted the concept of the co-equal divinity of the Son, and were by no means willing to admit the idea in terms of a third hypostasis. But many of them were not of the Arian party. The Homoousion of the Spirit was a concept that put heavy stress on the relatively recent alliance with the Nicene Homoiousians, and to that extent must have worried several theologians at the council of 381, not least the Antiochenes who sponsored it. Such pro-Nicene Pneumatomachians thought that the problems of the previous generation of the Church had largely been caused by the unfortunate word Homoousion and did not see why now it should be extended to the Spirit.

His remarks immediately precede what I think is a veiled allusion to Basil's treatise from 375, the *De Spiritu Sancto*. Gregory's silence about Basil's theological work has been almost "deafening" so far. Now Gregory characterizes it as one of those works of preparatory paideia, a preliminary treatise on words and meanings, which has benefitted him, but which he also contributed to, that can now be superseded by his latest treatment.[375] In this way the work of Basil is characterized as grammatikos in comparison to rhetorikos, a stepping place on the way somewhere else. The attitude is nothing new, Gregory more or less told Basil to his face while he was still alive that his pneumatology was insufficient, and that was one of the reasons they had so seriously fallen out.

The opening consideration of *Oration* 31 asks the audience to consider applying the selfsame designations to all three hypostases: not only the word "God" which some people seem to fear, but an example which connotes divine energy: the light. So, the biblical phrase: "He was the True Light enlightening everyone who comes

373. Orat. 31.2, PG 36.133.
374. Orat. 31.1, PG 36.133.
375. Orat. 31.2, PG 36.133. "We, however, shall now turn in this oration to more advanced issues."

into the world,"[376] can be read as applicable to any of the three hypostases. Since it
clearly refers to God, it is equally applicable to Father, Son, and Spirit, and when it
is so referred to the hypostases, all three enlightenments have a specific sense which
is harmonized in common by the relational force of convergence the individual
hypostases connote. Gregory loves to apply the image of light for the trinity, and
concludes here that each of the three enlightenments:

> Light, and light, and light again, all amount to one single light, since God is one. This
> is the meaning of David's prophetic revelation: "In your light we see light."[377] We re-
> ceive the Son's light from the Father's light, in the light of the Spirit. This is what "we
> too have seen and what we bear witness to in our preaching,"[378] a straightforward syn-
> opsis of the theology of the Trinity.[379]

Just as the Father, who is eternal, must have been eternally Father, so too the
Son must be eternally a Son, and as such is shown to be divine. Such a theology has
already been fully demonstrated, Gregory implies, and this is the logical basis of
the theology of the Spirit. For if to deny the eternity of the Son is to fall into
Arianism, so too is to deny the eternal holiness of the Spirit of God. If the Spirit is
not eternally holy, that is not hypostatically with God the Father from eternity, the
entire system of Godhead is damaged and the Spirit of God emerges as a creature,
pure and simple. The Spirit may be superior to human beings in terms of issuance
from God, but in no way can the Spirit be anything more than a creature. Not to
designate him God puts him in the ranks of the creatures, and deprives God of the
spirit of his own eternal holiness.[380] This is an extreme synopsis of the argument
he applied in regard to the Arian desire to profess the Son's essential "difference" to
God, and yet retain a strong sense of the Son's moral deity—or deity by proximity
in the divine plan of salvation. Gregory deliberately made the christological argument an "either-or" (as did Athanasios) so as to simplify the battle lines as much as
he could. He does the same from the very beginning of his argument over the
Spirit. The large ranks of pro-Nicenes who were still hesitant as to the Spirit's
divine title, he implies, are in the same position as the Arians were in regard to the
divinity of the Son.[381] But in this respect vague wavering does not amount to
orthodoxy. If the Spirit is not fully God, he can only be a creature, and a creature
cannot give sanctification in the manner in which it is ascribed to the divine

---

376. The Greek Johannine text (Jn 1:9) can be taken as referring the phrase "coming into the
    world" either to "everyone" or to the individual subject of the "True Light." Gregory here
    applies it to "everyone."
377. Ps 36:9.
378. Alluding to 1 Jn 1:1. Gregory as seer in the Johannine manner, completes what the prophet
    glimpsed.
379. Orat. 31.3, PG 36.136.
380. Orat. 31.4, PG 36.137.
381. It is clear from Orat. 31.13, PG 36.148, that Gregory is primarily addressing the wavering Nicenes,
    for he answers the accusation that he is a tritheist, with the reply "no more than you are ditheists."

Spirit—that is the deification of the human soul.[382] There follows a short "history of pneumatology."

The Sadducees denied the existence of a hypostatically distinct Spirit of God, just as they denied the resurrection of the souls, and the existence of angels. These, who "scornfully rejected so many scriptural proofs" are contrasted with the Hellenistic philosophers who even though they were outside Israel, still demonstrated a sense of the Divine Spirit, evoking it with titles such as the "Nous of the Universe." Among prior Christian thinkers some took it as a divine energy, others a creature of God, some saw it as divine, while others were "agnostic" about it on the grounds that scriptural revelation was unclear on the subject.[383] The latter party of agnostics, being the group which he is explicitly addressing in the present argument, he describes as "thoroughly pitiful" for taking up this halfway house. Their agnosticism offers neither guidance nor excuse. But "those who are wiser by far" have in the past recognized that the Spirit was indeed divine. They have tended to theologize in terms of three degrees of deity. The Father is infinite in essence and power, the Son is infinite in power but not essence, the Spirit is divinely majestic but finite in both essence and power. He is referring to Origen, without naming him, and he notes how this is a too overt reliance on the Neo-Platonic conception of the three degrees of divine extrapolation: Supreme Deity, Demiurge, and World Spirit. He says that he is not at all interested in arguing with Hellenistic philosophy (he will forego the luxury of the "oil of sinners")[384] and not going to waste his time with atheists who deny the Spirit's existence. But he will take issue with the prior tradition of Christian theologians who have done their work so badly. He makes a series of syllogisms to deal with each case he has mentioned. First, if the Spirit is a divine energy, he must be accidental to the deity, in the Aristotelian sense, and cannot be considered hypostatically existent. All the scriptural witness, however, attributes personality to the Spirit's action. It is not an impersonal force which is evoked by each one of the testimonies, but the most personal engagement possible, described in terms of subjectival agency. The Holy Spirit, he concludes, is a person, hypostatically existent according to the overall scope of the scriptural witness, and this returns him to the conclusion that if a person, the Spirit is either divine or non-divine, there cannot be a middle way.

After the opening statement he structures his attack as he did in *Orations* 29 and 30, by taking ten "objections" one by one.[385] He might have abstracted these from writings in advance, but I am of the opinion that he is actually responding *in extempore* to the critical questions of his audience. They amount to eight distinct positional critiques as follows: The scripture gives only categories of Ingenerate or

---

382. "If he has the same rank as myself how can he possibly divinize me?" Orat. 31.4, PG 36.137.
383. Orat. 31.5, PG 36.137.
384. Ps 141:5.
385. From Orat. 31.7-29, PG 36.140f.

Generate, so which one applies to the Spirit. If it is Generate will it not make him out to be the Son's younger brother? To what extent is the Spirit inferior to the Son if it is different from the Son? If the Spirit is divine does that imply it is Consubstantial too? How can two things from the same source be in union and yet distinct at the same time? What authority is there in the ancient tradition for worshipping the Spirit? Or, who ever prayed to the Spirit? Does not three divine persons imply a tritheist theology, because the image of three individuals sharing an abstract unity of essence is little different from polytheism? How can the words three and one be justified in their attribution without reducing trinitarian thought to mathematical nonsense? What biblical authority is there for elevating such a pneumatology?

He finds the first amusing. Those who think one can only describe God in terms of Father and Son, have taken the procreative gender analogy far too seriously. Do people really imagine God is a male because the language of fatherhood and sonship has masculine reference? Does the fact that the concept of Godhead is feminine in Greek suggest that it is really female deep down? Does the fact that Spirit is a Greek neuter term imply there is something wrong with the fertility of the third hypostasis?[386] It is obvious, he says, that strict logical application of gender analogies is inappropriate for the incorporeal God. And yet, these key terms are indicated in scriptural revelation, and signify theological verities that cannot be dismissed as merely accidental. What they signify, however, is not that God has gender, but that there is a divine process in the inner life of the Trinity. The careful exegete of these scriptural forms will see that Generacy and Ingeneracy are not the only two polarities that the scriptures use to describe the most mystical level of theology, but Jesus himself opens a new revelation when he describes the Spirit as "The One who proceeds from the Father."[387] Just as the Son is divine even though he is generated (at least for the Nicenes) so too the Spirit is divine in so far as it proceeds from the Father. But since it proceeds (on the authority of the Son, the only theologian who knows this truth, since it connotes something that is entirely outside of human comprehension) it is evidently not a generation, but a procession. His critic did not seem to be impressed, answering back and demanding a better explanation of what "procession" meant; to which Gregory replied that he would supply one if his critic could first supply a better definition of what generation means to the divine Son. Can he not see that the two of them "would go mad" if they pried any further into the ineffable inner life of God?[388]

This peremptory ending of the exchange, a recurring theme in Gregory's theology, has frustrated more than his first critic. It has often been taken as a preacher's avoidance of the argument. It is an easy prey to such a criticism, but Gregory is being

386. Orat. 31.7, PG 36.140-141.
387. Jn 15:26.
388. Orat. 31.8, PG 36.141.

consistent to the first premise he set out in his Constantinopolitan orations: that theology proper is radically restricted as far as human beings are concerned, and cannot be accessed by logic or illuminated by material analogies,[389] only given as a mystical insight to the few who have been chosen and have rigorously purified themselves for the revelation. Even so, some things, and in particular the inner life of God, are reserved behind the veil of the *Sanctum*, not known even to the archangels. Gregory, more positively than Wittgenstein in the *Tractatus*,[390] insists that "what cannot be spoken of must be passed over in silence." His silence, however, is not merely ignorance or inarticulation, for Gregory so heavily contextualizes it in the terms of mystery religion and temple-liturgy, that his implication is clearly that the silence initiates that religious wonder which takes up where theological confession has to end, in the act of the worship of the transcendent presence of the deity. It is the Spirit of God through which the Church prays and senses the divine presence. The Spirit is the inspiration, the medium and the end of worship. His critics who protest it is not within the Christian tradition to "pray to the Spirit"[391] have not understood the dynamic of revelation which the New Testament speaks about.[392] All prayer and worship is, *de facto*, "in the Spirit."

The simplest statement is the best, he thinks, and when it comes it emerges like a thunderclap in its historical context within this oration, yet it is given the least amount of fanfare:

> So what does all this mean? Is the Spirit God?
> Certainly.
> Is he Homoousion?
> If he is God, yes.[393]

This was indeed a new epoch in the history of Nicene theology. He will shortly go on to speak about it as seismic event, but here in the context, he seems to wish to introduce the idea as if it was the most ordinary thing in the world.

He goes on to argue a separate point: his critics who worry that a trinity must necessarily introduce number into the Godhead in such a way that monotheism degenerates into tritheism, can be accused in their own turn of the fundamental mistake of assessing the trinitarian life on terms of strict analogical parallelism with material forms. Such a theological process is no better than mythology[394] and contrary to the whole Christian religion. Numeration accounts for the *hypostases* but not for the Godhead:

389. Orat. 31.10, PG 36.144.
390. See Norris (1993b).
391. Orat. 31.12, PG 36.145.
392. Jn 4:24; Rom 8:26; 1 Cor 14:15.
393. Orat. 31.10, PG 36.144.
394. Orat. 31.16, PG 36.149-152.

We have One God, for the Godhead is One, and towards that One they all incline[395] who come from Him.[396] Yet we believe in the Three. One is not more, another less, than God. One is not first, another later. There is here no diversity of will, or distinction in power. There is here none of the qualities of divisible things. If I have to sum it up briefly, I would say that the Godhead is undivided in [three] who are distinct. There is one mingling of the Light as there would be if three suns joined together. If we consider the Godhead, or the First Cause, or the Monarchy, then it is revealed to us as One. When we consider those realities in whom there is the Godhead, however, who before all time derive their being from the First Cause and are of the same glory as it, then indeed we have three subjects for our veneration.[397]

The concept of numerical distinction within a class, such as is often appealed to in common estimations of the Christian trinity (three persons in one nature of godhead for example), is not what Gregory means here. Such a mathematical model drawn from material analogies cannot possibly explicate what the inner life of God is all about. Anything within the created order which could be conceived as related in a class, even if it were the most profound concept of unity that was being appealed to, does not draw near. Any image of related human persons also fails lamentably, "since humans are not merely composited beings but are also mutually opposed and even self-inconsistent, never staying the same for one day let alone a lifetime."[398] The union of the divine persons cannot be compared to this. Even to compare it to the unity which angels know falls short, even though the angels might be "non-composited, and more firmly stabilized by their proximity to the supreme beauty."

So, like most of Gregory's "simple solutions" the picture is complex. The concept of number applies to the Godhead and does not apply to the Godhead, like all corporeal analogies limping to an evocation of incorporeal mysteries. It is another partial approach to the inner life of God, and not the absolute referent of mathematics that some appeared to have thought it was. If a person applies number to the divinity it could be to list the three *hypostases*, each distinct as *prosopa* (or person/ subsistences) in the sense that we can name them singly, and recognize their divine

---

395. *Anaphora*—again a concept connoting relation that also has liturgical overtones.
396. This refers to the Father, the sole source of Godhead, and the Son and Spirit who issue from the Father in their respective relations, and constantly incline back to unity, rather than going away in differentiation. He elsewhere describes the motion of inner unifying relation as perichoresis: the (liturgical) dance of the persons around one another. This passage ought not to be read as inferring a single common abstract "Godhead" to which class three members belong; for this is what Gregory attacks in the following section of the Oration (ch. 15). For Gregory, the Godhead is that of the Father. He is the sole personal cause of the other hypostases. Godhead, in short, is never an abstraction in Gregory's thought, but is either considered from the point of view of its inner dynamic (the Father as *Aitios*/Cause) or its complex and dynamic tri-unity (the divine *hypostases* of Father, Son and Spirit) in a great mystery of diverse unification such as the words communion or *perichoresis* connote.
397. Orat. 31.14, PG 36.148-149.
398. Orat. 31.15, PG 36.149.

title and status singly. Equally, a person can enumerate the Godhead, and rightly say that the Godhead (the dynamic being of the Father) is simply One. As one, it cannot be rightly enumerated, just stated to be simple and single. To this extent number applies and does not apply to God. The paradox is useful in describing the three *hypostases*. The Father, as dynamic cause of the Godhead, timelessly, simultaneously, co-equally and consubstantially, emits the Son as a divine "generation," and the Spirit as a divine "procession." Both these generated and processed *hypostases* are God of God and, even though distinct (*hypostatically*), each *hypostasis* relates to the others in a manner that ontologically flows back to union; that union which is given not merely by a voluntary desire for communion, but substantively and essentially by virtue of having one dynamic of the Father's being common to all, and one will, one purpose, power and majesty, which also flows from that ontological unity. To say God is One is correct; to say God is three is correct; but each statement is only correct in the context of a vision of the deity which is complexly simple (though non-composite) and diverse in a manner that inherently "runs to" oneness. The Trinity, in short, cannot be defined mathematically, it can only be partially envisaged, through the mathematical paradoxes, as a mystical vision of *perichoresis* that exceeds anything that corporeality can conceive of as a complex union.[399] His best image is that of the stability and interpenetrability of the angelic ontology, and even this, as he often tells the reader, does not approach that ultimate mystery of the divine being which lies beyond the comprehension even of the angels, as that which is veiled from all the created orders within the innermost *Sanctum* of the holy of holies.

The other major critical objection which Gregory considered within this Oration, that the doctrine of the Spirit had no sufficient biblical sanction in the prior Christian tradition, he has partially admitted by agreeing that theologians before him did not really do a good enough job in setting out the tradition of pneumatology. To remedy this, Gregory is at pains to present the biblical evidence on the Spirit's hypostatic existence and functional role, which he does throughout his arguments. The Spirit is not "prayed to" in the scriptural record, since it is in and through the Spirit that all prayer takes place. At the end of the Oration, however, he comes back to this criticism in a comprehensive way, not merely supplying exegeses of the central texts, but considering why the proclamation of the full theology of the Spirit has been "reserved" until the present generation.

The entire economy of human salvation, stretching from the creation to the present day, has been subject, Gregory says, to two "seismic events": these are the giving of the Two Covenants, which sum up human history and give it its meaning. The first seismic crisis was the "transition from idolatry to the Law," the second was

399. "I have examined the questions so busily and so often, searching from every point of view for a suitable illustration of this profound matter. I have failed to find anything whatsoever in this world with which I might compare the divine nature." Orat. 31.31, PG 36.169.

the "transition from the Law to the Gospel."[400] There shall be a third, he says: the eschatological transformation which is spoken of in the Gospel, when the present order is transfigured into an order that "cannot be shaken,[401] beyond all present limitations. Each of the two transformations took place gradually and over a long time.[402] Even in Gregory's day there are those who worship idols, but the spiritually perceptive have been able to see the seismic events, and gather their import. He is implying too that certain key visionaries in the first seismic event, could even see on to the next, such as the prophets and visionaries of the Old Testament who foretold the coming of Christ. Paul was an example of a man in the transition point. He began life in the first "seismic order" and made the transition to the second when he accepted the revelation of Christ. "His earlier conduct was an accommodation to circumstance; his later conduct belonged to the full truth." This pattern of God's revelatory dealings with the cosmos can be discerned even in the present times. There are those like Paul who are still living in "accommodations" and others such as Gregory, who demonstrate the fullness of truth. In the Old Covenant the doctrine of God was revealed monistically. In the New Covenant the deity of the Son was progressively revealed as a more complete understanding of Godhead. It was not revealed openly at Sinai because the nuanced truth was dangerous at a time when the great majority of humankind were idolaters. Once the concept of the singleness of God's monarchy was firmly established the Second Person was revealed. The revelation of the deity of the Holy Spirit can only occur openly when the deity of the Son has itself been sufficiently established.[403] It all takes place like a gradual ascent of ascents,[404] a movement "from glory to glory."[405] This is the time: a new transition point in the seismic events that constitute the divine pattern of revelation in history. Gregory is the proclaimer. He does not say as much but he is undoubtedly implying that he, like Paul, is standing at the edge of the third seismic shaking. His age is the dawning of the apocalyptic end-stage. The last revelation of the Eschaton is the deity of the Divine Spirit whose coming at Pentecost inaugurated, in the Church, a society of the elect which would stand within history and not be ultimately subject to times and conditions, but would constitute by their destiny and progress the last revelation of the cosmic meaning: transformation into the heavenly Church in angelic glory, the liturgical chorus that saw the triune God face to face.

400. Orat. 31.25, PG 36.160-161.
401. Heb 12:18.
402. Orat. 31.25, PG 36.161.
403. Orat. 31.26, PG 36.161.
404. Another liturgical image from the psalms evoking the last processional climb of the pilgrims to the Temple at Jerusalem. For Gregory, the last stage of the ascent is the entrance to the Heavenly Jerusalem where the triune Godhead inhabits the sanctuary. He uses Ps 84 here to make the connection.
405. 2 Cor 3:18. The text celebrates the Spirit's final transformation of the destiny of humankind in the eschatological vision of God. Orat. 31.26, PG 36.164.

He cites, not himself, as an example of the "saint of the last ages" (though he is clearly associating himself in the notion), but Gregory Thaumaturgos,[406] the apostle of Cappadocia:

> Thus do I stand on these issues. Thus may I ever stand, and also all those I love; all of us able to worship the Father as God, the Son as God, the Holy Spirit as God: Three distinctions[407] in person, and one Godhead undivided as to honor or glory or essence or dominion, as one inspired saint of recent times so wisely expressed it.[408]

This is an extraordinary culmination to the *Theological Orations*. There is nothing comparable to it as a theory of revelatory process in the whole of patristic literature.[409] It is not anything like the theory of the "development of doctrine" later popularized in nineteenth-century Roman Catholicism after Newman. It is more akin, in Gregory, to the vast cosmological scheme of salvation manifested in the eschatological understanding of Origen. With him, as with Gregory, the eschaton is not (historically considered) an ending to present order, but the progressive spiritualization of the current order: the endless ascent to Divine Vision. Gregory has successfully, and in an incredible economy of words, compressed all of Origen's voluminous theory of spiritual progress (*prokope*) and finished off what the ancient teacher left undone: the correlation of the idea of eschatological ascent to the principle of divine revelation in history. In Origen's systematic the relation of the spiritual ascent of (pre-existent) souls is only loosely and accidentally connected to the incarnation within history. The Logos, for Origen, comes to human form merely as an emergency rescue for spirits fallen into corporeality. As far as Gregory is concerned, the corporeal form was destined for us from the outset by God, and was "assumed" into the divine revelation by the free choice of the Logos to become incarnate. The act of salvation in history, the Logos' assumption of flesh for its redemption, is at the same time the manifestation of the final mystery of the Trinitarian inner life of God. The economic revelation and the inner life are not to be confused, but they are mutually related. It was Gregory's genius to correct the Origenian system in this regard, without losing anything of the vast religious horizons of Origen's imagination. In this, as in many other aspects of his thought, Gregory reveals himself as the most consistently Origenian of the major Cappadocian thinkers after Gregory Thaumaturgos.

Typically, at the end of one of his most demanding and extensive "explanations," Gregory appeals for simplicity and the abandonment of relying on useless analogies. The gift of mystical illumination is the most reliable guide in such advanced matters, and Gregory's own mystical capacity will have to serve as a guide for others who are willing to follow him:

---

406. The identification of the otherwise unknown theologian is supplied by Elias of Crete. Cf. Norris.
407. *Idiotetas*.
408. Orat. 31.28, PG 36.164.
409. Cf. McGuckin (1998).

I resolved in the end that it was best to have done with images and shadows which are all deceptive and fall very short of the truth. Better to cling to a more reverent view and be content with paucity of words, using the guidance of the Holy Spirit, keeping to the very end as my true comrade and companion that enlightenment which I have received from the Spirit. As I make my way through this world I will try my best to persuade all others to worship Father, Son and Holy Spirit, One Godhead and Power. To Him belongs all glory and honor and might[410] to the Ages of Ages. Amen.[411]

This set of Orations represents a veritable Herculean labor in a short space of time. At the end of that summer in 380, Gregory tells us that his health was failing him once more.[412] He was fifty-one years of age, at a time when that was commonly regarded as old age, and he was very tired. Already he possibly had intelligence that the military campaign in Thessaloniki was progressing well. The Goths, already aimless after the first success at Adrianople, had been reined in, and could in all likelihood be brought back into a peaceful federation with the empire by Theodosius' strategies. Soon, then, the emperor would be making a progress to take charge of the capital, and then all manner of extra work would be required on the ecclesiastical front. We might suspect that immediately after giving this important series of lectures, Gregory was ready to take himself off for a rest in the country property near to Constantinople, which Theodosia his cousin also seems to have put at his disposal. Before he left he decided to honor Maximus the Egyptian Cynic orator who had helped him in his labors. He had heard that Maximus was thinking of returning home to Alexandria, and decided to give him a hero's farewell. It was to prove his single biggest political mistake. Years afterwards, when he sat at his scriptorium in the final retirement of old age, the remembrance of this event could bring him to put his head in his hands, lamenting the way that his love of talking remained his abiding weakness in an otherwise strictly disciplined and ascetic life.[413] It was this one oration he regretted most of all.

---

410. Rev 1:6.
411. Orat. 31.33, PG 36.172.
412. Orat. 25.1, PG 35.1197.
413. Carm. 2.1.34 (*On His Silence in the Time of Fasting*), vv. 160-178, PG 37.1318-1320.

6

ARCHBISHOP OF CONSTANTINOPLE

And he knew fears, whose entrance closed on one
Sudden and insurmountable as death.
His heart pushed slowly through with laboring breath;
He brought it up just like a son.

Ineffable necessities he knew,
Rayless as lumber-rooms where children cry;
Obediently he gave his soul up too,
When she reached womanhood, that she might lie

Beside her bridegroom and her lord; while he
Remained behind without her, in a place
Where loneliness increased fantastic'ly,
And never spoke and never showed his face.

But in return, after long time, the bands
Were loos'd, and he achieved the happiness
Of holding, with a piercing tenderness,
Himself, like the whole creation, in his hands.

Rainer Maria Rilke
The Life of a Saint

In the late summer of 380, when everyone was becoming restless to leave the city's heat, Gregory resolved to present Maximus with a special oration to thank him for all the assistance he had offered in the time he spent at the Anastasia. *Oration 25* is a very generous paean of praise, lauding him as a great hero of the Nicene faith.[1] He testifies before heaven how this man is a paragon of philosophic wisdom, of ethical transparency and purity of faith. He is no less than a mighty victor of the faith, an "old dog" of a Cynic, such was his faithful guarding of the house,[2] a faithful and fearless witness like the martyrs of old: in short, a veritable hero.[3] His long hair is the "sign of a Nazirite." Maximus is the "best of the best: the noblest of the noble." [4] He wins Gregory's great admiration for taking a "middle road," the path Gregory has always advocated, between solitary seclusion, and activity for

1. Maximus undoubtedly merited it: At least, in Gregory's eyes, until he turned against his patron, for he was an anti-Arian writer of no small ability to judge from Jerome's praises; cf. *De Vir. Ill.* 127. See also J. Mossay, "Note sur Héron-Maxime, écrivain ecclésiastique," *Analecta Bollandiana* 100 (1982), pp. 229-236.
2. Orat. 25.2, PG 35.1200.
3. *Agonistes*, Orat. 25.3, PG 35.1201.
4. Orat. 25.3, PG 35.1201.

the benefit of others, practicing philosophical detachment in the midst of the city.[5] One of his chief assistances, it seems, was supporting Gregory as a lawyer in the time when he was hauled before the hostile magistrate after the Pascha riot.[6] Gregory calls him up to the altar to be associated with him as he praises him, suggesting both that this was preached in the Anastasia Church, and was meant as a formal presentation of Maximus to the Anastasia congregation.[7] But presented for what? Could it be taken as Gregory advancing Maximus' claim to be considered as a new clerical leader for the Church? One might well have surmised that, if the claims of Gregory himself were not prior to those of any other. And yet, it also appeared to Maximus, and others perhaps, that Gregory was far too diffident about claiming the episcopal throne of Constantinople. Was it something that he really wanted or not? He had come to the capital as the bishop designated by the Antiochene council. That, in his mind, was something very different indeed to coming with a proprietorial claim to oust Demophilos. Even when Theodosius entered his city and wished to install Gregory as the official bishop in the church of the Holy Apostles in November a few months later, Gregory says he refused the offer,[8] indicating that it was his firm intention to have the successor to Demophilos formally recognized by the council that would meet in May 381. To Maximus this diffidence seemed odd—politically inept, and disloyal to the concerns of Alexandria which thought it had nominated Gregory by virtue of its own supremacy of jurisdiction in eastern ecclesiastical affairs. Maximus certainly wanted the see for himself, and the more Gregory appeared to be vacillating, the more he decided that for all practical purposes the bishops' throne should be regarded as vacant, and possibly ripe for the taking. Had not Gregory himself declared, in his other oration celebrating Alexandrian heroes of the faith,[9] that an orthodox Nicene taking the see from an Arian was no usurpation against canon law? More than Gregory's perennial indecision about whether he wanted the see for himself, it seemed to Maximus, and the Egyptian hierarchs who had recognized Gregory when they sent insignia and quasi-military support for his community, that he was failing in the one chief thing that the acceptance of the Alexandrian nomination signified: and that was the ancient canon law that subordinated Constantinople to the jurisdictional supervision of Alexandria. For Gregory to decide on his own initiative that he would obey the Antiochene synod above all else, meant that he increasingly revealed his hand to the Egyptian hierarchs who must have known from midsummer of 380 that he was no longer "their man" in the capital, if he had ever been so from the beginning. At this point Archbishop Peter, and his leading cleric Timothy, seem to have transferred all their expectations to Maximus, who cannot be exonerated of having plotted behind Gregory's back. Perhaps the crowning irony, of all the long list of strange events that transpired over this affair, was the strong likelihood that

---

5.   Orat. 25.5, PG 35.1204.
6.   Orat. 25.7, PG 35.1208.
7.   Orat. 25.2, PG 35.1200.
8.   Yet in all his city Orations thereafter he speaks proprietorially as bishop of the city.
9.   *In Praise of Athanasios*, Orat. 21.8, PG 35.1089.

Maximus took *Oration* 25 back as his personal reference from Gregory to Peter of Alexandria, and used it as the very basis of his claim for the candidacy as bishop of the Nicene party in Constantinople. Had not Gregory himself taken him to the front of the Church (his own Anastasia) and presented him to the congregation as the ideal man for the job?

While Gregory was praising him, of course, none of this was obvious, but the words he had so enthusiastically uttered in thanks for Maximus' efforts during the recent campaign would soon come back to haunt him in the most embarrassing way. As his list of praises subsides, Gregory concludes with a long synopsis of trinitarian orthodoxy which he presents to Maximus, to keep and sustain,[10] and then finishes with an extraordinarily ambiguous further "commendation." The confession of faith set out, and the commendation delivered to someone Gregory has explicitly called up to the altar of his Church, sounds for all the world like a commendation of a new priestly leader for the community. Gregory describes himself as having culled the harvest of the Anastasia faithful from the "gleanings of the field," that is the Arian majority when he came to the city. This is what he commends now to Maximus:

> You see the extent of all that we have harvested. For this reason come and make our barns even fuller and our wine-press even more abundant. Tell the tale of how we were called here and of our unbelievable time here, which we spent not in feasting but in sharing sufferings together, so that once the dangers were passed we could also share the glory together.[11]

Gregory left for the country[12] with a heart full of joy, sensing a real end to his labors. Maximus had sailed for Alexandria. The priests and deacons in charge of the liturgy at Anastasia would be perfectly able to do without him for a while. He could enjoy a well-earned convalescence in some peace. He spent a lot of time walking by the sea, either on the Euxine coast or the Propontis, or just possibly on the Princes Islands just out from the city. He watched the waves crash against the rocks on the shore and pondered.[13] It was a time of quiet solitude and leisure that was soon shattered. If his final words before he left the Anastasia had not, in their original intent, been meant to commend Maximus as the new episcopal candidate for the Nicene party at Constantinople, they were soon touted that way by the Egyptians who propagandized his cause in the community. Immediately on his arrival, Maximus communicated to Peter of Alexandria all of Gregory's ambivalences about taking the episcopal throne aggressively. Peter seems to have been outraged that Gregory's dilatoriness arose because he preferred canonical allegiance to Antioch over Alexandria, a blatant disregard of his own canonical primacy. So he gave Maximus his blessing to occupy the throne of the city for the Nicene cause.

10. Orat. 25.15-18, PG 35.1220-1224.
11. Orat. 25.19, PG 35.1225.
12. Orat. 26, PG 35.1228. Several of the mss. bear the title: "After his return from the country."
13. Orat. 26.8, PG 35.1237.

He sent consecrating bishops from Alexandria, with letters of appointment for Maximus, and instructed the Egyptian sailors who brought them to the city to ensure the successful completion of his schemes. This was regarded as an outrage by almost all the inhabitants of the capital: Nicenes, Arians, and pagans alike, for it was a slur on their honor, and even by this stage the see was attracting to itself a large ambit of influence, to the detriment of Alexandria's ancient jurisdictional claims. The tension between the two cities for prominence in Christian affairs would simmer on in several major crises to come. The Maximus affair is merely the first of a tumultuous series of events marking the slow decline of Alexandria as the primary political center of Church life in the East. Its role was inexorably passing over to the imperial city. The deposition of John Chrysostom by the Alexandrian archbishop Theophilos, disgracefully accomplished at the Chalcedon Synod of the Oak; the massive conflict between Cyril and Nestorios at the council of Ephesus 431; and the physical beating and deposition of Flavian at the synod of Ephesus 449; are all events marking the course of these continuing machinations against the stability of the Constantinopolitan archbishops, orchestrated by Alexandria, usually with the connivance of Rome.[14]

Gregory describes the fiasco most clearly in the poem *De Vita Sua*, which was meant in large part as an exercise in literary propaganda, to recover something of the large loss of reputation he suffered for his two great perceived breaches of judgment in the capital; first his lack of political sense in being duped by Maximus, and second his inability to handle the factions at the council of Constantinople.[15] There is no doubt that the Maximus affair cost him dearly, as it made him appear something of a liability to the Antiochene clergy who had heard noise of the controversy very soon after it; and also to the aristocrats at the court who were preparing for the entrance of Theodosius. If Gregory's primary role was to smooth over the path for the emperor before he took charge of a generally hostile capital and forced it to his religious will, then Gregory could not afford to be embroiled in any personal troubles of his own. If he had already attracted extensive ridicule for his part in the troubles he was a liability to the emperor's honor, and there seems to have been a cooling towards him from the political center after these events. As to the support of Alexandria, he knew this would never return, and the West generally had damned him by association with Meletios, to the extent that neither Damasus of Rome nor Ambrose of Milan

14. As was the case with Gregory, for Peter of Alexandria and Damasus of Rome were allied in their determination to oust Gregory. Damasus did not have any bone to pick with Gregory theologically speaking, but he had his face set against him since he was an appointee of Meletios, and Damasus was the main supporter of Meletios' rival Paulinus in the Antiochene schism. Gregory maintains a diplomatic silence about Damasus' hostility, though he knows it all too well from the attitudes of Acholius of Thessalonike and the Illyrian bishops who came later to the council of 381.

15. Which really means his refusal to be browbeaten by the Antiochene majority led by Diodore. He chose an unwilling retirement rather than compromise what he saw to be beneficial for the welfare of the Church internationally.

would ever recognize his claim to be legitimate bishop of the city, even after he had been formally assigned the charge by the Council in May 381. The pro-western bishops later called to be present at that council, from the province of Illyria, were equally obstructive to Gregory as can be seen in his remarks in the later autobiographical poem.[16]

In the *De Vita Sua,* Gregory gives a large account of the Maximus incident. He describes it as a new trouble coming cascading on all his difficulties caused by his Arian enemies. It was a "new plague from Egypt."[17] It was a prime example of "Egyptian fickleness." "An effeminate phantom from Egypt, a puppy, a streetwalker, a disaster of a dog (Cynic) with no sense of smell and a puny woof… plastered with cosmetics" fell into his life. The catalogue of insults, of course, refers to one and the same Maximus he had literally lauded to the skies—before the event. The long hair of the Nazirite and the philosophic clothes and the Cynic philosopher's staff which he found so noble and ascetic in *Oration* 25, are now seized on as dreadful signs of ambivalent gender:[18] girlish curls and a spinning distaff.[19] The police record which Gregory avers to and passes over quickly in regard to Maximus[20] is no mere invention of diatribe, but the result of "certain investigations" conducted into his previous behavior by the imperial secret agents in late 381, when he had once more appealed to the court for restitution, and gained the synodical support of the Italian and African bishops with Ambrose, at the council of Aquileia. This intelligence would have been communicated to Gregory from his family and court contacts, for it was certainly a large part of his activity in the early part of 382, not only to write apologetic poems in self-defense, but to prepare his case for a synodical review which he still thought might be forthcoming if the western bishops kept pursuing Maximus' claims for their own ends.

And yet the more he denounced Maximus as a dirty fraud, the more he threw a cold light onto his own naiveté, for being taken in to start with. Was such a simplicity suitable in someone who aspired to be the leader of the Nicenes in the capital city? Was it not an indication that the charges raised against him by Demophilos' clergy (which he tried to refute in *Oration* 33) were correct: that he really was a rustic from the provinces, who did not know how to conduct himself in the rough and tumble of the city? He knows he cannot escape the criticism and so admits to it frankly:

16. Cf. McGuckin, "Autobiography as Apologia," (2001). *De Vita Sua,* vv. 1800-1817, PG 37.1155-1156.
17. As recounted in Exodus 7:11. *De Vita Sua,* vv. 740-747, PG 37.1080.
18. A clear play to the gallery of the nobility, who were made very anxious by any suggestion they were unmanly, that is, related to the eunuch class, which connoted "servile" status in Gregory's context of diatribe. Gregory is consistently hostile to the eunuchs of Byzantium, perhaps mainly because here was the main locus of the Homoian opposition to his presence and theology. For more, cf. L. James (ed.) *Women, Men and Eunuchs: Gender in Byzantium* (NewYork, 1997).
19. *De Vita Sua,* vv. 750-772, PG 37.1081-1082. He may be making a learned pun, too, on the great Hercules, one of whose "labors" was to dress as a woman and sit spinning with them. The image of the hairy he-man demi-god in drag was a great joke in most Antique literature.
20. *De Vita Sua,* vv. 773-777, PG 37.1082-1083.

He was very clever for he built up his drama using me rather than strangers. What a
crafty sophist of wickedness he was. But I was inexperienced in such matters, a complete stranger to duplicity. It was my custom to value another sort of cleverness: how
to say something wise, and how to admire someone who could do this, and to seek the
inner meaning of the holy books...

If only everyone had an open and evident character... people would harm one another
less. But as it stands the good will always be a prey for the wicked...for the wicked
person will conceal himself by a thousand dev/ices... while the one who gravitates to
virtue is naturally slow and reluctant to believe ill of others. This is why kindness is
always an easy mark.[21]

Maximus evidently suborned accomplices apart from the Egyptian sailors and the
visiting hierarchs who came to consecrate him. Gregory regards the other two main
traitors in the camp as an otherwise unnamed deacon[22] and priest of the Anastasia
congregation. This was not the deacon Evagrios whom Gregory had brought with
him from Cappadocia, because the latter appears as still a loyal member of the entourage in late 381 when Gregory allocates him a good legacy in his last will and testament. The priest was "even more barbarian in mind than he was in his looks,"[23] and
Gregory cannot fathom his disloyalty, or the sudden revelation of all the hostility he
had been harboring against him, since he "had not been overlooked in any way, or ever
been treated unfairly, and still held the first place in the ranks of priests." The latter
phrase suggests, however, that jealousy may have been the motive—especially if Gregory had preferred the counsels of Maximus to all others, as he himself admits,[24] to the
detriment of those who had labored long and hard before he came to the city to maintain the Nicene faith there. It would have been an easy task for Maximus to alienate
the priest's attachments even more, and gain his loyalty by promises of close association with himself as the new bishop. The priest and deacon together with the candidate bishop formed the symbolic nucleus of clergy for a new local Church. More
significantly the incumbent clerics were able to admit or prohibit people from using
the altar at the Anastasia, where they habitually served the liturgy. Their agreement in
admitting the Egyptian bishops who came to consecrate Maximus was essential to the
success of the venture. Gregory, though he says he is bursting to spit it all out, is careful
in the poem to say nothing hostile about the Egyptian bishops themselves. He knows
that they merely acted in obedience to Peter of Alexandria,[25] the brother and successor of Athanasios, and the latter had, by the time Gregory was writing his diatribe,
already died and was, in Gregory's eyes, no longer a proper subject for attack. It was

21. *De Vita Sua*, vv. 784-806, PG 37.1083.
22. "He was once an angel, now a Belial." *De Vita Sua*, v. 823, PG 37.1086. The deacons took the
    role of the angelic orders in the celebration of the liturgy, and were close associates of the
    bishops, often controlling the fisc.
23. *De Vita Sua*, v. 825, PG 37.1086.
24. *De Vita Sua*, vv. 810-814, PG 37.1085.
25. *De Vita Sua*, vv. 845-855, PG 37.1087-1088.

also a time to be circumspect as the legal case between the court at Constantinople, the western sees of Rome and Aquileia, and Alexandria itself, was still "pending." It was inadvisable to attack them in such a public document in 382.

For Gregory the real villain is Maximus. He needed a large infusion of cash to advance his plans. This, we are told, he happily found from a priest who had sailed in recently from the Greek island of Thasos with a large amount of gold which his church had entrusted to him for the purchase of Prokonnesian[26] marble cut into sheets in the workshops of Constantinople for use in the flooring and cladding of buildings. The priest was induced to give the gold as an "advance" for a much greater return on his investment later when Maximus would be able to control the massive finances of the imperial Church. So much for dubious financial speculations in Byzantium. The Thasos Church never saw its marble floors, or its gold (or probably its priest) ever again.

Once he had secured the loyalties of a large number of Egyptian sailors to protect him and the clergy in attendance, Maximus marched for the Church (undoubtedly the Anastasia) and the consecration ceremony commenced. It was already late in the day, a fact which Gregory exaggerates, making it into "a nighttime affair"[27] to cast aspersions on its legitimacy on every level, both canonical (since nighttime ordinations without the acclaim of the people were contrary to Church custom) and civil (he describes them as nocturnal "thieves"). Gregory was well away from it all, because he was convalescing from illness he tells his readers, and nothing had been said to the lay leaders of the congregation[28] or to the members of the community who were not from Alexandria. Some of the clergy, however, lived next door and knew something was going on. Once they realized what it was they summoned help, and a large crowd quickly assembled to stop it. As the service of Matins[29] was being celebrated, a large crowd of Constantinopolitans burst in to stop the Egyptians consecrating a bishop for their city behind their backs. Gregory depicts it as a patriotic effort to stop an injustice, but his description on closer reading suggests it was a rerun of the very same forces that had earlier disrupted his own paschal services when he himself had appeared publicly at the Anastasia "as a bishop." He tells us that the crowd was composed of "high officials, outsiders (pagans), and those who were not even true Christians."[30] The latter must mean Arians. Gregory tells it as if they were one and all filled with outrage at the thought of the dishonor done to him, but this would only apply to the small core of Anastasia faithful. The very large crowd is clearly just disrupting the Nicene services once again and crushing their

26. The island was later renamed Marmara after its quarries.
27. *De Vita Sua*, v. 887, PG 37.1090.
28. "The rams of the church" *De Vita Sua*, v. 893, PG 37.1091.
29. "It was orthros." I take the latter to refer to the Church service rather than "dawn" per se. *Orthros*, the daydawn service of psalms, can on festive occasions take place on the evening before when combined liturgically with vespers. *De Vita Sua*, v. 898, PG 37.1091.
30. *De Vita Sua*, vv. 901-902, PG 37.1091.

pretensions to oust Demophilos, the legitimate incumbent as far as the court officials were concerned.

Maximus' party discovered that their sailors were simply insufficient to stop the
tidal wave of anger directed against them. Once again the ceremonies of the
Anastasia were smashed up, and the Egyptians had to retire into the safe surrounds
of the private house of a musician belonging to their party who lived and worked in
the city. White has put the best face on this in her recent translation of the *De Vita
Sua* by rendering "Choraulos" as "Choir-Master."[31] But Gregory and the other
Cappadocian fathers use the word "Chorostasia" to refer to the Church choir,[32] and
the choirmaster would then be Choriarchos, or Chorostates. No, Gregory has
chosen the word very carefully, and it means "flute player." It bears all the wide range
of opprobrious subtext that Gregory wants it to be ballasted with. The man is a flautist and lead dancer for a chorus of stage girls. His house may have been a safe haven
for the hierarchs (and might well have been very prestigious in reality), but for Gregory it is a "sad little hovel," and he pours all the scorn he can on it in a few choicely
sharpened verses to heighten the ridiculous aspect of a crowd of Egyptian hierarchs
having to finish off their solemn ceremony of consecration in the back bedroom of a
small-time hoofer from the red light district.[33] It is "a farce," and the "Cynic dog
with the lovely hair is sheared in a hurry." From a sheepdog he is made into a shepherd. Gregory makes much of the loss of his wonderful hair, finally suggesting he
should have it made into a wig to send as a present. But who would find it useful: the
church virgins or his friends on the stage? Gregory suggests he should send it to the
latter; the "Corinthian ladies"[34] he used to be "associated with in private mysteries."[35] He means, of course, to imply that Maximus' life was far from the paragon of
virtue he paraded before Gregory in the early days. It might be that he has access to
the file the imperial agents had amassed on his betrayer since the legal scrutiny
began between late summer of 380 and the early part of 382. Gregory seems to suggest he did have intelligence to this effect, when the man's deeds "were all made
public,"[36] or it may simply be a way of giving the worst of all possible readings to the
manner he celebrated the "mysteries" of his episcopal consecration in a
stage-dancer's house—a profession which at that time was commonly seen as synonymous with prostitution. Anyway, Gregory could not possibly tell the terrible deeds
of this man. His tact will be manifested in the way he simply "bites his lips with

---

31. *De Vita Sua*, v. 909, PG 37.1091.
32. Cf. G.W.H. Lampe, *A Patristic Greek Lexicon* (Oxford, 1978), p. 1527.
33. *De Vita Sua*, vv. 905-912, PG 37.1091-1092.
34. I.e., prostitutes.
35. *De Vita Sua*, v. 935, PG 37.1093.
36. *De Vita Sua*, v. 950, PG 37.1094. He also says that Maximus had suffered police penalties for
    his criminal behavior before coming to Constantinople, for which he received a sentence of
    exile (*De Vita Sua*, v. 976-977) though pretending to Gregory that he had suffered banishment on account of religious persecution for his orthodoxy.

shame." The passage in the *De Vita Sua* is a like giving a loud scream with shocked gesticulations, then telling people to pay no attention.

The point of it all at the end of this very funny but caustic section of the poem, is that Gregory asks his readers for forgiveness for his naiveté. "The man was a scoundrel: but to me he was a hero."[37] Gregory asks "the men of the jury" to pardon him as he has often made similar mistakes, being too generous in his estimation of people's characters. He knows that the chief reason why all this became so much more funny in the common estimation is the possible use of his own speech in praise of Maximus as the latter's evidence that he was fit to be the bishop over the head of his referee. Gregory says that he feels like "cutting off this own tongue of mine."[38] The poem, of course, is written in the year after the council of 381, when he was intent on restoring his honor in a city which now regarded this incident as prime evidence of his being unfit for high political office, and had told and re-told the story of the thrashing of the Egyptians as a moment of high farce. One of the chief players in that farce, as far as the Constantinopolitans were concerned, was the rustic old bishop from Cappadocia who had so praised the man to the heavens in a published discourse, and then denounced him as a traitor within weeks. As Gregory said, it was all fit material for a bad pantomime.[39] Perhaps it actually made its way to the stage, in a city that was always more than ready to ridicule the mighty and famous.[40] It took a great deal of effort to recover his reputation after this. Maybe he never did, but most of Gregory's literary efforts after 381 were dedicated to the cause of repairing his honor, and a large number of the poems have this motivation close to their core.

Maximus and his party made a strategic exit from the city straight afterwards. Gregory himself was informed of all that had been going on and had to cut his holiday short, returning to the Anastasia to salvage what he could on the home front (soon discovering the priest and deacon of his own sanctuary had abandoned him) and realizing that all his public propaganda work of the last year, trying to offset the Arian estimate of him as a bumbling fool, had been unraveled in one night. Even the large contingent of Egyptian sailors in the church had been unable to prevent another thrashing of the Anastasia from a determined Constantinopolitan mob. He realized that from now on he and his remaining community would have to be very circumspect until Theodosius arrived. His Egyptian "minders" might in the end have proved useless, but at least they had provide him with psychological security at the critical time he delivered the *Theological Orations*. Now, without them, he was in

37. *De Vita Sua*, v. 978, PG 37.1095.
38. *De Vita Sua*, vv. 984-989, PG 37.1097.
39. *De Vita Sua*, vv. 865-866, PG 37.1089.
40. Cf. Orat. 2, *Apol. de Fuga*. 84, PG 35.489. Though *Oration* 2 is an early piece, there are several interpolations about his griefs in Constantinople after his most recent "flight," inserted after 382. With the intimation of *De Vita Sua*, v. 865, PG 37.1089, it might be that Gregory knew he had been the subject of a mummer's farce.

a growing panic. His friends set a close guard about him and kept him out of the streets, for his own safety.[41]

He first decided to run for it. Flight was his usual response to crisis situations until he had considered his position. When he came back to the Anastasia he found criticism seething among his congregation. The community demanded to know what he had been up to. Where had the money come from to initiate Maximus' efforts? Gregory felt piqued that he was being asked by his own people to give an account of his financial dealings on behalf of the church at Constantinople. But he prepared an oration which would satisfy the faithful and assuage his desire to rub out the dreadful mistake of *Oration* 25 praising such a traitor as Maximus. *Oration* 26 was the result. Some commentators have read too much into the account he gives of his fiscal administration. This does not refer to the church at Constantinople at all; rather to the purses of the Anastasia congregation, which would have been considerably less extensive, although not inconsiderable, especially if Gregory had been financially patronized by pro-Theodosian aristocrats.

Oration 26 begins with Gregory telling his flock that he has missed them so much (and he knows they have missed him too) that he simply had to break short his convalescence and be back among them.[42] He has heard what has happened in his absence. There are many troubles, he says, in city life which is so worldly and corrupt, but what grieves him most is that this little oasis of holiness, the altar and sanctuary of the Anastasia, has been defiled by the approach to it of unworthy men.[43] Wolves (the Egyptian clergy) have tried to proselytize his church with their "fanatical doctrines" and he fears greatly, because he has been betrayed by someone who opened the door from the inside of the house (his own priest). Above all he fears the dog (Maximus) who tried to become a shepherd. How easy it is to take advantage of their small and weak condition, he says, but "those who unleashed their dogs against us" (the Egyptian hierarchs) cannot pretend that they did so for the benefit of the little flock. To let loose the dogs against the sheep is the work of a predator, not a friend.[44]

From section four onwards he admits that he has been the subject of criticism for his own part in the fiasco. He agrees that he is a timid soul, though not necessarily "cowardly," as he would prefer to see his timidity in the light of "cautious prudence." One thing he will not accept, however, is that he has profited from his pastoral charge. He flashes this back against the Egyptians[45] who seem to have originated the

---

41. *De Vita Sua*, vv. 1044-1051, PG 37.1101.
42. Orat. 26.1, PG 35.1228.
43. Orat. 26.1, PG 35.1229.
44. Orat. 26.3, PG 35.1232.
45. Christian hierarchs were already known for their distinguishing use of linen vestments (as was the case also with the Jewish and Egyptian pagan priesthoods); and those of Egypt, in particular, were known for their splendor in liturgical style. The episcopal insignia which Peter sent

charge, for he says that he, at least, cannot be accused of consuming the substance of the flock and "making lovely linen vestments by fleecing them."[46] He will give an account of how he has used all the money he has hitherto received as pastor in charge of the church. First of all he has been allowed, by their financial support, to be a full-time minister of the altar among them. He does not need to apologize for that. If they had not been willing to do this for him he would not have forced it upon them, and cannot be accused of imposing himself.[47] As to his recent spell in the country, well he has been exercising solitude. His rule of life is such that he regularly needs solitude and contemplative retreat, so that he can fall back into prayer and recollection after he has expended energy in public works for the church.[48] He has been walking a lot by the sea, and learning much from the way the waves crash against rocks. It has reinforced in him the lesson that the wise man, the really wise man, not specious philosophers such as Maximus, is one who is willing to bear all things with equanimity.[49] He is ready to tell them exactly what he has done with his church money: he has used it to feed the poor of the city, and arrange for the homeless some shelter for the night. In his own regard he has not used it for rich living. He has fasted as an ascetic. He was glad to disperse the money in this way, for charitable relief, for he felt that he applied the alms on behalf of all of them.[50]

What follows[51] is a chastened, and very fine encomium of the true philosopher. It lacks the rhetorical excess of his earlier praises of Maximus, and is clearly meant to be a sobered "rerun" of what he ought to have said. He still believes that the ascetic man, the true philosopher, is the highest vocation on earth. God is the First Nature, angels are the second, among human beings the highest rank of all is that of the true sophist.[52] The philosopher is defined here as one who remains above all assaults, who forgives readily like Christ forgave his enemies.[53] If he is a noble he adds noble conduct to that of his blood. If he is lowly born he achieves a higher nobility than all others by the ethical conduct he manifests. A young philosopher shows mastery over his desires. A rich philosopher shows disdain for personal possessions.[54] This is the model Gregory wishes to emulate. How can he now answer the charges of his critics outside the community on the basis of his philosophy? He has been called a stupid man—well, he will seek only the wisdom of God, which may not be the wisdom of

Gregory is an early example of this before marks of rank were generally distinguished among the clerical orders.
46. Orat. 26.4, PG 35.1232.
47. Orat. 26.6, PG 35.1236.
48. Orat. 26.7, PG 35.1237.
49. Orat. 26.8-9, PG 35.1237-1240.
50. Orat. 26.6, PG 35.1236.
51. Orat. 26.9-13, PG 35.1240-1245.
52. Orat. 26.13, PG 35.1245.
53. Orat. 26.12, PG 35.1244.
54. Orat. 26.11, PG 35.1241.

the world.[55] He has been called a ragged indigent. He feels no shame in this either. It has been his ascetical desire to be freed of the burden of his family wealth all along. He has been called a foreigner who ought to be deported immediately. What racist xenophobes his opponents are, he says. Is Maximus not also an expatriate and a foreigner? More importantly, is the true Christian at home anywhere in the world?[56] He has been criticized as an unfit leader for the community (here he seems to refer to internal criticism), since he is old and regularly ill, and not up to the demands of the job. He does not eat much, he admits, but his asceticism though it might have weakened him, has been the source of his knowledge, and this is cleverness enough for him. Those who criticize him on this score ought perhaps to gain a few more gray hairs themselves, and then they might show more wisdom in their judgments.[57]

The final sections of the oration turns to a series of threats that have been made against him. These are probably the tirades he mentions which the Egyptian party remaining in the capital raised against him in a howl of protests. Gregory attributes them all to Maximus in his later *De Vita Sua*:

> When he was cast out like the dog he was, he went off in a terrible rage, muttering oaths which made one shudder to hear them, before he packed off for Alexandria.[58]

In *Oration* 26 they are made more explicit. They are going to make sure that Gregory will be deposed from his episcopal throne. He replies to this that since he had never sought a throne for his own pleasure, merely sat in them uneasily for the service of others, he will not grow too worried about this threat.[59] The second (canonically the same as its predecessor) is that he shall be denied access to the altar, or in other words deposed from office. Gregory the priest, he says, knows and recognizes altars which are far above these earthly types. His opponents' threats cannot deprive him of those altars. Nor can he be exiled from his homeland, since it is heaven. In any case these are empty aggressions from posturers who could not achieve what they splutter they are going to do to him.[60] They shall seize all his property. What property? he asks. Does it mean his control of the fisc of the church? Ah, he sighs dramatically, here is the real cause of all the dissension. His enemies want to get their hands on ecclesiastical finances. Was it not the case that Jesus too was sold for thirty pieces of silver? Such a paltry sum too, though not the real value of the Lord, merely the worth of the traitor who betrayed him.[61] They will see to it that Gregory becomes a social leper. He will be refused invitations to the houses of the gentry; his friends will turn their backs on him. He sardonically replies that he will hardly miss

---

55. Orat. 26.14, PG 35.1245.
56. Orat. 26.14, PG 35.1245. Cf. Heb 13:14; 1 Pet 2:11.
57. Orat. 26.14, PG 35.1245.
58. *De Vita Sua*, vv. 1009-1013, PG 37.1098-1099.
59. Orat. 26.15, PG 35.1248.
60. Orat. 26.16, PG 35.1249. He was wrong. The Egyptians made good their threat to unseat him in the summer of 381 by their tactics at the council.
61. Orat. 26.16, PG 35.1249.

the great social whirl that has been offered to him since he first came to this unwelcoming city.[62] It is enough for him that he came to a strange place like the prophet Elias and the Shunamite woman of faith took him in with great charity (his cousin Theodosia). Gregory is suffering his own Passion, but even if all his friends and neighbors "look with dismay and stand far away" from him,[63] and "even if all were scandalized"[64] because of that night, he knows in whose steps he is following. Gregory presses the Passion parallels even further. As once before, a certain Peter has made a false denial. Gregory has little expectation that the latter day namesake in Alexandria will ever take the trouble to shed bitter tears of remorse over it.[65] He ends with a sense of grieved bemusement that so suddenly and so quickly the news of all this has spread to the East and West, and he has been turned into the hub of a violent polemic. What hurts him most, as usual, is the small detail, the one nearest the heart. How could friends who were once so close have turned so unexpectedly? How could they have so exploited his "simplicity"?[66] The Oration concludes with a prayer that the Trinity may bring back the faithless once more into his communion.

His time shuffling round the house in Constantinople, under armed protective guard, and unable to go outside, increased his panic despite his brave words in *Oration* 26 to the effect that his philosophical soul was "above all that sort of worry"; and in the course of the next week the tension was so great that he blurted out in a church service another speech. He has not preserved it except in digest, but members of his community later bore witness that he did utter such words, and they came back to haunt him during the council of 381.[67] Here, in the heat of the moment, he was so aggravated by the troubles coming upon troubles that he decided to clear off from the city. His work had been completed. He was going to slip away before the emperor came. They could find another bishop to defend orthodoxy, not him.[68]

His panic might have been accelerated by news that Maximus had gone back to Alexandria and on Peter's advice had gone straight on to find the Emperor in Thessalonike, to make his case there for recognition as the legitimate bishop of Constantinople. Since the edict *Cunctos Populos* of the previous February had elevated Damasus and Peter as the arbiters of catholic faith, it must have seemed reasonable to Gregory in late 380 that Theodosius would accede to Maximus' petition. As it

62. He notes in *Oration* 33 that he was socially excluded when he came.
63. Meaning the hierarchs of Antioch and Alexandria probably, who had both lost faith in Gregory's political skills, for various reasons, after this business. Orat. 26.17, PG 35.1249. He alludes to the psalm of the righteous man who suffers: Ps 3:11-12; a patristic typology for Jesus' Passion.
64. He alludes to Jesus' abandonment by his disciples in the disgrace of his arrest: Mt 26:31.
65. Mt 26:75. The Benedictine editors see a clear allusion to Peter of Alexandria in this, and I am sure they are right (PG 35.1250, fn. 7). Gregory still avoided explicit attacks on Peter even into 382, but made his point abundantly clear in lightly veiled references such as this.
66. Orat. 26.18, PG 35.1252.
67. Cf. *De Vita Sua*, vv. 1052-1073, PG 37.1102-1103.
68. *De Vita Sua*, vv. 1057-1058, PG 37.1102.

turned out, Theodosius knew better. Gregory had friends in high places, and the emperor was less than impressed by Maximus, ordering an enquiry to be initiated into the man's past history. After the failure of this venture Maximus returned to Alexandria and received, according to Gregory, no further help from an old and bewildered Peter whom he started to browbeat.[69] The reality is probably different. Maximus continued to receive Egyptian support in the council of 381, to the extent that Timothy (Peter's successor) continued to raise his claims against those of Gregory. Peter, also, was not the dim old man that Gregory paints in the poetry, rather, a shrewd and experienced operator. He most likely counseled Maximus, his protégé, to go on to the Western bishops, to Ambrose of Milan who could exercise some pressure on Theodosius, and re-present his case there. He did so in the following year, and was endorsed by Damasus and also by Ambrose and the synod of the Milanese bishops meeting at Aquileia in September 381. This cannot have happened without superlative references from Alexandria and their hierarchs' continued political support.

In retrospect, in the *De Vita Sua*, Gregory admits that his panic in October of 380 led him to make another "naïve mistake"[70] in suggesting that he might be leaving the Anastasia for good. He does not admit that he actually did resign, which was what his critics claimed, merely that he uttered words that "sounded like" a resignation, by telling them to defend the Trinity and remember all that he had done for them. Even so, he hurries on to tell his readers, once these words had escaped his lips, the congregation of the Anastasia was in an uproar. Gregory could not possibly leave them in the present condition. The Emperor was expected imminently. His abandonment of the ship now would be very detrimental. His speech was followed by the people "swarming like bees" demanding that he stay on as their legitimate leader. It was exactly that kind of extempore rhetorical pathos that could so usefully evoke "acclamation" from a reluctant audience. His own rhetorical professor in Athens had excelled in this kind of speech, and here, for once, it had actually served Gregory successfully. He would try it again in the middle of the council when he felt the bishops were wanting to get rid of him, but then it backfired badly, for the more cynical and worldly-wise clergy just decided to accept his tragically offered resignation, and so trumped his cards without recourse for any second gambit. The people of the Anastasia, however, genuinely seemed to have grown fond of him, and shouted out for him to stay.

69. *De Vita Sua*, vv. 1018-1020, PG 37.1099. Gregory tries to imply that Maximus was exiled from the city after trying to unseat Peter. This scenario is unbelievable, and the dismissal by the Governor of Alexandria which Gregory recounts is more like wishful thinking than anything else. A close reading of the words shows that he falls back from saying that Maximus actually was exiled, for which a legal record would have to exist. He was merely "sent away" in case the episode flared up further. This sending away was probably his commission to seek redress in the ecclesiastic courts of the West.
70. *De Vita Sua*, vv. 1053-1054, PG 37.1101.

At the sound of their abundant oaths and prayers and entreaties that I should stay to help them, and not hand my flock over to the wolves, how could I possibly have restrained my tears? O Anastasia! Most highly honored of churches...the Ark of Noah...

The heat was oppressive that evening as the sun went down. We were drenched in perspiration. The voices of all were growing tired from shouting. The women were frightened, especially the mothers of the young children who were bawling away. But all swore that they would not give in even if the church became their tomb, not until I had yielded to their demands. Then someone moved by desperation, finally took the floor. (Alas that I have the sense of hearing. I wish I had proven deaf on that day!). If you go, he said, you will throw out the Trinity along with you! This caused me to fear, in case a dangerous situation might result. So I gave an oath that I would stay until the advance party of the bishops arrived, who were expected at that time. (Well actually I gave my word, which was accepted as an oath because of my character, since I have never once since my baptism (If I may be allowed to boast a little) ever sworn a real oath). It was my hope that when they arrived I could free myself from all external cares. This was how we finally parted. Both sides thinking they had carried the day, and both deceived by their hopes. They thought I was now in their hands. I thought I only needed to stay on for a little while longer.[71]

It is a wonderfully vivid word-picture, but still does not alter the fact that the Maximus incident had cost Gregory dearly in terms of external support. The Egyptian hierarchy was now against him, and had carried the western bishops with them. The Antiochene clergy were dismayed at this political disaster. He had once had a powerful advocate in Eusebios of Samosata. But he had recently died as a result of Arian mob violence. Only Meletios was behind him, and the party of aristocrats who had first invited him to the city.[72] This was more than enough until that last pillar of support was knocked away. After the death of Meletios in the early part of the council, Gregory found he had very little groundswell of support indeed. His loving community at the Anastasia was simply not sufficient.

He only had a month to wait, probably still keeping to the house under guard. Theodosius entered his capital, fresh from his campaign in Macedonia against Gothic insurgents, on November 24, 380.[73] As Gregory already seemed to know he would,[74] the Emperor offered to Demophilos a continued occupation of the episcopal throne of the capital, if he would subscribe to the Nicene creed and its doctrine of the Homoousion. He stuck to his principles and refused, and two days later received an imperial sentence of exile and was escorted away with the inner circle of his entourage, though by no means all his clergy. Gregory received the imperial invitation to come with Theodosius in a state procession[75] to take control of the city,

71. *De Vita Sua*, vv. 1075-1112, PG 37.1103-1105.
72. "Those who regarded me as their own creation." *De Vita Sua*, v. 1128, PG 37.1106. Cf. v. 596, PG 37.1070.
73. *De Vita Sua*, vv. 1280-1281, PG 37.1117.
74. Orat. 33.15, PG 36.233.
75. An important propaganda exercise, considering the Gothic campaign was still undecided.

and (symbolically) its churches. Gregory would represent the Nicene cause the
emperor stood for. It was decided that the church of the Holy Apostles would be the
suitable venue for such a "statement": For Theodosius was at once claiming the
imperial mantle of the dynasty of Constantine, and imposing Constantine's creed
from 325. What more suitable place than Constantine's mausoleum-church?

Gregory, again with the hindsight of later reflection that his retirement after the
council brought him, thinks that Theodosius was:

> A good enough man as far as the faith goes, but he did not have that enthusiasm of
> spirit needed…to correct past errors using present opportunities… or perhaps it was
> his heroism or boldness that was lacking? Maybe some would refer this to his pru-
> dence, for he believed that persuasion, not repression was the right way forward.[76]

What this means, primarily, is his failure in Gregory's eyes to support him and
his two main items of agenda for the council of 381: the first being the settlement of
the Antiochene schism in a manner that would be acceptable to the western and
Alexandrian churches, and the second being the admission into the synodical statement of faith for the council of 381, of the explicit confession of the deity of the
Spirit as Homoousion with God. In late 381 Gregory knew that Theodosius had let
him down on these two cardinal matters of policy, and his enthusiasm for the supposed "defender of the faith" ebbed away very quickly.

As soon as the emperor arrived in his capital, however, Gregory was received in
audience and "treated with great respect both in the way he spoke to me, and in how
he listened." Gregory was delighted, and so sensible of his pleasure at finally coming
out into the light of day, that he reins in his description of his state audience, dismissing it as a "childishness" he should have risen above now that he is an old man.[77]
On the following day, the idea seems to have struck Theodosius that Gregory ought
to be in the state procession to the Holy Apostles:

> The emperor himself came to me in great joy and gave me such happiness… and the
> gist of it was he said: God hands the church through me to you because of your great
> efforts. I could hardly believe his words, until I saw them fulfilled, for the city was
> ready for revolt, so dreadful and terrible were the manifestations of its anger. They
> were refusing to give in even if they expected something unpleasant to happen,[78] but
> were determined to hold on tight to what they controlled. If they were forced out they
> had threatened to let loose their violent anger on me. The emperor's words made me
> shiver with delight, and also with the tremor of a fearful anticipation. I thought, O my
> Christ, of your invitations to those for whom you suffered, that they should often join
> you in suffering. Yet as once you led me into hardship, now you proved to be my com-
> forter in sorrows.[79]

76. *De Vita Sua*, vv. 12282-1293, PG 37.1117-1118.
77. *De Vita Sua*, vv. 1305-1310, PG 37.1119.
78. He means the Arian clergy primarily.
79. *De Vita Sua*, vv. 1305-1324, PG 37.1119-1120.

On Friday, November 27 Gregory found himself, suitably dressed up in splendid clothes for a change, accompanying the emperor to the church in a long royal parade of about a mile and a half down the great *Mese* of Constantinople from the palace, near to the hippodrome, to the church which was near the first city walls of Constantine, a spot now occupied by the Victory Mosque of Mehmed the Conqueror who demolished one of the most venerable sites in Christendom to build his own memorial.[80] An idea of the glory of what Holy Apostles was can be gained by its surviving "copy" in the beautiful Byzantine church of St Mark in Venice. In Gregory's time it was the principal church of the capital, surpassing in splendor the church of Hagia Sophia. Of the latter no trace remains of the building as it was in Gregory's time. Some fragments survive of the complete rebuilding which Theodosius II ordered in the fifth century, but only in the time of Justinian, after the fifth century building burned, did the present magnificent Hagia Sophia emerge, becoming thereafter the cathedral and imperial church. Holy Apostles was a basilica church with high marbled walls, all the way to the ceiling which was of gilded wood. It was in a cruciform shape like the other churches Constantine had built at Rome and Jerusalem.[81] Four porticoes surrounded the church and to the east of the apse was the annex of a rotunda, covered by an imposing cupola and containing the tomb of Constantine and the reliquary-sarcophagi of the twelve apostles.[82]

Armed soldiers were in place all down the route, and had stationed themselves already in the Holy Apostles for the emperor's reception. The procession passed through a generally noisy crowd, half protesting and half begging the emperor not to change their city's (Arian) faith. Gregory was an object of all the hostility they did not feel safe to direct at the emperor.[83] It was "like a town taken after a siege," he says[84] perhaps exaggerating by focusing on the religious aspect of that day's proceedings only, which touched him most nearly.[85] The colonnades and squares they passed through were full to overflowing. Gregory felt like a triumphant hero, carried away in the splendor of it all,[86] though his body was "feeble and broken with sickness." The day was overcast and gloomily dull. He could hear many people muttering, and obviously agreed with them internally that it was all "highly inauspicious." "To such people as this no visible sign is without significance, especially at a critical moment,

---

80. Fatih Mehmet Jami, on the Fevzi Pasha Caddesi. Roman columns from the Constantinian church survive in the mosque courtyard.
81. *Carmen de somnio Anastasiae*, vv. 59-60, PG 37.1258.
82. Cf. R. Janin (1969), pp. 46-55.
83. *De Vita Sua*, vv. 1325-1335, PG 37.1120.
84. *De Vita Sua*, v. 1335, PG 37.1121.
85. This should not be taken as a general attitude to the entry of Theodosius to Constantinople, for he appeared as their much hoped for deliverer from the Gothic menace.
86. *De Vita Sua*, v. 1336, PG 37.1121. A detail that belies the unremitting gloom of Theodosius' reception as if he had forcibly conquered the natives, something that Gregory has emphasized because he himself was the object of so much hostility. *De Vita Sua*, vv. 1331-1333, PG 37.1120-1121.

and I am not unconvinced by the argument too."[87] He just about made it to the church, he tells the reader, he was so exhausted by the walk. As the Nicenes took the buildings God seemed to have hidden his face in the skies, a cloud darkened the day even further. But, as they were actually passing through the great doors into the church itself, the cloud passed and dazzling rays of sunlight streamed through the windows to illuminate the shadowy building. To Gregory, and the members of the party, it was taken as a sign that God had sent his blessing on their work, and the psalms of praise commenced for morning service.[88] He tells us that the confidence of the worshippers (and the Anastasia congregation and Gregory's remaining clergy must have formed the core of the ministers present that day) was so uplifted by this regal "sign" in the heavens,[89] that they cried out in their enthusiasm that Gregory should there and then be nominated as the bishop of the capital.[90] The women were shouting this from the gallery, aristocrats were taking up the cry, until it became "an incredible thundering noise echoing off the walls." Gregory, now that he had received the highest "acclamation" of his whole career, was too weak to respond to it. He asked an officer to quieten the crowds, indicating the matter would be suitably decided on a later occasion, for now the prayers of thanksgiving had to be concluded properly. The congregation applauded him, and he received a sign of the emperor's approval too. When the service was over, and the imperial entourage left, Gregory felt immense relief. He had been terrified throughout the whole affair in case violence would break out. It had all passed off well, and despite his ambivalence about being involved in such a show of force he felt he had been vindicated righteously: "since the terrible sword had only been drawn for show and then allowed to fall back into the scabbard, meant only to check the wild behavior of the unruly crowds."[91]

The occupation of the church brought about more or less a common acceptance of the new state of affairs. Gregory says that the populace did not particularly like it, and kept on emitting groans like the giant Typhon imprisoned under volcanic Mount Aetna, but their "insolent behavior was ended" now that he was clearly under the imperial protection.[92] He himself remained very uneasy about the use of force to establish religious policy. It was something that he had denounced as one of the worst excesses of the Arian ascendancy. In this part of his autobiographical account he shows the signs of anxiety in being part of a new and arguably oppressive policy

---

87. *De Vita Sua*, vv. 1344-1346, PG 37.1121.
88. *De Vita Sua*, vv. 1355-1370, PG 37.1122.
89. Gregory is motivated to give the incident of the sun such a large place in the poem not only because signs were commonly looked for at that period (an imperial "taking of the auspices" as it were), but more specifically because it mirrors the sign in the heavens which blessed the beginning of the rule of Constantine, the founder of the church. The "sign in the sky" parallels Theodosius with Constantine: "In this you shall be victorious."
90. *De Vita Sua*, vv. 1372-1381, PG 37.1123-1124.
91. *De Vita Sua*, v. 1395, PG 37.1125.
92. *De Vita Sua*, vv. 1402-1406, PG 37.1126.

himself. He pressed for "moderation in all things"[93] and says that this was the emperor's first intention also, "much preferring persuasion to repression."[94] This would be a policy that Gregory would not renounce even now that he was in such a politically advantageous position. Equally, it was this, he admits, that called down on his head the most severe criticism from the "miserable crowd of young hotheads" who took it as another sign of his weakness.[95] Here, I think, he is referring to the group of younger bishops from the Antiochene metropolitanate, who so violently opposed his policies soon after when he was president of the council, after Meletios' death. The leader of the party was Diodore of Tarsus, and it is another sign that even his former Antiochene allies came to regard him as expendable once they arrived in the city in spring of 381. For them Gregory was just too gentle and accommodating to be of any use. Apart from these bishops, Gregory had great difficulties put in his way by the imperial eunuchs, who were in a new phase of excitement after the emperor arrived back into the palace, and making large sums of cash by accepting bribes to regulate admission to the chambers. Gregory was disgusted by their venality, and decided to:

> Withdraw with some vestige of self respect (for I would be rather missed than hated), and so I devoted the large part of my time to God, and to purification, abandoning the doors of the powerful to others.[96]

This probably indicates that Gregory did not have enough gold to ease his way into a regular communication with Theodosius and, even if he did, was not willing to play the politics of the game. It was another signal to the imperial court that here was an unusual man indeed, but perhaps not one who could fulfil the manifold roles required of the archbishop at the very seat of world power.

Yet Gregory was not entirely passive in this time around winter of 380, now the emperor was present. From the time he was installed in the Holy Apostles he knew that his orations would be heard by the court on the services of the Sundays and feast days, and he made some dramatic political moves of his own, from the basis of his real circle of influence, and his favored home ground, the church pulpit. This had suddenly been transformed from the makeshift bema of the little Anastasia, into the great gilded throne commanding the basilical nave of the emperor's own church. *Oration* 36 was the first large-scale rhetorical performance before the Emperor in the church of the Holy Apostles, probably on the first Sunday following his installation as imperial preacher, either November 29 or Sunday, December 7, 380.[97]

He begins by modestly acknowledging the plaudits of the people (it was the custom to applaud loudly when the orator was speaking in church), wondering aloud how they can so value such a "poor old foreigner." Moreschini is probably right in his

93. *De Vita Sua*, vv. 1412-1419, PG 37.1126-1127.
94. *De Vita Sua*, v. 1293, PG 37.1118.
95. *De Vita Sua*, vv. 1407-1411, PG 37.1126.
96. *De Vita Sua*, vv. 1432-1435, PG 37.1128.
97. Bernardi (1968), p. 192.

supposition that the words are tinged with a certain irony,[98] considering the way he
remembers how he had been ridiculed as a poor foreigner when he first came. He
wants to tell this larger crowd that he is by no means an innovator in the faith. He is
not the first to preach them orthodox doctrine, rather he is the successor of the truth
after a long time in abeyance. He succeeds the righteous Alexander, he says, "that
great defender and preacher of the trinity" whose disciples his congregation rightly
are. Alexander had been the Nicene bishop of Constantinople at the time when the
emperor Constantine had demanded that Arius be received back into the communion of the church. Alexander, in alliance with Athanasius, had not wished to signal
the reconciliation of Arius. The tale is told graphically by Athanasius.[99] As Arius was
being led by imperial escort to be received in the city, he was seized by an excruciat-
ing pain in the bowels. He had to make an emergency stop in a public latrine, where
"his bowels burst like those of Judas and he came to a wretched end." The manner of
his death (long a debating point whether it was a symptom of cancer or poison) was
used by the Nicenes as a propaganda coup. God had struck the arch-heretic down
on the very road to an enforced "communion" with the orthodox. Gregory uses references to Arius' death on other occasions in his works.[100] Here it serves to validate
his own claims to succession in the pulpit.[101] He is not an innovator, but the heir of
the Constantinopolitan Nicene Alexander. He intends to draw out the analogy for a
particular point: Once, long before, an emperor had determined to fix in place a
hierarch that had not been wanted by the bishop of the city. The cause was an
unrighteous one, and God had intervened to prevent it. No matter how powerful
the emperor's will, God had determined it would not happen. In his own case, the
people had determined not to accept such a hierarch as Gregory. The emperor had
determined to effect it. If God had not willed it to be so, however, no power on
earth could have brought Gregory to where he stood today. His presence, resuming
the true Nicene tradition of the Constantinopolitan church, is what God has
intended. So, he is not bringing them new "springs of doctrine" as an innovator;
rather, he is opening up for them the long-sealed wells in the desert which the servants of Isaac the patriarch opened up in ancient times.[102] Gregory uses the image of
the dramatic reversal of his fortunes at Constantinople, from his time when he was
decried as a fool, to the few days previously when he was loudly "acclaimed" as the
new bishop, to demonstrate that God is guiding his hand. Even so, the installation
of him as bishop by popular acclamation, he wonders, might be "more enthusiastic
than legal."[103] It is evident that even when he was in place as the *de facto* bishop of
the city, he still wished for the choice to be canonically validated by the council that

98. SC vol. 318 (1985), p. 241, n. 1.
99. Athanasius, *Letter to the Bishops of Egypt and Libya*, para. 19, PG 25.581; *Letter to Serapion*.
100. Orat. 21.13, PG 35.1096; Orat. 25.8, PG 35.1209.
101. Orat. 36.1, PG 36.235.
102. Orat. 36.2, PG 36.265.
103. Orat. 36.2, PG 36.268.

was soon to meet. His words seem to me an indication that Theodosius, after the events of November 27, did communicate to Gregory that he would support him in his position as Nicene archbishop. He swears before his audience that he never came to the city "coveting the spouse" of another bishop. He had no intention of taking this see for himself, merely of coming to preach for the orthodox faith.[104] If his opponents do not believe him, he has to appeal to God who "looks into the heart of men."[105] Gregory tells his audience that he is an old ascetic, his own man. He is like the undersea anemones who are not buffeted around by the crashing waves. He shall stand firm, and stand for the truth.[106]

Now he gives his episcopal "judgments" and first calls on the obedience of his "new flock."[107] He wants them merely to confess a true belief. Here, in contrast to the elaborated doctrine he set out in the *Five Theological Orations*, he sketches a confessional standard of the most generic type. The people need to give

> A firm and solid confession of the Father, Son and Holy Spirit; adding nothing, subtracting nothing, in no way diminishing the single Godhead...for it is a diminution when people introduce different degrees of nature in the Godhead. If they dare do this, send them packing as vermin in the church, as poisoners of the truth.[108]

This avoided uttering the keyword of the Homoousion, but it has clearly implied it for any who knew their theology; and for those who did not, it was an entirely moderate and reasonable sermon, such as would make them wonder what all the fuss was about in regard to accepting this new theologian. After speaking in this way to the people, Gregory addressed the emperor, on their behalf, as the spokesperson for the populace who could exercise *parrhesia* before the mighty. Gregory commands the emperor to "respect the purple" and makes the interesting case that the emperor is not above the law: "for my discourse shall set laws even to those who make them." The world has been given into Theodosius' hands by God, Gregory says, but he must always remember that God is above all. He shall be "as a god" before the face of his people, but must remember that: "God holds the heart of the king in his own hands,"[109] a text from Proverbs that Gregory seems to apply as much as a warning to the ruler, as any affirmation of his right to dominion.[110]

There follows a long series of episcopal instructions.[111] The courtiers must learn some humility and be loyal to their lord. The aristocracy must strive to be noble in

104. Orat. 36.6, PG 36.272-273.
105. 1 Sam 16:7; Orat. 36.7, PG 36.273.
106. Orat. 36.9, PG 36.276-277.
107. Orat. 36.9 shows that he was waiting only the confirmation of his episcopal appointment from the council, not its award. He has taken the acclamation and the imperial gift as canonically legitimate election to a new see.
108. Orat. 36.10, PG 36.277.
109. Prov 21:1.
110. Orat. 36.11, PG 36.277.
111. Orat. 36.11-12, PG 36.277-280.

behavior as well as birth. The intellectuals must not boast of their intelligence until they have learned the "first of all sciences," true belief.[112] The rich must learn from the psalms[113] not to set their heart on wealth, and even to "unballast the barges a little" so that they can get a better navigational control of their own lives, and come to the aid of the poor who surround them on every side, rather than bloating themselves with excessive feasting. Gregory ends with an appeal to the congregation of what he calls the primary church in the world. Nowhere is there any mention of Alexandria or its jurisdictional claims.

> You are the citizens of the great city. You are the first in rank immediately after that first-ranking city,[114] and perhaps do not even allow that the primacy lies there. Henceforth I want you to excel by a primacy in virtue, not in vices.[115]

If it was his unwillingness to pressure Theodosius for a more vigorous prosecution of the Nicene cause[116] that lost Gregory the support of the Antiochene bishops who were soon to arrive, it was words such as these that earned him the hostility of the Alexandrians and Romans, neither of whom would abandon their ecclesiastical pretensions to dominate the imperial city and its affairs. The conciliar canons of the council of 381, themselves to be heavily underlined by the canons of Chalcedon in 451, made steps to remedy this question of historical canonical precedence. It was, and remained, a flash point of church politics that initiated a long chain of internal Christian divisions lasting to the present day.

That month of December 380 saw another interesting politically motivated oration preached in the Holy Apostles. It is typical of Gregory to focus on something that had very close relation to the personal happiness of people, rather than on the grand scale. Of all the subjects he could set in motion for a lobbying of a change in the law, he seems to have asked for a reconsideration of marriage legislation. And to that end presented an extended consideration of the biblical basis of Christian marital law. It is the most extensive piece of biblical exegesis that has survived in his corpus, and occupies that place, probably as an example of practically orientated exegesis. The sermon has reference to four classes of people: the legislators, the virgins, the imperial eunuchs, and the wealthy or the aristocrats. It seems, therefore, that it was a discourse preached before the emperor as part of a chancery meeting for legislative consultation, rather than a generically addressed church homily.

Gregory has been consulted on the question of legal penalties suitable for adultery, and the legitimate causes for divorce. It is possibly one of the queries that Theodosius, who had been brought up under Latin canon law, raised immediately he came to the East and noticed that Greek Christian theologians were more willing to admit the

---

112. Orat. 36.12, PG 36.280.
113. Orat. 36.12; Ps 61:11.
114. I.e., Rome.
115. Orat. 36.12, PG 36.280.
116. A policy that was certainly advocated once they had removed Gregory.

ecclesiastical legitimacy of Roman state law concerning marriages than were their western colleagues.[117]

Gregory begins his consideration of the question of the relation of Roman to canon law on divorce by beginning with the wider Gospel context, not the immediate seeking for biblical proof texts, which he says is not a good way of resolving a truly theological question. His first starting point is the character of Christ's "law." This, he says, is philanthropic and inclusively merciful. Christ is like the fisherman who goes out with a wide drag net to bring all manner of fish into his boat. He is generously inclusive of all those fish, "that is human beings who are swimming in the turbulent and sorrowful waters of this life."[118] Throughout all his earthly life Christ consistently manifested this compassionate approach to human beings. It ought, therefore, to be the guiding premise that leads us to consider the specific question about marriage, but before reaching that Gregory takes the occasion to show how it relates to theological positions on the Arian question too—for many Arian exegetes have taken the sufferings and limitations of Jesus to be evidence that the Word cannot possibly be co-equal to the eternal deity.[119] Gregory answers that such a conclusion denigrates true theology, and mistakes his compassionate economy for revelations about theology. It is the standard answer he gave throughout the *Theological Orations*, that Arian exegetical attacks on the Nicene position make the fundamental category mistake of confusing *Theologia* and *Economia*. In regard to the question about marriage, here we have quintessentially a question about *Economia*: how God deals with the imposition of law over his creatures, and through law leads them to salvation.

As the starting point in the biblical text Gregory focuses on the pharisaic question to Jesus about the legitimate reasons for divorce,[120] a question he regards as a "tempting" of Jesus, since it is impertinent to ask the maker of marriage, the creative generator of all humankind, such paltry, narrowly focused questions.[121] In return Christ demonstrates his cosmic sense of the implications of the economia by giving them the answer which is a question in return: Do you not see how God made them in the beginning as male and female? Only in the context of this kind of cosmic economia can one rightly approach the question in hand, Gregory implies. But when he does turn to the issue, his is no theoretical generality. He comes into the precise issue with sharp focus and a finely honed agenda. Why, he asks, does Roman law punish the female adulteress with severe penalties, but a man who commits adultery has no penalty under the law? The answer is that the law was obviously made by men. "I do not accept this law. I cannot approve this custom," Gregory

117. Cf. H. Crouzel, *L'Église primitive face au divorce du Ier au Vième siècle* (Paris, 1971).
118. Orat. 37.1, PG 36.284.
119. Orat. 37.4, PG 36.285–288.
120. Mt 19:1–9; cf. also Mt 5:32.
121. Orat. 37.5, PG 36.288.

says. It is a legislation that is unjustly hard on women and children, who suffer from it while men are released with impunity. Such a law cannot reflect the God who is equitably even-handed to all.[122] What possible justification could be brought forward for this uneven treatment of women in a Christian context of legislation? Gregory raises some of the arguments he has heard advanced. Is woman not the cause of the fall? Well, he replies, Eve sinned, but Adam did no better, and have such thinkers not considered that Christ redeemed both Adam and Eve since those days—so how can such texts apply as paradigms of Christian behavior? Is not Christ honored primarily as a male, that is one coming "from the seed of David"? Certainly, Gregory says, this is a title of Christ, but it celebrates his ancestry purely from his mother's side. In contrast to all these weak biblical paradigms, one ought to consider the apostolic revelation that the husband in a marriage ought to reverence his wife as he would reverence Christ himself. It is the woman who is the icon of the Word of God in this case.[123]

Yet, if the latter is a strong biblical paradigm, he continues, it seems to suggest that second marriage is not permissible in the Church (an ancient prohibition of the Early Church's canon law that had been relaxed in later centuries in accordance with the prevailing secular law). And if second marriages are not legitimate, what does this say about third marriages, which were also tolerated by secular law? Gregory then gives his conclusion about the relation of the canon to the secular law in this matter. It is his first episcopal "judgment" as bishop of Constantinople, and was to have a determinative effect on Eastern canon law. First marriages are "according to the law," that is they reflect the exact intent of Christ's law of reverence for the icon. Second marriages are not exactly in accordance with Christ's law (though they do correspond to secular law), but they are not to be forbidden in the Church because they are "according to indulgence," that is they are permitted to Christians on account of an economy, so that their weaknesses will not close them off from grace. Christ's word of law, as Gregory implies, is seriously meant as the right way, and so marriage ought to be a unique lifelong event; but when it does not happen this way and the marriage bond is broken, the overarching principle of Christ's law also has to be invoked, that is the compassion which is the motivation for all his legislations and commandments, a compassion that seeks to rescue and save the mass of humankind. This is why the economy of indulgence in the second marriage, does not contradict the first law of single marriages, but refines it in the event of a lapse according to the deeper "intentionality" of the legislator. As to third marriages, Gregory does not forbid them either but advises they should be subject to some kind of penalty. If the first marriage is "legal," and the second "indulgential," the third is "transgressive." Anything beyond this, he says, is "swinish."[124] This very important "word of judgment" from the imperial bishop became, in all its constitutive elements, the canon law of the Eastern churches ever afterwards

122. Orat. 37.6, PG 36.289.
123. Orat. 37.7, PG 36.292.
124. Orat. 37.8, PG 36.292.

in regard to marriage. It is interesting to see Gregory's psychological character as a compassionate and carefully observant man (celibate ascetic though he was) so abundantly evidenced in that one area of society where so much joy and yet so much misery is evidenced in human affairs: intimate domestic relations. His concern is dominated by two equally marked principles: a remedy for an unjust and unequal treatment of women under the law, and a desire to inform Church law with compassionate realism, and take the stated laws of Christ beyond their fundamentalist significance to their ultimate goal, that is the mercifully economic salvation of men and women who are "swimming in a turbulent sea of grief."

The second point to consider once the legal principle has been established, is given for Gregory by the terms of the pharisaic question in the Gospel. Christ was asked if a woman could be set aside for "every cause" or not.[125] Here Gregory takes the strict view that Christ's intent was only to allow separation on the grounds of infidelity. In all other matters (and here Gregory evidences a perspective limited to a male view that seems predominantly concerned with nagging, aggressive wives) one ought "to endure patiently and seek to correct behavior by education." The secular law, he says, grants divorce for any reason at all. Christ does not do this, and so the secular law in this regard ought to be corrected by bringing it into harmony with the Gospel.[126] If, like the Pharisees, one replies that "it is better not to marry in this case" it is true, but not for such reasons. The truth is that the wise person will see that marrying is not a source of unalloyed bliss if only they take time to consider the evidence before their eyes: "the grief of widows and orphans, the dreadful funeral cortège that so often follows after the wedding,[127] and all the comedy and tragedy that is connected with it."[128] But this is the character of life, and men and women ought to be detached enough to set their sights on God's will not their own desires. Marriage is a good thing when followed according to God's law, and so is virginity, though the latter is even more honorable because it takes more account of the transience of all earthly joys.[129] It cannot be followed by everyone, as not everyone has the aptitude or the discipline necessary for the long prayers and fasts required to preserve chastity in this difficult way,[130] but the application of discipline, along with the gift of God, will allow the virgin to live surpassing nature, just as water when forced through a conduit pipe gains a force that can even make it run against gravity in a fountain. Like the splendid fountains of Constantinople, virginity is *contra naturam*,

125. The original context of the rabbinic dispute in the time of Jesus was the controversy between the schools of Shammai and Hillel, as to whether a wife could be divorced because of "any reason" or "solely for adultery."
126. Orat. 37.8, PG 36.292.
127. He is thinking, perhaps, of his own cousin, Euphemios, whose death occurred so soon after his own wedding feast in Cappadocia. Cf. *Epitaph* 29, PG 38.25; *Epitaph* 33, PG 38.27.
128. Orat. 37.9, PG 36.293.
129. Orat. 37.9-10, PG 36.293-296.
130. Orat. 37.13-15, PG 36.297-301.

but a spectacular sign of the Kingdom of God.[131] His oration finishes by referring to the other saying of Jesus, in reply to those who objected to his marriage advice: the recommendation of the state of being eunuchs for the Kingdom. Gregory has taken care not to apply the image of "eunuchs for the Kingdom" to refer to the "virgins of the Lord." He sees the term eunuch, almost always, as a term of disparagement. The words about eunuchs are, in this instance, addressed directly to the imperial eunuchs gathered in the room. From several earlier references we know that Gregory regarded them as his main continuing locus of opposition. He complains that they worked against him, and stirred up theological controversies. These, of course, were generally traditionalist Homoian Arians, still loyal to the exiled Demophilos, and probably still hoping (with good reason) that they could soon oust the Cappadocian and install another bishop closer to their way of thinking.

Gregory goes on the attack and tells them that the Savior's words about eunuchs made so by men[132] is no commendation of their state of life. What really matters is not a natural condition of sexlessness; rather, the desire to strive after spiritual chastity, and this amounts to theological orthodoxy. Even though it is late in the day, he says, it is time for the eunuchs to "show some manly intelligence" and stop scurrying around the women's quarters stirring up theological gossip.[133] There is a clear indication in the text at this point that there was some muttering in the ranks of the eunuchs. He defers to it, and says that he will end with something more positive to say for them. This is where his exegesis of "those who made themselves eunuchs for the kingdom" comes into play, for Gregory applies it purely to the question of orthodoxy, and concludes that some of the eunuchs manifested an extraordinary grace. Even without the teaching of real priests and bishops (so he dismisses the whole range of Arian incumbents of the see for the last forty years) some have manifested a purity of faith that is remarkable. Such men must continue to expunge their passions, and they will fulfil the Savior's commendatory remarks about eunuchs. The goal is to cast out all remnants of Arian and Sabellian heresy, he says, and confess the deity of the Son in a trinitarian faith.[134]

His next Oration was for the great winter feast of Christmas. It is not certain whether at this period Christmas was celebrated at Constantinople on December 25, which eventually became the standard Western date for the celebration, or on January 6, which for centuries was the Eastern Church's main Nativity festival. The late fourth century, when Gregory writes, was a time when the Eastern and Western Christian calendars were being increasingly standardized, and expanded into a range of other great feasts beyond the Paschal cycle.[135] The arrival of Theodosius, a Spanish

---

131. Orat. 37.12, PG 36.296-297.
132. Mt 19:12.
133. Orat. 37.16-18, PG 36.301-304.
134. Orat. 37.22, PG 36.308.
135. Mossay (1965) has shown that already in the late fourth century the Christmas feast of December 25 was being observed in Cappadocia. This does not answer what the tradition was at

Christian, might also have accelerated the Eastern adoption of the date of December 25, although I am of the opinion that Gregory's *Oration* 38, *On The Holy Theophany*, refers to the series of Nativity celebration held on January 6 (Theophany in the sense of the revelation of God to the nations, that is Epiphany day).[136] The Oration is thus the first of that momentous year 381,[137] and forms a liturgical series of festal orations (numbers 38-40 all making retrospective reference to the preceding discourse) concerned with the mysteries of the birth of Christ, and baptism. The latter connection is provided from the major focus of the celebration of the feast of Epiphany in the Eastern Church, which did not so much center around the western theme of the advent of the Magi, but more so the baptism of Christ in the waters of the Jordan, which was his "epiphany" to the world as the Son of God, vindicated as such by the divine voice that was heard as he emerged from the river. The sacrament of baptism, which was also celebrated at this time of year (not merely at Pascha or Pentecost) was known then as the Holy Illumination, which gives the point to *Oration* 39 being entitled "On the Holy Lights." The series culminated in an actual state ceremony of baptism, and *Oration* 40 is the oration delivered on that occasion, an event I take to be synonymous with the reception in January 381 of the aged Gothic chieftain Athanarich, into federation with the Roman empire.[138] At Athanarich's baptism Theodosius would have adopted the Gothic warlord as "his son" by standing as his sponsor. The ceremony held an immense military and political significance at a propaganda level, indicating the way in which the Gothic campaign could be brought to a positive resolution. At this time Theodosius still very much needed some propaganda victories. He elevated Athanarich, the Gothic leader before his present chief adversary Fritigern rose to dominate the Goths, as a symbol of how a solution by treaty could be achieved by subverting the current rebellious Gothic leaders.

Constantinople at this date, and Gregory would have conformed to local custom. Baumstark's thesis that he was the originator of the December 25 feast at the capital, based on his exegesis of the words: "I am the *exarchos* of the feast of his generation which we have just celebrated" (Orat. 39.14) is rightly dismissed by Gallay (SC vol. 358 [1990], pp. 14-15) as an over-exegesis of the significance of the word *exarchos*.

136. Jerome repeats what he might have heard from Gregory at this time, that the birth of Christ in the flesh is not an epiphany (manifestation) as such, since it is a hidden event. The epiphany proper is the feast of his revelation in the waters of the Jordan; cf. Jerome, Comm. in Ezek 1.

137. Gallay (1943), pp. 153-159, assigns it to 379, and lists the various opinions over dating which have generally hesitated over placing the discourse. Since Gregory came only to the city after the autumn of 379 by invitation of the synod of Antioch, and was gone by June of 381, winter of 380/381 is the only Christmas feast he celebrated publicly. The reference in the speech to his being a small and humble stranger, are not indications that he spoke before the arrival of Theodosius, but are uttered before a large congregation including many of his former opponents (especially the eunuchs) as ironic reminders of how they are now thronging to hear him since he was socially acceptable, but had formerly despised him before the emperor came.

138. Cf. Williams and Friell (1994), pp. 31-34; Ammianus, *Rerum Gestarum* 31.4.1; 31.4.13

Oration 38 invites his large congregation to celebrate the birth of Christ joyfully, but not so elaborately and expensively, with luxurious banquets exceeding good taste and moderation, that they fall into the trap of holding feasts in the "Hellenic manner," forgetting all about the poor who are scandalized by this excess. In Gregory's opinion the enjoyment of luxury while others are in want is "like holding dung precious."[139] The main section of his oration then proceeds to speak about the meaning of the birth of Christ. His concern is to clarify for the people who have been so used to Arianizing exegesis from the pulpit, that the events of Christ's birth do not mean that the Word of God is inferior to the Eternal Father. The distinction between Theology proper and the Economy of salvation has to be observed.[140] In its own nature the deity is completely simple. This means it is either completely comprehensible (as Eunomios taught) or completely incomprehensible. The latter is actually the case. In terms of God's proper nature, it is known only to Himself, not even the Seraphim can glimpse what it is, since it remains behind the veil of the Holy of Holies.[141] Arian exegesis, however, had generally taken the events of Christ's life such as his birth and sufferings to be explicit evidence that the Christ was far from "simple" in his ontology. By being involved in the vicissitudes of history he was, therefore, demonstrably "complex" and, by strict logical inference, unarguably not divine in the sense the Eternal and Changeless God was. Gregory wants, then, to use the episode of the birth of Christ in the present feast to demonstrate the flaw in this exegetical process. The Incarnation is not the doctrine of God, as such, but the doctrine of God's economy of salvation for humankind. To mistake the one for the other is a major category mistake. If his people wish to set the Christmas feast in its proper context they have to see it as part of the outreach of God to the world. It is his fundamental energy of "epiphany" that is at issue in this festival of the Theophany. For Gregory, the first movement of the epiphany is the creation of the first order of being: the angelic powers. These do not have absolute simplicity of being such as God possesses, but are close to it because they are simple spiritual natures. Like God they are spiritual lights, and stable in their ontology.[142] After the angelic orders comes the second creation which is humankind, composed of material and spiritual elements, a compound of earthly and heavenly creation, midway between angels and beasts: "set by the Word as a majestic smallness on the earth."[143] The human being is like a new kind of angel worshipping God in a tensile balance of spiritual aspiration and material limitation. Because of the material propensities of this unstable ontology, humankind fell away from the original pure obedience of God, and eventually came to a pitch of wickedness in human affairs that called out to the Word of God to effect the ontological rescue of the human race. This the Word decided to do by becoming

139. Orat. 38.5, PG 36.316.
140. Orat. 38.7-8, PG 36.317-320.
141. Orat. 38.8, PG 36.320.
142. Orat. 38.9, PG 36.320-321.
143. Orat. 38.11, PG 36.324.

intimately associated with his second creation (as he was already intimately associated with the angelic first creation) by being incarnate himself:

> Once I had a share in the divine image. I did not keep to it. So he assumed my flesh so that he might at one and the same time rescue the image and immortalize the flesh. He offered us a second communion, even more wonderful than the first.[144]

This movement of God's compassion, however, must be consistently referred to the context of his economic salvation. It does not reveal theological verities *per se*. In other words the long list of limitations, and involvements in relativized history, which Arian exegetes have taken as evidence for their denial of the Homoousion, do not prove that the Word of God is not a simple divine being, beyond all time and limit. On the contrary, the biblical evidence proves that he is a divine being who has a divinely expansive philanthropy and so assumes an active economy in time and space for the re-creation of his own handiwork.[145] Gregory applies a vivid allegorical exegesis: in coming in the incarnation for this economy, Christ is like the widow of the parable who "lit the candle of the flesh and swept out the whole household in search of the precious coin (of the lost image)."[146] All the references to Christ being sent, or being subordinate, or suchlike, must be taken in reference to the human nature the Word of God adopted.[147] He ends[148] with a passage that encapsulates much about his habitual approach to scriptural exegesis: his hearers must read the biblical stories as if they too were primary actors in the drama (for so they are). They must immerse themselves in the revealed truths and live out from them: flee into Egypt with Christ, even taste the gall of his vinegar. Finally, go so far as to die with God and be raised with him.[149]

Gregory argues that in such a true exegesis of the text, which is a correlation of the life of the believer and the ongoing work of the divine economy of salvation in the present age: "We shall contemplate the great God, and be looked at by him, the Lord who is worshipped and glorified in Trinity."[150] The theological content of this oration is a restatement of most of what he has said in all his speeches in the city from 380 onwards, but designed now in a most accessible way for a much larger audience of laity who have been accustomed for many years to a different approach to Christological exegesis altogether. Gregory emerges as a very good teacher indeed, shaping his message to the capacities of the many different audiences he had, and communicating it with vivid imagery and a great gift for graphically memorable synopsis.

144. Orat. 38.13, PG 36.325.
145. Orat. 38.14, PG 36.328.
146. Alluding to Lk 15:8-9.
147. Orat. 38.15, PG 36.328-329.
148. Orat. 38.18, PG 36.332-333.
149. The same idea of exegetical "immersion" is found in Orat. 39.14, PG 36.349.
150. Orat. 38.18, PG 36.333.

Oration 39 was the text he delivered on the vigil of the Epiphany, January 5, 381. The reference to it in *Oration* 38.16, as something that will "come very shortly," indicates that the earlier discourse for the Theophany (the birth of Christ) was given on the day before, and that which follows (40) is the main homily of the festival of "The Feast of Lights." The latter was a two-day liturgical celebration focused on the baptism of Christ in the Jordan, which began with a vesperal service and culminated on the second day (the third day of the triduum) with the celebration of the sacrament itself. Gregory had to prepare a series of Orations that would be suitable for the whole gathering of the imperial court, and for the retinue of Gothic warriors, which had all come together for the state occasion of the baptism of Athanarich, a cardinal point in the ceremonial enactment of the federation of this section of their old enemies. It was not only a propaganda exercise, it also marked the beginning of the end of the ascendancy of Fritigern the Gothic warlord who had spearheaded the recent rebellion of the Goths. The event signaled the success of that very old Roman politico-military strategy: divide and conquer. The suite of Orations, including the overall *tendenz* of *Oration* 38, is also concerned with giving a short synopsis of the whole gist of the Christian gospel. It was designed like this for traditional reasons, that the bishop had to present a preliminary catechesis of the Faith to those who were about to be baptized: the fact that Athanarich needed some explanation of what his new God would be is one part of Gregory's motivation. The chance to present a Nicene correction to Arianism, is another. And we may suppose that a third aspect is the desire of Theodosius, on the first liturgical occasion afforded by the calendar, to celebrate his own baptism by the rites and ceremonies which had necessarily been omitted when Acholius of Thessalonike had initiated him with the *clinicus* baptism, on what he thought was his deathbed.[151] Now that he was in his own capital, as undisputed emperor of the East, it was a fitting occasion to celebrate the event, and Gregory was called upon to supply the speeches. The "initiation" of a Christian emperor of the Romans had to have the ceremonies marked as well as any Hellene (such as Julian) who had signified the tenor of his proposed rule by the character of the initiations into mysteries which he chose to undergo. This social aspect of the imperial initiation was the reason Gregory spends so much time in the discourse talking about the other Mystery Initiations that were available to the non-Christian aristocracy, and demonstrating how inferior they all were to the sacrament of baptism.

Oration 39 shows a strong attention to mystery language. Gregory begins by explaining how this feast of lights is a celebration of the baptism of Christ, and recalls "the words from heaven" which surprisingly turn out to be not the expected verses of Mt 3:17, but the Johannine texts: "I am the Light of the World," and the prologue verses on the light that shines in the darkness; scriptural passages which are ideationally connected to baptism by their evangelical contexts of invitation to

151. February 380 according to Sozomen, HE 7.4; the less likely date of late in 380 is given by Socrates in HE 5.6.

rebirth and discipleship.[152] He asks at the end of his *exordium*: "Do you not see how powerful this mystery is? Are you not already exalted by my words?" He is very conscious that his logos will serve as the mystical purification for those approaching the Logos in this mystery initiation, and so casts himself as orator in the role of Hierophant.[153] The usual listing of extremes to be avoided follows, and he contrasts the celebrational method of feasts of "The Law," and those of the Hellenes. The Christian feasts are not like this at all. Though here he admits there are some similarities between baptism and the ancient Greek mysteries. The latter are "shameful goings-on" that vaguely mimic forms of the Christian mystery of salvation. The list he gives is very extensive: Zeus, Rhea, Demeter and Eleusis, Dionysian rituals, the cults of Semele, Aphrodite, Artemis, Hecate, Orpheus, Dodona, Delphi, the Magan sacrifices, Chaldaean astrology, Thracian rituals, the liturgies of Mithras, Isis and Osiris, and Apis at Memphis.[154] He will stop, however, at the worship of reptiles and other ridiculous things, or the even more stupid veneration of idols carved by masons.[155] The long list rhetorically relativizes the Greek Mysteries, and undermines their claims to social exclusivity, which was an important aspect to Gregory's purpose here, with such a prestigious audience in attendance. The whole catalogue of the Mysteries as the Greeks celebrate them is characterized as "the games of children at play."[156] Since they are subrational, one cannot discuss them with "men of sense,"[157] this is why they prefer to guard the mystical silence. But as the Christian mystery celebrates the divine Logos, Gregory will initiate rational mystics with the words of his discourse. The essence of the Christian mystery, he says, is to move on beyond the limitations of our present earthly form. This will take place in a progressive ascent. Its stages are the turning away from idols and demonic oppression which serves to deify the base passions in the cause of keeping rational beings enslaved to the lower senses.[158] Then follow the three stages of Christian ascent: the beginning of the observance of the commandments, the increasing purification of the soul, the strengthening of the illumination of the spirit. The final stage is the constant reaching out to the supreme good that transcends all earthly reality.[159]

Gregory's Oration is actually following the traditional structure of the episcopal prebaptismal catechesis, though in a highly original and personal form. The major elements of that traditional catechesis are all here: the act of renunciation of pagan cult, the instruction in moral behavior, and then the exorcisms that preceded the theological catechesis and the baptism proper. It is precisely here that Gregory too speaks of exorcism.

152. Jn 1:9; 8:12; 3:3; 1:5.
153. Orat. 39.2, PG 36.336.
154. Orat. 39.4-5, PG 36.337-140.
155. Orat. 39.6, PG 36.341.
156. Orat. 39.3, PG 36.337; Orat. 39.7, PG 36.341.
157. Orat. 39.3, PG 36.336-337.
158. Orat. 39.7, PG 36.341; Orat. 39.8, PG 36.341-344.
159. Orat. 39.8, PG 36.344.

This necessary activity will be accomplished by all who "sweep out their houses" and assiduously practice the discipline necessary to keep them morally clean. He alludes to the story of the woman possessed of seven demons, who is told to beware in case they return, and she finds herself in a worse state than before.[160] Having thus symbolically concluded all the three necessary preliminaries for baptism, (the renunciation rite, a moral *paranesis* and exorcism), Gregory ends the first part of his discourse by noting that his logos has served as the mental purification of the hearers.[161] Now that they are properly purified he will go ahead and reveal to them the mysteries of the inner initiation of Christian truth: how God enlightens the believer.

This is where his Trinitarian exposition commences. The threefold deity is the God in whom this bishop will baptize. The exposition that follows is another digest of his Trinitarian and Christological teaching, obviously designed for a common and mixed audience. God is three in hypostasis, or propriety, or prosopon (the words, he says, do not matter) and one in substance. The main thing is that the three lights add up to a single light

> divided without division, and united in distinction, if I may put it like this, for the Godhead is one in three, and the three are one in whom the Godhead is; or to speak more precisely, the three *are* the single Godhead.[162]

Gregory coins new technical terms. The Son comes from the Father "generatedly" if one considers that the Father is the First Cause of the Godhead, though this has to be understood as a timeless origination that does not necessitate priority and sequence, or superiority and inferiority. If one likes, Gregory says, one can also confess that the Son is "unoriginate" if that is taken to mean he is eternal and fully God, since he shares the character of the Father's unoriginateness, and himself has no origin in time.[163] "The Spirit comes forth from the Father not generatedly in the manner of the Son, but processionally, and here I must coin a word for the sake of clarity."[164] The Christological doctrines are then given, equally summatively. In describing the earthly incarnation, Gregory habitually leans on paradoxes to evoke the "two natures" so mystically brought into symbiosis. The Christological union is approached as a symbiosis that evokes a paradoxical "joint condition" of absolute freedom, and conditioned suffering. Gregory's Christological language is here leaning to the Athanasian tradition, and Cyril, in later centuries, will follow him in pressing the language of Christological paradox from a similar perspective of the

---

160. Orat. 39.10, PG 36.345.
161. Orat. 39.11, PG 36.345.
162. Orat. 39.11, PG 36.345-348.
163. Orat. 39.12, PG 36.348. This answers the chief objection of the Neo-Arian position that "Ingenerate" is a supreme title of divinity. Gregory agrees, in part, to attribute it in this sense to the Son also. It is an approach he takes to convince the large Arian contingent in the church. In the *Five Theological Orations* he preferred to demolish the initial premise: Ingenerateness is not the supreme descriptor of divinity.
164. He coins the adverb from *Ekporeusis*, his technical word drawn from Jn 15:26.

personalized unity of two different conditions. It was a language, however, that called for a much greater precision in following generations: "The Word became human, yet without change... The Unmingled was mingled...the Uncircumscribed was limited... the Impassible suffered...the Immortal One died."[165]

The Oration concludes its doctrinal initiation by calling for the candidates for baptism to present themselves. Gregory once more advises the need for correct preparation, and proper caution.[166] This indicates that he has just assumed control of the clergy, and has not previously been supervising the instruction of the candidates who are now ready to come forward. It must have been a strange thing for the Nicene preacher to accept the baptismal list of his Arian predecessor Demophilos, and it comes across in the number of times Gregory demands suitable purification, and the times in this oration when he seems to rebuke the catechists, or younger members of the Constantinopolitan clergy, insisting that they should conform themselves to the bishop's doctrine and leave aside their insolence.[167]

The presence of the emperor once more gives him an opportunity to plead for certain causes. A final description of the various types of baptism that are possible, from the rite Moses conducted[168] to baptisms of John and Jesus, and the blood baptism of the martyrs, leads him to conclude that there are four commonly regarded rituals, of which that of Jesus is the most sublime. Now he will also reveal to them that there is a fifth: the baptism of tears. It is that spiritual state of repentant readiness, that calls down the forgiveness of God. It is this evocation of the importance of repentance that leads him on to his precise point: an attack on the Novatianist sectarians, for their "pharisaic hard-heartedness" in making the church's penitential discipline difficult and rigorist. For Gregory the easy way should be preferred, as it is more fitting for a God whose philanthropy overflows onto humankind. All human beings are fallible by their very ontological constitution,[169] and for Gregory this is why the Church ought to be first and foremost a mediator of the generous forgiveness of God.[170] When considering who should or should not be reconciled, "in all cases of doubt charity must prevail."[171] Gregory was well aware when he made this attack on the old sect of puritans, still active in the capital from the disruptive days of the third century persecutions, that Theodosius was in the process of drawing up the edict he would issue only four days later,[172] listing the "heretics" who would be

---

165. Orat. 39.13, PG 36.349.
166. Orat. 39.14, PG 36.349-352.
167. "Do you presume to teach your elders, when you do not even have a beard, and have not reached maturity?" Orat. 39.14, PG 36.352.
168. Ex 19:14 and the various rituals of lustration.
169. Orat. 39.18, PG 36.356.
170. Further see McGuckin (1998).
171. Orat. 39.19, PG 36.357.
172. *Cod. Theod.* 116.5, 6. January 10, 381. This was the beginning of a long series of anti-heresy laws drawn up by Theodosius' administration; cf. King (1961) part 1, and relevant appendices for details.

forbidden use of the churches in the city from then onwards. It seems as if Gregory had an afterthought that this would be a good time to try to unseat the Novatians. They had a strong following, however, gaining much respect for their old-fashioned and rigorist stance, and had gained many protectors among the aristocracy. They survived as a presence in Constantinople until the fifth century, and Gregory's successor, Nektarios, held the Novatian bishop at Constantinople as his personal spiritual director. The edict, when it did appear, did not mention Novatians among the ranks of heretics, and this is a small indication that the religious legislation of Theodosius at this time might have used Gregory as a consultant, but was not emanating from Gregory himself.

His talk at the vigil service had gone on for a considerable time. He realized that it had better be terminated because of the hour, and accordingly he ends somewhat abruptly, a fact he explains in his opening remarks the next day.[173]

Oration 40 resumes his teaching on baptism at the morning service of the feast of January 6. This was the day when the waters were blessed and the sacrament of baptism was administered. It was possibly the day he received Athanarich, the Gothic chief as one of his candidates for entrance into the "Mysteries" as a high ranking *foederatus* of the empire. It also has a sidelong critical reference to Theodosius, it appears, for at one time Gregory cries out for people not to follow the bad practice of waiting until a fever brings them to the baptismal font,[174] surely knowing this was exactly how Theodosius had himself come to his initiation in Thessalonike. The Emperor was not present for this discourse, as it was given in the baptistery[175] to the collective gathering of the catechumens, before Gregory led those who had accepted the confession of faith and had been baptized into the main nave of the church for the "completion of the mysteries" at the Eucharistic altar. The text is an extraordinarily long moral *paranesis*, one of the longest of his surviving orations. It is predominantly concerned with answering a long series of supposed objections his audience might have to his episcopal invitation that they proceed for baptism. He rehearses all possible eventualities that might persuade someone to delay baptism, mainly averring to the common fear that since baptism was an unrepeatable purification, the sins of the flesh might later negate the effects of the sacrament if they took it too soon. Gregory wants to end this mentality of a lifelong belonging to the class of catechumens, calling it a "reckless caution."[176] He advocates the spiritual discipline of prayers and vigils, sleeping on the floor, and fasting and charitable almsgiving,[177] as more than capable of preserving a Christian on the right path if once given the "seal" of the grace of God in the sacrament. Gregory tells those who have no faith in their

173. Orat. 40.1, PG 36.360.
174. Orat. 40.12, PG 36.373.
175. Orat. 40.45, PG 36.425.
176. Orat. 40.16, PG 36.377.
177. Orat. 40.31, PG 36.404.

spiritual abilities to consider two characters of the bible who were praised for one single good thing in their lives: Rahab the harlot, and the publican who beat his breast before God as a sinner. If these people are honored by God because of a single good act, then those who are hesitating over committing themselves to baptism "should not so easily despair of themselves."[178] But those who put off their baptism until the very end are making a dreadful gamble, considering the fragile hold we humans have on life. Gregory sketches a vivid word picture of the man who has left his baptism until his deathbed, and the priest who comes to bring him the ritual but is kept out of the bedchamber by a grasping heir all too eager to get the will ratified, at the expense of the dying man's anxiety about his urgent spiritual needs.[179] The seal of baptism will be a far more reliable protection, Gregory says, than any amulet, for mothers who are frightened for the welfare of their babies.[180] Only wait until the child has reached its third year so that it can join in with the prayers.[181] The young and the old should hasten to their baptism.[182] Any counter-argument that Christ himself waited until his thirtieth year is inapplicable, Gregory says, since Christ had no need of baptism, but did it to show us the way, and consequently was in no danger for putting it off. Mimicry of Christ's life at this level of detail is not useful for, as his absolute fast for forty days shows, many of the things Christ did were unique to his divine condition, and only meant to be general examples to us who are weaker in our capacities.[183] The protective force of the sacrament will fend off demonic assaults, and give the security of a "precious shroud" far better than those "funeral rituals of the dead" (pagans) which try to secure the rest of the deceased by idolatrous libations.[184] Those who are married ought not to fear that they will be committed to celibacy thereafter. It is an interesting thing to note that Gregory has to disabuse them of this belief about Church discipline so late in the fourth century.[185] Marriage is an honorable thing "if only it avoids base lusts." This is as explicit as he is willing to be; an example of what Bernardi.[186] regards as a certain innocence of an old celibate allied with a very delicate sense of discretion in offering spiritual advice rather than "laws." The married ought only to undertake that they will, as baptized Christians, abstain from sexual relations at the fixed times of prayer;

178. Orat. 40.19, PG 36.384.
179. Orat. 40.11, PG 36.373.
180. Orat. 40.17, PG 36.381.
181. Orat. 40.28, PG 36.400.
182. Orat. 40.17, PG 36.380.
183. Orat. 40.29-30, PG 36.400-401.
184. Orat. 40.15, PG 36.377.
185. It had been a strict ascetical practice of the early Syrian church that baptism demanded life-long celibacy as a consequence. The catechumens were married. The baptized Ihidaya, children of the covenant, lived in celibacy.
186. Bernardi (1968), pp. 211-212. "L'imprécision de ce language pourrait bien n'avoir d'autre cause que la totale ignorance des réalités du mariage, et nous ne devons pas compter sur cet évêque pour nous renseigner sur la vie conjugale de ses fidèles."

that by mutual consent,[187] for Gregory wishes only to advise, not to lay down a commandment in this regard.

The *paranesis* completed, the time for baptism had finally arrived, and Gregory's latter part of the oration is the opening of the ceremony. He begins by the last initiation into theology that was traditionally given at the moment of baptism—the doctrine of the Spirit of God. Gregory chooses to deliver this as the:

> confession of the Father and the Son and the Holy Spirit. This I commit to you this day. Into this I shall baptize you for your growth. This I give to you to share and defend all the days of your life: the One Godhead and Single Power found in unity in the three, and comprising the three separately, with no inequality as to nature or substance, and never distinguished by superiorities or inferiorities, but in all respects coequal and the same. Just as the beauty and the greatness of the heavens amount to one thing, so is the infinite conjunction of the three infinites, each one God when considered in itself: the Father, the Son and the Holy Spirit. The three One God when contemplated together, yet each one God because they are Homoousios, and all One God because of the single Monarchy. No sooner do I conceive of the One than I am illumined by the radiance of the Three. No sooner do I distinguish them individually than I am pulled back again to the One.[188]

His last words to a list of catechumens largely prepared by the Arian clergy of the capital, is to encourage them to trust him. If they are afraid of tritheism, they should lay aside their fears. If they cling to Arian conceptions, they are committing themselves to the worship of a creature (the Word who is not fully God) and this is as bad as the worst excesses of those Syrians they look down on as crassly pagan, "the worshippers of Astarte or Chemosh that abomination of the Sidonians."[189] His candidates ought to have no fears, only trust their bishop who baptizes them. Using an image that must have been common to them as they were regularly ferried to and fro across the Golden Horn, Gregory says he will stand surety as the shipbuilder of this theology and this faith; they only have to trust in the soundness of his craft and rely on his skills as ferry man while he will take responsibility for them all, and for their salvation. They have no need to worry about the intricacies of the theological construct: it is not their concern as newly baptized Christians to be theologians, it is his affair as the bishop to ensure soundness of doctrine. All they need to know and confess is the principle of the Unity in Three.[190]

He tells them: "If your heart has been written up in another manner, come now and have the writing changed by me."[191] The baptismal rite itself was probably going to be altered by Gregory. The evidence of the Eunomian sect, and the *Apostolic Constitutions* which seems to have been edited by an Arian theologian at this time,

187. He is alluding to Paul; cf. 1 Cor 7:3-7.
188. Orat. 40.41, PG 36.417.
189. Orat. 40.42, PG 36.420.
190. Orat. 40.43, PG 36.420.
191. Orat. 40.44, PG 36.421.

suggests that the baptismal formula was a baptism "Into the death of the Son." Gregory is going to baptize in the evangelical manner,[192] in the threefold name. He refuses to perform the service in any other way, and those who insist upon the Arian traditional form, he says, must go elsewhere for a "sacrament of burial" for it will be the shipwreck of their salvation rather than a safe passage in his hands.[193] At this point he recites the Nicene Creed paraphrastically,[194] and tells the crowd gathered in the baptistery that: "this is now all that can be divulged about this mystery, all that is permitted for the ears of the many. The rest you shall learn within the church by the grace of the Holy Spirit, and those matters you must keep secret within yourselves, sealed and secure." Thus evidencing that the ancient discipline of the Arcana was still practiced in the late fourth century. His last word in the oration continues the theme of Mystery Initiation by letting slip one last instruction to the baptized (and of course doing so in the hearing of the rest of the catechumens for their "encourage-ment") that as they will now be led forward to the altar of the great church and be presented with further mysteries (the Eucharist) what they see and experience is to be taken as a type of their admission into the Kingdom of Heaven. As they have died with Christ in baptism, they will now be admitted to the mystery of the resurrection of Christ at the altar. This aspect Gregory compares to the eschatological coming of the Bridegroom.[195] The newly baptized stood alongside the bishop while the psalms were chanted and they themselves lit the numerous lamps hung in the church to sig-nify their newly found illumination, just as once the wise virgins of the parable did to celebrate the wedding feast of the Lord.[196]

It is, of course, difficult to judge, but one gains the sense from this long set of ora-tions, that the ceremonies involved large groups of the baptized, and considering the peculiar difficulties he had in changing the tenor of their whole prior catechesis, even to the point of publicly rebuking their catechists during the course of the services, Gregory must have felt, all in all, it was a triumph to be able to lead those candidates to the front of the church of the Holy Apostles that morning. If Athanarich and his retinue of Gothic warriors was among that procession, clad no longer in their war gear but in the splendid clothes of Roman nobility being admitted to the Mysteries under the sponsorship of the emperor, it must have been a splendid occasion indeed, and one that signaled more clearly even than the ceremonial procession into the city of eight weeks previously, that Gregory's position as imperial bishop was now assured.

Athanarich, however, was so old, and so worn down by the forced movements of his remaining tribes, that he died within a few weeks of his reception by the emperor. He was given a grand state funeral, at which Gregory must have presided, though he

192. Mt 28:19.
193. Orat. 40.44, PG 36.421.
194. Orat. 40.45, PG 36.424.
195. Mt 25:1-13.
196. Orat. 40.46, PG 36.425.

has left no trace of it whatsoever in his writings. Athanarich's soldiers were admitted into the Roman legions, more a symbolic gesture than a real military advantage, although the tide of the war had certainly changed, and the complete routing of the remaining Gothic insurgents would happen in the course of 382, when substantial reinforcements arrived from the West, and Fritigern's following melted away.

Four days after the baptismal celebrations, on January 10, when the feast was over and business resumed as usual, Theodosius issued a startling decree,[197] banning the Eunomian and Photinian heretics from any use of churches in Constantinople. The clergy who remained loyal to Demophilos, and therefore hostile to Gregory, were also deprived of their possession of the churches. The edict began to eject those clergy and Arian teachers who had thought they could survive the exile of their former bishop. The leader of the Neo-Arian teachers, Eunomios, was exiled from his villa at Chalcedon, and made his way back slowly into Cappadocia. Clergy loyal to the Nicene cause were installed in place of those who would not affirm their conversion.

Gregory's attention was now being taken up with the preparations for the council of bishops that would meet in May of that year. It was planned as the formal endorsement of the sketched out reconciliation that Meletios had brought about for the Antiochene schism, at his synod there in 379. By and large the same protagonists would be gathering. None of the bishops from the West were invited, and none from Illyricum (which was traditionally loyal to the West), and none from Alexandria. Gregory felt that he had little to worry about as far as his falling out on those fronts was concerned. Theodosius had already heard the appeal of Maximus, and rejected it out of hand, so as far as Gregory could see there was no way the Egyptians could touch him at the planned council. He placed his faith utterly in the emperor, and in this, like many another Archbishop of Constantinople after him, was disappointed.

Jerome was still in attendance in Gregory's circle. He says later that he engaged in biblical classes with Gregory, whom he calls his "teacher of exegesis."[198] It is noticeable that Gregory's interpretation of the scriptures witnessed in the Constantinopolitan orations begins to use more overtly allegorical exegeses than have hitherto been in evidence, although this is not unexpected in a lifelong disciple of Origen such as Gregory was. In one of his exchanges Jerome asked Gregory to explain for him the difficult textual reading of Luke 6:1, the "Second-First Sabbath."[199] It was a trick question, of course, for the word is one of those lexical oddities Jerome has taken delight in digging up for a master rhetorician's comment. Gregory's answer was to express surprise that Jerome did not know. If he really wanted to be instructed, Gregory says, he should stand near him in church the next time he preaches and he will be so carried away by the waves of applause that greet his interpretation of this passage that in

197. Gregory had intimated that it was coming in Orat. 37.23, PG 36.308.
198. *De Vir. Ill.* 117; Ep. 50.1; *In Isaiam* 3.
199. *En Sabbato Deuteroproto.* The reading is from the Uncial Mss. A C D K X etc. and entered the Byzantine Lectionary.

spite of himself he will be forced to admit that Gregory has the right answer (whatever it is). If Jerome insists on holding out, and does not applaud along with the others, everyone will take him for an *ignoramus*. This has sometimes been taken with some indignation by Victorian scholars who see in it evidence of Gregory's arrogance, and a less-than-serious approach to biblical exegesis. It is, what Jerome says it is in his letter, "an amiable joke." Gregory is actually admitting to Jerome that he too has no idea what such a barbarous word means, but he is willing to pull the wool over his eyes. The references to the waves of applause that greet his littlest remark are an ironic reference to the way his preaching is now applauded on every front, since the Emperor has arrived. Before November 380, Gregory was well aware that his preaching attracted hostility and even stones; after his installation in the Holy Apostles, the imperial church custom was to have claque-leaders open the applause for the bishop's orations, in much the same way as television studio managers hold up signs for the audience to applaud and laugh for recorded shows. Gregory's allusion to this practice is a source of high amusement to both him and Jerome, and when the latter remembers it and refers it to his correspondent, the priest Nepotianus, in the context of advising him how to preach in church, he uses it in the sense Gregory intended it: to demonstrate the folly of taking pride in popular acclaim from a fickle audience.[200]

When Gregory took over the administration of the budget for the church of Constantinople, he discovered that the account books had disappeared along with Demophilos. It was a covering of the tracks that might or might not indicate shady financial dealings. Gregory says that although he thought that vast sums were involved, he accepted the situation instead of prosecuting the case through an external auditor, in order not to give public scandal.[201] Most of the assets and income, however, cannot have been radically alienated, and Gregory was able to continue the administration of the numerous works of the church: the support of the indigents, the monastics, the foreign visitors (probably meaning in this instance the arrangements for the council) and the welfare of prisoners; tasks which he says kept him very busy indeed on top of his duties overseeing the liturgies and prayer services.[202]

Some time in the late spring of 381, Gregory of Nyssa and his brother Peter of Sebaste arrived at Constantinople, to take part in the council. Gregory arranged that his friend Gregory should give public readings of his latest work, the *Contra Eunomium*, which he had brought with him. The treatise had been written to defend his brother Basil's memory against the posthumous attacks made on it in Eunomios' *Second Apology*, and the performance was, to that extent, their common celebration of the memory of Basil the Great, whose funeral the elder Gregory had missed. Jerome was aware that he was present for a special occasion when he listened

200. For the text of Jerome's *Letter* 52, and commentary on it, see Gallay (1943), pp. 179-180.
201. *De Vita Sua*, vv. 1475-1494, PG 37.1131-1132.
202. *De Vita Sua*, vv. 1500-1505, PG 37.1133.

to those readings.[203] A room containing Gregory of Nyssa, Peter, Gregory
Nazianzen, Evagrios of Pontike, Jerome, and possibly Diodore of Tarsus all debating high points of metaphysics would have been a sight worth seeing. If the reading took place when the majority of the conciliar bishops had gathered, we could
even extend the audience to include Meletios of Antioch and his newly ordained
deacon John Chrysostom, Amphilokios of Ikonium Gregory's cousin, and Cyril of
Jerusalem.

The council opened in May 381.[204] It commenced with the intention of eccle-
siastically endorsing the imperial edict of January which called not only for the
ejection of heretics from the capital, but also the installation of only Nicene bishops in the sees of the Orient. This began a large-scale scramble for appointments
all over the East, and large benefactions were in the hands of the Nicene leaders
now gathered in the city. The other leading agenda item was to endorse the settlement to the schism promulgated at the Antiochene synod of 379. The first thing
that Theodosius wished confirmed, however, was his own judgment that Gregory
ought to be recognized as the Nicene bishop of the imperial city. Accordingly, the
claims of Maximus were quashed by an early session of the council, that met under
the presidency of Meletios of Antioch. The decision to reject Maximus was
enshrined in the fourth canon the council subsequently promulgated. By that
stage Gregory was no longer in residence, and so gains no mention, but the rejection of the one was originally meant as the formal endorsement of the other in the
original proceedings.[205]

Gregory has hardly anything at all good to say about the council. He looks back
on it with seething bitterness in his autobiographical poem, which is one of the main
sources we have for knowledge about the proceedings, since the meeting left no Acts
of its own. The historians Socrates and Sozomen[206] supplement what we know, and
it is clear from them that Gregory left out a considerable amount of things from the
proceedings. He does this from his usual custom of "passing over in silence things
that do not merit mention."[207] The jaundiced attitude to the council, however, rises
from events related to the later sessions, and derives from two main causes: first, the
rejection of Gregory's leadership in succession to Meletios, and the forced resignation this caused; secondly, the refusal of the council at large to endorse his theology
of the Homoousion of the Spirit, to which he had committed himself irrevocably.
Though he has a lot to say about the conciliar proceedings, his mind is predominantly focused on how badly the Syrian bishops behaved, and on the surprising turn
of events when the Egyptians also arrived. He has focused sharply on these matters

203. Jerome, De Vir. Ill. 128.
204. Socrates, HE 1.5.8.
205. "These men set me on the awesome throne." De Vita Sua, v. 1525, PG 37.1135.
206. Sozomen, HE 1.7.7; Socrates, HE 1.5.8.
207. Orat. 8.1, PG 35.792.

because the Council of Aquileia and Damasus of Rome continued to press for the cause of Maximus, and Gregory prepared this whole autobiographical poem as part of his legal apologia with the hindsight that distance by time and geography afforded him in 382.

Meletios, the president of the opening conciliar sessions, was someone whom Gregory regarded as a model bishop, and he describes him in terms redolent of the way he looked on his own father: righteous, innocent of heart, serene and modest.[208] Meletios encouraged Gregory to think he could use his influence as bishop of the imperial city to bring about a complete stabilisation of the Nicene party in the East, and Gregory was flattered enough to want to work for such a goal.[209]

It was at that point, just as Meletios was dreaming (like Athanarich five months before him) that all his difficulties had come to a resolution in the splendors of the capital city, that the old man died. A great cortège was gathered for the solemn transport of his body back home to Antioch for burial; a crowd which Gregory says had never before been gathered at the city gates to pay honor to any bishop (a commendation he also attributed to Athanasius in *Oration* 21). With Meletios' death Gregory's biggest problems began. The settlement which Meletios had arranged at the synod in 379 was very unpopular with his own party. It involved recognizing the validity of both contending bishops, Meletios and Paulinus, and at the death of one, to allow the other to continue as legitimate bishop of the city. The agreement had already been in place for two years, but no one particularly liked Paulinus, and his contingent was by far the smaller number of the Nicene faithful of Antioch. Similarly, no one had really expected Meletios to die so soon, and the prospect of seeing Paulinus recognized as leader of one of the most prestigious sees of the East was too much for the majority of the younger bishops who felt a deep bond of loyalty to their dead leader, but equally felt themselves at last free of his "settlement." They kept to the spirit of the agreement, however, and proposed to elect a younger member of Paulinus' clergy, the priest Flavian for whom they had a great deal of respect, and who had doubtless distinguished himself in the reconciliation process of 379. Flavian agreed to abandon Paulinus in return for elevation to the bishop's throne, and in this way it was felt that the situation at Antioch would be able to bring over all the Nicenes, while simultaneously excluding Paulinus who was regarded as an uncanonical puppet of the Western bishops who had no right to intrude him in the first place, but had added years of frustration to the Nicene cause in the East as a result of their interference.

Gregory was appalled at the proposition and, as he was canonically the next in line for the post of president, he tried to counsel the Syrian bishops to keep to the original agreement, and reconcile all parties at Antioch while simultaneously

208. *De Vita Sua*, vv. 1514-1524, PG 37.1134-1135.
209. *De Vita Sua*, vv. 1526-1540, PG 37.1135-1136.

restoring good relations with the West. This was probably his own sentiment anyway, a loyalty to the letter of Meletios' intentions, but it was also surely the advice of the Emperor, who was very anxious to secure better lines of communication with the Western churches.

Diodore of Tarsus became the leading spokesman for the Syrian metropolitanate, and exercised a massive influence over conciliar events from then on. He had been, before his consecration to the see of Tarsus, the administrator of the church at Antioch while Meletios was in exile, and was undoubtedly the sponsor for Flavian, just as he was the sponsor for Nektarios whose cause he strenuously advanced as someone dear to Theodosius' heart, a malleable and politically savvy aristocrat, who would not be so fussy about ecclesiastical procedure as the old and scrupulous Gregory was proving to be.[210] This growing mountain of dead-weight resistance to his new presidential policy Gregory describes with sharp scorn. He characterizes his opposition as having all the restless aggression of young men:

> Shouting, lobbying for friends, making accusations, and leaping about, grabbing hold of whoever they could to their side. Such was their frenzy for power. How can I suitably denounce such behavior?[211]

What had begun as a wonderful gathering to celebrate the Nicene ascendancy had developed into a nightmare, and now Gregory was expected to regulate it. He was approached by the Syrians and asked to validate their plan to consecrate Flavian. He would not listen to them.[212] The council rotated its sessions in various city churches, so where these events took place is not certain. The floor was taken by several bishops demanding Flavian be recognized as the new bishop of Antioch. Gregory intervened with a speech of his own, which is presented in a very long digest in verse form,[213] such was the importance it assumed in his mind. He gives the episode far more attention in the De Vita Sua than he does to the discussions of trinitarian theology which the council fathers initiated.[214] This is largely because he needs to offer evidence to critics in the capital in 382, who were still querying the legitimacy of his own title to the bishopric in the light of the legal objections the Egyptians had raised. He did not neglect the theological aspects, however, and if the issuing of the De Vita Sua is largely taken up with matters of episcopal succession, the publication of the Orations, which he arranges more or less from the same time was definitely intended to reaffirm his insistence that the Homoousion of the Spirit had to be confessed. That he so carefully neglected to minute the opposition of the council to his proposal, allowed him more space to "exegete" that council from a distance. In this latter theological propaganda he was eminently successful, for historically his

210. Cf. McGuckin, "Autobiography as Apologia" (2001).
211. De Vita Sua, vv. 1551-1557, PG 37.1137.
212. De Vita Sua, vv. 1583-1586, PG 37.1139.
213. De Vita Sua, vv. 1591-1679, PG 37.1140-1148.
214. De Vita Sua, vv. 1703-1744, PG 37.1148-1151.

orations came to be generally accepted as the "theological mind" of the council of 381. Gregory had his way after all, but probably only posthumously.

His speech decried Flavian, without naming him, as bad choice for teacher of such an important see.[215] He berated the gathering for being divided in their estimate over the succession,[216] and in any case losing sight of the larger cause of restoring doctrinal orthodoxy to the churches of the East, by becoming obsessed with one city.[217] However venerable the two bishops Meletios and Paulinus were in themselves, he argued, they were not worth the agitation of the whole Christian world when the communion of the Western churches was lying in the balance.[218] "Accept my advice," he said, "based as it is on careful thought, and wiser than the opinions of the younger men...Let the bishop's throne belong to the one (Paulinus) who has occupied it so far."[219] Paulinus can occupy the throne until he dies. The time could be suitably marked as a mourning period for Meletios, since this was his own policy, and then after the death of Paulinus let a council be gathered to settle the matter definitively.[220] It was a good plan, but he knew he had a long way to go to convince the party led by Diodore. Even hinting that anyone who opposed his solution should be regarded as suspect of simoniacal power-broking, did not clinch the case,[221] though it probably severed the last lines of loyalty between himself and the Syrians. He made a bad mistake here. Knowing that the resolution on the floor was barely winnable, he fastened himself to the mast and pushed it as a matter of personal loyalty to himself. As he had done on the occasion of the loss of confidence in the Anastasia church, he offered to resign if he was not accepted wholeheartedly:

> If some wicked person think I say these things to please someone, though it is he himself who has been bought off[222] ...then I leave the judgment to God's last fires. Give me a life, however that is free of a bishop's throne, inglorious perhaps, but at least no longer subject to such dangers. I will go off and settle far away from all these troubles, for it would be preferable than to stand in the midst of all this crowd, and be unable to win over any support. Let someone skilled in episcopal affairs come in my place. He will find himself in charge of a great crowd, including the worthy as well as wicked. Make up your minds. I have said all that I intend to say.[223]

215. *De Vita Sua*, vv. 1648-1652, PG 37.1144.
216. *De Vita Sua*, v. 1591, PG 37.1140.
217. *De Vita Sua*, vv. 1594-1607, PG 37.1140-1141.
218. *De Vita Sua*, vv. 1611-1620, PG 37.1141-1142.
219. *De Vita Sua*, vv. 1620-1624, PG 37.1142.
220. *De Vita Sua*, vv. 1625-1640, PG 37.1143-1144.
221. *De Vita Sua*, vv. 1663-1670, PG 37.1145-1146.
222. An indication perhaps that Diodore of Tarsus was very critical of Gregory preferring loyalty to the Emperor Theodosius, rather than his former patrons in the Metropolitanate of Antioch. Now that Gregory has received his "prize" of the capital (that is been "bought" by the emperor), he was felt to have betrayed the cause ungratefully. It is a charge which makes Gregory indignant. The counter charge that (Diodore) has been bought is more from passion than evidence.
223. *De Vita Sua*, vv. 1663-1679, PG 37.1145-1146.

This was, as is usually the case, a fatal political maneuver. At best it gains unwilling and sullen agreement; at worst it makes everyone, even one's moderate supporters, tempted to take the speaker at face value. Once someone has offered to resign over a point of principle, it is immensely difficult to regain the ground if the threat does not have the desired effect. In Gregory's case it did not. He lost control of the meeting. He describes the result as the party of younger bishops going into a fury over what he said "wheeling around like a flock of screeching jackdaws, making a whirlwind of dust."[224] Gregory noticed how Theodosius, who seems to have been present for the discussions, would not move to support him.[225] When he looked around the room to see how the "council of elders" was reacting, his heart sank to see how they too were rising to their feet to talk him down.[226] His discretion, as usual, does not identify the elder[227] who stood up and spoke against a pro-Western eirenic solution, but he does present the argument used, in order to hold it up as an imbecile example. The solution, it was argued, should follow the example of the Sun. As it rises in the East, the land which the Son of God chose as his birthplace, so the Eastern church should settle its own affairs. Gregory makes a muttering aside that it could also be argued that Christ chose the East because its wickedness called out to him all the more loudly.[228] But he could not repair the damage this loss of face had done. His presidency of the council continued in following sessions, but he knew that he had irremediably forfeited the leadership in losing the trust of the Antiochene majority.

In a subsequent session he came ready to discuss the theological confession the council ought to issue. He was appalled at the way in which the discussions were proceeding. Thirty-six bishops were present who had a very tenuous connection to the Nicene faith as represented by Athanasios. These were the so-called Macedonians,[229] who were willing to go so far as to admit the consubstantiality of the Son of God (though they thought the word had proved more of a trouble than a blessing to Christian theology) but they were certainly not willing to press on and apply it to the Spirit of God. Led by Eleusios of Cyzicus, they were determined opponents of an extrapolated theology of the Trinity, and Gregory represented to them all that they hated in the Alexandrian Nicene movement. It has to be admitted too, that a large number of Nicene stalwarts from the Antiochene side, shared many doubts about the radical pneumatology and co-equal Trinity such as Gregory had been preaching. The mutterings in his own Anastasia in his early orations on the subject

224. *De Vita Sua*, vv. 1681-1683, PG 37.1146-1147.
225. "They were out of control, and even an ruler with the authority of age and the power of fear behind him did not think it was proper to reason with them." *De Vita Sua*, vv. 1684-1686, PG 37.1141.
226. *De Vita Sua*, vv. 1688-1690, PG 37.1147.
227. I wonder if it was Cyril of Jerusalem, then a venerable old man.
228. *De Vita Sua*, 1690-1702, PG 37.1147-1148.
229. From Macedonios, a former bishop of Constantinople (352-362).

showed this fault line was equally unreliable. This large party of 36 disaffected bish-ops is known to us from Socrates and Sozomen only. Gregory has censored them from his account of the proceedings.[230] Early on in the theological discussions proper, they left the council. Gregory did not seem much to care. Theodosius, how-ever, was much exercised in the following year trying to arrange their reconciliation. It was not until later in 382 that he finally decided they were a lost cause. To see this large number walking out in protest must have alarmed the imperial retinue, and made them entertain further doubts about the suitability of Gregory as a midwife of reconciliation. A kind and accommodating personality he certainly was, but he lacked the desire to prevaricate about the faith, and refused to make compromises in regard to his "beloved Trinity."

Gregory watched the debates with growing dismay. He had little regard for the majority of opinions he heard there, and felt that too many bishops were either com-pletely ignorant of theology, or too ready to act as time-servers and agree to a compro-mise formula that was acceptable to authority.[231] He does not mention whose authority, but it is probably a veiled reference to the way the court was pressing for a generally accommodating statement that could be used broadly and generically to settle tensions in the Eastern Churches. Something as sharply focused as Gregory's trinitarian theology of the threefold Homoousion was anathema, and had to be sacrificed, along with him if necessary. His hostile description of his theological opponents, as "bishops who were still having to learn about God"[232] suggests strongly that it included the group of younger men led by Diodore of Tarsus, who were by no means antagonistic to Nicene faith, but neither were they keen to apply the Homoousion to the Spirit. So, after the walk-out by the thirty-six, here was Gregory having to do battle yet again with his Syrian colleagues. He knew exactly where their doctrine was tending: to that same generic vagueness he had years before berated in Basil. It is the theological vagueness about the divine Spirit that is still present in the words of the Niceno-Constantinopolitan creed, which proba-bly represents, substantively, the doctrinal settlement agreed on in the synod of 381. It is, in Gregory's eyes, fatally compromised for being silent on two issues he had prioritized as necessary for a completely orthodox confession: the ascription of the title God to the Spirit; and the admission that he is consubstantial with the Father and Son. Gregory felt the whole synod was becoming a pollution of the true faith:

> I stood and watched as the sweet and pristine spring of our ancient faith, which had joined that sacred and adorable nature of the Trinity in one, as formerly professed at Nicaea, was now wretchedly polluted by the flooding in of the brine of men of dubi-ous faith.[233]

230. Only obliquely referring to them as Moabites and Ammonites illegitimately permitted to enter with Israel. *De Vita Sua*, vv. 1737-1738, PG 37.1151.
231. *De Vita Sua*, v. 1709, PG 37.1149.
232. *De Vita Sua*, v. 1712, PG 37.1149.
233. *De Vita Sua*, vv. 1704-1708, PG 37.1148.

He intervened, presumably, by making his *Theological Orations* available to his colleagues, but he gives no mention of it. Apart from his *Farewell Oration* he has allowed no speech he gave on theology to the bishops to survive in his writings, except this highly caustic invitation that he must have given at the end of all the debates, which showed his disdain and scorn for them all with abundant clarity. His words are dripping with irony over the large number of them who had "revolved" theologically according to the prevailing winds:

> I stood in front of the Bema and made an announcement, addressing all the assembly in a loud voice. Come on roll up whoever wants to! Come, even if you have already changed your theology twice or even more times. The Theatre door is open. The Banquet is ready. I don't want anyone to go home from here without feeling they have had a part. If the dice fall differently (and as we all know there is nothing so fickle as chance) then don't forget the drill: just change direction again! It would be foolish, would it not, to represent one solid belief all one's life? Quite! One should explore many different paths![234]

He feared he was losing the theological argument. He knew he was losing control of the synod as a whole. It was now being carried from side to side without any regard to his authority.[235] What could he do in this new crisis when Moabites and Ammonites had been allowed into the assembly of Israel?[236] If it was ever a question of fight or flight, Gregory's habit was well enough known.

> At this point, thank heavens, illness came to my rescue, which usually kept me for the most part at home. I looked forward only to one thing, my exit which would bring me release from all my woes.[237]

He was surprised at how few were willing to sympathize with him, even among those whose theology he respected. Again he covers over names of individuals with a discreet veil, but the references to men who chose to close their eyes over the issues, those who were pressured into agreement with the conciliar policies, and friends who begged him to be reasonable and show some loyalty to the Antiochene cause,[238] all point to a certain criticism of Gregory of Nyssa, who advocated the policy of the council as a way of establishing the Nicene cause in the East. Gregory felt, on the contrary, that the theological policy was a mixing of "dung in the incense" and completely hostile to the faith evidenced at Nicaea.[239] Others began circulating that they had experienced revelatory dreams about him indicating he had to go. Gregory,

---

234. *De Vita Sua*, vv. 1724-1732, PG 37.1150.
235. *De Vita Sua*, vv. 1740-1744, PG 37.1151.
236. *De Vita Sua*, vv. 1736-1738. Cf. Dt 23:3. Those who were alien to Israel. It is probably a reference to the Macedonian party who had been admitted to the assembly, whose presence Gregory objected to, or a generic disparagement of the orthodoxy of the continuing opponents of the Homoousion of the Spirit.
237. *De Vita Sua*, vv. 1745-1748, PG 37.1151. He means his death.
238. *De Vita Sua*, vv. 1750-1755, 1766-1770, PG 37.1151-1153.
239. *De Vita Sua*, vv. 1755-1758, PG 37.1152.

normally an avid defender of the revelatory power of dreams, dismisses them in this case as mere projections of their wishful thinking.[240] Gregory could not, and would not, compromise: "How could I have agreed to work with them? Who could possibly have thought that a majority would ever lead me to a course of action, in preference to following the divine Word?"[241] And so, from that moment onwards, he gave directions for his belongings to be shifted back to the house his cousin had given for his use; and "barely dragged" himself back into private quarters, thereby symbolically renouncing the official residence of the archbishop of the city.[242]

One wonders whether this was again that technique of sham resignation he had learned from Himerios, his old rhetorical professor in Athens. In *Eclogue* 20 Himerios had shown how the trick worked by refusing to speak to his students gathered in the hall to hear him—and (of course) dedicating an entire rhetorical discourse to the silence afterwards (just as Gregory often dedicates poems and orations on the subject of an orator's silence).[243] On another occasion, and celebrated in Himerios' *Eclogue* 21, the rhetor made a pretence of abandoning the official throne of rhetoric to which he had been elected in 357 (he had been a private teacher before that time in Athens) and he was only persuaded to resume his status (as he tells us in the *Eclogue*) by the personal intervention of the Proconsul of Achaia Musonius, who came publicly to beg him not to abandon Athens. Gregory's mistake was to attempt both strategies (silent withdrawal followed by threatened resignation) in the highly conflicted time of the synod; and the complete failure of the technique to impress the bishops, is a large part of his subsequent scorn for lowborn ecclesiastical leaders who could not be expected to recognize the forms of subtle persuasion, or to follow the etiquette of polite behavior appropriate to those educated together in the higher echelons of society.

Gregory tries to show how the technique *should* have worked by reference to his reception back at the Anastasia. In words reminiscent of the reaction to his speech when he threatened to resign after the Maximus incident, he tells the reader that his disciples there tearfully begged him not to go. They wanted him to remain as their bishop until his death. The loyalty from his old little community, and the temptation to remain almost overcame him, he says,[244] but he decided that it would be best to slip away, if only he could find an excuse. All this was his state of mind when he was ill. It seems to have been a genuinely debilitating illness, not merely a convenient excuse to stay away from the council meetings, for he was advised to draw up his last will and testament[245] and did so on May 31,[246] having it

---

240. Carm. 2.1.19. *Lament on His Calamities*, vv. 75- 76, PG 37.1277; see also Carm. 2.1.9, v. 10, PG 37.1026.
241. *De Vita Sua*, vv. 1772-1773, PG 37.1153.
242. *De Vita Sua*, vv. 1777-1780, PG 37.1153-1154.
243. Cf. Carm. 2.1.34. *On the Lenten Silence*, PG 37.1307-1322.
244. *De Vita Sua*, vv. 1781-1796, PG 37.1154-1155.
245. *Exemplum Testamenti*, PG 37.389-396. Cf. Martroye (1924).
246. The ms. dates it to one day before the kalends of January in the consulship of Flavius Eucherius

witnessed by six episcopal friends[247] as the testament of the orthodox bishop of Constantinople. His primary and substantive donation of all his (fairly extensive) goods is designated to the church of Nazianzus for the relief and care of the poor.[248]

While he was still in this midway house, pleading sickness, and isolating himself from the conciliar business, the Emperor intervened to break the deadlock that had arisen once Gregory's leadership had been rejected by the Antiochenes. It was one thing to settle the Antiochene schism, and Theodosius certainly was willing enough to validate Flavian, but it was another matter to allow the whole agenda of reaching a common orthodox consensus flounder in the first great synod that had been held to restore Nicene belief in the Eastern Churches. As soon as the original participants collapsed into internal strife, the emperor seems to have acted decisively, and on his own counsel. He called for the bishops of Egypt, and Illyricum, to give extra weight to his pro-Western policies, hoping that the new influx of voting members would clear the log jam of the chaos of May's sessions.

The Alexandrians and Illyrians came some time in mid-June 381, hastily summoned by imperial command.[249] They immediately began deconstructing all the synodical process, to the intense annoyance of all the Eastern bishops already there. Gregory remained in seclusion, pleading illness, but news was brought to him of the proceedings, and he sarcastically describes the newcomers as "experts in the laws and mysteries of God,"[250] because of the way they were scrutinizing the proceedings like lawyers. The clash between the Westerners and the Easterners is ridiculed as a Euripidean fight between wild boars, clashing their tusks savagely.[251] In the course of the political tennis-playing, the Western bishops lodged a protest about the election of Gregory himself. It was the last painful insult he was willing to endure on this account.[252]

The Alexandrian Archbishop Peter had recently died, and his successor Timothy seems to have wished to press the cause of Maximus once more, or failing that, to insist that his own see had rights of primacy to nominate the successor to Constantinople. The Egyptians raised the canons of the council of Nicaea to argue the point that a bishop should not be translated from one see to another, but should stay in the see to which he had first been consecrated. Gregory was the bishop of

and Flavius Evagrius (382). By this time he was long back in Cappadocia, and Nektarios was the bishop of Constantinople. Tillemont argued that "January" was a scribal error for "June," giving the date of May 31, 381, which perfectly fits. Cf. Gallay (1943), pp. 205-206.

247. His cousin Amphilokios of Ikonium, Optimos the retired bishop of (Cilician) Antioch, Theodosius bishop of Ida, Theodoulos bishop of (Pisidian) Apamaea, Hilarios bishop of Isauria and Themistios bishop of Adrianople. Also present were Amphilokios' priest Cledonios, and Gregory's own notary and lector, John, PG 37.393-396.

248. *Exemplum Testamenti*, PG 37.389.

249. *De Vita Sua*, v. 1798, PG 37.1155.

250. *De Vita Sua*, vv. 1800-1801, PG 37.1155.

251. *De Vita Sua*, vv. 1803-1808, PG 37.1155-1156; Euripides, *Phoenissae*, 1380.

252. "They scrutinized a very painful matter as far as I was concerned." *De Vita Sua*, v. 1809.

Sasima, he ought to go back there. His installation at Constantinople was never legitimate. It seems that while they were pressing this cause they also sent messages of respectful acknowledgement to Gregory himself, telling him that they were not agitating out of any personal animosity, but because they wished to block the procedures of the Antiochenes.[253] Gregory says that the canons they cited were "long obsolete" and the charge "could not possibly apply as relevant" to him,[254] but that was a moot point indeed; and knowing very well that was so, he spends a great deal of time later in 382 composing the *De Vita Sua*, to defend the arcane position that he had never been either the legitimate bishop of Sasima, or the bishop of Nazianzus, all to clear his name and defend the legitimacy of his installation as archbishop at Constantinople.[255] The painful raking up of the Maximus affair, as well as his canonical behavior over Sasima, demanded his reappearance in the council meetings. He decided that he would not prosecute his case, but take the opposition as his excuse to go. It is fairly certain that by then his position was more or less intolerable. He had lost the confidence of the Antiochenes, he was being attacked by the Alexandrians, the Western sees of Rome and Milan refused to acknowledge his legitimacy, and the emperor himself had evidently lost confidence in his management by virtue of having so urgently called in the Egyptian and Illyrian bishops to resolve the mess his presidency had caused. Gregory puts the best face on it he can, insisting that he resigned and was not dismissed, but it was unarguably a forced resignation. He laments that his critics in retrospect still refuse to give him the benefit of the doubt, and mock him as someone who was thrown out for incompetence. His real feeling was that he was glad to be relieved of his duties, though he knows that he can: "never convince those who are hungry for power that this was so: though it is true."[256]

He appeared for one last time as president of the council and delivered a surprise speech of resignation. It appears it was listened to with great attention. The mess the council was in, Gregory says, was not his fault. It was a storm not of his making[257] but he is ready to do what Jonah did and volunteer himself as a sacrificial appeasement.[258] In that way his affairs and the legitimate succession to Constantinople will not further distract the council from its more essential business of restoring a unity of purpose to the Nicene cause in the East. If communion between the Eastern and Western churches was further disrupted on account of "strife over episcopal thrones," this council would have proved a disastrous beginning to the new policy of

253. *De Vita Sua*, vv. 1812-1817, PG 37.1156.
254. *De Vita Sua*, vv. 1810-1811, PG 37.1156.
255. He does not want rehabilitation, merely the "restoration of honor," and acknowledgement that he had been legitimately appointed to Constantinople, and had freely resigned.
256. *De Vita Sua*, vv. 1825-1826, PG 37.1157.
257. Though he had, in fact, refused to allow the nomination of Flavian under his presidency, and had thus caused the stalemate.
258. *De Vita Sua*, vv. 1838-1844, PG 37.1158.

Theodosius. Gregory is concerned only with one thing, he says, that the bishops who remain will defend the doctrine of the Trinity, and he worries aloud that with his departure no one will have either the skill or the necessary independence and courage to see this basic theological task through to the end.[259] With some irony he recommends them to read his work and then gave them his resignation and farewell. He notes with some amusement that they all sat in stunned silence after he had spoken, watching him make his procession out of the church, as we might imagine with high style and dignity. At once, he notes with disapproval, all the bishops were beating a path to his door; not to beg him to stay, but to tell him how much they individually valued him, and were sorry to be seeing him go. He described the last weeks of his time in Constantinople sardonically:

> Only God, and those people, know whether there were more things hidden in all this than ever appeared openly. Let others speak of such things. I shall remain silent, for I do not have the time needed to comprehend the twisting ways of wickedness. It is my study to practice simplicity of heart, the only source of salvation I am concerned about. But one thing I do know: those bishops immediately started to afford me honor with more alacrity than was proper and reached a common agreement surprisingly quickly. Well, so much for that. This was the way the city rewarded those it loves![260]

Gregory went straight over to the palace and asked for an audience with the Emperor, begging him for a personal favor, not the usual run of financial favors people normally requested, but to be allowed "to yield before envy." He pointed dramatically to his gray hairs (he specifically notes it because it must have struck him at the time he was giving a great performance) and reminded Theodosius of all his labors for the faith, comparing his efforts to the emperor's own recent conquest of the barbarians. Gregory petitioned Theodosius to insist on conciliar harmony: let this be the trophy he sets up in commemoration of his victory. Make the bishops disarm just as he did the insurgents. As for him, he could be expected to go on faithfully suffering for the sake of the world. He had been unwilling to be raised to the dignity when Theodosius came: the emperor can bear witness to it. Now he asks permission to resign.[261]

Gregory notes with pleasure that the emperor marked the end of his speech not with the stunned silence of his colleagues, but this time with the spontaneous applause that was far more appropriate for such a sterling performance. Once Theodosius started to clap, all the other courtiers joined in as well. At least the aristocrats had some sense of style in handling these difficult matters. Theodosius feigned great reluctance to let such a valuable person leave, and "only with great reluctance" did he grant the favor of a resignation. "But all the same, grant it he did," Gregory adds.[262]

259. *De Vita Sua*, vv. 1852-1855, PG 37.1159.
260. *De Vita Sua*, vv. 1861-1870, PG 37.1159-1160.
261. *De Vita Sua*, vv. 1879-1901, PG 37.1161-1162.
262. *De Vita Sua*, vv. 1902-1904, PG 37.1162.

He says that as he was preparing to depart, he was concerned whether his numerous supporters would be tempted to violent demonstrations to keep him in the city.[263] They were not. He adds too that several bishops when they heard the news ran away "clapping their hands loudly in disapproval and blocking their ears"[264] so that they would not hear such inauspicious sounds.[265] His college friend Philagrios represents the opinion of many other well-wishers in later years as the news of his resignation spread further afield, that he should not have so easily given in to his pressurizing opponents.[266] If he had only brazened it out, he would probably have remained as the archbishop of the capital. It was probably true. Whatever the ploys of the Westerners, their counsels as to the succession at Constantinople were destined to be rejected, both by the Antiochenes who resented their blocking tactics, and by the Constantinopolitans themselves who were well down to road of deconstructing Alexandria's pretensions to canonical jurisdiction over all the East. When Gregory's successor was chosen it was a candidate from the city itself, nominated by bishop Diodore of Tarsus in the name of the Antiochene metropolitanate. Gregory, most likely, could have weathered the storm if he had agreed to the election of Flavian. It was not so much this that stuck in his throat, I think, but the clear signals already given that the council was not going to endorse the Homoousion of the Spirit. It was this that broke his resolve, and made a political withdrawal more appealing. It is a remarkable testimony to his principles. Despite all that he so often says about being unwilling to accept the throne at Constantinople, he clearly regarded it as a wonderful honor, which had been taken from him in a shameful, ungrateful, and disparaging manner. He was not ready, however, to sacrifice the principles of what he believed to be just and right, and this stubborn defense of honor and pure theology cost him an old age at the height of fame. It was not a bargain he was willing to make. His soul was dearer to him than the kingdoms of the world.[267]

The digest of the farewell speech such as he gives in the *De Vita Sua* can be compared with the formal text of a "farewell speech" he later prepared for publication as *Oration* 42. The conciliar bishops would not let him slip away from the city without some rituals of honor, and decided to give him a series of celebratory orations to mark his departure. It is not surprising, considering the manner in which he rages against the duplicity of bishops in all his later poems, that he has preserved not a single one of them. To initiate the series, however, he agreed to appear one last time before the whole gathering of the bishops and first deliver a farewell oration of his own.[268] He presented it in the church of the Holy Apostles. The conciliar bishops

---

263. *De Vita Sua*, vv. 1905-1912, PG 37.1162-1163.
264. Not simultaneously, one presumes.
265. *De Vita Sua*, vv. 1913-1918, PG 37.1163.
266. Cf. Greg. Ep. 87, PG 37.160-161; Gallay (1964), pp. 108-109.
267. Mt 4:8-11. Tillemont called his resignation from that see, in those circumstances, "one of the most heroic gestures in the history of the church." *Mémoires*, vol. 9, pp. 479-480.
268. Bernardi (1968), p. 227, thinks that this was a fictive composition in Cappadocia: what he really wished he had said at the end rather than anything he did say. I do not think this follows.

were all in attendance, so too the monastics, and courtiers, and presumably the
Emperor, for he makes several asides which were pointedly relevant to him. It is
polite in the extreme, lacking the sardonic touches of the more "sharpened" autobiographical version he also wished to put on record. It is overall one of the finest
Orations he ever gave, at times very touching in the transparency of heart it achieves,
and a fine synopsis of trinitarian doctrine that strikes a good medium between the
generic synopses he offered to the laity, and that which he now wants to be used as
the basis for the credal statements of his colleagues.

He starts off by describing the bishops in fulsome terms as "heralds of peace."
He asks them whether they will accept him on trust, or do they demand from him a
formal accounting of his administration of Church affairs (doubtless hoping they
would accept his word as he had allowed the Arians to abscond with all the books).
But even so, knowing that they will take his word as having administered affairs
honorably, he will give them some general account of himself.[269] He has always been
a defender of orthodoxy, even to the point of suffering under the oppressions of the
evil king Nebuchadnezzar (Valens) along with many others (and many there present)[270] who became martyrs at that time.[271] He came to Constantinople to defend
Nicene orthodoxy and found it a desolate field, but he has worked assiduously to
cultivate it, and now the harvest is "indeed great in the eyes of the Lord of the harvest."[272] He can see in prophetic vision, for he too claims the charism, that the
Church at the capital will continue to grow and establish itself in orthodoxy from
now on,[273] like the dry bones of Ezekiel's vision coming back to life. Even when he
was shepherd of a tiny flock it did not matter to him, for God did not see numbers
but looked more at the faithfulness of the hearts of those who served him, and his
community contrasted with the luxury of a strongly walled city confident in its own
pride.[274] This glorious restoration of the city to orthodoxy is now his gift to the
assembled bishops: "For we have nothing more splendid or beautiful to offer you.
We have selected the greatest of our possessions so that you may see that (like Paul)

Bernardi thinks that his jibes at the bishops are too severe to let him get away with it in their
presence. A close scrutiny of the attacks shows that they are addressed to his "back-stabbing
enemies," and none of the bishops present would have wanted to own up to being one of
those. The Oration, though long, is not beyond the limit of his usual extempore performances, and his request for the bishops to begin their own commendations, at the end, suggests that it was delivered as part of a formal farewell celebration, probably ordered by the
Emperor (in whose direction Gregory throws several pieces of advice before he leaves).

269. Orat. 42.1, PG 36.457.
270. The point is important to him as one body of his critics had been bishops who were annoyed
    that he had not used his position at court to exact a more bitter vengeance on their Arian
    oppressors.
271. Orat. 42.3, PG 36.461.
272. Orat. 42.4, PG 36.464.
273. Orat. 42.6, PG 36.465.
274. Orat. 42.7, PG 36.465-468.

we were strangers but never in want, and though we were poor we brought riches to many."[275] Even the avowed enemies of Gregory, he tells the bishops, have grown peaceful towards him. The Arians attacked him when he first came, but he refused to reply in kind, and chose instead the way of the meek, offering them the example of the suffering Christ. It won him the respect even of bitter foes.[276] One wonders if he made this last remark with some degree of irony considering his meekness in the council had proved so disastrous in the presence of orthodox bishops. He was probably mentally contrasting the reception given to him by the Arians and by the Orthodox and wondering which proved the more bitter.

He goes on that if his audience wishes him to give an exposition of the faith he will do so, as far as he is able.[277] Sections 14-18 of the Oration represent his last words on how the bishops ought to conduct themselves. It was his last chance to influence the theological decisions of the Council. What follows is one of the clearest Trinitarian synopses he composed. Several bishops have been applying theological economy, keeping their ideas to themselves, and remaining silent as long as overt unorthodoxy is not being mooted. Gregory cannot be part of their number. He has to teach his faith in the open.[278] His faith is that not one of the three persons of the Trinity can be severed from the Godhead (he thus expresses the primary point he wishes observed, that "the Spirit is God," without demanding it in the straightforwardly bare terms that he had found scared off so many theologians). There is One God without beginning who is the beginning. The name of the one without beginning is the Father. The name of the beginning, is the Son. The name of the One who is with the beginning, is the Holy Spirit. All three have one nature: that of God. The Union of all is located in the Father from whom and to whom all the order, or taxonomy, of the persons runs its course in perichoresis. This divine union is not a confusion for it gains its cohesion in a synonymity of will, and power, and eternity. In material realities a plurality of individuals would necessarily be the result of confessing such a distinct triad, but in God this plural division does not apply, because in the case of the Trinity all the divine persons have but one and the selfsame simple, uncompounded, essence.[279] In simple terms, the orthodox thinker must steer a course between the extremes of Sabellian monism and Arian atomism in regard to the doctrine of God. The proper confession is of the Father, The Son and The Holy Spirit as one in substance and glory, who thereby must receive a single and undivided worship.[280] Whatever technical terms are used is not the chief matter, and disputes on technicalities should now be abandoned. Hypostasis or Prosopon makes no difference as

275. Orat. 42.10, PG 36.469; alluding to 2 Cor 6:10.
276. Orat. 42.13, PG 36.473.
277. Orat. 42.14, PG 36.473.
278. Orat. 42.14, PG 36.473.
279. Orat. 42.15, PG 36.476.
280. The terms of this "homodoxy" were adopted in the Conciliar creed: "Who is worshipped together with the Father and the Son."

long as the doctrine of essential unity with distinction of proprieties is observed.[281] If one needs to be precise, the proper titles of the persons are: Unbegotten, Begotten, and the One who Proceeds.[282] What is critically important is that heretical bishops, the Moabites and Ammonites that Moses once expelled from Israel's assembly,[283] should not be allowed in to the councils of the Church where they will devastate the discussion of Trinitarian theology, by "maliciously disputing the generation and the ineffable procession of God."[284] Gregory will not give any further elaboration of proper trinitarian thought as others have already written on the subject, and his own works cover it too. It would be a shameful thing, he says, to begin amassing proofs of the doctrine as if it was a novelty rather than the ancient faith of the Church. He admits that it would be a very useful thing for someone to give a coherent exegesis of all the biblical texts that expound pneumatological doctrine, but regrets that he is unable to do so now. This has to stand as his confession before them all.[285]

Now that he has given an account, how should he summarize his time in the city? He is sure that his efforts can not be taken in any way as an offense to the church.[286] Accordingly, should he claim a retirement reward to mark all his labors? He chooses the gift of peace. He slyly slips in that the bishops can elect another worthy man in his place, someone who is "clean of hand, and skilled in oratory, and ready to dance your pleasure in all matters." As for him, he is worn out. His body is sick and feeble, he even feels his mental powers may be deserting him, it is such a labor to keep his mind focused.[287] He is sick of being the subject of criticism because he acted too gently. His many assailants who come up to strike him on the breast, he says, are not so worrisome, as he is able to defend himself well enough. It is those who come up from behind to stab him in the back that have brought him down. He turns from the bitter reminiscence to a more sardonic mockery of his critics. Has he been a good pilot as far as his presidency of the conciliar meetings has been concerned? He is aware that he has attracted much criticism on this score, but even so he must insist that he has been an excellent ferryman all round. They all piled into his boat. The seas were raging in a frightful storm. Then the passengers started to panic and throw themselves about all over the boat. What more could the ferryman have

281. Orat. 42.16, PG 36.477.
282. Orat. 42.17, PG 36.477.
283. Dt 23:3.
284. Orat. 42.18, PG 36.480. Gregory here openly criticizes Theodosius' decision to admit the 36 Pneumatomachian bishops in the hope of effecting their reconciliation. It was their presence, and the desire to accommodate them, that led to the vagaries of the early sessions, Gregory implies, and resulted in spoiling a clear trinitarian confession for the sake of fruitless ecumenism. Theodosius did not abandon his hopes for their reconciliation, and for the council to produce a generally eirenical theological statement, until the end of the next year.
285. Orat. 42.18, PG 36.480.
286. Orat. 42.19, PG 36.480.
287. Another jab at the bishops, for when a highly intelligent man complains of being unable to follow the logic of a meeting one ought not to presume it is his fault.

done? It was a miracle they all did not sink. They should be grateful they reached the shore at all.[288] But he has to say that continuing the party divisions of previous generations, making claims for Meletians as against Paulinians, as in the Antioch affair, is a shameful business of the past that needs to be buried now for good.[289] Gregory cannot bear any more strife. He feels as if he has been at the hippodrome rather than at an ecclesiastical synod, with various contenders lashing one another from their chariots as they jockeyed for position. The truth is, he simply did not agree with what the majority thought. It has always been a problem of his, and no matter how many people call him stupid on account of it he cannot change his ways. He finds himself time and time again like the old man Democritos of Abdera, laughing at all that he sees, finding the behavior of his contemporaries so hilarious that they come to regard him as addled in the head.[290] One charge he is not ashamed to make public: He has been accused by several bishops present of being pusillanimous. They argued to him that he had the chance of the emperor's ear, and could have called down a suitable vengeance on the heads of all those who had been their oppressors in the time of the Arian ascendancy under Valens. Gregory had failed in his duty by being too soft. What have they to show for the six months he has been in charge? Gregory replies that the "wheel of fortune" has put their common enemies in his hands. He has chosen to treat them properly, even though they did not treat the Nicenes properly. He has insisted on showing them forbearance. What has been the result? The Nicene cause has flourished, for God has blessed them because they were merciful to their enemies. He refuses to apologize for it.[291] Should he answer other charges that he did not conduct himself in the proper manner of a bishop of such an important see? For this he will ask their pardon, and in a highly ironic confession, he asks them to forgive his stupidity for not realizing that he should have been a *bon viveur* instead of an ascetic. He will take himself back to his rustic simplicity as his penance. And when he goes, he admits, he shall really miss the stimulating intellectual life the capital offers. But he shall certainly not miss the agitation. The people really want rhetors to entertain them, not priests to serve them; they want someone who can amass gold, not claim souls. They do not want a pure offerer of sacrifice, as much as a powerful patron who can give them access to the mighty. He is not the right man for such a job.[292] And so, the bishops present should give him an "honorable discharge," good papers of dismissal that he can be proud of in his retirement. If they do not think he is even worthy of this, then it is of no matter. He knows that in the eyes of God he has done well. Now his colleagues can offer him their commendations; he offers them his last farewell.[293] The Oration concludes with a series of

288. Orat. 42.20, PG 36.481.
289. Orat. 42.21, PG 36.484.
290. Orat. 42.22, PG 36.485.
291. Orat. 42.23, PG 36.485.
292. Orat. 42.24, PG 36.488.
293. Orat. 42.25, PG 36.489.

Ave atque Vale. His first farewell is to his beloved Anastasia; it is that Shiloh where the Ark of the covenant finally came to rest in Israel after long years of wandering.[294] He bids farewell to the Church of the Holy Apostles. He wishes he had celebrated the liturgy in it more often, though his illness in the last months prevented him. He will remember with fondness the monastic singing of the psalms and the vigil services attended by the virgins and matrons, and the poor recipients of the church's aid. He recalls with fondness how many pressed in the great church to hear him speak, not even bothering to conceal the fact that they were taking down his speeches stenographically as he spoke.[295] He gives a last wave to the eunuchs gathered around the Emperor and, knowing that they were delighted to see him go, wonders aloud if they will be faithful to their new master, "for they are certainly not faithful to God." His words were a warning to Theodosius not to overlook the fact that here at his side was a large continuing faction defending the Homoian cause. Finally, he says that he shall cease speaking: "though I will not leave off the fight, by means of my writings."[296]

Gregory, finally feted and honored on every side, once he had been politically sidelined, left the city sometime in late June and made his way back to Cappadocia. He took with him the priest Cledonios, given to assist him by his cousin Amphilokios, to whom he had promised a country estate in his will. Cledonios was soon to take charge of the daily affairs of the church at Nazianzus so that Gregory himself would not have to be tied down. In his company were also his clergy and servants who had been with him throughout his time in the city, the deacon Evagrios, and the monk Eustathios. They were to be his chief companions at the hillside estate of Karbala near Arianzum, and he had already indicated in his will that he wanted them to possess the place after he died and continue running it as a monastic retreat.[297] With him were also the child Theophilos and the two brothers both called Eupraxios (probably because they were twins), and his notary-scribe Theodosius, all of whom were slaves of the Nazianzus estate who had been promised manumission as free men in his will. The road from the city gates ran straight through Nazianzus, but it was a long and hard journey, and he had a lot to turn over in his mind.

The council continued to meet throughout June, and confirmed Flavian as legitimate bishop of Antioch. Diodore's influence was very important at the remaining sessions, and he arranged that a rich, and so far unbaptized, married senator named Nektarios would accede to the throne of Constantinople. It was pleasing to Theodosius because he had a politician at his side whom he could rely on to put into place any policy he chose. It was useful to Diodore, because Nektarios had no knowledge at all about theology and would always be dependent on good advice he

294. Josh 18:8; Judg 18:31.
295. Orat. 42.26, PG 36.489–492.
296. Orat. 42.26, PG 36.492.
297. *Exemplum Testamenti*, PG 37.392.

himself hoped to supply. The selection of Nektarios was one of the most bitter pills that Gregory had to swallow: that he should have been unseated for a man of no theological, oratorical, or spiritual experience to speak of.[298] On July 9, 381, the conciliar business was concluded. The creed that is traditionally associated with this council is a most important confession in that it is now the creed that has ousted the Nicene symbol so as to be recited at every eucharistic service of the Orthodox and Catholic churches. Lack of any Acts for the council makes it difficult to correlate the text exactly with any conciliar business. Even so, it is certain that this creed fully represents all that Gregory took objection to in the high summer of 381.[299] It is not that it is unorthodox, if one gives it a circumspect exegesis, it is just that it represents what he denounced in *Oration* 42 as "unsuitable caution."

The christological clauses of the creed repeat the Nicene statement. The pneumatological clauses make an advance on the bare statement of Nicaea: "And we believe in the Holy Spirit." They go on to clarify the basis of Trinitarian theology as Gregory had insisted was necessary. The words are very carefully chosen, like a legal script where nothing is said, or left unsaid, without purpose:

> We believe in the Holy Spirit, the Lord and Life-Giver, who proceeds from the Father. Together with the Father and the Son he is worshipped and glorified. He spoke through the prophets

Ostensibly this clearly confesses the divinity of the Holy Spirit; or does it? It was a wonderful mixture of specific Nicene thought and Pneumatomachian ambivalence. It has universally come to be interpreted as professing the full deity of the Spirit of God, but that is largely attributable to the international acceptance of Gregory's theology as its exegesis. If we leave aside reading the credal intention through his lens for a moment (it was an irony he perhaps did not live to appreciate, though he certainly dedicated his last literary efforts to bringing it about), then certain things become abundantly obvious about this conciliar confession. It deliberately does not ascribe the title God to the Holy Spirit. It does not apply the notion of the Homoousion to the Holy Spirit. It studiously avoids any theology explicating the mystery of Trinitarian perichoresis. It makes only two statements to elucidate its positive confession: that the Spirit is "conglorified" with the Father and the Son, and that the Spirit "spoke through the prophets."

The latter confession is so vague as to be unarguable. The ascription of the right to "conglorification" with the Father and Son is a deliberate rejection of Gregory's Homoousion in preference for the concept of "Syndoxa." What is not said is that the Spirit of God is worthy of "Homotimia," which was what Athanasios and Basil had argued. For if one worships the Spirit as one worships God it is synonymous with confessing the Spirit to be God. Even this had drawn some criticism from Gregory

---

298. Cf. McGuckin, "Autobiography as Apologia" (2001).
299. Cf. Hanson (1988), pp. 812–820, who, following Ritter's critical study (1965), shows its connection to the council of 381.

when Basil had preferred it to his own insistence on proclaiming the Homoousion of the Spirit explicitly, but Gregory knew that Homotimia was essentially orthodox; a way of confessing the status of the divine Spirit through the liturgical confessions of the church. The confession of 381, however, argues only that "syndoxa" need be offered: that is veneration and glorification "along with God the Father and Son." This compromise of deliberately not specifying what that honor and worship should be (co-equal? or associative? or inferior?) was exactly the strategy that the Homoian Arians had long been pressing in regard to the divine status of the Son.

It was not as if the Homoians set out wanting to deny the Son's divinity, or erect this as the main premise of their school. This was the position that Gregory, their critic and opponent, wanted to push them to, in the footsteps of Athanasios and the other Nicenes who had argued passionately that the logical denial of the full co-equal deity of the Father and the Son deprived the Son of any entitlement whatsoever to divine rank. The Homoian position did not see the logic or the religious vague of this approach, and was happy with a vaguer confession that the Son was "like God in nature": different in some respects since he was not the Unoriginate God, but closely "associated with, and glorified with" the divine Father. Conglorification, not "co-equal glorification," was what was meant by the Arians here. For generations the Nicenes had fought them on the basis that this vagueness of confession of the full co-equal divinity was a denial of the faith. Now, in the cause of finding a vague enough commonality of confession that could unite the Neo-Nicenes, the old Homoiousians, and even the rump of the Macedonian party (later disparaged as the Pneumatomachians), the conciliar confession opted for a comparable vagueness in regard to the Spirit. The Nicene-Constantinopolitan creed is capable of being interpreted according to Gregory's theology only if "conglorification" is further specified into meaning "co-equal glory." The fact that the statement deliberately avoids this, while at the same time ignoring his pleas for the ascription of a clear divine title to the Spirit and the affirmation of the Homoousion of the Third Person of the Trinity, all amounts to a studied rebuttal of the terms of Gregory's Trinity doctrine set out in his *Five Theological Orations*, and even that of the last address he gave to the fathers before leaving the city. They did not only abandon him for his "gentleness" in dealing with their Arian enemies; it seems that the majority also jettisoned him because of his doctrine of God. Perhaps this is why he made his last remark to the assembly, at the very end of *Oration* 42, that though his tongue would henceforth be silent, he would carry on the fight unceasingly in his writings.

With continuing tact he never comes out and denounces his episcopal colleagues overtly for heresy. Equally he refused to come back to the capital to advise them in the further sessions of the council held in 382. He would have nothing to do with it. It was a briny pollution of the sweet spring of Nicene faith as far as he was concerned. It did not so much poison drinkers as make them sick. As he made his way into a self-imposed exile, it became more and more clear to him that he had to spend a lot of time polishing his literary works so that they could enjoy the largest and most "exemplary" circulation possible. He would transform them into a veritable compendium of writings and sermons needed in any future bishop's cabinet. It might take him the rest of his life, but this is basically the task he set himself. As with the Apostle Paul, his occasional sermons were destined to be elevated into a paradigmatic canon. He had a lot to do, and his failing health was against him. And so the carriage bumped its way back along the dusty summer roads to the familiar terrain of Cappadocia.

7

THE TWILIGHT OF A POET

And it was at that age that poetry came
Searching for me...
And I made my own way
Deciphering that fire,
And I wrote the first faint line...
The heavens unlocked and were laid open...
And I danced a circle with the stars,
My heart breaking loose on the wind.

Pablo Neruda

The more he began to think of the conduct of the bishops at the council, the more the need grew to vent his feelings. He wrote a series of poems on his way back home, and over the first few years of his time in Nazianzus, all aimed at episcopal hypocrisy. For several years, on and off, perhaps up to around 385, he would be concerned with apologetic writing, to offset the stories he heard that his reputation was being slighted in the city, and to make sure that he and the Trinity were not thrown out in one and the same movement.

The experience of the council had severely dented his belief that the bishops were the apostolic successors of the prophetic charism, and therefore should be the epitome of prayerfulness, kindness, and supreme theological wisdom. The chief exemplar of his anti-episcopal sentiment is the autobiographical poem the *De Vita Sua*, which he began to construct in this period. The short poem *A Farewell to My Enemies*,[1] shows both of his major apologetic motifs succinctly: his dismay at the hypocrisy of the clergy, and the sense that he abandoned the council because he was losing the battle over pneumatology.[2] He says that his enemies can applaud their success in getting rid of him, but it shall be a short-lived victory. He has got the better part, for having been forced to "share in error for a time, I have now escaped."[3] He had quite a few other poems to write before he got it all out of his system.[4] Every now and again he has to write a poem of particular lament, for his lost Anastasia. The early months when he first preached to that small congregation of faithful lodged as the best of times in his memory.[5]

---

1. Carm. 2.1.7, PG 37.1024.
2. Ibid. "Companions of my sacred office... I am leaving. Now applaud to your heart's content... For my part I am singing a hymn. The Spirit was always sacred to me. It was his honor I defended. But no more shall I have to jump in to separate those brawlers."
3. Carm. 2.1.9, vv. 11-12, PG 37.1026.
4. Carm. 2.1.8; 2.1.9; 2.1.10, PG 37.1025-1029; Carm. 2.1.12-15, PG 37.1166-1254; Carm. 2.1.17-18, PG 37.1262-1270; Carm. 2.1.40, PG 37.1337-1339.
5. Carm. 2.1.5, PG 37.1022-1023; Carm. 2.1.6, PG 37.1023-1024; Carm. 2.1.16, *Somnium de*

Most of his poetry from this period shows a high degree of self-examination of all that had gone on in the turbulent time of his administration. He feels that he has nothing to reproach himself for under the eyes of Christ. He suffered for noble reasons, even if in the eyes of the world his spiritual behavior appeared as political ineptitude. He tried his best not to belong to either party at war with the other, and for that he became the enemy of all.[6] He had to learn patience to suffer such a deep rejection,[7] which was a hard lesson. His thoughts turn also to asking solace from God; wondering where his life had gone, what were his ultimate accomplishments? The court, the city, the council of bishops, all had turned their backs on him. What was left to him now? Perhaps God had used the sorrowful events to call him back to the quiet life that had always been his deepest joy and his first calling, when God spoke to him directly[8] "in dreams of the night and through the terrors of the deeps" and first confirmed his Christian vocation. Now he has had to flee again from another storm, but this time in silence and contemplation he shall find a safe haven out of the swell of the sea.[9]

Hand in hand with his reflection on the perfidy of "modern bishops"[10] goes his decision to fulfil a debt of honor he must have promised to Gregory of Nyssa in Constantinople. His failure to attend the funeral ceremonies of Basil had been explained at the time on the grounds of ill health, and his convalescence in Seleukia. To signal that the old fallings-out were over (though there is a lot of resentment still apparent in his reminiscences), Gregory agreed to compose a funeral oration for Basil. It was designed for a present apologetic purpose too, for now that he had returned with his loyal monastic followers to Cappadocia, they had to find some *modus vivendi* with the larger monastic community based at Caesarea and fervently dedicated to Basil's memory and the defense of his reputation. Gregory knew that he had some bridges to build here, and this is one of the chief motivations of his *Oration* 43. Whether he delivered this text at Caesarea is a moot point, though it is probable.[11] He says that he gave the oration after many others had spoken before him,[12] which suggests that it was a large church festival of the martyrs or other such occasion that was also combined with memorials for Basil. The event could have been the twice yearly celebration of the Cappadocian

Anastasiae ecclesia, PG 37.1254-1261.
6. Carm. 2.1.10, vv. 18-20, PG 37.1028.
7. Carm. 2.1.12, PG 37.1166.
8. The image evokes God calling to the young prophet Samuel (1 Sam 3).
9. Carm. 2.1.10. vv. 25-33, PG 37.1029.
10. He has a section contrasting the hasty manufacture of a bishop (Nektarios) with the long ascetical preparation that the model bishop (Basil) underwent. Orat. 43. 26, PG 36.532.
11. Gallay (1943), p. 215, thinks he did, on the evidence of Gregory Presbyter's *Vita*, PG 35.301. But Gregory Nazianzen only says that he offers the speech in praise of Basil because he recognizes some of Basil's devotees in the audience (Orat. 43.2, PG 36.496.).
12. Orat. 43.2, PG 36.496.

martyr Mamas. This was a general occasion for large gatherings next to Caesarea[13] on September 1,[14] and also on the first Sunday after Easter.[15] It has generally been presumed that the funeral oration was preached on Basil's anniversary of death, January 1, but there is no pressing reason to suppose why this should be the case at this period, before calendrical celebrations of nonmartyr saints was fully established. It could, therefore, have been delivered at Caesarea at the town festival of the week after Easter 382, or that of September 383. The memorial oration for Basil is one of the most heavily worked-on of all his writings, and he drafted and redrafted it until in its final state it would have taken more than two and a half hours to deliver if preached as written.[16]

It has become one of the standard sources for Basil's life, and is the single greatest exemplar of Christian hagiographic writing, excelling even Athanasios' *Vita Antonii* and setting a standard, based on classical models of panegyric, that would be followed in the subsequent creation of the Byzantine genre of hagiography. The inner motivations, to re-establish a disrupted harmony between Basil's ascetics and himself, leads Gregory to devote much time to an idyllic period in Athens where his love for Basil was reciprocated in full, and Gregory himself was the initiator of Basil's ascetical interests.[17] This role he claims as ascetic guide stems from the fact that he himself was already baptized in his time at Athens whereas Basil was not. It also successfully removes Macrina and Eustathios of Sebaste, entirely and absolutely, from the picture as mentors. This is exactly what he wanted to do, to expunge the memory of Homoiousians who resisted the theology of the Trinity, and to claim back Basil himself purely and always as a trinitarian Homoousian. Armenians appear in the Athenian narrative as shady characters who unsettle and wound Basil, another sideways slight at Eustathios who came from Armenia.[18] He does not fail to remind everyone how his own father had been the leading protagonist of Basil's election even when the odds seemed stacked against him,[19] and how he himself had been Basil's right hand man in the time when the Arian Valens had[20] opened war against them. In all the hagiographic achievements of Basil which he recounts, the plural subject "we," rivets his own role to that of Basil at every step. Even the great falling-out, over the Sasima episode, is referred to as an unaccountable coldness and distrust that Basil (alone) began to entertain for Gregory.[21] It is all his fault. The

13. The basilica has been excavated in the village of Mamasios.
14. Cf. di Berardino (1992), p. 518, "St Mamas." Basil has left an Oration for St Mamas from this September festival.
15. This is the feast from which Gregory's own panegyric for St Mamas comes; cf. Orat. 44.12, PG 36.620-621.
16. Gallay (1943), p. 214.
17. Orat. 43.18-19, PG 36.520-521; Orat. 43.21, PG 36.524; Orat. 43.22, PG 36.525.
18. Orat. 43.17, PG 36.517.
19. Orat. 43.37, PG 36.545.
20. Orat. 43.44-54, PG 36.553-565.
21. Orat. 43.59, PG 36.573.

hearer could not possibly doubt that here was a devoted "Basilian" to judge from the passionate tenor of the panegyric. How easy it must have been to believe that perhaps it *was* all Basil's fault, given the latter's known tendency for pushing people round. The *Funeral Oration* ends with a last and most pressing concern of Gregory's: that Basil himself was, of course, a sworn follower of the doctrine of the Homoousion of the Spirit of God.[22] This might have been "unknown to the majority" but Gregory testifies to it from his own more intimate acquaintance with Basil's mind. This might well have been news to Basil's own followers, and to a reader of Basil's *De Spiritu Sancto*, but it is a way of Gregory catching up Basil into his own ongoing fight for Nicene orthodoxy. If Basil had once violently pressed Gregory into his service, Gregory now presses Basil into his. It was to be a standard element of hagiography ever afterwards, that the saint's doctrine was polished to contemporary standards. It certainly served its purposes in so eloquently persuading. For centuries afterwards it has been a major supposition that the thought of the "Cappadocian Fathers" is of a piece. So successfully did Gregory transform his old friend. Such a seamless unity is something that can only be sustained on the most careless and generic reading of the texts. Nicenes they may have been, but the details of what that meant both in Christology and Trinitarian thought calls for a far greater degree of shading. The homily also seemed to have had a contemporary success in reestablishing friendly relations among the local monks. He would be invited back next year to preach the paschal festal homily for St Mamas (*Oration* 44). And this time, perhaps, he would not be left to the end of a long series of previous speakers, surely a mark of their earlier disapproval.

Back home in Nazianzus, when Gregory heard the news of the election of Nektarios, a man who had no training and was not even baptized, and whose life hitherto had nothing to commend it in terms of his record for the defense of the Church, his rage was such that he composed a very long diatribe, and Diodore of Tarsus and Nektarios were two of the main objects of attack.[23] Against Diodore he even raises serious charges of heresy, in regard to the dualist tendency of his christological teaching, that he now feels free enough to give his genuine opinion about.[24] The subject of worldly young bishops is also much in evidence, especially the figure of a bishop who attended the theatre and who celebrated his wedding just before his election to a see (probably one of the numerous bishops appointed to replace ousted Arian incumbents in the conciliar business of 381). The exact identity of this bishop is not known, but he was certainly one of the young men of Antioch who shouted Gregory down vociferously and was rewarded with ecclesiastical preferment for his pains. Gregory's shock at his consecration so shortly after his

22. Orat. 43.69, PG 36.589.
23. Cf. McGuckin, "Autobiography as Apologia" (2001); material from which is used in this section.
24. Cf. *De Vita Sua*, vv. 609-651, PG 37.1071-1074; a charge repeated again in his heresiological list, ibid., vv. 1152-1207, esp. v. 1184 which attacks Diodore, PG 37.1108-1112.

courtship is colored by his own sense of having been a failure in the city because he was too ascetical, and too unworldly to oil the political wheels.

The choice of Nektarios, another married and wealthy socialite, the former Praetor of the city, is taken by him as yet one more slap in the face for ascetic bishops. He also includes in the hit list the Archbishop of Alexandria, Timothy, who had challenged his right to the throne. The catalogue of villains is given succinctly in the poem *On Himself and the Bishops*, vv. 397-710, which enumerates six main targets.[25] Chief among them all, surprisingly, is Nektarios. The motive of re-establishing himself as a theological standard-bearer for the Nicene cause, is surely a significant part of his intent in this vituperative defense of his honor, and his attention to Nektarios is an indication (if we needed one) that Constantinople was the intended destination for his major poetry.

He felt that his reputation had been badly damaged, not only by the ridicule he was suffering, but especially in the rejection of his doctrine of the Homoousion of the Spirit as an "innovation"[26] by the council fathers. Accordingly he must have felt the slighting of his qualifications by the Theodosian court in the manner in which Gregory of Nyssa and the current metropolitan of Caesarea Helladios (no great theological genius) were recognized by the emperor as Cappadocian arbiters of the faith, though he himself was passed over in silence. This was largely his own fault, since he had vehemently refused Theodosius' repeated requests that he should attend the subsequent session of the council at Constantinople in 382 as a theological *peritus*.[27] He was content to fire off a series of letters to bishops he thought would listen to him, pleading for a better regulation of conciliar affairs this time around.[28]

25. (a) Bishops who had had disgraceful pasts as stage mimes (Maximus the Cynic) *De seipso et de episcopis*, Carm. 2.1.12, vv. 397-404, PG 37.1195; (b) a horseracer, ibid., vv. 405-514 (I cannot relate this to any precise person); (c) a crooked lawyer, ibid., vv. 415-431 (I think this may be a reference to the late Peter of Alexandria whom he knows betrayed him [cf. *De Vita Sua*, vv. 858-864, PG 37.1088-1089] since he makes the joke of Simon Magus becoming Simon Peter); (d) A recently baptized courtier, *De seipso et de episcopis*, Carm. 2.1.12, vv. 432-619, PG 37.1197-1211 [Nektarios]; (e) a newly consecrated young bishop fresh from amorous dalliances, ibid., vv. 620-627, PG 37.1211 (and also see *De Vita Sua*, vv. 1407-1411 and vv. 1680-1687, PG 37.1126, 1148-1149). (One of the young agitators of the Antiochene party after Meletios' death who demanded Flavian's election in opposition to his own presidential agenda. Who this may be is uncertain. It is either one of those consecrated bishop at Meletios' Synod of Antioch in 379, or one of the new candidates appointed by the council itself, to oust Arian incumbents in outlying sees. The partial list for this council survives. Cf. Hanson. [1988], p. 803, fn. 63.)
26. *De Vita Sua*, v. 1760, PG 37.1152.
27. Cf. Ep. 130 which disparages councils as the worst way to resolve the difficulties of the Church, PG 37.225. Gregory pleads with the court officials to organize things better than they did in 381. Ep. 131 declined his second imperial summons too. Gregory was more interested in undermining the chicaneries of those he regarded as betrayers of the faith at the council, and in presenting a purer version of orthodoxy in the form of his *Theological Orations* which he was actively editing at this time.
28. Epp. 132-136, PG 37.228f; Gallay (1967), pp. 21f.

If he does not develop greatly on theological themes in the autobiographical texts he was writing at this time, it is only because he is already completing his editorial work on his *Theological Orations* for their publication, and dissemination back in the capital.

The large body of poems which Gregory wrote at this time contains much uneven work,[29] designed for a good deal of different reasons and crafted in diverse genres. Many of the pieces were didactic memory-verses written for the education of children in grammatical schools.[30] Many were epigrams or epitaph rhymes written idly, or as ascetical exercises in *memento mori*.[31] And many more were private prayers addressed from the heart to Christ, frequently in times of illness or depression.[32] The latter have often been elevated to provide the key signature for Gregory's last years.[33] The larger and more worked-on poems, however, do not fit into this category, and are robustly apologetic, above and beyond the personal hurt feelings Gregory manifests on his ejection from the capital. What they show is that he was very well aware that a propaganda battle was under way that was bent on claiming the Nicene inheritance and establishing the terms of reference for future orthodoxy; and he was determined not to allow the imperial court to get the upper hand in this movement. If the Nicene cause was finally in the ascendancy he was ready to continue working hard that it should be his version of it that triumphed. This is why these first years after 381, when he lived quietly back at home, demonstrate such a remarkable and continuing literary effort. He not only edited all his collection of Orations, he composed *de novo* apologetic poetry and anti-Apollinarist treatises. The image of Gregory slowly pining away in a depressed decline is a cliché that does not do justice to the evidence of the extant literature. The old lion still had a lot of roar left. He reminds me, in this time of his advanced age, of the poet Tennyson:

> Though much is taken, much abides; and though
> We are not now that strength which in old days
> Moved earth and heaven; that which we are, we are;
> One equal temper of heroic hearts,
> Made weak by time and fate, but strong in will
> To strive, to seek, to find, and not to yield.[34]

29. Like many another prolific poet he could churn out very dull pieces, as well as write vivid masterpieces. He carefully sifted through his *Orations* and *Letters* for publication, but does not seem to have done as much for his poetry.
30. Such as the verse synopses of the Old Testament miracles, and the Gospels. Carm. 1.1.12-28, PG 37.472f.
31. Such as the numerous examples in PG 38.11-130.
32. Such as Carm. 2.1.20-27; Carm. 2.1.33; Carm. 2.1.61-66 and 69-77, among others. A number of these smaller poems have been translated in McGuckin (1986, 1989). Other larger and more substantive poems can be found in translation in Moreschini and Sykes (1996), White (1996) and Gilbert (1994).
33. Cf. Rapisarda (1951).
34. Tennyson, *Ulysses*.

If most of the various motives for his postconciliar apologetic have long been recognized, the attack on Nektarios, I think, has not generally been discerned as dominantly operative within the poetic works from 382 to 385, and this for various reasons,[35] but it is, in my opinion, one of the chief spurs for his composition of the writings. One of the most bitter slights of all that had happened to him, he felt, was the election of Nektarios his successor whom he regarded (at least initially)[36] as a disastrous and unfitting choice, and a terrible slur on his honor as the de-selected predecessor.

Hanson describes the election of Nektarios as an example of the "ferocious coercion" Theodosius was to exercise on Church affairs, and calls it "an act to which the pro-Nicene party raised no objection."[37] This is hardly the case. Gregory Nazianzen at least regarded it as a dreadful precedent, and not merely for personal reasons of his own dispossession, but in relation to the Nicene cause which he certainly did not equate with the Theodosian policy that was launched under Nektarios' supervision. An archbishop who was devoid of theology, did not even know the basics of trinitarian thought until his hurried baptism days before his episcopal consecration, and who was a career politician, could only spell an ecclesiastical policy designed to be imposed as a state bureaucracy. If Gregory had little respect for Theodosius as a theologian, he had none at all for his choice of Church leader. It is none other than Nektarios, I am sure, who largely accounts for all the scorn poured in these late poems upon bishops who have not received any training,[38] and whose personal lives hitherto have not been models of ascetic piety. This, of course, conflicts with the generally received opinion, that Gregory more or less accepted Nektarios gracefully. The traditional view, which is repeated even into the modern critical edition of Gregory's *Letters*, is summed up elegantly in that venerable tome, the *Dictionary of Christian Biography*, as follows: "The good relations which subsisted between Nectarius and his illustrious predecessor are clear from six graceful letters which remain in the correspondence of Gregory."[39]

The *Letters to Nektarios* are Epp. 88, 91, 151, 185, 186 and 202 in the corpus.[40] If their tone is graceful and affable, how can this be reconciled with what appears from the autobiographical poems to be a determined assault on the worthiness of Nektarios to occupy the throne of the capital? We need to look more closely at the texts.

---

35. Meehan's (1987) footnotes to his translation of the *De Rebus*, p. 21, and fn. 62, p. 74, for example, presuppose no anti-Nektarian apologetic at all.
36. The later letters to Nektarios suggest he was moving to a grudging reconciliation in around 384-385, as he heard reports from the capital that Nektarios was doing a reasonably good job after all, and had actually been attacked by an Arian mob for his pains.
37. Hanson, (1988), p. 322.
38. The comic complaint that some bishops were still sooty with (slave-labor) smoke may perhaps be a jibe at Aetios who earned his living earlier as a "tinker"; but Aetios could hardly be dismissed as an unlearned man. Cf. *De seipso et de episcopis*, vv. 155f; Carm. 2.1.12, PG 37.1177.
39. W Smith and H Wace, *Dictionary of Christian Biography* (London, 1887), p. 12.
40. Cf. Hauser-Meury (1960), pp. 126-128.

The first letter in hand is 88. In it Gregory appears to express his delight in Nektarios' election, though bemoaning his own expulsion from the city. The letter, however, has several large question marks hanging over its authenticity. In the eleventh-century Cod. Vat. gr. 676 it appears as the work of the eleventh-century Byzantine writer John Mauropus, and is unknown to the six main families of Gregorian manuscripts. Gallay is inclined to think it is authentic on the somewhat circular argument that Gregory is known to have written to Nektarios (Ep. 91) and "it fits perfectly with the life of Gregory,"[41] but he admits that its place in the corpus remains dubious.[42] I propose that the letter is more than dubious, it is simply misascribed. Gregory supposedly praises Nektarios for his election as an ornament to the imperial city, and acclaims him for his oratorical ability, but the latter was a skill which Nektarios simply did not possess, and Gregory never attributes that particular encomium carelessly. Nektarios was neither a skilled speaker nor, even at the end of his long reign, sufficiently skilled as a theologian to be able to conduct doctrinal investigations without expert assistance.[43] At the end of *Epistle* 88, the writer professes eternal friendship—which accounts for the highly positive estimate of relations presumed by the traditional versions of the history—but at a stroke, with the removal of letter 88 from the hand of Gregory, all this is taken away, and we are left with a very different overall perspective on the remaining letters exchanged between Gregory and his successor, especially when they are read in the light of the poetic autobiographies.

The first of these is *Letter* 91. It is a very cool affair, where Gregory describes his situation (in reply to Nektarios evidently solicitous questions) as merely: "so, so." His tone is still highly defensive. He wishes Nektarios to "prosper and reign" as the psalmist says, sardonically omitting the remainder of the biblical phrase: "ride on in triumph." He pointedly makes his prayer that God, who has honored Nektarios with the priesthood, might keep him out of all calumny's way. He adds on to his letter a request. He asks Nektarios to advance his client Pancratios, but here he couches the request for patronage (a request which fills his other letters to the nobility of Cappadocia and Constantinople more or less as commonplaces, frequently warm and jovial in tone) with the rather frosty context of offering this "recommendation" as kind of "testing of the waters" between them.[44] He does not want any "human weakness" to affect their relationship, indicating, I suspect, that the feeling between them (at least on Gregory's side) was already more than colored by the

41. Gallay (1964), pp. xxxvi-xxxvii. See also idem. (1967) (re. epp. 103-249).
42. "En définitive, il reste un doute sur l'authenticité de la lettre 88." Gallay (1964), p. xxxvii.
43. That is, he always got others to do it for him. There is a highly ironic reference to Nektarios' capacity to recognize an important theological issue in Gregory's Ep. 202, PG 37.332, when Gregory tells Nektarios he is aware: "just how profoundly you have been instructed in the divine mysteries," and (accordingly) sends him his letter to explain what the Apollinarist issue is really about.
44. "I am addressing you this request so that we might give one another a mutual sign of confidence, not allowing any human weakness to affect us who stand in God's service."

bitter sentiments he still experienced in the aftermath of his departure from the city. It is also interesting to speculate as to whether Nektarios was so innocent and ignorant of his elevation as the common version of the story would have it. For two things are quite clear about that elevation, and ought not to be overshadowed by the myth of an unbaptized unknown who rose to prominence overnight. One is that Nektarios was clearly a choice of Theodosius who used him as a trusted state functionary in the task of bringing order to the ecclesiastical chaos, and the other is that Nektarios was a candidate proposed by Diodore of Tarsus, who was leading the Antiochene faction at the council, the bane of Gregory's life as president, and a man whose theology Gregory found verging on the heretical. The position of Nektarios is thus made triply problematic in Gregory's eyes: first as the successor to his own position which had been so rudely terminated, secondly as a candidate without any serious ecclesiastical training who was to serve as a functionary in the state promulgation of an orthodoxy Gregory deplored, and thirdly as a client of one of his most annoying conciliar opponents and theological enemies. Since Diodore had been the chief protagonist for the selection of Flavian, and thus the main leader of the opposition to Gregory's eirenical policy over the Meletian schism, Gregory increasingly came to regard him as the main agent of his fall from the throne of Constantinople.

Gregory's second letter to Nektarios[45] is couched in the same tone as the first and probably dates from the same time. He tells Nektarios that he is pleased by the general report he hears about Nektarios' good attitude which he (Gregory) has fostered among the influential, spreading a good report of how Nektarios is according Gregory honor and respect. In this light, he again sends Nektarios a young protégé of his, George, to see if he will do anything for him. The sense of testing the waters is still abundantly present,[46] although Gregory professes to be pleased at the way the relationship is working out. The observation about Nektarios' "good reputation" is a notable factor and occurs in other letters. This is indicative for, as we shall see, the harsh critique leveled against Nektarios in the autobiographical writings turns on the issue of a good reputation thoroughly undeserved.

Letter 185 is another appeal of Gregory's to Nektarios in his role as chief ecclesiastical judge of the Orient, and in it he intercedes for Bishop Bosporios,[47] who has been ousted from his throne on a charge of heresy. Gregory offers to stand surety for him on the basis of his own reputation for orthodoxy, and requests that trials of bishops should henceforth be restricted to a council of peers, something that was moved

---

45. Ep. 151, PG 37.256-257; Gallay (1967), p. 43.
46. "Grant him this favor he needs, if you are willing; or if you like grant it as if to us, for I know you have decided to be gracious to me in all things, as your deeds bear witness." Ep. 151, PG 37.257; Gallay (1967), p. 43.
47. A mark of his generosity of character for Bosporios had shown him only persistent aggravation when he returned to Cappadocia wanting to retire. Cf. Ep. 138, PG 37.233-236; Gallay (1967), pp. 26-27. He argues for Bosporios' cause also in Epp. 183 to Theodore of Tyana, PG 37.301; Gallay (1967), p. 74

to become imperial policy afterwards. In the preamble to the letter he again mentions how Nektarios is gaining a universal reputation for fulfilling his offices honorably[48] and once again (underlining for Nektarios' benefit how good are his sources of intelligence about life in the capital) ascribing this good reputation Nektarios is making with the latter's continuing policy of respecting Gregory's reputation and person,[49] and not merely offering respect but being willing to accept Gregory as his spiritual father and guide.

The same thing is seen in Ep. 186 which Gregory sends to Nektarios in the hands of his niece who wishes to have a case heard in the capital, and whom Gregory commends to Nektarios. Here he is sure Nektarios will assist her promptly, making the rather double-edged comparison to the Unjust Judge in the Gospel who even from his wicked heart acted promptly to help the widow.[50] All of these letters, 91, 151, and 185-186 are of a piece and may be dated closely together. They are written in an indeterminate time after Gregory's retirement but probably somewhere between 382 and mid-383. They certainly precede letter 202 which is from the end of that year.[51]

This last letter to Nektarios is more of an open complaint, spreading the news of Eunomios' the Neo-Arian's return to his native Cappadocia where he was still active; as Gregory says: "that grumbling bowel of the church." It probably was the spur for the issuing from Constantinople of an imperial sentence of exile against Eunomios. So far he had escaped more or less with impunity, clearing out of the capital when he knew the situation was most unfavorable. Now he received a formal exile to Moesia, and then was confined to the environs of Caesarea where his work could be curtailed by the archbishop. Finally, when he was perceived to have acceded to his silencing, he was allowed to spend his late years on his private estate in Cappadocia, dying sometime in 394, a few years after Gregory himself.

In the process of *Letter* 202 Gregory criticizes Nektarios for not doing enough to suppress the "even greater wickedness" of Apollinarism[52] which has unaccountably escaped the imperial proscriptions. This letter, a synoptic treatise on the evils of Apollinarism (like Ep. 101), is not a personal correspondence in any sense, rather a critical comment on the way in which the imperial policy of putting into effect the conciliar judgments of 381-382 has been handled by Nektarios' ecclesiastical bureau.

48. Ep. 185, PG 37.301; Gallay (1967), pp. 75-76.
49. "To their praises I add my own, and not as if lagging behind them either, for you have honored and respected us, and like a loving son have consoled your father's gray hairs." Ep. 185, PG 37.301; Gallay (1967), p. 75.
50. Ep. 186, PG 37.305; Gallay (1967), p. 77.
51. Ep. 202, PG 37.329-333.
52. Ep. 202, PG 37.332B. An extraordinary judgment from one who knew both systems intimately, but explicable, I think, on the grounds that it is better to err fundamentally in theology (as Eunomios did for Gregory) which exceeds our "capacity" anyway, than to err fundamentally in terms of the economy of salvation (which Apollinaris did) which destroys the evangelical hope more concretely and immediately.

The net result of all this is that, with the removal of *Letter* 88 from the corpus, we see a correspondence with his successor that shows Gregory is highly circumspect, offering, as it were, the exchange of clients as marks of goodwill and rapprochement between two gentlemen; men of the church who must not be seen to be divided "by human weakness." The tone is far from the hearty attitude signified by *Letter* 88 which for a long time falsified the general assessment of the relationship between the two. Nektarios certainly seems to have been trying to assuage Gregory, and he may have succeeded in establishing a distant kind of politeness by 384, but in the immediate aftermath of the council Gregory's feelings were very different indeed, and in the period between the council and the latter date, his hostility is given full tongue in the caricature of his successor in the autobiographical writings.

It is Nektarios, then, who is the paradigm of the uneducated bishop in these writings. As such he is a comic figure who is brought onstage many times The proems to both the *De Vita* and the *De seipso et de episcopis* set the rifle sights directly onto Nektarios.[53] In the *De Vita* he is the prime unnamed example of bishops appointed to lead others who do not know the way themselves, and Gregory ends with the extraordinarily subversive invitation to his readers: "not to follow such guides at all is my best advice." Even in the *De Rebus Suis*, which has a far more generic character of lament over the troubles of Gregory's life, the final edit has taken pains to include Nektarios into its remit. Here I propose that the reference to one of the greatest griefs in life being the way in which worthless people gain and sustain good reputations,[54] has direct bearing on the news which came to him from the capital that Nektarios was actually performing very well in office. The issue of Nektarios' good reputation (in contrast to his own honor which he thought was being impugned in the city)[55] is factor which he keeps alluding to, almost grudgingly, in the epistles.

In the poem *On Himself and the Bishops* it is Nektarios who is the dilettante who has been preferred to the hardworking ascetic. He picks up the specific attack shortly after he launches a sustained diatribe on the generally wretched state of bishops in the Church of his day.[56] This general review is written in the high satiric style of New Comedy, featuring a lot of the stock buffoon characters of the stage, especially the figure of the former slave who has risen to social prominence.[57] But one part of that generic tirade turns very precise and thus sharpens the satiric assault by cleverly drawing in the respected senator which Nektarios was into the ranks of the upwardly pretentious, for Gregory castigates an unnamed example in these terms: "Some were

53. Cf. *De seipso et de episcopis*, Carm. 2.1.12, vv. 25-69, PG 37.1168-1171; *De Vita Sua*, vv. 20-39, PG 37.1031-1032.
54. *De Rebus Suis*, Carm. 2.1.1, vv. 498-525, PG 37.1007-1009.
55. Cf. *De Vita Sua*, vv 1925-1929, PG 37.1164.
56. *De seipso et de episcopis*, Carm. 2.1.12, vv. 155-191, PG 37.1177-1180.
57. Such as, for example, the character of Trimalchio used to high comic effect in Petronius Arbiter's *Satyricon* (ETW) (Arrowsmith, NY, 1959).

the nephews of a tribune's accountant, whose only concern was the cooking of the books. Some have come to office straight from the tax bureau, and we know what kind of accounting is held in respect there."[58] It is too close to Nektarios' former office in the imperial impost bureau to leave much room for doubt. The diatribe is immediately followed by a lengthy set of "raised objections" which seem to refer to the case of a man called to episcopal rank by charismatic choice, on whom people were expecting the grace of consecration to do its work, and were justifying his lack of knowledge by the argument that the apostles were simple enough but effective.[59] Again the anonymous picture points unerringly to Nektarios. Gregory demolishes the claimed parallel by asking how the candidate in any sense demonstrates the miraculous charisms that characteri_ed the apostles by arguing that the apostles were skilled theological teachers; and by insisting that charismatic inspiration, in the case of a bishop, comes down first and foremost to the capacity to deliver skilled theological teaching. All of these things, he implies, Nektarios lacks, and thus his election remains dubious, his consecration remains unproven, and his effectiveness remains open to doubt.

This argument leads him on[60] to denounce the way bishops are selected so hastily. The stress on the "rashness" of choice of important leaders once again points directly to the case of Nektarios. He describes it as settling important business "by the method of a throw of the dice."[61] And this in turn leads him on to the structural heart of his apologetic in this poem, the long section[62] where he takes six examples of his contemporaries who make disastrous bishops and ridicules them one by one. The largest subsection[63] here is reserved for a supposedly anonymous character whose resemblance to Nektarios cannot be missed. This person is a recently baptized imperial official. His past is scrutinized. Gregory wants information on how he became so immensely wealthy while working in the imperial tax office.[64] It is a very funny, but devastating question. He resumes the argument he has obviously heard to the effect that Nektarios' baptism has wiped out all past offense, and concludes with the underwhelming comment: "we shall wait and see."[65] He then takes the attack to a new level by calling for Nektarios to prove his newly discovered conversion by following the path of that other tax fraudster Zaccheus, and by making restitution of wrongly acquired wealth. Only such a change will prove the episcopal consecration was effective.[66] It is a hard-hitting restatement of the earlier "suggestion" that

58. *De seipso et de episcopis,* Carm. 2.1.12, vv. 154-156, PG 37.1181.
59. *De seipso et de episcopis,* Carm. 2.1.12, vv. 193-329, PG 1180-1190.
60. *De seipso et de episcopis,* Carm. 2.1.12, vv. 371-394, PG 37.1193-1194.
61. *De seipso et de episcopis,* Carm. 2.1.12, v. 396, PG 37.1195.
62. *De seipso et de episcopis,* Carm. 2.1.12, vv. 397-786, PG 37.1195-1223.
63. *De seipso et de episcopis,* Carm. 2.1.12, vv. 432-619, PG 37.1197-1211.
64. *De seipso et de episcopis,* Carm. 2.1.12, vv. 432-441, PG 37.1197-1198.
65. *De seipso et de episcopis,* Carm. 2.1.12, vv. 442-454, PG 37.1198-1199.
66. *De seipso et de episcopis,* Carm. 2.1.12, vv. 455-463, PG 37.1199.

Nektarios' wealth was not all legally acquired. He then leads on to the closest he ever comes to a canonical charge:[67] For Nektarios not to divest himself of his money is tantamount to making his election simoniacal, and as Gregory and his readers well knew, this would have been grounds for securing his deposition. Once again it is a very subversive statement indeed. He has not finished yet, however, and goes on to argue that even if baptism wipes away past sins how can it possibly wipe away the kind of moral reputation this character had before his baptism, especially in the eyes of the non-Christians whose edification, Gregory proposes, is an important aspect of the bishop's role in a city?[68] He continues to pile on the criticism. Even if all else was satisfactory how could such a newly elevated bishop claim to be able to teach theology? Should he not be ashamed to have an audience that is more religiously literate than himself?[69] The tirade against Nektarios concludes with a highly pointed contrast drawn between this rich man used to living in luxury and careless of his religious duties, and the proper ideal of an ascetical, learned, and humble bishop (Gregory, that is) who is so unjustly passed over.[70] Can Nektarios see himself in this ideal model picture?[71] Certainly not, he says, for as everyone knows he still continues to live in his palatial villa with his lovely wife.

After this section of invective against his personal opponents is concluded[72] Gregory sums up, and clearly reveals who his central target really is, for in his summation he promptly forgets all about the other five characters, and focuses only on the recently baptized official who has supplanted him.[73] He reproduces for his readers two significant (and obviously hurtful) arguments which have reached him from the capital. Both of them confirm that it is obviously Nektarios who is meant. The first is that his successor, for all his lack of preparation, is actually far better at organizing his job than Gregory was. The second is that Nektarios is far more capable of negotiating with the imperial court (exercising *parrhesia*) than Gregory. His reply to this tries weakly to justify himself in regard to the first charge: Those who think that an ascetical archbishop was "useless to all but himself" have forgotten the power of a good example from a godly priest, he says. But elsewhere, in the *De Vita Sua*, he more or less admits that he was completely at a loss in the complex politics of the corridors of power.[74] His sense of honor and vindication of shame leads him on to a more robust argument answering the second charge, that Nektarios can plead before the emperor far more effectively than Gregory. He does it with characteristically brilliant wit, showing the

---

67. *De seipso et de episcopis*, Carm. 2.1.12, v. 464, PG 37.1199.
68. *De seipso et de episcopis*, Carm. 2.1.12, vv. 522-540, PG 37.1204-1205.
69. *De seipso et de episcopis*, Carm. 2.1.12, vv. 541-574, PG 37.1205-1207.
70. *De seipso et de episcopis*, Carm. 2.1.12, vv. 575-609, PG 37.1207-1210.
71. Gregory is inviting his readers to put names to the figures in the contrasting "anonymous" pictures he draws.
72. *De seipso et de episcopis*, Carm. 2.1.12, v. 708, PG 37.1217.
73. *De seipso et de episcopis*, Carm. 2.1.12, vv. 709-786, PG 37.1217-1223.
74. *De Vita Sua*, vv. 1424-1435, PG 37.1127-1128.

rhetorical skill for which he was justly renowned. A monkey's scream, he says, is still not as impressive as a lion's roar, although one may hear it far more often in the jungle.[75] And, finally, after this he leads into the general conclusion of his poem with a damning summative judgment against Nektarios: The man the conciliar fathers have elected as his successor is a no-mark who can shine only at state dinners. The polish of an urbanite is his only, and very dubious, distinction. It is clear, then, that there is little love lost, on Gregory's side, for the newly elevated Nektarios. He ends the poem, which he has intended from the start to be a controversial "farce" for the delectation of the capital, meant to restore his "honor," with the wickedly innocent disclaimer: If anyone gets angry at all this, it must be that they have recognized themselves in the strictly anonymous caricatures.[76] The culminative effect of it all is clear enough—in all three of the autobiographical poems Nektarios is a prime target for Gregory in what he sees as the necessary restitution of his personal honor.

Gregory presumably came back to lodge in his parents' home at Nazianzus. This meant that after a long interval he appeared once more in his father's place as bishop of the local church.[77] He wrote to this effect to the local metropolitan Theodore,[78] sending him a copy of the *Philocalia of Origen* to serve as a memento of himself and Basil. He had no intention of being left in charge of the episcopal duties when it had been this very reason which caused his flight to Seleukia, but he saw the need when he returned to repulse the roving bands of Apollinarists, one of which had its eyes on the long-vacant see of Nazianzus. So he instituted the priest Cledonios to be in charge of the church there, once more acting as bishop of the place without committing himself to be the resident bishop. It was a move that attracted some local criticism. In a letter he wrote to one of his persistent local critics, his contemporary the old bishop Bosporios,[79] Gregory mentions two reasons that have brought him to serve once more in his father's church: the complaints of local hierarchs (him foremost among them) that he has neglected his duty, and the (Apollinarist) "assailants" who are prowling in the area. Bosporios seems to have been one of those asked by the local synod to take over the administration of the church at Nazianzus, but he had already refused.[80]

Undoubtedly many of the local bishops still maintained their former view that Gregory had been legitimately appointed as suffragan to Nazianzus and ought now to take up his responsibilities fully. He composed a poem at this time to argue that he had never despised his father's church but in agreeing to assist him in his extreme

75. *De seipso et de episcopis*, Carm. 2.1.12, vv. 761-774, PG 37.1221-1222.
76. *De seipso et de episcopis*, Carm. 2.1.12, v. 810, PG 37.1225.
77. Ep. 138 to Bosporios of Colonia, PG 37.233-236; Gallay (1967), pp. 26-27. Also Carm. 2.1.19, vv. 101-102, PG 37.1279.
78. Epp. 115 and 121, PG 37.212, 216; Gallay (1967), pp. 9-10,
79. Ep. 138, PG 37.233-236; Gallay (1967), p. 26.
80. Gallay (1967), n. 2, p. 26.

old age he had never accepted the see either, and so was not subject to canonical obligation in regard to it now.[81] It was an old argument he had little interest in raking over. Whatever the merits of the different views, he says that ill health had forced his resignation from Constantinople, and ill health prevents him now from being the bishop of Nazianzus.[82] So he persevered with his petitions to have another bishop appointed. He had hopes that the new successor to the metropolitan Anthimos, Theodore of Tyana, would be more sympathetic to him, having written to give his support when he heard news that Gregory had been stoned by Arians in Constantinople. It seems that he was well-disposed to Gregory's position and allowed him to make his own arrangements for a successor. Gregory would make a clear and formal withdrawal from Nazianzus on the grounds of ill health, and then the successor could be recognized to everyone's satisfaction.

So it was that sometime around the winter of 383 Gregory's cousin, the ascetic Eulalios, was consecrated to the church.[83] This allowed him, as a kin relation, to enjoy the full benefit of Gregory's substantial property in the region, church and buildings included, which Gregory had already willed in his testamentary bequest to the "catholic church at Nazianzus."[84] Eulalios was very close to Gregory, and helped him in this period when he was editing his Orations. He also worked with Marcellus and Gregory, two monastic deacons, and the monk Eustathios, the core of the monastic community Gregory had instituted to serve at Nazianzus, for organizing poor relief in the church.[85] These moves indicate that Gregory had transformed both the buildings at Karbala, and the Nazianzus church administration, into a completely monastic establishment. The host of Byzantine churches and monasteries (now mainly neglected ruins) that still cluster round both the ancient sites of Arianzum (Sivrihisar), and Karbala (Guzelyurt) in Turkey, are a testimony that the monastic settlements flourished for a very long time indeed after Gregory's pioneering foundations.[86] Once Gregory had his own cousin installed as his successor and director of the church in Nazianzus he moved off back to the hillside villa at Karbala. One of his first letters was to invite Theodore of Tyana, as a mark of respect and gratitude, to come and visit them for the local saint's day on September 29, 383.[87] He

81. *Querela de suis calamitatibus,* Carm. 2.1.19, vv. 51-56, PG 37.1275.
82. Carm. 2.1.19, vv. 61-63, PG 37.1276.
83. G. Rauschen established the dating; cf. Gallay (1943), fn. 5, p. 227.
84. *Exemplum Testamenti,* PG 37.389.
85. *Exemplum Testamenti,* PG 37.389.
86. The two main loci of the monastic settlements are at Manastir Vadisi, within a few minutes walking distance from Karbala (Guzelyurt), and Peristremma (Ihlara Vadisi) which is in the adjoining valley. At Arianzum (Sivrihisar) the village retains rock-cut cells in the cliff, and in the valley below can be found the Red Church (Kizil Kilise). At Nazianzus no identifiable Christian remains are visible, although the extent of ancient pottery on the field surface calls out for a future excavation that might yield interesting results in more favorable times ahead.
87. Ep. 122, PG 37.216-217; Gallay (1967), pp. 13-14.

was delighted by the bishop's company, and wrote to tell him so after his departure.[88] When Theodore in turn invited him to Tyana, he sent a careful reply that he
would love to visit him any time—except when a synod was in progress.[89]

For the short time that he occupied the episcopal role in Nazianzus, and for Easter
of an undetermined date, though probably that of 383 (if we assign the *Funeral Oration*
for Basil to the post-paschal feast of Mamas of the previous year), he delivered the
Oration for Pascha. *Oration* 45 uses up a lot of material that previously appeared in
Oration 38, but he hardly suspected that any of the locals would know it.[90] The text
makes an early mention of the paschal fires that were lit on the vigil of the feast[91] as
"images of the Great Light." But his discourse was given on the morning of the next
day, the Sunday of Pascha itself. To his own people at Nazianzus he gives brief explanations of the eternity of God, and how this involves confession of the coequal Trinity.[92]
It moves through a long account of the plan of salvation, culminating in the incarnation and redemption Christ achieves. He tells his listeners to be patient, for all his
apparent digression has a direct reference to Pascha, though he may be taking a long
road to get there.[93] Then he turns into a typological exegesis of the word Pascha, by
reference to the Old Testament texts that formed the basis of the Vigil in the ancient
Liturgy (and still do): the sacrifice of the Passover lambs, and the Exodus events that
are spiritually consummated in the passion and death of Christ. Bernardi[94] sees in one
part of Gregory's exegesis of the spoliation of the Egyptians, a reference to Gratian's
law of May 383[95] that made Christian apostates unable to benefit from legal inheritance, or to leave their goods to others. The allusion seems to me rather dubious, and
would also require us to believe that this law was equally enforced in the East, for
which we have no evidence. Gregory ends with a simple "synopsis" of his recounting
of the story of salvation: "We were created in order to be happy. We were made happy
in the act of our creation. We were given paradise so that we might enjoy life."[96]

Oration 44 was delivered on the Sunday after Easter, probably of that same year 383,
and most likely in the basilica at Caesarea, which was the center for the celebrations in
honor of the great shepherd-martyr Mamas of Cappadocia. The Byzantine scholiast
Nicetas, commenting on this oration,[97] said that it was delivered in a martyrium of
St Mamas near to Nazianzus, but it is difficult to know whether he had any real idea of

88. Ep. 123, PG 37.217; Gallay (1967), p. 14.
89. Ep. 124, PG 37.217; Gallay (1967), pp. 14-15.
90. Cf. Gallay (1943), p. 159; Bernardi (1968), pp. 246-250.
91. Orat. 45.2, PG 36.624.
92. Orat. 45.4, PG 36.628.
93. Orat. 45.10, PG 36.636.
94. Bernardi (1968), p. 250, referring to Orat. 45.20. "Today the master takes the silver and gold
    and gives it to you," PG 36.652.
95. *Cod. Theodos.* 16.7.1-2.
96. Orat. 45.28, PG 36.661.
97. Cited in the *Monitum* to Orat. 44, PG 36.606.

the topography of Cappadocia Secunda, or whether he simply knew there was a shrine of Mamas in Cappadocia and Caesarea is "near enough" Nazianzus to serve his purpose. In the time of Nicetas, St Mamas was one of the great martyr saints of Constantinople. In the eleventh century, Symeon the New Theologian was the abbot of his monastery there, near the Theodosian walls beside the Studium monastery, and his cult was so thoroughly "appropriated" to the capital that his provincial origins then needed explanation. In the fourth century, however, it was the other way around. The great shrine for Mamas was his basilica near Caesarea which attracted many of the local orators. Gregory refers to the great crowd of several thousand that is present,[98] an indication that it is the martyr's tomb at Caesarea that is meant rather than a small chapel near Nazianzus. He also uses words which seem to suggest the martyr's relics are being carried in an open-air procession, which would only be appropriate at Caesarea.[99] In any case there is only a relatively small notice of St Mamas in this oration, which is predominantly given over to the idea of the Light of Pascha, indicating that his primary interest was the climactic celebration of paschal "Bright Week", the liturgical custom which is still observed in the Orthodox world. The light of this (Sunday) feast is an image of the light of the eternal Trinity for Gregory, and this is the subject of most of his opening remarks.[100] His ideas are drawn from other scriptural feasts of "new beginnings," and he elects seven examples to make his point.[101]

This turns into a long moral paranesis addressed to the crowd, calling for some kind of renewal in their moral life. The sins of the luxurious are denounced in a long list[102] and contrasted with the kind of behavior that is appropriate for making a new beginning. For all the forms of "arrogance" and "show of wealth" he has previously enumerated, Gregory lists the proper antitheses; such as "poor clothing," "sleeping on the ground," the "wearing of shabby clothes"; all of which indicates that he is holding up, in an encomium, the example of the local monks. It seems as if his Panegyric for Basil in the previous year had worked. Once more Gregory is the episcopal "patron" and defender of the Cappadocian monks.

Throughout 382 and 383 his sickness dragged him down. Increasingly debilitating ill health marked his slow decline in these years and was the subject of many of his last letters.[103] He was suffering from acute rheumatism,[104] and on account of it

98. Orat. 44.12, PG 36.620.
99. Orat. 44.12, PG 36.620; cf. Bernardi (1968), p. 251.
100. Orat. 44.1-7, PG 36.608-616.
101. Orat. 44.2f, PG 36.608.
102. Orat. 44.9f, PG 36.618.
103. Epp. 52, 129, 131, 133, 171, 172, and many others.
104. Ep. 193, PG 37.316; Gallay (1967), p. 84. His "podalgos" (rheumatism or gout), is the excuse he gives for not being able to come to the wedding of Olympias. The sight of him trying to dance, he says, would be a tragi-comic one. The letter is from an undetermined time, between 383 and 387 probably.

turned down invitations to come to the capital and celebrate the wedding of Olympias to Nebridios, Prefect of Constantinople. Olympias was one of the adopted children of Vitalianos and had been brought up by his cousin Theodosia, his aristo-cratic supporters when he was at the Anastasia church. He says he felt "like a new patriarch Job,"[105] and the local worries again started to obsess him to the point that he thought dogs were prowling round him ready to devour him.[106] The problems were not simply difficult standoffs with other members of the local Cappadocian synod, there seems to have been a more particular disturbance of his local church from the part of unnamed Apollinarists. When Gregory first returned and refused to claim the church at Nazianzus as the bishop, their aspirations to claim it for their party seem to have revived. In the autumn of 383 Gregory was absent from town, taking a healing cure at the hot springs at Xanxaris, near Tyana, in the volcanic region of Cappadocia. Cledonios wrote to him about moves that were being made to displace him, and Gregory recognized the time had come to move against the Apollinarists decisively. If he could demonstrate that they were dissidents in their faith as well as schismatics in their efforts to seize episcopal sees, he could call down on them a legal prohibition. It is for this reason that he wrote his short monographs on Apollinarist christology, *Letters* 101-102, and 202 especially, which were destined to become standard works of Christological soteriology, and important raw material that launched the great Christological debates of the fifth cen-tury. *Letter* 101 is the first document he produced in direct response to the troubles at Nazianzus in 383. *Letter* 202 was addressed later in 384 to Nektarios, trying to interest him and the court in the problem of Apollinarist dissidents. *Letter* 102 is the last part of the triptych again composed some short time afterwards, in 384 or 385.[107]

From the same period as *Letter* 101, and just after it, comes his *Letter* 125 addressed to Olympios, the local Prefect of Cappadocia Secunda. Here he complains that he has tried reasoning with them but to no avail. When some bishops were passing through the region on their way back from the second session of the council of Constantino-ple, this group took the opportunity of his absence at the springs at Xanxaris to have one of their number consecrated a bishop. Gregory is furious that they should con-tinue, in this way, to flout the clearly expressed will of the emperor, and he expects Olympios to do something about it.[108] It is not clear who the travelling bishops were who did the consecration. If they were on their way home after the council of Con-stantinople (382) they must have been Syrians, though if they were interested in Apollinarist dissidents, they could hardly have been the party loyal to Diodore of Tarsus, whose Christology was the opposite pole to all Apollinaris represented.

---

105. Carm. 2.1.19, v. 31, PG 37.1273.
106. Carm 2.1.22, vv. 20-21, PG 37.1282.
107. Ep. 102 refers to Pope Damasus as "blessed," a usual indication of decease. Damasus died in 384. Cf. Gallay (1943), p. 231.
108. Ep. 125, PG 37.217; Gallay (1967), pp. 15-16. The canons of the council of 381 had included a condemnation of Apollinarists.

It may be that Gregory's appeal to the Prefect comes simply from a general determination to stop a new resurgence of Apollinarist activity, but it is more likely that the bishop who had secured consecration then tried to claim the Nazianzus church as his base of operations. Gregory's *Letters* 101 and 102 show that he himself had been accused of heterodoxy, and his rival had tried to supplant him as a "purer Nicene" teacher; something that Gregory found preposterous. The rival had claimed to be a legitimate replacement, ousting a heretic. The matter touched close to home, because his opponents had not attacked him primarily on the grounds of Christology at all, but on his doctrine of the co-equality of the Spirit.[109] They themselves maintained a view of subordinationist relations of the persons in the Godhead: the Father being "Greatest," the Son "Greater," and the Spirit "Great" as he describes it. Gregory deliberately chooses not to engage them on the trinitarian level, perhaps sensing that the surrounding hierarchs in Cappadocia Secunda might themselves be generally sympathetic to such a subordinationist concept of Trinity, as it was evidenced in Origen and his disciple Gregory Thaumaturgos, the Cappadocian apostle. This is why the attack is mounted squarely on Christological grounds, to undermine their claim to represent Nicene faith honestly.

He also gives away, not entirely willingly, that at some stage, probably before he left for Seleukia in 375, he had enjoyed good relations with the Apollinarist monks of the region, and had even given his endorsement to the statement of faith offered by the bishop the party had tried to intrude into Antioch. This was the Apollinarist theologian Vitalios, who in 375 had been briefly acknowledged by Pope Damasus,[110] and had also received Roman endorsement of his written profession of faith. He was later condemned when it was discovered that the Apollinarists' real opinions were often masked by a flexible economy of language, a charge Gregory also repeats in *Letter* 102. In *Letter* 101[111] Gregory is outraged that they have been spreading "lying tales" that he himself was an adherent of their theology, and that he has now proved perfidious by reappearing in Cappadocia as an opponent. He calls this "the most shocking aspect of the affair." By the time of *Letter* 102, he has been forced to admit that he did in fact approve the confession of Vitalios at some stage, but was then simply deceived by the duplicitous words, just as Pope Damasus had been deceived when he first gave them his blessing.[112]

Letters 125 and 202 show Gregory in a new political light. In his early months in Constantinople, after Theodosius had taken possession of the city, he was very circumspect indeed about invoking the secular arm to prosecute heterodoxy. In the years following, when Theodosius was more and more vigorously applying his antiheretical legislation, Gregory seems more willing to take advantage of it. His prosecution of Eunomios and the Apollinarists bears this out.

109. Ep. 101, PG 37.192.
110. Jerome, Ep. 16.
111. Ep. 101, PG 37.176.
112. Ep. 102, PG 37.196, 200.

On September 3, 383,[113] a law was issued from the imperial capital particularly naming Apollinarists, and threatening them if they "conducted any further ordinations." The correspondence with Gregory's complaint seems remarkable, and his *Letter* 125 was probably his attempt to invoke the new law to defend his interests at Nazianzus.

The anti-Apollinarist triptych of *Letters* 101-102, and *Letter* 202, although they were occasional writings, became the standard "definition" of what Apollinarism was, and the classical patristic attack on what was wrong with it. They do not merely have a cardinal place in the catalogues of heresiology, however, but themselves became landmarks in Christological development, an important stepping place between the late writings of Athanasius of Alexandria, and the massive Christological disputes that arose in the fifth century between the Alexandrian tradition (as then represented by Cyril) and the Syrian tradition of Diodore of Tarsus (as then represented by Nestorius). Gregory of Nazianzus' Christological works seemed too vague to the theoreticians of the fifth century, though they were heavily used, and an unfortunate result of that was the polarization of the international ecumenical Christology between the Syrian and Alexandrian schools. This in turn resulted in the somewhat forced antitheses represented by the council of Chalcedon in 451 that have tended to make patristic Christology appear wooden and artificial ever since. In Gregory's hands Christology is never allowed to escape its proper context of reflection: the dynamic mystery of the economy of God's salvation of human kind. It was Gregory who underscored the inalienable connection of the Christ mystery to the doctrine of salvation. In short, for Gregory, if the soteriological principle could not be demonstrated at every turn, the Christology had to be suspect.

Apollinaris was a strong anti-Arian theologian in the time of Athanasius. His primary impulse was to present a mystical Christology that confessed the incarnate Christ as synonymous with the Divine Word who acted on earth to save humankind. To this extent he set himself to fight against the Arian exegeses which took the Gospel stories of the limitations and sufferings of Jesus as proof positive that the Word of God (the subject of the incarnation in both opposing schools) was himself limited, and thus inferior to the Father. Apollinaris insisted that the Word of God was in no way limited, and remained impassible in the Incarnation. To explain how this could be if he was, at one and the same time, the subject of Christ's actions, he devised a theory that the Word assumed only human flesh in the case of Jesus. In other words he did not assume a human person, through whom he worked, but inhabited a vessel of a human body through whom he lived. In assuming this "humanity" as opposed to a human, Apollinaris explained, the Word remained strictly the sole subject of all that Jesus did, and all that he accomplished in the flesh was the work of a God, and thus had infinite value. So, his death was the death of

113. *Cod. Theodos.* 16.5.12; Gallay (1943), pp. 221-222.

the immortal God, and had an infinite application, not merely an exemplarist significance, as it would had it been the death of a mere man.

The flaw in this strong theory of the Word of God's direct and unmediated subjectivity in the life of the incarnate Christ was the question of psychological subjectivity. Did Jesus have an infinite intelligence or a limited human intelligence? If the former, how could he be really a man? And if Christ was not fully and really man, was it not the case that their theory of incarnation became akin to Hellenistic ideas of a divine being giving a merely temporary epiphany in an illusory flesh? Apollinaris explained that God the Word was the direct source of all human wisdom. When he created a human being he put into the creature a small icon of his own divine wisdom so that each rational being would, by virtue of that inner wisdom, be "in the image and likeness of God." Human intelligence and wisdom (the Nous) was itself the divine "Image" in every human. In the case of the incarnation, however, there was no need for the Logos to put a small icon of his wisdom in the body of Jesus which he created specially, and specifically, in the Virgin for his own use. Having directly created the body of Jesus, he instilled within it his own Wisdom and Nous. The Divine Wisdom itself inhabited the flesh of Jesus so as to make an "incarnated deity." There was no need for a Soul (Psyche) or for a human Mind (Nous) in Jesus since the Word of God supplanted them. Apollinaris' idea was that this theory really improved matters. What need was there for a small imagistic prototype when the archetype himself was present? It was not a case, then, that the Divine Word was less than human: he was simply more than human. Even in his earthly Kenosis he remained divine as man. Apollinaris thought this was a highly reverent and mystical theology that rebutted Arian claims that Jesus' limitations in the Gospel narratives were signs that the Word of God was not absolutely divine. Others were less sure of the wisdom of his scheme. If the divine presence so supplanted the characteristics of human soul and human mental consciousness, was it not tantamount to suppressing the very essence of Jesus' humanity? Were human soul and human mind so peripheral that an idea of humanity could survive at all without them?

Gregory's anti-Apollinarist writings, it should be noted, are equally concerned to attack Diodore of Tarsus, who was already becoming known for his biblical exegesis and his "Two Sons" theory of Christology. This was Diodore's own answer to Apollinarist monism. In his triptych, Gregory evidently classes Apollinaris and Diodore together as the "two extremes" one ought to avoid in an orthodox confession. The same approach is found in digest in the *De Vita Sua*, written at the same time.[114] The denunciation of being "outside the faith" and "worthy of losing a place in the adoption promised" are some of the most severe denunciations Gregory ever fashioned, matching anything that he threw at the Eunomians. In *Letter* 101 it is a condemnation reserved for Diodore, who though he is not named specifically, is represented as a denier of the title *Theotokos* (Mother of God) and a proposer of

---

114. *De Vita Sua*, vv. 607-651, PG 37.1071-1074.

"Two Sons."[115] Against him Gregory offered the "correct" solution that would later be adopted as the basis for classical christological orthodoxy at the council of Chalcedon in 451: Christ was one person in two natures. Gregory puts it in a typically elegant phrase. Christ was: "allo kai allo, ouk allos kai allos": that is, one reality along with another reality, but not one person alongside another person; double in condition and single in personhood.[116] The Apollinarist chief theories are listed as: the denial of a human Nous in Christ, the doctrine that the flesh came from heaven, the impossibility of God's Wisdom and a human mind inhabiting the same being simultaneously.[117]

The idea of the flesh of Christ being in some way pre-existent and descending to earth as "heavenly flesh," is an idea Gregory attributes to them explicitly, though later scholars have wondered if it was not more part of his apologetic deconstruction than their original position.[118] He thinks that this position is based on a false interpretation of the Pauline words: "The Second Man is the Lord from heaven, and is heavenly"[119] but it is a "novel idea" and "anathema." It separates Christ's humanity from the common meaning of that word, and denies that he is a human "of us or from us, but makes it above us." Such a "humanity above humanity" is a logical nonsense, and misses the obvious fact that Paul is talking about the assumption of Christ, bodily, into heavenly glory, a fact which is clearly evidenced in other Gospel passages.[120]

Gregory argues that the Apollinarist theory that the human mind must give way to the Divine Wisdom, or otherwise merely a prophetic model of Christology would be possible,[121] is another example of foolish logic. A prophetic Christological model would be blasphemous, but it does not follow as a natural result of denying their theories, he says. They have set up false opposites as if one could not have sunlight and a house, for example. Why could one not have sunlight in a house?[122] Just so the archetypal Divine Wisdom does not cast out the possibility of seeing in Jesus a complete human consciousness and psyche. What is more, the logic of the issue considered more widely, in the context of the whole divine economy, makes such a position obviously necessary. Once again he has an eye for the sharp and memorable phrase to synopsize his position. He has attacked the Apollinarists for being more interested in

115. Ep. 101, PG 37.177-180.
116. Ep. 101, PG 37.180.
117. Ep. 101, PG 37.177-181.
118. The best general discussions, though now dated, are still C.E. Raven (1923) and Lietzmann (1904). Gregory does claim again, however, in Ep. 202 that he has an Apollinarist text in his hands that teaches a "garbling of the Gospels" by positing that he brought his flesh down from heaven, PG 37.332.
119. 1 Cor 15:47-48.
120. Ep. 101, PG 37.181.
121. The Word inhabiting a different man. This was also called Photinianism in the fourth century and was classed as an Arian position.
122. Ep. 101, PG 37.185.

snappy slogans[123] than accurate theology, but he has learned from them too. This letter is full of pithy phrases. Chief among them is a theological "rule" that became ever afterwards associated with his name, as much as his Trinity theology. It is the principle of soteriological Christology.

If Christ did not have a mind, Gregory says, or a human soul, he has accepted an incarnation that is deprived of the very factors in human life that stand most in need of redemption: the moral and spiritual lights in a human existence. Deprived of these things there is no humanity worth speaking of. But more importantly, since the entire incarnation has to be considered as a divine movement of healing and reconciliation—initiated not because God needed it, but because God was determined to use the incarnation as his healing medium for the salvation of humanity—then what possible reason would there be for arranging an incarnation that avoided the central areas of human life that stood most in need of help? To present an incarnate Christ without soul or *nous* is to offer a theory that has voided the whole purpose and dynamic of the Incarnation of the Logos understood as salvific act of healing. To put it succinctly, Gregory affirmed the rule: "What he has not assumed he has not healed."[124] Remembering his Origen, Gregory suggests that it is better to consider that the Divine Mind "mingles" with the human mind in Christ, as like to like, but the mingling is for the dynamic end of the deification of human existence.[125]

The incarnate Christ is one single person, then, but the divine person lives in an earthly existence which is authentically human. How the divine consciousness and human Nous coexist Gregory does not explain, other than suggesting the notions of commingling and deified transformation, both of which are mystically powerful images but ones that basically refuse to engage any further with the rival schools of Apollinaris and Diodore which, in different ways, had both called for greater precision in the explication of the Christological model. Once more Gregory had called for a mystical silence in preference to a syllogistic theology, but his appeal would fall on deaf ears. This further question (the "how" of the union) was to be the great battle ground of fifth-century Christology. In terms of what was to follow, it is clear that Gregory was by no means the last word in the Church's Christological settlement, but he certainly reinforced the main foundations of it, especially in his insistence (correcting the tendencies of Apollinaris and the early Athanasius) that a real acknowledgement of the full humanity of Jesus was in no way detrimental to the mystical force of a true and direct incarnation of the person of the divine Word himself. In the mid-fifth century, Cyril of Alexandria synthesized Gregory with Athanasius in his own study of their Christologies; and Gregory's role in formulating the Chalcedonian settlement was to be further acknowledged when the council of 451 awarded him the Ecumenical title of "Theologian."

123. Ep. 102, PG 37.200.
124. Ep. 101, PG 37.181. Here he quotes from Origen's *Dialogue with Heraclides.*
125. Ep. 101, PG 37.181, 185.

After this clash with Apollinarists, Gregory definitively decided to resign tenure at the Nazianzen church. At the end of 383, after Eulalios was installed as the new bishop in his place, Gregory moved to the villa at Karbala and lived in retirement with his close companions, his deacon Gregory and the monk Eustathios. He had willed the whole property to them, together with sufficient gold to maintain it as a monastic establishment in the future.[126] It is clear from this that he had no intention of moving again. The brusque *Letter* 203 which he wrote to one of his relatives who had moved into an adjoining property probably does not contradict this. Valentinianos had introduced women onto his grounds, and they were visible from the monastery at Karbala. Gregory writes a complaint that celibates must never be associated even with the rumor of the presence of women, as it would be a scandal. He is annoyed that Valentinianos, so soon after his taking possession of the property, has shown a disregard for those who have inhabited it for so long. He threatens that he will have to go on the road again, even at his age, because like Adam he has "been driven out of paradise by a woman." He knows that Valentinianos wanted to live beside him and have friendly relations, but in reality he has chased out an old man. So, he can have the place to himself, but he must not touch anything in the martyrium chapel or he will fall under a similar punishment from angry neighbors.[127] His annoyance is not so great, however, that he misses the opportunity for several literary jokes, which he includes for Valentinianos' benefit. The reply to his expostulations is not recorded, but it ought to be taken as another "inducement" by the old rhetorician for proper respect to be shown. Rather than imagining that he was in reality forced out of his home which he had occupied since he first tried out the monastic life after he came home from Athens, we ought to imagine as more likely that Valentinianos issued instructions to the women of his household to stay on the far side of the hill, and leave the cranky old men in peace.

His clash with the Apollinarists had reminded him of their custom of versifying to make catechesis easier. In *Letter* 101[128] he denounces their habit of replacing the holy psalms with hymns of their own composition, and in *Letter* 102 also complains about their love for catchy slogans,[129] but they probably gave him the idea of playing them at their own game. In his last retirement most of his poems were composed, and many of them were for a didactic reason. The doctrine he set out in his *Orations* is now given a more succinct form in meters. One of the poetic strategies was to present succinct anti-Arian[130] and anti-Apollinarist[131] christological poems.

126. *Exemplum Testamenti*, PG 37.392.
127. Ep. 203, PG 37; Gallay (1967), pp. 93-95. That is he will himself be chased away by the wrath of the martyrs.
128. Ep. 101, PG 37.193.
129. Ep. 102, PG 37.200.
130. Cf. Carm. 1.1.2, PG 37.401-408.
131. Carm. 1.1.10; 1.1.11, PG 37.464-471.

The defense of the doctrine of the Spirit is also a common theme.[132] After so many years his poetic theology is being taken seriously enough so that English translations are finally appearing.[133] The massive amount of poems he wrote at this time shows that the scholarly activities of writing and copying were the particular marks of the "ascesis" of Gregory's monastic establishment. In this he long predates the Studium that would set the standard Typikon for the scholarly monastic houses of the later Byzantine world.

Gregory's great-nephew Nicobulos was anxious to collate an edition of his Epistles, and the old man gives his opinions on how it should be arranged. Clarity, laconic wit, and grace are essential in a good letter, he says.[134] He also instructs Basil's letters to him to be placed at the head of the book,[135] saying that he has always admired them as models of style. Nicobulos was a regular visitor to Karbala at this time.[136] Gregory seems to have been very fond of the son of his little niece "the most sweet Alypiana."[137] He and other relatives had recently gone to Tyana for literary studies and Gregory interests himself in their training.[138] He intervened urgently for Nicobulos' father, who had been threatened with being sold into slavery[139] because of a crime committed by a member of his staff. Gregory got him off the charge by pleading with the imperial Prefect and his aide Asterios, and complaining that his treacherous accuser had himself only recently benefited from Gregory's letters of recommendation.[140] When Nicobulos the elder died, not long after this adventure, Gregory knew exactly the Magistrate who would smooth over all the matters of legal inheritance for the family.[141]

Bishop Eulalios was also helping Gregory in the editing of his Orations at this time.[142] He still kept up a regular correspondence with the great and the good,[143] but

132. Cf. Carm. 1.1.3, PG 37.408-415. Gilbert (Diss., 1994) gives a translation.
133. McGuckin (1989, 1996); Moreschini and Sykes (1996); and Gilbert (Diss. 1994).
134. Ep. 51, PG 37.105-108; Gallay (1964), pp. 67-68.
135. Ep. 53, PG 37.102; Gallay (1964), p. 70.
136. Epp. 52, 54-55, PG 37.108-109; Gallay (1964), pp. 68-71.
137. He mentions her in these terms in his will, in stark contrast to his other female relatives Eugenia and Nonna whose "reprehensible lives" he wants to criticize by not giving them anything. He does not give anything to Alypiana either, but this because he knew she was already well provided for; and he apologizes for it, saying that he wishes his money to go to those who need it, and to the Church. *Exemplum Testamenti*, PG 37.392.
138. Epp. 187-188, and 190-191, PG 37.305-313.
139. Hauser-Meury (1960), p. 130, n. 245 and p. 138, thinks that the reference to being enslaved refers to Nicobulos being drafted forcibly into curial service; but *Letter* 146.6 seems quite specific—the slavery must be for either Nicobulos or one of his children (who were still at the age of schooling at this time).
140. The elder Nicobulos was the husband of Alypiana, his sister Gorgonia's daughter.
141. Epp. 195-196, PG 37.317-321.
142. The title of *Oration* 13, PG 35.852, notes that it is a "Homily on the Consecration to Doara, as edited by Bishop Eulalios."
143. Such as his letters of recommendation of clients to the Cappadocian Governor (a well-disposed pagan) Nemesios. Epp. 198-201, PG 37.324-328; Gallay (1967), pp. 90-95. He also sent to him a verse composition inviting him to become a Christian. Carm. 2.2.7, PG 37.1551-1557.

there is more of an apologetic tone in evidence, a *leitmotif* of wondering whether anyone would want to take notice of such an old man in his last years.

He tried to intercede for an old friend the priest Sacerdos[144] who had been administering the Poor House at Caesarea, but had been removed in disgrace after his assistant, the monk Eudokios, had denounced him for some irregularity.[145] In this case his intercession did not prevail with the Caesarean bishop Helladios,[146] or Sacerdos' replacement Eudokios[147] who was annoyed at Gregory's intrusion. So Sacerdos received, instead, graceful supportive letters of condolence from Gregory.[148] He has to send letters of condolence also to Thecla, Sacerdos' ascetic sister, for soon afterwards the old priest died, still grieving over his disgrace.[149]

He held a lively correspondence with the Cappadocian Prefect Olympios who helped him in the Apollinarist dispute, even to the extent that he had to intervene once more on behalf of the rebellious people of Nazianzus, to save them from a second threat of a punitive military expedition.[150] Olympios had a return favor he wanted, and he sent on to Gregory one day a young frightened girl, asking for his judgment in a legal case that concerned her. Gregory received the young woman and questioned her about her troubles. She had been compelled by her father Verianos to return home, and to instigate proceedings to divorce her husband. The two families had seriously fallen out, and Verianos would not tolerate any further clan connection by marriage. Gregory sent his recommendation back to the Prefect not to allow the divorce to proceed,[151] and he wrote to the father to set him right too. Old celibate though he was he could read the heart and knew how to hear the soul-confessions of his people. The young girl had been strictly instructed by her father to demand a divorce for the sake of family honor. She rehearsed her speeches dutifully. Gregory commended her for it but also gave her what she dared not ask for. He told Verianos:

> It would not be lawful for me to accede to your requests on the basis of our mutual friendship... One day when she is free from the terror which you inspire in her, she will be able to speak the truth of the matter frankly. The words that dropped from her mouth were all for you, but the tears that dropped from her eyes were all for her husband.[152]

---

144. Epp. 169-170 to the Cappadocian noblemen Strategios and Palladios, PG 37.277-280; Gallay (1967), pp. 59-60.
145. Epp. 215-216, PG 37.352-353, 357; Gallay (1967), pp. 105-107.
146. Ep. 219, PG 37.357-360; Gallay (1967), pp. 109-111.
147. Epp. 216-218, PG 37.352-357; Gallay (1967), pp. 106-109.
148. Epp. 212-215, PG 37.349-352; Gallay (1967), pp. 104-106.
149. Epp. 222-223, PG 37.361-368; Gallay (1967), pp. 113-117.
150. Epp. 140-145, 146, PG 37.237f; Gallay (1967), pp. 28f. Ep. 141, on behalf of his town, thus parallels *Oration* 17 from the time just before he left for Seleukia about ten years earlier.
151. Ep. 144, PG 37.245; Gallay (1967), p. 35.
152. Ep. 145, PG 37.248; Gallay (1967), pp. 36-37.

He was becoming tired of talking. One Lent he decided to make an ascetical practice of keeping silence for the whole six weeks before Pascha. He would write out his experiences in a long, long poem, of course, as well as in numerous letters.[153] Having launched on the endeavor, he soon grievously missed that great delight of discourse that governed all his life; so he asked Cledonios the priest to come and at least talk *at* him.[154]

One of the last signs of his state of mind in his last days came in his letter to the eager young scholar Adamantios.[155] It is the last dispossession of an older man before a bright hopeful. In a sense, it is the ultimate farewell to the world a learned man makes[156] and a sure sign that Gregory knew his death was near: for he determined to sell his beloved books so that the money could be given to the poor as a final almsgiving. He wishes the young man well in all his journeys through the joys of study, but advises him not to lose sight of the real purpose of learning, which is Christian wisdom. Adamantios must never forget where his loyalties really lie: "Remember that you are one of us."

> Neither Eupraxios is of the noblest rank.
> They only have one name.
> They have but a single soul.
> Best of all the servants of Gregory the priest.
> Even now standing at his side.[157]

Newman[158] captured the general scene in his translation of a poem Gregory wrote in his last years,[159] telling local zealots and the eyebrow-raising aristocrats that he was as good a monk as anyone else, though he never had a taste for the ugly or excessive:

> Someone whispered yesterday
> Of the rich and fashionable:
> Gregory, in his own small way,
> Easy was, and comfortable.
>
> Had he not of wealth his fill,
> Whom a garden gay did bless,
> And gently trickling rill,
> And the sweets of idleness?
>
> I made the answer: Is it ease,
> Fasts to keep, and tears to shed?

---

153. Carm. 2.1.34, PG 37.1307 1322; Epp. 107-114, PG 37.208-212; Gallay (1967), pp. 5-9.
154. Ep. 109, PG 37.208; Gallay (1967), p. 5.
155. Ep. 235, PG 37.377-380; Gallay (1967), pp. 125-126.
156. Gallay (1967), p. 125 (n. 3) refers it to his "farewell to the world when he became a monk in 360. This is too soon. In his earlier study (1943), p. 237, he sets it to the end of Gregory's life.
157. *Epigram* 3, PG 38.83-84. They received manumission and a legacy of gold in his *Testament*, PG 37.392.
158. J.H. Newman, *The Church of the Fathers* (London, 1840).
159. Carm. 2.1.44, PG 37.1349-1353.

Vigil hours and wounded knees—
Call you such a pleasant bed?

Thus a veritable monk,
Does to death his fleshly frame;
But there who in sloth have sunk,
They have forfeited the name.

Gregory's last years were plagued by the worries of a man who had searched so deeply into his soul that he knew the paths and byways so intimately he could no longer mask himself from the eyes of God. His last years were spent in external peace and solitude, but the ascesis of the terrible insight into the soul, something he had dedicated all his writing to elucidate, made him, to the very end, a searcher and a struggler.

An Epilogue

In his poem *On Human Nature*[1] Gregory allows us a last glimpse of him in advanced age. He is sitting quietly under the trees, depressed and anxious, still trying to puzzle out the enigmas of human existence. His answer is not an easy one; no pious platitude has the strength to comfort him in the face of death. The old saint, sitting by the spring, finds his salvation in hope. It was his faith in God's mercy which was the praxis of his life-long philosophy; and he walks off out of our picture into the evening gloom, still puzzled but resilient in that same hope. He would find his answer in that love that long had formed the lodestone of his life's energies and all his mental actions:

> As before, a bitter grief still gnawed in me,
> I could not appreciate all this beauty,
> For when sorrows grip the mind,
> It finds it hard to sing its song.
> My mind was in a whirl of battling thoughts.
> Who was I? Who am I now? What shall I be?[2]
> I could see no clear answers to it all.
> Nor could I find anyone who knew any better than me...
>
> Divine terror has bowed me down,
> Worn out by worries night and day.
> The Proud One[3] thus steals my sleep from me,
> Crushing it underfoot...
>
> Already it was evening.
> And so from that shady grove
> I turned my steps homeward once again,
> Sometimes chuckling at how depressed I'd been,
> At other times feeling the embers of sadness
> shift and smolder in my heart:
> My mind still wrestling with itself.[4]

Gregory died at 61 years of age.

His death occurred around 390 according to Jerome,[5] and according to the

---

1. Carm. 1.2.14, PG 37.755-765.
2. The classical philosophical questions about the origins and goals of human existence. The answers to the riddles were: Water, Clay, and Dust (conception, flesh, and death). Gregory refers to it in verse 74, PG 37.761.
3. Satan.
4. Carm. 1.2.14, *De humana natura*, vv. 1-18, 43-45, 99-102, 124-132, PG 37.755-765.
5. *De Vir. Illustr.* 117. Jerome says that: "Gregory has died just three years or so before this." In Ep. 47.3, he tells his readers that his *De Viris* was composed in the fourteenth year of

Suida,[6] the great Byzantine encyclopaedia, "in the thirteenth year of Theodosius' reign," which makes it 391. Given Jerome's clear indication that he was speaking "round about," it is the *Suida* that ought to be preferred, even though the Lexicon then makes a mess about his birth date.[7] His body was laid in the family tomb near the Nazianzus church. No sign of this remains to the present, though it was a splendid stone octagonal building, erected by Gregory's father. The ruins of ancient Nazianzus lie a mile or so to the west of the modern village of Bekarlar (pre. 1922 name Nenizi) in Cappadocia. There is a beautiful Seljuk tomb (also octagonal) built over the site, and innumerable potsherds lie scattered in mute testimony on the surrounding fields. The emperor Constantine Porphyrogennitos ordered that his relics should be brought to Constantinople in the tenth century, writing a decree stating that since he had so assiduously defended the capital in his lifetime he ought now to: "come back to visit that people you once so graciously cared for and leave us orphans no longer."[8] It was the start of more, this time posthumous, journeys and adventures. Some of his relics remained in his birthplace, but were transferred from Nazianzus to the Byzantine "Kizil Kilise," the church in the valley beside Sivrihisar, the site of ancient Arianzum, because by the medieval period Karbala had become by far the larger settlement of Christians (reversing the situation that had existed in Gregory's day).

At Constantinople, his body for a long time lay beside that of John Chrysostom in the church of the Holy Apostles where he had once preached. The Benedictine editors of Gregory give a nicely eirenic version of how his relics came from there to Rome under "obscure circumstances"[9] and were lodged in the church of Santa Maria in the Campo Martio. The obscure circumstances were, of course, the pillaging of Constantinople by the mercenaries of the infamous Fourth Crusade in 1204 when, among the vast booty taken, were numerous "disappearances" of relics and shrines of the saints. The Venetians claimed to have taken the complete and intact relics of St Gregory, and lodged them in the church of St Zachary at Venice. The Bollandists wondered if this was not more likely the body of Gregory the Elder.[10] Pope Gregory XIII ordered a last translation of the relics that were lodged in the Campo Martio church to adorn the newly resplendent St Peter's, where they were carried with much ceremony on June 9, 1578, and where they still lie quietly near his new neighbour, St John Chrysostom.

Into modern times the head of Gregory was claimed by the Greek inhabitants of Gelvere (Guzelyurt), the site of Karbala near Arianzum (Sivrihisar) in Cappadocia.

Theodosius, that is 392; and three years in the antique manner of counting, including the beginning and end, thus gives 390. Cf. Nautin (1961) for this dating.

6. A. Adler (ed.), *Suidae Lexicon*, Pars. 1a, p. 541 (Leipzig, 1928); text also in PG 35.306-308.
7. Having him aged over ninety when he died. This was because it reckoned his time in Athens wrongly, and had worked backwards from the death date it knew, PG 35.308.
8. Text in PG 35.238.
9. PG 35.238-239.
10. PG 35.239.

There is a splendid empty medieval reliquary designed once to contain the head of St Gregory Nazianzen, made in copper gilt Champlève enameling, with carved walrus ivory. It is an exquisite and expensive piece dating from 1175, and is now kept in the Kunstgewerbemuseum in Berlin. The existence of this piece indicates that the relics of Gregory, probably from their first translation in the tenth century, were carefully divided. After the disastrous war of 1922, the Greeks of Cappadocian Gelvere had to abandon their churches, schools, and monasteries and made the long trek westwards. They settled just over the modern Greek border with Turkey, on the mainland to the west of Istanbul, and called their new domicile "New Karvala." Today it is a thriving settlement that still regards itself as Gregory's exiled flock. It has a Cappadocia Museum, now including ancient manuscripts of Gregory's work. In the old homeland, at Karbala, some of the memory of Gregory has been resurrected by the Turkish refugees from Kastoria who took the place of the exiled Greeks and renamed Gregory's estate as "Beautiful Place" (Guzelyurt). The nineteenth century Greek school has been renamed the Otel Karbala, and a handwritten sign in "Monastery Valley," that runs off the town square, quaintly points out to the occasional (and sensation-causing) tourist the kilise of "St Gregory the Ologian." It is a sadly declined building, Middle Byzantine in style, that was once the town's main Orthodox church. Apart from geography it has no connection with Gregory himself, though what pass for the local custodians try to claim it as a fourth-century building. After 1922 it served as the old town mosque, and the ninetheenth-century iconostasis was pried off the east end and nailed on to the south wall to indicate the direction of Mecca. The great bronze bell was carried off by the Greeks; only a massive "clapper" remains which is reverentially pointed out by the Imam to any visitor that finds their way there.

Gregory's hagiographers commenced work from the seventh century onwards. Gregory the Presbyter was the first. His *Vita* can be found in PG 35.243-304. Gregory Nazianzen, more than any other patristic writer, left abundant materials for any biographer. Niketas David the Paphlagonian (and thus his Cappadocian compatriot) also composed an *Encomium of St Gregory of Nazianzus* that was much admired in Byzantine times.[11] The tenth-century bishop Elias of Crete[12] was one among a series of Byzantine theologians, most notably including Maximus the Confessor,[13] who wrote commentaries on the theological works. Cosmas of Jerusalem[14] and Nicetas David were among the more important of the equally large number of

11. J. Rizzo (ed. and tr.), *The Encomium of St Gregory Nazianzen by Nicetas the Paphlagonian* (Brussels, 1976).
12. Elias' commentary can be found in PG 36.738-934.
13. Maximus wrote his *Ambigua* to comment on and explain difficult passages in the works of Gregory; cf. PG vols. 90-91.
14. The eighth-century poet and hymnographer. He and his adoptive brother John Damascene quarried Gregory Nazianzen extensively in their own hymns, and thus eased the way of many of Gregory's poetical ideas into the liturgical books of the Eastern Church, PG 38.339-679; cf. Sajdak (1912).

commentators on his poetry.[15] The brilliant and fiercely obscure statesman-scholar Theodore Metochites,[16] who built the wonderful church of the Holy Savior in Chora whose mosaics and frescoes are still the wonder of Istanbul, wrote a panegyrical *Laudatio* of Gregory, and the equally pedantic Byzantine scholar Manuel Philes even managed to turn the Orations into poetry (of sorts). Psellos called him the "Christian Demosthenes." Gregory's *Orations* were generally regarded as so valuable, that they remain the most copied genre of all Byzantine manuscripts after the Bible. Accordingly, the saint features very much in Greek manuscript illustrations. The twelfth-century Higumen of the Pantokrator monastery at Constantinople, Joseph Hagioglykerites, ordered a deluxe edition of Gregory's Orations, and it contains wonderful scenes of the saint sitting at his writing desk in Constantinople, scratching out the *Theological Orations*.[17] This is the manuscript now lodged at Sinai, and featured in the lavish catalogue of the Byzantine exhibition of the Metropolitan Museum in New York, in 1997.[18]

In most Byzantine manuscript illustrations Gregory is shown in the posture of an evangelist, iconically classed in the same rank as the other inspired "theologians" who composed the Gospels. In frescoes and portable icon panels he is depicted as a venerable old man wearing the robes of an archbishop. He features in many Eastern churches, both ancient and modern, as one of the "liturgical doctors" whose frescoes surround the altar behind the iconostasis. This is because a liturgy survives (one of the African Coptic families) which is attributed to his name,[19] and also because he defended the deity of the Holy Spirit. This, his mystical role, is celebrated in the company of the other liturgical doctors: Athanasios, Basil, and Chrysostom. The favored text, written onto the scroll he usually carries in his frescoes, is (oddly enough) not taken from his own works, nor does it refer to his Christology or pneumatology. Instead it celebrates Gregory the mystic, and reads: "God resting among his saints."

He would have wondered greatly to have thought he would be so often depicted, in so many churches across the world, standing in the company of his beloved Basil. He would have been delighted to have imagined that all his works would survive to have such an influence on the Byzantines, so that of all Christian writers he could claim the undisputed title of "Father of Greek Christian Letters." He would have been triumphant to have seen how his theological writings would eventually correct even an ecumenical council itself, so as to become the standard of subsequent Christian orthodoxy.

15. Nicetas' commentary on the *Arcana* (a series of selected theological poems of Gregory; further see Moreschini and Sykes [1996]) can be found in PG 38.682-842.
16. 1270-1332.
17. The ms. is: Sinai gr. 339, fol. 4v.
18. Catalogue: *The Glory of Byzantium*, H.C. Evans and W.D. Wixom, (eds.) (Metropolitan Museum of Art: New York, 1997), pp. 4, 109-110; see also O. Baddeley and E. Brunner (eds.), *The Monastery of St Catherine* (catalogue for an exhibition at the Foundation for Hellenic Culture) (London, 1996). An illustration of Sinai gr. 339, fol. 4v., is also found here on p. 84. See also Galavaris (1969), Der Nersessian (1962).
19. Though not from him historically; cf. PG 36.677f.

BIBLIOGRAPHY

ORATIONS AND LETTERS

The *Editio Princeps* of Gregory was published in Basel 1550.

Claude Morel issued a Paris edition in 1609, which was reissued in 1630 with a Latin translation supplied by Billius.

The Benedictine edition was prepared by Du Frische, Louvard, and Moran, and collated by Clémencet in Paris 1778. Its appearance was delayed because of the French Revolution, and it came to completion under Caillau only in 1840. It was this which was popularized as the edition in *Cursus Completus Patrologiae Graecae* (PG), vols. 35-38, ed. J. P. Migne (Paris, 1886). This is still the fullest and most complete edition, though a collection which, like many other parts of Migne, needs great care in its use (see Geerard, 1974). The task of identifying the *dubia* and *spuria*, and attaining a proper critical edition of Gregory has now been in process for over fifty years. The following represent the most important new editions, or select translations, in European languages:

Sources Chrétiennes (SC) Series (Paris, 1969-1995), vols. 149, 208, 247, 250, 270, 284, 309, 318, 358, 384, 406.

viz:

Tuilier A., "La Passion du Christ. Tragédie," SC 149 (Paris, 1969) (No longer generally regarded as authentically Gregorian).

Gallay P. & Jourjon M., *Lettres Théologiques.* SC 208 (Paris, 1974).

Bernardi J., *Discours* 1-3. SC 247 (Paris, 1978).

Gallay P. & Jourjon M., *Discours* Théologiques 27-31. SC 250 (Paris, 1978).

Mossay J., *Discours* 20-23. SC 270 (Paris, 1980).

Mossay J., *Discours* 24-26. SC 284 (Paris, 1981).

Bernardi J., *Discours* 4-5 Contre Julien. SC 309 (Paris, 1983).

Moreschini C., *Discours* 32-37. SC 318 (Paris, 1985).

Moreschini C., *Discours* 38-41. SC 358 (Paris, 1990).

Bernardi J., *Discours* 42-43. SC 384 (Paris, 1992).

Calvet-Sebasti M., *Discours* 6-12. SC 406 (Paris, 1995).

The critical edition of the *Letters* of Gregory has been prepared by:

Gallay P., *Gregor von Nazianz. Briefe.* GCS 53 (Berlin, 1969).

Idem, *S. Grégoire de Nazianze. Lettres.* 2 vols. (Paris, 1964, 1967).

Idem, *S. Gégoire de Nazianze. Lettres Théologiques.* SC 208 (Paris, 1974).

GREGORY'S ORATIONS

Orat. 1, *In Sanctum Pascha* [On the Holy Feast of Pascha].

Orat. 2, *Oratio Apologetica* [Apologia for his flight to Pontus].

Orat. 3, *Ad eos qui ipsum acciverant nec occurrerant* [In Response to Those Who Called For Him (to be a Priest) But Would Not Welcome Him].

Orat. 4, *Adversus Julianum imperatorem I* [First Invective Against Emperor Julian].

Orat. 5, *Adversus Julianum imperatorem II* [Second Invective Against Emperor Julian].

Orat. 6, *De Pace* [First Oration on Peace—or First Eirenika].

Orat. 7, *In Laudem Caesarii fratris* [Memorial Panegyric on His Brother Caesarios].

Orat. 8, *In laudem sororis suae Gorgoniae* [Memorial Panegyric on His Sister Gorgonia].

Orat. 9, *Apologeticus ad patrem suum* [Apologia To His Father on the Occasion of His Own Episcopal Ordination].

Orat. 10, *In seipsum... post reditum e fuga* [A Statement of His Position After Returning From His Flight].

Orat. 11, *Ad Gregorium Nyssenum* [To Gregory of Nyssa. (A composite piece also including an oration delivered on a festival of the local Cappadocian martyrs).

Orat. 12, *Ad patrem cum ei Nazianzenae ecclesiae curam commisisset* [To His Father After the Latter Had Inducted Him as Bishop at Nazianzus].

Orat. 13, *In consecratione Eulalii Doarensium Episcopi* [Address Given When He Consecrated a New Bishop at Doara. As Edited by his Cousin Bishop Eulalios]. (The Latin Migne title misreads the Greek and wrongly presumes Eulalios was the bishop consecrated.)

Orat. 14, *De pauperum amore* [On Love for the Poor].

Orat. 15, *In Macchabaeorum laudem* [Panegyrical Oration on the Maccabees].

Orat. 16, *In patrem tacentem* [Oration on His Father's Silence].

Orat. 17, *Ad cives Nazianzenos... et Praefectum irascentem* [Civic Address to Nazianzus. When the Prefect Was Enraged Against Them].

Orat. 18, *Funebris oratio in patrem* [*Funeral Oration* for His Father].

Orat. 19, *Ad Julianum tributorum exaequatorem* [To Julian the Moderator of Taxes].

Orat. 20, *De theologia et constitutione episcoporum* [On Theology and the Installation of Bishops]. (A composite from Orats. 2, 6, & 23. The original title was probably "An Exposition of Doctrine on the Occasion of a Reception of Bishops.")

Orat. 21, *In laudem Athanasii episcopi Alexandriae* [Panegyric on Athanasios the Bishop of Alexandria].

Orat. 22, *De pace III* [Third Oration on Peace—Third Eirenika].

Orat. 23, *De pace II* [Second Oration on Peace—Second Eirenika]. (The order of the titles is not in accordance with the Migne numerical listing because earlier editors had mistakenly assigned Orat. 23 to the same time as Orat. 6.)

Orat. 24, *In laudem sancti Cypriani* [Panegyric on St Cyprian].

Orat. 25, *In laudem Heronis philosophi* [Panegyric for the Philosopher Hero]. (Oration for Maximus the Cynic.)

Orat. 26, *In seipsum II* [A Second Statement of His Position]. (Cf. Orat. 10.)

Orat. 27, *Oratio theologica prima. Adversus Eunomianos praevia dissertatio* [First Theological Oration. An Initial Refutation of the Eunomians].

Orat. 28, *Oratio theologica secunda: de theologia* [Second Theological Oration. On the Nature of Theology].

Orat. 29, *Oratio theologica tertia: de Filio* [Third Theological Oration. On The Son].

Orat. 30, *Oratio theologica quarta: de Filio II* [Fourth Theological Oration. Second Oration on the Son].

Orat. 31, *Oratio theologica quinta: de Spiritu Sancto* [Fifth Theological Oration. On the Holy Spirit].

Orat. 32, *De moderatione in disputando* [On the Need for Moderation in Debate].

Orat. 33, *Adversus Arianos et de seipso* [Oration Against the Arians and On His Own Position].

Orat. 34, *In Aegyptiorum adventum* [Oration for the Arrival of the Egyptians].

Orat. 35, *Spurious Text. De martyribus et adversus Arianos* [On the Martyrs and Against the Arians].

Orat. 36, *De seipso et ad eos qui ipsum cathedram Constantinopolitanum, affectare dicebant* [On His Own Position. In Refutation of Those Who Maintained He Coveted the Throne of Constantinople].

Orat. 37, *In dictum Evangelii: Cum consummasset Jesus hos sermones* [On the Gospel Text: "When Jesus Had Finished These Words," Mt 19:1f].

Orat. 38, *In Theophania sive natalia Salvatoris* [On The Theophany, or the Birthday of the Savior].

Orat. 39, *In sanctum Lumina* [Oration on the Holy Lights].

Orat. 40, *In sanctum Baptisma* [Oration on Holy Baptism].

Orat. 41, *In Pentecosten* [Oration for Pentecost].

Orat. 42, *Supremum vale coram centum quinquaginta episcopis* [Final Farewell: Delivered in the Presence of the 150 Bishops].

Orat. 43, *In laudem Basilii magni* [Panegyric in Memory of Basil the Great].

Orat. 44, *In novam Dominicam* [On the New Lord's Day]. (Homily for the Sunday After Pascha.)

Orat. 45, *In sanctum Pascha* [Oration on the Holy Feast of Pascha]. (A re-edition of *Oration* 38.)

Other Translations & Editions

Boulenger, F., *Grégoire de Nazianze. Discours funèbres en l'honneur de son frère Césaire et de Basile de Cesarée* (Paris, 1908).

Browne, C.G. & Swallow, J.E. (eds.), *Gregory of Nazianzus.* The Nicene and Post-Nicene Fathers, 2nd series, vol. 7 (Oxford/New York, 1894; repr. T & T Clark, Edinburgh, 1989).

Gallay, P., *Grégoire de Nazianze* (Introduction and Fr. tr. of select passages) (Paris, 1959, 1993).

Hardy, E.R., "Christology of the Later Fathers." LCC, vol. 3 (1954) (*Theological Orations*).

King, C.W., *St Gregory of Nazianzus. Julian the Emperor: containing Gregory Nazianzen's Two Invectives and Libanius' Monody*, Bohn Classical Library (London, 1888).

Mason, A.J., *The Five Theological Orations of Gregory of Nazianzus* (Cambridge, 1899).

McCauley, L.P., Funeral Orations by S. Gregory Nazianzen and (Ed. et al.), S. Ambrose. FOTC, vol. 22 (Washington, 1953).

Metallenos, G.D., *Gregoriou tou Theologou Epitaphios eis ton Megan Basileion* (Text, Modern Gk. tr. & commentary) (Athens, 1968).

Moreschini, C., *I Cinque Discorsi Theologici,* CTP 58 (Rome, 1986).

Norris, F.W., *Faith Gives Fullness to Reasoning: The Five Theological Orations of S. Gregory Nazianzen* (Leiden, 1991); Commentary (Translation by F. Williams & L. Wickham).

Staniloae, D., *Cele Cinci Cuvintari Teologice* (Romanian text of *Orations* 27-31, with Intro. and notes) (Editura Anastasia: Bucharest, 1993).

Von Barbel, J., "Gregor von Nazianz: Die fünf theologische Reden" (Text. German tr. and commentary). *Testimonia Bd.* III (Düsseldorf, 1963).

The Poetic Works

The present state of the text of Gregory's poetry, particularly in Migne, is very regrettable. A complete critical edition is still awaited, although selected parts of the poetic corpus now have excellent editions.

Boyd, H.S., *Select Poems of Synesius and Gregory Nazianzen* (London, 1814).

Corsaro, F., *Poesie Scelte,* MSLC 6 (1955), pp. 1-42.

Dronke, E., *Carmina Selecta S. Gregorii Nazianzeni* (Göttingen, 1840).

Gallay, P., *Grégoire de Nazianze. Poèmes et Lettres Choisies* (Lyon/Paris, 1941).

Jungck, C., *De Vita Sua* (Text. German Tr. and Commentary) (Heidelberg, 1974).

McGuckin, J.A., *St Gregory Nazianzen: Selected Poems* (SLG Press: Oxford, 1986); repr. 1989.

Meehan, D., *St Gregory of Nazianzus. Three Poems,* FOTC, vol. 75 (Washington, 1987).

Moreschini, C. (ed.), *Gregory of Nazianzus: Poemata Arcana* (translation and commentary by D. Sykes) (Oxford, 1996).

Newman, J.H., *Historical Sketches,* vol. 2 (London, 1896).

Paton, W.R., "The Epigrams of St Gregory the Theologian. The Greek Anthology" (*Anthologia Palatina*), Book 8. *Loeb Classical Library* II (London, 1917).

Pellegrino, M., *Poesie Scelte* (Turin, 1939).

Peri, C., *S. Gregorio Nazianzeno: Epitaffi* (Anthologia Palatina VIII) (Milan, 1975).

Werhahn, H.M., *Gregorii Nazianzeni: "Synkrisis Bion"* (Wiesbaden, 1953).

White, C., *Gregory of Nazianzus: Autobiographical Poems* (Cambridge Medieval Classics, vol. 6) (Cambridge, 1996).

Other Related Classical Primary Texts

Aetios of Byzantium, "The Syntagmation of Aetius the Anomoean," L.R. Wickham, JTS 19 (1968).

Ammianus Marcellinus, *Opera.* LCL, 3 vols. (ET, J.C. Rolfe) (1950-52).

Apuleios of Madaura, *The Golden Ass* (*The Transformations of Lucius*) (ET, R. Graves) (Penguin Classics: London, 1950).

Basil of Caesarea, *Opera.* PG 29-32.
　Ascetical works (ET, M.M. Wagner). FOTC, vol. 9, 1950.
　Selected works (ET, B. Jackson). NPNF, vol. 8, 2nd series, 1895.
　Letters (a) (ET, A.C. Way). FOTC, vols. 13 & 28, 1951, 1955.
　Letters (b) (ET, R.J. Deferrari). LCL, 4 vols., 1950-53.
　Exegetical Works (ET, A.C. Way). FOTC, vol. 46, 1963.
　The Philocalia of Origen (with Gregory Nazianzus) (ET, G. Lewis) (Edinburgh, 1911).

Eunapios, *Eunapius: Vitae Philosophorum* (J. Giangrande, ed.) (Rome, 1956).
　Eunapii Historia. Fragmenta Historicorum Graecorum, vol. 4 (C. Muller, ed.) (Paris, 1951).
　Lives of the Philosophers and Sophists (ET, W.C. Wright). LCL (London, 1952).

Eunomios of Cyzicus, *Extant works* (ed., R.P. Vaggione) (Oxford, 1987).

Gregory of Nyssa, *Opera*. PG 44-46.
 Gregorii Nysseni Opera (ed., W. Jaeger et al) (Leiden, 1952).
 Selected Works (ET, W. Moore & H.A. Wilson). NPNF, 2nd series, vol. 5, 1893.
 On the Lord's Prayer: The Beatitudes (ET, H.C. Graef) (1954), *Ancient Christian Writers* [New York, 1946-]).
 Ascetical Works (ET, V.W. Callahan). FOTC, vol. 58 (1967).
 The Life of Moses (ET, A.J. Malherbe & E. Ferguson), CWS (1978).
 The Easter Sermons of Gregory of Nyssa (ET, A. Spira & C. Klock) (Cambridge, MA, 1978).
 Commentary on the Song of Songs (ET, C. McCambly) (Brookline, 1988).

Himerios, *Himerii declamationes et orationes cum deperditarum fragmentis* (ed., Aristides Colonna) (Rome, 1951).

Iamblichos, *De Mysteriis Aegyptiorum* (ed., E. des Places) (Paris, 1966).

Julian, *Works of the Emperor Julian* (ET, W.C. Wright). LCL, 3 vols. (1949, 1953, 1954).

Libanios, *Libanii Opera* (Ed. R. Foerster), vols. 1-12 (Leipzig, 1903-, 1912) (*Epistulae*. = *Opera*. vols. 10-11); repr. Hildesheim (Olms, 1963); *Selected Works* (ET, A.F. Norman), vol. 1, *The Julianic Orations*, LCL (1969).

Lucian of Samosata, *Satirical Sketches* (ET, P. Turner) (Penguin Classics: London, 1958).

Petronius Arbiter, *The Satyricon* (ET, W. Arrowsmith) (London, 1959).

Plato, *The Works of Plato* (ET, B. Jowett) (ed., I. Edman) (New York, 1956).

Porphyry, "The Life of Plotinus" (ET, A.H. Armstrong) in *Plotinus: The Enneads*, vol. 1. LCL (1966).

Themistios, *Themistii orationes quae supersunt*, 3 vols. (ed., H. Schenkl, completed by G. Downey) (Leipzig, 1965-1974).

A Select Bibliography of General Studies and Biographical Sources Relevant to the Subject

Anderson, G., *The Second Sophistic. A Cultural Phenomenon in the Roman Empire* (London, 1993).

Armstrong, A.H., *Plotinian and Christian Studies* (London, 1979).

Athanassiadi, P., *Julian: An Intellectual Biography* (London, 1992) (first issued as: *Julian and Hellenism* [Oxford, 1981]).

di Berardino, A. (ed.), *Encyclopedia of the Early Church*, 2 vols. (ET, Cambridge, 1992).

Berchman, R.M., *From Philo to Origen: Middle Platonism in Transition* (Scholars Press: Chico, CA, 1984).

Bidez, J., *La vie de l'empereur Julien* (Paris, 1930).

Bowersock, B.W., *Julian the Apostate* (Cambridge, MA, 1978) (1997).

Brennecke, H.C., *Studien zur Geschichte der Homoer. Der Osten bis zum Ende der homoische Reichskirche* (Tübingen, 1988).

Capes, W.W., *University Life in Ancient Athens* (New York, 1877).

Cochrane, C.N., *Christianity and Classical Culture* (Oxford, 1972).

Cox, P.L., *Biography in Late Antiquity: A Quest for the Holy Man* (Berkeley, 1983).

Dagron, G., *Naissance d'une capitale: Constantinople et ses institutions de 330 à 451* (Paris, 1974).

Elm, S., *Virgins of God: The Making of Asceticism in Late Antiquity* (Oxford, 1994).

Ensslin, W., *Die Religionspolitik des Kaisers Theodosios der Grosse* (Munich, 1953).

Fialon, E., *Étude historique et littéraire sur S. Basile, suivie de l'Hexaméron traduit en français* (Paris, 1865, 1899).

Gain, B., *L'Église de Cappadoce au IVe siècle, d'après la correspondance de Basile de Césarée*. OCA, 225 (Rome, 1985).

Giet, S., *Les idées et l'action sociale de S. Basile* (Paris, 1941).

Idem, "Le rigorisme de S. Basile," RSR (1949).

Hanson, R.P.C., *The Search for the Christian Doctrine of God* (Edinburgh, 1988).

Hefele, C.J.V, *Histoire des Conciles* (French Tr. and notes by H. Leclercq) (Paris, 1907).

Jaeger, W., *Paideia: The Ideals of Greek Culture*, vols. 1-3 (Oxford, 1939-1945).

Idem, *Early Christianity and Greek Paideia* (London, 1961).

Janin, R., *Constantinople byzantine: développement urbain et répertoire topographique* (Paris, 1964).

Idem, *La géographie ecclésiastique de l'empire byzantin*, Part 1 (Le siège de Constantinople et le patriarcat oecuménique, les églises et les monastères) (Paris, 1969).

Jones, A.H.M., *The Later Roman Empire*, vols. 1-2 (Oxford, 1964, 1986).

King, N.Q., *The Emperor Theodosius and the Establishment of Christianity* (London, 1961).

Kopecek, T.A., "Curial displacements and flight in later 4th century Cappadocia." *Historia* 23 (1974).

Idem, *A History of Neo-Arianism*, 2 vols. PMS 8 (Cambridge MA, 1979).

Laistner, M.L.W., *Christianity and Pagan Culture in the Later Roman Empire* (Cornell, 1967).

Lewy, H., "Chaldaean Oracles and Theurgy." *Mysticism, Magic, and Platonism in the Later Roman Empire* (ed., M. Tardieu) (Paris, 1978).

Lietzmann, H., "Apollinaris von Laodicea und seine Schule." TU 1 (Tübingen, 1904).

Lohr, W.A., *Die Enstehung der homoischen und homoiousianischen Kirchenparteien* (Bonn, 1986).

Lot, F., *Les Invasions germaniques* (Paris, 1905).

Mathews, T.F., *The Byzantine Churches of Istanbul: A Photographic Survey* (Pennsylvania State University Press, 1976).

Misch, G., *A History of Autobiography in Antiquity*, Part 2 (London, 1950).

Momigliano, A., *The Conflict Between Paganism and Christianity in the Fourth Century* (Oxford, 1963).

Ostrogorsky, G., *History of the Byzantine State* (ET, Oxford, 1989).

Puech, A., *Histoire de la Littérature grecque chrétienne* (Paris, 1930).

Ramsay, W.M., *The Historical Geography of Asia Minor* (London, 1890).

Raven, C.E., *Apollinarism. An Essay on the Christology of the Early Church* (Cambridge, 1923; repr. New York, 1978).

Reitzenstein, R., *Hellenistic Mystery Religions: Their Basic Ideas and Significance* (ET, J.E. Steely) (Pittsburgh, PA, 1978).

Ritter, A.M., *Das Konzil von Konstantinopel und sein Symbol. Studien zur Geschichte und Theologie des II Oekumenische Konzils* (Göttingen, 1965).

Rousseau, P., *Basil of Caesarea* (University of California Press: Berkeley and Oxford, 1994).

Scicolone, S., "Aspetti dell persecuzione giulianea." RSCI 33 (1979).

Seaver, J., "Julian the Apostate and the attempted rebuilding of the Temple of Jerusalem." RPL 1, (1978).

Trypanis, C.A., *The Penguin Book of Greek Verse* (London, 1971).

Idem, *Greek Poetry From Homer to Seferis* (Chicago, 1981).

Van der Meer, F., *Atlas de l'Antiquité chrétienne* (Paris, 1960).

Williams, S. & Friell, G., *Theodosius: The Empire at Bay* (London, 1994).

STUDIES ON THE THOUGHT AND STYLE OF ST GREGORY NAZIANZEN

Ackerman, W., *Die didaktische Poesie des Gregorius von Nazianz*. Diss. (Leipzig, 1903).

Adama, J.A., "La Tragedia Christus Patiens y la doctrina mariana en la Cappadocia del siglo IV." *Epektasis* (Mélanges patr. offerts à J. Daniélou; eds., J. Fontaine & C. Kannengiesser) (Paris, 1972).

Agathangelou, K., *To drama "Christos Paschon"* (Gk. text). *Orthodoxia* 20 (1945).

Idem, "Epi Gregoriou" (Gk. text) *Orthodoxia* 27 (1952); also 28 (1953).

Altaner, B., *Patrology* (ET, H. Graef) (New York, 1960).

Althaus, H., "Die Heilslehre des heiligen Gregor von Nazianz." *Münsterische Beitr. zur Theol.* 34 (Münster, 1972).

Armstrong, G.T., "The Cross in the Old Testament according to Athanasius, Cyril of Jerusalem, and the Cappadocian Fathers." *Theologia Crucis, Signum Crucis: Festschrift, E. Dinckler;* eds., C. von Andresen & G. Klein (Tübingen, 1979).

Asmus, J.R., "Gregor von Nazianz und sein Verhaltnis zum Kynismus." TSK 67 (1894).

Idem, "Die Invektiven des Gregorius von Nazianz im Lichte der Werke des Kaisers Julian," ZK 31 (1910).

Baldwin, B., "Gregory Nazianzen, Ammianus, Scurrae and the Historia Augusta." *Gymnasium* 93 (1986).

Baumstark, A., "Die Zeit der Einführung des Weihnachtsestes in Konstantinopel." *Oriens Christianus* 2 (1902).

Beck, H.G., "Rede als Kunstwerk und Bekenntnis: Gregor von Nazianz." *Bayerische Akademie der Wissenschaften,* phil. hist. Klasse (1977).

Begzou, M., "Philosophia Kai Theologia Ston Gregoriou Nazianzeno. Spoude ston Pateriko Eklektismo." *Synedrio Paterikes Theologias: Gregorios Ho Theologos* (ed., S.G. Papadopoulos) (Athens, 1990).

Bellini, E., "La chiesa nel mistero della salvezza in S. Gregorio Nazianzeno." *Varese Venegono Inferiore La Scuola Cattolica* (1970).

Idem, "Bibliografia su San Gregorio Nazianzeno." *La Scuola Cattolica*, supplemento bibliografico, 197.

Idem, "Il dogma trinitario nei primi discorsi di Gregorio Nazianzeno." *Augustinianum* 13 (1973).

Benoit, A., *St Grégoire de Nazianze: sa vie, ses oeuvres, et son époque* (Marseille/Paris, 1876; repr. Hildesheim/New York, 1973).

Bergmann, S., "Gregory of Nazianzen's Theological Interpretation of the Philosophy of Nature in the Doctrine of the Four Elements." *Geist, der lebendig macht: Lavierungen zur oekologischen Befreiungstheologie* (Frankfurt am Main, 1997).

Idem, "Die Welt als ware oder haushalt? Die Wegwahl der trinitärischen Kosmologie bei Gregor von Nazianz," *Geist, der lebendig macht: Lavierungen zur oekologischen Befreiungstheologie* (Frankfurt am Main, 1997).

Bernardi, J., *La Prédication des Pères cappadociens: Le Prédicateur et son auditoire.* PFLS 30, (Montpellier, 1968), Part II.

Idem, "Grégoire de Nazianze, critique de Julien." SP 14 (6th Int. Oxford Patristics Conf., 1971), TU 117 (Berlin, 1976).

Idem, (a) "Grégoire de Nazianze et le poète comique Anaxilas." *Pallas* 31 (1984).

Idem, (b) "Nouvelles perspectives sur la famille de Grégoire de Nazianze." VChr 38 (1984).

Idem, S. *Grégoire de Nazianze: Le théologien et son temps* (Paris, 1995).

Beuckmann, U., "Gregor von Nazianz: Gegen die Habsucht. Einleitung und Kommentar. Studien zur Geschichte und Kultur des Altertums." NF 2, Forsuchungen zu Gregor von Nazianz 6 (Paderborn, 1988).

Biedermann, H.M., "Die Bedeutung der drei Kappadozier und des Johannes Chrysostomos als fundament der byzantinischen Geisteshaltung." OS 32 (1983).

Bonis K.G., "Gregorios ho Theologos etoi to Genealogikon dendron Gregoriou tou Nazianzenou kai ho pros ton Amphilokion Ikonion suggenikos autou desmos. Patrologike kai genealogike melete." Theologia 21-23, 1950-1952 (Athens 1953) (Review: ByzZ 47, 1954).

Idem, *Gregorios ho Theologos. Bios kai erga* (Athens, 1982).

Bossi, F., "Note a Gregorio Nazianzeno." MCr 10-12, 1975-1977 [Carm. 1.2.1.547; 1.2.29.61f].

Bouteneff, P., "St Gregory Nazianzen and the Two-Nature Christology." SVTQ 38.3 (1994).

Bouyer, L., *The Spirituality of the New Testament and the Fathers* (History of Christian Spirituality, vol. 1) (New York, 1963).

Brou L., "S. Grégoire de Nazianze et l'antienne "Mirabile Mysterium" des Laudes de la Circoncision." Eph. Lit. 58 (1944).

Bruckmayr, P.A., *Untersuchungen über die Randscholien der 28 Reden des hl. Gregorios von Nazianz im Cod. Theol. Gr. 74 der Wiener Nationalbibliothek.* Diss. (Vienna, 1940).

Callahan, J.F., "Greek Philosophy and the Cappadocian Cosmology." DOP 12 (1958).

Calvet-Sebasti, M.A., *Grégoire de Nazianze, théoricien de la lettre. Actes du Colloque sur les lettres dans la Bible et la littérature* (Lyon, 1996).

Camelot T., "Amour des Lettres et désir de Dieu chez S. Grégoire de Nazianze: Les logoi au service du Logos." *Littérature et Religion, Mélanges offerts au chanoine J. Coppin*, MSR supplement 23 (Lille, 1966).

Cameron, A.D.E., "Gregory of Nazianzus and Apollo" (Carm. II, 2, 7, 253-255). JTS 20 (1969).

Capelle, B., "Les homélies de S. Grégoire sur le Cantique." RB (1929).

Cataldo, A., "Virtu è ricerca di Dio nell' epistolario di S. Gregorio di Nazianzo." *Sileno* 5-6 (1979-1980).

Idem, "Come l'oro nel crogiuolo" (Gregory's Ep. 214 and the Book of Wisdom 3, 5, 6). QILCL II (1983).

Cataudella, Q., "Derivazioni da Saffo in Gregorio Nazianzeno" (vv. 179 -205, Carm. Ad Vitalium, Carm. varia 51). BFC 33 (1926-27).

Idem, "Le poesie di Gregorio Nazianzeno." A&R 8, (1927).

Idem, "Kerkidas ho Philtatos" (Gregorio Nazianzeno De Virtute 598). *Convivium Dominicum* (Catania 1959).

Idem, "Cronologia e attribuzione del Christus Patiens." *Dioniso* 43 (1969).

Idem, "Influssi di poesia classica negli epigrammi." *Studi Colonna* (Perugia, 1982).

Cavallini, E., Gregorii Nazianzeni Carmen 1.2.1, 656f. Corolla Londiniensis I (ed., G. Giangrande), London Studies in Classical Philology, no. 8 (Amsterdam, 1981).

Chatillon, F., "De Gregorio Nazianzeno." RMAL 7 (1951).

Chelidze, E., "The two Georgian Translations of the Homilies of St Gregory Nazianzen."E.A. Livingstone (ed.), Acts of the 12th International Patristics Conference (Oxford,1995). SP 33 (Louvain, 1997).

Chrestou, P., "Gregorios Ho Theologos" (Gk. text). *Threskeutike kai Ethike Enkyklopaideia* 4 (1964).

Idem, *Gregory the Theologian: The Initiate of Divine Illumination* (Gk. text) (Thessalonike, 1990).

Colaclides, P., "Sur le modèle possible d'une épigramme de Grégoire de Nazianze" (PG 37.1449). C&M 30 (1969).

Coman, J., The genius of St Gregory Nazianzen (Romanian text). IRB III (Bucharest, 1937).

Idem, St Gregory Nazianzen's attitude to the Emperor Julian. An essay on Discourses 4 & 5 (Romanian text). IRB V (Bucharest, 1938).

Idem, "The Melancholic Character of St Gregory Nazianzen's Lyrical Poetry" (Romanian text). IRB VII (Bucharest, 1938).

Idem, "The Poetry of St Gregory Nazianzen" (Romanian text). *Studii teologice* 2:10 (Bucharest, 1958) (Cf. ByZ 52 [1959], and German resumé in *Bibliotheca Classica Orientis* 5 [1960].)

Idem, "Les deux Cypriens de S. Grégoire de Nazianze." SP 4, TU 79 (Berlin, 1961).

Idem, "Héllenisme et Christianisme dans le 25è discours de S. Grégoire de Nazianze." SP 14, TU 117 (Berlin, 1976).

Condamin, A., "Le texte de S. Grégoire de Nazianze sur Jonas." Rec SR (1922) (note on PG 35.505-508).

Conrotte, E.J., Isocrate et S. Grégoire de Nazianze; Le Panégyrique d'Evagoras et l'éloge funèbre de S. Basile (Musée Belge, 1897).

Cornitescu, C.I., "Sfintul Grigorie de Nazianz despre familia sa." Studii Teol. (Bucharest) 16, 5-6, 1964.

Corsaro, F., "Poesie Scelte di S. Gregorio Nazianzeno." MSLC 5 (1955).

Idem, "Gregorio Nazianzeno poeta." MSLC 6, 1956.

Costanza, S., "Su alcune risonanze classiche nel carme 1.2.10 di Gregorio di Nazianzo," Sileno 2 (1976).

Idem, La scelta della vita nel carmine 1.2.10 di Gregorio Nazianzeno. La priamel dei volori e delle professioni e il topos 'alloi me-ego de'. *Studi in onore del A. Ardizzoni* (Rome, 1978).

Coulie, B., "Chaines d'allusions dans les discours 4 & 5 de Grégoire de Nazianze." JOEByz 32, 3 (1982).

Idem, "Les richesses dans l'oeuvre de S. Grégoire de Nazianze. Étude littéraire et historique." PIOL 32 (Louvain La Neuve, 1985).

Courcelle, P., "Antecedents autobiographiques des Confessions de S. Augustin." RPLHA 31 (1957).

Cox, G.V., *Gregory of Nazianzus* (London, 1851) (ET of Ullmann).

Crimi, C. & Demoen, K., "Sulla cronologia del Commentario di Cosma di Gerusalemme ai carmi di Gregorio Nazianzeno." *Byzantion* 67 (1997).

Criscuolo, U., "Sull' epistola X di Gregorio di Nazianzo." *Koinonia* 9 (1985).

Idem, "Gregorio di Nazianzo e Giuliano. *Talariskos: (Studia Graeca A. Garzya).* Napoli d'Auria (1987).

Cummings, J.T., *A Critical Edition of the Carmen De Vita Sua of St Gregory Nazianzen,* Diss. Princeton University (1966).

Idem, "Towards a Critical Edition of the Carmen De Vita Sua of St Gregory Nazianzen." SP 7.1, TU 92 (Berlin, 1966).

Ibid., "Lexical Notes on St Gregory Nazianzen (De Vita Sua)." GRBS 9 (1968).

Davids, H.L., *De gnomologien van Sint Gregorios van Nazianze* (Nijmegen, 1940).

Idem, "De Gregorii Nazianzeni Epistula LXV." VChr 1 (1947).

Idem, "De Gregorii Nazianzeni Epistula CXCIX." VChr 2 (1948).

Davis, N.Z., "Gregory Nazianzen in the service of Humanist social reform." RQ 20 (1967).

De Jonge, L.F.M., *De S. Gregorii Nazianzeni carminibus quae inscribi solent "peri heautou,"* (Amsterdam, 1910).

Delekostante, K., "Ho Gregorios Theologos Kai To Problema Ton Skeseon Christianismou Kai Ellenikes Philosophias," *Synedrio Paterikes Theologias: Gregorios Ho Theologos* (ed., S.G. Papadopoulos) (Athens, 1990).

Delfgaauw, B., "Gregor von Nazianz. Antikes und Christliches Denken." *Eranos Jb.* 36 (1967).

Demoen, K., "Biblical versus non-Biblical vocabulary in Gregorius Nazianzenus: A Quantitative Approach," *Bible et Informatique: Méthodes, outils, résultats* (Jerusalem, [9-13 June] 1988).

Idem, "S. Pierre se régalant de lupins: à propos de quelques traces d'apocryphes concernant Pierre dans l'oeuvre de Grégoire de Nazianze." *Sacris Erudiri* 32 (1991).

Idem, "The Attitude towards Greek Poetry in the verse of Gregory Nazianzen," *Early Christian Poetry,* J. den Boeffe & A. Hilhortst (eds.). Series: *Suppl. to Vigiliae Christianae* 22 (Leiden, 1993).

Idem, "Pagan and Biblical Exempla in Gregory Nazianzen. A study in Rhetoric and Hermeneutics." CC, vol. 2 (*Lingua Patrum*) (Turnhout).

Idem, "Some remarks on the life and poems of Gregory Nazianzen." OCP 63 (1997).

Idem, "The philosopher, the call-girl and the icon: St Theodore the Studite's [ab]use of Gregory Nazianzen in the Iconoclastic controversy," in *La Spiritualité de l'univers byzantin dans le verbe et l'image* (Hommages offerts à E. Voordeckers), K. Demoen & J. Vereecken (eds.). *Instrumenta Patristica* 30 (Turnhout, 1997).

Idem, "Acteurs de pantomimes, trafiquants du Christ, flatteurs de femmes-Les éveques dans les poèmes autobiographiques de Grégoire de Nazianze," in *Vescovi e pastori in età teodosiana. Studia Ephemeridis Augustinianum* 58 (Rome, 1997).

Idem, "The paradigmatic prayer in Gregory Nazianzen," Acts of the 12th International Patristics Conference, Oxford, 1995, E.A. Livingstone (ed.). *Studia Patristica* 32 (Louvain, 1997).

Del Ton, I., "Ta Aporreta nel linguaggio di S. Gregorio Nazianzeno," *Augustinianum* 13 (1973).

Idem, "Natura e pregi della poetica di S. Gregorio di Nazianzo." QU 3 (1974).

Dennis, G.T., "Gregory of Nazianzus and the Byzantine Letter," T. Halton & J. Williman (eds.). *Diakonia* (1986).

Der Nersessian, S., "The Illustrations of the Homilies of Gregory of Nazianzus. Ms. Paris.Gr. 510. A study of the connection between text and images." DOP 16 (1962).

Devos, P., (a) "S. Grégoire de Nazianze et Héllade de Césarée, en Cappadoce." *Analecta Bollandiana* 79 (1961).

Idem, (b) "S. Pierre premier éveque de Sébaste, dans une lettre de S. Grégoire de Nazianze." *Analecta Bollandiana* 79 (1961).

Idem, (c) "Les deux Cypriens de S. Grégoire de Nazianze." SP 4 (1961).

Idem, "Grégoire de Nazianze; témoin du mariage de Grégoire de Nysse." *Sym. Naz.* (Paderborn, 1983).

Diobouniotou, K., "Niketas Herakleias: hermeneia eis Logous tou Gregoriou Nazianzenou" (Gk. text). *Theologia* 21 (1950).

Disdier, M.T., "Nouvelles études sur S. Grégoire de Nazianze." EO 34 (1931).

Doerrie, H., "Die Epiphanias-Predigt des Gregor von Nazianz (Or. 39) und ihre geistes-geschichtliche Bedeutung," *Kyriakon (Festschrift J. Quasten.* P. von Granfield & J.A Jungmann, eds.), vol. 1 (Münster, 1970).

Donders, A., *Der hl. Kirchenlehrer Gregor von Nazianz als Homilet* (Münster, 1909).

Idem, "Eine soziale Predigt des christlichen Altertums" (Orat. 14). *Kirche und Konzel* 3 (1920).

Idem, "Die hl. Schrift in den Predigten des Kirchenlehrers Gregor von Nazianz." KK 4 (1921).

Draeseke, J., "Gregorius von Nazianz und sein Verhaltnis zum Apollinarismus." TSK 65 (1892).

Idem, "Neu-platonisches in des Gregors von Nazianz Trinitatslehre." ByZ 15 (1906).

Dubedout, E., *De divi Gregorii Nazianzeni carminibus* (Paris, 1907).

Dziech, J., *De Gregorio Nazianzeno diatribae quae dicitur alumno* (Poznai, 1927).

Egan, J.P., "Gregory of Nazianzus and the Logos doctrine," *Word and Spirit,* J. Plevnik (ed.) (Willowdale, Ontario, 1975).

Idem, "The deceit of the devil according to St Gregory Nazianzen," in: Acts of the 10th International Patristics Conference, Oxford, 1987, E.A. Livingstone (ed.). *Studia Patristica* 22 (Louvain, 1989).

Idem, "Primal Cause and Trinitarian Perichoresis in Gregory Nazianzen's Oration," Acts of the 11th International Patristics Conference, Oxford, 1991, E.A. Livingstone (ed.), *Studia Patristica* 27 (Louvain, 1993).

Idem, "Toward Trinitarian Perichoresis: St Gregory the Theologian, Oration 31.14." GOTR 39, 1-2 (1994).

Idem, "Aitos (Author), Aitia (Cause), and Arche (Origin): Synonyms in selected texts of Gregory Nazianzen," E.A. Livingstone (ed.), Acts of the 12th International Patristics Conference, Oxford 1995, *Studia Patristica* 32 (Louvain, 1997).

Ellverson, A., "The Dual Nature of Man: A Study in the Theological Anthropology of Gregory of Nazianzus," Acta Univ. Upsal. *Studia doctrinae Christianae* 21 (Stockholm, 1981).

Elm, S., "Inventing the 'Father of the Church': Gregory of Nazianzus' Farewell to the Bishops (Or. 42) In its Historical Context." BHS 31 (Ordensstudien 13) (Berlin, 1999) (*Vita Religiosa im Mittelalter. Festschrift für Kaspar Elm* [herausgegeben: F.J. Felten & N. Jaspert].)

eadem, "The Diagnostic Gaze: Gregory of Nazianzus' Theory of the Ideal Orthodox Priest in His Orations 6 (*De Pace*) and 2 (*Apologia De Fuga sua*)." *Orthodoxie, Christianisme, Histoire*, S. Elm, E. Reillard & A. Romano (eds.) [Collection de l'École francaise de Rome] (Rome, 2000').

Engberding, H., "Die Kunstprosa des eucharistischen Hochgebetes der griechischen Gregoriusliturgie," *Mullus (Festschrift T. Klauser).* JbAC, Erg-Bd. I (Münster, 1964).

Ettlinger, G.H., "Theos de ouk outos (Orat. 37). The Dignity of the Human Person According to the Greek Fathers." SP 16 (1985).

Idem, "The Orations of Gregory of Nazianzus: A Study in Rhetoric and Personality." *Preaching in the Patristic Age,* D. Hunter (ed.) (1989).

Evenepoel, W., "The Early Christian Poets Gregory Nazianzen and Prudentius." *Philohistor. Miscellanea in honorem C. Laga*, A. Schoers (ed.) (Louvain, 1994).

Fantori, A., "L'Unita del cosmo nei discorsi di Gregorio Nazianzeno." SP 25 (1978).

Fellechner, E.L., *Askese und Caritas bei den drei Kappadokiern*. Diss. Heidelberg (1979).

Fernandez, M.N., "Observaciones sobre los Himnos de Gregorio Nacianceno," (With English synopsis), *Emerita* 36 (1968).

Fitzpatrick, G., "St Gregory Nazianzen: Education for Salvation." *Patristic and Byzantine Review* 10, 1-2 (1991).

Fleury, S., *Héllenisme et Christianisme. S.Grégoire de Nazianze et son temps* (Paris, 1930).

Focken, J., *De Gregorii Nazianzeni Orationum Carminum Dogmaticorum Argumentandi Ratione.* Diss. (Berlin, 1912).

Frangeskou, V.A., "Gregory Nazianzen's usage of the Homeric simile." *Hellenica* 36 (1985).

Idem, *The Hymns of St Gregory Nazianzen and their place in the history of Greek and Early Christian Hymnography.* Diss. University of Leeds, 1985 (Carm 1.1.29-38; & 2.1.38).

Frank, G.L.C., "The Incomprehensibility of God in the Theological, Orations of St. Gregory the Theologian and Its Implications for Contemporary debate about the fatherhood of God." GOTR 39, 1-2 (1994).

Freeland, J., "St Gregory Nazianzen from his Letters," *Dublin Review* 13 (1902), 333-354.

Gain, B., "L'Église de Cappadoce au 4è siècle d'après la correspondance de Basile de Césarée." OCA 225 (Rome, 1985).

Galavaris, G., "The Illustrations of the Liturgical Homilies of Gregory Nazianzen." *Studies in Ms. Illumination VI* (Princeton University Press, 1969) (Diss. Princeton, 1958).

Gallay, P., *Langue et style de S. Grégoire de Nazianze dans sa correspondance* (Paris, 1933).

Idem, *La Vie de S. Grégoire de Nazianze* (Lyon, Paris, 1943).

Idem, "Liste des manuscrits des lettres de S. Grégoire de Nazianze." REG (1944).

Idem, "Catalogue des manuscrits Parisiens des Lettres de S. Grégoire de Nazianze." Macon Protat (1945).

Idem, "Les Manuscrits des lettres de S. Grégoire de Nazianze," *Coll. des études anciennes* (Paris, 1957).

Idem, *S. Grégoire de Nazianze* (Église d'Hier et d'Aujourd'hui) (Paris, 1959; repr. 1993).

Idem, "La Bible dans l'oeuvre de Grégoire de Nazianze le Théologien," *Le Mond grec ancien et la bible,* C. Mondésert (ed.) (Paris, 1984).

Gangi, A., "Il De Vita Sua di Gregorio Nazianzeno." Diss Univ. of Catania (1947).

Garzya, A., "Per la cronologia del Christus Patiens." Studi Barigazzi 1, Sileno 10 (1984).

Geerard, M., *Clavis Patrum Graecorum*, vol. 2. *Gregorius Nazianzenus* (Turnhout, 1974) (authentic writings of Gregory listed and annotated, giving an extended bibliographical listing of other works relating to the Gregorian manuscript tradition).

Geoghegan, A.T., "The Attitude towards Labor in Early Christianity and Ancient Culture." *Studies in Christian Antiquity* 6 (Washington, 1945).

Ghedini, G., "La Poesia di S. Gregorio Nazianzeno." *Scuola Cattolica* (1932).

Ghellinck, J. de, "Quelques appréciations de la dialectique d'Aristote durant les conflits trinitaires du IVè siècle." RHE 26 (1930).

Giet, S., (a) *Sasimes; une méprise de S. Basile?* [Diss.] (Paris, 1941); (b) *Les idées et l'action sociales de S. Basile* (Paris, 1941).

Gilbert, P.L., "Person and Nature in the Theological Poems of St Gregory of Nazianzus." PhD. Diss. (Catholic University of America, 1994) (with translations of select poems).

Giudice-Rizzo, I., "Sul Christus Patiens e le Baccanti di Euripide." *Sic Gymn* 30 (1977).

Godet, P., "Grégoire de Nazianze." DTC 6.2 (1839-1844).

Gottwald, R., *De Gregorio Nazianzeno Platonico.* Diss. (Breslau, 1906).

Grabar, A., "Les miniatures de Grégoire de Nazianze de l'Ambrosienne (Ambrosianus 49-50), Coll. Orient. et Byzance." *Études d'Art mediéval*, vol. 1 (Paris, 1943).

Gregg, R.C., "Consolation Philosophy. Greek and Christian Paideia in the two Gregories." PMS III (Philadelphia, 1975).

Grenier, A., *La Vie et les poésies de S. Grégoire de Nazianze* (Clermont-Ferrand, 1858).

Gronau, K., "De Basilio, Gregorio Nazianzeno Nysennoque Platonis imitatoribus." Diss. (Göttingen, 1908).

Guida, A., "Un nuovo testo di Gregorio Nazianzeno." *Prometheus* 2 (1976).

Guignet, M., *S. Grégoire de Nazianze, orateur et epistolier*. Diss. (Paris, 1911) comprising:

Idem, (a) *Les procédés epistolaires de S. Grégoire de Nazianze comparés à ceux de ses contemporains* (Paris, 1911), and also:

Idem, (b) *S. Grégoire de Nazianze et la rhétorique* (Paris, 1911).

Hanriot-Coustet, A., "Grégoire de Nysse et un agraphon attribué à Barnabé." RHPhR 73 (1983) (note on Orat. 43).

Hanson, R.P.C., *The Search for the Christian Doctrine of God* (Edinburgh, 1988).

Harakas, S.S., "Ethical Teaching in St Gregory the Theologian." GOTR 39, 1-2 (1994).

Harkianakis, S., "Die Trinitatslehre Gregors von Nazianz" (with modern Greek synopsis), *Kleronomia* 1 (1969).

Harrison, V.E.F., "Some Aspects of S. Gregory the Theologian's Soteriology." GOTR 34 (1989).

eadem, "Poverty, Social Involvement and Life in Christ, according to St Gregory the Theologian." GOTR 39, 1-2 (1994).

eadem, "Gender, Generation, and Virginity in Cappadocian Theology." JTS 47 (1996).

Hauser-Meury, M. *Prosopographie zu den Schriften Gregors von Nazianzen*. Diss. Basel. *Theophaneia* 13 (Bonn, 1960).

Henry, R. de L., "The Late Greek Optative and its Use in the Writings of Gregory Nazianzen." *Patristic Studies* 68 (Catholic University of America: Washington, 1943).

Hergenroether, J., *Die Lehre von der gottlichen Dreieinigkeit nach dem hl. Gregorius von Nazianz* (Regensburg, 1850).

Hérouville, P. de "Quelques traces d'Aristotélianisme chez Grégoire de Nazianze." RSR 8 (1918).

Holl, K., *Amphilocius von Ikonium in seinem Verhaltnis zu den grossen Kappadokiern* (Tübingen-Leipzig, 1904).

Holman, S., "Healing the Social Leper in Gregory of Nyssa's and Gregory of Nazianzus' 'Peri Philoptochias'." HTR 92 (1999).

eadem, "Taxing Nazianzus: Gregory and the other Julian" (forthcoming). *Studia Patristica* (2001).

Hummer, F., *Des Heiligen Gregor von Nazianz, des Theologen, Lehre von der Gnade* (Kempten, 1890).

Hurth, X., "De Gregorii Nazianzeni orationibus funebris." Diss. Argentorati (1907).

Junod, E., "Rémarques sur la composition de la 'Philocalie' d'Origène par Basile et Grégoire de Nazianze." RHPhR 52 (1972).

Kakalaletre, D.P., "He Triadologia tou Gregoriou Theologou Me Emphase Stin Pneumatologia," *Synedrio Paterikes Theologias: Gregorios Ho Theologos*, S.G. Papadopoulos (ed.) (Athens, 1990).

Kalamakis, D., "Echoes of Pindar in Gregory the Theologian" (Gk text). *Athena* 79 (1983-1984).

Kambylis, A., "Gregor von Nazianz und Kallimachos," *Hermes* 90 (1982) (Carm. dogm. 1.8f).

Kantones, A., *Ho Hagios Gregorios Ho Nazianzenos* (Kavala, 1973).

Karmiris, J., *He Ekklesiologia tou Agiou Gregoriou tou Theologou* (Athens, 1960).

Keenan, M.E., "St Gregory of Nazianzen and Early Greek Medicine." *Bulletin of the History of Medicine* 9 (1941).

Kelly, J.N.D., *Early Christian Doctrines* (London, 1968).

Kennedy, G.A., *The Art of Persuasion in Greece* (Princeton, 1963).

Idem, *Greek Rhetoric Under the Christian Emperors* (Princeton, 1983).

Kertsch, M., "Gregor von Nazianz. Stellung zu Theoria und Praxis aus der Sicht seiner Reden." *Byzantion* 44 (1974).

Idem, "Begriffsgechichtliches aus den Grabreden Gregors von Nazianz." JOEByz 23 (1974).

Idem, "Bildersprache bei Gregor von Nazianz. Ein Beitrag zur spatantiken Rhetorik und popularen Philosophie." *Grazer theol. Studien* II, Grazer Inst. fur Okum. Theol. und Patrol. (Graz, 1978).

Idem, "Stilistische und literarische Untersuchungsergebnisse aus Gregors von Nazianz' Carmen de Virtute II." Sym. Naz. (Paderborn, 1983).

Idem, "Zur interschiedlichen ethischen Bewertung von 'Natur/ausserer Zwang' und 'freier Willensentschluss' bei Heiden und Christen im Hintergrund einer Aussage Gregors von Nazianz," WS 18 (1984) (note on Orat. 37.16).

Keydell, R., "Die Unechtheit der Gregor von Nazianz zugeschrieben Exhortatio ad Virgines." ByzZ 43 (1950).

Idem, "Ein dogmatisches Lehrgedicht Gregors von Nazianz." ByzZ 44 (1951) (Dölger Festschrift).

Idem, "Die literarhistorische Stellung der Gedichte Gregors von Nazianz," Atti dello 8o Congr. Int. di Studi bizantini. II. SBN vol. 7 (Rome, 1953).

Knecht, A., *Gegen die Putzsucht der Frauen* (Text and Commentary). *Wissenschaftliche Kommentare zu griechischen und lateinischen schriftstellen* (Heidelberg, 1972).

Kondothra, G., "The Word Human and Divine: An approach of Gregory Nazianzen." *Studia Patristica* 16.2, E.A. Livingstone (ed.) (Berlin, 1985).

Kopecek, T.A., "The Social Class of the Cappadocian Fathers." CH 42 (1973).

Idem, "The Cappadocian Fathers and Civic Patriotism." CH 43 (1974).

Idem, *A History of Neo-Arianism*, 2 vols. *Patristic Monograph Series,* vol. 8 (Cambridge, MA, 1979).

Koulits, P., "He Diadikasia Tou Theologein Kata Ton Agio Gregorio Ton Theologo." *Synedrio Paterikes Theologias: Gregorios Ho Theologos* (ed., S.G. Papadopoulos) (Athens, 1990).

Koster, W.J.W., "Sappho apud Gregorium Nazianzenum," *Mnemosyne* 17 (1964) (vv. 5-6, 10 of 1.2.14, PG 37.755).

Idem, "Sappho apud Gregorium bis detecta." Mnemosyne 18 (1965).

Kurmann, A., "Gregor von Nazianz. Oratio IV gegen Julian. Ein Kommentar," *Schweirische Beitrage zur Altertumswissenschaft* 19 (1988).

Lafontaine, G., "La Version copte des discours de Grégoire de Nazianze." *Muséon* 94 (1981).

Idem, "La tradition manuscrite de la version arménienne des discours de Grégoire de Nazianze. Prolégomènes à l'édition." *Muséon* 9 (1977).

Idem, (With B. Coulie) "La version arménienne des discours de Grégoire de Nazianze." CSCO 446, Subsidia 67 (Louvain, 1983).

Laga, C., "De Invectieven van Gregorius van Nazianze tegen Keizer Julian." Diss. (Louvain, 1952).

Le Clerc, J., *The Lives of Clemens Alexandrinus, Eusebius, Gregory Nazianzen, and Prudentius: Containing an impartial account of their lives and writings, together with several curious observations upon both* (London, 1696).

Leclercq, H., "Grégoire de Nazianze." DACL 6 (1925).

Lee, G.M., "Gregor von Nazianz. Oratio XV in Machabaeorum Laudem IV" (PG 35.916C). ZNTW 64 (1973).

Lefherz, F., *Studien zu Gregor von Nazianz: Mythologie, Überlieferung, Scholiasten.* Diss. (Bonn, 1958).

Lercher, J., *Die Personlichkeit des heiliges Gregorius von Nazianz und seine Stellung zur klassischen Bildung (aus seinen Briefen).* Diss. (Innsbruck, 1949).

Levy, P., *Michaelis Pselli de Gregorii Theologi judicium.* Diss. (Strasbourg, 1912).

Liebaert, J., *L'Incarnation*, vol. 1, *Des Origines au Concile de Chalcédoine* (Paris, 1966).

Idem, "L'Oeuvre de S. Grégoire de Nazianze. Publications récentes dans la Collection Sources Chrétiennes." MSR 36 (1979).

Lim, R., "*Polypragmosyne* and *Mysterion* in Gregory the Theologian's Orations 27-31: Knowledge and Community in Late Antique Constantinople." GOTR 39, 1-2 (1994).

List, J., "Zwei Zeugnisse für die Lobrede bei Gregor von Nazianz." ByJ 6 (1928).

Lloyd, G.E.R., *Polarity and Analogy. Two Types of Argumentation in Greek Thought* (Cambridge, 1966).

Lorenz, B., "Zur Seefahrt des Lebens in den Gedichten des Gregor von Nazianz." VChr. 33 (1979).

Louth, A., "St Gregory the Theologian and St Maximus the Confessor: The Shaping of Tradition," *The Making and Re-Making of Christian Doctrine: Essays in honor of Maurice Wiles*, S. Coakley and D.A. Pailin (eds.) (Oxford, 1993).

Idem, "St Gregory Nazianzen on bishops and the episcopate," in *Vescovi e pastori in epoca teodosiana. Studia Ephemeridis Augustinianum* 58 (Rome, 1997).

Ludwich, A., "Nachamer und Vorbilder des Dichters Gregorios von Nazianz." RM 42 (1887).

Lukinovich, A. (tr), *Grégoire de Nazianze. Le Dit de sa vie. Tradn. française. Mis en vers libres par C. Martingay.* Intr. par T. Spidlik (Geneva [edn. Ad Solem], 1997).

McGuckin, J.A., "Origen's Doctrine of the Priesthood." *Clergy Review* 70, 8 (August 1985); ibid., no. 9 (September 1985).

Idem, *St Gregory Nazianzen: Selected Poems* (Oxford: SLG Press, 1986; repr. 1989).

Idem, "Perceiving Light From Light in Light: The Trinitarian Theology of St Gregory the Theologian." GOTR 39, 1 (1994). (Acts of the Int. Colloquium commemorating the 16th Centenary of St Gregory Nazianzen, Brookline, MA, 1991.)

Idem, "Caesarea Maritima as Origen Knew It." *Origeniana Quinta*, R.J. Daly (ed.) (Leuven, 1992).

Idem, "Martyr Devotion in the Alexandrian School (Origen to Athanasius)." *Studies in Church History* 30 (Martyrs and Martyrologies) (Oxford, 1993). Reprinted in *Recent Studies in Church History* 5, E. Ferguson (ed.) (Garland Publishing: Hamden, CT, 1999).

Idem, "The Vision of God in S. Gregory Nazianzen" [Acts of the Oxford Int. Patristics Conference, 1995, ed., E.A. Livingstone. Peeters, Leuven]. SP 22, 1996.

Idem, "Eschaton and Kerygma: The Future of the Past in the Present Kairos (The Concept of Living Tradition in Orthodox Theology)." SVTQ 42, 3-4 (1998).

Idem, "St Gregory Nazianzen." *Encyclopedia of Monasticism*, W.M. Johnston (ed.) (Fitzroy-Dearborn: Chicago, 2000).

Idem, "Aliens and Citizens of Elsewhere: Xeniteia in East Christian Monastic Literature," in D. Smythe (ed.), *Strangers to Themselves: The Byzantine Outsider*. Variorum Press, London [Acts of the 32nd Symposium of the Society for Byzantine Studies. Brighton, 1998.] (London, 2000).

Idem, "Autobiography as Apologia in St Gregory Nazianzen" (Acts of the 13th Int. Oxford Patristics Conference, 1999). (Appearing in *Studia Patristica*, M.J. Edwards (ed.) [Peeters: Leuven, 2001]).

McLynn, N., "The Voice of Conscience: Gregory Nazianzen in Retirement." *Vescovi e pastori in epoca teodosiana*, vol 2. *Studia Ephemeridis Augustinianum* 58 (Rome, 1997).

Idem, (a) "A Self-Made Holy Man. The Case of Gregory Nazianzen." JECS 6.3 (1998).

Idem, (b) "The Other Olympias: Gregory Nazianzen and the family of Vitalianus." ZAC 2 (1998).

Idem, "Gregory of Nazianzus," in *Late Antiquity*, G.W. Bowersock, P. Brown & O. Grabar (eds.) (Cambridge: Harvard University Press, 1999).

Maier, J., *Die Eucharistielehre der drei grossen Kappadokier, des hl. Basilius, Gregor von Nazianz, und Gregor von Nyssa* (Freiburg, 1915).

Malin, N.A., *Hoi Epitaphioi Logoi Gregoriou Tou Nazianzenou* (Gk. text) (Athens, 1929).

Malunowiczowna, L., "La Consolation dans les lettres et orations de S. Grégoire de Nazianze" (Polish text with French synopsis), *Roczniki teol-kanon.* (Univ. of Lublin), 25 (1978), 4.

Maraval, P., "L'authenticité de la lettre 1 de Grégoire de Nysse," *L'Antiquité Classique* 102, 1984 (attributed to Gregory Nazianzen by E. Honigmann), cf. Mathieu, 1983.

Idem, "Un correspondant de Grégoire de Nazianze identifié: Pansophios d'Ibora." VChr 42 (1988) (Epp. 238-239).

Martland, T.R., "A Study of Cappadocian and Augustinian Trinitarian Methodology." *Anglican Theological Review* 47 (1965).

Martroye, F., "Le Testament de S. Grégoire de Nazianze." MSAF 76 (1924).

Masson, M.P., "Le discours 35 de Grégoire de Nazianze. Questions d'authenticité." *Pallas* 31 (1984).

Mathieu, J.M., *Structure et méthode de l'oeuvre doctrinale de Grégoire de Nazianze* (Diss. Sorbonne) (Paris, 1979).

Idem, "Remarques sur l'anthropologie de Grégoire de Nazianze (Poemata Dogmatica 8.22-32) et Porphyre." SP 17, part 3 (Oxford, 1982).

Idem, "L'authenticité de l'Exhortatio ad Virgines" (Carm. 1.2.3). Sym. Naz. (Paderborn, 1983).

Mayer, A., "Psellos Rede uber den rhetorischen Charakter des Gregorius von Nazianz." ByZ 20 (1911).

Meehan, D., "Editions of St Gregory of Nazianzus." ITQ 3 (1951).

Meijering, E.P., "The doctrine of the Will and of the Trinity in the Orations of Gregory Nazianzen." NTT 27 (1973); repr. in (Ibid.) *God Being History* (Amsterdam, 1975).

Memoli, A.F., "Eloquentia classica e sapientia cristiana nell'oratio funebris in laudem Basilii magni di Gregorio Nazianzeno." *Orpheus* 15 (1968).

Idem, "Testi biblici e compositio verborum nell'Oratio XLIII in laudem Basilii magni di Gregorio Nazianzeno." *La Buona Stampa* (Naples, 1969).

Idem, "Periodare ritmico nell'Oratio XLIII di Gregorio Nazianzeno." *La Buona Stampa* (Naples, 1969).

Menn, V., "Zur Pastoraltheologie Gregors von Nazianz." RITh 12 (1904).

Mercati, G., "Nuova Lettera di Gregorio Nazianzeno e riposta di Basilio Magno." *Studi e Testi* 11 (1903).

Meredith, A., "Gregory of Nazianzus and Gregory of Nyssa on Basil." SP 32 (1998).

Michaud, E., "L'Ecclésiologie de S. Grégoire de Nazianze." RITh 12 (1904).

Michopoulos, T.M., "Gregory the Theologian's Ontology of Compassion." GOTR 39, 1-2 (1994).

Misch, G., *A History of Autobiography in Antiquity*, vol. 2 (London, 1950).

Misko, C.D., *Democrite et Aristophane chez S. Grégoire de Nazianze. Problèmes de philologie classique, III.* Lvow University (1963) (*Letter* 64, PG 37.289-93).

Mitchell, J.F., "Consolatory Letters in Gregory Nazianzen." RTHP 34, 4th series (Louvain, 1966).

Momigliano, A., "Un termine post quem per il Christus Patiens." SIFC 10.

Montant, L., "Revue Critique de quelques questions historiques se rapportant à S. Grégoire de Nazianze et à son siècle." JTS 28 (1927).

Moreschini, C., "Luce e purificazione nella dottrine di Gregorio Nazianzeno." *Augustinianum* 13 (1973).

Idem, "Il Platonismo cristiano di Gregorio di Nazianzo." ASNP 3, ser. 4.4 (1974).

Idem, "L'opera e la personalità dell'imperatore Giuliano nelle due Invectivae di Gregorio Nazianzeno." *Forma Futuri (Festschrift M. Pellegrino)* (Turin, 1975).

Idem, "Influenze di Origene su Gregorio di Nazianzo." *Atti e Memorie dell' Accademia Toscana la Colombaria* 44 (1979).

Idem, "Aspetti della pneumatologia in Gregorio Nazianzeno e Basilio." *Atti del Congresso internazionale su Basilio di Cesarea* (Univ. di Messina, 1979) (Messina, 1983).

Idem, "La meditatio mortis e la spiritualità di Gregorio Nazianzeno." *Morte e immortalita nella catechesi dei Padri del 3-4 secolo*, S. Felici (ed.) (Rome, 1984).

Mossay, J., "La date de l'Oratio II de Grégoire de Nazianze et celle de son ordination." *Muséon* 77 (1964).

Idem, "Perspectives eschatologiques de S. Grégoire de Nazianze." QLP 45 (1964).

Idem, "La mort et l'au delà dans S. Grégoire de Nazianze." RTHP 34 (Louvain, 1966).

Idem, "Note littéraire sur la lettre 28 de Grégoire de Nazianze." *Muséon* 79 (1966).

Idem, "La predication 'liturgique' de Gregoire de Nazianze." SP 10.1, TU 107 (Berlin, 1970).

Idem, "Le Professeur Léon Sternbach, byzantiniste et patriote." RHE 65 (1970) (the Cracow project for a critical edition of the *Opera Gregoriana*).

Idem, "Notes sur l'herméneutique des sources littéraires de l'histoire byzantine." RecPhL 9 (1972) (Orat. 8.21-22).

Idem, "Note sur Grégoire de Nazianze: Orat. 8.21-22." SP 12 (Sixth International Oxford Patristics Conference, 1971), TU 115 (1975).

Idem, "L'Intervention angélique dans les funérailles de Constance II. Note sur Grégoire de Nazianze Orat. 5.16." *Mélanges Liturgiques offerts à B. Botte*. Abbaye du Mont César (Louvain, 1973).

Idem, "Grégoire de Nazianze. Travaux et projets récents. Chronique." *L'Antiquité Classique* 46 (1977).

Idem, "Gregor von Nazianz in Konstantinopel (379-381 AD)." *Byzantion* 47 (1977).

Idem, *Repertorium Nazianzenum, Orationes, Textus Graecus, 1. Codices Galliae* (Paderborn, 1981).

Idem, "Note sur Héron-Maxime, écrivain écclésiastique." *Analecta Bollandiana* 100, *Mélanges B. de Gaiffier & F. Halkin* (1982).

Idem (ed.), *Symposium Nazianzenum* (Louvain la Neuve, 25-28 Aout, 1981), *Actes du Colloque international*, SGKA. Gregor von Nazianz II (Paderborn, 1983).

Idem, *Discours 20-23, Sources Chrétiennes* 270 (Paris, 1980).

Idem, "Grégoire de Nazianze. Éditions grecques et orientales par l'université Cath. de Louvain," *Muséon* 93 (1980) [project for crit. edn. of poems & orations].

Mumrikov, A., "St Gregory of Nazianzus: For the 1600th anniversary of his demise." *Journal of the Moscow Patriarchate* 9 (1989).

Muraille, P., "L'église, peuple de l'oikoumene, d'après S. Grégoire de Nazianze. Notes sur l'unité et sur l'universalité." EThL 44 (1968).

Musurillo, H., "The Poetry of Gregory of Nazianzus," *Thought* 45 (Fordham Univ. Press, 1970).

Nau, F., "Receuil et explication des histoires mentionnées par S. Grégoire de Nazianze. La version Syriaque de l'écrit grec de Nonnus." ROC 7.

Nautin, P., "La date du De Viris Illustribus de Jérome, de la mort de Cyrille de Jérusalem, et celle de Grégoire de Nazianze." RHE 56 (1961).

Nicastri, L., "Richerche sull' elegia ellenistico-romana. La tradizione alessandrina nel carme 1.2.14 di Gregorio Nazianzeno." *Studi Cantarella* (University of Salerno, 1981).

Noble,T.A., *The Deity of the Holy Spirit according to Gregory of Nazianzen,* Diss. (Edinburgh, 1989).

Idem, "Paradox in Gregory Nazianzen's doctrine of the Trinity." Acts of the 11th International Patristics Conference, Oxford, 1991. E.A. Livingstone (ed.), *Studia Patristica* 27 (Louvain, 1993).

Norden, E., "Scholia inedita in Gregorii Nazianzeni Orationes." *Hermes* 27 (1892).

Idem, *Die Antike Kunstprosa* (I & II) (Leipzig, 1898, 1909).

Noret, J., "Les manuscrits sinaitiques de Grégoire de Nazianze. Première partie," *Byzantion* 48 (1978).

Idem, "Grégoire de Nazianze, l'auteur le plus cité après la Bible dans la littérature ecclésiastique byzantine." *Sym.Naz.* (Paderborn, 1983).

Idem, "Un fragment de Grégoire de Nazianze." *Analecta Bollandiana* 97 (1979).

Norris, F.W., *Gregory Nazianzen's Doctrine of Jesus Christ.* Diss. Yale University (1970), Synopsis Dissertation Abstracts 32 (1971) (529A).

Idem, "Of Thorns and Roses: The Logic of Belief in Gregory Nazianzen," *ChHist.* 53 (1984).

Idem, (a) "The Authenticity of Gregory Nazianzen's Five Theological Orations." *VChr* 39, (1985).

Idem, (b) "Gregory Nazianzen's Opponents in Or. 31," in: *Arianism: Historical and Theological Reassessments;* Papers from the 1983 Oxford Conference on Patristic Studies), ed., R. Gregg (*Philadelphia Patristic Foundation: Monograph Series*, no. 11 [Cambridge, MA, 1985]).

Idem, "The Tetragrammaton in Gregory Nazianzen, Or. 30.17." *VC* 41 (1989).

Idem, *Faith Gives Fullness to Reasoning. The Five Theological Orations of Gregory Nazianzen* (Leiden, 1991).

Idem, (a) "Gregory the Theologian." PE 2, 4 (1993).

Idem, (b) "Theology as Grammar: Gregory Nazianzen and Ludwig Wittgenstein." *Arianism After Arius*, eds., M. Barnes & D.H. Williams (Edinburgh, 1993).

Idem, "Gregory the Theologian and Other Religions." GOTR 39, 1-2 (1994).

Idem, "Gregory of Nazianzen: Constructing and Constructed by Scripture." P.M. Blowers (ed.), *The Bible in Greek Christian Antiquity* (Notre Dame, IN, 1997).

Idem, (a) "The Theologian and Technical Rhetoric: Gregory of Nazianzus and Hermogenes of Tarsus." *Festschrift for Thomas Halton*, ed., J. Petruccione (Washington, 1998).

Idem, (b) "Your Honor: My Reputation (Gregory's Orat. 43)." Greek *Biography and Panegyrics in Late Antiquity*, T. Hagg & P. Rousseau (eds.) (Berkeley, CA, 1998).

Oberhaus, M., "Gregor von Naziaz: Gegen den Zorn. Einleitung und Kommentar." Studien zur Geschichte und Kultur des Altertums. NF 2. Forsucuhngen zu Gregor von Nazianz, 8 (Paderborn, 1991).

Oehler, K., "Aristotle in Byzantium." GRBS 5 (1964).

Orlandi, T., "La traduzione copta dell'Encomio di Atanasio di Gregorio Nazianzeno." *Muséon* 83 (1970).

Otis, B., "Cappadocian Thought as a Coherent System." DOP 12 (1958).

Idem, "The Throne and the Mountain. An Essay on St Gregory Nazianzus." CJ 56 (1961).

Palla, R., "Sul testo di un epigramma di Gregorio Nazianzeno" (Epigr. 24). A&R 29 (1984).

Panagiotou, E., "Le trouble chez S. Grégoire de Nazianze." *Theologia*, vols. 65-66 (1995).

Papademetriou, G.C., "Gregory the Theologian: Patriarch of Constantinople." GOTR 39, 1-2 (1994).

Papadopoulos, S.G., *Gregorios Ho Theologos kai hai Prohypotheseis Pneumatologias autou* (Athens, 1971).

Pelikan, J., *Christianity and Classical Culture* (London, 1993).

Pellegrino, M., "La Poesia di S. Gregorio Nazianzeno." Pubbl. Della Univ. Cattol. del Sacro Cuore, *Vita e Pensiero* 13 (Milan, 1932).

Pépin, J., "Grégoire de Nazianze, lecteur de la littérature Hermétique" (PG 36.29C). VChr 36 (1982).

Petropoulou, N., *He teleutaia drasteriotes Gregoriou tou Theologou kata tas epistolas autou* (Thessalonike, 1962).

Phytrakes, A.J., *To poetikon ergon Gregoriou tou Nazianzenou* (Athens, 1968).

Piganiol, A., *L'Empire chrétien (325-395)* (Paris, 1947).

Pinault, H., *Le Platonisme de S. Grégoire de Nazianze: Essai sur les relations du Christianisme et de l'Hellénisme dans son oeuvre théologique* (La Roche-sur-Yon, 1925).

Peri, C., "Discorso 32 di Gregorio Nazianzeno: Una decantazi one della taxis cristiana." *La Scuola Cattolica* 103 (1975).

Plagnieux, J., S. *Grégoire de Nazianze Théologien: Études de Science religieuse* 7 (Paris, 1952).

Portmann, F.X., "Die göttliche Paidagogia bei Gregor von Nazianz. Eine dogmengeschichtliche Studie." KQS III (St Ottilien, 1954).

Pouchet, J.R., "Athanase d'Alexandria, modèle de l'évêque selon Grégoire de Nazianze, discours 21." Vescovi e pastori in epoca teodosiana. Studia Ephemeridis Augustinianum 58 (Rome, 1997).

Prestige, G.L., *God in Patristic Thought* (London, 1952).

Przychocki, G., *De Gregorii Nazianzeni epistulis quaestiones selectae.* Diss. Acad. Cracow. (1912) Sect. 1, Philolog. 248-392.

Puech, A., *Histoire de la littérature grecque chrétienne*, vol. 3 (Paris, 1930).

Quasten, J., *Patrology*, vol. 3 (Utrecht/Antwerp, 1975).

Queré, F., "Réflexions de Grégoire de Nazianze sur la parure feminine. Étude du poème sur la coquetterie I.II.29." RSR 42 (1968).

Queré-Jaulmes, F., "L'aumone chez Grégoire de Nysse et Grégoire de Nazianze." SP 8, TU 93 (Berlin, 1966).

Idem, "Les Pères sont-ils Jansénistes? Remarques sur la traduction classique de Grégoire de Nazianze." RSR 45 (1971).

Rapisarda, E., "Il Pessimismo di Gregorio Nazianzeno." MSLC 3 (1951).

Refoule, F., "La date de la lettre à Évagre." (PG 46.1101-1108), RecSR 69 (1961).

Regali, M., "Intenti programatici e datazione delle Invectivae in Julianum di Gregorio di Nazianzo." Cr.Stud. 1 (1980).

Riepl, R., "Des Heiligen Gregor von Nazianz Urteil über die Klassischen Studien und seine Berechtigung dazu," Progr. d. Obergymn. 4 (Linz, 1859).

Rizzo, J.J., *The Encomium of Gregory Nazianzen by Nicetas the Paphlagonian* (Brussels, 1976).

Rogich, D.M., "The Development of a Theologian according to St Gregory the Theologian." GOTR 39, 1-2 (1994).

Rose, H.J., "St Gregory Nazianzen and Pauline Rhythm." HThR (1933).

Rousse, J., "Les anges et leur ministère selon S. Grégoire de Nazianze." MSR 22 (1965).

Idem, "S. Grégoire de Nazianze." DS vol. 6 (Paris, 1967).

Rudasso, F., "La figura di Cristo in S. Gregorio Nazianzeno," *Bibliotheca Carmelitica*, Studia VIII, Ser. 2 (Ediz. del Teresianum: Rome, 1968).

Rudberg, S.Y., "Stelai ouk akinetoi: A Metaphor in Letter 154 of Gregory of Nazianzus. Kyriakon 1" (Festschrift J. Quasten, P. von Granfield and J.A. Jungmann [eds.] [Münster, 1970]).

Ruether, R.R., *Gregory of Nazianzus: Rhetor and Philosopher* (Oxford, 1969).

Rugé, W., "Nazianzos." RE, 16 (1935).

Russell, P.S., "St Gregory's Exegeses Against the Arians: Still a Viable Christian Tool." GOTR 39, 1-2.

Sajdak, J., "Nazianzenica" I. *Eos* 15 (1909).

Idem, "Nazianzenica" II. *Eos* 16 (1910).

Idem, "Quaestiones Nazianzenicae. Pars Prima: Quae ratio inter Gregorium Nazianzenum et Maximum Cynicum intercedat?" *Eos* 15 (1909).

Idem, "De Gregorio Nazianzeno poetarum Christianorum fonte." *Eos* 18 (1912).

Idem, "Historia critica scholastiarum et commentatorum Gregorii Nazianzeni." Pars Prima, *Meletemata Patristica* 1 (Cracow, 1914).

Idem, *Anonymi Oxoniensis lexicon in orationes Gregorii Nazianzeni* (Cracow, 1927).

Idem, "Die Scholastien der Reden des Gregor von Nazianz. Eine kurzgefasster Bericht über den jetzigen Stand der Forschung." ByZ 30 (1929-1930).

Salvatore, A., "Tradizione e originalità negli epigrammi di Gregorio Nazianzeno." Appendix to "Antologia di epigrammi gregoriani," *Collana di Studi greci* 33, Napoli Libr. Scientif. Ediz. (Naples, 1960).

Samuel, V.C., "God whom we worship: the teaching of Gregory Nazianzen," *Prayer and Contemplation*, C.M. Vadakkekara (ed.) (Asirvanam Benedictine Monastery: Bangalore, 1980).

Sandbach, F., "Five Textual Notes" [inter alia on Greg. Naz. Ep. 12]. ICS 2 (1977).

Sava, M., "Profilul teologului dup sfintul Grigorie de Nazianze." *Studii teologice* (Bucharest) 21 (1969).

Schultze, B., "S. Bulgakovs 'Utesitel' (Paraclete) und Gregor der Theologe über den Ausgang des Heiligen Geistes." OCP 39 (1973).

Schnayder, G., "Editionis Gregorianae ab Academia Litterarum Cracoviensi institutae fata quae fuerint." *Studia Theologica Varsaviensa* 9 (1971).

Serra, M., "La Carità pastorale in S. Gregorio Nazianzeno." OCP 21 (1955).

Sicherl, M. (et al.), "Vers une Édition critique de Grégoire de Nazianze." RHE 74 (1979).

Sinko, T., "De Gregorii Nazianzeni Laudibus Machaboeorum." *Eos* 13 (1907).

Idem, *De Cypriano martyre a Gregorio Nazianzeno laudato* (Cracow, 1916).

Idem, "De traditione orationum Gregorii Nazianzeni. I. De traditione directa." *Meletemata Patristica* 2 (Cracow, 1917).

Idem, Liryka sw Grzegorza z Nazjanzu. *Polonia Sacra* 1 (1918).

Idem, "De traditione orationum Gregorii Nazianzeni II, De traditione indirecta." *Meletemata Patristica* 3 (Cracow, 1923).

Idem, "Chronologia poezji sw Grzegorza z Nazjanzu. Sprawozdania z czynnosci i posiedzen." *Polska Akad. Um.* 48, 5 (1947).

Skimina, S., "De Gregorii Nazianzeni sermonum proprietatibus ad prosam rhythmicam pertinentibus." Acta II Congr. philol. class. slav (Prague, 1931).

Skurat, M., "St Gregory of Nazianzus on Philosophy and Knowledge of God: For the 1600th anniversary of his demise." *Journal of the Moscow Patriarchate* 10 (1989).

Smolak, K., "Interpretatorische Bemerkungen zum Hymnus *Pros Theon* des Gregor von Nazianz." *Studi Classici in onore di Q. Cataudella*, vol. 2 (Catania, 1972).

Snee, R.E., "St Gregory Nazianzen's Constantinopolitan career, AD 379-381." Diss. Univ. of Washington (1981).

Idem, "Valens Recalls the Nicene Exiles and Anti-Arian Propaganda." GRBS 26 (1985).

Soell, G., "Die Mariologie der Kappadozier im licht der Dogmengeschichte." ThQ 131 (1951).

Spidlik, T., "Grégoire de Nazianze. Introduction à l'étude de sa doctrine spirituelle." OCA 189 (Rome, 1971).

Idem, "La parola della lingua nativa nel servizio del Mistero inesprimabile; problema di Gregorio Nazianzeno." *Augustinianum* 14 (1974).

Idem, "La theoria et la praxis chez Grégoire de Nazianze." SP 14 (3) (1976).

Idem, "Per un rilettura di Gregorio Nazianzeno." *Koinonia* 5 (1981).

Idem, "Y-a-t-il un pluralisme théologique en Grégoire de Nazianze: La théologie est-elle une poésie ou une science?" SP 17, part 2 (Oxford, 1982).

Stephan, L., *Die Soteriologie des hl. Gregor von Nazianz.* Diss. (Rome, 1938) (Vienna, 1938).

Sternbach, L., "Dilucidationes Nazianzenicae" 1. *Eos* 16 (1910).

Idem, "Dilucidationes Nazianzenicae" 2. *Eos* 17 (1911).

Idem, *Prolegomena in carmina Gregorii Nazianzeni* (Cracow, 1926).

Strunk, O., "St Gregory of Nazianzus and the Proper Hymns for Easter." *Late Classical and Medieval Studies in honor of A.M. Friend,* K. Weitzmann (ed.), (Princeton, 1955).

Sykes, D.A., "The Poemata Arcana of St Gregory Nazianzen." JTS 21 (1970).

Idem, "The Poemata Arcana of St Gregory Nazianzen. Some Literary Questions." ByzZ 72 (1979).

Idem, "The Bible and Greek Classics in Gregory Nazianzen's Verse." SP 17, part 3 (Oxford, 1982).

Idem, "Understandings of the Church in the Cappadocians." *Studies of the Church in History* , H. Davies (ed.), Pittsburgh Theological Monographs, New Series 5 (Pittsburgh, 1983).

Idem, "Gregory Nazianzen as Didactic Poet." SP 16, part 2 (Berlin, 1985).

Idem, "Gregory Nazianzen: Poet of the Moral Life." Acts of the 10th International Patristics Conference, Oxford 1987. E.A. Livingstone (ed.), *Studia Patristica* 22 (Louvain, 1989).

Szymusiak, J., "L'Homme et son destin selon Grégoire le Théologien." Diss. (Paris, 1958).

Idem, *Éléments de théologie de l'homme selon S. Grégoire de Nazianze.* Diss. Pontif. Univ. Gregorianae (Rome, 1963).

Idem, "Pour un chronologie des discours de S. Grégoire de Nazianze." VChr. 20 (1966).

Idem, "Grégoire de Nazianze et le péché." SP 9 (4th International Patristics Conference, Oxford 1963), TU 101 (Berlin, 1966).

Idem, "Note sur l'amour des lettres au service de la foi chrétienne chez Grégoire de Nazianze." *Oikoumene,* Studi paleocristiani in onore del concilio ecumenico Vatican II (Univ. di Catania, 1964).

Idem, *Grzegorz Theolog* (Wojciecha, 1965).

Idem, "Les sites de Nazianze et Karbala." *Epektasis* (Mélanges Patristiques offerts à J. Daniélou. Eds. J. Fontaine & C. Kannengiesser) (Paris, 1972).

Idem, "Grégoire le Théologien disciple d'Athanase," in *Politique et Théologie chez Athanase d'Alexandrie.* Ed. C. Kannengiesser (Paris 1974).

Szymusiak-Affholder, C.M., "Psychologie et histoire dans le rêve initial de Grégoire Le Théologien." *Philologus* 115 (1971).

Tatakis, B., *The Contribution of Cappadocia to Christian Thought* (Gk. text) (Athens, 1960).

Teja, R., "Organizacion economica y social de Capadocia en el siglo IV segun los Padres Cappodocios." *Acta Salamanticensia. Fac. y Letras* 78 (Salamanca, 1974).

Telepneff, G., "Theopaschite language in the Soteriology of St Gregory the Theologian." GOTR 32 (1987).

Theodorou, A., "Light as Image and Symbol in the Theology of St Gregory of Nazianzus" (Gk. text). *Theologia* 47 (1976).

Thielman, F., "The Place of the Apocalypse in the Canon of St Gregory Nazianzen." *Tyndale Bulletin* 49 (1998).

Treu, K., "Philia und Agape. Zur Terminologie der Freundschaft bei Basilius und Gregor von Nazianz." *Stud. Clas.* III (1961).

Trembela, P., *Opoios emphanizetai en tais epistolais tou Gregorios ho Theologos* (Gk. text) (Athens, 1946).

Trisoglio, F., "Reminiscenze e consonanze classiche nella XIV orazione di S. Gregorio Nazianzeno." *Atti della Academia delle Scienze di Torino* 99 (1964-65).

Idem, "Sull interpolazioni nella XLV orazione di S. Gregorio Nazianzeno." *Aevum* 39 (1965).

Idem, "S. Gregorio di Nazianzo, scrittore e teologo in quaranta anni di ricerche (1925-1965)." RSLR 8 (1972).

Idem, "La poesia della Trinita nell' opera letteraria di S. Gregorio di Nazianzo." *Forma Futuri,* Studi in onore di M. Pellegrino (Turin, 1975).

Idem, "Il Christus Patiens. Rassegna delle attribuzioni." RSC 22 (1974).

Ibid, "I deuteragonisti del Christus Patiens." *Dioniso* 49 (1978).

Idem, "La Vergine ed il coro nel Christus Patiens." RSC 27 (1979).

Idem, "La Passione di Christo." *Coll. di testi patrist.* 16 (Rome, 1979).

Idem, "Filone Alessandrino e l'esegessi cristiana. Contributo all conoscenza dell' influsso esercitato da Filone sul IV secolo specificatamente in Gregorio di Nazianzo." ANRW 2, 21, 1 (Berlin, 1984).

Idem, "La figura dell'eretico in Gregorio di Nazianzo." *Augustinianum* 25 (1985).

Idem, "La Pace in S. Gregorio di Nazianzo." *Civilta classica e cristiana* 7 (1986).

Idem, "Uso ed effetti delle figurae elocutionis nei discorsi di Gregorio di Nazianzo." *Orpheus* 7 (1986).

Idem, "San Gregorio di Nazianzo e il Christus Patiens. Il problema dell'autenticità gregoriana del dramma." Univ. degli studi di Torino, Fondo Parini Chirio, Filologia, Testi e studi 7 (Firenze, 1996).

Idem, "Gregorio di Nazianzo il Teologo." *Studia Patristica Mediolanensia* 20, *Vita e Pensiero* (Milan, 1996).

Idem, "Il dramma dell'angoscia esistenziale nei carmi di Gregorio Nazianzeno." *Vescovi e pastori in età teodosiana, Studia Ephemeridis Augustinianum* 58 (Rome, 1997).

Trypanis, C.A., *Greek Poetry From Homer to Seferis* (London, 1981).

Tsames, D., (a) *He dialektike physis tes didaskalias Gregoriou tou Theologou* (Thessaloniki, 1969).

Idem, (b) "He peri Mesotetos didaskalia Gregoriou tou Theologou." *Kleronomia* 1 (1969).

Tsichlis, S.P., "The nature of theology in the Theological Orations of St Gregory of Nazianzus." *Diakonia* 16.3 (1981).

Tsirpanlis, C.N., "The doctrine of Katharsis, Contemplation, and Kenosis in St Gregory of Nazianzus." PBR 3 (1984).

Tuilier, A., "La datation et l'attribution du Christos Paschon et l'art du Centon." *Actes du 6è. Congrès Int. d'études byzantines*, vol. 1 (Paris, 1948).

Ullmann, C., *Gregorius von Nazianz der Theologe: Ein Beitrag zur Kirchen und Dogmengeschichte des vierten Jahrunderts* (1825; 2nd edn., Gotha, 1867) (First edn., pt. 1 [biographical] trans., C.V. Cox q.v.).

Unterstein, K., "Die naturliche Gotteserkenntnis nach der Lehre der Kappadozischen Kirchenväter, Basilius, Gregor von Nazianz, und Gregor von Nyssa." PGS 1-2, (1901-1902).

Vallianos, P.S., "The Attitude of the Three Hierarchs Towards Knowledge and Learning." GOTR 24, 1 (1979).

Van Dam, R., "Emperor, Bishops, and Friends in Late Antique Cappadocia." JTS 37 (1986).

Idem, "Self-representation in the Will of Gregory of Nazianzus." JTS 46 (1995).

Van Roey, A. and Moors, H., "Les Discours de S. Grégoire de Nazianze dans la littérature Syriaque." OLP 4 (1973); and ibid., 5 (1974).

Volk J., "Die Schutzrede des Gregor von Nazianz und die Schrift über das Priestertum von Johannes Chrysostomus." ZPT 17 (1895).

Wagner, M., "Rufinus the Translator: A study of his Theory and Practice as Illustrated by his Version of the Apologetica of St Gregory of Nazianzus." *Patr. Stud.* 73 (Catholic University of America: Washington, 1945).

Walter, C., "Liturgy and the illustration of Gregory of Nazianzen's homilies. An Essay in Iconographical Methodology." REByz 29, (1971) (Response to Galavaris).

Idem, "Un Commentaire enluminé des Homélies de Grégoire de Nazianze." C Arch 22 (1972).

Idem, "Biographical Scenes of the Three Hierarchs." REByz. 36 (1978).

Weijenborg, R., "Les cinq Discours Théologiques attribués a Grégoire de Nazianze, en partie oeuvre de Maxime Heron le Cynique, alias Evagre le Pontique d'Antioche." *Antonianum* 48 (1973).

Idem, "Some evidence of inauthenticity for discourse XI in honor of Gregory Nyssa, attributed to Gregory Nazianzen." SP 18, 3 (Oxford, 1982).

Idem, "L'origine evagriana dei Discorsi theologici III, IV, V (Discorsi 29-31) attribuiti a Gregorio di Nazianzio." *Augustinianum* 13 (1973).

Idem, "Prova dell' inautenticita del Discorso 25 attributo a S. Gregorio di Nazianzo." *Antonianum* 54 (1979).

Weiss, M., *Die Grossen Kappadozier: Basilius, Gregor von Nazianz und Gregor von Nyssa als Exegeten* (Braunsberg, 1872).

Werhahn, H.M., "Dubia und Spuria unter den Gedichten Gregors von Nazianz." SP 7 (4th International Patristics Conference, Oxford, 1963), TU 92 (Berlin, 1966).

Idem, *Die handschriftliche Überlieferung der Gedichte, Gregors von Nazianz* (Paderborn, 1985).

Wesche, K.P., "The Union of God and Man in Jesus Christ in the thought of Gregory of Nazianzus." SVTQ 28 (1984).

Idem, "Mind and Self in the Christology of St Gregory the Theologian. St Gregory's Contribution to Christology and Christian Anthropology." GOTR 39, 1-2 (1994).

White, C., *Christian Friendship of the Fourth Century* (Ch. 4) (Cambridge, 1992).

Whittaker, J., "Proclus, Procopius, Psellus and the Scholia on Gregory Nazianzen." VC 29, 4 (1975).

Williams, F., "Gregory Nazianzen and winter flowers" (Orat. 27.4; PG 36.16D). MPhL 4 (1981).

Wilson, A., "Centaurs and Synkrisis in Gregory Nazianzen." Acts of the 11th International Patristics Conference (Oxford 1991), E.A. Livingstone (ed.), *Studia Patristica* 27 (Louvain, 1993).

Winslow, D.F., "Gregory of Nazianzus and Love for the Poor." *Anglican Theological Review* 47 (1965).

Idem, "The Dynamics of Salvation." PMS 7 (Cambridge, MA, 1979).

Wittig, A., "Theologie als Erfahrung." Ostkirchliche Studien 35 (1986).

Wyss, B., "Gregorius Nazianzenus" (Or. 28.8, PG 36.36A). H (1938).
"Eine wenige beachtete Versreihe." Festschrift P. von der Muhl, *Phyllobolia* (Basel, 1946) (60 additional lines belonging to Carm.1.1.9).

Idem, "Gregor von Nazianz. Ein Griechisch-Christlicher Dichter des 4 Jahrhunderts." MH 6 (1949); repr. in series "Reihe Libelli." Bd. 73 (Darmstadt, 1962).

Idem, "Zu Gregor von Nazianz" (Notes on Or. 28.11, PG 36.10B; Ep. 178, PG 37.790-813). *Phyllobolia, Mélanges für P. von der Muhl* (ed., K. Meuli), vol. 1 (Basel, 1953).

Idem, *Gregor von Nazianz. Gestalten der Kirchengeschichte*, vol. II.2. M. von Greschat (ed.) (Stüttgart, 1984).

Idem, "Gregor von Nazianz oder Gregor von Nyssa?" (Authorship of Gregory Nazianzen's Ep. 49). Memorial A.J. Festugière, Antiquité païenne et chrétienne, E. Lucchesi and H. Saffrey (eds.), *Cahiers d'Orientalisme* 10 (Geneva, 1984).

Zehler, F.E., *Kommentar zu den 'Mahnungen an die Jungfrau.'* Carm. 1.2.2, vv. 1-354, Diss. (Münster, 1986).

Ziegler, A., "Gregor der Altere von Nazianz, seine Taufe und Weihe." MTZ 31 (1980).

Zincone, S., "L'anima come immagine di Dio nell'opera di Gregorio Nazianzeno." *Civilta classica e cristiana* 6 (1985).

A Thematic Guide to the Bibliography

1. *Gregory's Biography*
Benoit, Bernardi, Bonis, Cornitescu, Courcelles, Cox, Fleury, Freeland, Gallay, Hanson, Misch.

2. *Historical Questions*
Baldwin, Baumstark, Bernardi, Cameron, Criscuolo, Davids, Devos, Draseke, Elm, Gain, Gallay, Geoghegan Giet, Holman, Kopecek, Lim, Louth, McGuckin, McLynn, Montant, Mossay, Nautin, Otis, Panagiotou, Snee, Szymusiak, Van Dam, Weijenberg.

3. *Gregory and Julian the Apostate*
Asmus, Bernardi, Coman, Criscuolo, Kurmann, Laga, Moreschini, Scicolone, Seaver.

4. *Gregory and Philosophical Schools*
Asmus, Bergmann, Callahan, De Ghellinck, Delekonstante, Fantori, Gottwald, Gronau, d'Hérouville, Moreschini, Oehler, Pinault.

5. *Gregory's Poetic Work and its Allusions*

Achermann, Bernardi, Bossi, Cameron, Cataudella, Cavallini, Colacolides, Coman, Constanza, Corsaro, Crimi, Cummings, De Jonge, Del Ton, Demoen, Dubedout, Evenepoel, Fernandez, Frangeskou, Gangi, Ghedini, Giudice-Rizzo, Grenier, Kalamakis, Kambylis, Keydell, Knecht, Koster, Lukinovich, McGuckin, Mailin, Misko, Momigliano, Moreschini, Musurillo, Nicastri, Pellegrino, Phytrakes, Queré, Sajdak, Salvatore, Smolak, Sternbach, Sykes, Trisoglio, Trypanis, White, Zehler.

6. *Gregory and Classical Rhetoric / Hellenism*

Beck, Bernardi, Calvet-Sebasti, Camelot, Coman, Conrotte, Coulie, Engberding, Fleury, Focken, Frangeskou, Gallay, Gregg, Guignet, Hurth, Kennedy, Kertsch, Lercher, Memoli, Pelikan, Riepl, Ruether, Trisoglio.

7. *Gregory's Theological Doctrine*

(a) General Aspects:

Althaus, Begzou, Bergmann, Chrestou, Frank, Hergenroether, Kelly, Koulits, McGuckin, Mathieu, Papadopoulos, Plagnieux, Prestige, Skurat, Tsames, Tsichlis, Ullmann, Unterstein.

(b) Christology:

Bouteneff, Draeseke, Kandothra, Liebaert, Maier, Norris, Stauropoulos, Tsames, Wesche, Winslow.

(c) Trinitarian Theology:

Begmann, Bellini, Del Ton, Draeseke, de Ghellinck, Egan, Hanson, Harkianakis, Hergenroether, Kakaletre, McGuckin, Martland, Meijering, Moreschini, Noble, Norris, Papadopoulos, Schultze, Trisoglio.

(d) Soteriology:

Althaus, Harrison, Portmann, Stephan, Winslow.

(e) Theological Anthropology:

Bergmann, Ellverson, Gilbert, Mathieu, Menn, Michopoulos, Serra, Szymusiak, Trisoglio, Wesche, Winslow, Zincone.

(f) Scriptural Exegesis:

Capelle, Cataldo, Condamin, Demoen, Donders, Memoli, Norris, Thielman, Trisoglio, Weiss.

(g) Ecclesiology:

Bellini, Brou, Donders, Fitzpatrick, Karmiris, Michaud, Muraille, Pouchet.

(h) Mariology:

Adama, Soell.

(i) Spirituality:

Bouyer, Doerrie, Spidlik.

(j) Ascetical Theology:

Beuckmann, Cataldo, Coulie, Davis, Fellechner, Harakas, Harrison, Kertsch, Menn, Michopoulos, Moreschini, Plagnieux, Queré- Jaulmes, Serra, Sotiropoulos, Szymusiak.

8. *The Gregorian Manuscript and Textual Tradition*

Chelidze, Cummings, Der Nersessian, Galavaris, Gallay, Geerard, Lafontaine, Lefherz, Maraval, Masson, Mathieu, Meehan, Mossay, Noret, Sajdak, Sandbach, Sinko, Trisoglio, Walter, Werhahn, Wyss.

Index of Names and Places

Aaron 13-14, 25, 215, 245, 284.
Abourgios the Treasurer 162, 164.
Abraham 18-21, 287.
Acholius of Thessalonike 340.
Aetios 38, 99, 104, 106, 117, 131, 137,
    144-145, 181, 240, 261, 279-280, 283,
    289, 377.
Akakios of Beroea 261.
Akakios of Caesarea 37-38, 45, 105, 231.
Alexander of Constantinople 330.
Alypiana 6-7, 395.
Alypios 4-5, 26-27, 30.
Ambrose of Milan 157, 234, 314, 324.
Ammianus Marcellinus 126.
Amphilokios of Ikonium 7, 111, 127,
    133-134, 189, 223, 238, 350, 358, 366.
Amphilokios the Elder 7-8, 27, 35, 87, 101,
    133, 165.
Anastasia (church of) 241-243, 251-253,
    255-257, 262, 270, 311-313, 316, 319-320,
    324-325, 354, 357, 366, 371, 388.
Anaxilas 57.
Annesoi 88, 90-91, 93-95, 102, 133, 142.
Anthimos of Tyana 187-188, 195-196,
    198-202, 215, 226, 232-233.
Aphrodite 52-53.
Apollinaris of Laodicea 231, 262, 393. (+
    see Apollinarism in Subject Index)
Apollonios of Rhodes 57.
Apuleius of Madaura 64.
Aratos the Poet 57.
Arianzum 2, 93, 97, 139, 385, 400.
Aristophanes 57.
Aristotle 57, 98. (+ see Aristotelianism in
    the Subject Index).
Arius of Alexandria 330. (+ see Arianism
    in Subject Index).
Athanarich the Goth 337, 340, 344, 347-348.
Athanasios of Alexandria 38-41, 44-45, 56,

61, 92, 102, 113-114, 136, 138, 159,
    205-206, 221, 232, 234-235, 251, 260-261,
    266-269, 271-272, 290, 302, 330, 351,
    354, 367, 373, 390, 393.
Athene-Pallas 50, 53, 83.
Athens 85-87.
Basil of Ancyra 105.
Basil of Caesarea xxi, xxii, 7, 14, 33, 36, 44,
    46-47, 54-56, 61, 76-80, 88-98, 101-106,
    109-112, 114, 117, 127, 131-132, 134-135, 137,
    140-145, 147, 149-150, 156, 160, 162,
    167-198, 200-203, 205-206, 214, 216-219,
    221, 224, 226, 229-230, 234-236, 240,
    260-261, 271, 276, 280, 282, 301, 349, 355,
    367-368, 372-374, 387.
Bosporios of Colonia 379, 384.
Candidianos the Praeses 128-129, 133.
Caesarea Maritima 36, 41, 44, 62.
Caesarios (Gregory's brother) 3-4, 27,
    30-33, 35, 46-47, 55, 78, 85, 115-116, 118,
    127-128, 133, 155, 157-162, 164, 186, 259.
Caesarios the Magistrate 134.
Callimachos 57.
Cledonios the priest 358, 366, 384.
Constantius 100, 105, 112, 119, 135, 138, 181.
Cosmas of Jerusalem 401.
Cyprian of Antioch 251-253.
Cyprian of Carthage 251-252.
Cyril of Alexandria 297, 393.
Cyril of Jerusalem 40, 105, 350, 354.
Damasus of Rome 236, 238, 256, 314, 324,
    388-389.
Demeter 53.
Democritos of Abdera 365.
Demophilos of Constantinople 240-241,
    255, 257-258, 261, 266-267, 278, 312, 315,
    318, 336, 343, 348-349.
Demosthenes the Orator 57, 125.
Demosthenes the Eunuch 184-185, 221.

INDEX OF SUBJECTS

THE MEDITERRANEAN WORLD

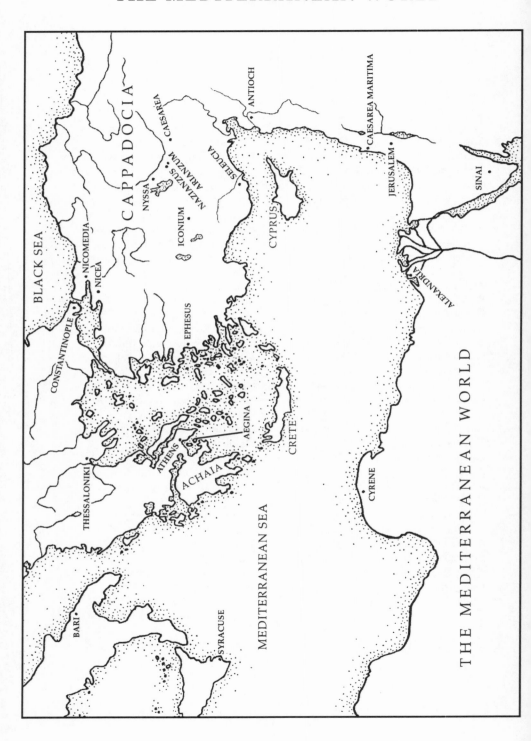

CONSTANTINOPLE AND CAPPADOCIA

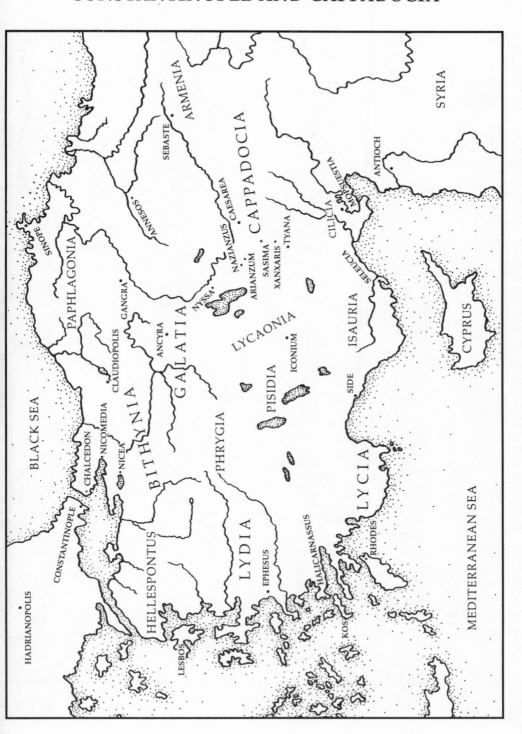

MAP OF CAPPADOCIAN LOCALITY

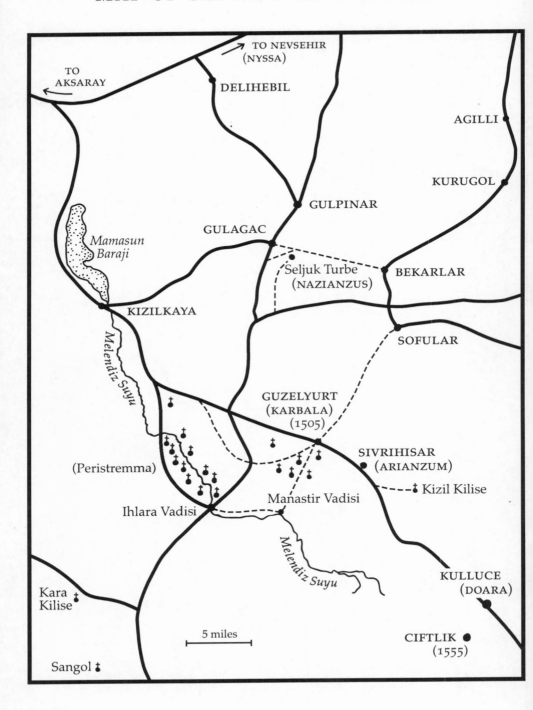